Frederick Paley, Sextus Propertius

The Elegies of Propertius

With English Notes

Frederick Paley, Sextus Propertius

The Elegies of Propertius
With English Notes

ISBN/EAN: 9783742807526

Manufactured in Europe, USA, Canada, Australia, Japa

Cover: Foto ©Andreas Hilbeck / pixelio.de

Manufactured and distributed by brebook publishing software
(www.brebook.com)

Frederick Paley, Sextus Propertius

The Elegies of Propertius

SEX. AURELII PROPERTII

CARMINA.

THE ELEGIES OF PROPERTIUS,

WITH ENGLISH NOTES,

BY

F. A. PALEY, M.A.,

EDITOR OF OVID'S *FASTI*, 'SELECT EPIGRAMS OF MARTIAL,' ETC.

SECOND EDITION, CAREFULLY REVISED.

LONDON:
BELL AND DALDY, YORK STREET, COVENT GARDEN.
CAMBRIDGE: DEIGHTON, BELL, AND CO.

MDCCCLXXII.

PREFACE TO THE SECOND EDITION.

THE former edition of Propertius, with English notes, was published in 1853. Though the work was composed under rather unfavourable circumstances, and with but few books available for reference or consultation; and though Propertius then was, as he even now is, but little read, compared with the contemporary poets Horace, Ovid, and Virgil, yet it gradually made its way, and in fact, has for some years been out of print. During the long interval since its first appearance, it may be supposed that I have been enabled to make many important improvements. To the fifth book especially, which is at once the most difficult and the most interesting, I have written nearly a new commentary, and with much fuller explanations than before. While I adhere to the opinion I formerly expressed, that it is "a reproach to the scholarship of this country that one of the most beautiful, interesting, and historically important of the Augustan Poets should remain unheeded and almost unknown,"[1] I may yet venture to think that some little advance has been made in the favourable estimate of the merits of Propertius by the mere fact of the poet having been edited in the present convenient form. I still feel some surprise that none of our English scholars have undertaken the work in a more thorough way, and with the painstaking minuteness that characterise the commentaries of Conington, Mayor, Ellis, and Munro. For I am not only quite unable myself to devote the necessary time and research even to the attempt at such a task, but I am now more fully aware of the extreme difficulties, both critical and exegetical, that beset this author. Of good MSS. there are but two, the Naples and the Groningen, neither of great antiquity, and both

[1] Preface to Ed. 1, p. i.

often very corrupt. The style of the poet too is obscure, abrupt, replete with affected Grecisms, and perplexed by sudden transitions and apostrophes. Some of the peculiarities in his Latinity may possibly be due to his Umbrian descent. For these and other reasons, (such as the great variety of the mythology, the large field of history and archæology, and the uncertainty as to the right division of the elegies, *lacunæ*, &c.,) a really complete edition of Propertius with English notes would form a much larger work than I have the power or the time to execute. I have therefore been content to record briefly the principal readings and conjectural emendations, and to offer in all cases the best explanation that I could give, avoiding superfluous discussion.

Of course I cannot expect that all students will have the same fondness for Propertius as a poet which I have long felt for him, and which only increases by time. There is truth in the remark of Lucian Mueller,[1] "Est sane difficilis Propertius, cujus sensus ac rationes nisi diligentissimo pariter ac longissimo studio perspicere non possis, sed ut eos quo magis penetraris, hoc vehementius te alliciant; plane sicut Tacitus, cum quo in quantum materiæ sinit diversitas, mirum in modum illi convenit." I can only wish he were more generally studied than he is; for though in some few places his elegies are, as may be expected, lax in their morality, they are nowhere coarsely indecent. And while Horace and Juvenal are read in schools, it is vain to exclude Propertius on that score.[2] He was a poet of thorough genius and (in spite of his fondness at a later period for Greek models) originality; a perfect master of *pathos*, which may be called the soul of elegy.

> Flebilis indignos Elegeia, solve capillos;
> Ah nimis ex vero nunc tibi nomen erit.[3]

As Horace boasted that he introduced the lyric, so Propertius claimed to be the Roman Callimachus,[4] and to have brought the elegiac Muse from her Heliconian heights into the Italian plains. Thus, though Catullus had used the elegiac verse to some

[1] Præf. ad Propert. ad init. (Lips. 1870).

[2] Selected Elegies from Propertius have been published, with brief notes for school-boys, by the Rev. A. H. Wratislaw, in the "Grammar-School Classics."

[3] Ovid, *Am.* iii. 9, 2.

[4] 'Umbria Romani patria Callimachi,' v. 1, 64.

extent before, and Tibullus had carried it to a high degree of perfection, to Propertius may fairly be attributed the first successful effort to take up this metre uniformly, as the best for narrative as well as for poetic sentiment.[1] It is rather singular that Propertius nowhere alludes to Tibullus; and it is probable that he was not acquainted with his writings. Neither Catullus nor Tibullus however,—nor indeed even Ovid,—used elegy *alone*.[2] Tibullus had exquisite taste, and very many of his verses are truly charming. But the elegiacs—not very numerous—of Catullus are so utterly rough and archaic,—I had almost said, semi-barbarous, but I must speak with respect of 'doctus Catullus,'—that they can bear no comparison with those of his successors. Take a brief example of his style:[3]

> Quem neque sancta Venus molli requiescere lecto
> Desertum in lecto cælibe perpetitur,
> Nec veterum dulci scriptorum carmine Musæ
> Oblectant, cum mens anxia pervigilat,
> Id gratum est mihi, me quoniam tibi dicis amicum,
> Muneraque et Musarum hinc petis et Veneris.

Propertius was not, perhaps, as popular among his contemporaries as Tibullus; probably because he was not so conversant with the great, though he seems to have known Mæcenas.[4] Yet he was evidently the model that Ovid proposed to himself, as is plain from the very numerous imitations that occur in his works.[5] Generally harmonious and smooth, he now and then adventures a word of four and even five syllables, or two spondees, at the

[1] In its origin, and in the hands of such early composers as Solon, Theognis, and Tyrtæus, elegy took rather a gnomic than a sentimental turn. Its use for epitaphs, in the hands of such a master as Simonides, perhaps tended to its after use for the expression of deep feeling. To the thoughtful student and practised composer, elegy will appear to be, as it is, a metre admirable for its versatility and almost endless power of combination and variety. A piece of English verse, given to 500 students at an examination, to turn into Latin elegiacs, would not be done by any two of them in precisely the same way. The genius of Martial shows to how many subjects, and with what success, it may be applied.

[2] The heroic poem in praise of Messalla, commonly given as the fourth book of Tibullus, is of rather uncertain authorship.

[3] Catull. 68, 5—10.

[4] See iv. 8, 57—60.

[5] These have been collected at considerable length by Dr. Anton Zingerle, in three parts. *Innsbruck*, 1871.

end of his hexameters.[1] As Pliny the younger said[2] of his friend Pompeius Saturninus, "inserit sane, sed data opera, mollibus levibusque duriusculos quosdam, et hoc quasi Catullus aut Calvus." His habit of using largely words of four, five, or even three syllables at the end of the pentameter gives a character (not, in my judgment, an unpleasing one) to the Propertian as contrasted with the more polished and equable Ovidian distich. Take the opening lines of the first book as an illustration:

Cynthia prima suis miserum me cepit ocellis,
  Contactum nullis ante cupidinibus.
Tum mihi constantis dejecit lumina fastus,
  Et caput impositis pressit Amor pedibus,
Donec me docuit castas odisse puellas
  Improbus, et nullo vivere consilio.

Here the fourth verse alone, metrically considered, is not pleasing. But let the following passage[3] be examined with attention, and it cannot fail to strike the reader of taste and judgment as singularly beautiful:

Ille sub extrema pendens secluditur ala,
  Et volucres ramo submovet insidias.
Jam Pandioniæ cessat genus Orithyiæ:
  Ah dolor! ibat Hylas, ibat Hamadryasin.
Hic erat Arganthi Pege sub vertice montis,
  Grata domus Nymphis humida Thyniasin:
Quam supra nullæ pendebant debita curæ
  Roscida purpureis poma sub arboribus;
Et circum irriguo surgebant lilia prato,
  Candida purpureis mixta papaveribus;
Quæ modo decerpens tenero pueriliter ungui
  Proposito florem prætulit officio;
Et modo formosis incumbens nescius undis
  Errorem blandis tardat imaginibus.

It cannot be doubted that the long words at the end of the pentameters in the above passage were studiously introduced. Every distich is elaborately constructed on that principle. And those who would object to such verses as inharmonious must have a very limited or a very erroneous conception of the capabilities of descriptive elegiac verse.

[1] See instances collected by L. Müller, De Propertii Arte Metrica, pp. xlvii—viii.
[2] *Ep.* i. 16.
[3] Book i. El. 20, 29—42.

But one of the chief beauties of Propertius' style consists in his habit of balancing the concluding noun of the pentameter by its epithet in the first half of the verse. The following lines are a good example :[1]

> Tu pedibus teneris positas fulcire pruinas,
> Tu potes insolitas, Cynthia, ferre nives?
> O utinam hibernæ duplicentur tempora brumæ,
> Et sit iners tardis navita Vergiliis,
> Nec tibi Tyrrhena solvatur funis harena,
> Neve inimica meas elevet aura preces,
> Et me defixum vacua patiatur in ora
> Crudelem infesta sæpe vocare manu.
> Atque ego non videam tales subsidere ventos,
> Cum tibi provectas auferet unda rates.
> Sed quocumque modo de me, perjura, mereris,
> Sit Galatea tuæ non aliena viæ,
> Ut te felici prævecta Ceraunia remo
> Accipiat placidis Oricos æquoribus.

It would seem, from the style of the historical poems in the fifth book, which appear to be amongst his earliest efforts, that the dissyllabic word at the end of the pentameter was generally preferred by him at first. These poems were professedly in imitation of the *Αἴτια* of Callimachus, but, the subjects being strictly national, they do not exhibit so much of the Greek learning as his later compositions.

Propertius began to write verses early in life, and as soon as he had taken the *toga virilis*, *i.e.* about 16.

> Mox ubi bulla rudi demissa est aurea collo,
> Matris et ante deos libera sumpta toga,
> Tum tibi pauca suo de carmine dictat Apollo,
> Et vetat insano verba tonare foro.[2]

Born *circa* 50 B.C., two or three years after Tibullus, and nearly forty after Catullus, he lived in the very best period of Roman literature. He has an interesting reference to the then forthcoming Æneid of Virgil,[3] which he appears to have heard pub-

[1] I. 8, 7—20. [2] v. 1. 131.

[3] iii. 26, 63. The ending of an hexameter in iv. 7, 49, *Oricia terebintho*, may have been borrowed, as L. Mueller suggests, Præf. p. xlviii., from Æn. x. 136, where the same words occur in the same position.

licly or privately recited. His first Book, entitled 'Cynthia,'—the first that was published, if not the first written,—is also a work of his early life, as indeed is attested by the ardour of feeling that pervades it. It is distinctly so called by Martial.[1]

> Cynthia, facundi carmen juvenile Properti,
> Accepit famam, nec minus ipsa dedit.

His birthplace was Mevania[2] (*Bevagna*) in the south of Umbria, near to Asisium and the sources of the Clitumnus. Pliny the younger twice mentions[3] Propertius in connection with one Passennus Paullus, a writer of elegies, and at once an imitator and a descendant, as well as fellow-townsman (municeps) of Propertius. It has hence been inferred that Propertius married and had legitimate children after Cynthia's death.[4] It seems that his position in life was what we call of middle class; for he supposes Cynthia to say of him (iii. 16, 21):

> Certus eras, heu heu, quamvis nec sanguine avito
> Nobilis, et quamvis haud ita dives eras.

The literary questions connected with the life and writings of Propertius have so fully been discussed by others[5] that I shall not here attempt to repeat them at length. An account of the numerous (but mostly late and interpolated) MSS. and early editions may also be found in the prefaces of Barth, Lachmann, Hertzberg, and others. L. Mueller, who again collated the Naples MS., hitherto regarded as of the xiiith century, inclines to think it is not really earlier than sec. xv.[6] In respect of its critical value, he comes to a conclusion opposed to the judgment of Lachmann, and says, "longe superat bonitate Groninganum." This latter, the Groningen MS., is thought to have been derived from an independent source; its readings are often unique, but

[1] *Ep.* xiv. 189.

[2] v. 1, 123—5. Plautus, also an Umbrian, but a very pure Latinist, was born at Sassina or Sarsina in the north of Umbria.

[3] *Ep.* vi. 15 and ix. 22. "In litteris veteres aemulatur, exprimit, reddit, Propertium in primis, a quo genus ducit, vera soboles, eoque simillima illi in quo ille praecipuus. Si elegos ejus in manum sumpseris, leges opus tersum, molle, jucundum, et plane in Propertii domo scriptum."

[4] His connexion with Cynthia (supposed to be *Hostia*, a descendant of Hostius, whose name is known as a poet), was illicit, and in ii. 7 he expresses his satisfaction at the relaxation of the law enforcing marriage on Roman citizens.

[5] Hertzberg and L. Mueller especially.

[6] Praef. p. ix.

whether or not due to an early emendator, it seems impossible to say.[1] But the Naples MS., according to Mueller, "est certe omnium qui jam extant longe optimus."[2] Lachmann[3] upholds the Groningen MS. as first in authority; "Codicem Groninganum, qui verum multorum locorum lectionem unus omnium indicat, proxime subsequuntur membranæ *Neapolitanæ*."

The German editions of Propertius are numerous; it is evident that the poet has long held a far higher place in their estimation than it has in our comparatively indolent universities. I have consulted throughout the following:

1. Frid. Gottlieb Barth, Lips. 1777, in 1 vol. 8vo., a laborious work, with a copious *apparatus criticus* and a full index; the text is a reprint from the second Gottingen edition of 1762.

2. Christian Theophilus Kuinoel, Lips. 1805. 2 vols. 8vo. The text of this edition, like the preceding, is founded too much on conjectural emendation and the readings of the interpolated MSS. The commentary however is copious, and often useful.

3. Car. Lachmann, Lips. 1816. 1 vol. 8vo. This, the first edition, was reprinted in 1829 with Catullus and Tibullus. The second edition I have not used; but of the first I have not formed quite so high an opinion as that generally held by his numerous admirers. Many of his alterations seem to indicate a want of poetic taste; but he was the first to reject a number of readings introduced since the time of the Scaligers, and to show what MSS. should be chiefly taken as a guide.

4. Frid. Jacob, Lips. 1827. 1 vol. 12mo. An unpretending, but excellent work, and the first that can be considered as founded wholly on MS. authority. The critical notes at the end of the volume are brief, but show sound judgment and knowledge of the idioms of the author. His tendency, like that of some of his successors, is to follow Lachmann.

5. Guil. Hertzberg, Halis, (*Halle*,) 1843. 4 vols. 8vo. This is by much the most complete edition that has appeared. It is furnished with a complete collation of all the good MSS., followed by an elaborate commentary, extending to about 500 pages, in two volumes. To these he has added a volume of *Quæstiones*, of

[1] See L. Mueller, Præf. p. v.—vii.
[2] *Ib.* Præf. p. 10.
[3] Præf. p. x. (ed. 1816).

great value and research, in which he treats of the personal history of the poet and his friends, his relations to Cynthia, the idioms, diction, genius and principles of his composition, the dates and historical allusions, the MSS., early editions, and other collateral points. To this work the present edition owes the greatest obligations.

6. Henr. Keil, Lips. 1850. 1 vol. 12mo. A carefully revised text, chiefly following Lachmann and Jacob. Some new emendations of his own or others are admitted; and the orthography is generally brought up to a uniform and more correct standard. Generally, he says,[1] he preferred to leave in the text readings which he felt sure were corrupt, rather than to adopt conjectures where several had a chance of being right.

7. Lucian Mueller, Lips. 1870. 1 vol. 12mo. This is an important edition, and I have made good use of it throughout. The text is carefully revised, and though the emendations introduced are rather frequent and violent, they are generally ingenious, and deserving of consideration. The volume contains also Catullus and Tibullus, each with a learned and useful Preface, and each accompanied by a brief critical commentary.

These seven editions—to which I might add Mr. Wratislaw's small volume as an eighth,—are all that I have regularly examined throughout. The editions of Weise, Haupt, and Rossbach, I have not had before me, though I have occasionally inspected that of Weise. In truth, the work of editing is so hard, and presses so severely on those whose time is fully occupied with other engagements, that I may hope for some consideration on the score both of errors and oversights, as well as of omissions.

So long as the writing of Latin verse is kept up in our public schools and colleges, Propertius ought to be, and will be, studied by some. I recommend him especially as a model for imitation; and I repeat that, as an Augustan poet of the earlier period, he deserves a great deal more attention than in this country he has hitherto obtained.

[1] Praef. p. iv. fin.

CAMBRIDGE,
October, 1872.

SEX. AURELII PROPERTII

ELEGIARUM

LIBER PRIMUS.

BOOK THE FIRST.

In most of the MSS. the first book is inscribed 'Cynthia, Monobiblos;' and under this title the poet himself appears to allude to it, iii. 15, 2: 'Et tua sit toto Cynthia lecta foro.' It was both written and published by its author A.U.C. 728, probably at the early age of twenty years. Hence Martial, xiv. 189: 'Cynthia, facundi carmen *juvenile* Properti.' *Ib.* viii. 7, 5: 'Cynthia te vatem fecit, lascive Properti.' It has all the freshness and ardour of early genius, before it suffered from the pedantry of the Greek learning that was becoming more and more fashionable. The fondness of the poet for Greek mythology is even here apparent; but he was not yet an avowed rival and imitator of Philetas and Callimachus (iv. 1, 1). The agnomen *Nauta* which is commonly given to the poet in the MSS. is thought to have originated from the false reading *Navita* for *non ita* in iii. 16, 22. So Plautus was sometimes known by the agnomen 'Asinius,' probably from his birthplace Sassina in Umbria.

PROPERTII

LIBER PRIMUS.

I.

CYNTHIA prima suis miserum me cepit ocellis,
  Contactum nullis ante cupidinibus.
Tum mihi constantis dejecit lumina fastus,
  Et caput impositis pressit Amor pedibus,
Donec me docuit castas odisse puellas

1.] *Cynthia.* That this name is feigned by the poet, as Delia was by Tibullus, and Lesbia by Catullus (Ovid, *Trist.* ii. 428: 'Femina, cui *falsum* Lesbia nomen erat,') is evident. Her real name is said to have been Hostia (Schol. ad Juven. *Sat.* vi. 7. Apuleius, *Apolog.* p. 279, quoted by Hertzberg). Of her birth and family nothing is known beyond the few hints to be collected here and there from the elegies, all which have been diligently examined by Hertzberg, *Quaestiones Propertianae*, p. 31—46. It is probable that she was a *libertina* (compare the details of her humble funeral, v. 7, 25, &c.), not indeed a woman of virtue, but highly accomplished, and even talented as a poetess (i. 2, 27). A particular description of her personal charms is given ii. 2, 5. She was, however, as may be supposed, faithless and profligate; and the poet's jealous temper continually finds in this a subject of complaint. See, for instance, ii. 5 and 6, and iii. 7. On a correct estimate of her character, which none of the editors before Hertzberg seem to have formed, the true interpretation of many passages depends. How, on any other supposition, could the poet with propriety introduce (ii. 6) the parallel between Cynthia and the most notorious courtesans of antiquity, Lais, Thais, and Phryne? And this circumstance was probably the real obstacle to their lawful union. See note on ii. 7, 1. Cynthia seems to have been by some years older than Propertius, iii. 9, 20, unless we should rather understand *anus futura haud longa die* of the mere transient nature of female beauty under a southern climate. The passage in iii. 24, 6, would be conclusive, were the reading *anum* certain.

ibid. *cepit*, 'took captive,' εἷλε. The metaphor is continued in the next three lines. —*contactum*, ἁλόντα, caught by none of the 'Veneris pueri,' v. 1, 138. The sense of this is determined by a circumstance in his early life recorded iv. 14, 6. Cynthia was his 'first love,' *i. e.* the first who had ever really possessed his affections.

3.] *lumina, etc.*, then Love made me cast down the eyes of resolute pride with which I had, as it were, bid him defiance. This appears to be the genitive of quality, but the expression is a remarkable one. *Fastus* is a word peculiarly used (1) as the boast of being superior to love, inf. i. 13, 27. (2) of those who reject the advances of others, as Penelope, iv. 12, 10. Compare iv. 18, 11; iii. 6, 13; iii. 17, 21. So Ovid, *Fast.* i. 419, 'Fastus inest pulcris, sequiturque superbia formam.'

4.] *Caput.* 'Trampled on my neck as a conqueror on a prostrate enemy.' This seems to have been a favourite subject in ancient paintings. (Kuinoel on ii. 30, 8). So Tac. *Germ.* § 37, 'infra Ventidium dejectus Oriens.'

5.] *Odisse*, to dislike chastity in women, to speak and think of it as mere prudery and affectation, and to disparage it as pre-

Improbus, et nullo vivere consilio.
Et mihi jam toto furor hic non deficit anno,
Cum tamen adversos cogor habere deos.
Milanion nullos fugiendo, Tulle, labores
Sævitiam duræ contudit Iasidos.
Nam modo Partheniis amens errabat in antris,
Ibat et hirsutas ille videre feras;
Ille etiam Hylæi percussus volnere rami
Saucius Arcadiis rupibus ingemuit.
Ergo velocem potuit domuisse puellam;—
Tantum in amore preces et benefacta valent.
In me tardus Amor non ullas cogitat artes,

senting an obstacle to possession.—*Nullo consilio*, *i.e.* temere, 'recklessly;' without any fixed object or principle; without regard to reputation or interests.

7.] The sense seems to be, 'And now a whole year has passed, and this madness ceases not, though all that time I have been unable to have the gods in my favour.' *Cum tamen*, el *sed*, even though I have had to endure the hard fate of not securing my mistress' affections. Inf. 31, 'quibus facili deus annuit aure.'

9.] *Tulle*, see on vi. 1. The argument is this. Some suitors, by persevering attentions and devotedness, have softened the obdurate hearts of their mistresses; but in my case Love is slow to suggest any such method of gaining my object (v. 17).—Milanion was the lover of Atalanta, daughter of Iasius. The form *Iasis* is, however, from *Iasus*, and this is the name given by Apollodorus, iii. cap. 9. Another form, used by Ælian, is *Iasion*. The history of Atalanta is given by the last-mentioned writer in a very beautiful narrative, *Var. Hist.* xiii. 1. He does not mention Milanion, but records her successful contest against two centaurs, Hylæus and Rhœcus, who came to serenade her. Apollodorus, l.c., is more concise: 'Ἰάσου καὶ Κλυμένης τῆς Μινύου Ἀταλάντη ἐγένετο. Ταύτης ὁ πατὴρ, ἀρρένων παίδων ἐπιθυμῶν, ἐξέθηκεν αὐτήν. Ἄρκτος δὲ φοιτῶσα πολλάκις θηλὴν ἐδίδου, μέχρις οὗ εὑρόντες κυνηγοὶ παρ' ἑαυτοῖς ἀνέτρεφον. Τελεία δὲ Ἀταλάντη γενομένη, παρθένον ἑαυτὴν ἐφύλαττε, καὶ θηρεύουσα ἐν ἐρημίᾳ καθωπλισμένη διετέλει. Βιάζεσθαι δὲ αὐτὴν ἐπιχειροῦντες Κένταυροι Ῥοῖκος καὶ Ὑλαῖος κατατοξευθέντες ὑπ' αὐτῆς ἀπέθανον.' According to this writer, Milanion obtained her in marriage by the well-known expedient of dropping golden apples when matched with her in a foot-race. See Theocr. iii. 40. The offspring was the Parthenopæus of Æschylus, *Theb.* 542. Other accounts represent him as attending on Atalanta in the chase, and as having been wounded by the centaur in her defence. Ovid, *Ars Amat.* ii. 185: 'Quid fuit asperius Nonacrina Atalanta? Succubuit meritis trux tamen illa viri. Sæpe suos casus, nec mitia facta puellæ, Flesse sub arboribus Milaniona ferunt.'

11.] *Partheniis in antris*. Ælian, *V. H.* xiii. 1. ὁ δὲ (πατὴρ) ἐκθεῖναι λαβὼν, οὐκ ἀπέκτεινεν, ἐλθὼν δὲ ἐπί τι Παρθένιον ὄρος, ἔθηκε πηγῆς πλησίον. Καὶ ἦν ἐνταῦθα ὕπαντρος πέτρα, καὶ ἐπέκειτο συνηρεφὴς δρυμών. This was a mountain in Arcadia—*ibat videre*. The Græcism is obvious. Cf. i. 6, 33. On *antrum* see v. 4, 3.

13.] The MSS. have *psili* or *psilli*. There can be no doubt of the truth of the correction made in the Ed. Rheg. 1481. Milanion, says the poet, was even wounded by a blow from the club of the Centaur Hylæus.

15.] *domuisse*, δαμάσαι, 'he was able to subdue the fleet-footed maid,' *i.e.* to overtake her in the race of love. In *velocem* there is an elegant allusion to her being matched with her lover in the foot-race, on which ancient custom see Pindar, *Pyth.* ix. 114—22. *Domare* would probably mean 'he might have vanquished her'; but the poets are not always consistent in the use of the present and the perfect infinitive.

16.] *benefacta*, viz. the assistance given against the Centaurs.

Nec meminit notas, ut prius, ire vias.
At vos, deductæ quibus est fallacia lunæ,
Et labor in magicis sacra piare focis,
En agedum, dominæ mentem convertite nostræ,
Et facite illa meo palleat ore magis.
Tunc ego crediderim vobis, et sidera et amnes
Posse Cytæeis ducere carminibus.
Et vos, qui sero lapsum revocatis, amici,
Quærite non sani pectoris auxilia.
Fortiter et ferrum, sævos patiemur et ignes;
Sit modo libertas, quæ velit ira, loqui.
Ferte per extremas gentes et ferte per undas,

18.] *Notas vias.* 'Sunt eæ, quibus ille deus insinuare se pectoribus puellarum solitus erat.' (Hertzberg).

19.] *At vos.* He appeals to magic aid, *i. e.* that of philtres and charms.—*fallacia*, *ars fallendi*. There seems no reason to alter this into *Adacia*, or in the next line *sacra* into *astra*, with Müller. As easy a guess would be *pellacia*, a word used by Lucretius.

20.] *Sacra piare.* An unusual expression, not signifying 'sacra facere expiandi causa,' but 'sacra pie solemnique ritu peragere. Nihil amplius.'—*Kuinoel*. '*Sacra* nostro loco significant res sacrificio oblatas, sive victimas, sive latices et herbas magicas, quæ certis carminibus certoque ritu Diis adolentur.'—*Hertzberg*. *Piare* is ἁγνίζειν, καθαγίζειν. Propertius frequently uses the word, as v. 1, 50; 7, 34; 9, 25.

21.] There is great difficulty about the reading of this verse. The ed. Rheg. has *cytheinis*; the best MSS. *cytalinis* or *cytheinis*. Jacob reads *Cyteinis*, Hertzberg and Müller *Cytinæis*, Kuinoel, Barth, and Lachmann *Cytæeis*, the conjecture of Guyet. Medea is supposed to be meant, so called from Κύτη or Κυταία, a town of Colchis; compare ii. 4, 7: 'non hic herba valet, non hic nocturna Cytæis.' The forms Κυταΐς and Κυταιεύς occur in Apoll. Rhod. ii. 399, 403, and Κυταίων ib. 1095; cf. iv. 511. But it does not appear by what analogy Κυταΐνης could be formed from Κύτη or Κυταία, with the ι long. Hertzberg compares Nerine (Virg. *Ecl.* vii. 37) from Nereus; but this fails, for Nerine is simply contracted from Νηρηΐνη or Νηρεΐνη. More appropriate would have been the feminine *Nereine* from *Nereus*. Cf. i. 19, 13. The termination in *inus* is generally used in the case of persons born in Greek towns, but out of Greece (especially of those in Magna Græcia). The only way of defending the long ι would be to compare Homer's use of ἄφθιτος for ἄφθιτος, on which see note on Æsch. *Cho.* 1038. Κυταιεύς might be formed from Κυταία, as Αἰαιεύς from Αἶα. The conjecture of Hertzberg is very plausible, '*Cytinæis*, i. e. Thessalicis. Steph. Byz. s. v. Κύτινα, inquit, πόλις Θεσσαλίας, ὡς Θέων ἐν ὑπομνήματι Λυκόφρονος (1389: Λαμπώνιον τε καὶ Κυτιναίου Κάδμου), ὁ πολίτης Κυτιναῖος.' The principal argument in his favour is that the *Thessalian* witches are especially mentioned by the Latin poets as being able to draw down the moon by their incantations. So perhaps 'Sinuessanumque Petrinum' in Hor. *Ep.* i. 5, 5, may have been so called from πέτρινος, 'rocky.'

25.] *Et vos*, *i. e.* vos etiam. *At*, the reading of one MS. (Groning.) seems objectionable from v. 19 beginning with *at vos*. I am surprised that Lachmann, Hertzberg, Müller, and Kuinoel should have admitted, and Jacob approved, *aut vos*, the conjecture of Hemsterhuis. With Barth, I follow the Naples MS.

27.] *Ferrum et ignes.* ἤτοι κέαντες ἢ τεμόντες εὐφρόνως πειρασόμεσθα πῆμ' ἀποστρέψαι νόσου.—Æsch. *Ag.* 832. 'Docte ab arte chirurgica metaphoram duxit.'—Hertz.

29.] The sense is, 'Nay, even banish me by way of cure, far from the sight of women.' There is much pathos in these beautiful lines. The only condition he imposes is freedom in expressing his sense of Cynthia's cruelty (v. 28); that is, he will not desist from writing verses to her.

Qua non ulla meum femina norit iter.
Vos remanete, quibus facili Deus annuit aure,
Sitis et in tuto semper amore pares.
In me nostra Venus noctes exercet amaras,
Et nullo vacuus tempore defit amor.
Hoc, moneo, vitate malum: sua quemque moretur
Cura, neque assueto mutet amore locum.
Quod si quis monitis tardas adverterit aures,
Heu, referet quanto verba dolore mea!

II.

Quid juvat ornato procedere, vita, capillo,
Et tenues Coa veste movere sinus?
Aut quid Orontea crines perfundere myrrha,
Teque peregrinis vendere muneribus,
Naturæque decus mercato perdere cultu,
Nec sinere in propriis membra nitere bonis?

31.] *Vos remanete.* This may mean, in opposition to the preceding, 'It is for you to stay at home, whose vows are heard by the gods' (sup. 8); but it may also be explained, 'remain constant to each other;' a sense peculiar to Propertius, and rather implied by the next verse. See below, el. 10, 29, and on ii. 9, 8.

33.] *amaras.* See v. 3, 29, 'at mihi cum noctes induxit vesper amaras.'

35.] *Hoc malum,* i.e. hoc extremum remedium, sc. exilium.—*Mutet amore locum,* i.e. discedat a domina sua. This distich contains advice to others to be constant, and so to avoid a quarrel (discidium) as the greatest of evils. But here also the sense is ambiguous; the lines may mean, 'stay at home, you who have gained the affection you aspired to.'

38.] *referet,* 'he will recal,' or, 'he will repeat to others.'

II. This beautiful elegy conveys advice to Cynthia not to be too fond of dress. We may suppose it written after meeting her in public more richly attired than he thought becoming her position. He cannot suppress a suspicion that she wishes to please others beside himself. Hence a tone of ill disguised jealousy throughout the poem.

2.] *Coa veste.* The silk from Cos was celebrated in the time of Aristotle, *Hist. An.* v. 19. ἐκ δὲ τούτου τοῦ ζῴου καὶ τὰ βομβύκια (*the cocoons*), ἀναλύουσι τῶν γυναικῶν τινὲς ἀναπηνιζόμεναι, κἄπειτα ὑφαίνουσιν· πρώτη δὲ λέγεται ὑφῆναι ἐν Κῷ Παμφίλη Πλάτεω θυγάτηρ. (Kuinoel).—*tenues,* so called from their thin and pellucid texture. Whence Martial, viii. 67, says, 'femineum lucet seu per bombycina corpus.' Infra. ii. 3, 15. 'Nec si qua Arabio lucet bombyce puella.' This distich is repeated in v. 5, 55. The ablative, *Coa veste,* is rather irregular; either *induta* may be supplied, or the ablative of material may be meant.—*movere sinus* alludes to the thin and fluttering folds of the dress, probably the tunica which the poet appears to have particularly admired in Cynthia: see ii. 3, 15; iii. 21, 25; iv. 9, 15. In this passage he speaks of it with a jealous dislike, as too fascinating to other eyes than his own.

3.] *Orontea,* with Syrian (eastern) perfumes.—*vendere,* 'to set yourself off by the produce of foreign lands,' perfumes and silk dresses, etc.

5.] *perdere,* to spoil nature's grace by purchased ornaments. The past participles of many deponent verbs are used both transitively and intransitively; as *meditatus, comitatus, expertus, sortitus, oblitus, partitus,* &c.

Crede mihi, non ulla tuæ est medicina figuræ:
  Nudus Amor formæ non amat artificem:
Aspice quos summittit humus formosa colores;
  Ut veniant hederæ sponte sua melius,
Surgat et in solis formosius arbutus antris,
  Et sciat indociles currere lympha vias.
Litora nativis collucent picta lapillis,
  Et volucres nulla dulcius arte canunt.
Non sic Leucippis succendit Castora Phœbe,

7.] *medicina*, 'there is no appliance that can improve your natural shape; Cupid is naked, and likes not the maker of an artificial beauty.'

8.] Kuinoel reads *formam*, which is a wanton corruption of the text. Compare ii. 1, 58; 'solus amor morbi non amat artificem.' Artifex does, however, occasionally mean *artificial*, as inf. iii. 23, 8; and *artificem vultum*, Pers. v. 40.

9.] *Submittat* is the reading of Kuinoel, from the Naples MS. Müller gives *quo submittat*. The others have *summittat*. In the next line all MSS. agree in *et*, for which Kuinoel, Barth, and Lachmann give *ut*. This is a question of considerable difficulty. The indicative in the first line may be taken either for *submittat*, according to the lax poetical usage sanctioned by Virgil, *Georg*. 1, 56, 'nonne vides croceos ut Tmolus odores, India mittit ebur?' cf. inf. 17, 6, and especially iii. 7, 29, and 26, 35; or we may understand *aspice flores, quos humus submittit*. Or again, if with Jacob and Lachmann we consider *sponte sua* to belong to *submittit* as well as to *veniant*, and so retain *et*, we must have recourse to the 'laxior orationis junctura' with which Jacob cuts the knot. I agree with Hertzberg in reading *ut*, and understanding *quos* as the relative, not as the indirect interrogative, and also in his judgment that '*et* hac sede non modo durum est, sed ne Latinum quidem.' *Submittere* is properly used of the earth which *sends up* (ἀναφύει) plants. So Lucretius, i. 7, 'tibi suaves dædala tellus submittit flores.'

11.] *Formosior* Kuinoel against all the MSS. *Felicius* Müller after Lachmann, as *formosa* occurred just before. In these beautiful verses the emphasis is of course to be placed on the words implying the absence of art; viz., *sponte sua*,—*solis*,—*indociles*,—*nativis*,—*nulla arte*, and the corresponding comparatives; *antris* is here used as i. 1, 11, *i.e.* 'mountain dells.'

12.] *indociles*, in reference to the water conducted in pipes from the aqueducts. So *nativis aquis*, v. 4, 4.

13.] *Collucent*. This is the reading of MS. Gron. and ed. Rheg. 1481. Cf. Cic. *de Nat. D.* ii. § 99, 'insulae litoraque collucent distincta tectis et urbibus.' The Naples MS. has *persuadent*, from which the ingenious and plausible reading *per se dent*, the correction of Scaliger, has been admitted by Barth and Kuinoel, with the change of *canunt* into *canant* in the next line. This, however, not only involves the correction of *lapillis* into *lapillos*, but introduces a sort of tautology by adding *per se* to *nativos*, as Lachmann has well remarked. The fact is, the construction here passes from the oblique to the direct, *i.e.* it no longer depends on *aspice*. *Persuadent* is not hastily to be rejected, since it is found in the oldest of all the existing copies. The sense would be, 'litora picta nativis lapillis persuadent tibi non nimis laborandum esse in cultu.' But the more regular word would be *suadent*; while *collucent* seems altogether appropriate and natural to the context. Palmer proposed *peraequalent*. Müller reads *praelucent* after Hertzberg.

15.] It was not thus, *i.e.* by dress, that Phœbe and Hilaira, daughters of Leucippus, attracted Castor and Pollux. Apollodor. iii. 10, 3. *Λευκίππου δὲ καὶ Φιλοδίκης τῆς Ἰνάχου θυγατέρες ἐγένοντο Ἱλάειρα καὶ Φοίβη. Ταύτας ἁρπάσαντες, ἔγημαν Διόσκουροι.* The maids had previously been betrothed to Lynceus and Idas. Ovid, *Fast*. v. 700. Apollodor. iii. 2. Theocrit. *Id*. xxii. According to Pausanias, lib. iii. cap. 16, there was a temple in Sparta to Hilaira and Phœbe, with certain priestesses attached who were called Λευκιππίδες.

Pollucem cultu non Hilaira soror,
Non, Idæ et cupido quondam discordia Phœbo,
Eveni patriis filia litoribus;
Nec Phrygium falso traxit candore maritum
Avecta externis Hippodamia rotis:
Sed facies aderat nullis obnoxia gemmis,
Qualis Apelleis est color in tabulis.
Non illis studium vulgo conquirere amantes;
Illis ampla satis forma pudicitia.
Non ego nunc vereor, ne sim tibi vilior istis:
Uni si qua placet, culta puella sat est.
Cum tibi præsertim Phœbus sua carmina donet,
Aoniamque libens Calliopea lyram;
Unica nec desit jocundis gratia verbis,
Omnia, quæque Venus quæque Minerva probat;
His tu semper eris nostræ gratissima vitæ,
Tædia dum miseræ sint tibi luxuriæ.

18.] *Eveni filia*, *i.e.* Marpessa. See Hom. *Il.* ix. 560, seq. Apollodor. i. 7, 8. *Εὐήνου μὲν οὖν ἐγένετο Μάρπησσα, ἣν, Ἀπόλλωνος μνηστευομένου, Ἴδας ὁ Ἀφαρέως ἥρπασε, λαβὼν παρὰ Ποσειδῶνος ἅρμα ὑπόπτερον. Ἴδας δὲ εἰς Μεσσήνην παραγίνεται, καὶ αὐτῷ ὁ Ἀπόλλων περιτυχὼν ἀφαιρεῖται τὴν κόρην.* It would seem, however, from an inscription on the carved chest of Cypselus, at Elis, preserved by Pausanias, lib. v. cap. xviii., that Idas eventually regained his bride, 'nothing loath:' *Ἴδας Μάρπησσαν καλλίσφυρον, ἅν οἱ Ἀπόλλων ἅρπασε, τὰν ἐκ ναοῦ ἄγει πάλιν οὐκ ἀέκουσαν.* *Patriis litoribus*, because the river Evenus was named after her father, who drowned himself therein, being unable to overtake Idas in the pursuit. *Litus* is therefore improperly used for *ripa*.

20.] *externis rotis*, by the stranger, Pelops in the chariot-race, Pind. *Ol.* i. 70.

21.] *Obnoxia*, 'indebted to.' So Virg. *Georg.* i. 396. 'Nec fratris radiis obnoxia surgere luna.'

22.] Apelles, the famous painter of Cos, is mentioned also in iv. 8, 11. 'In Veneris tabula summam sibi posuit Apelles.' This passage shows that his figures were admired for their simplicity and subdued colouring.

25.] *Ne sim tibi*. 'It is not that at present I have fear lest I should be held by you in less esteem than your other admirers are; (I only mean to remark) a girl is dressed well enough who pleases the eyes of one lover.' *Istis* is said with contempt of his real or supposed rivals. Cf. inf. 8, 3. ii. 9, 1. Kuinoel and Barth have perverted the sense by reading *ne sis mihi* with Scaliger and some later copies of no authority. But it may be questioned if we should not read interrogatively, 'Non ego nunc vereor, ne sim,' &c., 'Have I not now cause to fear, that I am held in less regard than those lovers of yours?' He thus goes on to say, '*If* you love me, dress only to please my eyes.'

27.] Especially, he adds, is dress unnecessary in the case of one who has such mental endowments as Cynthia. See ii. 3, 19—22. It seems best to connect these lines with 31—32, rather than with the preceding, which is the ordinary punctuation. Either however gives a fair sense.

32]. *dum*, dum modo, 'so long as (provided that) you hold in dislike finery that brings no happiness.' *Luxuriæ*. He indirectly warns her against being 'too gay,' *i. e.* inconstant to him. With all his romantic expression of regard, it is quite clear that neither Propertius was faithful to her (see next elegy, v. 36), nor she to Propertius (v. 8, 16, and ii. 6, 2).

III.

Qualis Thesea jacuit cedente carina
  Languida desertis Gnosia litoribus,
Qualis et accubuit primo Cepheia somno,
  Libera jam duris cotibus Andromede,
Nec minus assiduis Edonis fessa choreis
  Qualis in herboso concidit Apidano,
Talis visa mihi mollem spirare quietem
  Cynthia, non certis nixa caput manibus,
Ebria cum multo traherem vestigia Baccho,
  Et quaterent sera nocte facem pueri.
Hanc ego, nondum etiam sensus deperditus omnes,
  Molliter impresso conor adire toro.
Et quamvis duplici correptum ardore juberent
  Hac Amor hac Liber, durus uterque deus,
Subjecto leviter positam temptare lacerto,
  Osculaque admota sumere †et arma manu,
Non tamen ausus eram dominæ turbare quietem,

III. Few will have any difficulty in assenting to Kuinoel's introductory remark: 'Est profecto hæc elegia propter orationis directum et ornatum, pictorarum colorumque præstantiam, et dramaticam quasi repræsentationem suavissimis annumeranda.' It is an exquisite composition, and a finished picture. At the same time, it conveys the plainest proof that Propertius was a libertine, and that Cynthia knew it. He describes his feelings when, warmed with wine, he found his Cynthia asleep, and hesitated whether to wake or to watch her; not omitting to add her reproaches when she was aware of his late return to her.

2.] *Languida*, weary with watching and worn out with grief, as Andromeda was by terror and constraint.—*Gnosia*, the Cretan Ariadne.

4.] *Cotibus* is the reading of all good copies, and is here the same as *cautibus*, which Lachmann, Barth, and Kuinoel have edited. Compare *codex* and *caudex*. *Cautes* is a lengthened form of *cos* (*cotis*), as *plebes* is of *plebs*.

5.] *Edonis*, 'Ἠδωνίς, a Bacchanal.

10.] *Quaterent facem*. See on iv. 16, 16.

16.] The MSS. agree in reading *et arma*, except that one of the best (MS. Gron.) omits *et*. Kuinoel has admitted the ingenious, but violent correction of Gronovius, *ad ora*. This, as Lachmann remarks, would leave it ambiguous whether *manu* meant Cynthia's hand, kissed by Propertius, or that of the latter raised to the face of Cynthia. On the other hand, in v. 4, 34, 'dum captiva mei conspicer arma Tati,' we should probably read *ora* for *arma*. It must be confessed that *et arma* is difficult to explain. The best commentators agree in understanding it in a metaphorical sense; as a soldier *sumit arma* for battle, so the lover, who serves under the standard of Venus. Compare iv. 20, 20. 'Dulcia quam nobis concitet arma Venus.' *Sumere* must thus be taken in a slightly different sense, *i.e.* *carpere* oscula, *sumere* arma. Perhaps the original reading was some epithet as *larga*, or *amara*, a word which frequently bears the sense of *waspish*, *i.e.* 'kisses to my cost;' and this might be supported by v. 18. The obvious antithesis to the more natural epithet *dulcia*, would at once suggest this meaning. Müller reads *cara*, quoting from Tibull. i. 4, 53, 'rapies tum cara licebit oscula.'

Expertæ metuens jurgia sævitiæ:
Sed sic intentis hærebam fixus ocellis,
Argus ut ignotis cornibus Inachidos.
Et modo solvebam nostra de fronte corollas,
Ponebamque tuis, Cynthia, temporibus;
Et modo gaudebam lapsos formare capillos;
Nunc furtiva cavis poma dabam manibus,
Omniaque ingrato largibar munera somno,
Munera de prono sæpe voluta sinu.
Et quotiens raro duxti suspiria motu,
Obstupui vano credulus auspicio,
Ne qua tibi insolitos portarent visa timores,
Neve quis invitam cogeret esse suam.
Donec diversas percurrens luna fenestras,
Luna moraturis sedula luminibus,
Compositos levibus radiis patefecit ocellos.
Sic ait, in molli fixa toro cubitum:
Tandem te nostro referens injuria lecto

18.] *Verbera* is the reading of Kuinoel, from a late and worthless MS. All good copies agree in *jurgia*, which is perfectly unobjectionable.

21.] *Corollas*. Chaplets were worn at the banquet, and generally by the *comissantes* (κωμάζοντες) after a feast. In Plat. *Symph.* p. 213, A., Alcibiades in the same way takes the ribbands from his own chaplet and crowns the head of Socrates.

24.] *dabam*, etc., I stealthily placed apples in the hollow of her hand as she lay on the couch.

25.] *Munera*. Though *omnia* is poetically added, the apples are meant, which (as Kuinoel remarks) were the favourite offerings of lovers. The choice of epithets in this exquisite passage deserves attention.

27.] *Duxit* is the reading of the Naples MS. In any other poet than Propertius, who is fond of sudden transitions of this kind, the third person would be hardly compatible with *tibi* in v. 29. The meaning of the passage is this:—from Cynthia's sleeping sigh he derived a groundless omen that she was dreaming of violence offered to her by some importunate admirer, whom he supposes to be one of his rivals.

31.] *Diversas*, 'lectulo Cynthiae ex adverso oppositas,' Kuinoel. See inf. on 10, 16. Or it may mean, 'first one window and then another.' *Sedula*, 'officious;' in a bad sense, or possibly, 'lighting on,' ἐφιζάνουσα, in its literal sense from the root *sed*, ἑδ. Compare the use of *desidia*, 'a sitting down,' 15, 6. *Moritura lumina* are Cynthia's eyes, which would have slept on if the moonlight had not opened them. Compare 'victura rosaria Paesti,' v. 5, 61.

34.] *Fixa cubitum*, like *deperditus sensus* in v. 11, 'having my senses destroyed.' So *nixa caput*, v. 8, and *fusa brachia*, iii. 7, 24. This verse, like sup. 10, is faulty, not so much from ending with a word of three syllables, as from having no counterbalancing epithet in the former part. Cf. i. 4, ii. 22, vi. 16, 20, 22.

35.] The meaning appears to be,—'So then, you have only come to me at last, because you have been expelled by another.' *Injuria*, i. e. tibi ab alia puella illata. The editors find some difficulty in the word *expulit*, which may mean that he was excluded, or refused entrance, and so had to spend the night, as was the custom with importunate lovers, at the door in the open street, or (as the epithet *languidus* rather implies) that he was turned out, and the door shut against him, after having spent the greater part of the night in the house of another.

Alterius clausis expulit e foribus?
Namque ubi longa meæ consumpsti tempora noctis,
Languidus exactis, hei mihi, sideribus?
O utinam tales perducas, improbe, noctes,
Me miseram quales semper habere jubes!
Nam modo purpureo fallebam stamine somnum,
Rursus et Orpheæ carmine fessa lyræ;
Interdum leviter mecum deserta querebar
Externo longas sæpe in amore moras:
Dum me jocundis lapsam sopor impulit alis.
Illa fuit lacrimis ultima cura meis.

IV.

Quid mihi tam multas laudando, Basse, puellas
Mutatum domina cogis abire mea?
Quid me non pateris, vitæ quodcumque sequetur,
Hoc magis assueto ducere servitio?
Tu licet Antiopæ formam Nycteidos et tu
Spartanæ referas laudibus Hermionæ,
Et quascumque tulit formosi temporis ætas:
Cynthia non illas nomen habere sinet;
Nedum, si levibus fuerit collata figuris,

39.] Müller reads *producas* from the edition of 1661.

41.] *Purpureo stamine.* Cf. v. 3, 34. 'Et Tyria in radios vellera secta suos.' So Arete, the mother of the amiable Nausicaa, sate at the hearth ἠλάκατα στρωφῶσ' ἁλιπόρφυρα, *Od.* vi. 53.—*fessa*, i. e. when tired of spinning.

43.] *Leviter*, 'submissa et quasi suppressa voce.'—Hertzberg. This is the reading of all the good copies. Kuinoel and Lachmann give *graviter:* the latter, I think, rather through inadvertency than from deliberate choice.

46.] The meaning of this verse, as Hertzberg has explained it, is, that the last subject of care to her grief, before she fell asleep, was the infidelity of Propertius. Andrews, in his Dictionary, takes *cura* here for *medicina, curatio*. But the sense is simple and natural, 'sweet sleep at last brought an end to my cares;'—'beyond this, I had no care to cry about.'

IV. To Bassus. He was a man of noble birth, and a writer of iambics. Ovid. *Trist.* iv. 10, 47. 'Ponticus heroo, Bassus quoque clarus iambo.' It is probable that Bassus had endeavoured to draw away his friend from his infatuated attachment to Cynthia, by disparaging her charms, and that not from disinterested motives, as may be inferred from v. 20.

4.] *magis assueto.* Compare I. 26, 'neque assueto mutet amore locum.'—*Ducere* is the reading of the Naples MS., which Kuinoel and Hertzberg have adopted. Others give *vivere*.

5.] Antiope, daughter of Nycteus, was the mother of Amphion and Zethus, by Jupiter. She was ill-treated by Lycus, king of Thebes, and Dirce, his wife, and avenged by her sons. Apollodor. iii. 5, 5. Infra. iv. 15, 11. Hermione was the daughter of Menelaus and Helen. Hom. *Od.* iv. 14.

9.] 'Still less, if she should be compared with ordinary figures, would she

Inferior duro judice turpis eat.
Hæc sed forma mei pars est extrema furoris;
Sunt majora, quibus, Basse, perire juvat:
Ingenuus color et multis decus artibus et quæ
Gaudia sub tacita dicere veste libet.
Quo magis et nostros contendis solvere amores,
Hoc magis accepta fallit uterque fide.
Non impune feres: sciet hæc insana puella,
Et tibi non tacitis vocibus hostis erit.
Nec tibi me post hæc committet Cynthia, nec te
Quæret: erit tanti criminis illa memor;
Et te circum omnes alias irata puellas
Differet: heu nullo limine carus eris!
Nullas illa suis contemnet fletibus aras,
Et quicumque sacer, qualis ubique, lapis.
Non ullo gravius tentatur Cynthia damno,
Quam sibi cum rapto cessat amore deus,
Præcipue nostri: maneat sic semper, adoro;
Nec quicquam ex illa, quod querar, inveniam.

come off with discredit as inferior in the estimation of even a harsh judge.' *Figura* nearly corresponds with our familiar use of the word, as sup. 2, 7, iii. 17, 43. *Turpis*, like *αἰσχρός*, in its primary sense means 'ugly.' Kuinoel is scarcely correct in explaining it 'victa, pudore suffusa decedat.'—*duro judice*, even by a harsh and ungracious judgment.

13.] Keil and Müller read *calor* for *color*.—*artibus*, supply *quaestibus*, unless this be a rather harsh use of the ablative of quality, 'a grace of many winning ways.'

14.] *Sub tacita veste dicere*, 'to speak of with reserve.' *Dicere* is a probable emendation, preferred by most of the editors; though *libet* is rather in favour of the vulgate.

16.] 'Hoc magis uterque nostrum te fallet, constantes manebimus data acceptaque fide.'—*Kuinoel*.

19.] 'Non permittet ut tua in posterum consuetudine fruar.'—*Id*.

22.] *Differet*, i. e. diffamabit. Cf. inf. 16, 48; III. 14, 17. So the Greeks use *δυσφημεῖν* and *διαστρέφειν*.—*circum*, circumeundo.

22.] 'Nulla domo excipieris, janua cujusvis puellæ tibi claudetur.'—*Kuinoel*.

23.] Every altar and shrine, every *sacer lapis*, either Terminus or cippus, will be a witness to her denunciations of you. *Qualis ubique*, sc. in triviis stat. Cf. Tibull. I. 1, 12. So 'verbenis compita velo,' v. 3, 57. Keil and Müller read 'qualis, ubique, lapis,' *ὁποῖός τε καὶ ὅπου ἂν ᾖ*.

25.] 'Nothing distresses Cynthia so much as the feeling that she is slighted; and especially painful to her is the loss of my regard and the cessation of my visits.' *Rapto*, i. e. per rivalis artes subrepto.

27.] *nostro*, Keil and Müller.

28.] *Ex illa*. The English idiom is, *in her*. The Latin language in these cases expresses a part out of the whole. So Tacit. *Agric.* 4, 'retinuitque, quod est difficillimum ex sapientia, modum.' Where Ritter connects 'ex sapientia modum retinuit.' *inveniam* seems to be the future rather than the optative.

V.

Invide, tu tandem voces compesce molestas,
  Et sine nos cursu, quo sumus, ire pares.
Quid tibi vis, insane? meos sentire furores?
  Infelix, properas ultima nosse mala,
Et miser ignotos vestigia ferre per ignes,
  Et bibere e tota toxica Thessalia.
Non est illa vagis similis collata puellis;
  Molliter irasci non solet illa tibi.
Quod si forte tuis non est contraria votis,
  At tibi curarum milia quanta dabit!
Non tibi jam somnos, non illa relinquet ocellos:
  Illa feros animis alligat una viros.
Ah mea contemptus quotiens ad limina curres,
  Cum tibi singultu fortia verba cadent,
Et tremulus mæstis orietur fletibus horror,
  Et timor informem ducet in ore notam,

V. To Gallus. This man, who it appears from v. 23, was of noble birth, was a rival, if not a friend or relation of our poet. Hertzberg has a long and learned dissertation (Lib. i, cap. v. p. 21—2), to prove who he was not, which the reader may well be spared. Some have thought that he was the same as Ælius Gallus, whose wife is alluded to under the name of Arethusa, in the beautiful epistle to her husband, inf. v. 3. An estimate of his moral character may be formed from i. 13, 5. It would seem that he had made some proposals for an introduction to Cynthia, which were by no means agreeable to Propertius.

2.] *Pares*, *i. e.* sub æquo jugo. Cf. i. 1, 32.

3.] *meos furores*, the deep or mad attachment that I feel. Müller reads *meae*, *i. e.* dominae, after Hemsterhuis; but this seems a tame and very unnecessary change.

5.] *Ignotos per ignes.* 'To tread on hidden fire.' Hor. *Od.* ii. 1, 'incedis per ignes suppositos cineri doloso.' A danger familiar to those who lived in the volcanic regions of Italy.

6.] 'Thessalia ferax herbarum venenatarum. Cf. Tibull. ii. 4, 55, seqq.'—*Kuinoel.* (Quicquid habet Circe, quicquid Medea veneni, Quicquid et herbarum Thessala terra gerit).

7.] 'Do not infer, that because she is a mistress, she is therefore a common woman.' Such is clearly the meaning. See supr. on i. 1. For *non solet*, Barth gives *non sciet*, and so Kuinoel and Müller, from a MS. of no authority. *Tibi* (as Jacob has noticed), may be understood *ἠθικῶς*, *i. e.* acquisitively, you will find it in her way not to be gentle in her resentments. So iv. 9, 10, 'exactis Calamis se mihi jactat equis.'

10.] *Quanta*, more usually *quot milia*.

11.] *Relinquet ocellos*, *i. e.* tui juris esse non sinet. Cf. v. 1, 143. *Una* for unice, as frequently. So v. 6, 28, 'Nam tollit irates mobilis una Notos.' 'She has a peculiar power in enslaving and taming the fierce-minded.' The metaphor (as appears from *alligat*), is derived from a wild animal. See iii. 26, 48.

13.] *contemptus*, when on some occasion you have been slighted and spurned, *i. e.* even though at other times she is not *contraria votis*.

14.] *Cadent*, 'shall fail of utterance.' *Singultus* is the spasmodic stoppage of the voice, common in excitement.

16.] Hor. *Od.* iv. 2, 59, 'Qua notam duxit, niveus videri, cetera fulvus.' Fear will 'leave a mark,' as we say: but the Latins use *ducere* (*ἑλκύειν*) of anything extended in a line, as *fossam*, *murum*, &c.

Et quæcumque voles fugient tibi verba querenti,
  Nec poteris, qui sis aut ubi, nosse miser.
Tum grave servitium nostræ cogere puellæ
  Discere, et exclusum quid sit abire domum;
Nec jam pallorem totiens mirabere nostrum,
  Aut cur sim toto corpore nullus ego.
Nec tibi nobilitas poterit succurrere amanti:
  Nescit amor priscis cedere imaginibus.
Quod si parva tuæ dederis vestigia culpæ,
  Quam cito de tanto nomine rumor eris!
Non ego tum potero solatia ferre roganti,
  Cum mihi nulla mei sit medicina mali;
Sed pariter miseri socio cogemur amore
  Alter in alterius mutua flere sinu.
Quare, quid possit mea Cynthia, desine, Galle,
  Quærere; non impune illa rogata venit.

VI.

Non ego nunc Hadriæ vereor mare noscere tecum,
  Tulle, neque Ægæo ducere vela salo;
Cum quo Rhipæos possim conscendere montes,

20.] γιγνώσκειν οἷόν ἐστι τὸ ἀποκεκλῃμένον ἀπιέναι. Lachmann reads *domo*.

21.] *Nec jam....mirabere*, 'you will no longer, as so often before, express your surprise at,' &c.

22.] *Toto corpore nullus*. See iii. 13, 21.

24.] *Imaginibus*. See on iii. 4, 19.

25.] 'If the slightest clue is furnished to your evil practices, how soon will you be in everybody's mouth, and descend from your illustrious name.' 'De viro tanti nominis fies fabula et jocus.'—*Barth*. *Culpæ* may perhaps mean in particular his advances to Cynthia. *Rumor* appears to be opposed to *nomen*, but the precise meaning is a little obscure. The sense may be, 'how soon from that illustrious name you will become a subject of common gossip,' or, 'how soon your high reputation for success with women will be damaged by a repulse from Cynthia.' Inf. 13, 5, 'deceptis augetur fama puellis.'

31.] *Quid possit*, i. e. 'quas vires habeat accendendi amatores suos.'—*Barth*. *Non impune rogata venit*, i. e. venit et fert secum pœnam roganti, sollicitanti, tentanti, etc. But see inf. 10, 25, where *venit* is nearly a synonym of *est*. The elision of *impune* is remarkable, and indicates an early stage in the art of elegy-writing.

VI. To Tullus. Tullus was a friend and equal in age of Propertius; nephew of Lucius Volcatius Tullus, who was consul in the year 721 (*consule Tullo*, Hor. *Od.* iv. 8, 12), and proconsul of Asia. Hertzberg is inclined to think that the nephew was appointed legate in the province by his uncle. It is probable that this Tullus was one of the friends who endeavoured to divert Propertius from his attachment by recommending him to travel. See i. 1, 29. This is a beautiful elegy, and one that presents little difficulty to the student.

3.] *Rhipæos montes*, here put indefinitely for the extreme north, as *domos Memnonias*, Æthiopia, for the south. Hor. *Od.* i. 22, 6. 'Sive per syrtes iter æstuosas, sive facturus per inhospitalem Caucasum,'—a proverbial method of expressing the confidence of friendship, as Barth observes. Memnon is well known in mythology as the son of

Ulteriusque domos vadere Memnonias:
Sed me complexæ remorantur verba puellæ,
Mutatoque graves sæpe colore preces.
Illa mihi totis argutat noctibus ignes,
Et queritur nullos esse relicta deos;
Illa meam mihi jam se denegat; illa minatur,
Quæ solet ingrato tristis amica viro.
His ego non horam possum durare querellis;
Ah pereat, si quis lentus amare potest!
An mihi sit tanti doctas cognoscere Athenas,
Atque Asiæ veteres cernere divitias,
Ut mihi deducta faciat convicia puppi
Cynthia, et insanis ora notet manibus,
Osculaque opposito dicat sibi debita vento,
Et nihil infido durius esse viro?
Tu patrui meritas conare anteire secures,
Et vetera oblitis jura refer sociis.
Nam tua non ætas umquam cessavit amori,
Semper et armatæ cura fuit patriæ;

Aurora and Tithonus, *i.e.* 'a son of the east.'—*ulterius domos* is not a usual construction: the accusative appears to depend on the sense of *ultra*, while *ulterius quam ad domos* was in the mind of the poet. Or the sense may be, 'or even still further away to the far east.' Müller, after Haupt, reads *domo Memnonia*.—*nullos esse deos*, &c., 'complains that if she be deserted after all my promises, there are no gods the avengers of perfidy.'

7.] *Argutat*. Another form of this rare verb is *argutor*. Properly, 'speaks loudly of her love,' *i.e.* vehemently protests it, θρυλεῖ. From the analogy of *argutus*, it seems that the strictest sense is 'to talk in a shrill voice,' ἀπολαρυγγίζειν. See on el. 18, 30.

9.] The sense is, 'she tries various ways of moving me, by taunting me with indifference, and by the usual threats of an angry mistress.'—dicit mihi se non jam esse meam; she declares she is no longer mine, no longer reigns in my affections, if I relinquish her thus easily. Others understand *denegat se* 'Veneris gaudia negat;' but this would rather have been *denegat se mihi*, without *meam*.—*ingrato* is the reading of two inferior MSS. The better copies agree in *irato*, which seems destitute of any plausible sense.

16.] *Ora notet*, *i.e.* sua ora.

17.] *Oscula*, &c., 'And should declare that she owes (and will pay) kisses to any wind which shall prevent me from sailing.' Hertzberg correctly explains a passage about which difficulty has been causelessly made:—'Quid ait Cynthia? Oscula mea debentur a me vento, si se tibi opposuerit.'

19.] 'Do you endeavour to surpass the well-earned honours of your uncle (L. Volcatius Tullus), and in the capacity of legate, restore the laws to the allied cities in Asia which have forgotten them.' *Secures* is put for the proconsulship. Hertzberg understands *anteire* of the *præcedentis longi agminis officia*, Juven. x. 44, *i.e.* of the ceremonious respect paid to the proconsul by attendant friends and clients on public occasions. His note is a good one, as proving the custom; but the addition of *conare* seems fatal to this explanation, since there could be no *effort* in such service. The general sense is 'Do you, whose pursuits are so different from mine, go alone, and endeavour by your good conduct to rise to higher fame and dignity than even your uncle.'

22.] 'Patriæ armatæ, non Amori, servivisti; studium tuum omne in patria armis tuenda ac defendenda positum erat.' *Kuinoel*.—*cessavit*, vacavit, indulgebat.

Et tibi non umquam nostros puer iste labores
  Afferat, et lacrimis omnia nota meis.
Me sine, quem semper voluit Fortuna jacere,
  Hanc animam extremæ reddere nequitiæ.
Multi longinquo periere in amore libenter,
  In quorum numero me quoque terra tegat.
Non ego sum laudi, non natus idoneus armis;
  Hanc me militiam fata subire volunt.
At tu seu mollis qua tendit Ionia, seu qua
  Lydia Pactoli tingit arata liquor,
Seu pedibus terras, seu pontum carpere remis
  Ibis, et accepti pars eris imperii;
Tum tibi si qua mei veniet non immemor hora,
  Vivere me duro sidere certus eris.

VII.

Dum tibi Cadmeæ dicuntur, Pontice, Thebæ,
  Armaque fraternæ tristia militiæ,
Atque, ita sim felix, primo contendis Homero,—

23—30.] The depth of pathos contained in these fine verses shows the writer to have been a true poet. *puer iste*, Cupid; but *puer hic* is rather the sense required, and *iste* is sometimes laxly used in this sense, *e.g.* inf. viii. 46. 'Fortune,' says he, alluding to his comparatively humble birth (see iii. 16, 22, ib. 26, 55, v. i. 128) 'has willed that he should ever lie prostrate;' he begs, therefore, that his friends will not attempt to raise him. The metaphor is from a prostrate wrestler or gladiator.—*nequitiæ* implies a consciousness that the connection was illicit, and to be reprobated by his friends.

27.] *longinquo* is here for *longo*, *diuturno*; the confusion between words of *time* and *space* is sufficiently common.

30.] 'This is the only warfare fate has destined me to engage in,' *i.e.* amoris.

31.] *Tendit*, as extendit.—*tingit*, here in its proper use, being allied to the Greek τέγγει. Others refer it to the colour of the golden sands.

34.] *Ibis carpere*, see sup. i, 12. Hertzberg's explanation of the following words is satisfactory:—'pars eris imperii grati tibi, utpote viro bellicoso: unus imperantium eris.' Any one holding a situation—even a subordinate one—in a governor's retinue is *pars imperii*. Müller, in part following Lachmann, reads 'ut accepti sors erit imperii.' Compare inf. 21, 4.—*accepti* might perhaps be explained *accepti a te*, i.e. *tibi commissi*. So 'acceptas comas' (a villa) v. 11, 34.

VII. To Ponticus. This Ponticus was a writer of hexameter verses, and the author of a lost Thebaid. He is mentioned in Ovid. *Trist.* iv. 10, 47, already quoted on El. IV. The poem appears to be a reply to the exhortation of his friend to resign elegiac for epic composition.

2.] *Fraternæ militiæ*, Eteocles and Polynices, sons of Œdipus.—*tristia*, because fatal to themselves. The epithet is used however (as elsewhere *durus*) in opposition to *mollis versus* (v. 19). See inf. 9, 13, 'I, quæso, et *tristes* istos compone libellos, Et cane quod quævis nosse puella velit.'

Sint modo fata tuis mollia carminibus,—
Nos, ut consuemus, nostros agitamus amores,
  Atque aliquid duram quærimus in dominam;
Nec tantum ingenio, quantum servire dolori
  Cogor et ætatis tempora dura queri.
Hic mihi conteritur vitæ modus; hæc mea fama est;
  Hinc cupio nomen carminis ire mei.
Me laudent doctæ solum placuisse puellæ,
  Pontice, et injustas sæpe tulisse minas;
Me legat assidue post hæc neglectus amator,
  Et prosint illi cognita nostra mala.
Te quoque si certo puer hic concusserit arcu,
  Quod nolim nostros evolvisse deos!
Longe castra tibi, longe miser agmina septem
  Flebis in æterno surda jacere situ;
Et frustra cupies mollem componere versum,
  Nec tibi subiciet carmina serus Amor.
Tum me non humilem mirabere sæpe poetam;

4.] One might suspect a slight irony in this, as if in return for the *fastus* (v. 25) of Ponticus, and as a contrast to the prediction of his own immortality (v. 22). 'You rival Homer, if only your verses are destined to survive.' But the success of a poet is here spoken of as dependent on fate as much as on his own merits.

5.] *Consuemus* for *consuevimus* is probably a ἅπαξ λεγόμενον. Or is it an equally unique instance of contraction for *consuevimus*?—*in dominam*, i. e. ad expugnandam dominæ duritiem.

7.] 'I cannot, like you, indulge the bent of my poetical genius freely, but am obliged to make my verses (elegies) subservient to the expression of my grief, and in them to bewail my hard lot.'

11.] *Doctæ puellæ*, (dat.) i. e. Cynthia, herself a poetess and a musician, supra, 2, 27.—*solum placuisse*, to have been preferred to my rivals through the eloquence of my verses.—*laudent*, like *aiunt*, for *prædicent*.

16.] The MSS. agree in *evolasse*, which Jacob retains and attempts to explain. I cannot doubt that Lachmann, Barth, Hertz. and Kuinoel have rightly edited *evolvisse*. The sense is thus clear:—'If Cupid should hereafter strike you, as he has me; which however I trust that the gods who rule our destinies have not designed for you; then &c.' Müller reads, on his own conjecture, 'quo nolim nostros te violasse deos,' explaining *nostros deos* to mean 'Love and Venus.' Keil also retains *evolasse*. But the infinitive of *evolvo* is appropriate, the metaphor being taken from the thread spun by the Fates. Nor is there much force in Müller's remark, that Propertius does not elsewhere employ *diæresis* in the perfects of *solvo* and *volvo*.—*nostros deos* Barth and Kuinoel take for Venus and her attendant Cupidines. Rather, I think, the Fates who *in commune* govern the destinies of friends. Persius, *Sat.* iv. 45—50.

17—20.] 'You will then lament the late enslavement which forces you to lay aside your unfinished Thebaid, and to try, though without success, to write love ditties to your mistress.'—*longe*, i. e. longe absunt, in consequence of taking up a new subject.

18.] *Situ*, 'neglect.' Both *sinus* 'a nook,' and *situs* in its various senses, are from *sino* (*ἐᾶν* as opposed to *κινεῖν*). The 'site' of a building is the place where it is suffered to lie. The result of lying by is mouldiness or decay, the more usual sense of the latter word.

Tunc ego Romanis præferar ingeniis;
Nec poterunt juvenes nostro reticere sepulcro:
Ardoris nostri magne poeta jaces.
Tu cave nostra tuo contemnas carmina fastu:
Sæpe venit magno fenore tardus Amor.

VIII.

Tune igitur demens, nec te mea cura moratur?
An tibi sum gelida vilior Illyria?
Et tibi jam tanti, quicumque est, iste videtur,
Ut sine me vento quolibet ire velis?
Tune audire potes vesani murmura ponti?
Fortis et in dura nave jacere potes?
Tu pedibus teneris positas fulcire pruinas?
Tu potes insolitas, Cynthia, ferre nives?
O utinam hibernæ duplicentur tempora brumæ,
Et sit iners tardis navita Vergiliis,

22.] *Præferar*, i. e. tuo judicio. But, from the general sense which the words will bear, the poet passes to the prediction of his popularity with other youths in the same circumstances as Ponticus.

24.] *Jaces*. An expression of regret, like ὦ φίλε, κεῖσαι, Theocr. xxiii. 44.

25.] *Cave*. Similarly used i. 10, 21; iii. 4, 41. In v. 4, 48, 'tu cave spinosi rorida terga jugi,' there is a variant 'tu cape.'

VIII. This elegy, which is rather difficult, but very elegant, and full of feeling, is addressed to Cynthia (with what success appears from v. 27, &c.), to deter her from going a voyage to a half-civilised province with a certain Prætor, whom Propertius appears equally to hate and to fear as a rival. See on iii. 7, 1. 'Prætor ab Illyricis venit modo, Cynthia, terris.' *Ibid.* v. 8, he calls him 'stolidum pecus.' The circumstance affords us so clear an insight into Cynthia's real character, that it is surprising the editors should have generally failed to understand it.

3.] *Iste*, 'that lover of yours.' See sup. 2, 25. *Varronianus*, p. 311, ed. 2.

4.] *Vento quolibet*, i. e. without even waiting for a reasonable prospect of fair winds.

5.] *Tune.....potes?* 'Have you the courage to bear all the dangers and discomforts of such a voyage?' Cf. Pers. *Sat.* v. 146, 'Tun' mare transilias? tibi torta cannabe fulto Cena sit in transtro?'—*et*, for *etiam*. The editions, except Barth's, place no question at *ponti*.

7.] *Fulcire*, 'to press;' ἐρείδειν. This is a remarkable use of a word which usually means to 'support,' as a pillar props a roof. It may be explained on the statical principle that resistance is equal to thrust, i. e. if the roof presses on the pillar, the pillar presents the same counter-thrust both to the roof above and to the earth below. The explanation given by Barth is absurd:—'qui enim per pruinas nivesque incedunt, eorum pedes hauriuntur, atque ita recte pruinas superjectas fulcire dicuntur.' This double sense of a verb, arising from the association of ideas, is not without examples. Thus *arcere* to *keep off* or *away*, means to *keep in* (coercere) as a flock of sheep from a wolf: *arcendo* implies, as it were, the contrary action to *claudo*, not so much from its real meaning, as from the idea inseparable from it. Hertzberg reads *ruinas* with the best MSS. i. e. 'omne quod e caelo ruit.'

9.] *Hibernæ brumæ* is the stormy time of year at the winter solstice.

10.] 'That the sailor may remain inactive from the late rising of the Pleiads.' This constellation rises in spring and sets in autumn, so that while it is invisible the season is unfavourable for sailing.

Nec tibi Tyrrhena solvatur funis arena,
  Neve inimica meas elevet aura preces.
Atque ego non videam tales subsidere ventos,
  Cum tibi provectas auferet unda rates,
Et me defixum vacua patiatur in ora
  Crudelem infesta sæpe vocare manu.
Sed quocumque modo de me, perjura, mereris,
  Sit Galatea tuæ non aliena viæ;
Ut te felici prævecta Ceraunia remo
  Accipiat placidis Oricos æquoribus.
Nam me non ullæ poterunt corrumpere tædæ,
  Quin ego, vita, tuo limine verba querar;

11.] *Tyrrhena arena*, i. e. from the west side of Italy. The rhyming sound of these words induced Scaliger (followed, as usual, by Kuinoel), to introduce the correction *in ora*. They ought at least to have read *ab ora*. A similar instance is *absenti—venti*, I. 17. 5.

12.] *Elevet*, 'carry aloft,' i. e. irrita reddat. The use of this verb for 'to disparage,' Persius, *Sat.* 1, 6; inf. iii. 26, 58, is slightly different, being a metaphor from the lighter scale of the balance.

15.] *Patiatur*, i. e. unda. 'undam poeta precatur, ne committere velit, ut in litore desertus ipse—amicam crudelem frustra vocet.'—*Hertzberg*; who reads *patiatur* on the conjecture of Passerat. Nothing can be more awkward than 'non videam ventos subsidere, cum rates auferet unda et (cum) patiatur,' &c., nor is it easy to agree with him in explaining *infesta manu* by 'despecta et ludibrio habita' a Cynthia. It is quite natural, that a lover, when his mistress persists in leaving him in spite of all his entreaties, should make angry gestures to her with his hand, by way of finally denouncing her. The sense is:—'may the roar of the sea and the breakers allow my voice to be heard as I stand on the shore, to reproach you and call you cruel many times over (*sæpe vocare*), before the ship can get clear of the land.' Kuinoel's reading *ut me patiaris* is without authority. Müller, following Scaliger, transposes the couplet *atque ego* &c. to follow *vocare manu*; but it is difficult to see what advantage we get by this, which gives *ora* instead of *unda* as the subject of *patiatur*.

19.] *Prævecta* is the vocative; accipiat te, Cynthia, prævecta Ceraunia. This is more frequently substituted for the nominative than for the accusative, as Persius, v. 124, 'unde datum hoc sumis, tot subdite rebus!' *Id.* i, 123, 'audaci quicunque afflate Cratino Iratum Eupolidem prægrandi cum sene palles.' *Id.* iii. 29, 'Stemmate quod Tusco ramum millesime ducis, Censoremve tuum vel quod trabeate salutas.' Barth quotes Tibullus, i. 7, 53, 'sic venias hodierne.' Jacob, for once departing from the best MSS., admits the correction of Pucci, as possibly from the Valla MS., *per oras*. Müller, who objects to the vocative for the accusative, and still more to the perfect participle instead of the present, reads *post lecta Ceraunia*. It does not however follow, because *legere oram*, *litus*, &c., is in use, that *legere montem* would be correct. Oricos was a city of Epirus a little above Corcyra and the 'infames scopuli Acroceraunia.' (Hor. *Od.* i. 3, 20).—τὰ ἄκρα τῶν ὀρῶν ἃ Κεραύνια ὀνομάζουσι. Pausan. *Att.* 1, 13.

22.] The MSS. reading *verba querar* has been altered with much probability by Passerat, whom Müller follows, into *vera querar*, which Lachmann labours to refute, and corrects *fide* for *vita*. The meaning is, 'no new object shall engage my affections in your absence, or prevent me from throwing myself on your threshold and giving utterance to my grief.'—*verba queri* is thus opposed to *tacite queri*. We might, perhaps, read *acerba querar*, 'bitterly complain,' as we say. Hertzberg also admits *vera*; but his explanation of it is far-fetched:—'non alienus amor me ita corrumpet, ut tibi injuriam faciam, et ante tuas fores (ut solet improba turba) inique querar,' which, he adds, really means: 'querar quidem in limine, sed non nisi juste.' A simpler rendering would be, 'No other engagement shall prevent me from upbraiding you justly.' For a new love would induce him to resign a former one with indifference.

Nec me deficiet nautas rogitare citatos:
  Dicite, quo portu clausa puella mea est?
Et dicam, licet Autaricis considat in oris,
  Et licet Eleis, illa futura mea est.

Hic erit! Hic jurata manet! Rumpantur iniqui!
  Vicimus. Assiduas non tulit illa preces.
Falsa licet cupidus deponat gaudia livor:
  Destitit ire novas Cynthia nostra vias.
Illi carus ego, et per me carissima Roma
  Dicitur, et sine me dulcia regna negat.
Illa vel angusto mecum requiescere lecto,
  Et quocumque modo maluit esse mea,
Quam sibi dotatæ regnum vetus Hippodamiæ,
  Et quas Elis opes ante pararat equis.
Quamvis magna daret, quamvis majora daturus,
  Non tamen illa meos fugit avara sinus.
Hanc ego non auro, non Indis flectere conchis,
  Sed potui blandi carminis obsequio.
Sunt igitur Musæ, neque amanti tardus Apollo;
  Quis ego fretus amo: Cynthia rara mea est.
Nunc mihi summa licet contingere sidora plantis:
  Sive dies seu nox venerit, illa mea est;

23.] The impersonal use of *deficiet* is worthy of attention.—*citatos*, *i. e.* quamvis festinantes.—*Hertz.* Others understand it to mean *vocatos et compellatos*. I rather incline to the latter, on the ground of *tastem citare* being a conventional phrase.

25.] 'Whether she is staying, from stress of weather, among the Autarii in Illyria, or on the coast of Elis, she will yet be mine.' The common reading is *Atracis;* but as Atrax was a mountain in Thessaly, and the Autarii are mentioned by Strabo vii. v., Ἰλλυριῶν δὲ Αὐταριάται καὶ Ἀρδιαῖοι καὶ Δαρδάνιοι, Hertzberg is probably right in admitting the shrewd conjecture of Pucci in the edition of 1481. Müller reads *Autariis* and *Hylleis* (MSS. *hylsis*, or *hilsis*). With this verse Lachmann and others conclude the present elegy, though in all the MSS. it is continued as in the text. Jacob fancifully suggests that *jurata* in the next line appears to imply that the poet had just extorted from her own lips a promise to remain, as if the request had been preferred by him personally. The truth perhaps is, that the whole of the elegy was written after he had successfully dissuaded her, but in the former portion he sets forth the arguments used by him, in the form of a present appeal.

29.] 'My envious rivals may lay aside their mistaken joy at the expected separation.'

35.] *quam sibi*, sc. dari; though it is good Latin to say *nolo* or *malo mihi regnum*, &c.

37.] *Magna daret.* It is clear from III. 7, 43, that the Prætor, whoever he was, endeavoured to bribe Cynthia by his great wealth.

43.] *Contingere sidera.* A common way of expressing exultation. So Hor. *Od.* I. 1, ult. 'Sublimi feriam sidera vertice.' Theocr. v. 144, *ἐς οὐρανὸν ὔμμιν ἁλεῦμαι.*

Nec mihi rivalis certos subducet amores.
  Ista meam norit gloria canitiem.

IX.

Dicebam tibi venturos, irrisor, amores,
  Nec tibi perpetuo libera verba fore:
Ecce jaces, supplexque venis ad jura puellæ,
  Et tibi nunc quovis imperat empta modo.
Non me Chaoniæ vincant in amore columbæ
  Dicere, quos juvenes quæque puella domet.
Me dolor et lacrimæ merito fecere peritum:
  Atque utinam posito dicar amore rudis!
Quid tibi nunc misero prodest grave dicere carmen,
  Aut Amphioniæ mœnia flere lyræ?
Plus in amore valet Mimnermi versus Homero;
  Carmina mansuetus lenia quærit Amor.
I, quæso, et tristis istos compone libellos,

46.] *Ista, i. e.* hæc mea gloria. See sup. 6, 23.

IX. To Ponticus. This elegy announces the fulfilment of the prediction made in El. vii., that Ponticus with all his boasting would some day be overtaken by love. It appears that he was enamoured of a female slave of his own familia. This kind of attachment was considered peculiarly discreditable in an *ingenuus*. Hor. *Od.* i. 27, 15.

2.] *Libera verba.* 'That you would not always speak as freely and haughtily as you were wont.' The word *libera* introduces the metaphor which follows, and in which *jura* refers to the legal right of the master over the person of the slave. Cf. iv. 11, 2. 'Et trahit addictum sub sua jura virum.'

4.] Hertzberg alone defends the MSS. reading *quo vis* (*quævis*), understanding the sense to be 'quævis nuper empta nunc imperat tibi.' 'You are now so susceptible that the last female slave purchased into your family (*νεώνητος*) has an influence over you which makes her the mistress, you the slave.' Jacob and Lachmann, with Keil and Müller, adopt from Pucci *quovis modo*, 'to any extent,' 'ad arbitrium suum.'

5.] 'The very doves of Dodona are not better prophets than I in foretelling what youths each maiden is likely to enslave.'—*domet* must be for *domitura sit*, for otherwise there would be nothing to prophesy, but only something to observe.

7—8.] A beautiful couplet. 'I have learnt what love is in the school of adversity. O that I could unlearn it, and be again as a little child!'

9—10.] In allusion to the poem of the Thebaid which Ponticus was composing. See above, on El. vii.—*Amphioniæ lyræ.* Hor. *Od.* iii. 11, 2, 'movit Amphion lapides canendo.' *De Art. Poet.* 394. Infra, iv. i. 43, &c.—*flere*, flebiliter canere. K.

11.] 'Elegiac verses have more influence in love than heroic.' Mimnermus of Colophon lived about 600 B.C., and is said to have been the inventor of elegiac verse.

13.] Hertzberg has interpreted this verse, 'Go now and write those very poems (*i. e.* elegics) which you used to call contemptuously *tristes*.' Others take *compone* for 'lay aside,' *i. e.* in your scrinium, and *tristes libellos* for the dull Thebaid. But he well observes (1) that *componere* is the proper and conventional word for *scribere*, *συντιθέναι*; (2) that *i nunc* is often used in conveying a taunt; (3) that *istos* is the word of contempt formerly used by Ponticus to Propertius, and now retorted by the latter. There is weight in his arguments: nevertheless, I think the antithesis both here and elsewhere (see on iii.

Et cane, quod quævis nosse puella velit.
Quid si non esset facilis tibi copia? nunc tu
Insanus medio flumine quæris aquam.
Necdum etiam palles, vero nec tangeris igni;
Hæc est venturi prima favilla mali.
Tum magis Armenias cupies accedere tigres,
Et magis infernæ vincula nosse rotæ,
Quam pueri totiens arcum sentire medullis,
Et nihil iratæ posse negare tuæ.
Nullus Amor cuiquam facilis ita præbuit alas,
Ut non alterna presserit ille manu.
Nec te decipiat, quod sit satis illa parata:
Acrius illa subit, Pontice, si qua tua est;
Quippe ubi non liceat vacuos seducere ocellos,
Nec vigilare alio nomine cedat Amor;
Qui non ante patet, donec manus attigit ossa.
Quisquis es, assiduas ah fuge blanditias.
Illis et silices possunt et cedere quercus;

26, 44) between *tristis* or *durus* (epic) and *mollis* or *levis* (amatory elegiac verse), so marked, and the verses immediately preceding and following so strongly in favour of the old interpretation, '*sepone*, depone,' that I have not ventured to depart from it. Hertzberg admits that *omnes composui*, 'I have buried them all,' Hor. *Sat.* I. 9, 28, justifies such a sense.

15.] This seems a reply to a fancied objection made by Ponticus: '*You can't!* What would you do if a subject to write about were wanting, when even now you are puzzled what to say when over head and ears in love?'—*copia* here, as Hertzberg has shown, is *scribendi materies*. The passage is explained by 7, 19, 20, 'et frustra cupies mollem componere versum, nec tibi subiciet carmina serus amor.' Ponticus had been warned, that he had better practise elegy-writing against the time when he might require the aid of its persuasive eloquence.

17—18.] 'And even what you now feel is but a foretaste of the pangs of real love.'

22.] *Iratæ tuæ*, tuæ dominæ si quando tibi irascatur, iratam se ostendat.

23—4.] The meaning of these beautiful lines is well given by Kuinoel: 'nunquam Amor cuiquam amanti ita facilis est, ut non sæpius eum tormentis et cruciatibus afficiat.' The metaphor is taken from 'a wanton' who holds a bird in a silken thread, and lets it fly a little way only to pull it down again. I cannot believe that the poet had in mind the celebrated passage in the Phædrus, p. 251, B.—*alterna manu* does not mean *with the other hand*, but expresses the alternate action of the same hand which holds the string.

25.] 'Do not be deceived by the idea that possession will allay the anguish you are beginning to feel.'

27.] *Quippe ubi*, 'since in that case:' like *quippe qui*.—*vigilare alio nomine*, 'love does not allow you to be awake on any other account,' *i. e.* 'occupies all your waking as well as your sleeping hours with the thoughts of your mistress.' Hertzberg and others place an interrogation at the end of v. 28. 'Can love be expected to leave you, when your eyes hourly encounter the object of your regard?' thus making *vigilare* depend on *liceat*.

29.] *Manus attigit ossa*. Theocr. iii. 17, [illegible] καὶ ἐς ὀστίον ἄχρις ἰάπτει. Inf. v. 5, 64, 'per tenuem ossa mihi sunt numerata cutem.'—*patet*, viz. ipsi amanti.

30.] The MSS. have *aufuge*, which does not admit of an accusative case;—*ah fuge* Kuinoel, Lachmann, and Hertzberg, with the approval of Jacob.

31.] *Illis*. Not to the *blanditiæ*, but to the *assiduitas*;—cf. v. 5, 20.

Nedum tu possis, spiritus iste levis.
Quare, si pudor est, quam primum errata fatere:
Dicere quo pereas sæpe in amore levat.

X.

O jocunda quies, primo cum testis amori
Adfueram vestris conscius in lacrimis!
O noctem meminisse mihi jocunda voluptas!
O quotiens votis illa vocanda meis!
Cum te complexa morientem, Galle, puella
Vidimus, et longa ducere verba mora.
Quamvis labentes premeret mihi somnus ocellos,
Et mediis cœlo Luna ruberet equis,
Non tamen a vestro potui secedere lusu;
Tantus in alternis vocibus ardor erat.
Sed quoniam non es veritus concredere nobis,
Accipe commissæ munera lætitiæ:
Non solum vestros didici reticere dolores;
Est quiddam in nobis majus, amice, fide.
Possum ego diversos iterum conjungere amantes,

32.] *Spiritus . . . levis*, i. e. cum isto levi spiritu. So an ill-natured man is called σκαιαὶ φρένες, Theocr. xiv. 31.

33.] *Si pudor est.* 'If you are ashamed of loving a slave, and feel inclined to conceal the fact, be advised by me, and boldly avow it.'—*Errata*, a word properly used in this sense, like the Greek ἁμαρτίας, μάταν, Æsch. *Cho.* 904. Similarly *error* inf. 13, 35.

34.] *Quo in amore.* 'Conjungenda sunt hæc verba.'—*Hertzberg*. See on i. 13, 7, 'perditus in quadam.' Müller reads *quæ pereas*, i. e. *quæ puella*; and this seems very probable. 'To say, with whom you are enamoured, often brings relief in love.'

X. To Gallus. See above, on El. 5. It will be observed that Propertius speaks of him here as a friend, while before he assailed him with the bitterness of a rival. The ardent expressions in this elegy refer to an interview which Gallus had with his mistress, probably at a banquet, in presence of Propertius as a friend.

2.] *Conscius*, 'a witness,'—*lacrimis*, are 13, 15, 'vidi ego te—injectis flere diu manibus.'

5.] One MS. (Groning.) has *longam moram*. Perhaps the poet wrote 'vidimus in longam—moram.'

11.] 'Since you have not hesitated to make me a confidant, receive from me a return for having entrusted me with your joys.' This return is, the advice that Propertius thinks himself competent to give, should a quarrel occur between lovers.

13.] *Fide*, 'the power to keep a secret.'

15.] *Diversos*, 'separated.' Properly said of two persons who start from the same point in *opposite* directions; while *varius* or *varus* implies a path gradually diverging, like the letter Y. See Persius, *Sat.* iv. 12. Hor. *Sat.* i. 3, 47, 'hunc varum, distortis cruribus.' '*[illegible]*' Ovid, *Amor.* i. 8, 34. Hence *divaricare*, 'to stretch asunder,' as the legs of a compass; and *prævaricari*, said of a guide who deviates from the straight path, and so leads his follower wrong. 'Diversæ fenestræ' i. 3, 31, are 'opposite,' 'ex adverso patentes.' Tacit. *Ann.* iii. 2, 'etiam quo-

Et dominæ tardas possum aperire fores:
Et possum alterius curas sanare recentis,
Nec levis in verbis est medicina meis.
Cynthia me docuit semper quæcumque petenda
Quæque cavenda forent; non nihil egit Amor.
Tu cave ne tristi cupias pugnare puellæ,
Neve superba loqui, neve tacere diu;
Neu, si quid petiit, ingrata fronte negaris;
Neu tibi pro vano verba benigna cadant.
Irritata venit, quando contemnitur illa,
Nec meminit justas ponere læsa minas:
At quo sis humilis magis et subjectus amori,
Hoc magis effecto sæpe fruare bono.
Is poterit felix una remanere puella,
Qui numquam vacuo pectore liber erit.

XI.

Ecquid te mediis cessantem, Cynthia, Baiis,
Qua jacet Herculeis semita litoribus,
Et modo Thesproti mirantem subdita regno
Proxima Misenis æquora nobilibus,

rum diversa oppida, tamen obvii—dolorem testabantur,' *i.e.* towns *away from* which, rather than *towards* which, the funeral procession of Germanicus was directing its course.

19.] *quæ cuique petenda* Müller, who observes that the poet is here giving his own experience for the benefit of others.

21.] *tristi*, iratæ, when she happens to be cross or out of temper.

23.] *Verba benigna*, *i.e.* puellæ tuæ. 'Do not slight or treat with disregard her kind expressions towards you.'—*pro vano*, as if they had no sincerity in them. The whole passage probably refers to a *tristis puella*; and he here advises Gallus to meet with frankness any symptoms of returning tenderness, which his repentant mistress may exhibit.

25.] *Quando*, si quando, quotiens.—*venit*, see sup.

29.] 'That man will retain the object of his regard who shall prove himself at all times her devoted slave.' *Remanere*, noticed in El. 1, 31, is frequently *constans usus* in Propertius.

XI. Addressed to Cynthia while absent at Baiæ, and warning her, with all the earnestness of a jealous affection, to beware of the snares and gaities of that much frequented watering place.

1.] *Mediis Baiis*, midway between Misenum and Puteoli.—*semita*, &c. 'Semita illa Herculis montis jugum erat velut alta mole in mare jactum.'—*Hertz.* See iv. 18, 4. Strabo, lib. v. cap. iv., ὁ δὲ Λοκρῖνος κόλπος πλατύνεται μέχρι Βαιῶν, χώματι εἰργόμενος ἀπὸ τῆς ἔξω θαλάττης ὀκτασταδίῳ τὸ μῆκος, πλάτος δὲ ἁμαξιτοῦ πλατείας, ὅ φασιν Ἡρακλέα διαχῶσαι, τὰς βοῦς ἐλαύνοντα τὰς Γηρυόνου.

4.] For *proxima* Barth and Kuinoel read *et modo*, which was first introduced into the text by Scaliger from a late MS. Lachmann well observes that *subdita* is only applicable to *regna*. *Modo* would seem to imply that Cynthia occasionally made excursions from Baiæ to enjoy fine sea-views from other points. *Thesproti regno* is believed to be Puteoli; but the ancient historians afford no direct testimony in confirmation of the opinion. Müller

Nostri cura subit memores ah ducere noctes?
  Ecquis in extremo restat amore locus?
An te nescio quis simulatis ignibus hostis
  Sustulit e nostris, Cynthia, carminibus?
Atque utinam mago te remis confisa minutis
  Parvula Lucrina cymba moretur aqua;
Aut teneat clausam tenui Teuthrantis in unda
  Alternæ facilis cedere lympha manu,
Quam vacet alterius blandos audire susurros

reads *te Protei*, but *te* is certainly not wanted with the second participle, *ecquid te cessantem et te mirantem*, &c. Among the fifty sons of Lycaon, King of Arcadia, a Thesprotus is mentioned by Apollodorus, iii. 8, 1, but nothing further is recorded of him. The reader will probably be contented with the remark of Hertzberg: 'Itaque non tam testimonio egere, quam testem ipsum Propertium esse credam, illam Italiæ oram vel nescio cui Thesproto olim paruisse, vel a Thesprotis incolas accepisse, fontes vero, unde doctrinam eam hauserit, perditos esse.' The Roman poets, who delighted to exhibit their curious learning in Greek lore, had access to a number of writers whose works have long since perished, so that we can hardly expect to adduce direct proofs for every statement advanced by them. This remark is applicable, as we shall have occasion to notice, to many passages in Propertius.—A full account of Baiæ is given by Becker, *Gallus*, p. 85—97.

5.] The construction is, 'ecquid cura subit te, cessantem Baiis, ducere noctes memores nostri?' *i.e.* numquid curas ducere?—*ah ducere* is the correction of Scaliger for *adducere* or *educere* of the MSS.

6.] All the MSS. have *extremo*, which Passerat, followed by Kuinoel, has changed to *externo*, i.e. *alieno*. This alteration, however, gives a sense far from satisfactory; for not only does it too bluntly bring a charge of faithlessness against Cynthia, but it makes the poet ask the superfluous question, 'have you any room for me in your new regard for another?' Hertzberg suggests a meaning in which, in default of a better, I am inclined to acquiesce: 'have you any room left for me *in a corner of your love?*' 'In extremo certe angulo num sibi locus restet, modestius quærit.' Barth compares 'extrema linea amare.'—Ter. *Eun.* iv. 2, 12.

7.] *Nescio quis.* Said with marked contempt, as Kuinoel observes.—*sustulit*, has removed you from your place in my affections, and therefore from your place in my poems. Cf. v. 7, 50, where Cynthia says 'longa mea in libris regna fuere tuis.'

9.] Some commentators regard *confisa* as the vocative for the accusative, as supr. 8, 19. To me it appears clearly to agree with *cymba*, since a gondola 'relies' on its oars for safe guidance.—*moretur*, detineat, should amuse or engage your leisure-hours.

10—14.] 'I had rather you were cruising in the Lucrine bay, or indulging in the retired baths of Cumæ, than listening to whispered vows while softly seated on the shore of Baiæ.' It is altogether uncertain what is meant by *Teuthrantis in unda*: the reading itself is but a conjecture of Scaliger's for *trutantis* or *teutantis* of the MSS. Teuthras was a king of Mysia, where there was a city called Cumæ, which, together with that near Baiæ, was a colony of Chalcidians; hence both cities may have been called after this king. Hertzberg thinks Naples may be meant, which was originally a colony of Cumæans, (Strabo, v. iv. *μετὰ δὲ Δικαιαρχίαν ἐστὶ Νεάπολις Κυμαίων· ὕστερον δὲ καὶ Χαλκιδεῖς ἐπῴκησαν, καὶ Πιθηκουσσαίων τινὲς, καὶ Ἀθηναίων, ὥστε καὶ Νεάπολις ἐκλήθη διὰ τοῦτο*), and contained, according to the same authority, baths not inferior to Baiæ: whence *clausam* would mean 'within a covered swimming-bath.' This is by no means improbable; but I cannot concur in his opinion that Teuthrantis is an adjective, *Τευθραντίς*, agreeing with *lympha*. Kuinoel, without quoting any ancient authority, makes Teuthras the name of a small river some distance from Baiæ.

12.] *Manu* is for *manui*, the old, or rather the contracted, form of the dative, used occasionally even by Tacitus, as *Ann.* iii. 30, 33, 34; vi. 23, and others.

13.] *Susurros*, *ψιθυρισμούς*, *ψιθυρισμούς*. Words in both languages peculiarly used of lovers' converse.

Molliter in tacito litore compositam;
Ut solet amoto labi custode puella
Perfida, communes nec meminisse deos;
Non quia perspecta non es mihi cognita fama,
Sed quod in hac omnis parte timetur amor.
Ignosces igitur, si quid tibi triste libelli
Attulerint nostri: culpa timoris erit.
An mihi nunc major caræ custodia matris,
Aut sine te vitæ cura sit ulla meæ?
Tu mihi sola domus, tu, Cynthia, sola parentes,
Omnia tu nostræ tempora lætitiæ.
Seu tristis veniam, seu contra lætus amicis,
Quicquid ero, dicam: Cynthia causa fuit.
Tu modo quamprimum corruptas desere Baias;
Multis ista dabunt litora discidium;
Litora, quæ fuerant castis inimica puellis.
Ah pereant Baiæ crimen amoris aquæ!

16.] *Communes deos.* The gods mutually invoked as witnesses to vows made between two parties.

17.] The sense is; 'Not that my fears arise from any inconstancy in you; but in this place, *viz.* Baiæ, even the slightest attentions paid are to be dreaded.' *Amor* is here on the part of men, whom the poet hinted at in v. 13. Compare a similar irony supr. El. 2, 25. There seems no need to read *vereter* for *timetur*, with Lachmann and Müller.

21.] The best MSS. have *an mihi non*, which Pucci in the ed. 1481, altered to *aut mihi sit*, whence the corrected copies have *an mihi sit*—the reading of Kuinoel. Jacob gives from his own conjecture *haud mihi sit*, and in the next verse *haud sine te*, from one MS. (Groning.) Lachmann has *ah mihi non major*, and so Müller; but *ah non major sit*, &c. reads strangely to the ear. Keil gives *nunc mihi non major*, &c. The best correction, I think, is that of Hertzberg, who reads *nunc* for *non*, in the sense of the Greek enclitic *νῦν*. The direct interrogative use of *an*, it must be observed, is very rare. Professor Key (Latin Grammar, § 1421) denies that it ever is so used. It occurs however sup. 6, 18, and iii. 17, 23.

23.] *Parentes.* We know from v. 1, 127, that Propertius lost his father while quite a boy.

28.] All the MSS. have *dabunt*, which seems to bear the simplest sense, 'will give to many others beside myself.' Lachmann and Hertzberg read *debent* with Burmann from a late MS., and even Jacob approves. The ground of the alteration is, that the past tense, *fuerant*, immediately follows. But why not understand, 'Baiæ will yet cause many quarrels, as it *has heretofore*.'—*dissidium*, the reading of the Naples MS., seems more appropriate to *dabunt* than *discidium*, which the other editors prefer, Kuinoel excepted.

29.] On the pluperfect *fuerant* Hertzberg has a good note, in which he contends that the substantive verb may be so used, either alone or with a passive participle, for *erant*, but that the same licence does not extend to other verbs.—See inf. 12, 11.

30.] *Baiæ aquæ* for *Baianæ* is a bold expression. See note on v. 1, 36.—*crimen amoris*, 'of which love has so often had to complain.' Baiæ might be called *crimen* for *criminosæ*; but the genitive is added to show in what particular respect it deserves the bad character attributed to it. See an amusing epigram in Martial, I. lxiii.

XII.

Quid mihi desidiæ non cessas fingere crimen,
  Quod faciat nobis conscia Roma moram?
Tam multa illo meo divisa est milia lecto,
  Quantum Hypanis Veneto dissidet Eridano.
Nec mihi consuetos amplexu nutrit amores
  Cynthia, nec nostra dulcis in aure sonat.
Olim gratus eram: non illo tempore cuiquam
  Contigit, ut simili posset amare fide.
Invidiæ fuimus. Num me Deus obruit, an quæ
  Lecta Prometheis dividit herba jugis?
Non sum ego, qui fueram; mutat via longa puellas.
  Quantus in exiguo tempore fugit amor!
Nunc primum longas solus cognoscere noctes
  Cogor et ipse meis auribus esse gravis.

XII. To an anonymous friend, who had invited our poet into the country, and being unable to induce him to comply, had taunted him with his being a slave to Cynthia. The poet replies that she is far enough away, and laments that he has so far fallen from her affections.

2.] *Conscia Roma*, 'quæ amores meos, Cynthiam inclusam quasi habeat. *Conscia* enim sæpe poetis ea dicuntur, quæ aliquid in se continent, vel inclusum habent.'—*Kuinoel*. I am satisfied with this explanation. Not so Hertzberg, who by an error in judgment unusual with him, labours to prove, at some length, that the true reading is *conscia amore moram*, and he has actually introduced this alteration into the text. Müller so far follows him as to read *Cynthia amore moram*, the inferior MSS. giving *Cynthia* for *conscia*. The idea in the poet's mind was this: 'You accuse me of remaining in Rome from some secret motive which does not exist, and you call me 'a stay-at-home' (*deses*) for not leaving a mistress who all the time is far away.'

3.] *Illa*, Cynthia. Here again Hertzberg is at fault. *Illa*, says he, can only refer to Rome. The poet's mind was so full of Cynthia, that he most naturally speaks of her as *illa*.—*Hypanis*, a river of Scythia; (the Bog.)—*Eridanus*, a well-known name of the Po. The hyperbole in the distance is sufficiently manifest.

6.] 'Nor does the name Cynthia any longer sound sweet in my ears.' Others understand it: 'nor does she whisper sweetly in my ears,' *i.e.* prattle to me as before. Though this would more commonly be *dulce sonat*, there seems no reason why the feminine might not stand for the adverbial neuter. The poet however probably means, that he hears the name of his absent mistress with a pang, because it reminds him of lost affection. 'Non amplius mihi dulce est nomen Cynthiæ.'—*Barth*. Similarly ii. 1, 2, 'Unde meus veniat mollis in ore liber.' Hertzberg thinks it alludes to an *imaginary* sound of the name, for which he ingeniously quotes Lucretius, iv. 1058, 'si abest, quod ames, præsto simulacra tamen sunt Illius, et nomen dulce obversatur ad aureis.'

9.] *Invidiæ fuimus.* ἐβάσκηνεν ἡμᾶς ὁ θεός. This is generally read interrogatively,—the objection to which is that *num* would be out of place in the second question, 'an (obruit me) herba, quæ lecta &c., dividit (amantes)?' Plants gathered on Caucasus, on which Prometheus was chained, 'ex quo liquatæ solis ardore excidunt guttæ, quas saxa assidue instillant,' *Æsch. frag.* 179, were particularly used in incantations.

11.] Non sum *ille*, qui fueram.

13.] *Nunc primum*, &c., 'Now for the first time I am compelled to learn what it is to spend long nights alone, and to listen only to my own complainings.'

Felix, qui potuit præsenti flere puellæ;
  Nonnihil aspersis gaudet Amor lacrimis:
Aut si despectus potuit mutare calores;
  Sunt quoque translato gaudia servitio.
Mi neque amare aliam neque ab hac discedere fas est:
  Cynthia prima fuit, Cynthia finis erit.

XIII.

Tu, quod sæpe soles, nostro lætabere casu,
  Galle, quod abrepto solus amore vacem;
At non ipse tuas imitabor, perfide, voces;
  Fallere te numquam, Galle, puella velit!
Dum tibi deceptis augetur fama puellis,
  Certus et in nullo quæris amore moram;
Perditus in quadam tardis pallescere curis
  Incipis, et primo lapsus abire gradu.

15.] 'Happy he who has the chance of moving his mistress by the sight of a flood of tears.' Nonnihil, *i. e.* plurimum.—*Barth.* Lit. 'Love likes a few tears dropped.'

17.] 'Happy, too, if finding himself slighted, he can transfer his affections to another; for there is some pleasure even in a change of mistresses.' Kuinoel has a full stop at the end of v. 16, making *aut* commence a new sentiment: 'Or, (if that cannot be), should he be able to love another instead, there is some satisfaction,' &c.

19.] *Desistere* Müller, with Pucci, the Naples MS. giving *discedere*.

XIII. Addressed to Gallus (see on El. 5), on his having conceived an attachment for a woman of higher character than those with whom he had hitherto boasted of his acquaintance (v. 11). The person alluded to is the same as in El. 10, but certainly not Cynthia, as Hertzberg appears to suppose.

1.] *Lætabere*, 'will exult:' because Gallus had ridiculed the notion that Cynthia would prove as faithful to his friend as the latter had predicted. The absence of Cynthia at Baiæ is spoken of in the next verse, in which *abrepto* implies that a rival had supplanted him, in his (Gallus') imagination if not in reality.

3.] *Tuas voces.* The taunt alluded to, that she would soon leave him. These are the *voces molestæ* of El. 5, 1.

7.] *In quadam.* Hertzberg quotes many passages to prove that this is the usual form for expressing the strong devotion of a lover. He might have added Hor. *Od.* i. 17, 20, 'laborantes in uno Penelopen vitreamque Circen.' *Quidam* is here opposed to *quilibet;* a *particular* person to *any one*.

8.] Kuinoel and Lachmann with the inferior copies give *abire*. *Adire* is the reading of the good MSS. The sense would be, 'primo gradu lapsus, adis alteram pugnam, non victus discedis;' the *alteram* being naturally implied in the word *primo*. The metaphor is taken perhaps from the three throws which constituted a defeat in wrestling. So Gallus, once repulsed, again returns to the attack; so devoted is he to the new object of his affection. Hertzberg disapproves of this interpretation of *adire*, which is nearly that of Jacob, and says;—'hoc vult: Tu, qui antea in lubrica amoris via huc illuc desultare protervus solebas, nunc, dum adis puellam, primo gradu lapsus es, jaces, *ἀπεῖπας*,' (*i. e.* victus es). This however should rather have been 'incipis labi statim aggrediens,' not 'incipis aggredi statim lapsus.' It may be urged that *incipis* refers to *pallescere* rather than to *adire*,

Hæc erit illarum contempti pœna doloris:
  Multarum miseras exiget una vices.
Hæc tibi vulgares istos compescet amores;
  Nec nova quærendo semper amicus eris.
Hæc ego non rumore malo, non augure doctus;
  Vidi ego; me, quæso, teste negare potes?
Vidi ego te toto vinctum languescere collo
  Et flere injectis, Galle, diu manibus,
Et cupere optatis animam deponere labris,
  Et quæ deinde meus celat, amice, pudor.
Non ego complexus potui diducere vestros;
  Tantus erat demens inter utrosque furor.
Non sic Hæmonio Salmonida mixtus Enipeo
  Tænarius facili pressit amore deus;
Nec sic cœlestem flagrans amor Herculis Heben
  Sensit in Œtæis gaudia prima jugis.
Una dies omnes potuit præcurrere amantes;
  Nam tibi non tepidas subdidit illa faces,

which would have been *adis* had the metre allowed it. But this is so farfetched that I have preferred *abire*, 'to give up,' 'leave the arena.' And so both Keil and Müller have edited.

10.] *Multarum miseras vices*, 'retribution for the unhappiness of many.'

11.] *Compescet*, will check, put a stop to, those amours of yours with common women, πανδήμους ἔρωτας.

13.] *Rumore malo*, 'ill-natured gossip.'

15—17.] See above, 10, 5, &c. *Optatis labris* are simply the lips he had longed for, and of which he is unwilling, as it were, to resign the possession. If any alteration is necessary, *apertis* is perhaps more probable than *absentis*, Hertzberg's conjecture, who quotes against Burmann's emendation and in favour of his own, passages from the Greek poets which tell exactly the other way. The MSS. however agree in *verbis*, which is perplexing enough. But the sentiment is so familiar with the Greek epigrammatists and amatory writers, that Hertzberg seems to have judged rightly in reading *labris*, especially as Passerat professed to have found it 'in libro vetusto.' So also Keil and Müller.

21.] Neptune, assuming the form of the Thessalian river Enipeus, ravished Tyro, daughter of Salmoneus, who had been enamoured of the river-god. *Mixtus*, 'miscuisse se deum marinum fluvio egregie dicit, ad significandam liquidam deorum naturam.'—*Hertzberg*. Apollodor. i. 9, 8. Τυρὼ ἡ Σαλμωνέως θυγάτηρ καὶ Ἀλκιδίκης, παρὰ Κρηθεῖ τῷ Σαλμωνέως ἀδελφῷ τρεφομένη, ἔρωτα ἴσχει Ἐνιπέως τοῦ ποταμοῦ καὶ συνεχῶς ἐπὶ τὰ τούτου ῥεῖθρα φοιτῶσα, τούτοις ἐπωδύρετο. Ποσειδῶν δὲ εἰκασθεὶς Ἐνιπεῖ συγκατεκλίθη αὐτῇ. *Tænarius deus*, οὑπὶ Ταινάρῳ θεός, Arist. *Acharn.* 510. Pausan. iii. 12, 5. τούτων δ' οὐ πόρρω τέμενος Ποσειδῶνος Ταιναρίου. Ταινάριον γὰρ ἐπονομάζουσιν.

24.] *In Œtæis.* 'Sic libri omnes. Scaliger correxit *ab Œtæis*. At ista vis est. Recitius Propertium dices fabulam secutum esse, qua Hercules in ipso Œta, rogo evicto et mortalitate abdicata, Juventæ nuptiæ haud insulso commento narrarentur.'—*Hertzberg*. Müller reads *ab Œtæis —rogis*, the last word being a conjecture (a very needless one, I think,) of Schrader's.

25.] 'Sententia: Tu una hac die omnes superare amantes potuisti.'—*Hertzberg*. 'Eleganter tempori tribuit quod erat hominis.'—*Kuinoel*. For *amantes* Keil and Müller read *amores*, which seems the reading of the best copies.

Nec tibi præteritos passa est succedere fastus,
  Nec sinet abduci: te tuus ardor aget.
Nec mirum, cum sit Jove digna et proxima Ledæ,
  Et Ledæ partu, gratior una tribus,
Illa sit Inachiis et blandior heroinis,
  Illa suis verbis cogat amare Jovem.
Tu vero quoniam semel es periturus amore,
  Utere: non alio limine dignus eras.
Quæ tibi sit felix, quoniam novus incidit error;
  Et quodcumque voles, una sit ista tibi.

XIV.

Tu licet abjectus Tiberina molliter unda
  Lesbia Mentoreo vina bibas opere,

27.] *Fastus.* See on I, 8.—*succedere*, 'to come over you again,' *i. e.* she will not allow you to slight her as you have done others. Kuinoel takes the word in a very different sense: 'bene et prospere tibi evenire,' 'to succeed.'—*abduci*, to be drawn away by any new attachment.

30.] Müller adopts the reading of the Naples MS., *Jove digna proxima Ledæ.* Hertzberg's correction (*Ledæ e partu*) and explanation of this difficult passage appear to me equally unsuccessful. In defence of the former indeed he alleges the authority of one inferior MS., and argues that Propertius would have used the Greek genitive *Ledes* unless constrained by metrical necessity. The newly-found mistress of Gallus, whom he strangely conceives to be Cynthia herself, is called (he tells us) 'a second Helen' (una e Ledæ partu), who is handsomer than the real Helen, her sister Clytæmnestra, and their mother Leda. Nothing, as it seems to me, can be more awkward than this. The poet says she is worthy to be, what Leda was, the consort of Jove; coming next after Leda in deserving that honour, Leda's own offspring from Jove being of course excepted, and more *winning and agreeable* (he does not say *pulchrior*) than all three. It is probable, as Kuinoel observes, that Propertius here uses the very terms of commendation bestowed by his friend: 'and no wonder, since, as you say, &c.'—*partu* is for *partui*, as *manu* for *manui* sup. 11, 12. It is easy to account for the exaggerated praises the poet bestows on the lady of whom Gallus is enamoured. Knowing or suspecting his former partiality for Cynthia (see on El. 6), he is naturally anxious to extol the charms of any one else, in order to divert the fickle mind of his friend from thinking any more of Cynthia. And this seems the very point of vv. 33, 34, where *non alio limine dignus* clearly means 'Cynthia was no match for you in birth.'

31.] *Inachiis*, 'Grecian.' Inachus was the first king of Argos. Cf. inf. 16, 72.

34.] *Utere*, 'make the most of it.' Some earlier editions give *urere*.—*semel*, in the preceding verse, is 'for once at all events.'

35.] Lachmann, Hertzberg, Keil, Müller, and Jacob read—'Quæ tibi sit, felix' &c., which seems a perverse punctuation of a simple sentence: 'since you *have* at length found a worthy mistress, I wish you all happiness in the possession of her.'—*error*, see on *erravit* sup. 9, 33.

36.] *Quæcumque* Muller, after Dousa, the Naples MS. giving *quæcumque*. This is plausible, from the antithesis: 'may she alone be to you all (*i. e.* parents, sister, &c.) that you can wish.'

XIV. This elegant little poem is addressed to Tullus (see on El. 6) at his villa on the bank of the Tiber. The poet prefers his own happiness in the affection of Cynthia to the splendour and luxury of wealth.

2.] *Mentoreo opere.* Mentor was celebrated for designing and working cups and bowls in raised or embossed devices (*opus cælatum*). See inf. iv. 9, 13. Juven. viii. 104, 'raræ sine Mentore mensæ.' He lived B.C. 400—360.

Et modo tam celeres mireris currere lintres,
  Et modo tam tardas funibus ire rates,
Et nemus omne satas intendat vertice silvas,
  Urgetur quantis Caucasus arboribus:
Non tamen ista meo valeant contendere amori;
  Nescit Amor magnis cedere divitiis.
Nam sive optatam mecum trahit illa quietem,
  Seu facili totum ducit amore diem,
Tum mihi Pactoli veniunt sub tecta liquores,
  Et legitur rubris gemma sub æquoribus;
Tum mihi cessuros spondent mea gaudia reges;
  Quæ maneant, dum me fata perire volent!
Nam quis divitiis adverso gaudet Amore?
  Nulla mihi tristi præmia sint Venere.
Illa potest magnas heroum infringere vires;
  Illa etiam duris mentibus esse dolor:
Illa neque Arabium metuit transcendere limen,
  Nec timet ostrino, Tulle, subire toro,
Et miserum toto juvenem versare cubili:
  Quid relevant variis serica textilibus?
Quæ mihi dum placata aderit, non ulla verebor
  Regna nec Alcinoi munera despicere.

4.] *Funibus ire.* Towers of boats were called *helciarii*, Mart. ep. iv. 64, 22. The antithesis is 'tam celeres (remis), tam tardas funibus.'

5.] *Et* (licet) *omne nemus*, &c. 'Though all the woodland round you should wave with trees as large as those on Caucasus.' With *vertice* apply from the context *tam alto*. Kuinoel explains 'extendat, ut late conspicuum tollant verticem.'—*satæ silvæ* are *plantations*, as distinct from natural forests, with which he compares them in luxuriant growth.

7.] *Contendere*, 'all those charms that you enjoy cannot (in the happiness they confer) compete with my love.'—*nescit cedere*, i. e. non vult superari; feliciorem se prædicat.

11.] 'The gold-bearing waters of Pactolus seem to bring their wealth to my house.'

12.] *Gemma.* Perhaps the *concha Erycina*, inf. iv. 13, 6, pearls or mother-of-pearl. Hertzberg however well observes that the poet may mean jewels from the East, which the Romans fancied were washed up by the sea, and which even Gray has ventured to say that 'the dark unfathomed caves of ocean bear.'—*rubris æquore* means the Erythræan sea, or Indian ocean. So iii. 7, 17. 'Semper in Oceanum mittit me quærere gemmas.' Martial (v. ep. 37), speaks of 'lapilli Erythræi.' Cf. Tibull. ii. 2, 16.

13.] *Spondent*, &c. 'Assure me that kings themselves are less happy than I.'

15.] 'For who can take pleasure in riches, if unfortunate in his love?' *Nulla præmia*, i. e. nullæ opes.

19.] 'No self-control, no age, no amount of wealth secures the possessor against the assaults of love.' *Arabium limen*, made of a kind of precious onyx. The commentators refer to Pliny, *N. H.* xxxvi. 12.

21.] *toto cubili*, on both sides of the bed, the *pluteus* and *sponda*. See the note on v. 3, 31, 'et queror in toto non sidere pallia lecto.'—*serica*, the dyed or embroidered silken coverlets, *stragula*, often mentioned by Martial as very costly.

24.] For *nec* some copies have *vel*. Hence Müller reads *aut*, to the detriment of the verse and with no gain to the Latinity.

XV.

Sæpe ego multa tuæ levitatis dura timebam,
  Hac tamen excepta, Cynthia, perfidia.
Aspice me quanto rapiat Fortuna periclo:
  Tu tamen in nostro lenta timore venis;
Et potes hesternos manibus componere crines,
  Et longa faciem quærere desidia,
Nec minus Eois pectus variare lapillis,
  Ut formosa novo quæ parat ire viro.
At non sic Ithaci digressu mota Calypso
  Desertis olim fleverat æquoribus:
Multos illa dies incomptis mœsta capillis
  Sederat, injusto multa locuta salo;
Et, quamvis numquam posthac visura, dolebat
  Illa tamen longæ conscia lætitiæ.
Nec sic Æsoniden rapientibus anxia ventis
  Hypsipyle vacuo constitit in thalamo:

XV. Addressed to Cynthia, to upbraid her for indifference when the poet was on the eve of a voyage, probably that spoken of in El. 17. An elegy of great pathos, cleverness, and beauty, but of some difficulty.

1.] *Multa dura.* Cf. inf. 18, 13, 'multa aspera.' The MS. Groning. has *jura*.

5.] *Hesternos.* A beautiful expression, for 'quod ita mansit, ut heri erat.' *Hertz.*, who quotes, after Broukhusius, Ovid, *A. A.* iii. 154, 'Et neglecta decet multas coma: sæpe jacere hesternam credas; illa repexa modo est.' Martial, 'non hesterna sedet lunata lingula planta.'—An equally elegant term is *faciem quærere*, 'to adorn your person.' *Desidia* is here used literally, 'sitting at the toilet.'

7.] *Nec minus*, viz. than if I were to stay at home with you.—*Variare*, 'de smaragdi atque electri vicibus intelligo in monili conjunctorum.'—*Jacob.* The word is properly used (both actively and in a neuter sense) rather of *changing tints* (*e. g.* of ripening grapes, the hues of the clouds, sea, and foliage), than in the meaning either of *αἰόλλειν*, 'to diversify with alternate stripes,' or *ποικίλλειν*, 'to bespangle.'

9.] 'It was not after this fashion that Calypso bewailed the departure of Ulysses.' *Od.* vii. 244, &c. See iii. 12, 13.

10.] *Desertis æquoribus*, on the solitary shore, or on the shore of the desert sea.

11—12.] *Multos—multa*, 'Many days did she sit and many words did she utter.' Müller, whose poetic sense does not seem very high, says the repetition 'valde displicet,' and proposes *tenens* for *multa*.

12.] *Injusto, i. e.* sibi, 'cruel, inflicting a wrong on her,' by favouring the departure of Ulysses.

13—14.] 'Though about to lose him for ever, (and so having less concern in his safety than Cynthia has in mine) she wept from the recollection of past happiness.' He means to say that Cynthia ought to do the same if only from remembering the past, even though she had lost her regard for him henceforth.

15—16.] These verses ought probably to be placed after v. 20, or v. 22, as the commentators have perceived. For it is clear that *nec sic* in v. 17 should follow the example introduced by *at non sic* v. 9. and Keil and Müller have transferred them after v. 20. Alphesibœa had married Alcmæon, son of Eriphyle and Amphiaraus, who afterwards took Callirhoe for a second wife. The brothers of Alphesibœa killed

Hypsipyle nullos post illos sensit amores,
  Ut semel Hæmonio labuit hospitio.
Alphesibœa suos ulta est pro conjuge fratres,
  Sanguinis et cari vincula rupit Amor.
Conjugis Evadne miseros elata per ignes
  Occidit, Argivæ fama pudicitiæ.
Quarum nulla tuos potuit convertere mores,
  Tu quoque uti fieres nobilis historia.
Desine jam revocare tuis perjuria verbis,
  Cynthia, et oblitos parce movere deos:
Audax, ah nimium nostro dolitura periclo,
  Si quid forte tibi durius inciderit!
Multa prius vasto labentur flumina ponto,

Alcmæon for his perfidy, and were themselves put to death by her to avenge her faithless husband. See Ovid, *Met.* ix. 408. The story is somewhat differently told by Apollodorus iii. 7, 5.

17—20.] Hypsipyle, queen of Lemnos, was enamoured of Jason. The legend is well known from Ovid's Epistle 'Hypsipyle Jasoni,' (*Heroid.* vi.) Apollodor. I. 9, 17, *οὗτοι ναυαρχοῦντος Ἰάσονος ἀναχθέντες προσίσχουσι Λήμνῳ. Ἔτυχε δὲ ἡ Λῆμνος ἀνδρῶν τότε οὖσα ἔρημος, βασιλευομένη δὲ ὑπὸ Ὑψιπύλης τῆς Θόαντος.—Ὑψιπύλη δὲ Ἰάσονι συνευνάζεται, καὶ γεννᾷ παῖδας Εὔνηον καὶ Νεβροφόνον.*

21.] Evadne, the wife of Capaneus, who was killed by lightning in the siege of Thebes, threw herself on the burning pile of her husband. Apollod. iii. 7, 1, *τῆς δὲ Καπανέως καιομένης πυρᾶς, Εὐάδνη ἡ Καπανέως μὲν γυνὴ θυγάτηρ δὲ Ἴφιος, ἑαυτὴν βαλοῦσα συγκατεκαίετο.* See Eurip. *Suppl.* ad fin. *Elata per ignes*, *i. e.* mortem sibi consciscens inter ignes. See on iv. 13, 24, v. 4, 20. Hertzberg suspects that *elata* here means *insaniens*, *ἐμβακχιωσαμένη*. *Argivæ* is here put for *Grecian*, as sup. 13, 31; iii. 17, 43. Argos anciently comprised the greater part of Greece north of the Peloponnesus. See Æsch. *Suppl.* 250 and the note.

23.] 'Not one of whom could induce you to follow her example, viz. of constancy and devotion to one man, and render yourself illustrious in history.'

25.] 'Make no more vain professions of fidelity, which is but to revive the memory of your past perjuries (false oaths of affection), and cease to provoke the gods who have forgiven the past.'—*oblitos*, because the gods were supposed to take little heed of lovers' broken vows. 'Jupiter ex alto perjuria ridet amantum,' Ovid, *A. A.* I. 613. See iii. 7, 47.

27.] *Audax*, *i. e.* in tempting the gods.—*dolitura*, &c., 'dolebis laboribus nostris, si morbo forte aut alio malo tentabere; hoc enim tua in me injuria meritam sentias.'—*Lachmann.* 'Si perfidiam tuam dii, quos tu nimium audax irritas, punient, dolitura recordaberis mei periculi, desidiæ perfidiæque tuæ.'—*Kuinoel.*—*doleo* sometimes governs the ablative, as Virg. *Æn.* I. 669, 'nostro doluisti sæpe dolore.'—*nostro periclo* simply means the danger before alluded to in v. 3; and the poet says that Cynthia, now so coldly indifferent to it, will be sorry for it when she herself shall be in trouble, because she will reproach herself then for her heartlessness: her sympathy will be too late, and only given when she feels the want of it herself.

29.] The MSS. agree in *multa*. Kuinoel, Barth, Keil, Muller, and Lachmann adopt the unsatisfactory emendation of Muretus, *muta*. It is all but absurd to say, 'sooner shall rivers flow noisclessly to the sea, than,' &c., because that is what half the rivers in the world do already. Barth's brief note is amusing: 'De absurdo hujusmodi nihil attinet dicere.' I formerly felt convinced that *nulla* is right, the reading of Passerat, professedly from a 'vetus codex,' 'sooner shall no rivers flow,' *i. e.* as we should rather say, 'rivers shall cease to flow.' But I now think *multa* may be retained, and that the sense is *ἄνω ποταμῶν ἱερῶν χωροῦσι παγαί*, Eur. *Med.* 409, 'Many rivers shall sooner flow *from* the waste sea,' instead of into them,

Annus et inversas duxerit ante vices,
Quam tua sub nostro mutetur pectore cura;
Sis quodcumque voles, non aliena tamen.
Nam mihi ne viles isti videantur ocelli,
Per quos sæpe mihi credita perfidia est!
Hos tu jurabas, si quid mentita fuisses,
Ut tibi suppositis exciderent manibus.
Et contra magnum potes hos attollere Solem?
Nec tremis admissæ conscia nequitiæ?
Quis te cogebat multos pallere colores,
Et fletum invitis ducere luminibus?
Quis ego nunc pereo, similes moniturus amantes:
O nullis tutum credere blanditiis!

XVI.

Quæ fueram magnis olim patefacta triumphis,
Janua Tarpeiæ nota pudicitiæ,

'and the year shall sooner have the seasons go in inverted order,' *e.g.* summer shall succeed to autumn, and spring to summer.

32.] *Non aliena tamen*, supply *mihi amissa eris*.

33.] The MSS. have *ne*, which Pucci in the ed. 1481, corrected to *me*, *i.e. vel*. Lachmann gives *Nam mihi me*, &c., and so Keil and Müller. 'For never be it said that I hold cheap those dear eyes of yours, that have so often made me believe you when you swore falsely. You said, with an oath on them, that *if you had deceived me, you hoped they would fall out of their sockets into the hands held to catch them.*' Barth and Kuinoel read *Quamvis mihi*, which is perhaps right.

38.] *Admissæ nequitiæ* can hardly mean 'perjury' alone. He appears to charge Cynthia with having broken her promise to him by having granted her favours to another.

39.] 'You cannot say that I forced you to weep, and therefore when you so changed colour and shed tears, you did so from a consciousness at the time that you were deceiving me.'—*multos colores* refers to the sudden change from blushing to paleness, usual in strong excitement. This expression has been cavilled at by Markland as 'mire dictum.' There is severe truth in the rejoinder of Hertzberg: 'Non deesse scio, qui non licere posse credant, quod alius antea non dixerit.' See note on v. 7, 82.

41.] *Nunc*, etiam nunc, *i.e.* after all your frailties.—*similes*, equally credulous with myself.—*O nullis*, &c. is the *monitum*, in the form of a maxim, offered to all lovers. See 20, 3.

XVI. The *persona loquens* in this elegant poem is the door of a house, traditionally said to have been that of the Vestal Tarpeia (see v. 4), but now occupied by a female of no reputation. That *janua* cannot mean the triumphal gateway (*porta*) into the Capitol is evident, as the Commentators have observed, from the fact that the former term is confined to the door of a private house. It is not improbable that *indirectly*, *i.e.* by mentioning a different house, the poet may allude to Cynthia's obduracy. Such a house may have stood on the *sacra via*, and so, at least, have witnessed many processions to the Capitol.

1.] 'Patefactam januam triumphis interpretor, ut dominum læta familia exciperet a clientibus domum deductum, simul vero titulos spoliaque recepta, quibus atrium et vestibula ornaret.'—*Hertzberg*.

2.] 'The chastity of Tarpeia' is here put by a well-known figure for 'the chaste Tarpeia.' Whether this was the Vestal Virgin, whose broken vows and love for Titus Tatius, so beautifully described in the fourth elegy of the fifth book, scarcely

Cujus inaurati celebrarunt limina currus,
  Captorum lacrimis humida supplicibus,
Nunc ego, nocturnis potorum saucia rixis,
  Pulsata indignis sæpe queror manibus;
Et mihi non desunt turpes pendere corollæ
  Semper, et exclusi signa jacere faces.
Nec possum infamis dominæ defendere noctes
  Nobilis obscœnis tradita carminibus;—
Nec tamen illa suæ revocatur parcere famæ,
  Turpior et secli vivere luxuria.
Has inter gravibus cogor deflere querellis,

entitle her to the fame of *pudicitia*; or whether some other possessor of the Tarpeia gens is here meant, as Hertzberg supposes, is a question which it would be vain to discuss.

3—4.] *Cujus—limina*, the threshold of which was once crowded with gilt cars, and wet with the tears of suppliants. The triumphal car was deposited in front of the *janua*, in the vestibule of the house, which is here alluded to under the word *limina*. 'Stantes in curribus Æmilianos,' Juven. *Sat.* viii. 3, and vii. 125, 'alti Quadrijuges in vestibulo.' The word however retains its proper sense in the short verse, which Hertzberg well explains: 'Captivi supplices non reges sunt catenati, sed qui ex præda imperatori vel sorte evenerant, vel sub corona empti erant. Hi igitur ante limen prostrati ædem novi domini suæque servitutis inter lacrimas adorabant.'

7.] *Non desunt pendere.* Among many instances of this construction collected by the commentators the most appropriate is from Tacitus, *Hist.* iv. 11, 'nec deerat ipse, stipatus armatis,—vim principis amplecti, nomen remittere.' The custom of hanging on the doors of their mistresses the chaplets taken from the heads of the serenaders, is well illustrated by the fine verses of Lucretius, iv. 1171. 'At lacrymans exclusus amator limina sæpe Floribus et sertis operit, postesque superbos Ungit amaracino, et foribus miser oscula figit.'—*turpes*, 'disreputable.'—*faces*, the torches which had lighted the revellers, and which were tossed away before the house when burnt out, or when morning dawned.

9.] 'Non possum a domina mea infames noctes avertere, propulsare, nam ipsa famæ suæ non parcet. Virg. *Ecl.* vii. 47. *Solstitium pecori defendite.* Hor. *Od.* i. 17, 3.' —*Kuinoel.*

10.] *Tradita carminibus*, 'made the subject of song.' The revellers, anxious for admittance, addressed the door itself, as v. 17: 'Janua, vel domina penitus crudelior ipsa.'—*nobilis* either means, as Kuinoel thinks, 'notorious,' in a bad sense; or *quondam nobilis* is opposed to *nunc tradita*, &c., which seems better.

12.] *Vivere*, &c., 'from living worse than the debauchery of the day,' *i. e.* from even surpassing it in profligacy. The infinitive here takes a prohibitive sense (τοῦ μὴ ζῆν) which the former *parcere* (ὥστε φείδεσθαι) does not require. *Revocatur* seems susceptible of this double sense, viz. to be recalled *to* one act and *from* another. Others construe *non revocatur parcere vivere*, as *parce movere deos*, sup. 15, 26, and Müller contends this is the only legitimate construction.

13.] *Has inter*, *i. e.* has noctes, v. 9.—*deflere* seems here used for *flere*.—*tristior*, &c., 'made more sad by the long-continued appeals of the suppliant for admission.' Kuinoel reads with Broukhuis *ah longas excubias*, which Hertzberg approves. This certainly has the advantage of supplying an accusative case to *deflere*. So Ovid, 'Deflet Threiciam Daulias ales Ityn.' Many conjectures have been proposed on this obscure passage: *Hæc inter*, *has igitur*, *has mihi ter gravibus*, &c. I will add one more: *Interea gravibus*. For, *interea* being corruptly written *inter*, it was most natural, indeed, inevitable, to prefix the monosyllable *has*. It has also occurred to me to read 'supplicium longis tristius excubiis,' *i. e.* a beating (6) and an abuse (17, 37) more grievous to me than even the long nights spent on the threshold. Of course, *ille* (15) will then mean the lover, supplied from the context.—For *a longis* Hertzberg gives *ah! longis*, &c., and ex-

Supplicis a longis tristior excubiis.
Ille meos numquam patitur requiescere postes,
Arguta referens carmina blanditia:
'Janua, vel domina penitus crudelior ipsa,
Quid mihi tam duris clausa taces foribus?
Cur numquam reserata meos admittis amores,
Nescia furtivas reddere mota preces?
Nullane finis erit nostro concessa dolori?
Tristis et in tepido limine somnus erit?
Me mediæ noctes, me sidera prona jacentem,
Frigidaque Eoo me dolet aura gelu.
Tu sola humanos numquam miserata labores
Respondes tacitis mutua cardinibus.
O utinam trajecta cava mea vocula rima
Percussas dominæ vertat in auriculas!
Sit licet et saxo patientior illa Sicano,
Sit licet et ferro durior et chalybe,
Non tamen illa suos poterit compescere ocellos:
Surget et invitis spiritus in lacrimis.
Nunc jacet alterius felici nixa lacerto;
At mea nocturno verba cadunt Zephyro.
Sed tu sola mei, tu maxima causa doloris,
Victa meis numquam, janua, muneribus.
Te non ulla meæ læsit petulantia linguæ,
Quæ solet irato dicere turba joco,

plains it 'more sorrowful than even the suppliant lying outside,' *i.e.* supplice excubante. Müller (who always prints the interjection *o*, not *oh*,) takes the same view.

20.] 'Nescia moveri et preces meas, quas clam et furtim facio, ad dominam preferre.'—*Kuinoel.*—*reddere* is ἀποδοῦναι, 'to deliver the message.'

23.] 'The very stars as they set and the cold morning air feel for me as I lie; you alone, O door, have no compassion.' This is hyperbolical, but not absurd; nor does their seem good reason for the doubts and difficulties which have been raised about the passage.—*prona*, cf. v. 4, 64, 'ipsaque in oceanum sidera lapsa cadunt.'

26.] *Respondes mutua tacitis*, &c., 'answer me only by silence;' a sort of oxymoron. Kuinoel compares *mutua flere*, sup. 5, 30, as a similar construction.

27.] *Cava rima* is the ablative of the mode or *means* by which the voice is transmitted.

29.] 'More enduring than Sicilian rock,' *i.e.* than Ætna; if once she hears my voice, however hard-hearted she may be, she will be melted into tears.

32.] *Et invitis*, 'a sigh will arise with even involuntary tears.' So Müller, who compares Ovid, *Remed. Amor.* 268, 'longus et (al. *at*) invito pectore sedit amor.' The common reading however (a comma at *ocellos*) gives a good sense: 'non poterit non lacrimare, et in lacrimis, quamvis invita sint, surget spiritus.'

36.] *Muneribus*, *i.e.* osculis, corollis, unguentis, &c. See on v. 7, and inf. 41—4.

38.] The MSS. give 'quæ solet irato dicere tota loco,' which is obviously corrupt. —*turba* is the conjecture of Pucci in the ed. Rheg. Many corrections have been

Ut me tam longa raucum patiare querella
  Sollicitas trivio pervigilare moras.
At tibi sæpe novo deduxi carmina versu,
  Osculaque impressis nixa dedi gradibus.
Ante tuos quotiens verti me, perfida, postes,
  Debitaque occultis vota tuli manibus!'
Hæc ille, et si quæ miseri novistis amantes,
  Et matutinis obstrepit alitibus.
Sic ego nunc dominæ vitiis et semper amantis
  Fletibus æterna differor invidia.

XVII.

Et merito, quoniam potui fugisse puellam,
  Nunc ego desertas alloquor alcyonas.

proposed, of which the best perhaps is that adopted by Kuinoel, 'quæ solet ingrato dicere turba joco.' I have followed Hertzberg in admitting the two last words into the text.—*ingrato* and *irato* are similarly confused, El. 6, 10, but the latter epithet is consistent with *petulantia*.—*quæ* is here the same as *qualis*. Not much, I think, is to be said in favour of Müller's conjecture, which he introduces into the text, 'quæ solet ingrato figere theta loco.' He does not tell us what this can mean, but quotes in defence of it a well-known verse of the post-augustan writer Persius, iv. 13, 'et potis es nigrum vitiis præfigere theta.'

40.] *Sollicitas moras*, a long and anxious night-watch.

41.] *Deduxi*, 'spun.' See v. 1, 72.

42.] *Oscula nixa*, &c., for *ego nixus gradibus*, &c. The hypallage is a bold one; but the usage is frequent in Propertius. So *ebria vestigia* sup. 3, 9. This passage shows that the Roman houses had door-steps before them as in our own times.

44.] *Debita vota*, *i. e.* corollas, &c. See on v. 36. The expression is a brief one for 'dona ex voto debita.' From the addition of *occultis manibus* it would seem that *verti me ante postes* implies his turning round to face the street while he *secretly* affixed offerings to the door behind him. Or is *vertere* in this place ἐπιστρέφεσθαι?

45.] *Ille*, the *supplex* sup. 14.

46.] *Obstrepit*, 'out-bawls the morning cock.' The lover continues his doleful strain till the cock crows, and he raises his voice that it may be heard above it. See v. 4, 4. Kuinoel well quotes Theocr. vii. 123.

47.] *Semper—differor* must be connected, as Hertzberg observes. See sup. on 4, 22. The sense is, 'what with the frailties of the mistress within and the complaints of the lover without, the poor door is condemned to a perpetual infamy.' To avoid the pardonable tautology, Müller reads *alterna invidia*, with Markland.

XVII. It is by no means improbable that this exquisite elegy was written, as it professes to be, on board ship in the course of the voyage alluded to in El. xv. At all events the poet pictures to himself the dangers and incidents of a storm, that he may excite the sympathy of Cynthia by describing them.

1.] *Et merito*. *Et*, like *ergo*, used to introduce the subject at once, has a peculiar pathos. 'Here I am then and it serves me right' is the idea to be conveyed.—*potui*, ἔτλην, *sustinui*. Compare iii. 8, 14, and for *potui fugisse*, 1, 15.

2.] *Desertas*, *i. e.* solitarias. As the Halcyon was considered the 'bird of calm,' (Theocr. vii. 57. 'Αλκυόνες στορεσεῦντι τὰ κύματα), *alloquor* here implies perhaps an appeal to the birds to appear. The mistake of the Greeks, seldom correctly observant of facts of natural history, that certain sea-fowl floating buoyantly on the waves were sitting in their nests, cannot have escaped the attention of the thoughtful. According to Aristotle, *Hist. An.* viii.

Nec mihi Cassiope solito visura carinam est,
  Omniaque ingrato litore vota cadunt.
Quin etiam absenti prosunt tibi, Cynthia, venti:
  Aspice, quam sævas increpat aura minas.
Nullane placatæ veniet Fortuna procellæ?
  Hæccine parva meum funus arena teget?
Tu tamen in melius sævas converte querellas;
  Sat tibi sit pœnæ nox et iniqua vada.
An poteris siccis mea fata opponere ocellis,
  Ossaque nulla tuo nostra tenere sinu?
Ah pereat, quicumque rates et vela paravit
  Primus et invito gurgite fecit iter.

9, there were two species of Halcyon, one of which was vocal, the other *ἄφωνος*. In lib. ix. 14, he gives a minute description of what appears to be the Kingfisher. It is clear that the sea-bird must not be confounded with this.

3.] Cassiope, wife of Cepheus, was changed, like Ariadne and Callisto, into a star, which seems to have been regarded by sailors as the harbinger of a calm. The chief difficulty of this verse lies in *solito*, of which no other example can be adduced in this adverbial sense: for Kuinoel's reference to Ovid *Fast.* v. 547, where *solito citius* occurs, is not to the point. Perhaps we should read *solito visura carinam est omnino, et* &c. Or may there have been a phrase *ex solito*, *ἐκ τοῦ εἰωθότος*, like *ex more*?—*ingrato litore*, that is, thankless, *surdo*: regardless of the vows to build temples, offer sacrifices, &c. Hertzberg and Jacob understand Cassiope of a maritime town so called (*Κασσώπη* in Strab. vii. 7). The latter says: 'Solebant in Græciam a Brundisio navigantes Cassiopes portum in montibus Acroceraunüs situm ex more omnes petere.' Cf. Cic. *Ep. ad Fam.* xvi. 9, 'Corcyræ fuimus usque a. d. xvi. Kalend. Decembr. tempestatibus retenti. A. d. xv. Kalend. Decembr. in portum Corcyræorum ad Cassiopen stadia cxx processimus.' The Venice edition 1500 gives *solitam*. Hertzberg reads with Wyttenbach *solidam*, in the sense of 'Cassiope will not see my bark arrive safe.' Müller gives *salvam*, and in the next line *cadent*.

5.] 'The very winds, being adverse to me, take your side,' *i. e.* are taking vengeance on me. On the indicative *increpat* see sup. on 2, 9. The similarity of sound in *absenti* and *venti* is remarkable as being an apparent oversight in the best poets (so *Tyrrhena arena* sup. 8, 11), but a favourite and studied usage with the ecclesiastical poets of the middle and later latinity, from whom the modern poets have derived their practice of rhyming. Lachmann has collected many curious instances from our poet and others. Compare also II. 3, 27, 'Non, non humani partus sunt talia dona: Ista decem menses non peperere bona.'

7.] *Fortuna*, like the Τύχη Σωτὴρ of the Greeks (see on *Agam.* 647), was worshipped as a goddess *potens maris*. Hor. *Od.* i. 35, 6, where she is called *Domina æquoris*.—*meum funus*, *i. e.* meum corpus; but involving the notion of the exequiæ paid to it.

9.] 'Sensus: desine imprecari, et vota potius pro salute mea facias.'—*Kuinoel.*

11.] The good MSS. vary between *opponere* and *reponere*. The former is the reading of Jacob, Hertzberg, Keil, and Müller, the latter of Kuinoel, Barth, and Lachmann. I follow the more recent editors, who explain *opponere ocellis* &c., 'to present my fate to your (mind with tearless) eye,' *i. e.* to think of it without distress.

12.] As a token of especial affection, the urn containing the ashes or some small relic of a deceased relative was carried in the folds of the toga, *sinus*, clasped to the breast. Kuinoel quotes Tibullus, I. 3, 5, 'non hic mihi mater, quæ legat in mœstos ossa perusta sinus.' Compare also Tacit. *Ann.* ii. 75, 'At Agrippina—ascendit classem cum cineribus Germanici et liberis, miserantibus cunctis quod femina nobilitate princeps—tamo feralis reliquias sinu ferret.'

Nonne fuit levius dominæ pervincere mores,
  Quamvis dura, tamen rara puella fuit—
Quam sic ignotis circumdata litora silvis
  Cernere et optatos quærere Tyndaridas?
Illic siqua meum sepelissent fata dolorem,
  Ultimus et posito staret amore lapis,
Illa meo caros donasset funere crines,
  Molliter et tenera poneret ossa rosa:
Illa meum extremo clamasset pulvere nomen,
  Ut mihi non ullo pondere terra foret.
At vos æquoreæ formosa Doride natæ,
  Candida felici solvite vela choro:
Si quando vestras labens Amor attigit undas,
  Mansuetis socio parcite litoribus.

XVIII.

Hæc certe deserta loca et taciturna querenti,

15.] *Levius*, the reading of Hertzberg with Kuinoel and Lachmann, has the authority of the Naples MS. Jacob has edited *melius* from the ed. Rheg. and MS. Groning., and so Keil and Müller.

17.] 'Than thus to be gazing at the unknown forests which line the shore, and to wonder where I am.'—*Tyndaridas*: see Hor. *Od.* I. 3, 2, and on Æsch. *Agam.* 647, where the true explanation of this much wished-for apparition in a storm at sea is attempted. It is familiarly known in the Mediterranean as St. Elmo's fire.

19.] *Illic*, i. e. at home. *Sepelissent* implies the action done once for all and completed at the time; *staret*, the continued duration of the monument. But this distinction does not apply to *donasset* and *poneret* in the next distich.—*caros crines*, i. e. sibi; highly-prized, and therefore given only under the impulse of a deep affection. See Becker, Gallus, p. 518—20.

22.] 'She would lay my bones in the tomb softly on strewed rose-leaves.' The ablatives both here and in the next verse (*pulvere*), as indeed above in v. 21, and *nostro limine* 16, 11, have a locative sense, and furnish remarkable examples of the usage. Compare v. 8, 10, 'creditur ore manus.' But the exact sense of *extremo pulvere* is obscure. It may be an ablative of time, 'at the last dust,' i. e. when earth was thrown on the grave.

25.] Doris was wife of Nereus, and mother of the Nereids. 'unfurl the white sails with your propitious band;' i. e. by appearing on the surface, and portending calm weather, induce the sailors to spread before the breeze the sails which have been reefed in the gale.

27.] There is exquisite feeling and taste in this appeal to the chaste Nereid nymphs: 'if ever love has entered your cool watery realms, you can pity a lover, and will spare a fellow-slave by directing him to a sheltered shore.'—*litoribus*, as Hertzberg remarks, is the ablative 'quo simul modus et ratio significatur.'

XVIII. This elegy, as well as the last, is among the happiest efforts of our poet's genius. It exhibits an intensity of feeling by which Cynthia, unless more obdurate than the oaks it was addressed to, must have been moved. It is a soliloquy on Cynthia's cruelty, uttered to the winds and the birds in the depth of a forest. Kuinoel, who with all his faults has more heart than most of his critical co-editors, calls it 'elegantissimum carmen, et ad animum permovendum aptissimum. Tenerrimum,' (he adds), 'amoris sensum exprimit, et elocutionis suavitate ac simplicitate mirifice sese commendat.'

1.] *Taciturna*. This idea is more fully expressed in v. 4.

Et vacuum Zephyri possidet aura nemus.
Hic licet occultos proferre impune dolores,
  Si modo sola queant saxa tenere fidem.
Unde tuos primum repetam, mea Cynthia, fastus?
  Quod mihi das flendi, Cynthia, principium?
Qui modo felices inter numerabar amantes,
  Nunc in amore tuo cogor habere notam.
Quid tantum merui? quæ te mihi crimina mutant?
  An nova tristitiæ causa puella tuæ?
Sic mihi te referas, levis, ut non altera nostro
  Limine formosos intulit ulla pedes.
Quamvis multa tibi dolor hic meus aspera debet,
  Non ita sæva tamen venerit ira mea,
Ut tibi sim merito semper furor, et tua flendo
  Lumina dejectis turpia sint lacrymis.
An quia parva damus mutato signa colore,
  Et non ulla meo clamat in ore fides?
Vos eritis testes, si quos habet arbor amores,
  Fagus et Arcadio pinus amica deo.

5.] This verse is perhaps after Theocritus, ii. 64, *νῦν δὴ μούνη ἐοῖσα πόθεν τὸν ἔρωτα δακρυσῶ; ἐκ τίνος ἄρξωμαι;*

8.] *Habere notam*, 'to be degraded.' Allusion is made to the Censor's mark of infamy, attached to the names of those *qui senatu moverentur.*

9.] The MSS. have *carmina*, which can only be interpreted of magic verses. The editors, with some later copies, agree in reading *crimina*, Jacob excepted. Kuinoel however seems wrong in explaining *crimina a me commissa.* The word is rather used in its strict sense, '*accusations*,' *i. e.* slanders of enemies.—*mutant te mihi*, are changing or estranging your feelings towards me.

11.] *Sic—ut*, 'so surely—as &c.' This use of *sic* in protestations is too well known to require illustration.—*levis* is the vocative, 'fickle one.' But some explain it *leviter*, easily. This distich denies one of the charges, *crimina*, and the protestation extends over the next four. Then 17—18 reply to another *crimen*, that of *indifference;* and this also has four following in connexion. At 23—24, with the following distich, he denies the charge of suspicion, querulousness, and jealousy.

13—16. 'Though I have suffered much from you, yet I never will so resent it as to deserve your continual indignation by loving another.'—*furor*, *μῆνις*, the *object* of wrath.

17.] Kuinoel and Keil read *colore*, which has equal MS. authority. And certainly there is a naturalness and simplicity in this which can hardly be said to characterise *colore*. Compare sup. 1, 22, 'et facito illa meo palleat ore magis,' and 6, 6, 'mutatoque graves sæpe colore preces.' This latter verse did not occur to Hertzberg, when he raised the objection on the present passage, that *mutato colore* would only properly be used as 'primum nascentis amoris signum.' Though this might have been urged as the very point in its favour; for the poet asks, 'do you expect me continually to be changing colour, and do you think that, if I do not do so, my affection is mere pretence?' The other reading, *calore*, is explained by Hertzberg, not very successfully, as 'quod tam parva signa caloris det, unde mutatum eum necessario colligatur.' Nevertheless, Barth, Lachmann, Müller, and Jacob adopt *calore.*

20.] The loves of Pan and Pitys are here meant. The legend however is only recorded by a few of the less known authors, references to which are supplied by the commentators.

Ah quotiens teneras resonant mea verba sub umbras,
Scribitur et vestris CYNTHIA corticibus!
An tua quod peperit nobis injuria curas,
Quæ solum tacitis cognita sunt foribus?
Omnia consuevi timidus preferre superbæ
Jussa, neque arguto facta dolore queri.
Pro quo, divini Fontes, et frigida rupes
Et datur inculto tramite dura quies,
Et quodcumque meæ possunt narrare querellæ,
Cogor ad argutas dicere solus aves.
Sed qualiscumque es, resonent mihi CYNTHIA silvæ,
Nec deserta tuo nomine saxa vacent.

XIX.

Non ego nunc tristes vereor, mea Cynthia, Manes,
Nec moror extremo debita fata rogo;
Sed ne forte tuo careat mihi funus amore,
Hic timor est ipsis durior exequiis.
Non adeo leviter nostris puer hæsit ocellis,

21.] Both Lachmann and Hertzberg have a page of notes on the precise meaning of *teneras umbras*. What can be more appropriate than *tenera* to the delicate foliage which forms the shade in a wood? Müller accords a very ingenious correction of Schrader, *vestras—umbras*, and *teneris—corticibus*.

23.] *Ah tua quot nobis* &c.—*Kuinoel*. But Barth explains the vulgate rightly: 'or is the reason of your estrangement the consciousness of having wronged me? Of *that* I have never complained except to the doors.' More precisely, 'Or are you vexed with me because I have been distressed by your slights?' Müller reads *en tua quot peperit*, and says that *an* "sensu caret." The note on 11 sup. will show that he did not understand the passage.

24.] *Cognita foribus*. See sup. 16, 17, seq.

26.] *Fata* Kuinoel after Passeius; a conjecture not worth refuting.—*facta* is 'your treatment of me,' opposed to *jussa* as ἔργον is to λόγος.

27.] *Divini* is the reading of all the MSS., nor is there much reason in the objections which have been raised against it. Since a divinity was believed to reside in every tree and fountain, it was natural to call them *divinos*. The passage in Theocr. viii. 33, ἄγκεα καὶ ποταμοί, θεῖον γένος, is very much to the purpose. Müller admits the needless alteration of N. Heinsius, 'pro quo dumosi montes' &c.

30.] *Argutas*, vocales. Any *distinct* and especially *piercing* sound is so called, as in Virgil *argutum pecten*, *arguta hirundo*, *arguta serra* &c. See above v. 26. *arguto dolore*, and on El. 6, 7.

32.] *Nec saxa vacent*, i. e. may the echo respond.

XIX. That this elegy was not written, as might be conjectured from the commencement of it, in a time of sickness or danger, appears from the concluding distich. It is full of deep feeling and tenderness to Cynthia, assuring her of his love even in the nether world.

2.] *Nec moror*, 'nor do I care for.'—'*fata* pro cadavere, mortuo,' says Kuinoel; but the expression, though not without a parallel, seems merely a periphrasis for *fatum rogi*.

5.] *Hæsit*. The metaphor, according to Hertzberg, who quotes from the Greek Anthology to prove it, is taken from an-

Ut meus oblito pulvis amore vacet.
Illic Phylacides jocundæ conjugis heros
Non potuit cæcis immemor esse locis;
Sed cupidus falsis attingere gaudia palmis
Thessalis antiquam venerat umbra domum.
Illic, quicquid ero, semper tua dicar imago:
Trajicit et fati litora magnus Amor.
Illic formosæ veniant chorus heroïnæ,
Quas dedit Argivis Dardana præda viris:
Quarum nulla tua fuerit mihi, Cynthia, forma
Gratior; et Tellus hoc ita justa sinat.
Quamvis te longæ remorentur fata senectæ,
Cara tamen lacrimis ossa futura meis:
Quæ tu viva mea possis sentire favilla!
Tum mihi non ullo mors sit amara loco.

captum by birdlime. This is perhaps correct, and the image is worth attention. The lover goes about with his eyes smeared to catch Cupid as he flies, and so is unable to shake him off again. A less attentive consideration of the passage might suggest the simple notion of a bird lighting (ἐφ-ιζάνειν) and remaining on its perch.—*oblito* is here used in a passive sense. See on El. 2, 6. If taken as the ablative absolute, *vacet* will mean *vacivus* (or *vacivus*) *sit*, 'that my shade will have nothing to engage or occupy it.'

7.] *Phylacides.* Protesilaus, Ἰφίκλου υἱὸς πολυμήλου Φυλακίδαο (Hom. *Il.* B. 705), who was so attached to his wife Laodamia that he obtained leave from the gods below to return to his former abode (*antiqua domus*) for a single day. See Ovid *Her.* xiii.—*Illic—cæcis locis*, 'there in the gloomy realms of the dead:' a pleonasm common in Greek, as αὐτοῦ ἐνὶ Τροίῃ, ὑπ' Ἴλιον αὐτοῦ etc. in Homer. So iii. 1, 32, 'hic—ante pedes.'

9.] *Falsis palmis*, 'utpote umbra,' Kuinoel; who makes *cupidus* refer to *umbra* by a well-known Greek idiom, βίη Ἡρακληείη etc. But Hertzberg says, '*cupidus* ad *Phylacides* referendum, umbra Thessalis vero non subjectum est, sed prædicato additum.' I think he is right. *Thessalis* is the correction of Pucci for *Thessalus*.

11.] This passage recals to mind the fine parallel in Eur. *Alcest.* 363, ἀλλ' οὖν ἐκεῖσε προσδόκα μ', ὅταν θάνω, καὶ δῶμ' ἑτοίμαζ' ὡς συνοικήσουσά μοι. K. compares inf. iii. 6, 36, 'hujus ero vivus, mortuus hujus ero.'—*magnus amor* (emphatic), *i. e.* extraordinary attachments continue even in the other world.

13.] 'Neque formosissimæ heroinæ tibi animum meum mutabunt, nulla earum mihi jucundior te ipsa formosa erit. Intelliguntur Cassandra, Andromache, Helena, aliæ feminæ Trojanæ, quæ in prædæ divisione Græcis victoribus contigerant.'—*Kuinoel.* See Eur. *Troad.* 241—277.

16.] *Ita justa*, 'in eo justa, si id, quod jure fit, tribuit atque concedit.' Ast, quoted by Hertzberg. Or perhaps, 'ita (esse) sinat.' Lachmann, 'justos inferos sperat ut se Cynthiam heroinis præferre patiantur.' Kuinoel follows Burmann in the portentous alteration, 'et Venus hoc si dea justa sinat.'

17—20.] There is some obscurity in these four verses, which have been recklessly altered and perverted by the earlier editors. Müller marks them severally with an obelus, but has no comment on them. Following the best MSS. with Jacob and Hertzberg, we may thus paraphrase: 'However long you, Cynthia, may survive me, your death will ever be looked for to console my grief in Hades. And may you feel the same regard for me, while yet you remain on earth after I am burnt on the pyre, which I shall feel for you in the shades. If assured of this, death will not be bitter to me wherever I may meet it.' Lachmann (on iii. 13, 44) interprets this verse: 'mortem amaram nullius sibi momenti et nequaquam gravem fore dicit, si

Quam vereor, ne te contempto, Cynthia, busto,
  Abstrahat heu! nostro pulvere iniquus Amor,
Cogat et invitam lacrimas siccare cadentes!
  Flectitur assiduis certa puella minis.
Quare, dum licet, inter nos lætemur amantes:
  Non satis est ullo tempore longus amor.

XX.

Hoc pro continuo te, Galle, monemus amore,
  Id tibi ne vacuo defluat ex animo:
Sæpe imprudenti fortuna occurrit amanti.
  Crudelis Minyis dixerit Ascanius.
Est tibi non infra speciem, non nomine dispar
  Thiodamanteo proximus ardor Hylæ:

puellam sibi fidelem sciat.' *Nullo loco amara*, 'in no respect bitter,' is a plausible translation; but it is not very easy to defend it by the phrase *nullo loco numerare* (Cic. *de Fin.* ii. 28, 90, quoted by Lachmann), which seems to be a version of the Greek *οὐδαμοῦ τίθεσθαι*. Hertzberg is more successful: 'Ubicunque moriar, mors non amara mihi erit.' *Quamvis*, in v. 17, certainly governs *removeatur*, because *tamen* in the next verse depends directly on such a sense. It is strange that Hertzberg should make *removeatur* an optative, like *possis*, for no other reason than that a prose writer would more accurately have written *removeatura sint*.—*Ossa*, i.e. *umbra tua*; but the allusion evidently is to a survivor on earth clasping the bones of a deceased relative and bedewing them with tears; which action is poetically transferred to the part of him who has previously deceased, and is expecting his partner in Hades. See on iii. 4, 39.

22.] *Heu!* is the reading of Hertzberg for *e*, which he shows to be a common compendium with transcribers for the former interjection. The other editors have *e*, with the ed. Rheg.—*busto* is, of course, for *meo busto*.

23.] The words *cogat* and *invitam* are used in reference to *minis*, threats being the last resource adopted in overcoming the fidelity of a woman. So Ovid, *Fast.* ii. 806, 'nec prece, nec pretio, nec movet ille minis.' There is no need, therefore, with Markland and Kuinoel to understand *promissis* as applied in *minis*.—*certa*, i.e. quamvis constans.

XX. Addressed to Gallus (supra El. v.), with the advice that he should take good care of a youth on whom he had bestowed his regards, called, probably by Gallus himself, *Hylas*.—The poem is a very elegant one, though not one of the easiest. 'Judice Broukhusio,' says Barth, 'non extat in toto Latio venustior.'

1.] Hoc monemus te, ne id (illud) defluat, excidat tibi, 'Fortunam sæpe adversam esse' &c. The third line is given as a maxim: cf. 15, 42.—*pro continuo amore*, by (for the sake of) our long uninterrupted regard. Compare 22, 2.

3.] 'Fortune often proves adverse to a lover when least expecting it.'

4.] *Dixerit* is the reading of the Naples MS. The rest have *dixerat*. The former is clearly right: it represents the Greek optative with ἄν, but has no precise English equivalent.—*crudelis Minyis*; the river Ascanius, in Bithynia, is called *pitiless* to the Argonauts, because it occasioned the loss of Hercules: see Theocr. *Id.* xiii. The sense of the whole passage is well given by Hertzberg: 'imprudenti amanti fortunam nocere Ascanius, crudelis olim Minyis, docuerit vel doceat.'—*imprudens* (improvidens) is for *incautus*: cf. Virg. *Georg.* i. 373, 'nunquam imprudentibus imber obfuit.'

6.] 'Est tibi puer amatus simillimus et facie et nomine Hylæ.'—*Hertzberg*.

Hunc tu, sive leges umbrosæ flumina silvæ,
 Sive Aniena tuos tinxerit unda pedes,
Sive Gigantea spatiabere litoris ora,
 Sive ubicumque vago fluminis hospitio,
Nympharum semper cupidis defende rapinis,—
 Non minor Ausoniis est amor Adryasin.
Ne tibi sit—durum!—montes et frigida saxa,
 Galle, neque experto semper adire lacus,
Quæ miser ignotis error perpessus in oris
 Herculis indomito fleverat Ascanio.

Compare *gravima Leda*, sup. xiii. 29. Apollodor. i. 9, 19, Ὕλας, ὁ Θειοδάμαντος παῖς, Ἡρακλέους δὲ ἐρώμενος, ἀποσταλεὶς ὑδρεύσασθαι, διὰ κάλλος ὑπὸ Νυμφῶν ἡρπάγη.

7.] *Sila* for *silva* is the ingenious correction of Scaliger, approved by Jacob and Lachmann, and adopted by both Keil and Müller. This was a mountainous forest in the district of the Bruttii, in the foot of Italy. Virg. *Georg.* iii. 219, 'pascitur in magna Sila formosa juvenca,' where the common reading is *silva*. *Æn.* xii. 715, 'Ac velut ingenti Sila summove Taburno,' &c. Both words, in fact, are the same, the insertion of the digamma in the one causing the apparent difference. Hertzberg objects that the mention of such an out-of-the-way place would be little to the purpose, and doubts whether there is any stream there which could have been navigable even for a boat. He appears to be right in explaining the sense thus: 'sive tu fluminis ripam cymba leges, sive ipso flumine natabis, sive spatiaberis in litore; perinde cavendum a rapinis nympharum.' —On *legere* see v. 4, 42.

9.] *Gigantea ora*, i. e. Cumæ. The district known to the ancients as the Phlegræan plains, (φλεγραία πλάξ, Æsch. *Eum.* 295), was the scene of the battle between the gods and the rebel giants. It derives its name from some outbreak of the volcanic fires, which ever since the historic period have been more or less active in that district.

10.] *ubicumque*, sc. spatiabere, Gr. ὅπου ἂν ἀλλαχοῦ or ἄλλοθι.

11.] *Cupidis rapinis* is the reading of Jacob and Hertzberg from MS. Groning. The other have *cupidas rapinas*, which involves the necessity of altering *hunc* into *huic* in v. 7, with Lachmann, Barth, Müller, and Kuinoel. In point of construction, there is nothing to choose. Virg. *Georg.* iii. 164, 'hunc arcebis gravido pecori.' *Ecl.* vii. 47; Hor. *Od.* i. 17, 3.

12.] The MSS. have *adriacis*, or *hadriacis*. Scaliger and Kuinoel give *ah! Dryasin*; Jacob, *a Dryasin*. Lachmann's conjecture is ingenious and appropriate, *Hydriasin*. Were there more authority than there appears to be for calling the water-nymphs Ὑδριάδες, (a name only found in two late epigrams in the Greek anthology), no judicious critic would hesitate to adopt this reading. Hertzberg gives *Adryasin*, which he tells us Lachmann himself subsequently preferred. So also Keil and Müller. Nymphs of trees were called indifferently Dryades, Adryades, Hamadryades.

13.] *Durum!* σχέτλιον, an interjection, as Lachmann, Jacob, and Hertzberg agree in printing it, while Kuinoel reads *durus* with Lipsius. The construction is, *ne tibi sit adire*; and *durum* is added as a dissuasive;—'you will find it a hard task.' Lachmann explains 'Nympharum fraudes vita, ne tibi per montes et saxa lacusque errandum sit, quemadmodum Herculi olim Hylam amissum quærenti;' and he appositely quotes Theocr. xiii. 66, ἀλώμενος ὅσσ' ἐμόγησεν ὄρεα καὶ δρυμώς.

14.] Hertzberg is right, I think, in reading *experto* for *expertos*. The construction is continued into the next distich; 'experto (ea) quæ errans Hercules perpessus fleverat ad indomitum (i. e. crudelem, flecti nescium) Ascanium.' *Expertos* is improbably explained by Barth, 'quos noxios et Nympharum insidiis plenos semper experti sunt amantes.' The accusative however is retained by Lachmann, Keil, and Müller. Perhaps *expertos* is corrupt, and the next distich was meant as an exclamation.

Namque ferunt olim Pagasæ navalibus Argon
  Egressam longe Phasidos isse viam;
Et jam præteritis labentem Athamantidos undis
  Mysorum scopulis adplicuisse ratem.
Hic manus heroum placidis ut constitit oris,
  Mollia composita litora fronde tegit.
At comes invicti juvenis processerat ultra
  Raram sepositi quærere fontis aquam.
Hunc duo sectati fratres, Aquilonia proles,
  Hunc super et Zetes, hunc super et Calais,
Oscula suspensis instabant carpere palmis,
  Oscula et alterna ferre supina fuga.
Ille sub extrema pendens secluditur ala,
  Et volucres ramo submovet insidias.
Jam Pandioniæ cessit genus Orithyiæ:
  Ah dolor! ibat Hylas, ibat Hamadryasin.

17.] *Pagasæ*, the port in Thessaly whence the Argonauts set sail, and from which Jason is called *Pagasæus* in Ovid. *Fast.* i. 491. Müller reads *Pagasa*, with Lachmann (MSS. *pagase*), and *Argon* with the old copies.

18.] *Longe isse*, 'had gone far on its voyage to the Phasis,' viz. to the east of the Euxine.

20.] 'Applicuisse (eos) ratem labentem,' &c., seems a better construction than that adopted by Hertzberg, 'ferunt Argo—applicuisse ratem.' *Athamantidos undis*, i. e. the Hellespont. Helle was daughter of Athamas. Apollodor. i. 9, 1, τῶν δὲ Αἰόλου παίδων Ἀθάμας, δυναστεύων Βοιωτίας ἐκ Νεφέλης τεκνοῖ μὲν παῖδα Φρίξον, θυγατέρα δὲ Ἕλλην. *Mysorum scopulis*: Apollon. Rhod. i. 1177, ἦμος δ' οἵ γ' ἀφίκοντο Κιανίδος ἤθεα γαίης,—τοὺς μὲν ἐυξείνως Μυσοὶ φιλότητι κιόντας δειδέχατ', ἐνναέται κείνης χθονός.

22.] *Composita fronde.* Theocr. xiii. 32, λειμὼν γάρ σφιν ἔκειτο μέγας, στιβάδεσσιν ὄνειαρ.

23.] *Processerat quærere.* Compare sup. i. 12, *ibat videre.*

25.] *Sectati*, i. e. Hylæ amore incensi. *Kuinoel.* Calais and Zetes, *οἱ Βορέαι*, are enumerated among the Argonauts by Apollodorus, i. 9, 16. *Suspensis palmis*, 'with their hands while balanced in the air.' Most commentators have explained *palmis* by *pennis*. But Hertzberg aptly quotes sup. 3. 16, 'oscula sumere admota manu.' Barth reads *plumis*. It is evident that the whole account is taken from some picture; and indeed the rape of Hylas was a favourite subject for vase-paintings and frescos. (A very beautiful fresco from Herculaneum is engraved in Pl. 47 of *Raccolta de più belli dipinti di Ercolano*, &c., Naples, 1854). The two winged brothers are here supposed to be hovering over Hylas, with their arms hanging down to grasp his neck, while the coy youth hides his head under his arm (ala), and tries to beat off his assailants with a branch. So Mr. Wratislaw has rightly explained the passage. He thinks *pendens* (29) does not mean 'raised aloft,' but either 'on tip-toe' or 'in anxious fear.'

27.] *Ferre* I take for φέρεσθαι rather than for φέρειν, 'to steal kisses from his upturned face, descending to snatch them with alternate flight,' i. e. first one and then the other. Compare Tibullus i. 1, 20, '*fertis munera vestra, Lares.*' Ovid, *Fast.* iii. 506, 'Hei mihi! pro cœlo qualia dona fero.' 'Hoc novum, quod oscula quæ Boreades *proni* ferebant, *supina* dicuntur, quippe rapta supino Hylæ.'—*Hertzberg.*

31.] *Genus Orithyiæ*, i. e. Calais and Zetes, Boreas having carried away Orithyia for his wife. Inf. iv. 7, 13, 'infelix Aquilo, raptæ timor Orithyiæ.'

32.] *Hamadryasin* is the correction of Scaliger for *amadrias hine* or *hamadrias hine*. *Ah dolor!* may be compared with 'proh pudor!' Kuinoel and others join

Hic erat Arganthi Pege sub vertice montis
  Grata domus Nymphis humida Thyniasin,
Quam supra nullæ pendebant debita curæ
  Roscida desertis poma sub arboribus,
Et circum irriguo surgebant lilia prato
  Candida, purpureis mixta papaveribus.
Quæ modo decerpens tenero pueriliter ungui
  Proposito florem prætulit officio;
Et modo formosis incumbens nescius undis
  Errorem blandis tardat imaginibus.
Tandem haurire parat demissis flumina palmis
  Innixus dextro plena trahens humero:
Cujus ut accensæ Dryades candore puellæ
  Miratæ solitos destituere choros,
Prolapsum leviter facili traxere liquore:
  Tum sonitum rapto corpore fecit Hylas.
Cui procul Alcides iterat responsa: sed illi

ibat dolor (i.e. causa amoris cum dolore conjuncta) *Hamadryasin*; and so Hertzberg. The sense is, 'No sooner has Hylas escaped from one danger, than he falls into another.'—*ibat*, he went on merely to become theirs.

33.] *Pege*. The singular number *erat* excuses the use of πηγὴ for πηγαί, or rather Πηγαί, as Hertzberg observes. Apollon. *Rhod*. i. 1222, αἶψα δ' ὅγε κρήνην μετεκίαθεν, ἣν καλέουσι Πηγὰς ἀγχίγυοι περιναιέται. The word is corruptly written in the MSS.

35—42.] The singular beauty of these verses depends in great measure on their simplicity, but in part also in the choice and appropriate epithets. Those who condemn the use of words of more than two syllables at the end of the pentameter will do well to study this passage.

35.] The MSS. and editors agree in *nullæ*, an old and rare form for *nulli*.

42.] *Blandis imaginibus*. By looking at the pleasing shadows of himself in the clear water.

44.] *Plena trahens*, 'as he drew a pitcher full.'

45.] *Dryades*. According to Apollonius, in a very beautiful passage, i. 1224—39, not only the water-nymphs, but those of the woods and mountains were celebrating a nightly dance to Artemis when Hylas came by moonlight to draw water from the spring.—*cujus* refers to *humero*. The nymphs saw the white-armed shoulder projecting over the bank, and left the dance to gaze at it; a highly poetical image. The apodosis to the sentence as *traxere* &c.

48.] *Sonitum fecit*. 'Dum cadit Hylas, sonum corpore lapso dedit: ad hunc sonum proclamavit Hercules sæpius; cui nullum tamen responsum datum, nisi ab Echo.'—*Barth*. Mr. Wratislaw says, 'Hylas appears to have made a splash, not as he slipped into the water, but as he disappeared under it. It is to this splash that Hercules *iterat responsa*.' Apollonius and Theocritus represent Hylas as calling out while under the water. Propertius does not express this, but leaves the cry for aid to be implied, by stating that Hercules answered him from afar. Whether *sonitum* or *Hylas* is the antecedent to *cui*, is not very clear.—*illi*, Herculi, aura reddit nomen (Hylæ) ab extremis fontibus. The hero called 'Hylas!' but only the echo, not the living voice of the ravished boy, gave the reply. Theocrit. xiii. 58: τρὶς μὲν Ὕλαν ἄυσεν, ὅσον βαθὺς ἤρυγε λαιμός· Τρὶς δ' ἄρ' ὁ παῖς ὑπάκουσεν· ἀραιὰ δ' ἵκετο φωνὰ ἐξ ὕδατος.—*extremis* appears to signify *longinquis*; or we must supply *aditum* if *nomen* means the name of Hercules uttered from the depth of the water. Müller admits an alteration of Haupt's, which seems very unsuited to the genius of elegy, *iterat*

Nomen ab extremis fontibus aura refert.
His, o Galle, tuos monitus servabis amores
Formosum Nymphis credere visus Hylan.

XXI.

Tu, qui consortem properas evadere casum,
Miles, ab Etruscis saucius aggeribus,
Quid nostro gemitu turgentia lumina torques?
Pars ego sum vestræ proxima militiæ.
Sic te servato possint gaudere parentes,
Hæc soror acta tuis sentiat e lacrimis:

responset: ut illis &c. Lachmann had before proposed, with no better success, *iterat, responsa det: illi* &c.

52.] *Visus.* 'Who have hitherto been so careless of your Hylas, that one might suppose you intended to entrust him to the very parties who were most likely to carry him off.' Kuinoel and Barth read *tutus*, with Scaliger, from one inferior MS. and explain it, 'nihil sollicitus credere.' Lachmann's conjecture, *fisus*, is perhaps more probable.

XXI. This Gallus, whom the reader will not confound with the high-born friend of the same name addressed in El. v., nor with Gallus the poet in iii. 26, 91, was related to Propertius, as appears from v. 7 of the next elegy, and seems to have been waylaid and killed by banditti in the Perusine war, having joined the side of Antony against Octavian. He is here represented as giving his dying request to a comrade, to convey to his sister. There is great pathos in these brief verses, which have an epigrammatic character not unlike the *ἐπιτύμβια* of the Greek Anthology.

1.] *Consortem casum*, 'casum consortium.'—*Hertzberg.* He appeals to a soldier retreating from Perusia to escape the fate of so many of his comrades.

2.] *Etruscis aggeribus*, the walls and fortifications of Perusia (Perugia), an important town of Etruria, which was taken by siege from L. Antony's forces by Octavian, B.C. 40. See ii. 1, 29. Tac. *Hist.* i. 50. Suet. *Oct.* § 14.

3.] The meaning seems to be, 'quid torques oculos ad gemitum meum, ita ut turgeant lacrymis præ miseratione?' If *torques* could be used for *detorques*, we might be tempted to translate, 'Why do you turn away your eyes, filled with tears at my moans?'

4.] *Proxima* both Kuinoel and Hertzberg understand as *proxime*, i. e. *modo*, *nuper*. But he was *still* a part, being a soldier on the same side, though wounded and dying. Why should it not mean 'closely connected by common ties,' as the chorus in the Agamemnon says of itself, ὡς θέλει τόδ' ἄγχιστον Ἀπίας γαίας μονόφρουρον ἕρκος, v. 246. Compare sup. 6, 34, 'accepti pars eris imperii.' inf. ii. 1, 73, 'pars juventæ.'

5—6.] There is much difficulty about the reading and sense of these lines. The MSS. have *ut possint*, (though *ut* appears to have been erased from MS. Groning.) and in v. 6 *nec* or *ne*. *Hæc* is from Pucci; the ed. Rheg. has *hec*. Lachmann and Hertzberg read thus:—

> Sic te servato, ut possint gaudere parentes,
> Nec soror acta tuis sentiat e lacrimis;

where *servato* is the imperative. He is followed by Keil and Müller. I much prefer the reading of Jacob, as given in the text. *Sic te* &c., is the usual form of adjuration, like Horace's 'sic te diva potens Cypri,' and *sentiat hæc acta* may be rendered 'let her be apprised of what has been done to me.' *Tuis e lacrymis* will then signify, 'let her know my fate from the silent testimony of your tears;' the *particulars* which follow being supposed to be learned from a subsequent verbal account. But, as the word *acta* refers also to the last instructions about burial, as in iii. 4, 16, 'Accipe quæ serves funeris acta mei,' this will suit the sense very well; for in v. 9 a request to look for his remains is clearly conveyed. The reading of Kuinoel, *hæc soror Acca* &c., is the conjecture of Scaliger.

Gallum per medios ereptum Cæsaris enses
  Effugere ignotas non potuisse manus,
Et quæcumque super dispersa invenerit ossa
  Montibus Etruscis, hæc sciat esse mea.

XXII.

Qualis, et unde genus, qui sint mihi, Tulle, Penates,
  Quæris pro nostra semper amicitia.
Si Perusina tibi patriæ sunt nota sepulcra,
  Italiæ duris funera temporibus,
Cum Romana suos egit discordia cives,—
  Sit mihi præcipue, pulvis Etrusca, dolor:
Tu projecta mei perpessa es membra propinqui,
  Tu nullo miseri contegis ossa solo,—
Proxima subposito contingens Umbria campo
  Me genuit, terris fertilis uberibus.

7.] *Per medios enses*, 'from amidst the weapons.' Propertius occasionally uses *per* for *inter*, as iv. 1, 4, and v. 4, 20.—*ignotas manus*, the hands of some barbarous spoiler.

8.] 'Tell her this, that she may not search in vain for my corpse among the slain, but may know that my body was mangled and my bones scattered over the mountain passes.'

XXII. To Tullus. This is probably the same Tullus to whom the first, sixth, and fourteenth elegies were addressed. The present reply to his oft-repeated (*semper*, v. 2) question, as to the birth and country of the poet, would seem to show that Tullus stood in the relation of a powerful patron rather than in that of an intimate acquaintance.

2.] *Pro amicitia*, as *pro continuo amore*, sup. 20, 1.

3.] *Perusina patriæ sepulcra*, i. e. the number of your own citizens (Romans) who found their graves at the siege of Perusia.—*sepultæ* is the correction of Scaliger.

6.] *Pulvis Etrusca*, for terra Etrusca, but used with peculiar elegance from the allusion in the next verse to the unburied bones of Gallus. The construction is, sit mihi dolor (propter te), pulvis Etrusca, quia tu perpessa es &c.—*projecta*, sc. *jacere*; an idiom like *nolim factum*. *Sis* Barth and Kuinoel after Scaliger. Müller, after Lachmann, reads *sis* for *sit*. A neater reading, but further from the copies, would be *tu mihi*.

9.] *Proxima contingens*, &c., 'joining close with the champaign country beneath it.' See lib. v. l. 121, where the poet mentions Mevania as in the immediate vicinity of his birth-place, which was probably *Asisium* (Asisi). The Umbrian, like the Etrurian, towns, seem to have been built on rocky eminences, to which allusion is made in v. 1, 125, 'scandentisque Asis consurgit vertice murus,' and *ibid.* 65, 'scandentes siquis cernet de vallibus arces.' Virg. *Georg.* ii. 156, 'Tot congesta manu præruptis oppida saxis.'

PROPERTII

LIBER SECUNDUS.

I.

QUÆRITIS, unde mihi totiens scribantur amores,
  Unde meus veniat mollis in ore liber.
Non hæc Calliope, non hæc mihi cantat Apollo:
  Ingenium nobis ipsa puella facit.
Sive illam Cois fulgentem incedere coccis,

I. Addressed to Mæcenas, who appears to have urged our poet to attempt nobler strains, and to sing *res egregii Cæsaris* (Hor. *Od.* i. 6, 11). To which exhortation he replies that his genius is not adapted for any but elegiac composition, and that Cynthia is his perpetual theme.

2.] *In ore.* 'Dum in ore versatur et legitur versus, mollis apparet.'—*Hertzberg.* In this sense we have in Ar. *Ach.* 198, *κἂν τῷ στόματι λέγωσι, βαῖν' ὅπῃ θέλεις.* Others, as Keil and Müller, have *in ora*, with the ed. Rheg.

5—10.] The order of these three distichs has been reversed by Lachmann, with the approval of Jacob and Hertzberg, followed by both Keil and Müller. Lachmann objects to the apodosis following the protasis in the first verse, while the construction of that protasis itself depends on the third (*vidi*). Were the reading of the fifth verse certain, it would be more easy to give a definite opinion on the necessity of the transposition. The MSS. however give *cavis* or *chois*, and *togis* at the end of the line; for which Lachmann conjectured *coccis*, and this has been received by both Jacob and Hertzberg. Kuinoel gives *incedere vidi*, which removes the difficulty of the construction at the expense of probability, *vidi* being only found in two late and corrected copies. Barth has 'sive togis illam—Cois,' with the Aldine. It seems to me that this principle of transposition is rather a violent remedy; and granting that the order in the text is somewhat harsh, we cannot say that it is unintelligible, or tie Roman poetry strictly to rules drawn up by ourselves. Lachmann also reads *in Coa veste* for *e*, but the latter may surely mean that a whole book is composed *out of*, *i. e.* on the subject of, Cynthia's dress and varied accomplishments. The *toga* was the dress of a *meretrix*; but there is good reason to doubt whether Cynthia would have assumed that degrading habit: see on i. 2, 2. It is certainly harsh to anticipate *vidi* in v. 5, from *seu vidi* in v. 7: see however iii. 15, 11—3, though even this leaves the principal difficulty, the apodosis following the ellipse, undefended. On the whole, it seems best to follow Jacob and Hertzberg in retaining the common order, and admitting *coccis*. Coccum is a a dye extracted from an insect on the quercus coccifera, or Kermes oak; it must not be confounded with Tyrian dye, as Martial combines 'Tyriasque coccinasque,' iv. 28. Compare Hor. *Sat.* ii. 6, 102, 'rubro ubi cocco picta super lectos canderet vestis eburnos.' Juvenal, *Sat.* iii. 283, 'coccina læna.' In the present passage, it means not only the dye, but the dyed stola. See on i. 2, 2, and compare ii. 3, 15; iii. 21, 25; iv. 10, 15, whence it will appear that the poet had conceived a particular admiration for this silk dress of Cynthia's.

Hoc totum e Coa veste volumen erit;
Seu vidi ad frontem sparsos errare capillos,
Gaudet laudatis ire superba comis;
Sive lyræ carmen digitis percussit eburnis,
Miramur, faciles ut premat arte manus;
Seu cum poscentes somnum declinat ocellos,
Invenio causas mille poeta novas;
Seu nuda erepto mecum luctatur amictu,
Tum vero longas condimus Iliadas;
Seu quicquid fecit, sive est quodcumque locuta,
Maxima de nihilo nascitur historia.
Quod mihi si tantum, Mæcenas, fata dedissent,
Ut possem heroas ducere in arma manus,
Non ego Titanas canerem, non Ossan Olympo
Impositum, ut cæli Pelion esset iter;
Non veteres Thebas, nec Pergama, nomen Homeri,
Xerxis et imperio bina coisse vada;
Regnave prima Remi, aut animos Carthaginis altæ,
Cimbrorumque minas, et benefacta Mari;
Bellaque resque tui memorarem Cæsaris, et tu
Cæsare sub magno cura secunda fores.
Nam quotiens Mutinam, aut civilia busta Philippos,

10.] *Premat.* 'Comprimat manus, casque chordis imprimat.' Kuinoel, absurdly. Of the two interpretations here combined, the latter appears the true one.

11.] Kuinoel reads *somnos* from the MS. Gron. in defence of *poscentes* quoting iv. 10, 12, 'Surge, et poscentes justa precare deos,' *i. e.* poscentes invocari.

15.] *Seu quicquid* &c. Supply *mulier*, or *scribo de ea*, quicquid fecit.—*de nihilo*, a whole story grows out of the most trifling incidents.

17.] 'Had nature given me the talent of writing epic poetry, I should not have selected mythological subjects for my theme, but the exploits of Cæsar, and your connexion with them.'—*heroas manus*, *i. e.* heroum copias, which the poet himself is said *ducere in arma* by singing of their achievements. A similar figure occurs in Horace, *Od.* ii. 1, 17.

18.] *Heroas manus*, for *heroicas*, like *heroas manus afferre*, Persius i. 69. Cf. i. 6, 29, 'non ego sum laudi, non natus idoneus armis.'

20.] The MSS. vary between *impositam* and *impositum*. Lachmann alone has preferred the latter, which, being the more obvious construction, is probably due to a correction. Understand *Ossam montem*, as Ossa is feminine in Ovid, *Am.* ii. 1, 14, quoted by Lachmann.

22.] There is truth in Hertzberg's remark, that *bina coisse vada* cannot possibly signify the union of two continents by a bridge over the Hellespont, since *vada* would here stand for *litora*, which is absurd. He understands it therefore of the canal said to have been cut through Athos, Herod. vii. 21, quoting Juven. x. 173, 'creditur olim velificatus Athos.' Lachmann, objecting to the form of genitive *Xerxis*, reads *Xerxive imperio*.

24.] *Benefacta Mari*, τὰ καλῶς πεπραγμένα, the victory of Marius over the Cimbri, and his other military and political achievements. Similarly Tac. *Ann.* iii. 40, 'majorum bona facta.'

27.] *Civilia busta*, ubi sepulti jacent tot cives. Compare 'patria sepulcra' i. 22, 3.

Aut canerem Siculæ classica bella fugæ,
Eversosque focos antiquæ gentis Etruscæ,
Aut Ptolemæei litora capta Phari,
Aut canerem Cyprum et Nilum, cum tractus in urbem
Septem captivis debilis ibat aquis,
Aut regum auratis circumdata colla catenis,
Actiaque in Sacra currere rostra Via;
Te mea Musa illis semper contexeret armis,
Et sumpta et posita pace fidele caput.
Theseus infernis, superis testatur Achilles,

—*classica bella*, i. e. navalia. He alludes to the defeat of Pompey by Octavian off the coast of Sicily, A.U.C. 718. Hor. *Epod.* ix. 7, 'ut nuper, actus cum freto Neptunius dux fugit ustis navibus,' &c. An event at which it would seem from *Epod.* i. 1—4, that Mæcenas was present.

29.] *Focos Etruscæ gentis.* The siege of Perusia. See on i. 21—2.

30.] Hertzberg is probably right in reading *Ptolemæei*, on the analogy of Ὁμήρειος from Ὅμηρος, Πτολεμαιεῖος from Πτολεμαῖος. Jacob gives *Ptolemæe*, Lachmann *Ptolemæïa*, Müller *Ptolemæei*. Compare *Menelaeus*, iii. 6, 14. The MSS. agree in the masculine form, in defence of which Hertzberg quotes *Alexandrini Phari* from Suet. Claud. 20. The capture of Alexandria by Augustus is the historical event alluded to. See Hor. *Od.* iv. 14, 35.

31.] *Cyprum* is the reading of Hertzberg from MS. Gron. Kuinoel and Jacob give *Ægyptum* from the ed. Rheg. The Naples MS. has *cyptum*, which is about equally in favour of both. 'Cyprum inter titulos triumphi referri ne mireris: hanc provinciam Antonius Cleopatræ gratificatus regno Ægyptiaco addiderat, non sine maxima sui invidia. Testes Plutarch. Anton. 36, 54. Strabo xiv. 6, extr.—*Hertzberg.* Müller approves of Baehrens' correction *Coptum*, citing 'Mareotica Coptos' from Statius, *Th.* i. 264. Lachmann reads aut *canerem ereptum et Nilum.* The metaphor of the Nile enchained, and dragged to Rome as a captive with its seven mouths, is a happy one, expressive of Egypt being reduced to a Roman province by Augustus. Compare Ovid, *Fast.* i. 286, 'Tradiderat famulas jam tibi Rhenus aquas.'

33.] 'Reges, ante currum triumphalem ducti—intelliguntur qui Antonio Bruto Sexto Pompeio et aliis Augusti hostibus faverant.'—*Kuinoel.* For *aut* (in 33) Lachmann reads *et*, observing that 31—4 describe the details of the triumph, the former verses the events preceding it. But the poet may well be supposed to have selected some special characteristic of the procession, and dwelt on that in particular.

34.] The prows or rather the beaks of ships destroyed in the battle of Actium seem to have been carried in the triumphal procession along the Via Sacra to the Capitol.

35.] In celebrating the above exploits, the poet declares that his Muse should inweave the name of Mæcenas, as having taken an active part in them; but whether merely by his counsels, or by having been personally present in some of the engagements, as Kuinoel thinks, it is not easy to decide, in the absence of direct historical testimony.

37.] Having alluded to the fidelity of Mæcenas to his friend and patron Augustus, the poet passes by a somewhat abrupt transition to illustrate it by the example of Theseus and Pirithous, Achilles and Patroclus. We must therefore simply supply *sic* before *testatur*, the sense being, 'So Theseus makes Pirithous a witness to his friendship among the shades below, and Achilles makes Patroclus among those on earth,' (or, the gods above). It is probable that this distich was added as an afterthought by way of compliment to Mæcenas, and that it was intended to illustrate the double relation of the friend to the patron, *et sumpta et posita pace*, by instances of fidelity *apud infernos et superos*; a clumsy and pointless comparison, it must be admitted. In the short verse, it will be observed that the usual rule in the use of *hic* and *ille* is violated from the necessity of the metre. See iii. 13, 38; iv. 14, 18.

Hic Ixioniden, ille Menœtiaden.
Sed neque Phlegræos Jovis Enceladique tumultus
Intonet angusto pectore Callimachus;
Nec mea conveniunt duro præcordia versu
Cæsaris in Phrygios condere nomen avos.
Navita de ventis, de tauris narrat arator,
Enumerat miles vulnera, pastor oves;
Nos contra angusto versantis prœlia lecto:
Qua pote quisque, in ea conterat arte diem.
Laus in amore mori; laus altera, si datur uno
Posse frui. Fruar o solus amore meo!
Si memini, solet illa leves culpare puellas,
Et totam ex Helena non probat Iliada.
Seu mihi sint tangenda novercæ pocula Phædræ,
Pocula privigno non nocitura suo,
Seu mihi Circæo pereundum est gramine, sive

39.] 'But, as Callimachus, whom I propose to myself as a model, would not have lungs enough (so to say) to thunder forth the battle of the giants, so neither have I the genius to treat of *Julius a magno demissum nomen Iulo.*' (Virg. Æn. i. 288).—'*Nomen condere in avos* est, Cæsaris nomen ad Trojanorum gentem transferre, et celebrare inde a prima gentis origine.' *Kuinoel.*—'Celebrando Augusti nomen usque in Phrygios avos carmine ascendere,' *Hertzberg*: i. e. to trace it back till lost in the dim obscure of antiquity.—*duro versu* (dative) is opposed to *molli*, epic contrasted with elegiac, as has been pointed out on i. 9, 12. The ordinary construction would be *conveniunt præcordiis versu condere* &c.

45.] *angusto*, opposed to the *latus campus* of real warfare.—*versantis*, amatoria prœlia versantis se in lecto &c. This is Müller's reading and explanation for *versantes*. The construction, according to Hertzberg, is, *nos contra* (narramus) *versantes* &c., the accusative *versantes* depending on a verb implied in *enumerat*, v. 44. This, though rather harsh, is better than cutting the knot by reading *versamus* with Passow and Kuinoel.—*Qua pote.* See on iv. 7, 10.

47.] In this verse the poet anticipates an objection which he feels will be raised against his profession of an amatory poet, and maintains that there is credit in an attachment which, like his own, is constant to one object. For *uno* Hertzberg reads *uni*, and explains the sense thus: 'Pulchrum est, in amore mori, pulchrum hoc quoque, si contingat ut semotis remotis uni fruaris amore; quod ut mihi contingat non modo opto, sed futurum esse etiam spero.' This is not improbable; but I cannot enter into his elaborate objections to *uno*, the sense being sufficiently simple, 'it is likewise a credit, if a man is privileged to have one and not more than one love.' It is something to boast of, that is, to keep the object of your affection exclusively to yourself. And he proceeds in v. 49 to extol Cynthia's fidelity to him.

50.] *Ex Helena*, δι' Ἑλένην. She does not approve of the whole of the Iliad, in consequence of Helen's character as therein depicted.

51—6.] 'Ne efficacissimis quidem veneficarum potationibus adigar ut dominam prodam. Moriar potius, dum ultra vires resisto, quam seduci me patiar. Nam contra amorem Venere irata pertinaciter obnitentibus mortem certam futuram omnis antiquitas credidit.'—*Hertzberg.*

52.] *Privigno*, her step-son Hippolytus. The story here alluded to may have been given in the original play of Euripides, that which we now have being a second and altered edition, Ἱππόλυτος Στεφανηφόρος.

Colchis Iolciacis urat aëna focis:
Una meos quoniam prædata est femina sensus,
Ex hac ducentur funera nostra domo.
Omnes humanos sanat medicina dolores:
Solus amor morbi non amat artificem.
Tarda Philoctetæ sanavit crura Machaon,
Phœnicis Chiron lumina Phillyrides;
Et deus extinctum Cressis Epidaurius herbis
Restituit patriis Androgeona focis;
Mysus et Hæmonia juvenis qua cuspide volnus
Senserat, hac ipsa cuspide sensit opem.
Hoc si quis vitium poterit mihi demere, solus
Tantaleæ poterit tradere poma manu.
Dolia virgineis idem ille repleverit urnis,
Ne tenera assidua colla graventur aqua.
Idem Caucasia solvet de rupe Promethei
Brachia, et a medio pectore pellet avem.
Quandocumque igitur vitam mea fata reposcent,
Et breve in exiguo marmore nomen ero,
Mæcenas, nostræ pars invidiosa juventæ,

54.] The MSS. reading *Colchiacis* appears to me so intolerable, that I have here followed Lachmann in admitting Scaliger's correction.—*urat aena*, *i. e.* subjecto igne calefaciat, ad me recoquendum et renovandum.—*Barth.* So 'urit officinas' Hor. *Od.* i. 4, 8.

56.] '*Ex hac domo.* Latet, quod nemo sensit, 'in hujus amplexu moriar.''—*Hertzberg.*

57—62.] The general sense is, 'All maladies may be cured but love.' For the particular instances adduced, see Ovid, *Met.* xiii. 329; viii. 307. *Deus Epidaurius* is Æsculapius, who restored Androgeos, son of Minos king of Crete, to life, with some others, for which he was punished by Jupiter. See on Æsch. *Agam.* 992. Propertius is the only writer who records this legend of Androgeos.

63.] *Mysus juvenis*, Telephus, who was wounded by Achilles, and afterwards cured by the rust from his brazen spear, according to Pliny, *N. H.* xxv. 5, quoted by Kuinoel.

65.] *Hoc vitium*, this weakness, *vices*, viz. the love of women.

66.] The MSS. have *Tantalea*, which both Jacob and Hertzberg retain, though the latter strongly approves the conjecture of Beroaldus, *Tantaleæ*; and this Barth, Lachmann, and Kuinoel have admitted. The error naturally arose from the copyists misunderstanding the contracted form of the dative *manu*: see on i. 11, 12. Nevertheless, the frequent use which Propertius makes of the ablative under the most unusual conditions renders it possible that the vulgate may be right, and may signify *ita tradere ut ponantur in manu*. Compare 'cum temere anguino creditur ore manus,' v. 8, 10. The sense in either case is clear; 'he who can cure me of love, can also put the apples in the hand of Tantalus, and fill the leaking tubs of the Danaids with their urns.' *assidua aqua*, 'by the waterpots always resting on them,' to fill the *dolium*, or large earthenware jars, by water carried to it in the *urnæ*. For *urnis* Müller gives *umbris* after Baehrens. What he says of the vulgate, that it is *ineptum*, might surely be retorted on the emendation. —*ero*, i. e. *ut non*, [illegible].

71.] *Reposcent*, shall demand back the span of life they gave me to enjoy for a time.

73.] Hertzberg, Jacob, and Müller read *pars invidiosa* with the MS. Groning. Kui-

Et vitæ et morti gloria justa meæ,
Si te forte meo ducet via proxima busto,
Esseda cælatis siste Britanna jugis,
Taliaque illacrimans mutæ jace verba favillæ:
Huic misero fatum dura puella fuit.

II.

Liber eram, et vacuo meditabar vivere lecto;
At me composita pace fefellit Amor.
Cur hæc in terris facies humana moratur?
Juppiter, ignoro pristina furta tua.
Fulva coma est, longæque manus, et maxima toto

noel, Lachmann, and Keil give *oper* from the Naples MS. and the ed. Rheg. I think Hertzberg gives a satisfactory explanation: '*nostra juventa* erit *Romana*;—*pars* autem *invidiosa juventæ Romanæ*, invidia dignus juvenis Romanus Mæcenas dicitur, ut *pars militiæ*, pars imperii.' (i. 21, 4; *ib.* 6, 34). The use of *invidiosus* in a good sense may be illustrated by Æsch. *Ag.* 912, ὁ δ' ἀφθόνητός γ' οὐκ ἐπίζηλος πέλει. Allusion is at the same time intended to the Equites, who were distinctively called *juvenes*, and to whom Mæcenas prided himself in belonging. Compare iv. 9, 1, 'Mæcenas, eques Etrusco de sanguine regum.' Hor. *Od.* iii. 16, 20, 'Mæcenas, Equitum decus.'

76.] *Esseda Britanna*, for *Britannica*, as *Liburna* for *Liburnica*, iv. 11, 44. *Juno Pelasga* iii. 20, 11. *Inda* for *Indica*, iv. 13, 5. *esseda* were properly the Celtic war-chariots, which were introduced at Rome for the purposes of travelling,—with certain modifications from their barbarous form, we are bound to suppose. Kuinoel refers to Cæsar, *Bell. Gall.* iv. 24. Sueton. *Calig.* 51. Virg. *Georg.* iii. 204.

II. This short but elegant elegy describes in glowing terms his admiration of Cynthia's beauty, and is a kind of apology for his having become so deeply enamoured of her, in violation of a solemn resolution to leave her.

1.] *Quærebam*, Kuinoel, which has no MS. authority, and is supposed by Lachmann to have arisen from an oversight on the part of Scaliger. It is not nearly so elegant as *meditabar*.—*composita pace* is explained by Kuinoel *ficta, simulata*, as *componis insidias* iii. 24, 19; *componere fraudes* ii. 9, 31. But Lachmann (Præf. p. xxv.) understands 'pacem integrato amore cum Cynthia factam,' quoting from Livy ii. 13, 'his conditionibus composita pace,' and Æn. viii. 339, 'Disjice compositam pacem.' Thus the sense seems rather to be, 'I vainly flattered myself, that having made a truce with love, I should live for the future unmolested by him. Compare v. i. 138, 'Et Veneris pueris utilis hostis eris.' The peace is that made with Love, not that with Cynthia, as Lachmann thought. From ii. 3, 3, it seems that his resolution to live apart only lasted a month.

3.] 'Why does so fair a form still linger on earth?' I think nothing of those famous charms with which you made free, O Jupiter, when I compare them with Cynthia.' *Ignoro* approaches closely to the English use; 'I ignore them;' *i.e.* I do not take any account of them, [illegible].—*ignosco*, which is written above the word in the Naples MS., not only changes the sense materially but absolutely requires another construction. The meaning is, if Jupiter were really as amorous as he is represented in the legends, he certainly would have carried Cynthia up to the sky. We might, however, suggest either *ignores* or *ignoras*, 'you disown them,' will not admit their reality, now that so much more beautiful a woman lives on earth.

5.] *Longæ manus*, 'taper hands.' A well-shaped hand is a part of a portrait which is especially regarded; and it is well known how proud the possessors of such a feature are wont to be. Cf. iii. 8, 23.—*Jove digna soror*, a brief expression

Corpore, et incedit vel Jove digna soror.
Aut cum Dulichias Pallas spatiatur ad aras,
Gorgonis anguiferæ pectus operta comis.
Qualis et Ischomache, Lapithæ genus, heroïne,
Centauris medio grata rapina mero,
Mercurio et Sais fertur Bœbeïdos undis
Virgineum primo composuisse latus.
Cedite jam, divæ, quas pastor viderat olim
Idæis tunicas ponere verticibus.
Hanc utinam faciem nolit mutare senectus,
Etsi Cumææ secula vatis aget.

for *quæ sit Jovis soror*; 'worthy of Jove as his sister.'—*incedit*, cf. Virg. Æn. i. 46. *Fulva coma est.* The light flaxen hair of the Teutonic type, so common in those of Saxon descent in our country, but so rare among the black-haired and olive-complexioned natives of the south of Europe, was greatly admired by both Greeks and Romans. The former called it ξανθή, a word difficult to disconnect with ξουθός, on the analogy of our word *flaxen*. οὔλη κόμη was crisp, woolly hair, as opposed to hair which could be plaited or woven from its soft and pliant nature, and the word ξανθή may have passed into the secondary signification of the *colour* of such hair.

7.] The epithet *Dulichias* appears to refer to some cultus of Pallas in the island of Dulichium (one of the Echinades), of which no account has come down to us. As this goddess was the especial patroness of Ulysses, in whose dominions the island lay, (see iii. 5, 4), it seems rash to alter the word to *Munychias*, as Kuinoel has done with some of the corrected copies. The next line describes the ægis: see on v. 9, 58. For *aut cum* Hertzberg and others suggest *ut cum*, with great probability. But the idea in the poet's mind may have been 'Cynthia is as fair as Juno *or* Pallas.'

9.] I quite agree with Hertzberg, that the common reading, *Lapithæ genus heroinæ*, cannot be defended. As the good copies agree in *heroïne*, it seems better to consider it as the Greek form of the nominative. *Lapithæ* is the genitive singular of *Lapithas*, the hero or eponym of the Lapithæ. Ischomache (called also Hippodamia) was the wife of Peirithous, king of the Lapithæ; and it was at her nuptials, and in consequence of her being carried off by a Centaur, that the battle between the Centaurs and the Lapithæ arose. See inf. ii. 6, 18.

11.] The Naples and Groning. MSS. have *Mercurio satis*. Lachmann, Kuinoel, and Keil edit *sanctis* from an interpolated copy; Jacob *Saitis*, from his own conjecture: Hertzberg with Pucci, *Mercurio et Sais*. Müller, with Aldus, *Mercurioque* &c. For *primo* in the pentameter Lachmann and Kuinoel, followed by Keil and Müller, give *Brimo* (Βριμώ) a name of Proserpine, who is said to have been assaulted by Mercury near the Bœbian lake in Thessaly; for which legend reference is given to several grammarians in Kuinoel's note. The correction, which is Turnebe's, is exceedingly ingenious and probable. On the other hand, Minerva is called Σάις κατὰ τὴν Αἰγυπτίων φωνὴν in Pausanias, ix. 12, 2, (the reference in Hertzberg's note to the Schol. on Æsch. *Sept. c. Theb.* 169 is a mistake), and all accounts represent Proserpine not only as having successfully resisted the advances of Mercury, but even as having derived her name *Brimo* from the terrible fury she displayed on this very occasion. But Jacob and Hertzberg incline to the opinion that the Egyptian Minerva was essentially the same in her attributes as Proserpine, and that Propertius has followed (as in so many other instances) a somewhat different legend from any which is known to us. A verse of Hesiod preserved by Strabo, ix. 5, is believed to refer to this legend, νίψατο Βοιβιάδος λίμνης πόδα παρθένος ἀδμής.

16.] *Et sic* Kuinoel, contrary to the good copies, and with great detriment to the sense, which is obvious: 'may her beauty never be spoiled by age, though she live as long as the Sibyl.'

III.

Qui nullam tibi dicebas jam posse nocere,
  Hæsisti: cecidit spiritus ille tuus.
Vix unum potes, infelix, requiescere mensem,
  Et turpis de te jam liber alter erit.
Quærebam, sicca si posset piscis arena,
  Nec solitus ponto vivere torvus aper,
Aut ego si possem studiis vigilare severis:
  Differtur, numquam tollitur ullus amor.
Nec me tam facies, quamvis sit candida, cepit,—
  Lilia non domina sint magis alba mea:
Ut Mæotica nix minio si certet Hibero,
  Utque rosæ puro lacte natant folia;—
Nec de more comæ per levia colla fluentes,
  Non oculi, geminæ, sidera nostra, faces;
Nec si qua Arabio lucet bombyce puella,—
  Non sum de nihilo blandus amator ego,—
Quantum quod posito formose saltat Iaccho,
  Egit ut euantes dux Ariadna choros,

III. The subject is much the same as the last. The poet admits, while he alleges the reasons of, his complete enslavement to his mistress.

1.] The MSS. have *nullum*, which Jacob alone retains, while he assents to the correction of Heinsius, *nullam*. The poet addresses himself: 'This then, is the end of all your boasting and *fastus*' (i. 1, 3).

4.] *Liber alter*. The first book was therefore already published, and only a month before the commencement of the second.—*de te*, viz. as containing a confession and exposure of your frailties.

5.] *Quærebam*, etc. 'In this resolve' (see v. 1 of the preceding) 'I was in fact expecting the impossibility of an animal living out of its own element.' On *nec solitus* see iii. 20, 52.

7—8.] 'Or whether I myself could give my attention to severe studies: (but alas! in vain:) love may be put off for a time, but is never entirely removed.' Here *ego* is emphatic, as in contrast with *piscis* and *aper*.

9.] *cepit*, cf. i. 1, 1.

11.] *Minio Hibero*, 'vermilion from Spain,' *i. e.* cinnabar, or ore of Mercury. K. refers to Pliny *N.H.* 33, 7. The μίλτος of Homer proves its use as a colouring matter from very early times.

12.] The elegant comparison of rose-leaves in milk with the delicate contrasts of colour in a youthful face occurs also in *Æn.* xii. 68, 'aut mixta rubent ubi lilia multa alba rosa.' (K.)

15.] '*Si qua*, *i. e.* si forte vel quandocunque.' Jacob; which Hertzberg approves of, comparing *Æn.* i. 18, 'Si qua fata sinant.' He might have added ib. vi. 883, 'si qua fata aspera rumpas,' *&c.* But I think *siqua* is for *si aliqua*, and that the meaning is this: 'nor is it from the mere accident of a girl dressing in silk: I am not a man to become a devoted lover on such trifling grounds.' So iii. 4, 10, 'Nec siqua illustres femina jactat avos.'—*blandus amator*, *i. e.* qui blanditias adhibet, qui capere studet. Jacob draws a refined distinction between '*quia pulcra est et quod saltat*,' and '*si forte et quum*;' the causal and the conditional. On the silk dresses of the Roman ladies see on i. 2, 2. Becker, *Gallus*, p. 442 &c.

17.] From this verse (and inf. 33) the true character of Cynthia (*i.e.* as a meretrix) is sufficiently apparent. For her polite accomplishments see i. 2, 27.

Et quantum, Æolio cum tentat carmina plectro,
  Par Aganippeæ ludere docta lyræ,
Et sua cum antiquæ committit scripta Corinnæ,
  Carminaque Erinnes non putat æqua suis.
Num tibi nascenti primis, mea vita, diebus
  Candidus argutum sternuit omen Amor?
Hæc tibi contulerunt cælestia munera divi;
  Hæc tibi ne matrem forte dedisse putes.
Non, non humani sunt partus talia dona;
  Ista decem menses non peperere bona.
Gloria Romanis una es tu nata puellis;
  Romana accumbes prima puella Jovi.
Nec semper nobiscum humana cubilia vises;
  Post Helenam hæc terris forma secunda redit.
Hac ego nunc mirer si flagrat nostra juventus?
  Pulchrius hac fuerat, Troja, perire tibi.
Olim mirabar, quod tanti ad Pergama belli

19.] For *Æolio* Müller conjectures *Aonio*.

20.] *Aganippeæ lyræ*, the Muses.—*par* appears to be the nominative.

21.] *Et cum*, 'and when &c.' Hertzberg rightly observes that Corinnæ is the dative, being used for *scriptis Corinnæ* by a well-known idiom. Otherwise the construction might have been *cum* (scriptis) *Corinnæ*, σὺν ταῖς τῆς &c., but that the poet would have written *Corinnes*, as Hertzberg remarks. Compare II. 6, 23, 'Et sua cum miseræ permiscuit ossa puellæ.'

22.] The MSS. generally have *carmina quæ quivis* (evidently a correction), or *quæ lyrnes*. The latter (in MS. Gron.) retains a vestige of the true reading, which was restored by Beroaldus.—Corinna was a Bœotian poetess, contemporary with Pindar. Erinna lived still earlier (about B.C. 600). Both composed in the Æolic dialect, whence *Æolio plectro*, v. 19. There can be no doubt that in the Augustan age the ancient lyric poetry of Greece was extant, and extensively read and imitated.—The sentiment, perhaps, is not intended to be so boastful as it appears at first sight: 'she vies with the poetesses of old' is what the poet wished to express. There is an hyperbole however in either case.

24.] The MSS. have *ardens* or *ardidus*. Kuinoel gives *aureus* from Heinsius. Jacob and Lachmann *candidus*, which, being preserved by Macrobius, who quotes this verse (though with the error of *augusta* for *argutum*), seems evidently the true reading, especially as the accidental omission or obliteration of the initial *C* would account for the reading *ardidus*. Hertzberg's usual good judgment fails him here, when he says there is no reason why we should reject *ardidus*, (which he gives in the text), since it *may have been* formed from *ardeo* after the analogy of *timidus*, *tumidus*, *fervidus*, &c. The appeal to *what may have been* is always unsafe in a critic, who has only to deal with *what is*, in the state in which a language exists as known to him. The omen of sneezing was considered lucky even from the time of Homer (*Od.* xvii. 541), and a similar passage to the present is quoted from Theocr. vii. 96, Σιμιχίδᾳ μὲν Ἔρωτες ἐπέπταρον.

26.] *Forte* (*i.e.* fortuito) *dedisse* are to be connected, though *ne forte putes* is defensible if we suppose an ellipse, as ('which I say) lest' &c. On the rhyme in the following distich see I. 17, 5.

30.] The MSS. have *accumbens*. With some probability Lachmann and Jacob propose to change the order of these lines, so that *nec semper* &c. should be followed by *Romana accumbes* &c.

33.] *Flagrat* Keil and Müller for *flagret*. —*hac*, sc. quam Helena, *i.e.* propter Helenam.

Europæ atque Asiæ causa puella fuit:
Nunc, Pari, tu sapiens, et tu, Menelae, fuisti,
Tu, quia poscebas, tu, quia lentus eras.
Digna quidem facies, pro qua vel obiret Achilles;
Vel Priamo belli causa probanda fuit.
Si quis vult fama tabulas anteire vetustas,
Hic dominam exemplo ponat in arte meam:
Sive illam Hesperiis, sive illam ostendet Eois,
Uret et Eoos, uret et Hesperios.
His saltem ut tenear jam finibus; at mihi siquis,

38.] *Lentus*, sc. in reddendo quam injuria rapuisti. This is a clever distich.

39.] 'Beauty (in the abstract) I now feel to have been worth dying for, even if it cost the life of an Achilles; nay, it was deserving of approval (*probari debebat*) as a motive for war even by the aged Priam.' Lachmann reads *foret* with the MS. Groning. But this would imply the awkward ellipse of *vel* (quæ) *foret*, &c., the subjunctive depending on *digna*. The same MS. has *Priamus*. The verse has evidently been tampered with. Allusion is made to that fine scene, *Il.* iii. 154.

42.] 'Let that man portray my mistress.'—*ponere in arte* is so natural and correct an expression, that it seems surprising how Jacob and Lachmann should have preferred *in ante*, the reading of the Naples and Groning. MSS. Of the confusion between *a* and *r* we have had an instance in *ardidus* for (*c*)*andidus* sup. v. 24. Lachmann says, '*ante* verissimum est:—id est, ante quam alias tabulas ponat, pro exemplo pingat dominam nostram.' Truly, a most meagre sentiment.—*exemplo*, as an original to copy.

43.] 'Omnes quicunque Cynthiæ imaginem viderint, sive sint Eoi, sive Hesperii, eam deperibunt.'—*Kuinoel*. 'If the artist shall but exhibit the portrait of Cynthia to the nations of the east or the west, they will all be enamoured of her beauty.' Lachmann has a long note on this passage, of more curious learning than of practical utility, in which he collects from the best poets many examples of words *repeated with a change of the ictus*, as in the present instance, 'sive illam Hesperiis, sive illam ostendet Eois.'

45.] With this verse Keil and Müller with Jacob and Lachmann commence a new elegy, and print it in continuation with the next, contrary to the authority of the MSS. Lachmann writes at great length, but by no means convincingly, in favour of his new arrangement. 'Cum neque illi decem versus' (he says) '*His saltem* etc. prioribus commode conjungi queant, et hi versus *Multo prius* etc. in carminis principio positi difficiles intellectus habeant, quid probabilius est quam illos decem versus ad hoc posterius carmen pertinere?' But, if the sentiment here enunciated seems abrupt, is it not still more so at the beginning of another poem? Hertzberg appears to judge more correctly in the following words (*Quæst.* Lib. ii. cap. v. p. 66), 'Non raro poemata diversi illa quidem argumenti, sed quæ una eademque occasione nata exiguo temporis spatio interjecto scripta aut essent aut fingerentur, ab ipso poeta ita sunt conjuncta, ut, quomodo ab artificibus plures sæpe statuas in unum argumentum compositas esse videmus, sic in unius quodammodo corporis membra coirent.' He therefore places a mark of separation in this and other instances, to show the addition of an afterthought, or rather a postscript, to the poem as originally completed. The idea in the poet's mind seems to have been this: Cynthia's charms are such, that my former vows to live *vacuo lecto* were not broken without some excuse. My object now is to keep within the limits of this one new affection; for, since I experience such pangs in this, what should I suffer were another and still more ardent passion to possess me?' For *aut mihi si quis* Lachmann and Keil give *heu mihi, si quis*, Müller *si mihi*, Hertzberg *ah mihi, si quis* &c. I have some confidence in restoring *at mihi si quis*, which, like the Greek ἀλλ' εἰ, 'but what if,' furnishes the exact sense required. Compare Ovid, *Fast.* ii. 899, 'at si quis vestræ deus esset originis auctor,' if some fastidious critic should require an example of the

Acrius ut moriar, venerit alter amor!
Ac veluti primo taurus detrectat aratra,
Post venit assueto mollis ad arva jugo,
Sic primo juvenes trepidant in amore feroces,
Dehinc domiti post hæc æqua et iniqua ferunt.
Turpia perpessus vates est vincla Melampus,
Cognitus Iphicli subripuisse boves;
Quem non lucra, magis Pero formosa coegit,
Mox Amythaonia nupta futura domo.

IV.

Multa prius dominæ delicta queraris oportet,
Sæpe roges aliquid, sæpe repulsus eas,
Et sæpe immeritos corrumpas dentibus ungues,
Et crepitum dubio suscitet ira pede.
Nequicquam perfusa meis unguenta capillis,
Ibat et expenso planta morata gradu.
Non hic herba valet, non hic nocturna Cytæis,

concurrence of these words. At the same time I am aware that *ut* is not commonly used in interrogative sentences, and therefore it seems best to regard it as interjectional.—*acrius ut moriar*, like *peream*, must be understood metaphorically, of the distresses of love; as indeed *acriter mori* would have no meaning taken literally.

50.] *Ferunt*, sc. quæ sibi imperat domina.

51.] Melampus, son of Amythaon and brother of Bias, according to the common legend, undertook to drive the herd of Iphiclus for Neleus, the father of the fair Pero, that Bias might possess her as a wife. See Theocr. iii. 43; Hom. *Od.* xi. 290, xv. 225. Melampus however was caught in the attempt, and imprisoned for a time by Iphiclus. Being a seer, *προεῖπεν ὅτι φωραθήσεται, καὶ δεθεὶς ἐνιαυτὸν, οὕτω τὰς βοῦς λήψεται*, Apollodor. i. 9, 12. But, as Hertzberg remarks, our poet clearly represents Melampus himself to have been enamoured of Pero; otherwise there would be no point whatever in the illustration. The context shows, that Melampus had refused the offer of bribes, but yielded through love of Pero, though destined to be his brother's bride.

IV. Under the form of counsel and warning to a friend, the poet describes his own experience in love. He appears to have written this elegy when smarting under some provocation or disappointment.

1—4.] 'You will have to complain of many wrongs and many refusals; you will give way to much ill-temper and impatience, before the course of love becomes smooth for you.'—*immeritos*, you will gnaw the nails which deserved no such vengeance; cf. v. 3, 10, and *ib.* 4, 23.—*crepitum suscitet* (oportet), the *creaking* of the shoe from hasty and irresolute steps seems intended. Others explain it of the noise made by stamping on the ground. The latter is the more natural action, the former the more correct meaning of the word. *Crepare* however is used even of the notes of a pipe, v. 7, 25. *increpare* of the sharp ringing sound of a bow, ib. 3, 66, *fragor increpat*, *Æn.* viii. 527.

5.] 'I found it of no avail to perfume my hair and to walk with slow and measured step,' *ἁβρὸν βαίνειν*, *i.e.* in attempting to win the favour of Cynthia. The commentators compare the Greek expression *μετὰ ῥυθμοῦ βαίνειν*.

7—14.] 'Nor can love be treated as an ordinary malady, and cured by diet or drugs,' (as some think *φίλτρα* will cure it). —*Cytæis*, *i.e.* Medea: see on I. 1, 24.—*nocturna*, because spells were practised at

Non Perimedeæ gramina cocta manus.
Quippe ubi nec causas nec apertos cernimus ictus,
Unde tamen veniant tot mala, cæca via est.
Non eget hic medicis, non lectis mollibus æger;
Huic nullum cæli tempus et aura nocet.
Ambulat, et subito mirantur funus amici:
Sic est incautum, quicquid habetur amor.
Nam cui non ego sum fallaci præmia vati?
Quæ mea non decies somnia versat anus?
Hostis si quis erit nobis, amet ille puellas;
Gaudeat in puero, si quis amicus erit.
Tranquillo tuta descendis flumine cymba:
Quid tibi tam parvi litoris unda nocet?
Alter sæpe uno mutat præcordia verbo,
Altera vix ipso sanguine mollis erit.

night, by the aid of Hecate and in presence of the moon. Perimede was a celebrated enchantress, mentioned in connexion with Medea by Theocritus ii. 16. Apollodorus (i. 7, 3) records the name of Perimede daughter of Æolus king of Thessaly, who is perhaps the same, that country being renowned for witches.—The MSS. give *per Medeæ*, which Beroaldus corrected from a late MS. Lachmann and Hertzberg explain *manus* by *herbæ*,—i. e. *remedies* in general; in which opinion I cannot follow them. Why should not 'herbs distilled (*coctæ*) by the *hand* of Perimede' be allowed to signify philtres made after her recipe?

10.] *Tamen.* The sense is, 'For, where we cannot see the cause of the malady, the course of all these evils (*which nevertheless do spring from some source*) is uncertain, and their treatment empirical.' Hertzberg well compares v. 5 of the next elegy, and Ovid, *Fast.* i. 495, 'Nec fera tempestas toto tamen horret in anno,' though he has added other passages which are not to the point.

11.] 'It is no bodily affection; neither the season nor malaria has hurt him: he walks about in apparent health, and—drops down dead.' He means to express the perplexing nature of the malady of love, by comparing it with some obscure ailment (as disease of the heart) in which nothing does the patient any good, and by which he is suddenly carried off without, as it were, being actually ill.

14.] *Incautum*, ἀφύλακτον, i. e. non præcavendum. — *quicquid habetur amor*, quicquid illud est quod dicitur amare, 'the thing men call Love.' So Ovid, *Her.* xi. 32, 'Nec noram quid amans esset; at illud eram.' Eur. *Hippol.* τί τοῦθ', ὃ δὴ λέγουσιν ἀνθρώπους ἐρᾶν;

15.] 'How many seers and beldames have I not paid to interpret my dreams and tell me my fortune!' Theocr. ii. 90, καὶ ἐς τίνος οὐκ ἐπέρασα, ἢ ποίας ἔλιπον γραίας δόμον, ἅτις ἐπᾷδεν;

18.] *In puero*, in amasio. So v. 8, 63, 'Cynthia gaudet in exuviis victrixque recurrit.' 'My worst wish to an enemy is that he may be captivated by women; to a friend I would say, fix your regard upon a youth, where (inf. 19—22) the course of affection is smooth, and safe from rocks and shoals. The one is mollified by a word; the other is scarcely appeased by your very life-blood.' On *in puero* see on i. 13, 7. v. 8, 63.

20.] *Unda parvi litoris*, 'you will receive no harm from sailing in a small creek, which has none of the dangers of a great sea.' Either *litus* here means *ripa*, or *flumine* means *æstus*, the current or motion of the sea.

V.

Hoc verum est, tota te ferri Cynthia, Roma,
  Et non ignota vivere nequitia?
Hæc merui sperare? dabis mihi, perfida, pœnas;
  Et nobis aliquo, Cynthia, ventus erit.
Inveniam tamen e multis fallacibus unam,
  Quæ fieri nostro carmine nota velit,
Nec mihi tam duris insultet moribus, et te
  Vellicet. Heu sero flebis amatu diu!
Nunc est ira recens, nunc est discedere tempus:
  Si dolor abfuerit, crede, redibit amor.
Non ita Carpathiæ variant Aquilonibus undæ,
  Nec dubio nubes vertitur atra Noto,
Quam facile irati verbo mutantur amantes:
  Dum licet, injusto subtrahe colla jugo.
Nec tu non aliquid, sed prima nocte dolebis:
  Omne in amore malum, si patiare, leve est.
At tu, per dominæ Junonis dulcia jura,

V. He upbraids Cynthia with an inconstancy which was so notorious as to have become common gossip; and threatens to leave her, and write verses in praise of one more deserving of the honour. It is clear he feels himself piqued as a poet, as well as aggrieved as a man.

1.] *Ferri*, 'differri, diffamari.'—*Kuinoel.*

4.] The MSS. agree in *et nobis Aquilo*, a reading which, as Hertzberg pleasantly remarks, 'immanes tempestates interpretibus movit.' Accordingly, he admits *aliquo*, which is the almost certain correction of Lachmann, (or rather, his improvement upon Burmann's emendation *alio*). The sense will then be, 'We too will sail somewhere else,' *i.e.* I will attach myself to some other mistress. The metaphor we have just seen in the preceding elegy, vv. 19, 20. Jacob, while he retains the vulgate, assents to the correction. Should any one insist on the MSS. reading, perhaps *eris* for *erit* would afford the best solution of the difficulty; 'I too (like other disappointed lovers) shall hold you as fickle as the wind.' And this well suits not only inf. 11, but also the following distich: 'Yet, fickle as women are, I shall find some one who will be faithful to me, and will like to become known through my verse,' *i.e.* who will be grateful for the compliment. Otherwise (viz. reading *aliquo*) we must refer *tamen* to the use noticed above, 4, 10.

8.] *Vellicet.* 'Verbum vindictæ feminem in rivalem alteram apprime conveniens; te insectabitur, per ora hominum traducet. Horat. *Serm.* i. 10, 79, *vellicet absentem Demetrius.*'—*Kuinoel.* It may mean, 'vex and annoy you by the contrast of her attachment with your levity.'

11.] *Non ita*, supply *facile.*—*variant*, 'change colour.' See v. 2, 13, and on i. 15, 7.

14.] *Subtrahe.* He addresses himself, (as also, perhaps, in 9—10) and argues the necessity of immediate separation, having felt his own weakness in keeping resolutions before, ii. 3, 4.—*injusto*, *iniquo*, 'ill-matched.' Virg. *Georg.* iii. 347, 'Non secus ac patriis acer Romanus in armis Injusto sub fasce viam quum carpit.'

15.] 'Dolebis, sed iste dolor non ultra primæ noctis spatium protendetur.'—*Kuinoel.* Here also the poet addresses himself.

17.] After threatening Cynthia that he will abandon her for ever, he relents, and has recourse to the most gentle and winning expostulation. Propertius is eminently a poet of the heart. He carries with him the whole sympathy of the reader; and

Parce tuis animis, vita, nocere tibi.
Non solum taurus ferit uncis cornibus hostem,
Verum etiam instanti læsa repugnat ovis.
Nec tibi perjuro scindam de corpore vestem,
Nec mea præclusas fregerit ira fores;
Nec tibi connexos iratus carpere crines,
Nec duris ausim lædere pollicibus:
Rusticus hæc aliquis tam turpia prælia quærat,
Cujus non hederæ circuiere caput.
Scribam igitur, quod non umquam tua deleat ætas:
CYNTHIA FORMA POTENS, CYNTHIA VERBA LEVIS.
Crede mihi, quamvis contemnas murmura famæ,
Hic tibi pallori, Cynthia, versus erit.

VI.

Non ita complebant Ephyreæ Laïdos ædes,
Ad cujus jacuit Græcia tota fores,
Turba Menandreæ fuerat nec Thaïdos olim

the singular charm of his verses consists in their intense feeling, while Ovid is more indebted to his art in versification for making an impression on the affections.—*tuis animis*, 'through your own waywardness.'

18.] *Tuis animis*, ista ferocia, 'by that high spirit of yours.'

19—20.] 'Even a naturally harmless and quiet disposition can resent, if irritated beyond endurance.'

21.] *Nec*, i. e. *nec tamen*, 'Not that my revenge shall consist of vulgar violence. No! I am a poet, and you shall be punished by a verse' (28).

23.] *Connexos*, put together by a comb or hair-pins. Cf. v. 5, 31, 'si tibi forte comas vexaverit utilis ira.'

27.] *Quod non umquam* &c., 'which will be remembered as long as you live.' The subjunctive expresses the nature and quality of the verse. Cf. 5, 28.

28.] *Verba levis*, *i. e.* false in her professions of fidelity. Kuinoel and Barth read *forma levis*, inferior in sense (if indeed, it has any meaning at all, except that in i. 4, 9, quoted by Lachmann), and contrary to the authentic copies. Of all the absurdities (and they are not few) inflicted by Scaliger on Propertius, his emendation of this verse bears the palm: 'Cynthia formipotens, Cynthia verbilevis.'

29.] *Contemnis* Kuinoel and Barth, contrary to the MSS. and the usage of the best writers. Not that *quamvis*, when used for *quamquam* (*etsi*), may not be followed by an indicative, (as Virg. *Ecl.* iii. 84, inf. 8, 27), but that in this case it bears its proper sense of *however much*, and therefore requires the conjunctive.

VI. The subject of this elegy is so intimately connected with the last, that it is surprising that no adventurous editor has proposed to print it continuously. Jacob and Lachmann, (whom Keil and Müller more or less closely follow) have introduced marks of lacunæ in several places (after v. 24, 26, 34, 36), though there is no proof of anything having been lost except a certain abruptness, more imaginary than real,—certainly not greater than the excitement of the writer's mind would fairly account for. Of this propensity to 'disjunctiveness' we shall have many other instances to discuss in the present and succeeding books.

1—3.] Lais of Corinth and Thais of Alexandria were celebrated courtesans, whose beauty and accomplishments captivated the richest and greatest men of their day. The first lived in the time of the Peloponnesian war: the second was con-

Tanta, in qua populus lusit Erichthonius,
Nec quæ deletas potuit componere Thebas
  Phryne, tam multis facta beata viris.
Quin etiam falsos fingis tibi sæpe propinquos,
  Oscula nec desunt qui tibi jure ferant.
Me juvenum pictæ facies, me nomina lædunt,
  Me tener in cunis et sine voce puer;
Me lædit, si multa tibi dedit oscula mater,
  Me soror, et cum qua dormit amica simul.
Omnia me lædunt;—timidus sum; ignosce timori;—
  Et miser in tunica suspicor esse virum.

temporary with Alexander and the Ptolemies, who are said not to have been insensible to her charms. She is called 'Thais pretiosa Menandri' in v. 1, 43, from that poet having inscribed a play with her name.

4.] *Lusit*, 'disported itself,' 'found amusement.' Others render it, 'who was the object of their amours.' See iii. 9, 24, and i. 10, 9.—*in qua*, 'in the drama called after her name.' See note on i. 13, 7.—*populus Erichthonius*, the Athenians.

5.] Phryne, a contemporary of Thais, was a renowned beauty born in Bœotia, and so popular with the gay and the wealthy that she offered to rebuild Thebes at her own expense on condition that Alexander who destroyed it would consent to allow an inscription to record the facts.—*componere*, 'to put together,' *i.e.* rebuild. There is, of course, nothing in the word which of itself can imply *reponere*. This sense is derived from the epithet *deletas*. Kuinoel endeavours to elicit such a meaning from 'urbem componere terra,' *Æn.* iii. 387, and 'componere templa,' Ovid, *Fast.* 1, 708. With the latter passage the sense of v. 9, 74, accords better than the verse before us. In the first six lines we notice the compliment paid to Cynthia, by comparing her successes with those of the most celebrated ἑταῖραι of antiquity, together with a reproach for her shameless infidelity. The poet proceeds to express his jealous fears lest every pretended relation of Cynthia should prove a lover in disguise, and every portrait a souvenir of some favoured admirer.

6.] *Facta beata*, made rich by the costly presents of so many admirers.

8.] *Nec desunt*. There is a slight irony in this: 'you say they are only cousins, who have a right to salute you.' Jacob (probably by an oversight) has edited with Kuinoel and the emendated copies *ne desint*.

9.] *Numina*, Kuinoel, with one or two of the interpolated copies. This reading Hertzberg thinks 'non inficetum,' supposing with others that portraits of the gods may be meant, made to represent, according to a custom not unusual, likenesses of friends and admirers. But *nomina* (*i. e.* juvenum) pronounced by Cynthia as if speaking of her relations, is far more simple and natural, and has all the good copies in its favour.

10.] *Puer*. Cynthia had no child of her own. (See iii. 9, 33, 'cum tibi nec frater, nec sit tibi filius ullus.') The child alluded to does not therefore imply any fear that it was Cynthia's by another father, but simply that the poet is jealous of the kisses bestowed even on a child in the cradle: an hyperbole, as in the following distich.

12.] *Cum qua*, &c., et ea, cum qua amica dormit, *i. e.* even though my suspicions might fairly be removed by the circumstance. The two sleeping together would at least not indicate a lover's cunning device to obtain Cynthia. *Amica* is not Cynthia, but any friend or attendant; the idea uppermost in the poet's mind being, that a lover is lurking under this or that character, even though a female one. *Cum quæ*, the correction of Dousa, *i. e.* *cum aliqua*, for *si qua*, has received the approbation of Lachmann, Hertzberg, Jacob, Keil, and Müller.

14.] *In tunica*. Although this garment was worn by men, as was the toga under certain circumstances by women, it is clear from this passage that the two words, in a general sense, represent the distinctive dresses of the sexes. Compare v. 2, 23.

His olim, ut fama est, vitiis ad prœlia ventum est:
  His Trojana vides funera principiis.
Aspera Centauros eadem dementia jussit
  Frangere in adversum pocula Pirithoum.
Cur exempla petam Graium? tu criminis auctor,
  Nutritus duro, Romule, lacte lupæ.
Tu rapere intactas docuisti impune Sabinas;
  Per te nunc Romæ quidlibet audet Amor.
Felix Admeti conjunx et lectus Ulixis,
  Et quæcumque viri femina limen amat.
Templa Pudicitiæ quid opus statuisse puellis,
  Si cuivis nuptæ quidlibet esse licet?
Quæ manus obscenas depinxit prima tabellas,
  Et posuit casta turpia visa domo,
Illa puellarum ingenuos corrupit ocellos,
  Nequitiæque suæ noluit esse rudes.
Ah gemat, in terris ista qui protulit arte
  Jurgia sub tacita condita lætitia.

15—24.] The connexion of these verses with the preceding seems to be this: 'Such indeed are the frauds which women have ever practised, and such are the jealousies of men consequent upon them.' Of the latter he proceeds to give examples. 'De mulierum libidine accipias, quam efficere dicit, ut jure meritoque aliquis timeat.'—*Lachm.*

17.] 'The same infatuation led the Centaurs to break embossed beakers over the head of Pirithous.' See note on ii. 2, 9.

20.] *Dura*, Lachmann, Müller, and Kuinoel, with one late MS. Hertzberg compares v. 4, 52, 'dura papilla lupæ.'

21.] Compare v. 4, 57, 'at raptæ ne sint impune Sabinæ, me rape.'

23.] *Ulyxis.* According to analogy, this word should be written *Olixis*, and so (if I remember aright) Dr. C. Wordsworth copied it from the walls of Pompeii. Lachmann gives *Ulixi.* The Greek δ passes into the Latin *l*, as in *δάκρυ*, *lacrima*, &c.

25.] *Templa.* There were two, dedicated to P. patricia, in the forum boarium, and to P. plebeia, in the Vicus Longus. Livy, x. 23. The poet shows the absurdity and the mockery of public temples to Chastity, while every private house tended to a violation of that virtue by its internal decorations. The passage 27—36 is a very fine one; and it is curious to remark the ideas of morality which could induce a Propertius so feelingly to bewail the depravity of the women, unconscious of his own delinquencies.

26.] *Quidlibet*, *i. e.* not only a wife to her husband but a concubine to others. There seems no need of Lachmann's reading *cuilibet*, found in inferior copies. He thinks *nupta* is here not confined to the meaning of 'lawful wife,' but 'de illegitimo quoque amore dicitur.'

27.] *Tabellas.* From v. 34 it seems clear that the *fresco* paintings are meant, which were very frequently of the most amorous, not to say indecent description. To them perhaps Juvenal alludes in the celebrated lines, 'Nil dictu fœdum visuque hæc limina tangat, intra quæ puer est.' I scarcely comprehend on what ground Hertzberg, on v. 34, after Welcker, says, 'non picturas tectorias, sed tabellas parietibus inclusas,' comparing the present verse.

31.] *Gemat*, *[illegible]*. *In terris* for *sub terris*, says Kuinoel. There is no ground for such an interpretation: it is better to connect *in terris* with what follows.

32.] *Jurgia.* The quarrels and disputes of lovers, originating from what was meant tacitly to please the eye. The latter being the secret source of the former, are said *condere*, to conceal them. *Jurgia* are the same as the Greek *[illegible]*, a word peculiarly applied to disputes caused by jealousy.

Non istis olim variabant tecta figuris:
  Tum paries nullo crimine pictus erat.
Sed non immerito velavit aranea fanum,
  Et mala desertos occupat herba Deos.
Quæ igitur tibi custodes, quæ limina ponam,
  Quæ numquam supra pes inimicus eat?
Nam nihil invitæ tristis custodia prodest:
  Quam peccare pudet, Cynthia, tuta sat est.
Nos uxor numquam, numquam diducet amica:
  Semper amica mihi, semper et uxor eris.

VII.

Gavisa est certe sublatam Cynthia legem,
  Qua quondam edicta flemus uterque diu,

35.] 'Hoc distichon, præsertim hoc loco positum, intelligi nullo modo potest,' Lachmann; who places the mark of a lacuna before it. Hertzberg would read *sed nunc immerito*. It is difficult to see what the editors object to in the vulgate, of which the sense is by no means obscure: 'But now religion has fled; the temples (viz. of Mens, Fides, Pudicitia &c.) are deserted; vice and immorality prevail, and the gods are neglected. How *therefore* (v. 37) shall I keep my Cynthia virtuous, apart from her moral sense?'—*non immerito*, 'not without good reason,' *i.e.* no wonder the temples are deserted when all regard for piety is lost.

37.] *Quæ limina*, he should rather have said *ostium*, but he uses *ponam* in direct reference to *custodes*. Lachmann reads *quæ ad limina*, which makes an awkward elision, and is not necessary for the sense. —*eat*, see sup. 5, 27.

39.] *Nihil prodest invitæ*, *i.e.* nolenti pudicam esse non opus est custodem imponere: 'persuasæ fallere rima sat est,' v. 1, 146.

42.] 'For my part, I can assert that neither wife nor mistress shall ever draw me away from my Cynthia.' Keil and Müller mark a *lacuna* before the final distich. The point of it appears to be, that Propertius will remain faithful, though Cynthia be unfaithful. Such professions, made on the ardour of the moment or for a purpose, are hardly to be expected to possess the close coherence which a less impassioned reasoning might claim. But it is probable the allusion to *uxor* is the same as in the following elegy. The MSS. give *me ducet*. To avoid the change of *nos* and *me*, Lachmann gives *diducet*, (the Roman edition of 1482 having *deducet*), Kuinoel *uxor me numquam*.

VII. He congratulates Cynthia on his not being compelled by the law to take a wife, and so obliged to desert his mistress. A poem remarkable for its pathos and tenderness.

1.] *Gavisa es* Lachmann, Keil, Müller with Burmann.

Ibid. *Sublatam legem.* Tacit. *Ann.* III. 25: 'Relatum deinde de moderanda Papia Poppæa, quam senior Augustus, post Julias rogationes, incitandis cælibum pœnis et augendo ærario sanxerat. Nec ideo conjugia et educationes liberum frequentabantur, prævalida orbitate: ceterum multitudo periclitantium gliscebat, cum omnis domus delatorum interpretationibus subverteretur; utque antehac flagitiis, ita tunc legibus laborabatur.' See on this passage the excellent note of the last editor, Ritter. The Julian law alluded to he considers to have been revived in the year of the city 736; and certainly it was in force in 737, when Horace speaks of the 'patrum decreta super jugandis feminis,' *Carm. Sæc.* 17; but it was found so impracticable that it had to be modified shortly afterwards. An historical difficulty occurs in the discrepancy of dates, since the present book is shewn by Hertzberg to have been written in 728, and he is therefore driven to the supposition

Ni nos divideret; quamvis diducere amantes
  Non queat invitos Juppiter ipse duos.
At magnus Cæsar;—sed magnus Cæsar in armis:
  Devictæ gentes nil in amore valent.
Nam citius paterer caput hoc discedere collo,
  Quam possem nuptæ perdere amore faces,
Aut ego transirem tua limina clausa maritus,
  Respiciens udis prodita luminibus.
Ah mea tum qualis caneret tibi, Cynthia, somnos
  Tibia, funesta tristior illa tuba!
Unde mihi patriis gnatos præbere triumphis?

that some previous attempt of Augustus must be alluded to, (see *Quæst. Prop.* p. 224 seq.) and that the 'Juliæ rogationes' of Tacitus must be understood of a bill founded on Julius Cæsar's edict by Augustus, but which never passed into a law. The Lex Papia Poppæa was not carried till the year 762, or A.D. 9. The reason why Propertius could not have married Cynthia was that she was a *meretrix*; and such were not allowed by the Roman law to marry with *ingenui*. See Hertzberg, *Quæst.* lib. I. cap. vi. p. 36. Kuinoel's introductory note contains some errors from a misconception of the real character of Cynthia, whom he regards, and often describes in his commentary, as a lady of high birth.

3.] *Ni nos divideret.* The sense is, 'Sentire timebamus ne nos divideret.' *Ni* is an old usage for *ne*, which latter is the reading of the Groning. MS. Hertzberg rightly shows that since 'quicunque flet, aut doleat aut metuat necesse est,' the construction is sometimes adapted to both of these meanings. (*Quæst.* p. 156). In *dividere* and *diducere* a difference of sense seems intended: 'the law might *separate* us, though Jove himself could not break the bonds of mutual affection.'

5.] It is not very clear whether we should understand *at magnus* (est) *Cæsar*, or *at magnus Cæsar diducere potest* or *poterat*. The latter is the construction adopted by Lachmann and Kuinoel, and also by Hertzberg, who considers the flattery of making Augustus superior to Jove not too gross for the age: and he is right. But the poet may be supposed to correct himself after making an apparently disparaging remark on Cæsar's law; 'I admit indeed that he is great; but his greatness is in arms, not in controlling affections: and I say that neither he nor Jove himself can do this.'—*devictæ gentes*, &c. for 'devictæ gentes nil valet.' Cf. *Æn.* xi. 268, 'devictam Asiam subsedit adulter.'

8.] *Faces.* 'Intellige flammas amoris ingenuas, quas matrimonio perdere verebatur poeta.' Hertzberg; who compares i. 13, 26, and i. 18, 21. The earlier commentators absurdly explained this 'faces nuptiales inutili sumptu dispendioque frustra prodigendas.'

9.] The construction is, *aut* (quam) *transirem* &c. 'I would sooner die than have to pass by your house, and see it abandoned and closed, as I proceed to my home in the marriage procession.' The editors however agree in placing a full stop at *faces*, and commencing a new *interrogative* sentence with *aut ego* or *aute ego*.—*prodita*, *i.e.* a me: in the sense of *uproditis*.

11.] 'What sort of sleep would my pipers play to *you* in the same procession, as it passed by night conducting the bride to her husband? Would it not sound more doleful than the trumpets in a funeral?' For *Cynthia* the Naples MS. has *tybia*. In Kuinoel's and Barth's editions the verse is read *ah mea tum qualis faceret tibi tibia cantus*. The reader will notice the antithesis in *mea* and *tibi*. For the allusion in *tibia* and *tuba* compare Ovid, *Her.* xii. 140, 'Tibiaque effudit socialia carmina vobis, At mihi funesta flebiliora tuba.' In this, as in so many other instances, it is difficult to acquit Ovid of plagiarism. See also *inf.* v. 11, 9, 'Sic mæstæ cecinere tubæ.'

13.] *Unde mihi*, *i.e.* quo mihi? quid prodest? In most of the copies a new elegy commences with this verse. Lachmann and Jacob, followed by Keil and Müller, put a mark of a lacuna. But the

Nullus de nostro sanguine miles erit.
Quod si vera meæ comitarem castra puellæ,
Non mihi sat magnus Castoris iret equus.
Hinc etenim tantum meruit mea gloria nomen,
Gloria ad hibernos lata Borysthenidas.
Tu mihi sola places: placeam tibi, Cynthia, solus:
Hic erit et patrio sanguine pluris amor.

VIII.

Eripitur nobis jam pridem cara puella;

connexion is complete. 'Why should I marry, merely to furnish sons to grace the triumphal processions?' A general way of saying, 'to supply my country with soldiers.' Müller follows Lachmann in reading *Parthis* for *patriis*, *i.e.* 'triumphis e Parthis agendis.' This verse supplies a clear hint of the real motive in passing the laws *de maritandis ordinibus*: which indeed is known from other sources, viz., to supply the deficiency in the population caused by the civil wars, which rendered it difficult to procure a sufficient number of recruits. See Hor. *Od.* i. 2, 'vitio parentum rara juventus.'

15.] Compare v. 3, 45, 'Romanis utinam patuissent castra puellis.' Tacitus (*Ann.* iii. 33—4) records an interesting debate on a measure proposed in the senate 'ne quem magistratum, cui provincia obvenisset, uxor comitaretur;' which was negatived rather as an indulgence than on military principles.—For the obscure words *vera meæ*, Scaliger, followed as usual by Kuinoel, reads *Romanæ*; a most improbable conjecture on any known principles of palæography. Hertzberg, who reads *comitarent* with the MSS., thus explains it: 'Quamquam si castra, quæ puellæ meæ sequuntur, *i.e.* dulcis illa amoris militia (i. 6, 30) vera militia verumque bellum esset; summus miles par mihi non esset futurus.' Propertius (like most of the elegiac poets) constantly speaks of the *castra amoris*, as again v. 1, 138, so that it became almost necessary, if he wished to be understood in speaking of *real* warfare, to add *vera*.—*meæ puellæ*, in the plural, is used (as Hertzberg thinks) not only because 'one mistress does not make a camp,' but because the poet elsewhere openly boasts, as in iii. 28, 37, of the favour of several mistresses, 'ut regnet mixtas inter conviva puellas.' This is surely unsatisfactory. For it is obvious that Cynthia must be principally and in particular meant, since, taken literally, the plural involves an absurdity, as it would convert a compliment into an insult. But Keil and Müller follow Lachmann in retaining *comitarent*, and for *vera* Müller proposes *sera*, Lachmann *cura—comitari*. The whole passage is very obscure, and perhaps as Lachmann thinks, corrupt. He gives the general meaning nearly thus: 'Si Cynthia se comitaretur, non filios se militatum missurum esse, sed ipsum cum illa in castra profecturum; hanc enim solam carminis sui, hanc gloriæ causam esse, hanc unam præ omnibus sibi placere.' Jacob gives *comitarer* from the excerpta of Pucci, and perhaps on the whole this is the simpler sense: 'Were I in reality (*i.e.* not only as a *miles amoris*) to follow my Cynthia in the field, I would rush to battle as quickly as the best steed could carry me.' The horse of Castor,—as renowned for the equestrian as his brother for the pugilistic art,—was called *Cyllarus*, Virg. *Georg.* iii. 90.

17.] *Etenim.* There is an ellipse which must be supplied to connect the sense. ('But I do not fight, for I am by profession a poet:) it is from this, not from deeds of arms, that my fame lives.'

20.] *Patrio sanguine.* A singular expression for *procreandis liberis*, as Hertzberg appears rightly to explain it, referring it to the Julian law. *Patrio* is either for *paterno*, 'I prefer illicit love to the honours of paternity,' or it signifies the Roman race in a general sense. Compare *patriis triumphis*, 'national triumphs,' v. 13.

VIII. A singularly elegant and eloquent composition, lamenting the success of a rival, and threatening vengeance against both him and the faithless Cynthia. The parties alluded to in vv. 3 and 5 are un-

Et tu me lacrimas fundere, amice, vetas!
Nullæ sunt inimicitiæ, nisi amoris, acerbæ;
Ipsum me jugula, lenior hostis ero.
Possum ego in alterius positam spectare lacerto?
Nec mea dicetur, quæ modo dicta mea est?
Omnia vertuntur; certe vertuntur amores:
Vinceris, aut vincis; hæc in amore rota est.
Magni sæpe duces, magni cecidere tyranni,
Et Thebæ steterunt, altaque Troja fuit.
Munera quanta dedi, vel qualia carmina feci!
Illa tamen numquam ferrea dixit: Amo.
Ergo jam multos nimium temerarius annos,
Improba, qui tulerim teque tuamque domum.
Ecquandone tibi liber sum visus? an usque
In nostrum jacies verba superba caput?

known. Lachmann divides this elegy into two at v. 17, and prints the first part as lacunose, in which he is followed by Jacob and Müller. Having a decided opinion on the unity and integrity of the whole, as arranged in all the MSS., I have not hesitated to restore the old way, with Hertzberg, Kuinoel, and Keil.

1.] *Jam pridem cara* must be construed together. He means to express his prior claims to possession arising from long attachment.—*jampridem eripitur* would mean 'has this long time been gradually leaving me,' and is less consistent with the outburst of grief implied in the next verse.

3.] *Acerbæ*, 'implacable.'—*amoris*, resulting from, or on the subject of, love.

8.] *Rota*, 'the turn of fortune,' in reference to *vertuntur*. Müller, after Scaliger, places this distich after v. 10. This seems to pervert the sense entirely, since *magni sæpe duces* &c. are cited as an example of the fickleness of fortune.

10.] The MSS. have *steterant*, which Jacob alone retains in the text, though approving of Scaliger's correction. It is not so certain that Propertius would have preferred *steterunt* to a lax use of the pluperfect, were the alternative to choose between them.

11.] *Vel*. 'cum levi correctione copulat.'—*Jacob*. Hertzberg has this good note: 'cum *aut* non posse simul esse duas res significet; *et* vero simpliciter, esse simul; *vel* in medio positum non debere quidem simul esse, sed posse ita cogitari, indicat.' For example: *aut vir, aut femina* (but not both): *et vir et femina* (both at once): *vel vir vel femina* (either one or the other, *or possibly both*). So below, v. 39, *inferior vel matre vel armis*, 'certainly in one or the other, probably in both.' Here we may translate, 'and I might say, how many verses have I composed.' For *vel* Lachmann reads *seu*.

13—16.] These lines admirably express the roused spirit of a wronged man. The poet suddenly addresses himself, almost fiercely, to Cynthia, and asks if he has not been infatuated in so long bearing with her and her family. It is easier to understand *sum* with *temerarius* (and perhaps it is not too much to say that its omission imparts a tone of abruptness and indignation), than to suppose a distich lost, while v. 15 so closely continues the sense. Hertzberg, by placing only a comma after *domum*, (in which he is followed by Müller), makes the construction to be, 'ecquando ego temerarius—visus sum liber?' But *ergo ecquandone!* do not well agree; on the other hand *ergo* is used in making admissions or confessions: 'so then I have been rash,' &c. There is probability in Lachmann's proposed reading *Ergo ego tam multos* &c. He gives the general sense thus: 'Ergo ego nimis temerarius? egone audax, qui amorem tuum poscam? cum tamen tam multos annos imperium tuum patienter tulerim. Jam dubito, sitne tibi umquam liber visus, an usque me pro servo tuo habitura sis.' 'Do you suppose I am for ever to be your slave?'

Sic igitur prima moriere ætate, Properti?
  Sed morere; interitu gaudeat illa tuo;
Exagitet nostros Manes, sectetur et umbras,
  Insultetque rogis, calcet et ossa mea.
Quid? non Antigonæ tumulo Bœotius Hæmon
  Corruit ipse suo saucius ense latus,
Et sua cum miseræ permiscuit ossa puellæ,
  Qua sine Thebanam noluit ire domum?
Sed non effugies: mecum moriaris oportet;
  Hoc eodem ferro stillet uterque cruor.
Quamvis ista mihi mors est inhonesta futura;
  Mors inhonesta quidem; tu moriere tamen.
Ille etiam abrepta desertus conjuge Achilles
  Cessare in tectis pertulit arma sua.
Viderat ille fugas, tractos in litore Achivos,
  Fervere et Hectorea Dorica castra face;
Viderat informem multa Patroclon arena
  Porrectum et sparsas cæde jacere comas;
Omnia formosam propter Briseïda passus:
  Tantus in erepto sævit amore dolor.
At postquam sera captiva est reddita pœna,
  Fortem illum Hæmoniis Hectora traxit equis.

17.] 'Shall I then die without an effort to escape? Yes: die, as Hæmon died of love for Antigone, (Soph. *Ant.* 1235,) die, that she may exult in her victory.' There is something fine in the sudden despair with which he resigns his resolution to resist as soon as he has made it. Kuinoel well says in his terse way, 'splendidus locus.'

23.] *Cum* (ossibus) *puellæ*. See on II. 3, 21.

24.] Müller reads *noluit inire*; but *ire* may well stand for *redire*.

26.] *Eodem*. On the synizesis see v. 7, 7.

30.] *In tectis*, 'in his tent.' Kuinoel has *in Teucros*, from the later and interpolated copies. Barth has the bad taste to read *in thecis*, and Müller follows him. The allusion is probably to some lost epic, as inf. 10, 9, seqq.

31.] *Fugas*. Thus Lachmann, Hertzberg, and Jacob, with the Naples MS. The Groning. MS. and ed. Rheg. give *fuga tractos* (*fractos*, Kuinoel). Lachmann has *fugas, fractos* &c., but suggests *pyras*; Müller *fuga stratas*, Keil *fuga fractos*.—In the next verse the burning of the Grecian fleet by Hector is alluded to.

33.] Kuinoel and Barth edit *Patroclon*, which is a false quantity. The MSS. agree in *Patroclon*. Both Πάτροκλος and Πατροκλῆς occur.—*multa arena porrectum*, ἐν κονίῃσι μέγας μεγαλωστὶ τανυσθείς, *Il.* xviii. 27.

36.] *In erepto dolore*. These words, compared with the first line *eripitur nobis* &c., go far to show that the whole of this is really one connected elegy.

37.] *Sera pœna*, 'by a late retribution,' ποινῇ, as K. remarks. If, says the poet, the loss of his love could so completely subdue even the hero Achilles, who only regained his valour on her restoration, it is not to be wondered at if love has still greater power over one so inferior to him.

38.] *Fortem illum*, 'that brave Hector,' τὸν ἐσθλόν, is simple and natural. Müller needlessly reads *fortem idem* &c.—*Hæmoniis*, Thessalian, viz. from Phthiotis.

Inferior multo cum sim vel matre vel armis,
  Mirum, si de me jure triumphat Amor?

IX.

Iste quod est, ego sæpe fui; sed fors et in hora,
  Hoc ipso ejecto, carior alter erit.
Penelope poterat bis denos salva per annos
  Vivere, tam multis femina digna procis;
Conjugium falsa poterat differre Minerva,
  Nocturno solvens texta diurno dolo;
Visura et quamvis numquam speraret Ulixem,
  Illum expectando facta remansit anus.
Nec non exanimem amplectens Briseïs Achillem
  Candida vesana verberat ora manu,

39.] *Matre.* Because a goddess was the mother of Achilles. Most of the copies have *Marte.* On *vel—vel*, see above on v. 11.

40.] There is some confusion in this verse between *mirum, si triumphat*, and *jure triumphat.*

IX. Like the last, this is a very charming poem; but like it also, it has been disfigured by being printed in a mutilated and lacunose form in the editions of Jacob, Lachmann, and Müller. Even Hertzberg has a gap between v. 40 and 41. No stronger presumption of the fallacy, or at least, the utter uncertainty, of these opinions need be adduced, than the fact that the editors themselves do not agree as to *where* the supposed abruptness exists; for while Jacob ignores one of Lachmann's *lacunæ* (after v. 24), Hertzberg ignores those of both, except after v. 40.—The subject of this elegy is the same as the preceding, and probably in reference to the same rival. He upbraids Cynthia with ingratitude, and asserts his unchanged affection in the most moving terms.

1.] *Iste.* On the contemptuous use of this pronoun applied to a rival, see on I. 2, 25.—'The same inconstancy which induced you to reject me for this man, will perhaps in an hour supply his place by a third.' The natural sentiment of one who tries to persuade himself that his rival is not *really* beloved—*fervit* is the not improbable reading in Barth's edition.

3—16.] 'Women were constant in times of old, and waited with unchanged affection for their husbands even until death; whereas Cynthia could not wait for a single day or a night' (19—20).

5.] *Falsa Minerva*, 'by pretending to weave,' and undoing at night the web she had completed in the day, *Od.* ii. 104. Plat. *Phædo*, p. 84, A., ἀνήνυτον ἔργον πράττειν, Πηνελόπης τινὰ ἐναντίως ἱστὸν μεταχειριζομένης.

7.] *Visura speraret.* A very remarkable construction, to which it is not easy to find an exact parallel in either language. The Greeks do not say ἤλπιζεν ὀψόμενος for ὄψεσθαι, and Virgil's well-known 'sensit medios delapsus in hostes' pertains to an idiom restricted to verbs of sense and perception. The present may, perhaps, be regarded as an attempt at a Græcism, made on unsound principles. He intended to express *speraret se visuram esse*, and thought himself at liberty to substitute *visura*,—if, indeed, *visuram*, with the ellipse of *se*, be not the true reading. The instance given by Hertzberg, from iv. 6, 40, 'jurabo et bis sex integer esse dies,' is not strictly to the purpose, being a simple rendering of ὄμνυμαι ἦ μὴν ἐγνωκέναι, or ἐγνωκὼς εἶναι.

8.] *Remansit*, i.e. in ejus conjugio: 'perduravit,' *Hertzberg.* Lachmann quotes iii. 11, 17, 'me tibi ad extremas mansurum, vita, tenebras,' and Homer's use of μένειν in several passages relating to Penelope, as well as Eur. *Orest.* 583 (590). Compare i. 1, 31, and 10, 29. There is no difficulty in *facta anus expectando illum.* Lachmann needlessly proposes *illi* and *casta.*

Et dominum lavit mœrens captiva cruentum,
  Appositum flavis in Simoënta vadis;
Fœdavitque comas, et tanti corpus Achilli
  Maximaque in parva sustulit ossa manu,
Cum tibi nec Peleus aderat nec cærula mater,
  Scyria nec viduo Deidamia viro.
Tunc igitur veris gaudebat Græcia natis;
  Tunc etiam felix inter et arma pudor.
At tu non una potuisti nocte vacare,
  Impia, non unum sola manere diem.
Quin etiam multo duxistis pocula risu,
  Forsitan et de me verba fuere mala.
Hic etiam petitur, qui te prius ipse reliquit;—
  Di faciant, isto capta fruare viro!
Hæc mihi vota tuam propter suscepta salutem?

12.] This verse is probably corrupt. The MSS. agree in *flaviis*, which Jacob and Hertzberg retain; the latter however alone attempts to defend *flaviis vadis*, which he thinks intended to express a shallow pool of *running* water, the epithet, or rather attribute, implying the virtue believed to reside in such water for the purposes of lustration. It is difficult to believe that the usage is good Latin. Is it conceivable that *flavius vadum* could have been used in the nominative? With Lachmann and Kuinoel I have admitted Heinsius' conjecture, *flavis*, for which Horace's 'flavum Tiberim,' furnishes sufficient authority. It has, however, this objection, though to some it may appear a fanciful one, that the word expresses the name of the second Trojan stream, *Xanthus*. If *vadis* could mean (and why should it not?) the sandy puddles formed at the estuary of a river, *fulvis* would be an obvious suggestion, from Virgil's use of *fulva arena*, *Georg.* iii. 110.—*in Simoenta*, as the Greeks say τιθέναι εἰς τόπον, 'brought to the river and laid there.' Hertzberg suggests that it may mean 'so placed as to lie in the water in part.' Perhaps however *in Simoenta* was meant to depend on some word (as *fusis* or *fluxis*) now lost in the corrupt *flaviis*, or else we should read *ad Simoenta*, i. e. *ad ripas Simoentis*.

13.] *Fœdavit*, ᾔσχυνε. The poet imitates *Il.* xviii. 23, as the commentators have pointed out. There is something touching and beautiful in Briseis holding 'the large bones (*i. e.* the ashes of them) in her *little* hand.' It is the happy stroke of an artist to a picture.—*tanti*, 'so huge a man.' So Achilles is called τοσοῦτον, 'so big,' by Phœnix in *Il.* ix. 485. It is strange that Müller should not have seen this, but marked the passage as corrupt, and proposed the tasteless reading *ad fumati corpus Achilli*.

15.] *Tibi.* Achilles is addressed, though the apostrophe is harsh and strange, especially as Cynthia is so soon after appealed to, v. 19. 'All this Briseis did through her affection for you, when others stood aloof.'—*viduo viro*, χηρεύοντι σοι, 'when thus left a widower,' *i. e.* by the absence of Deidamia, by whom, when in the island of Scyros, the hero had had a son Pyrrhus (or Neoptolemus).—Lachmann, Kuinoel, and the more recent editors have *toro* for *viro*, from a late MS.

18.] *Felix* &c. 'Then also virtue throve even in the camp.'—*etiam* is to be taken with *tunc*, so that *et arma* has its own independent force.

21.] *Duxistis*, viz. you and your lover, the *iste* of v. 1. So 'ducere Nectaris succos' Hor. *Carm.* iii. 3, 34.

23.] *Prius*, 'on a former occasion.' For *ipse* Müller and Keil, against the copies, give *ante*, 'before you deserted him.' Or should we read *prior*?—*fruare*, ὄναιο, ἀπολαύσειας, 'may you have a benefit of him,' as we say.

25.] I have placed the interrogation at the end of this verse rather than after v. 27, with most of the editors, because *cum*—*tum* seem to be natural correlatives.

Cum capite hoc Stygiæ jam poterentur aquæ,
Et lectum flentes circum staremus amici,
Hic ubi tum, pro di, perfida, quisve fuit?
Quid, si longinquos retinerer miles ad Indos?
Aut mea si staret navis in Oceano?
Sed vobis facile est, verba et componere fraudes:
Hoc unum didicit femina semper opus.
Non sic incerto mutantur flamine Syrtes,
Nec folia hiberno tam tremefacta Noto,
Quam cito feminea non constat fœdus in ira,
Sive ea causa gravis, sive ea causa levis.
Nunc, quoniam ista tibi placuit sententia, cedam:
Tela, precor, Pueri, promite acuta magis!
Figite certantes, atque hanc mihi solvite vitam:
Sanguis erit vobis maxima palma meus.
Sidera sunt testes, et matutina pruina,
Et furtim misero janua aperta mihi,
Te nihil in vita nobis acceptius umquam;
Nunc quoque eris, quamvis sis inimica mihi;

For *hæc* Kuinoel has *quæ*, with an exclamation at *amici* v. 27. Lachmann needlessly proposes *et*. The sense is, 'Are these the vows I made for your recovery, when you were despaired of?' *i. e.* is this the gratitude you showed for all my concern? Hertzberg well compares v. 3, 11, 'haecne merita fides?' &c. The dangerous illness and recovery of Cynthia are described again iii. 20, but if we follow Hertzberg (*Quæst.* p. 224), in his chronological arrangement of the poems, the present elegy was written A.U.C. 728, the other later than 729, but before 732.

28.] *Hic*, 'where *then* was this lover of your's, or who was he to you?' *i. e.* a stranger, or a friend, or false lover and a traitor.

29.] *Quid si* &c. 'If you leave me so easily when I am present, what might I expect if (like Ulysses) I were detained far away from home?'

33.] *Mutantur*, *i. e.* by the shifting of the sands: an event common to all shoals, and constituting their chief dangers.

34.] *Tam*, i. e. *tam cito*.

38.] *Pueri*, 'O Cupids.' Compare v. 1, 138, 'Et Veneris pueris utilis hostis eris.' iii. 21, 3, 'obvia nescio quot pueri mihi turba minuta.' Kuinoel, following Burmann, strangely understands the slaves;—'alloquitur pueros, servos, eosque cohortatur ut ipsi ferro mortem inferant.' Barth is here quite right: 'alloquitur Cupidines cum desperatione.'

40.] *Palma*, see v. 1, 140.

41—52.] Here Jacob, Lachmann, Hertzberg, (as stated at the beginning of the elegy) Müller and Keil place a mark of severance, as if the concluding lines had no intelligible connexion with the preceding. Hertzberg does not hesitate to call it 'pannus ordine præpostero hic assutus, ad El. xiii. (iii. 4) referendus.' It is hard that the poet may not end his appeal to Cynthia by the simple and natural sentiment, 'The very stars can bear witness how I have ever loved you,' without being so capriciously used. By placing a colon at the end of v. 42, and thus making v. 43 an independent sentence, an incoherence (if such it can be called) is created, which is at once removed by adopting the construction *sidera sunt testes —te nihil umquam acceptius fuisse.* But, since Hertzberg adds, 'Lachmannus non posse post absolutum jam carmen hunc exitum tolerari certissimis argumentis evicit,' it is due to these learned men briefly to examine these cogent reasons. 'Hither-

Nec domina ulla meo ponet vestigia lecto:
  Solus ero, quoniam non licet esse tuum.
Atque utinam, si forte pios eduximus annos,
  Ille vir in medio fiat amore lapis!
Non ob regna magis diris cecidere sub armis
  Thebani media non sine matre duces,
Quam, mihi si media liceat pugnare puella,
  Mortem ego non fugiam morte subire tua.

to,' says Lachmann, 'the poet has despaired—given in—invoked the Cupids to kill him. *Now* he declares he will never live with another.' Truly, an invincible argument! Let the reader compare the perfectly parallel *μετάνοια* in ii. 5, 17, where, after asserting that he will instantly leave her, he begs her to relent, and think of her own interest. Similarly, he now offers to receive her again into his favour, and declares that he will have her or no one.

45.] *Vestigia*. This word, like *στίβοι φιλάνορες* in Æsch. *Ag*. 401, appears to mean the mark or impression left by a sleeper on the couch. Compare iii. 21, 35, 'apparent non ulla toro vestigia presso,' and Ovid, *Her*. x. 53. Hertzberg, in a long note, endeavours to show that *ponere vestigia* is the same as *ponere pedes*, i. e. *adire*, *ingredi*. Such appears commonly to be the true meaning; nor is it necessary to quote fifty passages to prove that a person who plants a footstep also plants his foot.

47.] *Si forte* &c., if the affection (or dutifulness) of our former years has entitled the prayer to be heard.—*ille vir*, the rival alluded to at the beginning of the elegy.

49—52.] 'Not more fatal were the arms by which Eteocles and Polynices slew each other, when their mother Jocasta vainly interfered to separate them, than those should be with which I would fight my rival were Cynthia placed between us as the prize in the contest.' The simile is rather irregularly worked out; such however seems to be the poet's meaning. The last four lines are marked off by a space in the later editions, after Lachmann; but the connexion does not seem broken; 'I would die for you,' adds the poet, after declaring that he will have none other than Cynthia.

PROPERTII

LIBER TERTIUS.

I.

SED tempus lustrare aliis Helicona choreis,
  Et campum Hæmonio jam dare tempus equo.
Jam libet et fortes memorare ad prœlia turmas,
  Et Romana mei dicere castra ducis.

I. It is difficult to resist the arguments of Lachmann (*Præf.* pp. xxi—iii.) that with the present elegy a new Book commences, whether we assent to his opinion or not, that a large portion of the Second Book has been lost. The elegy now before us is decidedly introductory in its character. It is strictly a prœmium, like those with which Books II. and IV. respectively open. The poet changes his style and tone, and bethinks himself of acting on the often-urged advice of his friends, to sing of wars, that is, in fact, of the exploits of Augustus: for this is what the Augustan poets always mean when they talk of turning martial. 'Bella Canam,' he says, v. 8, 'quando scripta puella mea est.' More conclusive still is v. 25 of the fourth elegy, in which the poet says 'sat mea sat magna est, si tres sint pompa libelli,' proving that *two* had already been published, and that this therefore was part of the third. Nevertheless, Hertzberg, who follows the MSS. in continuing the second book up to the conclusion of the third of the present volume, while he admits (*Quæst.* lib. iii. cap. ii. p. 216) that Lachmann's new arrangement is 'satis probabilis,' is of opinion that a counter-testimony to the above verse may be drawn from iii. 15, 1. 'Tu loqueris, cum sis jam noto fabula libro, as if only one book had hitherto been published. It is not perhaps very easy to reconcile the two passages: but Lachmann suggests that the third may have been *written* before the second book was *published*; or again, that all the poems collectively, written to and on Cynthia, may be called generally 'a book,' (Præf. p. xxvii.) There are reasons too for believing (Hertzberg, *Quæst.* p. 220) that the first book was dedicated to Cynthia, and as such published as a distinct work with all the care and polish the poet could bestow upon it; and if this verse (iii. 15, 1) be taken, as it must, in strict connexion with its pentameter, 'Et tua sit toto Cynthia lecta foro,' it is almost certain that the first book alone is alluded to. To the ordinary reader, it is a matter of such little importance and even interest whether there are five or only four books of elegies, that I have purposely avoided a long discussion of the subtle and intricate arguments by which the contrary opinions are respectively maintained, and contented myself with following Lachmann, Jacob, Keil, and Müller, as on the whole the more plausible view.

1.] *Sed tempus.* Lachmann and Jacob consider the commencement abrupt, and that something has been lost. Barth and Kuinoel read *jam* for *sed*. But Hertzberg rightly observes that the idea in the poet's mind was this: 'Hucusque equidem cecini puellarum amores; sed tempus &c.—*lustrare*, to go over, visit; so Virg. *Æn.* ii. 528, 'vacua atria lustrat saucius.'—*Hæmonio*, i. e. Thessalico, the horses of that country being noted for their breed. See ii. 8, 38. Müller reads *Emathio*. 'To give the field' to the steed, is to give him wider space, as well as to urge him to full speed. For the well-known metaphor compare *Georgic* iii. ult.

3.] Construe *fortes ad prælia*, i. e. equitem ad pugnandum promptum, audacem.

4.] *Mei ducis*, Augustus. There is allusion to the military title of Imperator.

Quod si deficient vires, audacia certe
  Laus erit: in magnis et voluisse sat est.
Ætas prima canat Veneres, extrema tumultus;
  Bella canam, quando scripta puella mea est.
Nunc volo subducto gravior procedere vultu:
  Nunc aliam citharam me mea Musa docet.
Surge, anima, ex humili jam carmine sumite vires,
  Pierides: magni nunc erit oris opus.
Jam negat Euphrates equitem post terga tueri
  Parthorum, et Crassos se tenuisse dolet;
India quin, Auguste, tuo dat colla triumpho,
  Et domus intactæ te tremit Arabiæ;
Et, si qua extremis tellus se subtrahit oris,
  Sentiet illa tuas postmodo capta manus.
Hæc ego castra sequar; vates tua castra canendo
  Magnus ero; servent hunc mihi fata diem!
Ut caput in magnis ubi non est tangere signis,

5.] *Audacia*, fiducia, 'courage to make the attempt.' The word is rarely found in a good sense.—*in magnis*, ἐν τοῖς χαλεποῖς, in subjects great and difficult.

7.] The apparent antithesis in *prima* and *extrema ætas* is much greater than is really intended, or than the dates of the poems will admit of. See on iv. 25, 3. The poet merely means that youth is fit for singing of love, maturer age of war (*tumultus*).

8.] *Quando*, quandoquidem, ἐπειδή.

9.] *Subducto vultu*, 'withdrawn into itself,' *i. e.* sober and demure.

11.] Lachmann punctuates thus: 'Surge, anima, ex humili: jam carmine sumite vires, Pierides.' This appears to me to be an alteration without improvement, though he is followed by Jacob and Hertzberg. Barth and Keil, 'surge, anima, ex humili jam carmine, sumite vires.—*ex* is here 'after.' Kuinoel and Lachmann give *anima* with Burmann.

13.] The sense is, 'The Euphrates no longer boasts of its Parthian horseman, *fidentem fuga versisque sagittis*.' *Georg.* iii. 31.—*post terga tueri*, *i. e.* to watch for the opportunity of turning round and discharging a fatal arrow at the pursuer. *Crassos tenuisse*, non remisisse. Both father and son were killed in that unfortunate expedition, B.C. 53—4. Whence Ovid, *A. A.* i, 179, 'Crassi gaudete sepulti.' See inf. v. 6, 83.

16.] *Intactæ Arabiæ*. From this verse Hertzberg (*Quæst.* p. 217) deduces the date of the poem. The allusion is to the expedition of Ælius Gallus (see on v. 3) in 730, which was miserably defeated and destroyed. Now he rightly argues that had this unfortunate termination already occurred, the poet would not have mentioned it, as reflecting discredit rather than praise on Augustus: and therefore that this was written when the expedition was contemplated, B.C. 25, or in 729. Arabia is called *intacta* because the Roman arms were first brought against it on this occasion. Barth compares 'intactis opulentior Thesauris Arabum,' *Hor. Od.* iii. 24, 1. The lengthening of ā in *Arabia* is one of the many instances of the metrical licence taken by both Greek and Latin poets in proper names. Similarly Arabium limen i. 14, 19: and ii. 3, 15.

19.] *Castra sequar*, *i. e.* as if a bard attached to the expedition on purpose to celebrate its victories. Hertzberg compares iv. 9, 43, 'prosequar et currus utroque ab litore ovantes:' but this refers rather to following the triumphal car in the procession to the capitol.

21—4.] The simile is a very original one. 'As, when we cannot reach the head

Ponitur hic imos ante corona pedes,
Sic nos nunc, inopes laudis conscendere carmen,
Pauperibus sacris vilia tura damus.
Nondum etiam Ascræos norunt mea carmina fontes,
Sed modo Permessi flumine lavit Amor.

II.

Scribant de te alii, vel sis ignota licebit;
Laudet, qui sterili semina ponit humo.
Omnia, crede mihi, secum uno munera lecto
Auferet extremi funeris atra dies.
Et tua transibit contemnens ossa viator,
Nec dicet: Cinis hic docta puella fuit.

III.

Quicumque ille fuit, puerum qui pinxit Amorem,
Nonne putas miras hunc habuisse manus?

of a lofty statue, we are compelled to lay at its feet the crown we have brought as an offering: so I, at a loss to rise to the height of heroic song, am content to give a trifling tribute.' Kuinoel misinterprets *hic ante pedes* (v. 22) by '*tunc, ubi non licet.*' It is rather the Greek *αὐτοῦ ὑπὸ ποσίν*, as if the place where to lay the crown were *pointed out* to the party offering it. See on i. 19, 7.—*laudis conscendere carmen*, 'illud assequi culmen, quo epici poetæ perveniunt carminibus suis.'—*Barth.* Müller reads *culmen* after Heinsius. So v. 10, 3, 'Magnum iter ascendo.' Or we might suggest *currum*.—*sacris*, see on v. 6, 1, 'sacra facit vates,' and iv. 1, 3, 'primus ego ingredior puro de fonte *sacerdos*' &c.—*vilia tura*, cheap and common: compare *nulla mercede hyacinthos* v. 7, 33. v. 1, 'Vesta coronatis pauper gaudebat asellis; Ducebant macræ vilia sacra boves.'

25.] For *etiam* Müller reads *etenim*, and says the vulgate *omni vacat sensu*.

25—6.] 'I am not yet a Hesiod: the only skill I have attained in versification was taught me by Love.' Permessus (Hesiod. *Theog.* 5) was a spring near to Hippocrene, and sacred to the Muses. The antithesis is not so much between a greater and a less fountain, as between heroic and amatory subjects. On *lavit*, i. e. *lavit me*, Hertzberg remarks, that bathing in, as well as drinking of, the sacred well was thought to inspire poetic rapture.—*modo*, *i. e.* tantummodo.

II. This isolated and perhaps fragmentary *ἐπύλλιον* was probably written under the excitement of some momentary vexation, perhaps caused by the indifference Cynthia had manifested towards some of the poet's verses. He warns her not to rely too much on her present popularity, which, he intimates, arises from his praises, and that she possesses no quality which will cause her name to be known to posterity. Jacob (who in this particular respect almost always echoes Lachmann's dictum) too confidently writes, 'Neque elegiam primam finitam esse, et hujus initium desiderari, *certum est*.'

2.] 'Let him praise you henceforth who is willing to undertake a vain task.'

3.] *Omnia munera.* 'Carmina illa, quæ laudes tuas celebrant.'—*Kuinoel.* Rather, I think, 'all your accomplishments,' *i. e.* beauty and mental endowments, the latter of which are alluded to in v. 6.—*uno lecto*, the bier on which the body was carried to the pyre. See on v. 11, 12.

III. An elegant but difficult little poem on the symbolism embodied in the popular representations of love.

Hic primum vidit sine sensu vivere amantes,
 Et levibus curis magna perire bona.
Idem non frustra ventosas addidit alas,
 Fecit et humano corde volare deum;
Scilicet alterna quoniam jactamur in unda,
 Nostraque non ullis permanet aura locis.
Et merito hamatis manus est armata sagittis,
 Et pharetra ex humero Gnosia utroque jacet;
Ante ferit quoniam, tuti quam cernimus hostem,
 Nec quisquam ex illo vulnere sanus abit.
In me tela manent, manet et puerilis imago;
 Sed certe pennas perdidit ille suas,
Evolat heu! nostro quoniam de pectore nusquam,
 Assiduusque meo sanguine bella gerit.
Quid tibi jocundum est siccis habitare medullis?
 Si pudor est, alio trajice tela tua.
Intactos isto satius tentare veneno:
 Non ego, sed tenuis vapulat umbra mea;
Quam si perdideris, quis erit qui talia cantet?

3.] *Sine sensu*, ἀναισθήτως, ἀφροντίστως. Is the allusion to Love being blind? Theocr. ix. 19, τυφλὸς δ' οὐκ αὐτὸς ὁ Πλοῦτος, ἀλλὰ καὶ ὡφρόντιστος Ἔρως.—*levibus curis*, i. e. *prae negligentia*; or, perhaps, 'with indifference,' οὐ φροντίζων ἀπολλυμένης τῆς οὐσίας.

5.] *Humano corde*. These words have been very variously interpreted. Hertzberg seems right in considering them the ablative of place, 'to flit *in* the human heart.' If it can be shown from ancient art that love was represented as a heart with wings affixed, such an image would be well expressed by the words in the text, where *humano corde* would be the ablative of the mode. In the next verse, *scilicet* is in explanation of the epithet *ventosas*. The wings, says the poet, typify our ever-changing destinies, and the fickleness of the gales by which we are driven, as it were, this way and that.—*alterna unda*, 'modo tranquilla, modo commota.'—*Barth*. This is not satisfactory. Probably it means 'up and down,' *i. e.* now on the crest, now in the trough of the wave. So *alterna manu*, I. 9, 24.

10.] *Ex humero utroque*. Not that he had *two* quivers, as Hertzberg remarks, but that the quiver with its strap (amentum) may be said to hang from both shoulders. But I have some suspicion that the sense is this: the quiver, when not in use, hung at the back, from *both* shoulders; when used, it was pulled to one side, and so was suspended only from the opposite shoulder. In this case, Love holds the barbed arrow ready in his hand, *because* (quoniam) he aims instantaneously, before we can see his movements from a position of security, and does not wait to draw the arrow from the quiver. I agree with Hertzberg in rejecting Jacob's emendation, *jacit*.

13.] *Puerilis imago*. He appears to mean Cupid himself, but uses the word *imago* because he is describing the details of his image or picture.

17.] Müller reads *qui* for *quid*, and in the next verse, *i, puer, en, alio* &c., the Naples MS. giving *puer* for *pudor*.

20.] *Tenuis umbra*. The commentators observe that the poets (as Theocr. ii. 55) speak of love as draining the life-blood of its votaries. At the same time the poet probably alludes to his own attenuated frame, iii. 18, 21.

21.] *Si perdideris*, 'If you utterly destroy the poor lover, who will equally well sing your (Cupid's) praises?'

Hæc mea Musa levis gloria magna tua est,
Quæ caput et digitos et lumina nigra puellæ,
Et canit, ut soleant molliter ire pedes.

IV.

Non tot Achæmeniis armatur Itura sagittis,
Spicula quot nostro pectore fixit Amor.
Hic me tam graciles vetuit contemnere Musas,
Jussit et Ascræum sic habitare nemus:
Non ut Pieriæ quercus mea verba sequantur,
Aut possim Ismaria ducere valle feras,
Sed magis ut nostro stupefiat Cynthia versu:
Tunc ego sim Inachio notior arte Lino.
Non ego sum formæ tantum mirator honestæ,
Nec si qua illustres femina jactat avos;

23—4.] Müller and Keil, with Lachmann and Hertzberg, read *qui caput—, et canit—*, from the Naples MS., regarding the preceding verse as parenthetical, and thus continuing the construction from *qui talia cantat* in v. 21. The authority for the two readings being about equal, the sense of that given in the text seems preferable: 'This muse of mine, humble as it is, is a great glory to you, in extolling as it does the various perfections of my mistress,' i. 2, 27.—*digitos*; see on ii. 2, 8.

IV. There does not appear to be sufficient reason for following those editors who would divide the present long elegy into three, viz. at v. 17, and v. 43. Here again, as remarked on ii. 9, there is a discrepancy of opinion which goes far to invalidate the whole theory. For while Lachmann and Kuinoel, after others, break the continuity of the poem at the points mentioned, Hertzberg makes no stop at v. 17, and Jacob none at v. 43. I hope to shew at the proper place that the elegy may fairly be regarded as a whole and complete composition. The subject is, that the poet's memory will survive in his poems; to which are added some general, but by no means desultory or unconnected, reflections on his death.

1.] The authentic copies have *etrusca* or *hetrusca*, for which Barth, Lachmann, Kuinoel, Jacob, Keil, and Müller, give *Susa*, after Beroaldus, who professed to have found it in a MS., though doubtless a corrected one. Hertzberg follows the conjectural correction of Fontanus, *Itura*; and this seems the most plausible emendation, from the celebrity of the Ituræans in archery: compare *Georg.* ii. 448, 'Ituræos taxi torquentur in arcus.' The epithet *Achæmeniis* (*Persian*) may very well arise, Hertzberg observes, from the imperfect geographical knowledge and confusion between the names of eastern nations which prevailed in the Augustan age. Itura, or Ituræa, was situated on the N.E. of Palestine, and was an Arabian tribe. See Tac. *Ann.* xii. 23.

2.] *Spicula.* The metaphor seems to show that the present was written soon after, or in continuation of, the preceding elegy, of which cf. v. 13.

3.] *Graciles*, slight and slender, opposed to *graves*, amatory to heroic verse.

4.] *Sic.* 'Love compelled me to be a poet *to this end*, viz. not to make the Thracian oaks and wild beasts follow me like a second Orpheus, but in order to captivate Cynthia.' Kuinoel, by placing a full stop at *versus*, v. 4, shows that he misunderstood the sense.

8.] *Tunc.* 'Then, and then only,' viz. if I succeed in this, 'should I surpass the fame of the Grecian Linus.' *Sim* appears to be *εἴην ἄν*, not the expression of a wish. See on i. 13. 31, 'Inachiis et blandior heroinis.'

10.] *Nec si qua.* The sentiment appears to be a general one. But see on iv. 20, 8.

Me juvet in gremio doctæ legisse puellæ,
  Auribus et puris scripta probasse mea.
Hæc ubi contigerint, populi confusa valeto
  Fabula; nam domina judice tutus ero.
Quæ si forte bonas ad pacem verterit aures,
  Possum inimicitias tunc ego ferre Jovis.
Quandocumque igitur nostros nox claudet ocellos,
  Accipe quæ serves funeris acta mei;
Nec mea tunc longa spatietur imagine pompa,
  Nec tuba sit fati vana querella mei;
Nec mihi tunc fulcro sternatur lectus eburno,
  Nec sit in Attalico mors mea nixa toro.
Desit odoriferis ordo mihi lancibus; adsint

11.] *Juvat* Kuinoel, with some inferior copies. Lachmann acutely observes that *hæc ubi contigerint*, v. 13, implies that such a result as her critical approbation was yet to come.—*auribus puris*, καθαροῖς, properly *purgatis* in a physical sense, Hor. *Ep.* i. 1, 7. Pers. *Sat.* v. 63; then, such as are capable of appreciating harmony, &c.—*doctæ*. The emphasis is on this word: ''Tis not only beauty and rank, but talent and judgment which captivate me.' Compare with this passage ii. 3, 9—22.—*probasse*, to make them acceptable to, *commendasse*.

13.] *Confusa fabula*. 'The vague and contradictory talk.' We may infer from this that the poet had his calumniators. To this probably v. 16 alludes.

15.] *Ad pacem*. If she listens to the proposals of peace offered in my poems, I care not if Jupiter himself is my enemy.

17.] Having spoken of his verses with some slight self-congratulation, he proceeds to say, that he wishes for no other honour to be paid to his memory, than that they should be carried in his funeral procession; and accordingly, he leaves instructions to that effect. I do not think it necessary to add a word in refutation of Kuinoel's remark, even though echoed by both Lachmann and Jacob, 'Quæ inde a v. 17 leguntur, neutiquam cum antecedentibus cohærere jam Broukhusius, Hemsterhusius, Burmannus, alii, monuerunt.'

18.] 'Hear' (this is said to Cynthia) 'the instructions which you are to observe in conducting my funeral.' On this peculiar use of *acta*, see i. 21, 6.

19.] '*Longa imagine*. Pro longa imaginum serie dixit.'—*Hertzberg*. *querella*, see on v. 11, 9. The Romans had a singular custom of preserving waxen masks or likenesses of their ancestors, arranged in order round the *atrium*, and used only on the occasion of funerals. They are called 'picti vultus majorum,' Juven. viii. 2, who alludes to them also *ibid.* 19, 'Tota licet veteres exornent undique ceræ Atria, nobilitas sola est atque unica virtus.' Ovid, *Fast.* i. 591, 'Perlege dispositas generosa per atria ceras.' *Amor.* i. 8, 65, 'Nec te decipiant veteres quinquatria ceræ: Tolle tuos tecum, pauper amator, avos.' See Becker, *Gallus*, p. 512: 'Men, resembling in size and figure the persons to be represented, placed these masks before their faces, and marched along in front of the *lectus*, clad in the dress appropriate to each, with all the insignia appertaining; whence also Hor. *Epod* viii. 2, 'Esto beata: funus atque imagines ducant triumphales tuum.' Thus the whole row of ancestors swept along, represented by living individuals in proper costume, in front of the corpse; and this was not confined to those in direct ascent, but the collateral branches also sent their *imagines* to the cavalcade; as is seen from Polybius. This is what Pliny xxxv. 2 calls '*gentilitia funera*.' *Supra*, i. 5, 24, 'Nescit amor priscis cedere imaginibus.' From this the more modern, though now nearly obsolete, practice of heraldic pursuivants and blazonry has originated.

22.] *Mors mea*, i. e. cadaver meum. *Attalico*: see on v. 5, 24. 'Sertaque ab Attalicis putria signa toris.'

Plebei parvæ funeris exequiæ.
Sat mea sat magna est, si tres sint pompa libelli,
Quos ego Persephonæ maxima dona feram.
Tu vero nudum pectus lacerata sequeris,
Nec fueris nomen lassa vocare meum,
Osculaque in gelidis pones suprema labellis,
Cum dabitur Syrio munere plenus onyx.
Deinde, ubi suppositus cinerem me fecerit ardor,
Accipiat Manes parvula testa meos,
Et sit in exiguo laurus superaddita busto,
Quæ tegat extincti funeris umbra locum.
Et duo sint versus: QUI NUNC JACET HORRIDA PULVIS,
UNIUS HIC QUONDAM SERVUS AMORIS ERAT.
Nec minus hæc nostri notescet fama sepulcri,
Quam fuerant Phthii busta cruenta viri.
Tu quoque si quando venies ad fata (memento
Hoc iter) ad lapides cana veni memores.

24.] The *lances* here spoken of seem to be small metallic pans, containing frankincense, and carried in front of the procession. These are not to be confounded with the perfumes placed with the burnt bones in the urn; see i. 17, 23. Among the articles consumed on the pyre Virgil (Æn. vi. 224) enumerates 'thurea dona, dapes, fuso crateres olivo.' The immense quantity of perfumes used in funerals may be inferred from Juvenal, iv. 109.

25.] See introductory note to the first elegy of this Book. The construction is: 'sat magna est mea pompa, si sint tres libelli,' &c. The best copies give *sat mea sit magni si* &c.

29.] *Pones.* In the imperative sense, like *sequeris* v. 27. Kuinoel has *ponas*, from some inferior copies, which likewise give *sequare*. This use of the future is principally confined to *persons*, being an imitation of the Greek optative with ἄν. On this principle the poet writes *accipiat* rather than *accipiet*, v. 32. On [illegible] for [illegible], see note on v. 11, 1.

33.] *Busto* is used in the proper sense, for the spot on which the body was burnt.

35.] All the good copies agree in *horrida*. Kuinoel and even Jacob give *arida* from the corrected MSS. Hertzberg well observes on the vulgate: 'Tristes et deformes mortui reliquias compto illi et eleganti quondam Veneris hominis cultui oppositas posita.' The first part of the distich may have been *siste, viator, iter*, or some such familiar formula of address.

38.] *Phthii viri*, i.e. of Achilles, over whose tomb Polyxena was sacrificed. The construction is remarkable: *nec minus notescet quam busta fuerant* (nota). On the inchoative form of the substantive verb *esco*, like the Greek ἔσκον for ἦν, Hertzberg has a good note: but the limits of the present work only allow a reference to it. See *Varronianus*, p. 396.

39.] 'Hoc ait:' Tu quoque aliquando morieris—nec unquam velim hoc oblivisci are—sed opto, ut diu etiam in vivis sis, neve nisi anus ad inferos et sepulcra venias; illic ego semper tui memor ero.'—*Hertzberg*. 'When you too shall come to die, come (*i.e.* may you come) at a ripe age to join me in Hades, where be sure that I shall expect your arrival.' See on i. 19, 17.—*lapides*, i.e. *me sepultum*. Supra, v. 32, where see note. There is an antithesis in *cana* and *memores*, rather implied than expressed. Compare i. 19, 17. 'Quamvis te longae remorentur fata senectae, Cara tamen lacrymis ossa futura meis.' But the verse is probably corrupt. No other pentameter in the elegy ends with three syllables; and the correction 'memento—cara venire meos' is plausible.

Interea cave sis nos aspernata sepultos:
  Nonnihil ad verum conscia terra sapit.
Atque utinam primis animam me ponere cunis
  Jussisset quævis de tribus una soror!
Nam quo tam dubiæ servetur spiritus horæ?
  Nestoris est visus post tria secla cinis;
Cui si longævæ minuisset fata senectæ
  Gallicus Iliacis miles in aggeribus,
Non ille Antilochi vidisset corpus humari,
  Diceret aut: O mors, cur mihi sera venis?
Tu tamen amisso non numquam flebis amico:
  Fas est præteritos semper amare viros.
Testis, cui niveum quondam percussit Adonin
  Venantem Idalio vertice durus aper.
Illis formosum jacuisse paludibus, illuc

41.] *Interea*, between the present time and your yet remote decease. The sense is, 'slight me not in the grave, for the dead have some perception of what is passing on earth, and therefore can be pained by being forgotten.' The pantheistic doctrine of earth itself being a divinity possessed of consciousness and volition, is here enunciated. Whether we should construe *ad verum sapit* or *ad verum conscia*, seems uncertain.

43.] Having spoken of the uncertainty of the time of death, he passes into a natural reflection, that it would be better to die young than to live long in a state of suspense and anxiety. In a word, the subject of death is followed out to the conclusion of the elegy in a manner, to say the least, not inconsistent with the sentiments already expressed. Hertzberg calls these verses 'pannus infeliciter assutus.' See however the introductory note.

45.] 'For to what purpose should life be preserved for an event so unforeseen and uncertain as death?'

47.] The best copies read *Quis tam longævæ* &c., of which it seems impossible to make any plausible sense, though it is retained by Keil. With Lachmann, I have admitted an anonymous conjecture *Cui si*, approved also by Jacob. Hertzberg, loath to part with *tam*, gives *Cui tam longævæ*, understanding *si*; which is very awkward and unsatisfactory. Barth reads *si tam longævæ* &c. When *Cui si* had been corrupted into *quis*, it was natural to add *tam* to prop up the metre.

48.] The word *Gallicus* seems corrupt: nor has any very probable conjecture been proposed. Lachmann reads *Ilius Iliacis*, 'me probante,'—says Jacob. It appears to me to be liable to the same objection as *Colchis Colchiacis* ii. 1, 54. Kuinoel explains: 'Gallicus miles, Phrygius, Trojanus, a Gallo Phrygiæ fluvio, de quo v. Ovid, *Fast.* iv. 364. Stephanus de urbibus: Γάλλος ποταμὸς Φρυγίας.' Hertzberg thinks it barely possible that Propertius may have borrowed the name from some Alexandrine or Cyclic poet, or even from Callimachus, referred to by Pliny, *N. H.* vi. 1.

49.] *Antilochi.* A remarkably parallel passage occurs in Juvenal, x. 250, 'Attendas, quantum de legibus ipse queratur Fatorum, et nimio de stamine, cum videt acris Antilochi barbam ardentem,' &c.

51.] 'Yet you will be sorry to lose me, and if you long survive me, will regret for the rest of your life that you loved me so little.'—*præteritos*, οἰχομένους. 'It is usual to love when too late.'—*fas est*, i. e. mos hominum.

53.] Testis (Venus) cui &c. The MSS. and early edd. have *Testis qui*, which introduces the manifest absurdity of a boar being a witness to a moral truth. Hertzberg, Lachmann, and the later editors have admitted *cui* from the conjecture of Huschk. Kuinoel gives *Testis, quem niveum quondam percussit, Adonis*, &c.

55.] The construction is, 'illis paludibus (dicitur eum) formosum jacuisse; illic tu diceris isse' &c. Kuinoel has *flevisse* for

Diceris effusa tu, Venus, isse coma.
Sed frustra mutos revocabis, Cynthia, Manes:
Nam mea quid poterunt ossa minuta loqui?

V.

Non ita Dardanio gavisus Atrida triumpho est,
Cum caderent magnæ Laomedontis opes;
Nec sic errore exacto lætatus Ulixes,
Cum tetigit caræ litora Dulichiæ,
Nec sic Electra, salvum cum vidit Oresten,
Cujus falsa tenens fleverat ossa soror,
Nec sic incolumem Minoïs Thesea vidit,
Dædaleum lino cum duce rexit iter,
Quanta ego præterita collegi gaudia nocte:
Immortalis ero, si altera talis erit.
At dum demissis supplex cervicibus ibam,

jaceatis, from some of the early editions. Lachmann, from his own conjecture, *illis formosis jaceatis* &c. The construction of the vulgate reading is so harsh that its correctness cannot be relied upon. Müller's emendation, *[illegible]* for *jaceatis*, seems to have but small probability.

57—8.] 'You will vainly call on me in the grave. Shew your affection for me while I have the faculty of speech, and can return it.'—*loqui*, i. e. respondere. cf. 28, 'nec fueris nomen lassa vocare meum.'—*minuta*, when reduced to fragments on the pyre.

V. 'Lætitia exultat, quod amica tandem et præter opinionem suam potitus fuerit. Lætitiam suam inde perceptam affirmat majorem fuisse et esse, (1—8) lætitia Agamemnonis, Troja capta; Ulyssis, cum finito errore in patriam revenisset; Electræ, cum salvum adspexisset Orestem; Ariadnæ, cum Thesea sospitem vidisset. Duo priora exempla (1—4) gaudium indicant post longum temporis spatium perceptum; posteriora, (5—8) nec opinatum.'—*Kuinoel.*

4.] *Dulichiæ*. See on ii. 2, 7. In Homer, the name is always written Δουλίχιον, nor does any passage in either of his poems imply that this island was part of Ulysses' dominions. On the contrary, each of the adjacent group seems to have had its *regulus* or hero-chief. Here, however, (and compare iii. 12, 13), *Dulichia* stands for Ithaca; or rather, a part of the dominions is put for the whole. The word is perhaps a form of δολιχός, 'Long Island.'

6.] *Falsa ossa*, the urn with the pretended ashes of Orestes, as described in the Choephoroe and in the Electra of Sophocles.

7.] *Nec sic*, i. e. *læta* or *lætatus*.—*cum rexit* &c., when she had guided his steps safely out of the labyrinth of Dædalus by the clue of a thread.

11.] *Demissis cervicibus*, i. e. *demisso capite*, humiliated and forlorn as one rejected.—The expression *sicco lacu vilior* can only be understood by reference to local customs. In volcanic districts, where water is at once bad and scarce, tanks were, and still are, used (the λάκκοι of the Greeks: see on v. 1, 124) for collecting and preserving the precious gift of nature. The well-known epigram of Martial (iii. 57) is thus to be explained: 'Callidus imposuit nuper mihi caupo Ravennæ; Cum peterem mixtum, vendidit ille merum;' that is, water was dearer than wine, as the preceding epigram distinctly asserts: 'Sit cisterna mihi quam vinea malo Ravennæ, Cum possim multo vendere pluris aquam.' When these tanks were dry, the disappointment of the thirsty traveller who had expected a supply from them, induced him to turn away with disgust, and originated the proverb 'more worthless than a dry tank.' The tanks in Rome, supplied by the aqueducts, can hardly be meant, since

Dicebar sicco vilior esse lacu.
Nec mihi jam fastus opponere quærit iniquos,
Nec mihi ploranti lenta sedere potest.
Atque utinam non tam sero mihi nota fuisset
Conditio! cineri nunc medicina datur.
Ante pedes cæcis lucebat semita nobis;
Scilicet insano nemo in amore videt.
Hoc sensi prodesse magis: Contemnite, amantes;
Sic hodie veniet, si qua negavit heri.
Pulsabant alii frustra dominamque vocabant;
Mecum habuit positum lenta puella caput.
Hæc mihi devictis potior victoria Parthis,
Hæc spolia, hæc reges, hæc mihi currus erunt.
Magna ego dona tua figam, Cytherea, columna,
Taleque sub nostro nomine carmen erit:
HAS PONO ANTE TUAS TIBI, DIVA, PROPERTIUS ÆDES
EXUVIAS, TOTA NOCTE RECEPTUS AMANS.
Nunc in te, mea lux, veniat mea litore navis

these were never *sicci*. Compare ili. 14, 2 'Ipsa petita lacu nunc mihi dulcis aqua est.'

13.] *Fastus*. See note on i. 1, 3.—*opponere mihi*, i. e. 'to reply to my entreaties by a cold refusal.'

14.] *Potest*, 'has she the heart.'—*lenta*, apathetic, heartless, indifferent, as inf. 22, sc. *lenta aliis*. Cf. i. 15, 4.

16.] *Conditio*. That the way to overcome contempt in a mistress is to show contempt for her in return. This appears from v. 19, where some have perverted the sense of the whole passage (15—20) by reading *contendite* from an interpolated MS.—*cineri medicina datur*, i. e. the remedy is known too late. A proverb, perhaps; ''tis too late to give drugs to dead men.'

17.] *Ante pedes* &c. 'The road lay clear and bright before us as we walked, but we were blind and saw it not; people never *do* see, when madly in love.' Hence the saying that Cupid is blind. The *meaning* is, that the poet did not perceive, blinded by his love, that the best way of treating Cynthia was to requite her with affected indifference.

24.] *Hæc* &c. The more usual idiom is '*hi* reges, *hi* mihi currus erunt.'

25.] *Tua columna*. On the pillars of the temples it was the custom to hang votive verses: see iii. 20, 43. 'Pro quibus optatis sacro me carmine damno.' In the present instance, probably always, some gift was attached, like the 'gilt palm' in Tibullus, i. 9, 82. See also Ovid, *Am.* ii. 13, 25 (quoted by Kuinoel). The *votivæ tabulæ* affixed to the walls are well known from Hor. *Od.* i. 5, 14.—*sub nostro nomine*. Kuinoel gives *munere* on the authority of a late MS. We must suppose that the gift was accompanied with the dedicatory words 'Propertius posuit,' and that *under* the name the distich was written.—*Exuviæ* must be understood in continuation of the metaphor in v. 23, *i. e.* Cynthia's favours wrested from his rivals, and represented by some offering to Venus.

27.] The use of the plural *ædes* (meaning a temple and not a house) is remarkable. Kuinoel and even Lachmann read *ædem* from Scaliger's correction.

29.] 'Henceforth it depends on you whether my bark is to come safe to shore, or to be stranded on the shoals.' The MSS. and editions have *ad te*, which I have ventured, with Heinsius, to alter to *in te*. The vulgate is retained by Keil and Müller, who think the difficulty removed by an interrogation at *vadis*. *In te* was altered to *ad te*, as I conceive, in consequence of *veniat*. Kuinoel adopts (in his note; for he retains *ad te* in his text, by an oversight), *a te* from one MS., which

Servata, an mediis sidat onusta vadia.
Quod si forte aliqua nobis mutabere culpa,
  Vestibulum jaceam mortuus ante tuum.

VI.

O me felicem! o nox mihi candida! et o tu
  Lectule, deliciis facte beate meis!
Quam multa apposita narramus verba lucerna,
  Quantaque sublato lumine rixa fuit!
Nam modo nudatis mecum est luctata papillis,
  Interdum tunica duxit operta moram.
Illa meos somno lapsos patefecit ocellos
  Ore suo, et dixit: Siccine, lente, jaces?
Quam vario amplexu mutamus brachia! quantum
  Oscula sunt labris nostra morata tuis!
Non juvat in cæco Venerem corrumpere motu:
  Si nescis, oculi sunt in amore duces.
Ipse Paris nuda fertur periisse Lacæna,
  Cum Menelaëo surgeret e thalamo;
Nudus et Endymion Phœbi cepisse sororem
  Dicitur et nudæ concubuisse deæ.
Quod si pertendens animo vestita cubaris,
  Scissa veste meas experiere manus;
Quin etiam, si me ulterius provexerit ira,
  Ostendes matri brachia læsa tuæ.

he explains by a questionable ellipse, *a te pendet*. Lachmann reads 'nunc da te, mea lux, venit mea litore navis servata: an mediis sidat onusta vadis?'—For *sidat* Jacob has given *sistat* from the Groning. MS.; but the common reading seems much more appropriate. Jacob indeed maintains the reverse, but on grounds not connected with the reading given in the text. Cf. iv. 24, 16.

31.] 'If you should unfortunately change your feelings towards me through any fault of mine, my wish then is that I may be found dead before your door, and so give a proof of my affection to the last.' See i. 16, 17 seqq. On *vestibulum* see Becker, *Gallus*, p. 237.

VI. The subject is continued from the last, and probably refers to the same occasion. He reiterates his profession of ardent attachment and fidelity to Cynthia.

1.] *Felicem.* The *hiatus*, or non-elision of the final *m*, is remarkable. In Plautus it seems often to occur, where modern editors thrust in some word to evade it. In this case it would be easy to read *o te nox mihi candida.*

7.] *Illa* has the same emphasis as if he had said *illa ipsa suo suavissimo ore* &c.

13.] *Fertur.* Some lost 'Homeric' or 'Cyclic' account is clearly alluded to.

17.] *Cubaris.* We may notice here and inf. 7, 23, the archaism *cubavi* for the more usual *cubui*. The address to Cynthia is sudden, but this is a common practice with the poet, *e. g.* ii. 9, 15.

Necdum inclinatæ prohibent te ludere mammæ;
  Viderit hæc, si quam jam peperisse pudet.
Dum nos fata sinunt, oculos satiemus amore:
  Nox tibi longa venit, nec reditura dies.
Atque utinam hærentes sic nos vincire catena
  Velles, ut numquam solveret ulla dies!
Exemplo junctæ tibi sint in amore columbæ,
  Masculus et totum femina conjugium.
Errat, qui finem vesani quærit amoris:
  Verus amor nullum novit habere modum.
Terra prius falso partu deludet arantes,
  Et citius nigros Sol agitabit equos,
Fluminaque ad caput incipient revocare liquores,
  Aridus et sicco gurgite piscis erit,
Quam possim nostros alio transferre dolores:
  Hujus ero vivus, mortuus hujus ero.
Quod mihi si secum tales concedere noctes
  Illa velit, vitæ longus et annus erit;
Si dabit hæc multas, fiam immortalis in illis:
  Nocte una quivis vel deus esse potest.
Qualem si cuncti cuperent decurrere vitam,
  Et pressi multo membra jacere mero,
Non ferrum crudele neque esset bellica navis,

21.] *Necdum*, 'et nondum.' 'Besides, such *lusus* befits your youth,' τῷ νέῳ τε καὶ σφριγῶντι σώματι, Eur. *Androm.* 196. —*viderit hæc* &c., 'let that be the concern of those who regret they are past child-bearing,' which you are not. See inf. 9, 20.

25.] *Catena*, 'jugo Veneris.' *Jacob.*—*velles*, addressed to Cynthia, 'I would that you might consent,' &c. Kuinoel has *vellent*, i. e. *fata*; the conjecture of Burmann. The allusion in *catena* is to the well-known legend of Mars and Venus in Hom. *Od.* viii. 275, &c.

28.] *Totum conjugium*, *i. e.* qui solo suo conjugio fruantur; qui toti sibi, non aliis, dediti sunt. The order of the words is, 'masculus et femina, totum (in se ipsis) conjugium.' 'Unus columbus non nisi unam columbam in conjugio habet.'—*Barth.*

31.] *Falso partu*, monstroso, 'unnatural.' Juvenal, *Sat.* xiii. 64, 'Egregium sanctumque virum si cerno, bimembri Hoc monstrum puero, vel miranti sub aratro Piscibus inventis, aut fetæ comparo mulæ.'

33.] *Revocare.* See i. 15, 29.—*piscis erit*, *i. e.* live fishes will be found in the dry bed of a river. That this, here spoken of as a prodigy, is literally true under certain circumstances, is asserted by Sir Emerson Tennent in his Natural History of Ceylon, chap. x.

35.] Jacob and Lachmann, with Barth and Kuinoel, read *calores* from the Aldine. —*dolores* is much more elegant, and may easily bear the same sense.

39.] 'Even a single year will seem long for my life.' With the next verse compare v. 10 of the preceding: 'immortalis ero, si altera talis erit.'

41.] Jacob alone has *decurrere* from the Groning. MS. The sense is, 'If all mankind would worship Venus and Bacchus, the service of Mars would soon cease.'

Nec nostra Actiacum verteret ossa mare,
Nec totiens propriis circum oppugnata triumphis
  Lassa foret crines solvere Roma suos.
Hæc certe merito poterunt laudare minores:
  Læserunt nullos pocula nostra deos.
Tu modo, dum lucet, fructum ne desere vitæ:
  Omnia si dederis oscula, pauca dabis.
Ac veluti folia arentes liquere corollas,
  Quæ passim calathis strata natare vides,
Sic nobis, qui nunc magnum speramus amantes,
  Forsitan includet crastina fata dies.

44.] *Verteret*, Barth and Kuinoel with Scaliger. Lachmann defends the vulgate by Virgil's use of *volvere*, *Georg.* iv. 525, to which Hertzberg adds *Æn.* i. 100, 'scuta virum galeasque et fortia corpora volvit.' But *volvo* and *verto* are not synonymous; and the conjecture of Scaliger has much to commend it.

46.] 'Rome beset all around by its own victories' is a bold figure. *Propriis triumphis* is interpreted by Kuinoel *civilibus victoriis*; and perhaps *propriis* may signify *de se ipsa reportatis*. The idea however is, that its victories have been but so many defeats, and that it has been wearied in weeping for its own citizens. *Solvere crines* refers to the dishevelled hair of captives. See v. 11, 56. 'Africa tonsa,' which relates to the same custom, since either *cutting off* or *letting fall* the long hair implies the same disregard of personal adornment. So Livy, i. 26, 'Solvit crines, et flebiliter nomine mortuum sponsum appellat.'—*Lassa solvere*, as *lassa vocare*, iii. 4, 28.

47.] *Hæc*, sc. what he avows in the next verse, that the gods have never been outraged by his intemperance. See v. 42. It is probable that there is an allusion to Antony's well-known propensity, since this would be in keeping with the reference to the battle of Actium v. 44. This however is mere supposition, the sense being complete in itself, 'Whatever posterity shall say of our pleasures, they cannot charge us with the crime of provoking the gods to take vengeance on our country.'

49.] *Dum lucet*, i. e. antequam advesperascit. Compare supr. v. 2. Lachmann and Kuinoel give *dum licet*, *hunc* &c. The Groning. MS. has *dum licet*, the ed. Rheg. *dum licet*, the Naples MS. alone *dum lucet*. Müller reads *dum licet, o fructum* &c., the good copies omitting *hunc*.—*ne desere*, noli deserere, μὴ προδῷς, do not relinquish or resign it.

51.] A very choice and original simile, or rather, a new way of expressing an old one. 'Life is as frail as the leaves which fall from the garlands on the heads of the guests, into the goblets.' This sense of *calathus* (usually 'a flower-basket') is found in Virg. *Eclog.* v. 71, 'Vina novum fundam calathis Arvisia nectar.' Compare iii. 25, 37.

53.] Lachmann and Kuinoel prefer *spiramus*; a conjecture, though a probable one, of Scaliger's. It is adopted also by Keil and Müller, and by Barth, who compares μέγα πνεῖν and μέγα φρονεῖν. Yet with *magnum* we may understand *fructum* from v. 49.

54.] *Includet fata*. This is generally interpreted 'finiet vitam.' Hertzberg has suggested a more natural meaning of the words, 'crastina dies nos mortuos Orcino thesauro tradet,' and he ingeniously explains from this verse the obscure one in Hor. *Od.* i. 24, 17, 'Non lenis precibus fata recludere.' In fine, *fata* being used for *mortuos*, the notion of *inclosing* in the tomb is so natural a one, that it is found under some form or other in many passages, *e.g.* v. 11, 2, 'Panditur ad nullas janua nigra preces.'

VII.

Prætor ab Illyricis venit modo, Cynthia, terris,
  Maxima præda tibi, maxima cura mihi.
Non potuit saxo vitam posuisse Cerauno?
  Ah, Neptune, tibi qualia dona darem!
Nunc sine me plena fiunt convivia mensa,
  Nunc sine me tota janua nocte patet.
Quare, si sapis, oblatas ne desere messes,
  Et stolidum pleno vellere carpe pecus.
Deinde, ubi consumpto restabit munere pauper,
  Dic alias iterum naviget Illyrias.
Cynthia non sequitur fasces, nec curat honores;
  Semper amatorum ponderat illa sinus.
At tu nunc nostro, Venus, o succurre dolori,
  Rumpat ut assiduis membra libidinibus.
Ergo muneribus quivis mercatur amorem?
  Juppiter, indigna merce puella perit.

VII. Written to upbraid Cynthia for renewing a connexion with a certain wealthy but unintellectual official, already alluded to i. 8. He will not allow himself to suppose she cares for anything but his money; hence he directs his reproaches rather against her avarice than the fickleness of her attachment.

1.] *Illyricis.* From i. 8, 2, it appears that the prætor was governor of the province of Illyricum; and as on a former occasion he had proposed to carry Cynthia with him from Rome, so now on his return he desires to renew an old acquaintance. It may appear strange that the poet should dare to speak so insolently (v. 8 and 24) of a dignity like the Prætorian presidency of a province. Yet Tacit. *Ann.* iv. 52, calls Domitius Afer, 'recens prætura, modicus dignationis:' whence it may be inferred that *prætores* (to whom under Augustus the provinces were generally assigned, Asia and Africa being proconsular appointments), were of no very high rank. The student will refer to the 'Dictionary of Antiquities,' under *Provincia*, for a full account of their administrative powers. That the government of a province was a most lucrative appointment is certain from abundant testimonies. See Juvenal, viii. 87—122.

7.] *Si sapis* &c., said, of course, in bitter irony.

8.] *Pleno vellere.* 'Pluck him while his fleece hangs thick upon him,' *i. e.* before he is stripped of it by those who are ready and willing to plunder him. There is perhaps an allusion to the golden fleece, so that *pleno* might mean, 'full of gold dust.' So Caligula called Junius Silanus, proconsul of Asia, 'pecus aureum,' Tac. *Ann.* xiii. 1.

10.] *Alias* &c., that he may get rich by plundering another province.

11.] Having told Cynthia, in a taunting manner, to make the most of her prize, he adds, in the same strain, ''tis not so much rank and honour that my Cynthia cares for, as money. She always feels the pockets of her lovers to see if they are heavy.' There is perhaps a double sense in *sinus*, the folds of the toga and the feelings of the heart; and if so, he ironically means that Cynthia does not care for the devotion of lovers, but only for their wealth.

14.] *Rumpat ut*, *i. e.* faciendo ut &c.

16.] *Indigna merce*, 'for an inadequate price.' Lachmann reads, *Juppiter, indignum! merce puella perit!* But he rightly explains the vulgate, 'indigna hercle ista merx est, qua puella veneat,' while he less correctly objects that such a sense should have followed a *specific* mention of gold

Semper in Oceanum mittit me quærere gemmas,
  Et jubet ex ipsa tollere dona Tyro.
Atque utinam Romæ nemo esset dives, et ipse
  Straminea posset dux habitare casa!
Numquam venales essent ad munus amicæ,
  Atque una fieret cana puella domo.
Non, quia septenas noctes sejuncta cubaris,
  Candida tam fœdo brachia fusa viro;
Non quia peccaris, testor te, sed quia vulgo
  Formosis levitas semper amica fuit.
Barbarus excussis agitat vestigia lumbis,
  Et subito felix nunc mea regna tenet.
Aspice quid donis Eriphyla invenit amaris,
  Arserit et quantis nupta Creusa malis.
Nullane sedabit nostros injuria fletus?
  An dolor hic vitiis nescit abesse tuis?

and gems, and not a general enumeration, *muneribus*. Hertzberg gives a sufficient reply to this: 'puella merce perit, indigna (re) qua puella pereat. *Semper* enim indigna mors, qua puella talis pereat.'—*perit*, 'is thrown away,' 'is lost,' *perditur*.

17.] *Mittit me*. The connexion is, 'I now see that it was from her natural avarice that she was ever asking me for gifts.' The expression is of course hyperbolical. See on i. 14, 12.

20.] 'I would that the emperor himself could have lived, like Romulus of old, in a thatched hut.' There is an allusion to the *casa Romuli*, on which see v. 1, 9.

23.] *Septenas*. Here used for *septem*.—*fusa brachia*, a Græcism like *flores inscripti nomina*. Virg. *Ec*. 3, 106. περιπεπλεγμένη ὠλένας. See on i. 8, 34.

25.] The editors agree in *peccaris*, which (according to Jacob, but not to Lachmann and Hertzberg), is the reading of the MS. Groning. The rest give *peccarim*. 'Philippus Beroaldus correxit.' *Lachmann*. 'Non te testem appello tui unius peccati, sed communis formosarum mulierum levitatis, *i. e.* non tantum indignarer, si sola tu hoc commisisses scelus, quantum quod jam nulli puellæ confidere licet.'—*Hertzberg*. The sense is, 'I make this appeal to *your* feelings, not so much from offence at *your* fault in particular, but because frailty seems inseparable from beauty.' These verses contain in fact an apology for her conduct rather than a reproof. Jacob has adopted a punctuation which destroys wholly the even tenour of the passage; *sed quia—barbarus* &c., the intermediate words being taken as parenthetical.

27.] For *excussis* Müller suggests *exossis*.

28.] *Mea regna*, 'the queen of my heart.' Cf. v. 7, 50, 'longa mea in libris regna fuere tuis.'

29.] *Aspice—quid invenit*. See on i. 2, 9. The story of Eriphyle, wife of Amphiaraus, who betrayed her husband for the bribe of a necklace from Polynices, and was put to death in consequence by Alcmæon, Apollodor. iii. 6, 2, is familiar to most.—To Creusa, *alias* Glauce, daughter of Creon king of Corinth, Medea sent an embroidered robe besmeared with phosphorus. Hertzberg objects that this is not a case in point, since it does not appear that Creusa was *bribed*; and he supposes the poet to have followed, as elsewhere, an account now lost. But the general idea in view is the evil arising from *gifts*, and the danger of women receiving them under any circumstances.

31.] '*Sedabit fletus*, efficiet ut Cynthiam contemnam, ab eaque discedam.'—*Kuinoel*.

32.] 'Am I to grieve for ever at your perfidious conduct, or shall I not cast you off if you continue to offend?' *i. e.* 'an ego, quamvis dolens, nunquam potero a te vitiosa decedere?' For *tuis* Kuinoel gives *suis*, with the Naples MS. and ed. Rheg. Lachmann reads *ah dolor* from his own

Tot jam abiere dies, cum me nec cura theatri,
  Nec tetigit Campi, nec mea Musa juvat.
At pudeat certe, pudeat: nisi forte, quod aiunt,
  Turpis amor surdis auribus esse solet.
Cerne ducem, modo qui fremitu complevit inani
  Actia damnatis æquora militibus.
Hunc infamis amor versis dare terga carinis
  Jussit, et extremo quærere in orbe fugam.
Cæsaris hæc virtus et gloria Cæsaris hæc est:
  Illa, qua vicit, condidit arma manu.
Sed quascumque tibi vestes, quoscumque smaragdos,
  Quosve dedit flavo lumine chrysolithos,
Hæc videam rapidas in vanum ferre procellas,
  Quæ tibi terra, velim, quæ tibi fiat aqua.
Non semper placidus perjuros ridet amantes
  Juppiter, et surda negligit aure preces.
Vidistis toto sonitus percurrere cælo
  Fulminaque ætheria desiluisse domo:
Non hæc Pleiades faciunt, neque aquosus Orion,
  Nec sic de nihilo fulminis ira cadit:

conjecture. (Hertzberg is wrong in attributing *ab* to MS. Gron. the mistake arising from confounding this with v. 35).

35.] *Pudeat*, αἰσχυνθείην ἄν. This is said in respect of the advice so often tendered by his friends. See i. 1, 25. a, *pudeat arte*, Müller, with MS. Gron.

36.] *Turpis amor*, i. e. *infamis*, 'disreputable attachments refuse to hear the advice of friends.'

37.] 'Look at the case of Antony, and his infatuated attachment, and then say if it is easy to pause in the career of love before it has brought ruin.'

38.] *Damnatis*, cf. v. 6, 21, 'altera classis erat Teucro damnata Quirino.' *Ib.* 11, 15, 'damnatæ noctes, et vos, vada lenta, paludes.' The construction is not very clear; probably *damnatis militibus* is the ablative absolute, 'when his crew were condemned to defeat by the deified Romulus.' Barth explains it, 'quos senatus cum duce Antonio hostes judicaverat.'

39.] *Insanus amor* Müller, with the inferior copies. He says these words are sometimes confused by transcribers.—*amor*, viz. Cleopatra.

40.] *Extremo orbe*, i. e. by making sail for Egypt, v. 6, 63.

42.] *Condidit*, he sheathed the sword with the same hand by which he conquered. For, as Aristotle says, *Eth. N.* x. 7, πολεμοῦμεν ἵνα εἰρήνην ἄγωμεν.

43.] *Smaragdos*. On the metrical peculiarity see on v. 4, 48.

44.] *Dedit*, sc. prætor iste.

46.] *Fiat*. So all the editors but Jacob, who gives *fiet* from the MSS. while he admits the necessity of the correction. The meaning of vv. 43—6 is, 'Perish the gifts he has given you! May they turn to vile earth and water in your possession!' The expression is proverbial. Kuinoel quotes Hom. *Il.* vii. 99, ἀλλ' ὑμεῖς μὲν πάντες ὕδωρ καὶ γαῖα γένοισθε. Tibull. i. 10, 11, 'At deus illa In cinerem et liquidas munera vertat aquas.'

47—52.] See on i. 15, 25, and compare Juvenal, xiii. 228; Persius i. 24; Aristoph. *Nub.* 399, from which it is clear that the ancients thought death by lightning the proper and peculiar punishment of perjury. Kuinoel refers to Tibull. iii. 6, 49, 'perjuria ridet amantum Jupiter, et ventos irrita ferre jubet.'

52.] For *fulminis ira cadit* Müller conjectures *numinis ira cadit*. Compare however Æsch. *Theb.* 424, οὐδὲ τὴν Διὸς ἔριν πέδῳ σκήψασαν ἐμποδὼν σχεθεῖν.

Perjuras tunc ille solet punire puellas,
  Deceptus quoniam flevit et ipse deus.
Quare ne tibi sit tanti Sidonia vestis,
  Ut timeas, quotiens nubilus Auster erit.

VIII.

Mentiri noctem, promissis ducere amantem,
  Hoc erit infectas sanguine habere manus.
Horum ego sum vates, quotiens desertus amaras
  Explevi noctes, fractus utroque toro.
Vel tu Tantalea moveare ad flumina sorte,
  Ut liquor arenti fallat ab ore sitim;
Vel tu Sisyphios licet admirere labores,
  Difficile ut toto monte volutet onus:
Durius in terris nihil est, quod vivat, amante,
  Nec, modo si sapias, quod minus esse velis.
Quem modo felicem, invidia admirante, ferebant,
  Nunc decimo admittor vix ego quoque die.
Nunc jacere e duro corpus juvat, impia, saxo,

53.] *Tunc*, *i. e.* quoties fulminat.

55.] 'A Tyrian garment is an uneasy possession, if the owner has to fear every storm;'—'exanimis primo quoque murmure coeli,' Juven. xiii. 224.

VIII. He complains of having been deceived by a promise of admittance.

1—2.] 'To disappoint a lover is as bad as to be a murderess.' This alludes to v. 13, where he threatens to kill himself. Hence 'hoc *erit*,' *i. e.* you will be answerable for my death. Compare for the sentiment iii. 13, 45.

3.] *Horum ego sum vates.* 'I foretell that such an event will happen, (*i. e.* I think of suicide) whenever I have to pass the night alone.' 'Per utrumque torum intelligitur utraque tori pars, sc. sponda interior et exterior.' Ovid, *Am.* 1, 14, 32. 'Cur pressus prior est interiorque torus? *fractus*, nam qui somno frui non potest, membra huc et illuc versat.'—*Kuinoel.* Compare v. 3, 31, 'tum queror in toto non sidere pallia lecto,' and on i. 14, 21, 'et miserum toto juvenem versare cubili.' He means both *sponda* and *pluteus* (Becker, *Gallus*, p. 291). For *fractus*, *i. e.* fatigatus, Müller feebly reads *stratus*, a conjecture of Keil's. Hertzberg has a long note in explanation of *utroque torus* for *utraque pars tori*, which he defends on the principle that adjectives of number are often added to singular substantives to express the component parts of a whole, as *sex severis moveor*, *multa aqua* &c., and perhaps he might have added *totum conjugium*, iii. 6, 28.

5—10.] 'You may commiserate Tantalus and Sisyphus, but a lover is more truly deserving of your pity.' The construction is, 'licet vel moveare Tantali sorte ad flumina (stantis), quomodo liquor ab ore (recedens) fallat sitim, *i. e.* sitientem.'

11.] *Invidia admirante*, 'Envy herself standing aghast at my good fortune.' Martial, ep. v. 6, 5, 'et sic Invidia favente felix.'

13.] *Nunc—juvat.* 'Now I am disposed to commit suicide.' I doubt if the reader would stop to raise an objection against this passage, were he not told 'corruptum locum critici omnes senserunt,' and that Lachmann, in a note of two pages in length, defends his conjectural reading *jubet* for *juvat*, while Hertzberg devotes more than a page to prove that the two distichs 13—16 should be transposed, and *licet* substituted for *juvat*; both of which

Sumere et in nostras trita venena manus.
Nec licet in triviis sicca requiescere luna,
Aut per rimosas mittere verba fores.
Quod quamvis ita sit, dominam mutare cavebo.
Tum flebit, cum in me senserit esse fidem.

IX.

Assiduæ multis odium peperere querellæ:
Frangitur in tacito femina sæpe viro.
Si quid vidisti, semper vidisse negato;
Aut si quid doluit forte, dolere nega.
Quid si jam canis ætas mea candeat annis,

corrections he admits into the text. But the chief seat of the corruption is presumed to be in v. 15, where all the MSS. have *nec licet*. Kuinoel gives *nunc licet*, Hertzberg *nec juvat*. Rejecting these alterations as altogether uncertain and by no means necessary, we may translate, 'Nor is it possible to sleep in the streets when the moon is waning, and so to whisper through a chink in the door.' Probably (at least the hypothesis is not an extravagant one) the Romans thought the night air peculiarly unwholesome when the moon was waning; and every one knows what danger there is in the malaria of an Italian night. *Sicca luna*, a singular expression, derived from a popular notion that the apparent expansion and diminution of the moon's disk arose from the vapours which it imbibed or parted with. The commentators refer to Anacreon xix. 6, and Pliny, *N. H.* xvii. 9. Lachmann supposes *nec licet* to refer to the care taken by his rival the Prætor, mentioned in the foregoing elegy, and probably alluded to in this, to prevent his access to Cynthia: to which Hertzberg objects that *decimo quoque die* he was permitted to see her, which would hardly have been the case under such circumstances.

14.] *Trita*. So the Groning. and Naples MSS. Hertzberg supposes there is a reference intended to the *embrocades* (ἐγχριστά) of the ancient pharmacy. Kuinoel's *tetra* has but little authority.

17—18.] 'However, I shall take good care not to leave her for another; and perhaps in the end my constancy will move her to relent.'

IX. In this elegy the poet grows not only impatient of Cynthia's cruelty, but so unpolite as to taunt her with becoming old, and dyeing her hair. There is something amusing in the pettish spite with which he denounces this innocent article of the toilet (v. 27). It seems extraordinary, since the two taunts are so naturally connected, that Lachmann and Jacob, and even Kuinoel, Keil, and Müller (who, however, generally follow Lachmann), should suppose a new elegy commences with v. 23. There is no more reason for thinking with Jacob and Kuinoel that something may have been lost after v. 32: and here Lachmann holds the contrary opinion.

1—2.] 'Too much complaining often engender dislike; while keeping silence (*i. e.* enduring in silence) often regains an estranged mistress.' Hertzberg shrewdly remarks on this, 'Ipse secum agit poeta, et dum in rebus amatoriis vulgaris sapientiæ præceptis in ordinem redigere ipsum se fingit, figurata hac et composita oratione falsam istam doctrinam irridere se significat.'

3.] *Vidisse negato*. Compare Juvenal, I, 56, 'doctus spectare lacunar, Doctus et ad calicem vigilanti stertere naso.'

4.] *Doluit*, ἐλύπησε, used transitively, as in I. 16, 24.—*dolere*, *i. e.* nega id tibi dolori esse.

5.] Lachmann, Jacob, and Hertzberg adopt the reading of MS. Gron. and ed. Rheg., as given in the text. Kuinoel and Müller have *quid mea si canis ætas canduerit annis*, in which they follow the Naples MS., except that the latter has *canuerit*. Some of the latter MSS. give

Et faciat scissas languida ruga genas?
At non Tithoni spernens Auroræ senectam
Desertum Eoa passa jacere domo est.
Illum sæpe suis decedens fovit in undis,
Quam prius adjunctos sedula lavit equos.
Illum ad vicinos cum amplexa quiesceret Indos,
Maturos iterum est questa redire dies,
Illa deos currum conscendens dixit iniquos,
Invitum et terris præstitit officium;
Cui majora senis Tithoni gaudia vivi,
Quam gravis amisso Memnone luctus erat.
Cum sene non puduit talem dormire puellam,
Et canæ totiens oscula ferre comæ.
At tu etiam juvenem odisti me, perfida, cum sis
Ipsa anus haud longa curva futura die.
Quin ego deminuo curam, quod sæpe Cupido

canueret. Barth ventures to edit 'quid si jam canis ætas mea caneret annis?' Hertzberg thinks the passage corrupt, on the ground that *candeo* 'de splendido maxime colore dicitur.' The argument does not seem worth much, especially as he quotes Tibull. i. 10, 43, where it is used of grey hair. Anyhow, the meaning of the poet is perfectly clear: 'If you slight me in my youth, how would you treat me as an old man?'

6.] *Languida*, 'attesting the feebleness of age.'

7.] 'Aurora could love Tithonus, old as he was; whereas I (v. 19) am still in the prime of manhood.' These verses are very beautiful, and by no means difficult, though much altered and perplexed by the commentators. *Eoa domo*, 'in Oriente, ubi sol surgere visus.' The 'abode' of Aurora is in the East. When she was obliged to depart to perform her duties of giving light to the world (v. 14), she did not leave him without a parting embrace, but *fovit*, ἠγάπησε, 'hugged him,' and that *suis in undis*, where, as the dawn first rises (to an Italian) over the sea, her chamber was feigned to lie. Jacob quotes Hom. *Hymn. in Ven.* 227, where it is said that Tithonus, while young, ναῖε παρ' Ὠκεανοῖο ῥοῇς ἐπὶ πείρασι γαίης, but when old he was petted by the goddess in her home, αὐτὸν δ' αὖτ' ἀτίταλλεν ἐνὶ μεγάροισιν ἔχουσα. *Lavit equos* refers to the plunge through the sea from the submarine *stabulum* in which they had passed the night. Kuinoel, Barth, and even Lachmann, totally pervert the meaning of these lines by reading *ulnis* and *adjunctos*. Keil and Müller also read *ulnis*, retaining *adjunctos*.

10.] *Quam prius*. For priusquam. Surely this is a remarkable usage. For to compare, as Kuinoel does, Ovid, *Trist.* iv. 9, 31, 'hoc quoque, quam volui, plus est,' is clearly nothing to the purpose. It would only have been applicable had the present passage been 'quam lavit, prius fovit;' a construction by no means without examples. The peculiarity here is the placing the particle of comparison *quam*, *without the action compared*, before the comparative adverb *prius*. The commentators generally pass it over without remark. See however on iii. 17, 26.

12.] *Maturos*, 'all too soon.'

16.] *Amisso Memnone*. This is not mentioned by Homer, who only records the name *Od.* xi. 522.

20.] *Anus futura*. From this verse, and perhaps we may add, from the fact that she was childless (v. 33), it might be inferred that Cynthia was somewhat advanced in life. See however iii. 6, 21. The word *juvenis* is so indefinite that it is not clear whether she was older than the poet.

21.] *Quin ego diminuo curam*. 'Let me however console myself with the reflection, that Cupid is fickle, and often punishes

Huic malus esse solet, cui bonus ante fuit.
Nunc etiam infectos demens imitare Britannos,
Ludis et externo tincta nitore caput?
Ut natura dedit, sic omnis recta figura est:
Turpis Romano Belgicus ore color.
Illi sub terris fiant mala multa puellæ,
Quæ mentita suas vertit inepta comas!
De me, mi certe poteris formosa videri:
Mi formosa satis, si modo sæpe venis.
An si cæruleo quædam sua tempora fuco
Tinxerit, idcirco cærula forma bona est?
Cum tibi nec frater nec sit tibi filius ullus,
Frater ego et tibi sim filius unus ego,

those whom he before favoured.' This use of *quin*, properly asking a question, 'Why do I not?' and thence in a hortatory sense, is familiar to every scholar.

23.] *Infectos*, 'stained with woad.' *nunc etiam*, i. e. at your time of life, when these follies might reasonably cease. Though perhaps in Cynthia's view it was just the time to begin them. From the practice of dyeing the hair, the poet draws an exaggerated comparison of staining the whole body.—*Ludis*, ἀφροδισιάζεις: compare *lusus*, iii. 24, 29. The ancient Britons are said to have stained themselves with woad (*isatis tinctoria*), to which colour he alludes in *cærulea*, v. 31. Compare Martial, ep. xi. 53. The Eastern practice of staining the eyes, nails, &c. with henna probably led to the adoption of similar customs in Rome. See the curious fragment of Ovid, *Medicamina Faciei*, which contains the recipes for various cosmetics. Id *Rem. Amor.* 351, 'Tum quoque, cum positis sua collinet ora venenis, Ad dominæ vultus, nec pudor obstet, eas. Pyxidas invenies, et rerum mille colores,' &c. Dyeing the hair is frequently alluded to: cf. Ovid, *Amor.* i. 14, 1, 'Dicebam, medicare tuos desiste capillos: Tingere quam possis, jam tibi nulla coma est.' Tibull. i. 8, 43, 'Tum studium formæ: coma tum mutatur, ut annos Dissimulet viridi cortice tincta nucis;' which appears to refer to the peel of fresh walnuts.

24.] *Nitor* is here the glossy colour of the *flavi crines* of which the Romans were so fond. See ii. 2, 5.

25.] *Recta est*, καλῶς ἔχει. On *figura* see i. 4, 9.

26.] *Belgicus color*. There is some doubt as to the precise meaning of this expression. Both Kuinoel and Hertzberg agree with D'Orville that 'Dutch soap,' *spuma Batava*, Martial, viii. 33, 20, is meant, a preparation with which the ancient German tribes inhabiting that country used to dye their hair red, the 'flava cæsaries' (Juven. 13, 165) of that people being well known. Compare also Martial, xiv. 26, 'Caustica Teutonicos accendit spuma capillos.' The same writer (iii. 43) mentions the practice of staining gray hair: 'Mentiris juvenem tinctis, Lentine, capillis; Tam subito corvus, qui modo cygnus eras.' See also lib. iv. ep. 36.

29.] *De me*, 'quod ad me attinet.' Kuinoel, who refers to iii. 24, 21, not quite appositely. Compare Martial, ep. i. 16, 6, 'de nobis facile est; scelus est jugulare Falernum.'—*poteris*, i. e. sæpe veniendo.

30.] *Sat es* for *satis* Müller after Lachmann and Heinsius. But it is easy to supply *videris* from the preceding.

31.] 'Supposing it were the fashion to dye the hair blue; would it be becoming merely because it was fashionable?' By an absurd supposition he endeavours to throw ridicule upon the custom.

34.] The editors, by placing a full stop at *ego* have made out a plausible excuse for the supposed lacuna after v. 32. The sense however is clear enough, and closely connected with the preceding verses: 'Since you have no relations to dress for, and only me to please, keep to your own engagements, and do not study personal adornment so much.' In *custodis* he alludes to the keepers (see i. 11, 15; iii. 14,

Ipse tuus semper tibi sit custodia lectus,
Nec nimis ornata fronte sedere velis.
Credam ego narranti, noli committere, famæ:
Et terram rumor transilit et maria.

X.

Etsi me invito discedis, Cynthia, Roma,
Lætor quod sine me devia rura colis.
Nullus erit castis juvenis corruptor in agris,
Qui te blanditiis non sinat esse probam;
Nulla neque ante tuas orietur rixa fenestras,
Nec tibi clamatæ somnus amarus erit:
Sola eris, et solos spectabis, Cynthia, montes,
Et pecus et fines pauperis agricolæ.
Illic te nulli poterunt corrumpere ludi,
Fanaque peccatis plurima causa tuis.
Illic assidue tauros spectabis arantes,
Et vitem docta ponere falce comas;
Atque ibi rara feres inculto tura sacello,
Hædus ubi agrestis corruet ante focos;

14) who were appointed to protect and watch the actions of women in Cynthia's position.—*tuus lectus*, i. e. your pledges to me.—*nimis ornata*, cf. i. 2, 1 seqq.

37.] The meaning appears to be, 'noli committere ut ego credam famæ de te male narranti.' Kuinoel explains the verse very differently: 'Credam ego famæ de te narranti, propterea noli committere, noli peccare, nam nihil tegetur.' Nor is this in itself objectionable.—*narranti*, 'gossiping.'

38.] *Terras* Lachmann.

X. Addressed to Cynthia on her contemplated excursion into the country, and written in a cheerful and affectionate tone, which presents a strong contrast with his anxiety at her absence at Baiæ, i. 11. A very elegant poem, and displaying a fine sense of the beauties of nature, to which Humboldt (*Cosmos*, vol. ii. p. 16) considers the Romans in general to have been but little sensitive.

2.] *Quod sine me*, i. e. quod, quum me præsto non habeas, &c. For *colis*, the reading of the authentic copies, Lachmann, Hertzberg, and Müller give *coles* from one or two of the later MSS. It is true that Cynthia is about to depart, and therefore that *colis* must be taken for *cultura es*; but there seems no great difficulty in such a use of the present.

3.] *Juvenis corruptor*. See i. 11, 13.

9.] *Ludi*, i. e. theatrales.—*fana*, because under pretence of religion these places were made the scenes of secret meetings &c. Compare v. 8, 16. Juvenal, ix. 24, 'Nam quo non prostat femina templo?'

12.] *Docta falce*, 'skilful,' because on the art of the pruner the crop of fruit in great measure depends. From the judgment required in selecting proper *surculi*, and cutting away the rest, *putare*, 'to prune,' and *amputare* (ἀμφὶ), 'to cut away on both sides, leaving a central twig,' suggested the cognate meaning of rejecting all superfluous and intrusive ideas, and fixing the mind on one subject, i. e. of *thinking*.

13.] *Rara*, 'only now and then,' i. e. your dreaded visits to temples will be few and far between. So *raris Kalendis*, v. 3, 53.

Protinus et nuda choreas imitabere sura,
  Omnia ab externo sint modo tuta viro.
Ipsa ego venabor. Jam nunc me sacra Dianæ
  Suscipere, et Veneri ponere vota juvat.
Incipiam captare feras, et reddere pinu
  Cornua, et audaces ipse monere canes.
Non tamen ut vastos ausim temptare leones,
  Aut celer agrestes cominus ire sues:
Hæc igitur mihi sit lepores audacia molles
  Excipere et stricto figere avem calamo,
Qua formosa suo Clitumnus flumina luco
  Integit, et niveos abluit unda boves.
Tu quotiens aliquid conabere, vita, memento
  Venturum paucis me tibi Luciferis.

15.] 'There you shall dance forthwith,' (*protinus*, without let or hindrance from me) 'with bared leg in the festive dance of the rustics, so long as no rival is there as a spectator.'

17.] *Sacra*. Hertzberg regards this as an adjective agreeing with *vota*. The passage, which is obscure, is thus explained by him: 'Jam recuperato Cynthiæ amore, Veneri gratus vota pono suscepta; jam nova Dianæ suscipio, et si propitia mihi fuerit in venando, in delubris ejus (hæ autem sunt silvæ) prædæ partem, cornua excelsa, suspensurum me voto damno.' *Ponere vota* is *solvere*, *ἀνατιθέναι*, *suspendere*. But the simpler sense is, 'I will now make my vows (for success) to the goddess of the chase, and lay aside the vows I have hitherto made to the goddess of love.' A contrast seems intended between the two infinitives, the one to *take up*, the other as it were to *lay down*, or get quit of certain vows. The custom of hanging the spoils of the chase on the forest trees is interesting, as showing the origin of that ancient and chivalrous adornment of baronial halls, horns and heads of beasts captured in hunting. See Plutarch, *Quæst. Rom.* § iv.; Virg. *Ecl.* vii. 30. Kuinoel, who misinterprets the whole passage 17—20, reads *reddere pennis* on Burmann's improbable conjecture.

21.] The MS. Gron. has *temerare*, the Naples and ed. Rheg. *temptare*.—*vastos*, 'huge,' as 'vasti ducis,' v. 10, 40.—*Leones* must be taken as an hyperbolical expression, unless any one will seriously maintain that the Italian woods sheltered that creature in the Augustan age. Yet lions once existed in Britain; they are found to this day in Asia Minor, and the upper part of Greece seems to have been infested with them even in the time of Pausanias, who says (vi. 5, 3) *εἶναι πολλάκις οἱ λέοντες καὶ ἐς τὴν περὶ τὸν Ὄλυμπον πλανῶνται χώραν*. The question, perhaps, deserves investigation. See *Georgic* ii. 151; Martial, xiv. 30.—The accusative follows *cominus ire*, as if *aggredi* was the word he had intended.

23.] *Mihi*, emphatic; 'let this then be my venture, to lay in wait for the harmless hare.'—*Excipere*, a word used of the hunter who lies in waiting near his nets, *λινοπτάμενος*.—*stricto calamo*, i. e. sagitta ad jaculandum parata.

25.] *Clitumnus*. See on v. i. 124. *Georg.* ii. 146-7.—*niveos abluit*, a Græcism, 'washes them white;' because by drinking the water of that river cows were believed to produce white calves, so much required for sacrifices. The shady banks of the river, where it passed through or near the poet's paternal estate, are spoken of as 'hiding the stream in its own woods.'

27.] *Aliquid conabere*. The commentators understand by this 'aliquid nefandi,' so that *venturum me* would imply a kind of threat,—an argument against the hope of wronging him with impunity. They are perhaps right, though the tender expression *vita* does not seem well to accord with this view. May not the poet mean 'aliquid in venando'?

Sic me nec solæ poterunt avertere silvæ,
  Nec vaga muscosis flumina fusa jugis,
†Quin ego in assidua mutem tua nomina lingua;
  Absenti nemo non nocuisse velit.

XI.

Quid fles abducta gravius Briseïde? quid fles
  Anxia captiva tristius Andromacha?
Quidve mea de fraude deos, insana, fatigas?
  Quid quereris nostram sic cecidisse fidem?
Non tam nocturna volucris funesta querella
  Attica Cecropiis obstrepit in foliis,
Nec tantum Niobe bis sex ad busta superba

29.] *Solæ silvæ.* Not those of his own retirement at home, but Cynthia's country abode. 'Not even your present seclusion can prevent me from having your name continually on my tongue,' (i. 18, 31), *i. e.* from anxieties and fears on your behalf. Hertzberg, in a very long note, maintains that *mutare* is for *mussitare*; and that in this passage it is to be taken literally in the latter sense, as in Virgil, *Ecl.* v. 5, 'Zephyris mutantibus umbras,' and vi. 28. *Æn.* v. 707, where *mutare* has less MS. authority than *mussare*. Jacob ingeniously suggests *metuam*, 'from fearing your name on everybody's tongue,' (*i. e.* the frequent mention of you, and your celebrity for talent and beauty, which will render your real seclusion a difficult matter), 'lest some one should wrong me while absent,' or should try to withdraw your affections from me. Perhaps we should read *mussem*, (a word that occurs Virg. *Æn.* xii. 657 and elsewhere,) *i. e.* 'mutter,' 'secretly invoke.' Barth gives the sense thus: 'silvas. flumina, formosam Cynthiam resonare assidue docebo, atque ita linguis fascinantibus et male laudantibus obstrepere non desinam, ne tibi nocere possint.'

32.] Hertzberg with good reason objects to *ne nemo velit* for *ne quis velit*, as false Latinity. He himself reads *non* for *ne*, with the Naples MS., placing a colon at the end of the preceding verse;—'any one will be willing to wrong me in my absence from you.' Müller follows Lachmann in reading *ne*. Keil edits as given in the text above. 'Lest no one should be willing' can only imply a wish that some one should be willing; whereas *nemo non* is *quivis*, 'any one may wish' &c., *i. e.* any rival of mine. The passage is difficult, and both of these interpretations make considerable demands on one's faith in the integrity of the MSS. One of the later copies has *ut* for *ne*. May *mi* for *mihi* have been the true reading? The sense would then be optative, 'may no one wrong me' &c. Compare *utinam nolit*, ii. 2, 15; *utinam velles*, iii. 6, 25.

XI. Kuinoel says, 'Hæc elegia est una ex illis, quas poeta ante omnes reliquas, etiam primi libri, scripsit.' It is difficult to say wherein he finds the proof of this; in fact, he is generally content to re-echo the statements of his predecessors. That neither Propertius nor Cynthia observed strict fidelity to each other is certain from many passages already noticed; and the recrimination of the one, followed by protestations of regard from the other, may be supposed to have been frequent during the whole course of their connexion. In this instance the poet seems to have been the offender; for the present elegy is manifestly a reply to her expostulations (v. 33).

5.] *Funesta volucris Attica*, Philomel, daughter of Pandion.—*obstrepit*, properly ἀντιφωνεῖ, sings against other birds: see on i. 16, 46.

7.] *Niobe—superba* are to be taken together. The epithet refers to her conceit in preferring the beauty of her own offspring to that of Latona, for which offence she was punished by the loss of her twelve children.—*bis sex ad busta* affords a curious

Sollicito †lacrimas defluit a Sipylo.
Me licet æratis astringant brachia nodis,
Sint mea vel Danaës condita membra domo;
In te ego et æratas rumpam, mea vita, catenas,
Ferratam Danaës transiliamque domum.
De te quodcumque ad surdas mihi dicitur aures;
Tu modo ne dubita de gravitate mea.
Ossa tibi juro per matris et ossa parentis,—
Si fallo, cinis heu sit mihi uterque gravis!—
Me tibi ad extremas mansurum, vita, tenebras:
Ambos una fides auferet, una dies.
Quod si nec nomen, nec me tua forma teneret,
Posset servitium mite tenere tuum.

instance of the want of the article in the Latin tongue (τῶν δακρύων).—*tantum*, following *tam*, need not create any difficulty, as some have thought. Compare Moschus, *Id.* III. 37—44, οὐ τόσον εἰναλίαισι παρ' ᾀόσι μύρατο δελφίν, κ.τ.λ.

8.] Lachmann, Jacob, Keil, Müller, and Hertzberg, retain the MSS. reading *defluit*. Kuinoel and Barth have *deplui*t, the probable conjecture of Scaliger. For the active use of *defluere* Lachmann adduces no more satisfactory authority than two passages from Claudian. Hertzberg adds the transitive construction of ῥεῖν in Eur. *Herc.* 628. Müller adopts the correction of the older Burmann, *lacrimae*, i. e. 'nec tantum lacrimae defluit a Sipylo ad busta his sua (liberorum superbae Niobae.' But *lacrimae* is too far removed from *tantum*; and the singular is strangely used for *tantum lacrimarum*. Lachmann reads *superbae* for *superbis* or *superbe*, i. e. *superbae defluit*. Even this seems unsatisfactory. Perhaps *lacrimis*, as the poets use *fluere sanguine*, *sudore*, *mero* &c. The beautiful legend of Niobe turned to stone manifestly arose from a water-dropping crag, which at a distance resembled the human form. Pausan. Lib. I. cap. 21, 3, ταύτην τὴν Νιόβην καὶ αὐτὸς εἶδον ἀνελθὼν ἐς τὸν Σίπυλον τὸ ὄρος· ἡ δὲ πλησίον μὲν πέτρα καὶ κρημνός ἐστιν, οὐδὲν παρόντι σχῆμα παρεχόμενος γυναικὸς, οὔτε ἄλλως, οὔτε πενθούσῃ· εἰ δέ γε πορρωτέρω γένοιο, δεδακρυμένην δόξεις ὁρᾷν καὶ κατηφῆ γυναῖκα. The 'Group of Niobe,' in the Florence collection, is engraved in p. 552 of Smith's *History of Greece*.

10.] *Domo*, the 'turris aënea,' Hor. *Carm.* III. 16, 1, in which Danae was confined by her father Acrisius.

11.] *In te*, 'in your case,' i. e. propter te.

13.] The construction is, 'quodcunque de te dicitur, id dicitur mihi ad surdas aures.' Cynthia, as Kuinoel observes, had evidently offered some explanation for a rumour which had reached the poet respecting her conduct. He ingeniously turns aside the complaints against himself, by assuring Cynthia he never listens to what people say of *her*; implying that she ought equally to disregard evil reports respecting himself. —*gravitas* in the pentameter is opposed to *levitas*, and therefore means *constantia*.

15.] From this verse we learn that both the poet's parents were dead. Hence the allusion in I. 11, 23. His father died when he was very young: see v. 1, 127. The use of *parentis* for *patris*, as opposed to *matris*, is, as Hertzberg observes, remarkable, and the more so because it is properly ἡ τίκτουσα. The impossibility of misunderstanding its meaning is a sufficient excuse; nor is *paternae*, which some have proposed, likely to be the true reading.

17.] *Mansurum*, constantem futurum; or supply *fidum* or *in fide*.

18.] *Una fides auferet*. A poetic way of saying *in una eademque fide* (cf. v. 34) *emoriemur*.

19.] *Nomen*. 'Genus, nobilitas.'—*Kuinoel*. This is clearly wrong: see note on I. 1, 1. We must understand her reputation for beauty and talent, so often alluded to before.—*mite servitium tuum*, 'the influence which you possess, and so gently exercise over me, might have retained me,' —an elegant way of saying *mitis imperia tua*, the apparent contrary; but *servitium tuum* is τὸ ἐμὲ δουλεύειν σοι.

Septima jam plenæ deducitur orbita lunæ,
Cum de me et de te compita nulla tacent;
Interea nobis non numquam janua mollis,
Non numquam lecti copia facta tui;
Nec mihi muneribus nox ulla est empta beatis;
Quicquid eram, hoc animi gratia magna tui.
Cum te tam multi peterent, tu me una petisti;
Possum ego naturæ non meminisse tuæ?
Tum me vel tragicæ vexetis Erinyes, et me
Inferno damnes, Æace, judicio,
Atque inter Tityi volucres mea pœna vagetur,
Tumque ego Sisyphio saxa labore geram.
Nec tu supplicibus me sis venerata tabellis:
Ultima talis erit, quæ mea prima fides.
Hoc mihi perpetuo jus est, quod solus amator
Nec cito desisto, nec temere incipio.

XII.

Ah quantum de me Panthi tibi pagina finxit,
Tantum illi Pantho ne sit amica Venus!
Sed tibi jam videor Dodona verior augur?
Uxorem ille tuus pulcher amator habet.
Tot noctes periere! Nihil pudet? aspice, cantat

21.] *Deducitur*. 'Recte Jacobs. confert Ovid, *Met.* vii. 530, "Luna quater plenum tenuata retexuit orbem." Nam *deducere* proprium de opere textorio verbum.'—*Hertzberg*. See i. 16, 41; inf. 26, 38.

23—4.] Jacob is inclined to prefer *non unquam* with the Naples MS. But the sense is obvious: 'during the last seven months all the world has been talking of us, (*i. e.* saying things to our discredit) and yet *many times* has your door been opened to me, and that from regard, not for gifts received from me.' Compare *nonnihil* for *plurimum*, i. 12, 16.—*mollis*, opposed to *dura, crudelis*, i. 16, 17—8.

26.] *Quicquid eram* (tibi), 'tam benivolentiæ acceptum debeo.'—*Kuinoel*.

28.] *Naturæ tuæ*, *i. e.* indolis, 'your kindness.'

29.] *Tunc*, *i. e.* si quando obliviscar.

30.] *Æace*, see v. 11, 19.

31.] *Mea pœna vagetur*, inter vagas volucres sit.

33.] 'Write me no more supplicatory letters; my affection will never change; I am not as other lovers, fickle and capricious; but my way is not to be easily smitten nor soon tired.'—*hoc jus est*, hanc legem habeo, hunc morem sequor.—The last distich is omitted in MS. Gron.

XII. He boasts of having *foreseen* the true character of one Panthus, a rival, who had deceived Cynthia and married another.

1—2.] 'In the same degree as Panthus has misrepresented and slandered me in his correspondence with you, may Venus prove adverse,' *i. e.* may his recent marriage be an unhappy one. For *ah*, MS. Gron. has *en*. Barth and Kuinoel edit *at*, the conjecture (a probable one) of Heinsius.

3.] 'Do I now seem to have predicted truly, when I told you he did not really love you? Behold, he has married a wife.'

5.] *Periere*, 'have been thrown away.'—*cantat liber*, i. e. *vacuus*, tui amore non

Liber; tu nimium credula sola jaces.
Et nunc inter eos tu sermo es; te ille superbus
Dicit se invito sæpe fuisse domi.
Dispeream, si quicquam aliud quam gloria de te
Quæritur; has laudes ille maritus habet.
Colchida sic hospes quondam decepit Iason:
Ejecta est; tenuit namque Creusa domum.
Sic a Dulichio juvene est elusa Calypso:
Vidit amatorem pandere vela suum.
Ah nimium faciles aurem præbere puellæ,
Discite desertæ non temere esse bonæ.
Huic quoque, qui restat, jam pridem quæritur alter.
Experta in primo, stulta, cavere potes.
Nos quocumque loco, nos omni tempore tecum
Sive ægra pariter sive valente sumus.

obligatus.—*cessare* implies the indifference of one who has no other concern to occupy his thoughts. *Tu sola jaces*, i. e. illo conjuge non potiris.

7—8.] 'At this very time Panthus and his wife are talking about you, and he is trying to persuade her that it was not by *his* desire that you so often remained at home, but that you were so fond of him' &c. *Esse domi*, like our familiar phrase, implied the intention of admitting a visitor. 'Ait te domi fuisse, non quod ille jusserit et condixerit, sed quod tu volueris.'—*Barth*.

9.] *Gloria*. Compare i. 13, 8, 'dum tibi deceptis augetur fama puellis.'—*has laudes*. 'Now that he is married, he boasts of your affection for him: he glories in having deceived you, just as Jason deceived Medea and married Creusa: or as Ulysses won the regard of Calypso and then left her.'—*ille maritus*, ironical; ὁ πόσις ὁ καλός.

12.] *Tenuit namque Creusa domum*. So Lachmann, Jacob, Hertzberg, with the MS. Groning. The common reading is *tenuis domo*. Kuinoel gives *ejecta tenuit namque Creusa domum*. Barth reads 'Electa est tenui namque Creusa domo.' Müller 'ejectæ tenuit' &c., after Ruhnken, who also proposed *locum* for *domum*. The sense however is sufficiently clear: 'she was cast off because Creusa became the wife.'—On *Dulichius juvenis*, see iii. 5, 4.

16.] *Non temere esse bonæ*, 'not on such slight grounds to earn the title of *bonæ*,' i. e. faciles, from your admirers. The construction of the nominative is a Græcism: see on ii. 9, 7. Hertzberg's note is rather obscure; '*Discite* hic quasi imperativus verbi *posse* est.' Rather the verb assumes the construction of *volo*, *incipio*, *desino* &c.

17.] *Nunc quoque*, Kuinoel. *Hinc quoque* MS. Gron. Keil reads *huic quoque qui restat*; Barth, *nunc quoque, qui restet*; Müller, *hinc quoque qui restat?* Lachmann, *huic quoque qui restat!* Hertzberg appears to be right in his view of the passage, which has perplexed the commentators not a little: 'Hæc quoque, (i. e. puella nostra, Cynthia,) modo repudiata nihil pœna sua didicit; jam enim quærit alterum amatorem eum, qui restat, quemque in talem eventum sibi quodammodo reservaverat. In quo idem eam periculum, quod in priore modo experta sit, manere ait Propertius.'—*huic quoque*, i. e. puellæ, Cynthiæ; in reference to *puellæ* used generally in 15.—*qui restat* probably refers to the Prætor, supr. El. 7.

19—20.] 'You can rely on my devotion to you both in health and in sickness.' 'Videtur ille rivalis Cynthiam ægram neglexisse.'—*Kuinoel*. This view is justified by ii. 9, 25.—*pariter*, i. e. sive ægra sis sive valeas. The argument is, 'since therefore you can depend upon me alone, resign all others and attach yourself to me.'

XIII.

Scis here mi multas pariter placuisse puellas,
  Scis mihi, Demophoon, multa venire mala.
Nulla meis frustra lustrantur compita plantis;
  O nimis exitio nata theatra meo!
Sive aliquis molli diducit candida gestu
  Brachia, seu varios incinit ore modos,
Interea nostri quærunt sibi vulnus ocelli,
  Candida non tecto pectore si qua sedet,
Sive vagi crines puris in frontibus errant,
  Indica quos medio vertice gemma tenet.
Quæ si forte aliquid vultu mihi dura negarat,
  Frigida de tota fronte cadebat aqua.
Quæris, Demophoon, cur sim tam mollis in omnes?
  Quod quæris QUARE non habet ullus amor.

XIII. In an epistle to a feigned friend the poet describes his own temperament, and confesses his weaknesses in a very ingenuous strain. It may be inferred from v. 20—1, that he had been reproached with injuring his health by his follies; he calls such reproofs *invidia*, and, as usual, quotes precedents in his favour from Grecian antiquity. This elegy is concluded by Jacob and Lachmann with v. 42.

1.] *Here*. The day before he seems to have been at the theatre, and expressed his admiration for *multas puellas* whom he saw there.—*venire*, i.e. ea ex causa. Lachmann awkwardly and unnecessarily inserts *hinc*, 'scis mi hinc, Demophoon,' &c.—*mala* means nothing more than *amoris vulnera*, as iii. 17, 46.

3.] *Lustrantur*, 'are traversed,' iii. 1, 1. No allusion seems intended to the Compitalia, which would be quite out of place.

4.] *O nimis* &c. 'And as for the theatres—alas! they were made for my ruin.' Such is the sense of this verse. Kuinoel and Barth, following the interpolated copies, give *omnis in exitium—meum*. The reading, as Jacob observes, seems to have arisen from a mistake, afterwards corrected, of the transcriber of the Groning. MS. *O nimis in exitio*. Lachmann, followed by Keil and Müller, place a comma at *meo*, and a note of admiration at *modos*. But this would make Propertius an admirer of the actors; whereas he says that while the acting is going on (*interea*), he is looking at the women in the theatre. Lachmann explains *interea* by 'dum puellæ illos artifices spectant.'

5.] *Diducit* Lachmann and Hertzberg with Passerat. The MSS. have *deducit*. He speaks of dancers gracefully extending their arms, *gesticulantes*, while performing in the lewd farces called *mimes*, and professes his indifference to the acting, however good.

9.] *Puris*, 'apertis et splendentibus.'—*Barth*.

10.] *Medio vertice*. The top-knot, *κρώβυλος* (apparently the English word *crope* or *crop*), which appears to have been fastened with a jewelled pin, perhaps after the fashion of the modern Italian women (Martial, xiv. 24). This (Roman) method of dressing the hair is described in the article on *acus* in the Dictionary of Antiquities. An engraving (art. *coma*, p. 266), is given of a top-knot from the head of Diana, and this is perhaps the costume alluded to. Compare Ovid, *A. A.* iii. 143, 'altera succinctæ religetur more Dianæ.'

14.] The true meaning of this verse was first seen by Lachmann; 'hoc Quare, quod tu quæris, rationem *cur* aliquis amet, non habet ullus amor.' *Cur* and *quare* (quâ re, quar, quor, cur) being different forms of the same word, or rather words, this repetition is quite appropriate. Hertzberg has collected several instances of this custom of *quoting* a word (which the Greeks so neatly express by prefixing the neuter

Cur aliquis sacris laniat sua brachia cultris,
  Et Phrygis insanos cæditur ad numeros?
Unicuique dedit vitium natura creato;
  Mi fortuna aliquid semper amare dedit.
Me licet et Thamyræ cantoris fata sequantur,
  Numquam ad formosas, invide, cæcus ero.
Sed tibi si exiles videor tenuatus in artus,
  Falleris: haud umquam est culta labore Venus.
Percontere licet; sæpe est experta puella
  Officium tota nocte valere meum.
Juppiter Alcmenæ geminas requieverat Arctos,
  Et cælum noctu bis sine rege fuit:
Nec tamen idcirco languens ad fulmina venit:
  Nullus amor vires eripit ipse suas.
Quid? cum e complexu Briseïdos iret Achilles,
  Num fugere minus Thessala tela Phryges?
Quid? ferus Andromachæ lecto cum surgeret Hector,

article), among which that from Persius, v. 87, is the best, '*licet* illud et *ut volo* tolle,' *i.e.* ἔασον τὸ ἔξεστι καὶ τὸ ὅπως θέλω. Compare also *Antig.* 567, ἀλλ' ἥδε μέντοι μὴ λέγε. See inf. iii. 17, 2. Müller reads *cura* with Haupt, *i. e. amor non curat;* and Lachmann thinks the correction plausible.

15.] 'You may as well ask the reason of the infatuation which makes some votary of Cybele cut himself with knives at the sound of the Phrygian flute.'

17.] *Creato*, 'at his birth,' γενομένῳ. For *fortuna* Barth and Kuinoel repeat *natura*, following as usual a late MS. There is no reason for supposing, with Lachmann, that *fortuna* is the ablative, and understanding *natura* from the preceding verse, —'ut semper forte fortuna aliquid amet.' The influence of Fortune in love is mentioned ii. 5, 6.

19.] The sentiment seems a singular one, 'Though I should be struck blind like Thamyras or Thamyris (*Il.* ii. 595—9), I shall never be blind to beauty.' He means, however, 'Though I should be blind to all *other* objects,' &c.

25.] *Geminas Arctos*, *i. e.* duas noctes. Kuinoel's idea that *requieverat* is for *requiescere fecerat*, is refuted by Jacob at great length. A fact so obvious as that *requiesco* is and can be only an intransitive verb scarcely requires five pages in the way of proof. The notion of its active sense seems principally to have arisen from an unsound remark of Servius on Virg. *Ecl.* viii. 4, 'Et mutata suos requierunt flumina cursus,' where the accusative depends on *mutata*. But the same learned critic is less happy in his brief note: 'Ceterum *Alcmenæ* genitivus est, qui dependet a Jovis nomine, ut *Alcmenæ Juppiter* ex amantium more dicatur.' It is the dative 'acquisitively' used, *in gratiam Alcmenæ*. See Plautus, *Amphitryo*, Prolog. 113, 'et hæc ob eam rem nox est facta longior, Dum cum illa quacum volt voluptatem capit.'—*geminas Arctos*, *i. e.* duas noctes dum se vertunt ea sidera.

31.] *Andromachæ*. This is the reading of all the good copies. Hertzberg, who has examined the question with great minuteness, (*Quæst.* p. 163—4), contends that Propertius always prefers the Greek genitive in *es*, rather than the Latin in *æ*, in Greek names of this declension, and that if in certain instances the MSS. agree in the latter, some reason must be looked for, or some corruption be suspected. Hence in i. 13, 30, he reads 'et Ledes e partu,' and in the present passage 'Andromaches e lecto.' I am not sufficiently convinced of the certainty of the fact, to which there are several exceptions, the authority of the MSS., or the consistency of the poet in such details, either to follow him or to

Bella Mycenææ non timuere rates?
Ille vel hic classes poterat, vel perdere muros.
Hic ego Pelides, hic ferus Hector ego.
Aspice uti cælo modo sol, modo luna ministret:
Sic etiam nobis una puella parum est.
Altera me cupidis teneat foveatque lacertis,
Altera si quando non sinit esse locum:
Aut, si forte irata meo sit facta ministro,
Ut sciat esse aliam, quæ velit esse mea.
Nam melius duo defendunt retinacula navim,
Tutius et geminos anxia mater alit.
Aut, si es dura, nega: sin es non dura, venito!
Quid juvat et nullo ponere verba loco?

write *Andromache* with Lachmann. This learned scholar is of opinion that the names *Andromede*, *Clytæmnestra*, *Leda*, *Cinara*, and generally *Electra*, forming the Greek nominative in *a*, not in *e*, always form the genitive in *æ*. But not even this rule can be considered an absolute one: he admits the occurrence of *Hypermnestre* and *Andromede* in Ovid, and also supr. i. 3, 4; v. 7, 63, and 67.

33.] A confused expression for *vel ille* (Hector) *classes*, *vel hic muros perdere poterat*: where the usual rule for the use of *hic* and *ille* is not observed. See on ii. 1, 37.—'*hic ego* nempe in amoris militia.'—*Kuinoel*. For the concluding *ego* perhaps we should read with MS. Gron. *ero*. In either case *hic* is the adverb, sc. in hac nostra militia.

36.] *Sic etiam*, viz. by change and rotation.

39.] *Meo ministro*. See on v. 2, of the next elegy. He appears to allude to some offence given to Cynthia by his servant. Jacob proposes *mero*, i. e. *inter vina*. There is no necessity for the change, were it better than it is.—*aut—ut sciat* gives a second reason why another girl should be held, as it were, in reserve; the first being *si quando non sinit*, &c. 'Or that she may know I have another girl who will consent to be mine, if *she* should pout and show ill temper.' By placing full stops at the end of 37 and 38, with Barth, Kuinoel shows that he did not understand the poet's meaning.

41.] *Duo retinacula*, i. e. duæ anchoræ, or, which is much the same thing, duo funes (πρυμνήσια). The Greek proverb is well known. See Pindar, *Ol.* vi. 100, ἀγαθαὶ δὲ πέλοντ' ἐν χειμερίᾳ νυκτὶ θοᾶς ἐκ ναὸς ἀπεσκίμφθαι δύ' ἄγκυραι. 'To have two strings to your bow' is the equivalent modern proverb.

42.] A mother was supposed to have more care for each child, when she had several, than for an only child. The opinion is not confirmed by modern experience. Kuinoel quotes two beautiful lines from Ovid, *Remed. Am.* 463, 'Fortius e multis mater desiderat unum, Quam quæ flens dicit, Tu mihi solus eras.'

43.] Lachmann and Jacob, followed by Keil and Müller, commence a new elegy with this verse. Hertzberg however (*Quæst.* p. 113 &c.) has remarked that Propertius is peculiarly apt to apostrophise persons of whom he was before speaking in the third person. This being admitted, it is clear that the poet is pursuing the idea in v. 38. The general sense is, 'Refuse or assent as you please; it matters not to me, who have another in reserve.' This is not said to Cynthia in particular, but to any one of his acquaintances indefinitely. The construction is rather irregular for *aut nega*, *aut venito*.

44.] *Ponere verba nullo loco*, 'hic debet esse, nullius auctoritatis vel ponderis verba proloqui: *et random* quod Angli aiunt.'—*Jacob*. Müller reads *a*, *nullo* &c. (*i. e.* ah!) 'Cur nihili facis verba, id est, promissa tua?'—*Lachmann*. See on i. 19, 17—20. Barth and Kuinoel follow Beroaldus, *in nullo pondere verba loqui*, and tells his readers, 'præpositio *in* redundat.' The expression (in this sense) is unusual. Perhaps he had in view οὐδαμοῦ τίθεσθαι. Hertzberg considers that 'not to value words,' and 'to throw away or waste words,' are correlative ideas. Yet it

Hic unus dolor est ex omnibus acer amanti,
  Speranti subito si qua venire negat.
Quanta illum toto versant suspiria lecto,
  Cum recipi, quem non noverit illa, putat.
Et rursus puerum quærendo audita fatigat,
  Quem, quæ scire timet, dicere plura jubet.

XIV.

Cui fuit indocti fugienda hæc semita vulgi,
  Ipsa petita lacu nunc mihi dulcis aqua est.
Ingenuus quisquam alterius dat munera servo,
  Ut promissa suæ verba ferat dominæ?
Et quærit totiens: Quænam nunc porticus illam

scarcely follows that they are convertible terms. The poet's meaning is this: 'What is the good of promising, merely to keep peace for a time, when you do not intend to perform?' He proceeds to show the annoyance arising from such conduct.

46.] Kuinoel joins *subito venire*. Rather, I should say, *subito negat*, which alludes to sending a sudden excuse.

48.] *Cum recipi*, &c. 'Cum sibi praeferri alium ignotum amatorem putat.'—*Kuinoel*, who reads *quem non noverit ille*. This 'vexatissimus versiculus,' as Lachmann calls it, is variously read in the MSS. The best copies have *cur* for *cum*, *quæ* and *ille* for *quem* and *illa*; and *vetat* for *putat*. The reading in the text is that of Lachmann and Jacob, with Keil and Müller, from the excerpta of Pucci. The sense is, 'he is tortured with jealousy, believing she has admitted some one else, to whom in fact she is a perfect stranger.'

49.] *Rursus quærendo audita*, 'by repeating questions already answered.'

50.] This verse is wanting in the Naples MS., whence there is some reason to suspect that the conclusion is imperfect. The sense appears to be, 'whom (*i.e.* the slave) he urges to tell him more fully the circumstances of which he (the expectant) fears to be informed.' In a few words, 'he implores him to tell the worst.' But *quærere plura* is the reading of the MSS. and most of the edd. Lachmann says: 'puerum, qui se causam, cur puella non veniat, scire negavit, plura, quæ ipse timet scire, quærere jubet.' And he marks the loss of some verses next following.

XIV. He compares the pride of high-born women with the facile compliance of the humbler classes. This, like the next, is a difficult elegy; both have given much trouble to critics and commentators.

1—2.] 'I, who formerly thought that I ought to shun the vulgar path, now find the water sweet drawn from the common tank.' That is, I who once thought myself too clever to act like others, now discover my error, and find satisfaction in returning to the old ways. He blames himself for aspiring to the favour of Roman ladies above his position in life. For the metaphor in v. 2, see note on iii. 5, 12.—'*semita vulgi*, alludit ad semitarias meretriculas.'—*Barth*. Cynthia, it will be remembered, was not one of these.

3—4.] 'Is a gentleman to bribe the servant of another to carry the message which he has engaged to convey (and therefore is bound to convey without a gift) to his mistress?' Or *promissa* may mean, 'promised by the lover at some former interview.' It is probable that services of this description formed a regular trade at Rome. To be a 'go-between' was to make a handsome livelihood. Juvenal, *Sat.* iii. 45.

5—8.] 'Is he to put himself to endless trouble to find out in what piazza or in what part of the Campus Martius she takes her walk, merely to be favoured with a note from her, asking for a present?' On the peculiar construction *quisquam dat*, where we should expect the subjunctive, see iii. 26, 1.

Integit? et: Campo quo movet illa pedes?
Deinde, ubi pertuleris, quos dicit fama, labores
Herculis, ut scribat: Muneris ecquid habes?
Cernere uti possis vultum custodis amari,
Captus et immunda sæpe latere casa?
Quam care semel in toto nox vertitur anno!
Ah pereant, si quos janua clausa juvat!
Contra, rejecto quæ libera vadit amictu,
Custodum et nullo sæpta timore, placet;
Cui sæpe immundo Sacra conteritur Via socco,
Nec sinit esse moram, si quis adire velit.
Differet hæc numquam, nec poscet garrula, quod te
Astrictus ploret sæpe dedisse pater;
Nec dicet: Timeo: propera jam surgere, quæso:
Infelix, hodie vir mihi rure venit!
Et quas Euphrates et quas mihi misit Orontes,
Me juerint: nolim furta pudica tori.

9.] *Amari*, 'cross.' Kuinoel and Barth give *avari* from the Aldine.

10.] *Captus*, metuens ne deprehendatur marito superveniente.—*casa*, the wooden shed of some slave, the porter, perhaps. Hor. *Sat.* i. 2, 132, 'discincta tunica fugiendum est ac pede nudo; Deprendi miserum est.'

11.] *Quam care*, 'at how high a price a single night in the whole year comes round to your turn!' The MS. Gron. has *verterit*. Kuinoel *venditur*, the conjecture of Hemsterhusius.—*nox*, i.e. noctis fructus.—*janua clausa*, aditu difficilis; si quos juvat sæpius excludi quam admitti.

13.] *Libera*, ad suum arbitrium; ubicunque et quandocunque vult; mariti timore non impedita, &c.—*rejecto amictu*. These words naturally refer to the custom of muffling the face for fear of being recognised. Hertzberg explains it, 'domi relicta toga a meretrice,' comparing the *tunicatus popellus* of Horace, *Ep.* i. 7, 65, which however probably refers only to males,—as we should say, 'in shirt-sleeves.' Another interpretation proposed by him is that the *ricinium* (*Festus*, p. 274, Müller), or dress of the *nobiles feminae*, marked with the laticlave, is meant; a word supposed to be derived a *rejiciendo* (παρὰ τὸ ἀναβάλλεσθαι). Varro, *L. L.* v. § 132, 'Antiquissimis amictui ricinium. Id, quod eo utebantur duplici, ab eo quod dimidiam partem retrorsum jaciebant, ab rejiciendo ricinium dictum.' Perhaps the *domino* or mask of more recent times. *Libera* must then mean *secura*, for he is speaking not of ladies, but '*contra*,' of those who are in common life.—*Timore custodum*, i. e. custodibus timendis. Kuinoel and Barth read *tumore*, from the Aldine; i. e. the *ὄγκος*, or 'parade' of attendants.

15.] *Soccus* was the loose overshoe used by both sexes in their ordinary out-of-door avocations. Hence *immundus*, lutulentus. Ladies were carried in their lecticæ.

17.] *Differet*, 'abuse you.' See on i. 4, 22.—'Promulgabit'—*Barth*.

20.] *Infelix*, supply *sum*.—*rure venit*, *redit*; cf. Hor. *Sat.* i. 2, 127, 'nec metuo ne—vir rure recurrat.'

21.] Juven. iii. 62—5, 'Jam pridem Syrus in Tiberim defluxit Orontes, et linguam et mores, et cum tibicine chordas—Vexit, et ad Circum jussas prostare puellas.'—*juerint*, i. e. juverint. So Hertzberg from the Naples MS., which gives *iuerint*. The rest have *capiant*. One reading or the other is manifestly a correction; and as a question of probability, the chances are in favour of the least usual form being the genuine one. *Juerint* occurs Catull. lxvi. 18.—*furta pudica tori*, i. e. pudici tori, nuptarum.

Libertas quoniam nulli jam restat amanti,
  Nullus liber erit, si quis amare volet.

XV.

'Tu loqueris, cum sis jam noto fabula libro,
  Et tua sit toto Cynthia lecta foro?'
Cui non his verbis aspergat tempora sudor?
  Aut pudor ingenuis, aut reticendus amor.
Quod si tam facilis spiraret Cynthia nobis,
  Non ego nequitiae dicerer esse caput;
Nec sic per totam infamis traducerer urbem,
  Urerer et quamvis, nomine verba darem.

23—4.] 'Since every lover of necessity loses his liberty, none must love who wish to be free.' Jacob places a colon at v. 22, and a full stop at v. 23, 'ne in protasi idem esset quod in apodosi: Quoniam nemo amans liber, nemo amans liber est.' Hertzberg rightly restores the old punctuation. Müller follows Fischer in regarding the last verse as 'ab interpolatore conflatum.' Perhaps *volet* may be rendered, 'if he shall persist in loving,' *i. e.* free women.

XV. The same subject is continued. He excuses himself for his faithlessness to Cynthia, on the plea that she acts towards him the capricious part before described as peculiar to the ladies of Rome. This elegy is difficult, nor do the commentators agree either as to sense, reading, or punctuation in many places.

1.] *Tu loqueris?* As in El. 9, supr. he commences with a quotation, and is replying to an imaginary rebuke: 'Do *you* talk of having abandoned your pursuit of women in the better rank of life, when all the world knows, by your published poems, your attachment to Cynthia?'—*noto libro*, See introductory note on iii. 1.

2.] *Cynthia lecta.* The first book of Elegies was inscribed 'Cynthia,' as has been already stated. Hence, *lecta* must be taken literally.

3.] 'Is there not some reason to feel distressed at the just reproach?' *i. e.* Have I not subjected myself to just ridicule? With Jacob and Lachmann I have followed the reading of all the MSS. in retaining *sudor*, which in fact the sense of the verse almost imperatively demands. Hertzberg, Barth, and Kuinoel give *sordes* from Scaliger's conjecture, and make *pudor* and *amor* the nominatives to *aspergat*, v. 3. The whole passage is very obscure, and has been variously interpreted. One difficulty is, whether the second distich continues the reproach, or contains the poet's reply. The fourth verse is commonly read thus: *aut pudor ingenuus, aut reticendus amor*. For the first *aut* the MS. Gron. has *et*, which Jacob admits. Lachmann incloses the whole verse in brackets, as 'spurius et subditivus;' a supposition extremely improbable. None of the editors seem to have taken offence at the metrical licence at the end of the first penthemimer, which is in some degree justified by *cineris* in ii. 8, 8. Nevertheless, *ingenuis* is surely the true reading. The sense is, 'men of good birth must either expect to be put to the blush, or they must keep secret their love.' Or thus: 'if young nobles have any shame, they will not talk of their loves.' In plain words, 'If a man will write verses on his mistress, (he being *ingenuus* and she a *meretrix*), he cannot avoid becoming *fabula in toto foro*.' Müller reads *haut pudor ingenuis, haud* &c.' with Haupt, and makes this distich to continue the speech or address of the first two lines.

5.] 'Were Cynthia a little less cruel, I should never have been called a profligate,' *i. e.* I should not have exposed myself by writing verses. *tam facilis*, 'as compliant as you say that she is.' On *spiraret* see iii. 3, 8.

8.] *Nomine*, by concealing my name. If, he says, Cynthia were less obdurate, I would not make myself notorious by writing verses about her; however much I was in love (*urerer*), I would not let out the secret, *reticerem amorem*, sup. 4. From *infamem* however (10) it might be surmised

Quare ne tibi sit mirum me quærere viles:
  Parcius infamant; num tibi causa levis?
Et modo pavonis caudæ flabella superbæ,
  Et manibus dura frigus habere pila,
Et cupit iratum talos me poscere eburnos,
  Quæque nitent Sacra vilia dona Via.
Ah peream, si me ista movent dispendia; sed me
  Fallaci dominæ jam pudet esse jocum.

XVI.

Hoc erat in primis, quod me gaudere jubebas?
  Tam te formosam non pudet esse levem?
Una aut altera nox nondum est in amore peracta,
  Et dicor lecto jam gravis esse tuo.
Me modo laudabas, et carmina nostra legebas:
  Ille tuus pennas tam cito vertit amor?

that Cynthia had spoken against him to his rivals.

11.] He passes to another objection, alluded to in v. 8 of the preceding elegy. 'Besides, she is extravagant, and is ever wishing to possess a flapper (fan) of peacock's feathers, or a ball for cooling her hands; and she requires me, already exasperated by her demands, to beg for her (*emere*, Hertzberg) ivory dice.' The *flabellum* was used, as it now is in hot countries, for making a cool breeze: Martial, iii. 82. Plautus, *Trinum.* 252 enumerates the *flabelliferæ* among the many attendants of fashionable courtesans. What the *pila* was, alluded to in v. 12, appears to be hitherto unexplained. Kuinoel says, 'pila ex crystallo, quam matronæ delicatiores æstivo tempore ad calorem frigore ejus mitigandum manibus tenere solebant. Vide Pliny, *N. H.* xxxvii. 2; Martial, xi. 8,' (v. 37), where mention is made of amber, but in a manner not applicable to the present passage. A conjecture may be hazarded, in the absence of any direct testimony. Claudian has a series of epigrams (vi—xiv.) 'de crystallo cui aqua inerat,' which the Romans appear to have considered (or rather perhaps, poetically to have represented) as ice, partly congealed to stone, partly liquified in the interior. The *cold* sensation to the touch is more than once alluded to: ep. viii. 'Solibus indomitam glaciem Alpina rigorem Induerat, nimio jam pretiosa gelu;' and ep. xi. 'Dum crystalla puer contingere lubrica gaudet, Et gelidum tenero pollice versat onus' &c. Pieces of rock-crystal may be seen in museums in which water or globules of air are enclosed. To this day ignorant vendors of minerals tell their customers that quartz, sulphate of lime, and fluor spar, are 'congealed water.' And from the same erroneous idea, perhaps, the epithet *aquosa* is applied to crystal in v. 3, 52. The cold feel, attributed to crystal, arose from the notion of its being mineralised ice. It is common to see in toy-shops glass globes containing water with bubbles or particles of light matter which float within on being shaken.

XVI. This elegy is a continuation of the preceding in all the MSS. There can be no reasonable doubt that the editors have rightly separated it. It is addressed to Cynthia, and the subject is a comparison of his own fidelity with the insincerity of his rivals. 'Mollissimus regnat in hoc carmine sensus, qui et ad commiserationem mirifice animum movet.'—*Kuinoel.*

1.] *Hoc erat* &c. 'Haeccine tua promissa, quæ meum animum lætitia perfundebant? itane constans es in amore?' *Kuinoel.*—*gaudeo* not unfrequently governs an accusative, like the Greek ἥδεσθαί τι.—*in primis gaudere*, 'so greatly to congratulate myself upon.'

Contendat mecum ingenio, contendat et arte,
  In primis una discat amare domo;
Si libitum tibi erit, Lernæas pugnet ad hydras,
  Et tibi ab Hesperio mala dracone ferat;
Tetra venena libens, et naufragus ebibat undas,
  Et numquam pro te deneget esse miser;
Quos utinam in nobis, vita, experiare labores!
  Jam tibi de timidis iste superbus erit,
Qui nunc in tumidum jactando venit honorem;
  Discidium vobis proximus annus erit.
At me non ætas mutabit tota Sibyllæ,
  Non labor Alcidæ, non niger ille dies.
Tu mea compones, et dices: 'Ossa, Properti,
  Hæc tua sunt; heu heu, tu mihi certus eras.
Certus eras heu heu, quamvis nec sanguine avito
  Nobilis, et quamvis haud ita dives eras.'
Nil ego non patiar; numquam me injuria mutat;

7—12.] 'Let my favoured rival shew himself as clever, as patient, as obedient to your behests as I, before he makes the same pretensions to your esteem.' — *in primis discat &c.* 'Above all, let him learn to be constant to one.' The connexion with the preceding seems sufficiently plain: but Müller marks a *lacuna* after v. 6, 'oratione aperte hiante,' as he says.

10.] 'Let him prove his devotion by performing at your will some Herculean task.' Barth remarks that this verse is taken from Theocritus, *Id.* 25, 37:

νῦν μὲν [illegible] τὰ χρήματα μᾶλλ' ἕνεκεν [illegible]
βαίνω, καὶ φύλακες [illegible] Κέρβερον.

Ibid.] *Ebibat.* Lachmann raises a groundless objection to this word as if it could only mean 'let him *drink up* the sea,' and reads *imbibat*. From iv. 7, 52, it will be seen that nothing more is meant, than 'let him brave shipwreck, and gulp the briny wave.' *Epotus* however means 'drunk up,' Juven. x. 177.

11.] *Trita* for *tetra* Müller, who shows that these words are sometimes confused.

13—16.] 'And then try the same toils and troubles in me, and you will find, by the contrast, that your proud and boastful lover is a coward.' All the editors adopt a punctuation of v. 13 which appears to me completely to pervert the sense. Keil and Müller, with Barth and Kuinoel, inclose it as a parenthesis; the others regard it as an abrupt and interpolated exclamation. Yet the general sense seems sufficiently clear. *Utinam experiare in nobis eosdem labores*, may certainly signify, 'I only wish you would put me to the test in performing the same task.'

15.] *In tumidum honorem* is both an unusual and a questionable expression. Kuinoel explains, 'honor qui tumidum et inflatum reddit.' The editors give *qui nunc se in tumidum &c.*, but the MS. Gron. omits *se*, and so Hertzberg (in his commentary): *jactando* will thus be used absolutely for *jactantia*. But perhaps we should read, *Qui nunc se tumidum* (i.e. tumide) *jactando invenit honorem*.

16.] *Dissidium*, Kuinoel with the Naples MS. and ed. Rheg.

22.] *Non ita* is the conjecture of Beroaldus. The MSS. have *navita*, which seems to have arisen from the agnomen *Nauta* attached in most copies to the names Sextus Aurelius Propertius; or conversely (as Hertzberg and others think), the corruption of the present passage suggested the addition of the name. Jacob, with Heinsius, prefers *haud ita*; and this is nearer to Nevita, *haud* or *haut* being sometimes written *hau*, according to Gronovius on Tac. *Ann.* vi. 43, quoted by Hertzberg, (where the Medicean MS. has *haci*.)—On the birth and fortune of the poet, see on v. 1, 128; iii. 26, 56.

Ferre ego formosam nullum onus esse puto.
Credo ego non paucos ista periisse figura;
Credo ego sed multos non habuisse fidem.
Parvo dilexit spatio Minoïda Theseus,
Phyllida Demophoon, hospes uterque malus;
Jam tibi Iasonia amota est Medea carina,
Et modo servato sola relicta viro.
Dura est, quæ multis simulatum fingit amorem,
Et se [illegible]uni si qua parare potest.
Noli nobili[illegible], noli conferre beatis:
Vix ve[illegible] extremo qui legat ossa die.
Ii tibi nos [illegible]rimus; sed tu potius precor ut me
Demissis plangas, pectora nuda, comis.

XVII.

Unica nata meo pulcherrima cura dolori,

24.] *Ferre formosam.* There is a play on the verb between the literal sense and that of 'putting up with the caprices of' &c.

26.] *Fidem,* sc. quam ego habeo.

29.] The MSS. and early editions give *nota est.* 'Jam artius conjunge cum *Iasonia carina,* et vide an satis apta hæc evasura sit sententia: 'Notum est tibi, Medeam jam fuisse in nave Iasonis: et tamen mox perfide desertam.''—*Hertzberg.* *Jam fuisse in nave* he explains as equivalent to *jam ab illo tanquam uxorem avectam.* The omission of *fuisse* is a grave objection to such an interpretation. There is less difficulty in *et* for *et tamen,* with the defence of which the greater part of the learned commentator's note is occupied. Lachmann, with Jacob's approval (!) reads *Jam tibi Iasonia votum est, Medea, carina,* i.e. 'habes quod optabas in nave Iasonis;' and he quotes some passages where *votum* means 'one's wish.' Jacob says: '*nota est* erit: modo innotuit nobis illuc venisse, et jam deseri eam videmus.' None of these views appear tenable. The context seems to require *amota est,* which accordingly I have ventured to restore. 'Then again, you have (in story) Medea carried off by Jason in his ship, and deserted by a husband whose life she had so lately saved.' The sense of *jam* may also be, that she was no sooner carried off than she was deserted. For the acquisitive use of *tibi* see on i. 5, 5.

32.] *Parare se.* So the Greeks use ἑτοιμάζειν of preparing for nuptial purposes, Eur. *Suppl.* 454.

33.] *Conferre,* 'to draw comparisons with the noble and the wealthy.' Barth thinks it may mean 'confer your favour on,' χαρίζεσθαι.

34.] *Vix venit,* raro inventus est.

36.] *Pectora nuda.* Kuinoel reads *pectore* with Scaliger. *Nuda* is of course the nominative. The sense is, 'I hope however that you will survive me.' This is said, as it were, *avertendi ominis gratia,* since in v. 34 allusion is made, though in a general sentiment, to Cynthia's death.

XVII. He asserts that though there is a time for all things to cease, yet he can never cease to love; and (v. 21) warns his rivals not to rely on the permanence of the favour they now enjoy. This is one of the more difficult of the elegies.

1.] 'O tu, quæ pulcherrima mihi cura nata, quamvis dolenti, quod tam raro admittor, unica tamen cura es.'—*Hertzberg;* who rightly connects *quamvis* in the second verse with *meo dolori.*—*cura nata,* τὸ καλλίστην ἐκφῦσαν. See on iii. 13, 14. This explanation is due to Jacob, before whose edition the most extravagant alterations and interpretations had been proposed. Lachmann on his own conjecture reads 'excludi quoniam sors mea sæpe vehit;' Barth, 'excludi quoniam sors mea sæpe, venis.' Müller and Keil edit as in the text.

Excludit quoniam sors mea SÆPE VENI;
Ista meis fiet notissima forma libellis,
Calve, tua venia, pace, Catulle, tua.
Miles depositis annosus secubat armis,
Grandævique negant ducere aratra boves,
Putris et in vacua requiescit navis arena,
Et vetus in templo bellica parma vacat;
At me ab amore tuo deducet nulla senectus,
Sive ego Tithonus, sive ego Nestor ero.
Nonne fuit satius duro servire tyranno,
Et gemere in tauro, sæve Perille, tuo?
Gorgonis et satius fuit obdurescere vultu;
Caucasias etiam si pateremur aves.
Sed tamen obsistam: teritur rubigine mucro
Ferreus, et parvo sæpe liquore silex;
At nullo dominæ teritur †sub limine amor, qui
Restat et immerita sustinet aure minas.
Ultro contemptus rogat, et peccasse fatetur

4.] Calvus was the friend of Catullus, and like him a writer of amatory verses. Ovid, *Am.* iii. 9, 62. 'Obvius huic venias, hedera juvenilis cinctus Tempora, cum Calvo, docte Catulle, tuo.' He apologizes to them for having used the superlative, *notissima*, etiam notior vestris; implying that Cynthia's celebrity would be greater than the mistresses of either of those poets, viz. Quintilia and Lesbia, inf. iii. 26, 87—90.

5—10.] 'The soldier lies by when aged, the ox at length leaves off ploughing, the old ship and the old shield become useless; but of my love there will be no end, if I live as long as Nestor.'

9.] Lachmann reads *diducet*. See on iii. 13, 5. In this instance there is no reason for altering the reading of all good copies.

11.] 'And yet have I not endured more torture than? &c. Still, I will not give in. The obduracy even of a rock is worn down by the continued efforts of the unceasing water-drop.'—*Perillus* was the maker of the brazen bull for the tyrant Phalaris, and was himself burnt alive in it. 'Et Phalaris tauro violenti membra Perilli Torruit: infelix imbuit auctor opus.'—*Ovid*.

13.] *Obdurescere*, to be changed into stone by looking at the head of Medusa.—*Caucasias aves*, the vulture of Prometheus. With *etiam* understand *satius fuit*.

17.] 'Desperatus versus.'—*Jacob*; who gives the reading of the MS. Gron., '*At nullo de me teritur sub limine amor qui*,' and proposes to read *at nullo dominæ teritur ipse limine, amorque Restat* &c. interpreting *nullo limine* by *nulla exclusione*. As may be anticipated, he has not found a follower in Hertzberg, who retains the vulgate, and explains *limen* of the *lintel*, ὑπέρθυρον. Müller reads *teritur molimine amator*, from Davis and Heins, but he doubts the genuineness of *teritur*. Possibly *sub nullo dominæ limine* may mean, as Barth has explained it, 'dominæ limen in quo jaceo pernox, non potest amorem meum terere et consumere.' *Sub limine* must be taken literally, but elliptically, for *excubando sub limine*, i. e. 'close under,' and *nullo* gives the sense of *nunquam* to the whole verse. But if any should prefer to take *sub limine* for *sub domo*, there would be no difficulty, especially if for *amor qui* we read *amator*. *Restat* will thus mean 'he holds out,' *empeni*, 'remains obstinate,' even though he is forced to listen to threats which he thinks he has not deserved.

19.] *Ultro* is properly used when anything is done *proprio motu*; unasked, unchallenged, unprovoked: properly, *beyond* what the laws of *par pari referto* require.

Læsus, et invitis ipse redit pedibus.
Tu quoque, qui pleno fastus adsumis amore,
Credule, nulla diu femina pondus habet.
An quisquam in mediis persolvit vota procellis,
Cum sæpe in portu fracta carina natet?
Aut prius infecto deposcit præmia cursu,
Septima quam metam triverit ante rota?
Mendaces ludunt flatus in amore secundi.
Si qua venit sero, magna ruina venit.
Tu tamen interea, quamvis te diligat illa,
In tacito cohibe gaudia clausa sinu;
Namque in amore suo semper sua maxima cuique
Nescio quo pacto verba nocere solent.

Thus, *ultro bellum inferre* is to commence hostilities without any previous injury. In the case of separated lovers, the party who first makes overtures for a reconciliation is said *ultro venire*. Hence Persius, v. 172, 'ne nunc, cum accersor, et *ultro supplicet*, accedam?'—*peccasse fatetur læsus*, *i. e.* when the lover, though the fault is not really on his side, is willing to bear it in his anxiety to make up the quarrel. The editors place a full stop at *minas*. Possibly the construction is continued from *natat*, viz. *amator*.

21.] He warns his rival, in a very elegant couplet, that he will not give up his claims to Cynthia because he has been rejected; but may yet supplant him in the contest for her regard.—*fastus*. See on i. 1, 3.

23—6.] 'No one reckons on safety in a storm, or victory in a race, before he has realised it: do you therefore not presume too much on your fancied success.'—*cum sæpe, &c.*, *i. e.* when even in the harbour itself ships are sometimes lost: 'fallit portus et ipse fidem,' iv. 7, 36.—*natet*, 'floats helpless,' or 'water-logged.' A singular meaning of the word, which seems so used in v. 1, 116, 'et natat exuviis Græcia pressa suis.'—*septima rota*, septimo cursu. Both in the Greek stadium and the Roman circus, the racers took twelve turns round the pillar. Soph. *El.* 726, τελοῦντες ἕκτον ἕβδομόν τ' ἤδη δρόμον. The charioteer was said *radere*, *stringere*, or *terere metam*, words signifying the actual scraping of the wheel against the pillar, but implying only the close proximity.—*prius-quam ante triverit* seems to be the construction intended, *ante* being redundant by a well-known use, as Æsch. *S. c. Theb.* 694, λέγουσα κέρδος πρότερον ὑστέρου μόρου. Hertzberg joins *quam-ante*, for *antequam*; see on iii. 9, 10, 'Quam prius adjunctos sedula lavit equos.' The examples he adduces from Tibull. i. 3, 9; iv. 1, 33, Ovid, *Trist.* iv. 9, 31, are not really to the point for the reason mentioned on the former passage. But that from the Copa, commonly attributed to Virgil, v. 4, is appropriate: 'Quid juvat æstivo defessum pulvere abesse, Quam potius bibulo decubuisse toro;' *i. e.* potius quam. The redundance of *ante* after *prius* is well defended by Kuinoel from Virg. *Æn.* iv. 24—7, 'Sed mihi vel tellus optem prius ima dehiscat, —ante, Pudor, quam te violo.'

27.] *Secundi*. Kuinoel, with Heinsius, reads *secundo*. Hertzberg rightly approves of Lachmann's explanation: 'mendaces isti venti sunt, si qui propitii amantibus flare videntur.' 'In love, fair gales play but to deceive.'

29.] *Tu tamen*. That is, quamvis te diligat, tu tamen cohibe &c. 'Do not boast of your good fortune lest you should be put to the blush when it leaves you.' The evils arising from proud words are well expressed in the following distich; 'in speaking of his own success in love, some how or other it happens that his own big words are ever wont to bring a lover his bane.'

32.] From *speaking* with too much boldness and freedom, the poet passes to the danger of *acting* in such a way as to excite *invidia*. Both the Greeks and the Romans considered that it was easy to provoke the gods to withdraw the *felicity* bestowed on those who made an unworthy or thankless

Quamvis te persæpe vocet, semel ire memento:
  Invidiam quod habet, non solet esse diu.
At si sæcla forent antiquis grata puellis,
  Essem ego, quod nunc tu; tempore vincor ego.
Non tamen ista meos mutabunt sæcula mores:
  Unusquisque sua noverit ire via.
At vos, qui officia in multos revocatis amores,
  Quantum sic cruciat lumina vestra dolor!
Vidistis pleno teneram candore puellam,
  Vidistis fusco: ducit uterque color.
Vidistis quandam Argiva prodire figura,
  Vidistis nostras: utraque forma rapit.
Illaque plebeio, vel sit sandicis amictu:
  Hæc atque illa mali vulneris una via est;
Cum satis una tuis insomnia portet ocellis,
  Una sit et cuivis femina multa mala.

use of it. Lachmann singularly misunderstood this doctrine: 'ineptum hoc est, immo putidum, quod quamvis sæpe a puella vocetur, semel tantum, neque amplius, ire jubetur.' Jacob pronounces *semel* 'ridiculum,' and would read *simulare momenta*. Kuinoel's explanation appears perfectly right:—'ne abutaris benignitate dominæ, sed parce utere ea, ut decet circumspectum.'

35—6.] The meaning of this distich, which has much perplexed the editors, and which Lachmann and Müller regard as corrupt, appears to be this: 'But if the times now were, which the girls of the olden time so much liked, (*i. e.* the times when lovers were constant, and did not trust to bribes,) I should be what you now are (viz. in favour with Cynthia;) it is by the custom of the age (not by your merits) that I am beaten in the contest.' He goes on in the same strain: 'However, this fashion of yours,' *i. e.* of bribing, 'shall not change my manners; every man will know best how to pursue his own way,'—you by gifts, I by my constancy.

39.] *Revocatis*, 'withdraw from one to bestow upon another.'—'You who set your fickle affections on many women, what pain do you inflict on your own eyes by this conduct!' This uneasiness, which he here assigns to others, the poet avows to be his own habitual malady, supr. El. 13.

42.] *Fusco*, sc. colore. Müller reads *fuscam* on his own conjecture.

43.] *Argiva figura*, 'of Grecian form.' ('Grecian [illegible],' we might almost render it in modern phrase). See on i. 15, 22, and i. 4, 9.

45.] *Sandicis*, 'of purple.'—*[illegible]*, (Virg. *Ecl.* iv. 45) or *[illegible]* was a dye extracted from a plant. Others (Pliny, *N.H.* 35, 23) make it a bright red mineral colour.

46.] *Hæc atque illa* &c. 'Each of these individually inflicts a wound.' Hertzberg observes on this: 'mirum, quod puella ipsa *via* vulneris dicitur, quam pro *causa* Latine poni nego.' He therefore thinks that the *vulnus* spoken of is from the darts of Cupid, who 'pulchris excubat in genis' puellæ. And this seems a reasonable view. Cupid inflicts the wound, which comes *through* the girl by whose beauty the party is struck.

48.] *Et cuivis*, supply *alii*, sc. *mihi*. 'As one woman causes sleeplessness enough to *your* eyes, so one woman may well be the cause of many evils to any one else,'—that is, Cynthia to me.

XVIII.

Vidi te in somnis fracta, mea vita, carina
  Ionio lassas ducere rore manus,
Et quæcumque in me fueras mentita fateri,
  Nec jam humore graves tollere posse comas,
Qualem purpureis agitatam fluctibus Hellen,
  Aurea quam molli tergore vexit ovis.
Quam timui, ne forte tuum mare nomen haberet,
  Atque tua labens navita fleret aqua!
Quæ tum ego Neptuno, quæ tum cum Castore fratri,
  Quæque tibi excepi, jam dea Leucothoë?
At tu, vix primas extollens gurgite palmas,
  Sæpe meum nomen jam peritura vocas.

XVIII. He endeavours, by relating a feigned dream, to deter Cynthia from a voyage she was about to make (v. 29); but concludes by professing his readiness to follow her, should she adhere to her resolution. From not sufficiently attending to the poet's custom of relenting and unsaying at the end what he had threatened or predicted at the beginning, most of the editors have commenced a new elegy at v. 21. Hertzberg has followed the arrangement in the MSS., observing that it would be absurd to relate a dream without following it up by some conclusion. He regards it as an allegory, implying the favour of the gods towards a poet, (v. 16; but this is said of Cynthia, not of Propertius); and his own fidelity, symbolized by leaping after her from a rock, v. 19.—It is a most elegant poem.

5.] *Qualem Hellen.* More usually *qualis Helle;* but the accusative is by attraction to *te* preceding. Barth is clearly wrong in construing *qualem ovis auream vidit Hellen.* Hertzberg remarks on *purpureis* (the Homeric *πορφύρεον κῦμα*), that the southern seas do under certain circumstances assume a purple tint; arising, of course, from the reflection of the sky. See on v. 2, 13.—*tergus*, it is proper to remark, differs from *tergum;* though the latter is used for the former by Tacit. *Ann.* iv. 72, and xv. 44. Virg. *Æn.* i. 368.

7.] *Tuum nomen.* The elegance of the compliment is enhanced by *quam timui*, as if he could not lose her even for the geographical immortality of a 'Mare Cynthiacum.'—For *atque* Hertzberg proposes *tecum*, observing that out of 43 places where the poet has used the word, in one other only (v. 2, 52) it occurs without elision. The reluctance of the Roman poets generally to place *atque* before a consonant is well known: perhaps *nunc* would be a still more probable correction.

9.] *Quæ* (vota) *excepi*, i. e. suscepi Neptuno. So iii. 7, 4. 'Ah! Neptune, tibi qualia dona darem!'—*jam dea*, 'once a mortal, now a goddess,' *Jacob.* Keil and Müller, with Kuinoel and Lachmann, read *tum dea*, after Beroaldus. Hertzberg is more successful; 'jam ad te me converti, Leucothoe, quæ simili quondam periculo per undas jactata misera mulier, dea facta sis naufragis propitia;' though this amounts to nothing more than making *jam* equivalent to *tum*. The same critic retains the MSS. reading *Leucothoe*. The others change it to *Leucothea*, a questionable form. The Greeks used either *Λευκοθόη* or *Λευκοθέη*, the Latins appear to have preferred *Leucothea*. The derivation of both is from *θέειν*, *θεὸς*, as Hertzberg remarks. Compare *Cymothoe* v. 16.—Ino, the daughter of Cadmus, was enamoured of Athamas, and threw herself into the sea with the body of her son Melicertes, Learchus, the brother of the latter, having been killed by his father Athamas in a fit of madness. See Apollodor. iii. 4, 3, who writes the word *Λευκοθέα*. Inf. El. 20, 19.

11—12.] Müller, after Baehrens, transposes this distich to follow 18. He thinks it absurd that the poet should wish to assist Cynthia, when the dolphin was at hand to help her, unless some new cause

Quod si forte tuos vidisset Glaucus ocellos,
  Esses Ionii facta puella maris,
Et tibi ob invidiam Nereides increpitarent,
  Candida Nesæë, cærula Cymothoë.
Sed tibi subsidio delphinum currere vidi,
  Qui, puto, Arioniam vexerat ante lyram.
Jamque ego conabar summo me mittere saxo,
  Cum mihi discussit talia visa metus.
Nunc admirentur, quod tam mihi pulchra puella
  Serviat, et tota dicar in urbe potens.
Non, si Cambysæ redeant et flumina Crœsi,
  Dicat: De nostro surge, poeta, toro.
Nam mea cum recitat, dicit se odisse beatos:
  Carmina tam sancte nulla puella colit.
Multum in amore fides, multum constantia prodest:
  Qui dare multa potest, multa et amare potest.
Seu mare per longum mea cogitet ire puella,
  Hanc sequar, et fidos una aget aura duos.
Unum litus erit sopitis, unaque tecto
  Arbor, et ex una sæpe bibemus aqua,
Et tabula una duos poterit componere amantes,
  Prora cubile mihi, seu mihi puppis erit.
Omnia perpetiar; sævus licet urgeat Eurus,

of alarm had occurred. But this argument does not seem a cogent one. The idea of the description is borrowed from Helle when drowning stretching out her hand to her brother Phrixus.

13.] *Quod si* &c. If some sea-god had then seen you, my aid, as well as that of the dolphin, would have been useless; you would have been carried off to be made queen of the sea, and to excite the jealousy of the Nereids.

15.] *Ob invidiam. Præ invidia* Barth and Kuinoel, the reading of the inferior copies.

18.] *Lyram.* Hertzberg remarks on the use of this word to express the musician himself. He should have used this verse in defence of the much more singular expression *imbellis lyra* for 'the Muse,' in v. 6, 36. But nothing more is conveyed by the phrase than 'Arion and his lute.'

21.] *Nunc admirentur.* He proceeds to show, that it is through fondness for his verses, and not for money, that Cynthia attaches herself to him. 'Not for all the gold of Pactolus' (he adds, v. 23) 'would she reject me to the admission of a rival.' Probably he has in view his enemy the Prætor, iii. 7.

23.] *Jam Gyges*, for *Cambysæ* Müller, after Schrader.

24.] *Poeta, i. e.* 'qui carmina tantum, non nummos, mihi das.' Cf. v. 5, 57, 'Qui versus, Coa dederit nec munera vestis, Istius tibi sit surda sine ære lyra.'

27.] 'There is much, too, in a constant lover, who is with good reason preferred to a rich one, inasmuch as his very riches supply the means of tampering with the affections of many.'

28.] *Multa amare*, 'multas puellas nulla constantia.'—*Kuinoel.*

31—4.] These beautiful lines evidently allude to some voyage which Cynthia was about to make.'—*tabula una*, &c. 'A single plank shall form our common couch.'—*componere* is συγκοιμίζειν. Compare Æsch. *Ag.* 1417, ναυτίλων δὲ σελμάτων ἰσοτριβής.

Velaque in incertum frigidus Auster agat,
Quotcumque et venti miserum vexastis Ulixen,
Et Danaum Euboico litore mille rates,
Et qui movistis duo litora, cum rudis Argus
Dux erat ignoto missa columba mari;
Illa meis tantum non umquam desit ocellis,
Incendat navem Juppiter ipse licet.
Certe isdem nudi pariter jactabimur oris.
Me licet unda ferat, te modo terra tegat.
Sed non Neptunus tanto crudelis amori;
Neptunus fratri par in amore Jovi.
Testis Amymone, latices dum ferret, in Argis
Compressa, et Lerne pulsa tridente palus.
Jam Deus amplexu votum persolvit; at illi
Aurea divinas urna profudit aquas.
Crudelem et Boream rapta Orithyia negavit;
Hic deus et terras et maria alta domat.
Crede mihi, nobis mitescet Scylla, nec umquam

37.] The Groning. MS. alone gives *quodcumque*; the rest *quicumque*, and so Kuinoel and Lachmann, and the later editors. Hertzberg *quotcumque*; which is a happy restoration of the true reading.—*Euboico litore*. See on v. 1, 116.

39.] *Duo litora*. The Symplegades. See on v. 6, 27. Müller thinks *litora* (*littora*) has crept in from the preceding verse, but he suggests no substitute.—*movistis*, 'qui venti concurrere fecistis.'—*Herzb.*—*rudis Argus* is a correction of *ratis Argo* first made in the edition of 1488. Apollon. Rhod. ii. 562.

ὁ δ' ἀίξας πτερύγεσσιν
Εὔφημος προΐησι πελειάδα· τοὶ δ' ἅμα πάντες
ἤειραν κεφαλὰς ἐσορώμενοι· ἡ δὲ δι' αὐτῶν
ἔπτατο.

41—4.] In fine, lightning may strike the ship, provided only I do not lose sight of you: and if we are to be cast on the waters, I will not leave you, alive or dead. I shall be content to float on the wave, provided you are covered with a little sand.'—*certe*, 'be assured that I shall not leave you; if we are cast ashore, it shall be in each others arms.'

47.] *Testis*, sc. Neptunum amori esse deditum. Hertzberg follows Jacob in reading *dum* for *cum* from the Naples MS., and interpreting, 'on condition of receiving water.' On this use of *ferre* (*φέρεσθαι*) see on i. 20, 28. Apollodor. ii. 1, 4, *μία δὲ αὐτῶν* (sc. *Δαναΐδων*) *Ἀμυμώνη ζητοῦσα ὕδωρ ῥίπτει βέλος ἐπὶ ἔλαφον, καὶ κοιμωμένου Σατύρου τυγχάνει· κἀκεῖνος περιαναστὰς ἐπεθύμει συγγενέσθαι. Ποσειδῶνος δὲ ἐπιφανέντος ὁ Σάτυρος μὲν ἔφυγεν, Ἀμυμώνη δὲ τούτῳ συνευνάζεται, καὶ αὐτῇ Ποσειδῶν τὰς ἐν Λέρνῃ πηγὰς ἐμήνυσεν.* See Ovid, *Met.* i. 283.

48.] *Lerne* Hertzberg, with the Naples MS., and so Kuinoel. *Lernae* Lachmann, *Lerna* Jacob, Keil, and Müller.

49.] *Amplexu*. 'Non dativum pro amplexui, sed ablativum pretii.'—*Hertzberg*.

51.] Kuinoel gives *negabit*. The later editors have rightly restored *negavit* from the MSS. 'Amymone Neptunum amori facilem testificata est, Boream Orithyia.'—*Lachmann*. The argument is, that lovers need not fear either winds or waves, since both these elements can sympathise with them.

53.] *Nec umquam Scylla vorans*. i. e. et Scylla (mitescet) nunquam vorans sc. naves main absorbens. Hertzberg is the only one who has rightly understood this passage. He compares iii. 20, 52, 'Vobiscum Europe, nec proba Pasiphae,' i. e. et non proba Pasiphae. Kuinoel, with one or two interpolated copies, reads *alternas revomet*; which Lachmann in a long note shows to

Alternante vorans vasta Charybdis aqua.
Ipsaque sidera erunt nullis obscura tenebris;
Purus et Orion, purus et Hœdus erit.
Quod mihi si ponenda tuo sit corpore vita,
Exitus hic nobis non inhonestus erit.

XIX.

At vos incertam, mortales, funeris horam
Quæritis, et qua sit mors aditura via;
Quæritis et cælo, Phœnicum inventa, sereno,
Quæ sit stella homini commoda quæque mala,
Seu pedibus Parthos sequitur seu classe Britannos,
Et maris et terræ cæca pericla viæ.
Rursus et objectum fletis capiti esse tumultum,
Cum Mavors dubias miscet utrimque manus;
Præterea domibus flammas, †domibusque ruinas,
Neu subeant labris pocula nigra tuis.
Solus amans novit, quando periturus et a qua
Morte; neque hic Boreæ flabra neque arma timet;
Jam licet et Stygia sedeat sub arundine remex,
Cernat et infernæ tristia vela ratis:

be wrong, though he himself understands *erit*, and Jacob follows him. Müller reads *vacuus* for *serenus*, after Haupt. But Lachmann well compares Ovid, *Met.* xiii. 731, 'vorat hæc raptas revomitque carinas.'

57.] *Tuo corpore.* The sense is, if I am to be drowned in your embrace, *i.e.* in trying to save you, it will be an honourable death. On the ablative see i. 17, 21.

XIX. The manner of death is uncertain to all but the lover, who alone knows that the ardour of his affection must bring him to the grave. This sentiment seems connected with some popular superstition on the 'charmed life' of a lover. See v. 1, 147—9.

3.] *Phœnicum inventa.* The accusative in apposition to the sentence *quæ sit stella &c.* He attributes to the Phœnicians the art of astrology, perhaps confounding them with the Chaldæans from the well-known skill of the former in navigating by observation of the stars. Cf v. 1, 83, 'felicesque Jovis stellas Martisque rapacis, Et grave Saturni sidus in omne caput.'

5.] *Sequitur* Kuinoel, with the Naples MS. and ed. Rheg. In either case the transition to *fletis* in v. 7, is rather harsh, though much more so by the ordinary punctuation, which places a full stop at *mala*, v. 4, and only a colon or semicolon at *viæ*, v. 6. The nominative *homo* is implied from the preceding verse.—*viæ maris et terræ*, *i.e.* itineris mari vel terra facti.

7.] *Caput esse tumultu* (i. e. *tumultui*) Müller, who gives *caput* on the authority of 'optimus liber' without naming it.

9.] *Ruinas*, *i.e.* casus. The fall of a house, an event so rare in modern times, seems to have been a danger constantly dreaded in Rome. See Juvenal *Sat.* iii. 190—6, 'Quis timet aut timuit gelida Præneste ruinam,' &c.—For *domibusque*, which appears to be corrupt, Lachmann reads *dominisque*, Müller, on his own conjecture, which is probable, *natisque*.

13.] *Remex*, 'with oar in hand.' Virg. *Æn.* vi. 320; Arist. *Ran.* 201 &c. Virgil also (*Georg.* iv. 478) describes the 'limus niger et deformis arundo Cocyti.'

Si modo damnatum revocaverit aura puellæ,
  Concessum nulla lege redibit iter.

XX.

Juppiter, affectæ tandem miserere puellæ!
  Tam formosa tuum mortua crimen erit.
Venit enim tempus, quo torridus æstuat aer,
  Incipit et sicco fervere terra Cane.
Sed non tam ardoris culpa est, neque crimina cæli,
  Quam totiens sanctos non habuisse deos.
Hoc perdit miseras, hoc perdidit ante puellas:
  Quicquid jurarunt, ventus et unda rapit.
Num sibi collatam doluit Venus ipsa paremque?
  Præ se formosis invidiosa dea est.
An contempta tibi Junonis templa Pelasgæ,

15.] 'Amator vel morti vicinus reviviscet, si modo fugientem animam revocaverit puella amata.'—*Kuinoel*. Compare v. 7, 23, 'At mihi non oculos quisquam inclamavit euntes: Unum impetrassem, te revocante, diem.'—The reading *damnatum* (*i. e.* morti addictum) is only found in the MS. Groning. Kuinoel, Barth, and Lachmann give *clamantis* with the other copies. Apart from the question of authority, *damnatum*, or perhaps *clamatum* appears the preferable word.—*aura* is obscure: Hertzberg seems to be right in understanding it of the flashing light or *glimpse* of a passing object; comparing, with Jacob, Hor. *Od.* ii. 8, 24, 'tua ne retardet aura maritos.' Perhaps *aura* and *aurum* may be considered cognate, as 'that which flashes' has the same connexion with 'that which passes quickly by,' as *coruscare*, *micare*, &c., in their double meaning of *to shine* and *to move quickly*. It is at least remarkable that Virgil combines these two words, *Æn.* vi. 204, 'Discolor unde auri per ramos aura refulsit.' See, however, *Varronianus*, p. 113, ed. 2.

XX. This beautiful poem was written on an occasion of Cynthia's dangerous illness. Nothing can be more refined and tasteful than the mythological allusions by which he at once compliments and consoles her. At the same time he warns her that sickness is sent as a punishment for broken vows. On the date of the elegy, see on ii. 6, 25.

1.] *Affectæ*, sc. morbo, ægrotanti.—*tam formosa mortua*, τὸ τὴν τοιαύτην ἀποθανεῖν, *crimen erit tibi*, sc. dedecus tibi, utpote in formosas propenso.

3.] The unhealthiness of Rome in summer and autumn is well known. Hence *enim* refers to *mortua*, and implies that the hopes of her recovery were but slight at that season. The MS. Gron. has *Incipiunt siccos fervere terra canes*; which none of the editors have preferred, though it appears fully as good as *Incipit et* &c.

5.] *Tam* would not be missed if the MSS. ignored it.

9.] The Groning. MS. alone preserves the true reading *ipsa paremque*. The rest give *per æquas* or *peræque*. 'Num forte, inquit, cum ipsa Venere tuam formam contulisti? Hoc malum tibi dolor deæ parem te sibi agnoscentis immisit.'—*Lachmann*.

10.] *Præ se formosis*, i. e. se formosioribus. Lachmann's objection is scarcely fair, that this is incompatible with *paremque* in the hexameter. It is merely, as it were, improving upon it: 'Venus is ever jealous of equal and superior charms.' Lachmann reads *per se*, and Müller follows him. Hertzberg proposes *semper*, believing the vulgate corrupt. I entertain no doubt of its being the true reading.

11.] *Juno Pelasga* (see on ii. 1, 78. Here was κατ' ἐξοχὴν the goddess of the Argive or Pelasgic race. Inf. v. 8, 3. Æsch. *Suppl.* 287.—*honos*, sc. pulchros; in allusion to some foolish discussion of the

Palladis aut oculos ausa negare bonos?
Semper, formosæ, non nostis parcere verbis.
Hoc tibi lingua nocens, hoc tibi forma dedit.
Sed tibi, vexatæ per multa pericula vitæ,
Extremo veniet mollior hora die.
Io versa caput primos mugiverat annos:
Nunc dea, quæ Nili flumina vacca bibit.
Ino etiam prima terris ætate vagata est:
Hanc miser implorat navita Leucothoën.
Andromede monstris fuerat devota marinis:
Hæc eadem Persei nobilis uxor erat.
Callisto Arcadios erraverat ursa per agros:
Hæc nocturna suo sidere vela regit.
Quod si forte tibi properarint fata quietem,
Illa sepulturæ fata beata tuæ:
Narrabis Semelæ, quo sit formosa periclo;
Credet et illa suo docta puella malo;
Et tibi Mæonias interque Heroïdas omnis

day whether γλωσσώδης was a complimentary epithet or the reverse.—*sane*, supply *es*.

14.] *Hoc*, 'hunc morbum.'—*Kuinoel*. *lingua nocens* alludes to the supposed offence against Juno and Pallas; *forma* to the comparison with Venus, v. 9. Barth refers to a similar verse in Ovid, *Heroid.* xv. 68, 'hoc mihi libertas, hoc pia lingua dedit.' The transition here from the plural to the singular is in accordance with the poet's habit of suddenly apostrophising. For the danger of proud words, see iii. 17, 31.

15.] *Vexata—vita* Jacob, from Pucci's excerpta, to avoid the ambiguity of the common reading, *vexatæ* being the dative, *vitæ* the genitive. The sense is, 'If you die, you will not only be released from the dangers and vexations of life, but will receive the consolation of being honoured as the most beautiful of women in the other world.' And the poet gives examples of mortal women who have become goddesses.

17.] *Versa caput.* Hertzberg denies that Io was represented either by Æschylus or others *as a cow*, and considers that she was simply a woman with horns on her head. He appeals in proof of this to ancient paintings where she is so represented. That such was the idea which Propertius entertained there can be no doubt; but it is far from certain that he is right with respect to Æschylus. At all events, *Suppl.* 294—6 can only be understood of the *body* of a cow. See note on v. 564 of that play.—*nunc dea*, sc. Isis.

19.] *Terras* Kuinoel, with some early editions; which is correct Latinity, like Virgil's *maria omnia vecti*, *Æn.* i. 524, but the good copies agree in *terris*. Müller reads *prima Thebis ætate fugatast*. On the form of the word *Leucothoen* see on iii. 18, 9.

25.] *Properarint quietem*, i. e. prematuram mortem voluerint.—*fata sepulturæ*, sc. fatum quod post mortem te manet, *beata erunt*.

28.] *Docta suo malo*. Semele was killed by lightning Ζῆν᾽ ὅτι γάμους ἐψεύσατο, Eur. *Bacch.* 15. He therefore means to express the danger of beauty combined with falsehood and perjury.

29.] The Groning. MS. alone has *interque*. The rest *inter*, which the editors have preferred. The conjunction seems less objectionable than the metrical licence. For it is easy to understand *omnes alias heroidas*, i. e. *heroinas*.—*Mæonias*, 'ab Homero celebratas.' Others understand *Asiaticas*, which is less appropriate to the sense; or specifically *Trojanas*; which has i. 19, 13—15 in its favour. Kuinoel compares Ovid, *Trist.* i. 6, 33, 'Prima locum sanctas Heroidas inter haberes.'

Primus erit, nulla non tribuente, locus.
Nunc, utcumque potes, fato gere saucia morem:
  Et deus et durus vertitur ipse dies.
Hoc tibi vel poterit conjunx ignoscere Juno:
  Frangitur et Juno, si qua puella perit.
Deficiunt magico torti sub carmine rhombi,
  Et jacet extincto laurus adusta foco,
Et jam Luna negat totiens descendere cælo;
  Nigraque funestum concinit omen avis.
Una ratis fati nostros portabit amores
  Cærula ad infernos velificata lacus.
Si non unius, quæso, miserere duorum.
  Vivam, si vivet; si cadet illa, cadam.

31.] 'Now that you are struck with illness, submit, as best you may, to fate,' *i. e.* to whatever is in store for you, be it death or recovery.—*durus dies vertitur*, 'even the decree of death when it has gone forth is not irrevocable,' since persons have recovered even when despaired of. From all these expressions it must be inferred that Cynthia was or had been in great danger.

33.] Keil and Müller, with Lachmann and Hertzberg, regard *conjunx* as the vocative, sc. tibi, O Jupiter. Jacob considers *hoc* as the ablative, 'on this condition,' (*i. e.* si morem geris), but proposes to read *sic*. *Hoc* however is clearly the accusative, namely the sparing Cynthia's life. *Ignosco* is properly identical with *ignoro*: 'ignoscere alicui aliquid' is, 'to know nothing about a thing in reference to a particular party;' the Greek *περιιδεῖν*, 'to overlook it,' 'ignore its existence.' *Conjunx Juno*, also 'Juno sacris præfecta maritis,' Ovid, *Her.* 12, 87, Ἥρα τελεία, hence called simply γαμετή, 'the wife,' in Æsch. *Suppl.* 170.—*tibi*, again a sudden apostrophe, sc. *O Jupiter.* Müller inclines to the view of some who would place this distich after v. 2; but Lachmann observes that *miserere* in 41 would be unintelligible unless Jupiter were before appealed to.

35.] At this verse a new elegy commences in the Naples MS. Jacob, Keil, and Müller, follow this arrangement, and Hertzberg prints it detached from the preceding. But I cannot see any just reason for questioning its continuity. 'We have done all that we can,' says the poet, 'for Cynthia's recovery, and have tried magic arts in vain; the rest must be left to Jupiter.' Moreover, (as above remarked), *tibi* in v. 33, and *miserere* in v. 41, are alike addressed to Jupiter; consequently the whole passage inclusive must be regarded as one and the same appeal to him for pity.—*torti sub carmine rhombi*, 'præeunte carmine ac rhombi vertiginem moderante.'—*Barth.* An imitation of a well-known use of *ἴυγξ*.

36.] *Et tacet* Lachmann, and so Barth.

37.] *Negat totiens*, 'refuses any longer to descend to our incantations.' The connexion of the moon with sudden affections, according to the ancient philosophy, while it accounts for the word *lunaticus*, 'moon-struck,' explains the reason why Artemis was so often said εἰς ἀγανοῖς βελέεσσιν ἐποιχομένη κατεπέφνειν, and why Cynthia is urged (v. 60) to institute a chorus in honour of Diana. Hence witches seem to have been engaged 'to draw down the moon' in cases of serious illness. The notion of the temporary absence of that satellite from the sky must of course have arisen from its frequent eclipses.

38.] *Nigra avis.* This is generally explained *infelix, infausta*, and understood of the owl: see v. 3, 59. Why not the raven? The croaking of this bird is believed by some to portend death in a family even to this day. K. cites Ovid, *Amor.* iii. 12, 2., 'Omina non albæ concinuistis aves.'

39.] *Ratis fati*, for fatalis cymba.—*velificata* &c., 'sailing for the Stygian waters,' *i. e.* to cross them. See v. 9, 6, 'Nauta per urbanas velificabat aquas,' Juven. x. 174, 'velificatus Athos.'

Pro quibus optatis sacro me carmine damno:
  Scribam ego: PER MAGNUM SALVA PUELLA JOVEM.
Ante tuæque pedes illa ipsa adoperta sedebit.
  Narrabitque sedens longa pericla sua.
Hæc tua, Persephone, maneat clementia, nec tu,
  Persephones conjunx, sævior esse velis.
Sunt apud infernos tot milia formosarum:
  Pulchra sit in superis, si licet, una locis.
Vobiscum est Iope, vobiscum candida Tyro,
  Vobiscum Europe, nec proba Pasiphaë,
Et quot Troja tulit vetus et quot Achaïa formas,
  †Et Phœbi et Priami diruta regna senis:
Et quæcumque erat in numero Romana puella,
  Occidit. Has omnes ignis avarus habet;
Nec forma æternum, aut cuiquam est fortuna perennis:
  Longius aut proprius mors sua quemque manet.
Tu quoniam es, mea lux, magno dimissa periclo,

43.] *Damno me carmine*, 'I undertake to offer verses in the temple.' See iii. 5, 25. *Voti reus* and *voti* (or *votis*) *damnatus*, Virgil, *Ecl.* v. 80, are said of those who are under obligation to pay what they have promised to the gods.

44.] *Salva &c.* Cf. v. 3, 72, 'subscribam, salvo grata puella viro.'

45.] *Adoperta*, capite velato. To sit at the feet of the statute and express *viva voce* gratitude for deliverance seems to have been considered an act of greater piety than to suspend a votive tablet on the wall.

47.] Jacob and Lachmann, followed by Keil and Müller, make this the beginning of a new elegy. The MSS. agree in connecting it with the preceding. Having spoken of what he will do in the event of her recovery, he proceeds to speak of it as realised, and begs of Proserpine and Pluto not to withdraw the boon they have granted. Perhaps these lines were added as an afterthought, on the illness taking a favourable turn. Barth's explanation is not probable: 'etiam tua clementia expectet vota similia iis quæ Jovi solvet.'

51.] *Iope.* So Jacob and Hertzberg with the Naples MS. and ed. Rheg. The MS. Gron. has *Iole*, which Lachmann prefers; Barth and others edit *Antiope*. *Iope* is said to have been the wife of Cepheus.—*nec proba Pasiphae*, i. e. *et improba Pasiphae*. See supr. iii. 18, 53.

53.] *Troja.* The MSS. agree in this reading, which gives a perfectly natural sense in connexion with *Achaia*, since the Trojan and Grecian heroine are elsewhere mentioned by the poet, *e.g.* i. 13, 31; i. 19, 14. Scaliger, however, finding in one copy *hios*, and in the margin *hiona*, (apparently a misspelt word clumsily corrected by a late scribe), conjectured *Iona*, in which he is followed by Barth and Kuinoel, though the word is contrary to all analogy. Hertzberg gives *Eoa*, and in the next verse *Phœbei et muri*,—both rather violent and by no means plausible alterations, though of the latter he does not fear to say, 'Certum est, Propertium scripsisse quod dedimus.' The only objection that can be raised against the reading *Troja* is that the next verse implies a repetition. Perhaps however we may allow a poet to amplify a particular city by adding, in a wider sense, the entire dominions of its king. The word *Phœbi* is more probably corrupt. Jacob proposes *et Beli*, Scaliger *et Thebæ*. Hence Müller gives *Thebe*. Lachmann incloses the distich in brackets, 'ne legentem moretur.'

59.] Jacob makes the last four lines a separate elegy: the improbability of which must strike every reader of judgment.—*dimissa* is the reading of Hertzberg and Lachmann for *demissa*.

Munera Dianæ debita redde choros;
Redde etiam excubias divæ nunc, ante juvencæ;
Votivas noctes et mihi solve decem.

XXI.

Extrema, mea lux, cum potus nocte vagarer,
Nec me servorum duceret ulla manus,
Obvia nescio quot pueri mihi turba minuta
Venerat;—hos vetuit me numerare timor,—
Quorum alii faculas, alii retinere sagittas,
Pars etiam visa est vincla parare mihi.
Sed nudi fuerant. Quorum lascivior unus,
'Arripite hunc,' inquit, 'nam bene nostis eum;
Hic erat, hunc mulier nobis irata locavit.'
Dixit, et in collo jam mihi nodus erat.
Hic alter jubet in medium propellere, at alter:
'Intereat, qui nos non putat esse deos!
Hæc te non meritum totas expectat in horas;

60.] *Dianæ*. See supra on v. 37.

61.] *Excubias*, i.e. vigilias. Isis, or Io, (see supra v. 17) seems to have brought with her to Rome some admixture of Phœnician or Jewish rites, (see iii. 25, 2), one of which was the abstinence from conjugal rights for ten nights, to which he evidently alludes in the *decem votivæ noctes sibi potius quam Isidi solvendæ*.

XXI. In this elegy the poet offers a playful excuse for having wrongly suspected, and jealously tested, the fidelity of Cynthia, by acting as a spy on her privacy. He now pretends that it was the result of a drunken frolic, and laments the consequent loss of her regard.

1.] The MSS. give *hesterna*. As it is impossible to reconcile with this reading the last verse of the elegy, where the poet declares that since then he has never spent a happy night, I have followed Lachmann and Hertzberg in admitting Heinsius' correction *Extrema*. So also Keil and Müller. 'Late at night,' is when night is coming to an end, and morning is approaching. Hertzberg remarks that *extrema* and *hesterna* are often confused in the MSS.

2.] *Servorum manus*. The slaves of a family used to attend their masters home with torches: Juvenal, iii. 284.

3.] *Minuta*. When anything is broken into small pieces, each particle becomes 'minute,' i.e. small. This is one of a class of verbal adjectives, (commonly called passive participles), which have become by use mere adjectives, as *rectus*, *salsus*, (*salio*), *altus*, *certus* (for *cirtus*, *cerno*), &c. So 'remis confisa minutis,' i. 11, 9.

5.] *Retinere*, 'to have in store for me,' i.e. to *keep back* for the present. This seems more correct than Kuinoel's 'retinere pro tenere.'

7.] *Fuerant* for *fuerunt* Müller, with Heins.

9.] *Locavit*, 'pretio proposito excruciandum tradidit.' *Locare* and *conducere*, the reader is aware, are terms used of letting and accepting contracts, expressed in Greek by μισθῶσαι and μισθώσασθαι.

11.] *In medium*, ἐς μέσον, as if before a court or public assembly. Hertzberg gives *at alter* from the Naples MS. The editors generally prefer *et alter*.

13.] *Totas in horas*, 'for whole hours together.' Similarly 'totis noctibus,' i. 6, 7.

At tu nescio quas quæris, inepte, forea
Quæ cum Sidoniæ nocturna ligamina mitræ
Solverit, atque oculos moverit illa graves,
Adflabunt tibi non Arabum de gramine odores,
Sed quos ipse suis fecit Amor manibus.
Parcite jam, fratres; jam certos spondet amores;
Et jam ad mandatam venimus ecce domum.'
Atque ita me injecto duxerunt rursus amictu:
'I nunc, et noctes disce manere domi!'
Mane erat, et volui, si sola quiesceret illa,
Visere: at in lecto Cynthia sola fuit.
Obstupui; non illa mihi formosior umquam
Visa, neque ostrina cum fuit in tunica,

14.] *Ineptè.* 'Stuporem poetæ exprobrant Cupidines, quod cum pulcherrimam puellam gratis habere possit, alterius fastus ferre malit.'—*Hertzberg.*—For *forea* Müller reads *foris*, with Dousa, in allusion to *vagarer* sup. l. Thus *nescio quas* means *puellas*. But there is no sufficient reason for altering the vulgate. If indeed, we read *nescio quam*, the *quæ* in 15 would refer to this meretrix, to whom *mitra* was appropriate (Juv. iii. 66, 'picta lupa barbara mitra,') and *illa* in 16 will mean Cynthia: and this will alter the whole tone and meaning of the passage.

15.] *Quæ cum*, &c. 'When Cynthia rises in the morning, the most delicate fragrance will play around you, and remind you of your folly in slighting her charms.' *Sidonia mitra*, the night-cap of Tyrian dye; rather, perhaps, of Tyrian embroidery or imagery. The *mitra* is usually spoken of as the head-tire of *old* women, as in v. 5, 72. It was worn like a kerchief folded round the head. Thus 'ligamina mitræ' does not mean 'the night-cap strings,' but *mitram circumligatam*.

18.] Love himself is represented as possessing a recipe for the perfumes which attend the presence of Cynthia. But Hertzberg seems to be correct in explaining the verse of the *natural* freshness of health and youth as opposed to the artificial eastern perfumes, of which the poet professes himself to be no admirer, i. 2, 3.

19.] *Spondet*, 'he (our captive) promises to be constant for the future.' Jacob reads *spondere* from Pucci. This alteration is metrically inelegant, and supported by an argument of little weight, that the leader of the Loves ought rather to give his guaranty for the poet, than the latter for himself, 'in ingenti pavore Propertio obmutescente.'

21.] *Me—duxerunt.* I have retained the reading of the MSS. against the united judgment of the best editors, who adopt the conjecture of Heinsius *mi—duxerunt*. *Rursus injecto* implies that they had stripped off his outer garment. '*Duxerunt rursus*' (reversum) might imply that they took him at once back to his own house: but the point of the story seems to be that the Loves brought him first to Cynthia's house that he might see with his own eyes the groundlessness of his suspicions. What follows, *mane erat* &c., implies that in the morning, *i. e.* when he was sober and the dream had fled, he wished to go and visit Cynthia. This would be from his own house; and therefore it was more natural to represent that he had been conducted back again by the Loves.

23.] *Si sola quiesceret*, si aliquem secum haberet. Compare with this visit the beautiful account in i. 3.

24.] Hertzberg and Jacob give *et* with the Groning. MS., the others *at*. I do not feel the force of Jacob's remark, that the poet ought not to express *surprise* at her being alone, but satisfaction at his suspicion proving groundless. For the very fact of his going to see, implied a doubt of her being faithful; which doubt is properly followed by *at*.

26.] *Ostrina tunica.* Lachmann refers this to the particular dress which Cynthia wore when the poet first beheld her; see iv. 10, 15. 'Dein qua primum oculos cepisti veste Properti, Indue, nec vacuum flore relinque caput.' The general sense and

Ibat et hinc castæ narratum somnia Vestæ,
 Neu sibi, neve mihi quæ nocitura forent:
Talis visa mihi somno dimissa recenti;
 Heu quantum per se candida forma valet!
'Quo tu matutinus,' ait, 'speculator amicæ?
 Me similem vestris moribus esse putas?
Non ego tam facilis: sat erit mihi cognitus unus,
 Vel tu, vel si quis verior esse potest.
Apparent non ulla toro vestigia presso,
 Signa voluptatis, nec jacuisse duos.
Aspice, ut in toto nullus mihi corpore surgat
 Spiritus, admisso notus adulterio.'
Dixit, et opposita propellens savia dextra,
 Prosilit in laxa nixa pedem solea.
Sic ego tam sancti †custos excludor amoris.
 Ex illo felix nox mihi nulla fuit.

connexion are thus given in Hertzberg's paraphrase: 'nunquam formosior visa est, ne tum quidem cum, quantum memini, pulcherrima mihi videretur, quo tempore purpurea tunica induta ex hoc ipso cubiculo (*hinc*) prodiens ad Vestæ ibat. Nec aliter (*talis*, v. 29) nunc recens experrecta.' But, if *ibat* depends upon *cum*, and the poet's *first* sight of Cynthia is referred to the time when she was going to relate her dreams (*primum cepisti*,) to Vesta, it is difficult to understand her motive in praying that they might prove harmless to herself *and to Propertius* (v. 28), with whom she could have had no acquaintance. On the other hand, if *ibat* describes her action on the present occasion, *in lecto fuit et exire parabat*, *talis visa mihi* in v. 29 must be referred back to v. 26, which is certainly awkward. The tunic however may well have been the same as that which first captivated the poet on her appearance in it before the time here spoken of. Lachmann gives *ibat ut hinc* &c., adding 'illo ipso tempore, quo ad Vestæ templum in tunica purpurea iverat, primum ocellis suis amatorem ceperat.'

28.] *Neu—neve*. For neque (i. 3, 29). *Neu—neve* here follow the analogy of *seu—sive*,—both being, as the student is aware, different forms of the same words,—whereas *neu* generally follows *ut*, and may be considered in translating as equivalent to *et ne*.

29.] *Dimissa*. The MSS. have *demissa*, as in v. 59 of the preceding elegy.

30.] *Eu quantum* Müller, on his own conjecture.

31.] *Quo*. 'Qua mente? quo consilio?' *Barth*.

32.] *Vestris moribus*, *i. e.* moribus hominum qualis tu es.

33.] *Tam facilis*, sc. quam putas.

34.] *Verior*. Not *constantior*, but *minus mendax*, according to Hertzberg. *Certus* is the word generally used for 'constant,' as iii. 16, 20, and v. 19 of this elegy.

35.] *Vestigia*. See on ii. 9, 45.

38.] *Notus*, *i. e.* ut vulgo fieri notum est.

39.] *Propellere*, used in its proper sense sup. 11, here means *repellere*.

40.] *Nixa pedem*. Compare i. 3, 8, 'Cynthia non certis nixa caput manibus.' —*prosilit*, e lecto, sup. 24.

41.] The reading of this verse is very uncertain. The MS. Groning. gives *custode reludor*, the Naples MS. *custodis reludor*, the ed. Rheg. *custodis rector*. Kuinoel and Lachmann follow Broukhuis, *custos excludor*, understanding *custos* as *speculator*, *explorator*, *observator*. Hertzberg gives *custos reludor*, which appears from his commentary to be a misprint for *excludor*. Keil reads *custode recludor*, Müller *custodi excludor*, after Heins. Lachmann conjectures *cultu excludor*, 'nihil promittens de veritate conjecturæ.' The reading of ed. Rheg. points to *custos rejector*, the correction of Pucci; but *rejecto* is a rare word, and in Lucretius ii. 827, it

XXII.

Quo fugis? ah, demens, nulla est fuga! tu licet usque
  Ad Tanain fugias, usque sequetur Amor.
Non si Pegaseo vecteris in aëre dorso,
  Nec tibi si Persei moverit ala pedes;
Vel si te sectæ rapiant talaribus auræ,
  Nil tibi Mercurii proderit alta via.
Instat semper Amor supra caput; instat amanti,
  Et gravis ipse super libera colla sedet.
Excubat ille acer custos, et tollere numquam
  Te patietur humo lumina capta semel.
Et jam si pecces, deus exorabilis ille est,
  Si modo præsentes viderit esse preces.
Ista senes licet accusent convivia duri:

means to 're-echo.' Perhaps *custodi ludor*, 'I am baffled by one who so virtuously keeps her affections for me,' *tam sancte amores custodit*. When the dative was corrupted into the ablative (which would have been *a custode*), *ludor* was not unnaturally changed to *eludor*. Compare 'tibi luditur,' 'the game is played by you,' Persius, *Sat*. iii. 20.

XXII. This is a difficult elegy. Kuinoel, with the earlier commentators, wrongly imagined that the poet was addressing Cynthia, and dissuading her from undertaking a voyage 'ad Parthos vel Indos,' (!) on the plea of withdrawing herself from the calumnies of her enemies. Barth is even more absurd: 'Cynthiam lucri studio in bellum (!) proficisci cupientem revocat ab incepto,' &c. The poet however speaks of himself in the second person, or in other words, holds a dialogue with himself, to show the impossibility of escaping from the thraldom of love, and the expediency of acquiescing in his present fate. He assumes the Bacchic frenzy, and invites Cynthia to join him in a revel in the wild woods (25, 39), resolving to indulge in gaiety and pleasure, since it is distasteful to him to follow the precepts of dull virtue (16). Neither Lachmann, who divides the present elegy into two at v. 23, nor Jacob, who seems to think the first part of the poem addressed to a friend, has rightly seen the purport of the whole, the chief obscurity in which depends on the sudden transitions from one person to another, which will be pointed out in their proper places.

3—6.] There is a slight confusion in the disposition of the negatives, if we follow the explanation commonly proposed, *non—nil tibi proderit*, in which case *vel* in v. 5, must be taken for *nec*. But may we not rather understand *non* (proderit) *si vecteris, nec si ala* &c., *vel, si auræ te rapiant, nil tibi via Mercurii proderit*: where *vel—nil* in the last distich is equivalent to *nec quicquam*. Or thus: 'non (fuga est) si Pegaso vecteris; si te vel Mercurii talaria te rapiant, nihil proderit ejus via.'

8.] *Ipse*. Lachmann and Hertzberg approve of the correction of Beroaldus, *ipsa*, i. e. *etiam super libera colla*, sc. amore vacua. But *ipse* may mean *in person*, not *per custodem*, nor by mere mental anxieties &c.

11.] *Et*. Lachmann follows Burmann in reading *sed*, with the approval of Jacob. Perhaps *et* may have the sense of *et tamen*; 'And yet, if any indiscretion shall have alienated you for a time from your mistress, the quarrel may be made up by a prompt confession.' Indeed, *etiam* is only another way of writing *et jam*; and other passages occur where the meaning is identical, as *Georg*. iii. 189. —*præsentes*, παρ' αὐτὸ τὸ ἁμάρτημα. 'Quamprimum errata fatere,' i. 9, 33.

13.] *Ista convivia* may mean *hos convivas*; or *tua convivia*, if we suppose the poet addresses Cynthia as a part of himself.

Nos modo propositum, vita, teramus iter.
Illorum antiquis onerentur legibus aures:
Hic locus est, in quo, tibia docta, sones,
Quæ non jure vado Mæandri jacta natasti,
Turpia cum faceret Palladis ora tumor.
Num jam, dure, paras Phrygias nunc ire per undas,
Et petere Hyrcani litora nauta maris?
Spargere et alterna communes cæde Penates,
Et ferre ad patrios præmia dira Lares?
Una contentum pudeat me vivere amica?
Hoc si crimen erit, crimen Amoris erit;

Equally ambiguous is *modo* in the next line. It may mean *super propositum*, or *nos modo teramus*, i. e. nihil curantes amorum præcepta.

15.] Construe, *illorum aures onerentur* &c., 'Let them (the *senes*) be bored with old-fashioned rules; this is the school for wine and music;' cf. inf. 37.

17.] *Quæ non jure* &c. 'Quæ immerito a Minerva abjecta es in Mæandrum, cum te inflasset et vidisset genas intumuisse.'—*Kuinoel*. Ovid, *Art. Amat.* iii. 505, 'I procul hinc, dixit, non es mihi, tibia, tanti, Ut vidit vultus Pallas in amne suos.' Cf. *Fast.* vi. 700; Pind. *Pyth.* xii.

19.] Lachmann, Kuinoel, and Keil give *num jam, dure, paras* &c. Jacob and Müller *nam jam, dure, paras*, Hertzberg *nunc jam, dure* &c. *Dure* is the reading of the MS. Groning., and seems to have arisen from the mistaken idea that it was Cynthia and not Propertius who was contemplating the journey. The same MS. has *nunc* with the Naples MS. and ed. Rheg. But *nunc paras, nunc ire* is a repetition which could only be defended on the ground that the instant urgency of the journey (perhaps such a journey as his friends had advised him to take, i. 1, 29), was the point in question, which does not seem to be the case; to say nothing of the awkward *nunc jam* for *jam nunc*. The sense is, 'Do you still intend?' &c., *i.e.* after the considerations just enumerated against it. The reading of the MS. Naples is remarkable: *non* (*sic a pr. m.*) *tamen immerito*. This, taken in combination with 21—2, might be considered as ironically said; 'truly, you have good reason for wishing to go abroad and fight against enemies who ought rather to be friends of Rome' &c. But it does not appear by what doctrine of ellipse the infinitives could be explained.

20.] The MSS. have *nota*, except one of the inferior copies, which gives *mota*. Hertzberg's correction is so probable that I have ventured to admit it. He compares Hor. *Od.* i. 1, 13, 'ut trabe Cypria Myrtoum pavidus nauta secet mare,' and *ib.* iii. 4, 30, 'insanientem navita Bosporum tentabo,' while he shows that so far from the shores of the Caspian sea being *nota* to the Romans, they were the very reverse. Müller reads *littora Eoa*.

21.] *Communes Penates*. Hertzberg ridicules, and with good reason, the absurd explanation of preceding commentators, 'Cynthiæ et Propertii ædes,' and compares i. 11, 16, 'communes nec meminisse deos,' the gods common to two sides or parties, and similarly Virg. *Æn.* viii. 275; xii. 118. Allusion is made (Hertzberg, *Quæst.* p. 225) to a treaty ratified in the year of the city 728 between the Romans and Polemo king of Pontus, apparently against the rebellious and quarrelsome nation of the Parthi. 'Itaque *communes Penates* aut erunt *publici penates* ejus regionis quam bello petitura erat expeditio Romana, aut quod multo magis placet, quos uterque populus colit.'—*Hertzberg*. What particular gods the Parthians worshipped in common with Rome, the learned editor is unable to state.

23.] With this verse Lachmann commences a new elegy; but he is not followed by the recent editors. 'My severe censors say that I ought to be ashamed of living with Cynthia. Ashamed of being faithful to one! That is but nature, and therefore no sin.' Compare ii. 1, 47, 'Laus in amore mori; laus altera, si datur uno Posse frui.'

Mi nemo obiciat. Libeat tibi, Cynthia, mecum
  Roscida muscosis antra tenere jugis.
Illic aspicies scopulis hærere Sorores,
  Et canere antiqui dulcia furta Jovis:
Ut Semela est combustus, ut est deperditus Io,
  Denique ut ad Trojæ tecta volarit avis.
Quod si nemo extat, qui vicerit Alitis arma,
  Communis culpæ cur reus unus agor?
Nec tu Virginibus reverentia moveris ora:
  Hic quoque non nescit quid sit amare chorus;
Si tamen Œagri quædam compressa figura
  Bistoniis olim rupibus accubuit.
Hic ubi te prima statuent in parte choreæ,
  Et medius docta cuspide Bacchus erit,
Tum capiti sacros patiar pendere corymbos:
  Nam sine te nostrum nil valet ingenium.

25.] *Mihi* &c. 'Let no one charge *me* with a crime for which Love alone is responsible.' He adds, somewhat abruptly, 'If we cannot live without these reproaches at Rome, retire with me into the country, and cultivate literature and poetry (i. 2, 27) in peace.'

29.] *Io* (Ἰοῖ) seems to be the ablative. Otherwise the accusative (Ἰὼ) might have been defended, as *deperditus est* = *amavit*: compare *ardebat Alexim*, Virg. *Ecl.* ii. 1.—*avis*, *i. e.* in avim, sc. aquilam, mutatus, ad rapiendum Ganymedem. The construction is similar to *Ecl.* vi. 64, 'Tum canit, errantem Permessi ad flumina Gallum Aonas in montes ut duxerit una sororum.'

31.] *Alitis*, *h. e.* Cupidinis.

33.] 'Nor will you put the Virgin Muses to the blush: for they also know well what it is to love. *Reverentia*, αἰδεῖα, verecunda. The sense is, 'Be not deterred by their well-known attributes of *Virginitas* and *verecundia* from invoking them in composing love-songs.'

35.] *Si tamen*. 'If, in spite of the alleged chastity' &c. See on ii. 4, 10.—*Œagri figura*, 'by one in the form of Œagrus;' thus leaving it indefinite whether he were really Œagrus or a god. Apollodor. i. 3, 2, Καλλιόπης μὲν οὖν καὶ Οἰάγρου, κατ' ἐπίκλησιν δὲ Ἀπόλλωνος, Λῖνος, ὃν Ἡρακλῆς ἀπέκτεινε. There is a similar story of Terpsichore and the river Strymon, Eur. *Rhes.* 920.

37.] Lachmann, with the approval of Jacob, reads *te* for *me* from one of the inferior MS. Both Keil and Müller retain *me*. Hertzberg is scarcely successful in his explanation:—'hic, (*i. e.* tecum in patriis montibus, non saeculatis Hyrcanis), si mihi Musæ et Bacchus carmina dederint, lubens ego me furore poetico rapi patiar,—vel si te præsente, gelidum nemus fontesque salubres et vinum ad carmina pangenda paratum me reddiderint, non refragabor. Nam sine te nostrum non valet ingenium.'—He rightly compares, in illustration of *prima in parte choreæ*, iv. 6, 19. But *hic* seems rather to refer to *hic locus*, sup. 16.

38.] *Bacchus*. On his connexion with poetry, see on v. 1, 62.—*docta cuspide*, *i. e.* thyrso, quo docte moderatur choro. Compare *docta falce* iii. 10, 12. Scaliger, followed by Kuinoel, reads *tecta cuspide*, comparing Catull. lxiv. 257, *i. e.* velata.—In *medius erit* there is a double allusion, both to wine being placed on the table before Cynthia and Propertius, and to the god Bacchus acting as arbiter and exarch of the chorus.

40.] *Sine te*. Can this refer to Bacchus? The change in the person from v. 38, presents little difficulty in Propertius. In this case, of course, the MSS. reading *me* would be retained in v. 37. But all the commentators understand this verse of Cynthia, who as it were inspires the poet to sing. Compare ii. 1, 4, 'Ingenium nobis ipsa puella facit.'

XXIII.

Quæris, cur veniam tibi tardior? Aurea Phœbo
  Porticus a magno Cæsare aperta fuit.
Tota erat in speciem Pœnis digesta columnis,
  Inter quas Danai femina turba senis.
Hic equidem Phœbo visus mihi pulchrior ipso
  Marmoreus tacita carmen hiare lyra;
Atque aram circum steterant armenta Myronis,
  Quattuor artificis, vivida signa, boves.
Tum medium claro surgebat marmore templum,

XXIII. This elegy is one of the poet's earlier productions. The date is determined by the circumstances alluded to, the solemn dedication and opening of the new temple of Apollo on the Palatine, Oct. 24, A.U.C. 726, by Augustus in memory of his victory at Actium. The same event is commemorated by Horace, *Od.* i. 31. The poet excuses his delay in visiting Cynthia on the plea of having been present at the ceremony. Some have thought this a mere fragment of a longer poem describing the spectacle in detail: but Lachmann acutely remarks that *cur veniam*, v. 1, would have been *cur venerim*, had the poet taken time to compose a long account.

2.] *Magno*, cf. ii. 7, 5, 'at magnus Cæsar.'

3.] *In speciem*, *speciose*, 'with a view to effect;' the architect had laid out the whole design (not only the façade) with columns for the purpose of presenting a magnificent appearance, not merely for structural use.—*Pœnis columnis*, of the marble now called '*giallo antico*;' *Hertzberg*. See the commentators on Hor. *Od.* ii. 18, 4, 'non trabes Hymettiæ premunt columnas ultima recisas Africa.' Ovid, *Am.* ii. 2, 3, 'Hesterna vidi spatiantem luce puellam, Illa quæ Danai porticus agmen habet.' *Trist.* iii. 1, 59, 'Inde tenore pari gradibus sublimia celsis Ducor ad intonsi candida templa dei; Signa peregrinis ubi sunt *alterna columnis* Belides, et stricto barbarus ense pater.' Opposite to these were the *fratres aheni*, or equestrian statues of the sons of Ægyptus. Persius, *Sat.* ii. 56.

4.] *Turba*, as v. 11, 76, 'omnis erit collo turba ferenda tuo,' *i. e.* omnes liberi.

5.] *Equidem*. A remarkable instance of the use of this word in a writer of the Augustan age, which tends to disprove its alleged derivation from *ego quidem*. Lachmann reads *hic quidem*, after Markland. It is not easy to assent to the opinion of Dr. Donaldson, *Varron.* p. 443, that the initial *ē* is long, and that it must therefore have been pronounced in verse *ēqu'dem*, and that in Persius, i. 110, 'per me equidem sint omnia protinus alba,' we must read *me quidem* and pronounce it *per me qu'dem*. Hertzberg transposes vv. 5—8 to the end of the elegy, on the ground that the same statue is here described as in v. 15. Granting this to be the case, and that it would have been better to have arranged the subject otherwise, the common order is sufficiently justified by the haste and brevity of what was, perhaps, little better than an extempore composition. In truth, the four verses in question do not harmonise in continuation with v. 16.

6.] *Tacita lyra*, an elegant expression for a mute statue. This statue is said to have been the work of Scopas (Pliny, *N. H.* xxxvi. 4, 7), and is distinguished by Hertzberg from another colossal one of bronze, said to have represented Augustus himself, and to have stood in the Palatine library. Hor. *Ep.* i. 3, 17, 'et tangere vitet scripta, Palatinus quæcunque recepit Apollo.' A copy of this statue, 'Apollo Citharœdus,' is in the Vatican collection, and is engraved in Dr. Smith's *Student's History of Greece*, p. 551, 580. The mouth is opened, as in singing; hence the propriety of *carmen hiare*.

8.] The MSS. give *artificis*, which may stand, if taken for *artificem*. See note on i. 2, 8. But most editors prefer the latter form. What particular mythical event (if any) the four cows represented, is not known.

9.] *Medium*. The temple itself appears to have stood between two, if not four porticos. Hertzberg shows from Sueton. *Oct.* § 29, that more than one were dedicated

Et patria Phœbo carius Ortygia.
In quo Solis erat supra fastigia currus,
Et valvæ, Libyci nobile dentis opus,
Altera dejectos Parnasi vertice Gallos,
Altera mœrebat funera Tantalidos.
Deinde inter matrem deus ipse interque sororem
Pythius in longa carmina veste sonat.

XXIV.

Qui videt, is peccat: qui te non viderit ergo,
Non cupiet; facti lumina crimen habent.
Nam quid Prænesti dubias, o Cynthia, sortes,

by Augustus.—*claro marmore*, *i. e.* bright, polished. Scaliger, followed by Kuinoel, reads *clario*.—*et patria Ortygia*, 'even than his native Ortygia,' *i. e.* than the temple in Delos, or as some think, near Ephesus (Tac. *Ann.* iii. 61). That the gods had a particular partiality for certain temples is well known, and easily explained from the jealousies incidental to rival pretensions.

11.] The MSS. have *in quo*, which Keil and Müller retain. Hertzberg reads *et duo*, and *erant* for *erat*, proving from ancient examples that the figures on the pediment were two, one on each side of the highest point, as on the Mausoleum in Caria. Cf. Ovid, *Fast.* v. 560. Others have proposed *aurea*, or *ergo*, and read *erat*.

12.] This verse is nearly identical with one of Martial's, xiv. 3, 'Eacumus Libyci nobile dentis opus.'

14.] *Mœrebat.* One of the great doors represented sculptured in ivory the retreat of the Gauls from the temple at Delphi, scared by earthquakes and a storm of thunder and lightning; the other *mourned*, *i. e.* set forth in moving imagery, the death of Niobe's children, slain by Apollo and Diana. With *Gallos* we may supply from the context some verb like *pingebat*.—*funera*, 'the dead children;' so v. 1. 97, 'fatales pueri, duo funera matris avaræ.' On the former event see on iv. 13, 53.

15.] The god stands between Latona and Diana, wearing the long dress (*palla*, Tibull. iii. 4, 35) peculiar to the citharœdi. It was this which Arion put on before he leapt into the waves, Ovid, *Fast.* ii. 107, 'Induerat Tyrio bis tinctam murice pallam.' *Deinde* means, 'after passing through the portico.'

XXIV. Written in a fit of jealous alarm to upbraid Cynthia for her frequent absence from Rome under various pretences, which he suspects are but vain excuses for getting out of his sight, and seeking the company of more favoured lovers.

1—2.] Hertzberg considers *Qui videt is peccat*, as the words of Cynthia excusing her conduct, by alleging that she cannot help the notice which she attracts. 'Tu frequentiam amatorum eo excusas, quod quicunque te viderit, te tentet. Non equidem nego factum. Sed causam facti præcidere te jubeo. Fac ne videaris.' *Lumen* he accordingly interprets 'quod semper illa in publico et lumine versetur,' while others explain it of *the eyes* of Cynthia's admirers, which are in fault rather than themselves. In the vulg. *facti crimina lumen habet*, *lumen* may mean 'your frequently exhibiting yourself in open day;' but the first words seem to be not Cynthia's, but the poet's. 'To see you,' he says, in a half angry, half expostulatory strain, 'is to be enamoured. Therefore avoid being seen, which is the cause of your misbehaviour.' Müller, with Heins and Lachmann, reads *facti lumina crimen habent*, the Naples MS. giving *crimina lumen habent*. And they are probably right: 'the eyes have the guilt of the deed.' For, as Shakespeare says, 'how oft the sight of means to do ill deeds makes ill deeds done.'

3.] The reading of the MSS. Gron. and Naples is rightly retained by Hertzberg, who shews (what seems obvious enough) that it is the locative, *i. e.* 'at Præneste.' So also Keil and Müller. Jacob and Kuinoel give *Prænestis*; Lachmann, very improbably, *Nam quid Prænesti in dubias*,

Quid petis Ææi mœnia Telegoni?
Curve te in Herculeum deportant esseda Tibur?
Appia cur totiens te via ducit anum?
Hoc utinam spatiere loco, quodcumque vacabis,
Cynthia! sed tibi me credere turba vetat,
Cum videt accensis devotam currere tædis
In nemus et Triviæ lumina ferre deæ.
Scilicet umbrosis sordet Pompeia columnis
Porticus aulæis nobilis Attalicis,
Et creber platanis pariter surgentibus ordo,

&c., *i. e.* 'Quid Præneste tendis, illas dubias sortes quæsitum?' The *ablative* is *Præneste*, which misled the commentators. Juven. iii. 190, 'Quis timet aut timuit gelida Præneste ruinam?' There was a temple of Fortune at Præneste, and the reader will find in Cic. *de Div.* ii. 41, a curious account of the sortes Prænestinæ. For a similar and equally questionable trip of Cynthia to Lanuvium, see v. 8, 15.

4.] Tusculum is here called the 'fort of Telegonus,' as in Horace, *Od.* iii. 29, 8, 'Telegoni juga parricidæ.' Telegonus was the son of Ulysses by Circe, hence called the *Ææan*: Hom. *Od.* x. 135, Αἰαίην δ' ἐς νῆσον ἀφικόμεθ'· ἔνθα δ' ἔναιε Κίρκη ἐϋπλόκαμος.

5.] *Herculeum Tibur.* See on v. 7, 82. These two last mentioned places, Frascati and Tivoli, were favourite resorts of the Romans in the summer. This verse is corruptly written in the MSS., but so as to leave little doubt of the true reading. Müller gives 'Cur aut te' &c. The MS. Gron. has *cum vetera*, others *cur vetera*. The Naples MS., by a curious corruption, 'curva te herculeum deportantes sed abitur.'

6.] The better copies agree in *anum*, which can only mean 'old woman as you are;' for the suggestion of an old commentator 'ducit te toties ad anum,' *i. e.* ad sagam,' is scarcely admissible. Lachmann, Jacob, Hertzberg, and the latest editors, read *anus*, which is found in three of the inferior copies. Authority however is clearly for *anum*. Is it then less harsh and unusual to call a public highway *anus via*, than to taunt Cynthia with vanity in being so fond of displaying her charms when she was becoming *passée*? This very fact she is reminded of in terms nearly as blunt and undisguised in iii. 9, 20, 'cum sis ipsa anus haud longa curva futura die.' On a careful consideration of the passage I have not hesitated to retain *anum*, though Hertzberg quotes *terra anus*, *charta anus*, *testa anus*, &c., in defence of *anus via*, which the Appian road is conceived to be called, because it was the first constructed of all the Roman roads. See v. 8, 17.

8.] Keil and Müller, with Jacob and Lachmann, read *nam* for *sed*, from the MS. Groning. The sense is equally good.—*turba*, *i. e.* the crowd who come to see you. 'In illa turba hominum, quæ in ea via semper versatur, vereor ne plures insint qui te visam depereant.'—*Lachmann.*

10.] *Triviæ deæ.* To Diana worshipped at Aricia, called on that account 'nemoralis Aricia' by Ovid, *Fast.* vi. 59. *Ibid.* iii. 263, 'Vallis Aricinæ sylva præcinctus opaca Est locus, antiqua religione sacer.—Sæpe potens voti, frontem redimita coronis, Femina lucentes portat ab urbe faces.' This worship was connected with the infernal attributes of Diana as Hecate. She was the goddess of *light*, Lucina, *i. e.* Luna, and as such may have claimed the offering of torches; but *Trivia* is synonymous with Hecate. Ovid gives an explanation, though an absurd one, of this ancient custom, *Fast.* iv. 493, viz. that Ceres lighted her torch at the crater of Etna in her search for Proserpine: 'Illic accendit geminas pro lampade tædas: Hinc Cereris sacris nunc quoque tæda datur.'

11.] *Scilicet.* 'I suppose, forsooth,' &c. The piazza of Pompey was a favourite and fashionable promenade. See v. 8, 75, 'Tu neque Pompeia spatiabere cultus in umbra.' Ovid, *A. A.* i. 67; Mart. ii. 14, 10.

12.] Tapestry of eastern manufacture, professedly or really bequeathed to the Romans by king Attalus (see v. 5, 24), appears to have been suspended in the Portico to shade it from the sun. Hence, perhaps, (in part at least) the columns are called *umbrosæ*.

Flumina sopito quæque Marone cadunt,
Et leviter lymphis tota crepitantibus urbe,
Cum subito Triton ore recondit aquam.
Falleris; ista tui furtum via monstrat amoris:
Non urbem, demens, lumina nostra fugis;
Nil agis; insidias in me componis inanes;
Tendis iners docto retia nota mihi.
Sed de me minus est: famæ jactura pudicæ
Tanta tibi miseræ, quanta mereris, erit.
Nuper enim de te nostras me lædit ad aures
Rumor, et in tota non bonus urbe fuit.
Sed tu non debes inimicæ credere linguæ:
Semper formosis fabula pœna fuit.
Non tua deprenso damnata est fama veneno;
Testis eris puras, Phœbe, videre manus:
Sin autem longo nox una aut altera lusu
Consumpta est, non me crimina parva movent.
Tyndaris externo patriam mutavit amore,

14.] *Sopito Marone*, 'from a statue of the sleeping Maro.' Maro is variously represented as Silenus, a son of Silenus, and a son of Bacchus: see Hertzberg, who shows in a very excellent note that these figures of Silenus, teeming water from a jar, were so common in Italy that the conduits formed in that fashion were called *Sileni*. Hence Lucretius, vi. 1262, speaking of the thirst occasioned by the plague, says 'corpora *silenos* ad aquarum strata jacebant.' Kuinoel's brief note is right, though he was probably at a loss for details: '*Marone*, intell. statua sc. signum Maronis, e quo aquæ cadebant.' Keil and Müller read *Anione* for *Marone*, and in the next verse *tot leviter* &c., 'when so many fountains may be heard plashing in Rome.'

16.] *Triton*. A similar fountain to the above is here described, probably spouting out water from a shell. For *lymphis* the Naples MS. has *nimphis*, whence Kuinoel *Nymphis*. In either case it must be understood of the babbling of water. The argument of the poet is this: 'You pretend to seek for cool shade and refreshing streams at Tibur and Tusculum, when you may have both in Rome.' Hence *falleris* (v. 16) is, 'You are mistaken if you think to deceive me by that plea.'

20.] *Iners*, ἄτεχνος, contrasted with *docto mihi*.

22.] *Quanta mereris*, 'in proportion to your deserts.' The meaning is, 'I do not care so much about myself, as about the discredit you are incurring by your misconduct.'

23.] *Me lædit*. The Groning. MS. has *pervenit*, which appears to be a correction. The ellipse of *perlatus* is awkward, and the present tense following *nuper* suspicious. Compare however iii. 8, 6. Müller marks the verse with an *obelus*.

25.] 'But' (you will say to me) 'you ought not to trust report, which has ever been unjust to the fair. Granted, that you are not accused of poisoning; that you can say, 'Bear witness, O sun, that my hands are pure;' nay, I am not disposed to take you to task for spending one or two nights in gaiety; it is not a little cause that moves my wrath.'

29.] *Luxu* Jacob and Keil, from the MS. Groning. This word means more than 'luxury' in the best authors, and is equivalent to our term 'debauchery.'—*lusu*, 'pastime,' here means the same, but is a less coarse and criminatory expression. See iii. 9, 24.

31.] 'Helen left husband and home, and yet was taken back without formal condemnation being passed upon her,' *sine decreto*, perhaps a ἅπαξ λεγόμενον for *sine supplicio*. The sense is, other persons have

Et sine decreto viva reducta domum est;
Ipsa Venus quamvis corrupta libidine Martis,
Non minus in cælo semper honesta fuit;
Quamvis Ida Parim pastorem dicat amasse
Atque inter pecudes accubuisse deam.
Hoc et Hamadryadum spectavit turba sororum,
Silenique senes, et pater ipse chori,
Cum quibus Idæo legisti poma sub antro,
Supposita excipiens Naïca dona manu.
An quisquam in tanto stuprorum examine quærit:
Cur hæc tam dives? quis dedit? unde dedit?
O nimium nostro felicem tempore Romam,
Si contra mores una puella facit!
Hæc eadem ante illam impune et Lesbia fecit:
Quæ sequitur, certe est invidiosa minus.
Qui quærit Tatios veteres durosque Sabinos,
Hic posuit nostra nuper in urbe pedem.
Tu prius et fluctus poteris siccare marinos,
Altaque mortali deligere astra manu,
Quam facere, ut nostræ nolint peccare puellæ:
Hic mos Saturno regna tenente fuit,

committed greater crimes and been forgiven.

34.] *Non minus.* I have followed Jacob, Hertzberg, and Keil, in the reading of this passage. For *quamvis* (v. 33), the Naples MS. gives *fertur*, which Lachmann has edited, and both that and MS. Groning. have *nec minus, non* being from Pucci. If *nec* be understood as *nec tamen*, there is no reason for rejecting *fertur*. But it is a difficult critical question to decide between the merits of these two MSS., neither of which is altogether free from the suspicion of conjectural emendation.

35.] 'No, not even though mount Ida can attest that the goddess was enamoured of Paris, and was his consort among the flocks of his fold.' The construction is, *dicat deam amasse Parim*. This legend, it must be observed, is not recorded by any other writer. It is not impossible that the poet, who has elsewhere erred in his mythology (see on v. 4, 40) has confounded Paris with Anchises. Müller reads *palam* for *Parim*, after Haupt.

39.] *Legisti*, i.e. O Pari.—*Naica dona*, gifts offered by the Naid Œnone; apples gathered by her for you and dropped into your hands.

41.] 'Where all are unchaste, does any one express surprise or curiosity at the magnificent gifts received? Rome were too happy if (i.e. it cannot be expected that) one girl should act otherwise than the rest.' *Stuprorum examen*, i.e. turba impudicarum.

45.] *Lesbia*, the mistress of Catullus. '*She* was not blamed for infidelity: why should I expect Cynthia to be more faithful?' For the non-elision in *illam* see iii. 7, 1. Perhaps *ante illas*, alluding to *stuprorum turba* in 41.

47.] *Latias veteres*, 'Latin girls of the olden time,' Müller, after Schrader, retaining the vulgate *durasque Sabinas*, which Lachmann altered to *durosque Sabinos*. 'He who expects to find the primitive virtue of the Sabines in Rome, must have arrived *fresh* in the city.'

50.] *Deripere astra* Müller, after Burmann. It is difficult to defend the vulgate.

52.] *Hic mos*, sc. 'non peccandi.' So Juv. *Sat.* 6, 1, 'Credo pudicitiam Saturno Rege moratam In terris.'—*nostræ*, by contrast, means 'nostri temporis puellæ.'

Et cum Deucalionis aquæ fluxere per orbem,
  Et post antiquas Deucalionis aquas.
Dic mihi, quis potuit lectum servare pudicum?
  Quæ dea cum solo vivere sola deo?
Uxorem quondam magni Minois, ut aiunt,
  Corrupit torvi candida forma bovis.
Nec minus ærato Danaë circumdata muro
  Non potuit magno casta negare Jovi.
Quod si tu Graias, tuque es mirata Latinas,
  Semper vive meo libera judicio.

XXV.

Tristia jam redeunt iterum sollemnia nobis;
  Cynthia jam noctes est operata decem.
Atque utinam pereat, Nilo quæ sacra tepente
  Misit matronis Inachis Ausoniis!

53.] *At* for *et* Müller, as Beroaldus had proposed, with a comma after *aquæ*. But Lachmann objects, 'deos ante diluvium Deucalionis amoribus non studuisse falsum est, si vera narravit Clymene Virg. *Georg.* iv. 347,' 'aque Chao densos divum numerabat amores.'

57.] *Uxorem Minois*, Pasiphäe, whose amour resulted in the birth of the Minotaur.

60.] *Casta*, i.e. quamvis casta. For *Jovi* Jacob has *deo*, apparently by a misprint.

61.] The best MSS. have *imitata*, which Keil retains. Hertzberg seems right in editing *mirata* from two or three of the inferior MSS., on metrical grounds. Lachmann reads *æquas* (æque es), and Müller *æquasque imitata*. The sense is, 'if you profess to be an admirer and follower of the profligate heroines of Greece and Rome, I will not be your judge: follow the bent of your own inclination, and suffer for it.'

XXV. The poet complains of Cynthia's too rigid observance of certain foreign rites, enjoining strict continence for a stated period. (See iii. 20, 61; v. 5, 34). With an inconsistency not uncommon in profligate persons, she appears to have paid scrupulous attention to the ceremonies of religion, while she spent her nights in drinking and loose company.

2.] *Operata est.* The meaning evidently is, 'has engaged to keep,' &c., for if the time had elapsed there would have been little to complain of; if it had not yet commenced, the perfect tense could not have been used. The word *sacris* must be supplied. Compare Juvenal, vi. 535, 'Ille petit veniam, quoties non abstinet uxor Concubitu sacris observandisque diebus.' See the whole passage, 526—541. The same rite was strictly kept by Delia. Tibullus, i. 3, 25; cf. Ovid. *Am.* iii. 9, 34, and 10, 2.

4.] In his contempt for Egyptian customs, he does not hesitate to ridicule the cow-goddess (for Isis was the same as Io) who has imported from the tropical Nile into Rome so much of superstitious novelty. The facility with which the Romans enlarged their mythological creed to admit all sects and professions has often caused surprise, and been attributed to various motives. The explanation of it is probably to be sought in the immense number of resident foreigners who were allowed, from the necessity of the case, to exercise their own religion without restraint. The state had no particular fondness for innovation, for it could enact stringent laws against *externas superstitiones*, and enforce them too, when Christians or Jews were the subjects. We find the Emperor Claudius complaining of the rapid spread of foreign rites, Tac. *Ann.* xi. 15. It may be questioned if a national or established religion is ever tolerant but from motives of policy. Pas-

Quæ dea tam cupidos totiens divisit amantes,
  Quæcumque illa fuit, semper amara fuit.
Tu certe Jovis occultis in amoribus, Io,
  Sensisti, multas quid sit inire vias,
Cum te jussit habere puellam cornua Juno,
  Et pecoris duro perdere verba sono.
Ah quotiens quernis læsisti frondibus ora!
  Mansisti stabulis abdita pasta tuis!
An, quoniam agrestem detraxit ab ore figuram
  Juppiter, idcirco facta superba dea es?
An tibi non satis est fuscis Ægyptus alumnis?
  Cur tibi tam longa Roma petita via est?
Quidve tibi prodest viduas dormire puellas?
  Sed tibi, crede mihi, cornua rursus erunt;
At nos e nostra te, sæva, fugabimus urbe:
  Cum Tiberi Nilo gratia nulla fuit.
At tu, quæ nostro nimium placata dolore es,

sages like the present show the contempt in which the genuine Romans held the worship of strange divinities. Augustus held in respect only such as were of ancient repute in other countries, 'ceteras contemptui habuit.'—Sueton. *Oct.* § 93. Tiberius 'externas ceremonias compescuit, Id. *Tib.* § 36. Infra v. 1, 17, 'Nulli cura fuit externos quærere divos.'

6.] *Quæcumque illa fuit.* ἥτις ποτ' ἦν, implying contemptuous disregard who and what she really was, *i. e.* whether identical with Io or not. Keil and Müller place a mark of interrogation at *amantes*, Lachmann a mark of admiration.

7.] The sense is, 'you at least should be the last to cause in others the pain of separation which you so bitterly experienced in your own case.' Any one may be said *inire multas vias* who enters on many routes but pursues none; that is, who wanders vaguely and without purpose. Lachmann and others seem wrong in attributing a less delicate meaning to the words: unless indeed we are to regard the whole passage (7—12) as a coarse insult rather than a peevish banter. But the logical sequence is clearer on the other view.

12.] *Mansisti.*—*ah quotiens* must be repeated, though the ellipse is harsh even for Propertius. Perhaps *et* has been lost. Lachmann reads *mansisti ut.* 'How often,' he says in ridicule, 'after a dinner on oak-leaves, were you shut up all alone to digest it?' How often you experienced solitude and separation, and that too in a manner and under circumstances not the most agreeable. We might suggest *et quotiens* &c., 'but when you had dined off rough oak-leaves, you had to stay concealed in your stall, and secluded from converse with your lover.'

13.] *Agrestem figuram*, μορφὴν βοηδόν. 'Have you become proud as a goddess for no other reason than that you did not always remain a cow?'

18—19.] He continues to banter the unfortunate Isis. 'You seem, from your savage temper, likely to wear your cast-off horns again. Methinks it were better for us to turn you out of our city at once.' Barth observes, on the authority of Dio, that Agrippa, as prefect of the city, did in fact prohibit the worship of Isis at Rome in 733. This threat therefore has an historical import. *Sæva* belongs rather to v. 18.

21.] *Nostro placata dolore.* 'Cui placandæ nimium operam sumsi, quæ nimis duram te præbuisti.'—*Barth.* Lachmann reads *implacata* with Heinsius.—Perhaps *placanda*. *Noctibus his vacui, i. e.* when the period of abstinence shall have been completed.—*iter* is the 'cursus amoris.'—*ter* seems to be added, as if the temporary suspension of endearments justified a more

Noctibus his vacui ter faciamus iter.
Non audis, et verba sinis mea ludere, cum jam
Flectant Icarii sidera tarda boves.
Lenta bibis; mediæ nequeunt te frangere noctes.
An nondum est talos mittere lassa manus?
Ah pereat, quicumque meracas repperit uvas,
Corrupitque bonas nectare primus aquas!
Icare, Cecropiis merito jugulate colonis,
Pampineus nosti quam sit amarus odor.
Tuque o Eurytion vino Centaure peristi,
Nec non Ismario tu, Polypheme, mero.
Vino forma perit, vino corrumpitur ætas,
Vino sæpe suum nescit amica virum.
Me miserum, ut multo nihil est mutata Lyæo!
Jam bibe; formosa es: nil tibi vina nocent,
Cum tua præpendent demissæ in pocula sertæ,

frequent renewal. Scaliger's portentous emendation, *refaciamus*, though a barbarous form, has found its way into Barth's generally judicious text.

23.] Before this verse Hertzberg, after a peculiar fashion of his own, places the marks of a lacuna, regarding the remainder of the elegy as an afterthought. There is perhaps more probability in Kuinoel's view, that it is a scrap of an amorous ditty sung in a serenade, like i. 16. But neither of these suppositions is necessary. The poet, having proposed his visit, immediately pictures to himself the exclusion he has too much reason to expect. This sudden transition of thought and scene is common in Propertius, and is the key to the right understanding of many very abrupt passages.—*ludere*, ludibrio fieri.

24.] *Icarii boves.* Kuinoel wrongly joins *Icarii sidera;* but Hertzberg is unnecessarily severe upon him, for both forms, *Icarus* and *Icarius*, were in use, and the poet seems to have adopted both indifferently (see v. 29). Besides, *Icarius* may here be an adjective from *Icarus*. Apollod. iii. 14, 7. Δήμητρα μὲν Κελεὸς εἰς τὴν Ἐλευσῖνα ὑπεδέξατο, Διόνυσον δὲ Ἰκάριος, καὶ λαμβάνει παρ' αὐτοῦ κλῆμα ἀμπέλου. Καὶ τὰ περὶ τὴν οἰνοποιίαν μανθάνων, καὶ τὰς τοῦ θεοῦ δωρήσασθαι θέλων χάριτας ἀνθρώποις, ἀφικνεῖται πρός τινας ποιμένας, οἳ γευσάμενοι τοῦ ποτοῦ, καὶ χωρὶς ὕδατος δι' ἡδονὴν ἀφειδῶς ἑλκύσαντες, πεφαρμάχθαι νομίζοντες, ἀπέκτειναν αὐτόν. He was made a star in Bootes by Bacchus. Tibullus, iv. 1, 9, 'cunctis Baccho jucundior hospes Icarus, ut puro testantur sidera cœlo.' It appears to be another name for Arcturus or Bootes, *Charles' wain* (*i. e.* 'churl's waggon'), and the meaning is, 'you keep me here offering a vain petition while the slow-moving stars of the pole are making their descent towards the morning.'

25.] *Frangere*, fatigare.

27.] *Merum*, vinum meracum, ἄκρατον, was only used by drunkards. There is a sort of confusion in expressing two distinct ideas: 'Perish he who introduced neat wine, and even he who used it in the less objectionable mixture with water.' It is not quite clear whether *corrumpere* is simply for *miscere* (cf. *Georg.* II. 466), or in the literal sense of *spoiling* good water: the epithet rather suggests the latter.

31.] *Eurytion.* He was killed in the fight of the Centaurs at the marriage of Pirithous: see ii. 6. 17.—*Ismario mero.* Hom. *Od.* ix. 198.

35.] *Nihil es mutata* Barth, against the best copies. The ed. Rheg. has *es*, the other copies *est*.

36.] *Jam bibe.* πίνοις ἂν ἤδη, 'Well, go on drinking. Wine has no ill effect on you: you look the handsomer for it when,' &c.

37.] The Naples MS. gives *sertæ*, the others *serta*. And the former reading is quoted by Charisius, a grammarian who

Et mea deducta carmina voce legis.
Largius effuso madeat tibi mensa Falerno,
Spumet et aurato mollius in calice!
Nulla tamen lecto recipit se sola libenter;
Est quiddam, quod vos quærere cogat Amor.
Semper in absentis felicior æstus amantes:
Elevat assiduos copia longa viros.

XXVI.

Cur quisquam faciem dominæ jam credit amori?
Sic erepta mihi pæne puella mea est.

lived circa A.D. 400. 'Propertius feminine extulit: Cum tua præpendent demissæ in pocula sertæ.' The same MS. also has *proependent*, while the others give *propendent* or *prependent*. This is a testimony of some value to the integrity of the oldest MS. extant of Propertius. See note on iii. 8, 29.

38.] *Deducta voce.* As these verses are evidently intended to express a half-intoxicated condition, the meaning of the words must be determined by the circumstances of the case. Hertzberg explains, 'voce molliter in muliebrem modum fracta et cum plasmate cantui simili flexa,' quoting *vocem deducere* and *vox deducta* from fragments of Lucilius and other writers, where the sense seems to be, 'submiss,' 'gentle,' 'winning.' Others understand, 'a drawling tone of voice,' deriving the metaphor from spinning. This certainly seems to suit the context. See iii. 11, 21. There is something very graphic, as Kuinoel remarks, and almost picturesque, in the description of Cynthia sitting at a banquet and reading to others the verses of him whom she has slighted, and looking the more lovely from the drooping garlands and the flush of the wine.

39.] 'Let the wine flow more freely, that you may drown the thoughts of me which will arise amidst your forced gaiety.' This is said with something of spiteful vexation.—'Yet the time will come when you will regret a lover's absence. Possession cloys, absence enhances desire.' *Sola* refers to v. 2. Barth explains *absentes* of some rival, as opposed to *assiduos*, implying the attentions of the poet. But the sense seems rather to be, 'You will miss me when you find your loss.'—*felicior æstus*, 'warmer passion,' or 'more favourable disposition towards,' &c.—*elevat*, parvi facit.

41.] *Lecto*, for *ad lectum*, is remarkable. Perhaps *reficit se*.

XXVI. This elegy, which in the MSS. is continuous with the preceding, is addressed to Lynceus, a friend and fellow-poet, who seems to have so far abused the confidence of Propertius as to have attempted to ingratiate himself with Cynthia at a banquet (v. 22). Of Lynceus as a poet nothing is recorded. He appears (from v. 29-41) to have composed a tragedy on the model of the Seven against Thebes. The first part of the present poem (1—26) is devoted to an expostulation and reproof; the middle portion (27—46) conveys advice, that since he (Lynceus) has at length succumbed to love, he should change the style of his writings and the course of his studies for others more congenial to his circumstances; and the conclusion contains a fine eulogy on Virgil, and an exhortation to tread in the steps of other poets who have sung the praises of their mistresses. Hertzberg (*Quæst.* p. 95) remarks on the general composition, 'Si quis singulas iterum hujus elegiæ partes excutere et ad suum quamque locum referre tentaverit, tantam dispositionis varietatem agnoscet, quantam in nullo alio carmine.' It may be added, few elegies exhibit greater critical difficulties than the present.

1.] *Credit.* The Naples MS. has *credet*, and so Lachmann and Kuinoel. It is by no means clear that they are wrong. The usual construction of *quisquam* interrogatively is with the indicative, as iii. 14, 3, 'Ingenuus quisquam alterius dat munera servo?' Martial, *Ep.* i. 56, 5, 'Quisquam picta colit Spartani frigora saxi?' and the

Expertus dico, nemo est in amore fidelis:
  Formosam raro non sibi quisque petit.
Polluit ille deus cognatos, solvit amicos,
  Et bene concordes tristia ad arma vocat.
Hospes in hospitium Menelai venit adulter:
  Colchis et ignotum nonne secuta virum est?
Lynceu, tune meam potuisti, perfide, curam
  Tangere? nonne tuæ tum cecidere manus?
Quid, si non constans illa et tam certa fuisset?
  Posses in tanto vivere flagitio?
Tu mihi vel ferro pectus, vel perde veneno:
  A domina tantum te modo tolle mea.
Te socium vitæ, te corporis esse licebit,
  Te dominum admitto rebus, amice, meis:
Lecto te solum, lecto te deprecor uno;
  Rivalem possum non ego ferre Jovem.

reason is, that when we say 'quisquam hoc facit?' we mean, 'nemo hoc facit.' But the addition of *cur* makes some difference in this case; nor is the passage which Hertzberg quotes from Hor. *Sat.* ii. 2, 103, 'Cur eget indignus quisquam te divite?' really parallel to the present. For in that verse a fact is stated, and the reason of it is asked. We may, however, understand *cur quisquam credit?* in this sense: 'On what principle of reason do men continue to entrust, as we daily see them doing, beauty to the tender mercies of Love?' *Amor* is here represented as a treacherous *custos*, who is sure to betray his charge. The MS. Gron. has *amori*. Jacob edits *amico* from Passl. This, though adopted also by Weise, Müller, and Keil, reads rather like a correction; though, on the other hand, *ille deus* (in 5) may have caused *amico* to be corrupted into *Amori*.—*sic*, *i.e.* sic temere credendo. The poet seems to have allowed Cynthia to be escorted to a banquet by his sober old friend, as he thought him; but wine and beauty fairly overcame the veteran.

3.] *In amore*, *i.e.* sibi commisso.

5.] *Polluit cognatos*, 'sets at defiance natural laws of relationship.' Æsch. *Suppl.* 221, ἐχθρῶν ὁμαίμων καὶ μιαινόντων γένος. Inf. v. 9, 8, 'furto polluit ille Jovem.' Hor. *Od.* iii. 6, 18, 'inquinavere et genus et domos.'

7.] 'Paris, to whom as a stranger Menelaus entrusted the honour of his wife, proved himself a false guest.' Æsch. *Agam.* 399, οἷος καὶ Πάρις, ἐλθὼν ἐς δόμον τὸν Ἀτρειδᾶν, ᾔσχυνε ξενίαν τράπεζαν κλοπαῖσι γυναικός.—*ignotum virum*, *i.e.* hospitem, peregrinum. 'A gallant gay came as a guest to be entertained by Menelaus; and did not Medea in like manner go off with a stranger?' For *hospes* Müller reads *Tros et*.

9.] *Perfide, curam tangere?* Others, as Barth and Keil, read *tangere—perfide*, but against the best copies.—*meam curam*, 'the object of my care,' ἐμὸν μέλημα.—*cecidere manus*, as in Virg. *Æn.* vi. 33, 'bis patriæ cecidere manus,' sc. defecere, victæ sunt.

12.] *Posses*, 'could you have consented to live (or gone on living) under the consciousness of so great a crime,' viz. of having succeeded in the seduction.

13.] *Perde* &c. 'Vel fodi pectus ferro, vel perde (vitam) veneno.'

14.] *Modo* following *tantum* seems a tautology; 'all I ask is, that you do but take yourself off from my mistress.' Müller proposes *te tibi tolle*.

15.] 'Corporis socius est is, qui continuus comes lateri adhæret.'—*Kuinoel*. *dominum admitto*, in reference to the proverb κοινὰ τὰ τῶν φίλων.

17.] *Solum—uno*. You are the only man I would refuse, and the only thing I would refuse you is my Cynthia.

Ipse meas solus, quod nil est, æmulor umbras,
  Stultus, quod stulto sæpe timore tremo.
Una tamen causa est, qua crimina tanta remitto,
  Errabant multo quod tua verba mero.
Sed numquam vitæ fallet me ruga severæ:
  Omnes jam norunt, quam sit amare bonum.
Lynceus ipse meus seros insanit amores.
  Solum te nostros lætor adire deos.
Quid tua Socraticis tibi nunc sapientia libris
  Proderit, aut rerum dicere posse vias?
Aut quid †Erechthei tibi prosunt carmina lecta?
  Nil juvat in magno vester amore senex.
Tu satius †memorem Musis imitere Philetam,
  Et non inflati somnia Callimachi.

19.] 'I am jealous even of my own unsubstantial shadow; much more so of a friend who, though no longer young, is still flesh and blood.' This use of *æmulor* with an accusative is worth attention.—*solus*, *i.e.* when none else is near to be jealous of.

24.] *Jam norunt*, a satire, perhaps, on the results of philosophy, when philosophers themselves set the example of going astray.

25.] *Seros*. This word shows that Lynceus was advanced in life.—*nostros deos*, Venus and Cupid. 'My only consolation and hope of revenge is, that you are become a votary of my deities,' *i.e.* a lover at last, like myself.

27—8.] This distich explains 51—54. Lynceus was not only a poet, but a student of both moral and natural philosophy.

29.] *Erechthei*. This is the emendation of Hertzberg, who does not seem to have been aware that Heinsius had anticipated him. The Naples MS. gives *Erechti*, the MS. Gron. *Erethei*, with *vatis* for *lecta*; the ed. Rheg. *cretei*, and later copies *creteri* or *Erethei*. Pucci reads *eritei*, but conjectures *Tirtei* (Tyrtæi). Lachmann, with Scaliger, edits *Lenæi*, Jacob and Kuinoel *Cretæi*, supposing the word to mean Epimenides of Crete. Both these are very improbable. *Erechtheus* is taken to mean *Atheniensis*, that is, Æschylus. The objection to this is, that *Æschyleo cothurno* occurs inf. 41. Müller reads *ope Chii*, on his own conjecture, 'the epics of the Chian bard,' Homer. *Vester senex* in the next verse is not inappropriately applied to the same poet; and Hertzberg well refers to Arist. *Ran.* 1053 as a witness to his avowed indifference to the emotions of love. *Vester* however should rather apply to the philosophers generally.

31.] There is much reason to fear that this verse is corrupt. The copies give either *memorem Musis* or *Musis memorem*. Hertzberg adopts Scaliger's correction, *Musis meliorem*, but proposes a better himself, 'Tu socius Musis Mimnermi imitere Philetam.' Whether *satius* can be used adverbially for *potius*, does not seem certain: the dictionaries however attribute the usage to Cicero. Hertzberg and Müller evade the difficulty by explaining it *satius est te imitari*, i.e. *satius est ut imitere*. Cf. iii. 3, 19. Perhaps the suggestion of Pucci is worth some attention, that *memorem* is used passively for *curam Musarum*. Something similar is *docilis sonus*, v. 2, 63. Philetas *may* have spoken of himself as Μούσαις μεμναμένος, or used some similar expression constructed with the dative. Müller gives *tuus* for *Musis*, on the ingenious correction of Eldik. Keil, *Tu Latiis Memorem Musis* &c., which has but slight probability.

32.] *Non inflati*. The epithet is perhaps intended as a defence of his favourite poet against the common and not altogether unjust charge of being inclined to bombast. Compare ii. 1, 40, 'Intonet *angusto pectore* Callimachus,' which expresses precisely the same idea. The lost epic, *Aitia*, is called *somnia*, 'quia Callimachus finxerat, somniasse aliquando se intervenisse Musis, quae postea literis mandavit.'—*Barth.*

Nam cursus licet Ætoli referas Acheloi,
  Fluxerit ut magno fractus amore liquor,
Atque etiam ut Phrygio fallax Mæandria campo
  Errat et ipsa suas decipit unda vias,
Qualis et Adrasti fuerit vocalis Arion
  Tristis ad Archemori funera victor equus;
Amphiaraëæ non prosunt fata quadrigæ,
  Aut Capanei magno grata ruina Jovi.
Desine et Æschyleo componere verba cothurno,
  Desine, et ad molles membra resolve choros.
Incipe jam angusto versus includere torno,

33.] *Cursus.* The Naples MS. with some inferior copies give *recursus*, but the reading is not deserving of much consideration. Barth has *non cursus licet*, Kuinoel *non cursus* &c., *non* being from Scaliger. But none of them understood the poet's meaning. 'You may, if you please,' (he says) 'imitate Callimachus, and take up the same mythical narratives which he treated of in his *Αἴτια* (viz. 33—8), but your present tragedy of the Seven against Thebes will not tend to alleviate your distress' (v. 39).

34.] *Fluxerit.* So all the MSS. He alludes to the defeat of the river by Hercules (*μνηστὴρ γὰρ ἦν μοι ποταμός*, Ἀχελῷον λέγω, *Trach.* 9), and to the consequent reduction of speed in the vanquished current. Some, as Barth and Weise, read *luxerit*.

35.] *Ut errat.* On the construction see i. 2. 9. The river Mæander is mentioned, as Hertzberg plausibly suggests, in connexion with Hercules' enslavement to Omphale, Ovid, *Her.* ix. 55.—*decipit suas vias*, an elegant expression applied to a winding stream which continually thwarts its own progress by returning back upon itself.

37.] The order of the words is, 'Et qualis tristis victor ad Archemori funera fuerit Arion, vocalis ille equus Adrasti.' As a victor is usually *lætus*, *ovans*, so here Arion was *tristis*, because the games at which he conquered were instituted in memory of Archemorus, son of Lycurgus, king of Nemea. Lachmann and Weise, with Barth, read *tristia*. This horse is said to have carried Adrastus safe out of the battle-field (Apollodor. iii. 6, 8. See also iii. § 4), and to have been gifted with human voice and more than human foresight. He is called 'præsagus Arion' by Statius, *Theb.* vi. 424, &c. where a long account of his conduct in a race is given.

39.] This verse has suffered from the clumsy attempts of metrical transcribers. The MSS. prefix *non* to *Amphiareae*, which is variously written. The copyists evidently supposed its scansion was the same as *Amphionia*, i. 9, 10. Barth and Kuinoel give *A. nil prosunt*, &c. Jacob *A. haud prosunt tibi*, and Hertzberg *A. haud prosunt fata*, leaving the hiatus to take care of itself. In the pentameter the MS. Gron. omits *magno*, which error has given rise to some extravagant conjectures, among which that of Lachmann must be enumerated. He edits the distich thus:—

> 'Non magnæ Amphiaraëæ prosunt tibi fata
> Quadrigæ, aut Capanei grata ruina Jovi.'

Müller gives a verse hardly less inharmonious, 'non prosint tibi quadrigæ fata Amphiareæ.' Keil, 'non magnæ Amphiareæ tibi fata quadrigæ prosint, aut' &c. In all probability, the verse requires no other alteration than to restore *non* to its place after *Amphiareae*.

41.] *Æschyleo.* The quantity of this word is to be remarked. The Naples MS. has *aeschileo*, whence Scaliger conjectured *desine Achilleo*, and so it is printed in Barth's edition.—*resolve*, 'unbend your limbs, *i. e.* your stiff attitude, to take part in the pliant dance.'

43.] *Angusto torno*, 'a limited theme,' *i. e.* one of love, and not of heroic deeds, which present so wide and varied a field. 'Quod angustiori elegiacæ poesis spiritui accommodatius est.'—*Hertzberg*. Similarly, but more literally, Barth; 'elegos scribere, ubi singulis distichis sententia includitur.' —*tornus* is an instrument for bringing objects to a true circular outline, by which they are said *includi*. Müller reads [illegible], which introduces a different metaphor.

Inque tuos ignes, dure poeta, veni.
Tu non Antimacho, non tutior ibis Homero:
Despicit et magnos recta puella deos.
Sed non ante gravi taurus succumbit aratro,
Cornua quam validis haeserit in laqueis;
Nec tu tam duros per te patieris amores;
Trux tamen a nobis ante domandus eris.
Harum nulla solet rationem quaerere mundi,
Nec cur fraternis Luna laboret equis,
Nec si post Stygias aliquid restabimus undas,
Nec si consulto fulmina missa tonent.
Aspice me, cui parva domi fortuna relicta est,
Nullus et antiquo Marte triumphus avi,
Ut regnem mixtas inter conviva puellas

44.] *Durus poeta* is opposed to *mollis* (v. 42) as epic or tragic is contrasted with elegiac verse. Compare ii. 1, 2, and 41; and note on i. 9, 13, *inf.* iv. 1, 19—20.

45.] Antimachus of Colophon was a celebrated epic poet, who is said to have edited a Homer, and to have written a Thebaid and also an elegy on the death of one Lyde, his mistress. Ovid, *Trist.* i. 6, 1, 'Nec tantum Clario Lyde dilecta poetae.' He was contemporary with Aristophanes. Hertzberg rightly gives the sense, which some editors have greatly misunderstood: 'Tu, quamvis magnus poeta, eadem quae maximi ante te passi sunt ne opera evitaturum esse. Nam Homerum et Antimachum, utrumque amoris vinculis irretitum fuisse, Hermesianax auctor est.' The argument is, 'Think not to conquer your love by pursuing epic and heroic themes, on the vain notion that epic-poets are superior to love.'

46.] *Recta puella*, i. e. puella rectae figurae. Cf. iii. 9, 25, '*Recta puella* est ita comparata, ut recte et vere eo nomine digna sit,—*une fille comme il faut*.'—*Hertz.* '*deos*, nedum poetas heroicos et philosophos, qualis tu es.'—*Kuinoel*: who wrongly explains *recta* by *superba*.—*despicit* is *καταφρονεῖ*, facile vincit.

47.] 'But, as the sturdy bull is not brought to the yoke without being first caught and thrown by the lasso, so you, inexperienced and restive in love, must take a preparatory lesson from me,' (55). Kuinoel has *artis*, which is not improbable, in v. 50.

49.] *Per te*, sponte tua, sine alterius disciplina.—*trux tamen*, i. e. quamvis modo captus ferocias, tamen jugum per me tibi imponendum erit.

51—4.] The meaning is, 'you must not expect to captivate your mistress by your philosophy.' But it is not quite clear to what *harum* refers. If, as most commentators think, the mistresses of the above-mentioned poets are meant, *solet* for *solebat* is awkwardly used. Müller transposes 51—4 to follow 46, apparently acquiescing in this view. Probably he means *harum*, *inter quas ego regno*, v. 57, and he points to his own success as an elegiac poet, and how *he* is toasted by the fair, though without wealth, or philosophic wit, by way of exhorting Lynceus to follow his example. Compare with the present passage iv. 5, 25—46, and especially Tibullus, ii. 4, 17—20.

53.] This verse also is corrupt in the MSS., which vary between *restaverit undas* and *restabit erumnas*. In the Naples MS. the verse stops short with *restabit*. Hertzberg has admitted Jacob's conjecture, *aliquis sedet arbiter undas*, comparing iv. 19, 27, 'Minos sedet arbiter Orci.' Müller, following Haupt, reads *aliquid restabimus*, i. e. si aliquid de nobis post mortem restabit.' Prof. Munro ingeniously conjectures 'aliquis re est arbiter,' i. e. *berus*, 'if there really is a judge of the nether world.' Lachmann and Barth give *aliquid restabit ad undas*, in which case *post* must be taken for *posthac*.

54.] *Consulto*. Opposed to *fortuito*.

55.] See note on v. 1, 127, and iii. 16, 21.

Hoc ego, quo tibi nunc elevor, ingenio.
Me juvet hesternis positum languere corollis,
Quem tetigit jactu certus ad ossa Deus:
Actia Vergilium custodis litora Phœbi,
Cæsaris et fortes dicere posse rates:
Qui nunc Æneæ Trojani suscitat arma,
Jactaque Lavinis mœnia litoribus.
Cedite Romani scriptores, cedite Graii:
Nescio quid majus nascitur Iliade.
Tu canis umbrosi subter pineta Galæsi
Thyrsin, et attritis Daphnin arundinibus,
Utque decem possint corrumpere mala puellas,
Missus et impressis hædus ab uberibus.
Felix, qui viles pomis mercaris amores!
Huic licet ingratæ Tityrus ipse canat.
Felix, intactum Corydon qui tentat Alexin

58.] *Ego* is emphatic, 'how *I* hold role' &c. Barth and Weise read *hoc, ego quo* &c.

59—61.] 'Be it mine to spend whole nights at the banquet, and to lie at my ease crowned with the flowers of yesterday's feast; let others, if they prefer it, write epic poems in praise of Cæsar.'

61.] *Virgilio* MS. Naples and ed. Rheg., and so Jacob, who understands *fas est*.

63.] *Trojanaque* Jacob with the MS. Gron. The rest have *Trojani*. From the words *nunc suscitat* it is clear that Virgil was known to be engaged on the composition of the Æneid, which is generally believed to have been commenced B.C. 27. The date of this elegy is B.C. 24.

65—6.] These often-quoted lines refer to the expectation which was generally entertained of the surpassing merits of the forthcoming Æneid. It is very probable that some parts of it had already been heard at public recitations.

67.] With this verse commences a difficult yet very interesting and beautiful part of the poem. There is some truth in Lachmann's complaint that the sense is incoherent. *Tu* is, of course, addressed to Virgil, not to Lynceus, and he appears to mean, 'Not that Virgil confines himself to epic poetry, since he has written not only distinctively amorous poems in the Bucolics, but also others (the Georgics) which occupy a kind of middle place between the two, and are adapted for all tastes' (v. 81—2). Thus *tu canis* will mean 'etiam tu, Virgili, non solum Philetas et Callimachus.' The inference therefore is, that Lynceus might attempt more than one style with the like success.—*Galæsus* was a river near Tarentum, called by Horace 'dulce pellitis ovibus flumen,' *Od.* ii. 6, 10, where Virgil was then residing. See *Georgic* iv. 126. The particular allusions in the following lines are to *Eclog.* v. and vii., iii. 70, and perhaps ii. 34.

69.] *Puellas.* The 'aurea mala decem,' *Ecl.* iii. 70, were in fact sent by Menalcas to his favourite boy. Compare Lucret. v. 964, 'vel pretium (amoris) glandes atque arbuta vel pira lecta.' Lachmann reads *puellam*. But by using the plural our poet means to apply a particular gift to the influence of presents generally. In v. 71, *felix* &c. is addressed to Menalcas, and so returns, as it were, to the point.

70.] *Impressis*, non pressis, πημάλαστοις. Compare *immoror*, i.e. non moror, iv. 8, 21.

72.] *Huic.* Galatea, the mistress of Tityrus, *Ecl.* i. 32. The sense is, 'happy those who by a few apples or a tune on the pipe can soften the anger of their favourites.'—*licet canat* is for *canere possit*, cf. 83; and *ipse* implies that he does it in person, while others, who are *exclusi*, can only *send* verses &c. Cf. i. 12, 15. Lachmann reads *huic, licet ingratæ, Tityrus ipse canens*.

Agricolæ domini carpere delicias!
Quamvis ille sua lassus requiescat avena,
Laudatur facilis inter Hamadryadas.
Tu canis Ascræi veteris præcepta poetæ,
Quo seges in campo, quo viret uva jugo.
Tale facis carmen, docta testudine quale
Cynthius impositis temperat articulis.
Non tamen hæc ulli venient ingrata legenti,
Sive in amore rudis, sive peritus erit.
Nec minor his animis, aut si minor, ore canorus
Anseris indocto carmine cessit olor.
Hæc quoque perfecto ludebat Iasone Varro,
Varro Leucadiæ maxima flamma suæ.
Hæc quoque lascivi cantarunt scripta Catulli,
Lesbia quis ipsa notior est Helena.
Hæc etiam docti confessa est pagina Calvi,

74.] *Delicias domini* is borrowed from *Ecl.* ii. 2.—*carpere Alexin*, as *carpere fructum* &c.

75.] *Ille.* Another sudden transition. 'Though Virgil should throw aside the bucolic reed, he gains equal reputation by singing of forest trees,' *i.e.* by the Georgics. He pleases the compliant wood-nymphs, and therefore knows how to win woman's favour. The following distich is added to make the allusion to the Georgics more definite and intelligible.—*tu*, *i.e.* O Virgil.

81.] See on v. 67.

83.] By a witty application of the name of a bad poet, Anser, to the lines of Virgil, *Ecl.* ix. 35, 'Nam neque adhuc Vario videor, nec dicere Cinna Digna, sed argutos inter strepere anser olores,' Propertius pays his friend an elegant compliment. A goose as opposed to a swan (the bird of song: see on *Æsch. Agam.* 1419), is as a bad poet compared with a good one; hence *olor*, Virgil, is said not to be silenced by the unskilful verse of Anser. The passage is obscure, and Müller, who marks it with an *obelus*, says 'hæc nondum cuiquam expedire contigit.' The sense is thus given by Hertzberg after Weichert, though the latter reads *animis*, *aut si minor*. 'Nec minor est his, *i.e.* Eclogis et Georgicis, Virgilii spiritus, aut si minor est, non tamen hic olor ore canorus cessit indocto carmini Anseris, *i.e.* non tamen ab Ansere, indocto carminis auctore, superatus est.' Hertzberg adds, '*hi animi* animi erant, qui his carminibus apparent.' Barth and Kuinoel read *at minor*. The best copies give *sim minor*. The Naples MS. omits *minor ore canorus*. Lachmann has transposed this distich to follow v. 66. The reservation implied in *aut si minor* is well explained in the brief words of Hertzberg: 'ut concessa majore carminis heroici laude, tamen his etiam Virgilii lusibus aliquam laureolam relinqui dicatur.—The poet Anser is mentioned by Ovid, *Trist.* ii. 435, 'Cinna quoque his comes est, Cinnaque procacior Anser, Et leve Cornifici, parque Catonis opus,' where *procacior* shows, as do the other passages where the unfortunate name occurs, that his contemporaries delighted to banter the luckless owner of it.—On *carmine* see iv. 6, 24.

85.] *Hæc quoque*, *i.e.* the subject of love.—*Varro*, called *Atacinus* from having been born near the river Atax in Gallia Narbonensis, B.C. 82, translated the Argonautica of Apollonius. Ovid appears to allude to him, *Trist.* ii. 439, 'Is quoque, Phasiacas Argo qui duxit in undas, Non potuit Veneris furta tacere suæ.' Hor. *Sat.* i. 10, 46, 'experto frustra Varrone Atacino.' Hence *perfecto Iasone* means, 'carmine de Iasone absoluto.' Perhaps indeed the poem was entitled *Jason*.

89.] *Confessa est*, 'the same *confession* of devoted attachment is found in the writings of Calvus, when he sang the fate of his poor dear Quintilia.' He was a friend of Catullus: see on iii. 17, 4.

Cum caneret miseræ funera Quintiliæ.
Et modo formosa quam multa Lycoride Gallus
Mortuus inferna vulnera lavit aqua!
Cynthia quin etiam versu laudata Properti,
Hos inter si me ponere Fama volet.

91.] *Modo.* Cornelius Gallus the poet (a different person from the Gallus of i. 21, &c.) killed himself in the year 728. 'He not only wrote,' says the poet, 'but he even died for love.' He had been appointed by Augustus to the prefecture of Egypt, but fell under suspicion of mal-administration and treason. This is the Gallus who has furnished the subject of Becker's celebrated narrative of that name. Ovid, *Amor.* iii. 9, 64, 'Sanguinis atque animæ prodige, Galle, tuæ.' Elsewhere these poets are mentioned together, as *Art. Am.* iii. 333—6; *Amor.* i. 15, 21—30.—*formosa Lycoride* may be called a Propertian ablative absolute, 'cum ei esset formosa Lycoris.' Lachmann is certainly wrong in construing *mortuus Lycoride*. There is some probability in Wakker's conjecture, *qui multa Lycoride passus*, since the poet may well have suppressed the name in consideration of his melancholy end. In *vulnera* (*i. e.* amoris) there is no allusion to that event.

93.] *Cynthia.* Either *nota erit* must be supplied from v. 88, or *laudata erit* was intended. Either ellipse is sufficiently harsh.

PROPERTII

LIBER QUARTUS.

I.

CALLIMACHI Manes et Coi sacra Philetæ,
  In vestrum, quæso, me sinite ire nemus.
Primus ego ingredior puro de fonte sacerdos
  Itala per Graios orgia ferre choros.
Dicite, quo pariter carmen tenuastis in antro?
  Quove pede ingressi? quamve bibistis aquam?

This book comprises elegies written A.U.C. 731—2. The historical proofs will be noticed as they occur. The subject of the present elegy is one which the poet repeatedly treats of, and shortly below, El. 3, viz. his reasons for adhering to elegiac composition, and declining to attempt heroic strains: from the former alone he looks for an immortality of fame.

1.] *Sacra.* He represents himself as a priest, and consistently with the metaphor addresses the sacred rites and sacred grove of Philetas of Cos, asking to be allowed admittance thereto. Compare v. 6, 1, 'Sacra facit vates; sint ora faventia sacris.' Hor. *Od.* iii. 1, 3, 'carmina non prius audita Musarum sacerdos Virginibus puerisque canto.' There really is nothing in the expression to require the pages of notes which the commentators have devoted to its explanation. Instead of saying, 'O Philetas, admit me to your sacred rites,' he changes the ordinary expression to, 'Ye sacred rites of Philetas, admit me to your grove,' *i.e.* to the grove in which you are celebrated. Some have attempted to explain *sacra* by *Manes*—a mere tautology. By invoking the 'Spirit of Callimachus' he shows that the rites meant are those offered to the dead.

3.] *Ingredior.* He uses this word in reference to *nemus.* The infinitive in the next verse may be compared with *dat videre*, i. 1, 12, 'I am the first who have entered that grove for the purpose of introducing Roman poetry, from a source not yet made turbid by the crowd of ordinary poets, to take its place among Greek compositions.' In *orgia* and *choros* the metaphor is continued from *sacra*, v. 1. *Per* is not unfrequently used for *inter*, as i. 21, 7; iv. 14, 5; v. 4, 20. Hertzberg thinks *Itala per* must be joined; but the ambiguity of this is too great to be attributed to Propertius, even though he does occasionally misplace his words in a very awkward manner, as remarked on iii. 17, 35. Similarly inf. El. 4, 18, 'subter captos arma sedere duces,' for *subter arma.* *Primus* is evidently used with a consciousness that he can rightly claim that honour. The fact is that Catullus and Tibullus, who preceded Propertius, cannot compete with him in this respect. Catullus wrote but few elegiacs, and those of Tibullus are not derived from any acquaintance with the pedantic Alexandrine learning of the Augustan age.

5.] *Carmen tenuastis, i.e.* carmen molle ac tenue fecistis. 'To spin a *fine* verse,' or rather, 'to spin it fine,' as opposed to the rough and bold sounds of the heroic foot, seems more naturally the poet's idea than *levigare, polire,* which Hertzberg attributes to him from *tenui pumice* in v. 8.

6.] *Quo pede ingressi.* The usual explanation of this passage, *dextro an laevo,* which is defended by Becker, Gallus, p. 57,

Ah valeat, Phœbum quicumque moratur in armis!
  Exactus tenui pumice versus eat,
Quo me Fama levat terra sublimis, et a me
  Nata coronatis Musa triumphat equis,
Et mecum in curru parvi vectantur Amores,
  Scriptorumque meas turba secuta rotas.
Quid frustra missis in me certatis habenis?
  Non datur ad Musas currere lata via.
Multi, Roma, tuas laudes annalibus addent,
  Qui finem imperii Bactra futura canent:
Sed, quod pace legas, opus hoc de monte Sororum
  Detulit intacta pagina nostra via.
Mollia, Pegasides, date vestro serta poetæ:

(English ed. 1849) is rejected by Hertzberg as 'absurdum, ac ne Latinum quidem.' Barth also prefers to understand, 'quam viam, quam rationem inieritis?' Juvenal's *quid tam dextro pede concipis* &c. (x. 5) is well known to allude to the popular superstition of 'putting the best leg foremost,' or entering a place with the right foot first. The objection, that this would have *utro pede*, is hypercritical in a poet like Propertius. It is not, however, a very appropriate question to put to successful and celebrated poets, 'did you enter the grotto of the Muses with the right or the left foot first?' for the former would be understood as a matter of course. The words may indeed mean, 'quo pedibus ingressi estis?' The general idea is evidently this: 'tell me where you sate, and from what inspiring fount you drank, that I may closely follow your example.'

7.] *Phœbum moratur in armis*, 'employs his genius on heroic verse.' The epithet *tenui* in the next verse applies virtually to *versus*, and gives the sense of *mollis*: see on ii. 1, 41. The application of *pumice* to the external finishing of the parchment is borrowed to express the careful composition of the verses. Hence also *eat*, in allusion to publication.

9.] *Quo me levat*. 'Let that verse be elegiac *by which* fame is to raise me to the triumphal car.'—The indicatives which follow *eat* are rather irregular. He seems to have meant, 'ille versus, qui me levaturus est, et per quem Musa triumphat, eat,' &c.

10.] *Musa a me nata*, 'a style of poetry originating from me.' Lachmann reads *nota*, an unfortunate change.

12.] *Rotas*. He continues the simile of a triumphal procession, in which he represents himself as the victor in the chariot, the Loves as his children borne with him (a custom which Hertzberg proves from Livy, xlv. 40), and the inferior poets following him. Sueton. *Tib.* § 6, 'Dehinc pubescens (Tiberius) Actiaco triumpho currum Augusti comitatus est sinisteriore funali equo, quum Marcellus, Octaviæ filius, dexteriore veheretur.'

13.] *Certatis*, i. e. O scriptorum turba. He suddenly changes the metaphor to the race-course. *Lata via* implies the attempt to pass his chariot. 'The road to poetic fame is narrow; you cannot get before me without a collision.'

15.] 'There will be no lack of poets to sing the military glories of Rome: I therefore prefer to follow a new track, and to write for the amusement of my countrymen in times of peace.' It is clear that *tuas laudes*, i. e. bellicas virtutes, is opposed to *pace*, and *multi* to *intacta via*. 'But *this* work, to be read in a time of peace, my Muse hath brought down from Helicon by a route as yet untrodden.'—*Bactra futura*, the expedition against the Parthians undertaken A.U.C. 734, B.C. 20, was contemplated even at this time: see inf. El. 4.

19.] The usual antithesis between *mollis* and *dura*, elegiac and epic, has already been pointed out, iii. 26, 44. So *hirsuta corona*, of the archaic language of Ennius, v. 1, 86. The more common idiom is *facere ad*, as Ovid, *Her.* xv. 8, 'Non facit ad lacrimas barbitos ulla meas.' But the dative closely represents the English use, 'will not do for my head.' Compare v. 1, 61.

Non faciet capiti dura corona meo.
At mihi quod vivo detraxerit invida turba,
Post obitum duplici fenore reddit Honos.
Omnia post obitum fingit majora vetustas:
Majus ab exequiis nomen in ora venit.
Nam quis equo pulsas abiegno nosceret arces,
Fluminaque Hæmonio cominus isse viro,
Idæum Simoenta Jovis cunabula parvi,
Hectora per campos ter maculasse rotas?
Deïphobumque Helenumque et Pulydamantas in armis?
Qualemcumque Parin vix sua nosset humus.
Exiguo sermone fores nunc Ilion, et tu
Troja, bis Œtæi numine capta dei.
Nec non ille tui casus memorator Homerus
Posteritate suum crescere sensit opus;
Meque inter seros laudabit Roma nepotes:

21.] An ellipse must be mentally supplied. '(True it is, that detractors are never wanting when a poet attempts a new and unbeaten track;) yet' &c.

23.] The *prospective* use of *vetustas* is remarkable. It illustrates the well-known ἀρχαῖον γάνος, *olim antiquum futurum*, Æsch. *Ag.* 579. The sense is, 'when poems become old, they are always more valued than when new.'

25.] 'For, (if poetry did not survive to late posterity), who at the present day would have heard of Troy taken by the wooden horse, or the fight between the river Xanthus and Achilles?'—*pulsas arces*, because some writers considered the δουράτεος ἵππος to have been used for battering the walls, as indeed the Greek epithet not unnaturally implies; or rather, perhaps, it was contrived as a pent-house for concealing and covering the ram. See Pausan. i. 23.

27.] *Jovis cunabula*. There is a confusion between the mount Ida of Crete, fabled as the birth-place of Jove, and the Ida of Troas. Lachmann in a long note, not very creditable to his critical judgment, condemns the whole verse. The legends of the Cretans and the Phrygians probably had the same eastern origin, and therefore were naturally mixed up together, as Hertzberg shows that in fact they frequently were. It is singular that the words *cunabula parvi* are omitted in the Naples MS. Probably the scribe could not decipher them in his copy, and had intended to supply the omission afterwards. See on iii. 26, 83.

28.] *Per*. Lachmann, Barth, and Kuinoel, read *ter*, the conjecture of Fruter. But it is easy to supply *tractum*; 'aut Hectora, ter tractum per campos, rotas currus maculasse.'

29.] The MSS. give *Polydamantas* (more or less correctly written) *in armis*. Lachmann and Jacob read *Polydamanta, et in armis* &c. Kuinoel and Barth *P. sine armis*. There is no reason for altering the vulgata. The plural seems used to express the Trojan heroes generally. *In armis* is a common use for *armis indutus*. See v. 2, 28, 'Corbis in imposito pondere messor eram.'—The form *Pulydamas* is to be preferred, as representing the Greek Πουλυδάμας. Persius, *Sat.* 1, 4, 'Ne mihi Polydamas et Troiades Labeonem prætulerint.'

30.] *Vix*, *i.e.* nisi carminibus celebratus esset.

32.] *Bis capta*. 'Primum ab Hercule ipso, sub Laomedonte, qui ei equos promissos denegarat, deinde sub Priamo, ope sagittarum Herculis, quæ Philoctetæ obtigerant.'—*Kuinoel*.

34.] I have removed the full stop usually placed at the end of this verse. The sense appears to be, 'both Homer gained greater renown after the lapse of time, and I shall in like manner be held in repute by future generations.'

Illum post cineres auguror ipse diem.
Ne mea contempto lapis indicet ossa sepulcro
Provisum est, Lycio vota probante deo.
Carminis interea nostri redeamus in orbem,
Gaudeat ut solito tacta puella sono.

II.

Orphea detinuisse feras et concita dicunt
Flumina Threïcia sustinuisse lyra;
Saxa Cithæronis Thebas agitata per artem
Sponte sua in muri membra coisse ferunt;
Quin etiam, Polypheme, fera Galatea sub Ætna
Ad tua rorantes carmina flexit equos.
Miremur, nobis et Baccho et Apolline dextro,
Turba puellarum si mea verba colit?
Quod non Tænariis domus est mihi fulta columnis,

36.] *Illum diem*, *i.e.* illam vitam. The MS. Gron. has *eam*, which might stand by a lax use for *futuram esse*.

38.] *Provisum est*, sc. a me, votis Apollini susceptis et ab eo probatis. He alludes, as Barth thinks, to his poems being admitted into the Palatine library.

39.] *Orbem*, 'routine.' 'Ita redit, ut cum ab initio puellis amantibus potius placere quam magno heroum facta celebrando famam quaerere se professus esset, postquam inde a v. 21, alio digressa est oratio, puellam suam sono solito delectaturum se promittat.' Hertzberg, *Quaest.* p. 65.—The Naples MS. gives *insolito*, whence Lachmann, with Burmann, reads *in solito sono*. But on *gaudeat in puero*, II. 4, 28, which they adduce in defence of this reading, see the note. See also v. 8, 63.

II. He speaks of the influence of poetry over the female mind, and attributes his own success not to any wealth or splendour, but solely to his verses. This elegant little elegy is connected with the preceding by Lachmann, and even Jacob inclines to follow him, on the authority of Muretus. So also Keil and Müller. The break in most of the MSS. is at v. 39, of the preceding.

1.] *Detinuisse*, 'to have arrested,' 'amused,' 'kept fixed to the spot.' Kuinoel has *Orphea, te lenisse feras* &c. Lachmann, *Orphea delenisse*; Müller, *delenisse*; others, *Orphea, te tenuisse*. But the good copies agree in the reading in the text.—*sustinuisse* is, 'tenuisse ne deorsum fluerent,' 'to have kept back.' Ovid, *Fast.* v. 660, 'cursum sustinuistis, aquae.'

3.] *Per artem*, *i.e.* non vi tracta, sed Amphionis lyra delenita. Compare 'Amphioniae moenia flere lyrae,' i. 9, 10.—*agitata*, coacta, ad Thebas convecta; or *ἀγερθέντα*, perhaps, implying the frequent repetition of the act.

5.] See Theocr. *Id.* vi. where however no mention is made of ocean steeds. Probably therefore the poet has other Greek authorities in view, who made even the sea to have yielded up its denizens to hear the magic strains. These imaginary sea-monsters, half fish and half horse, are commonly represented in the train of ocean deities. Cf. *Georg.* iv. 388.

7.] On the poetical connexion of Bacchus with Apollo, see on v. 6, 76, and iii. 22, 36.

9.] *Quod non* &c. 'As for the fact that,' &c. Perhaps (as *si non* would be simpler in this sense,) we should read *non quod*, i. e. *non eo colunt quia* &c. It is easy however to supply an ellipse, such as *hoc quidem nihil est*.

Nec camera auratas inter eburna trabes;
Nec mea Phæacas æquant pomaria silvas,
Non operosa rigat Martius antra liquor:
At Musæ comites, et carmina cara legenti,
Et defessa choris Calliopea meis.
Fortunata, meo si qua es celebrata libello!
Carmina erunt formæ tot monumenta tuæ.
Nam neque Pyramidum sumptus ad sidera ducti,
Nec Jovis Elei cœlum imitata domus,
Nec Mausolei dives fortuna sepulcri
Mortis ab extrema conditione vacant.
Aut illis flamma aut imber subducet honores,
Annorum aut ictu pondera victa ruent;
At non ingenio quæsitum nomen ab ævo
Excidet: ingenio stat sine morte decus.

10.] *Cameræ eburnæ.* The sunken panels of white stucco forming rectangular compartments between the gilded beams, otherwise called *lacunaria*. Kuinoel refers to Pliny, *N. H.* xxxiii. 3, to prove that these were actually overlaid with ivory. See also Hor. *Od.* ii. 18, 1, 'Non ebur neque aureum Mea renidet in domo lacunar,' where however *ebur* does not necessarily apply to the ceiling. The Tænarian marble, according to Becker (Gallus, p. 16), was *verde antico*, or green porphyry.

11.] *Nec mea pomaria* &c. 'And that I have no orchards to vie with the Phæacian plantations.' Hertzberg well remarks, that *mea* does not imply that the poet really possessed any orchards at all.—The MSS. and early edd. have *Phæacias*. If *Phæaæ silvæ* be the nominative, the final syllable should be short. It appears therefore to be from *Phæacus*.

12.] *Operosa antra.* 'Artificial grottos.' The water from the aqueduct built by Q. Martius Rex, who was prætor B.C. 144, some arches of which are still standing, was held in especial esteem for its clearness. It was supplied to private houses and gardens by leaden pipes, as we are perhaps justified in inferring from a curious passage in Ovid, *Met.* iv. 121. To this Strabo seems to allude, lib. v. cap. iii. *τοσοῦτον δ' ἐστὶ τὸ εἰσαγόμενον ὕδωρ διὰ τῶν ὑδραγωγείων, ὥστε ποταμοὺς διὰ τῆς πόλεως καὶ τῶν ὑπονόμων ῥεῖν· ἅπασαν δὲ οἰκίαν σχεδὸν δεξαμενὰς καὶ σίφωνας καὶ κρουνοὺς ἔχειν ἀφθόνους.* Cf. Hor. *Epist.* i. 10, 20; Martial, *Ep.* vi. 42, 18, and ix. 18, 6; Tac. *Ann.* xiv. 22.

13.] *Cara.* Jacob gives *grata* from the MS. Groning.

15.] *Est* Hertzberg and Lachmann with the Naples and Groning. MSS. The others give *es* from Puccl. Cynthia is obviously meant under the indefinite *si qua*.

18.] *Cœlum imitata*, *i.e.* bespangled with stars.

19.] The tomb of Mausolus, king of Caria, erected by his surviving queen, Artemisia, at Halicarnassus, B.C. 353, was celebrated as one of the seven wonders of the world. Though partly recovered by modern research, under the care of Mr. Newton, its overthrow, by an earthquake or by human violence, verifies the poet's prediction.

23.] *Ab ævo.* The preposition is added because *excidet* is equivalent to *extinguetur*, and *ævum* is regarded as the agent rather than the instrument. In the same way the Greeks say *πάσχειν τι ὑπό τινος.*

III.

Visus eram molli recubans Heliconis in umbra,
  Bellerophontei qua fluit humor equi,
Reges, Alba, tuos et regum facta tuorum,
  Tantum operis, nervis hiscere posse meis;
Parvaque iam magnis admoram fontibus ora,
  Unde pater sitiens Ennius ante bibit,
Et cecinit Curios fratres, et Horatia pila,
  Regiaque Æmilia vecta tropæa rate,
Victricesque moras Fabii, pugnamque sinistram
  Cannensem et versos ad pia vota deos,
Hannibalemque Lares Romana sede fugantes,

III. The poet pleads the injunctions of Apollo and the Muses for continuing to write elegies, and for not essaying heroic verse. Frequently as this theme is repeated, there is ever novelty and ingenuity in the treatment of it, which prevents sameness and monotony.

1.] *Visus eram*, *ἐδόκουν ἐμοί*, 'I had fancied myself able.' As the infinitive *posse*, v. 4, depends on this verb, the strict notion of *videbar mihi in somniis* seems scarcely applicable. We do not dream of a mere *possibility*, but of some action, though the action itself may be impossible. It may, indeed, be questioned if the title ordinarily prefixed to this elegy, 'Propertii somnium,' is correct. There is no indication throughout the poem that he intends to describe a dream. It is rather an allegory than a vision: while expatiating in the regions of poetry he had ventured to think himself capable of higher efforts, but received a rebuke from Apollo. The editors seem to attribute too much weight to Hesiod's narrative, that he became a poet while feeding his flocks on Helicon.

4.] *Tantum operis*, 'great as was the task.'

5.] For the common reading *tam* I have ventured to read *jam*, on account of *cum* inf. 13. 'Already I had essayed heroic subjects, when Phœbus rebuked me, and bade me turn to another kind of verse.' He had already tried historical poems, those in the fifth book being among the earliest in date. See on v. 1, introductory note.

8.] *Æmilia rate*. By a singular anachronism, pointed out by Hertzberg, the commentators have referred these words to the return of Lucius Æmilius Paullus, after the defeat of Perseus, king of Macedonia, in 486, (B.C. 167), whereas Ennius died B.C. 169, or nearly two years before that event. The allusion is therefore to the defeat of Demetrius, governor of the island of Pharos, in the Adriatic, by Lucius Æmilius Paullus the consul, B.C. 219. It may be remarked that we have here an authentic enumeration of some of the subjects on which Ennius wrote in his Roman Annals. But Keil and Müller read *cerni* for *cecinit*.—The short form *Curii* for Curiatii, the three champions of Alba, is said to occur only in this passage. For a theory of the meaning of the names see *Varronianus*, p. 76. 'The fight between the Horatii and Curiatii probably refers to a contest between the *κουρῆτες*, 'men of the *Curis*,' and wielders of the spear, or wearers of the helmet, and the *χερῆτες*, or 'handicraftsmen,' *i. e.* the lower order, in which contest, as usual, the latter succeeded in maintaining their just rights.' We may notice too *Horatia* used for *Horatiana*. So *Partha* for *Parthica*, inf. 4, 6.

9.] *Moras Fabii*, *i. e.* the policy of Q. Fabius Maximus, who obtained the agnomen of Cunctator in his contest with Hannibal.

10.] *Versos deos*. He alludes to the public supplications, by which it was believed that the gods diverted Hannibal from attacking Rome after the battle of Cannæ.

11.] *Lares*. Hertzberg shows from Varro that a Lar was called *Tutanus* from the supposed influence of his fraternity in keeping Hannibal away from the city.—*anseris voce*: the cackling of the geese in

Anseris et tutum voce fuisse Jovem;
Cum me Castalia speculans ex arbore Phœbus
Sic ait aurata nixus ad antra lyra:
Quid tibi cum tali, demens, est flumine? quis te
Carminis heroi tangere jussit opus?
Non hinc ulla tibi speranda est fama, Properti:
Mollia sunt parvis prata terenda rotis,
Ut tuus in scamno jactetur sæpe libellus,
Quem legat expectans sola puella virum.
Cur tua præscriptos evecta est pagina gyros?
Non est ingenii cymba gravanda tui.
Alter remus aquas, alter tibi radat arenas;
Tutus eris: medio maxima turba mari est.
Dixerat, et plectro sedem mihi monstrat eburno,
Qua nova muscoso semita facta solo est.
Hic erat affixis viridis spelunca lapillis,
Pendebantque cavis tympana pumicibus.

the Capitol, by which M. Manlius, consul B.C. 392, was aroused when it was attempted by the Gauls under Brennus.—*Jovem*, i. e. Jovis Capitolini templum.

13.] *Castalia.* The fountain, and perhaps grove, so called, were on Parnassus, not on Helicon. But Hertzberg rightly observes that the names of these sacred localities are indifferently used, as the narrative is only allegorical.—*ex arbore*, ex silva.—*ad antra*, prope ad, juxta. Apollo presented himself as watching my movements, sheltered by trees and leaning on his lute at the entrance of a sacred grot (γύαλον) concealed by bay-trees. And he pointed out a new retreat which the Muses were just adorning and furnishing for themselves and their votaries, inf. 33.

17.] *Non hinc.* Non ex eo loco quo nunc versaris. *Hinc* is from the edition of Volscus. The MSS. give *hic*.

18—20.] 'You must enter a smoother course, with less aspiring effort, and write ditties for the desultory reading of a forlorn mistress.'

21.] From the slight error (presuming it to be such) of the MSS. *præscripto evecta* for *præscriptos evecta*, which would, as a matter of course, be the cause of changing *gyros* into *gyro*, Lachmann, Jacob, Hertzberg, Keil, and Müller have ventured to enrich the Latin language with the otherwise unknown and improbable compound *erveho*. Lachmann's objection is futile, 'quis ita locutus est, *evehi gyros*, pro ex gyris, vel extra gyros?' The idiom is, in fact, very common, as *egredi flumen*, *evadere sylvas* &c. So *fines exire*, iv. 5, 37.—*gyros*, like *orbis*, iii. 1, 39, is the usual routine of composition. At the same time, allusion is made to the turnings of the race-course.

23.] *Alter remus* &c. Hug the shore in your course, and do not venture far out to sea, where the waters are raging.

27.] *Affixis lapillis.* Hertzberg well observes that the poet had in view the artificial grottos (*operosa antra*, supr. 2, 12) common in the gardens of the wealthy Romans. It may be suggested, that the Romans called volcanic rocks in general by the terms *pumex* and *silex*. In the cindery precipices of the Canary Islands, I have seen hundreds of natural caves of this description; whereas pumice-stone, properly so called, only occurs in isolated pieces or stratified beds. It is clear that we must understand Horace's 'Quæ nunc oppositis debilitat pumicibus mare Tyrrhenum,' *Od.* i. 11, 5, according to the above general explanation.—*tympana*, the Bacchic instrument, τύμπανον, the tambourine, was hanging on the walls of the cave, or from the vaulted roof.

Ergo Musarum et Sileni patris imago
  Fictilis, et calami, Pan Tegeæe, tui;
Et Veneris dominæ volucres, mea turba, columbæ
  Tingunt Gorgoneo punica rostra lacu;
Diversæque novem sortitæ rura puellæ
  Exercent teneras in sua dona manus.
Hæc hederas legit in thyrsos, hæc carmina nervis
  Aptat, at illa manu texit utraque rosam.
E quarum numero me contigit una dearum,—
  Ut reor a facie, Calliopea fuit:
Contentus niveis semper vectabere cycnis,
  Nec te fortis equi ducet ad arma sonus.
Nil tibi sit rauco præconia classica cornu
  Flare, nec Aonium cingere Marte nemus,
Aut quibus in campis Mariano prœlia signo
  Stent et Teutonicas Roma refringat opes:

29.] He describes the grotto as sacred to Pan, Silenus, the Muses, and Venus; the instruments of one, the terra-cotta image of another, and the doves of the last, respectively indicating the joint possessors.—*ergo* is used in a rare sense: 'conjeceram Musas tibi futuras: en vero ipsas' *Hertzberg*; 'and so in fact,' *i. e.* as might have been anticipated from the general appearance. Or perhaps for *deinde*, like *igitur* (*Varronianus*, p. 149). Lachmann reads *ergo hic Musarum*, and explains it of effigies or statues of the Muses made of terra-cotta. Müller adopts the rather ingenious, but surely unnecessary, corrections of Heins and Unger, *Orgia mustarum* (*mystarum*, μυστῶν).

31.] *Mea turba*, *i. e.* meæ deliciæ, mihi amatæ.—*Gorgoneo lacu*, Hippocrene; Pegasus having sprung from the Gorgon Medusa, whence he is called *Medusæus equus* by Ovid, *Fast.* v. 7. Allusion is probably made to a well-known classical design of doves drinking out of a basin.—*tingunt*, τέγγουσι, as elsewhere.—*punica rostra*, red or rose-coloured, Ovid, *Am.* ii. 6, 22. Euripides attributes to these birds φοινικοσκελεῖς χηλαί, *Ion*, v. 1207.

33.] *Diversæ*, χωρίς, each apart from the others.—*rura* here represent the different departments of poetry and fine art which the Muses cultivated; λειμῶνα Μουσῶν ἱερόν, Arist. *Ran.* 1300.—*in sua dona*, to prepare the different gifts for different classes of poets, *e. g.* the thyrsus for writers of dithyrambs, the crown of roses for elegiac authors.

38.] *A facie*, as if the name were from καλή and ὄψις.

39.] 'Recte cycnis vectum ideo fingi interpretes perspexerunt, quod ea avi Venus quoque in curribus utatur.'—*Hertz.*

41.] *Nil tibi sit.* 'Let it not be your part.' So the Greek occasionally use οὐδὲν and μηδὲν for οὐ and μή, Æsch. *Ag.* 1462. But in the following distich it bears a slightly different sense, 'Let it be nothing to you,' 'let it not concern you.'—*præconia classica*, *i. e.* navalium bellorum laudes.—*classica* is here used precisely as in 'classica bella,' ii. 1, 28. Barth has adopted *prætoria* from Beroaldus. For *flare* the MSS. give *flere*, which was first corrected by Dousa. Lachmann well refers to Martial, xiii. 3, 'Quantaque Pieria prœlia flare tuba;' but he is scarcely justified in saying of this distich, 'singula fere verba hic dubitationi obnoxia sunt.'—*cingere Marte nemus*, *i. e.* 'arma et bellum ipsum in poesin inferre, hujusque mollitiem strepitu dissono perdere.'—*Hertzberg*. 'To beset with armed force the Grove of the Muses' is a rather inflated way of saying 'to disturb its peacefulness by singing of wars.'

43—4.] Marius' defeat of the Cimbri and Teutones is alluded to, B.C. 102—1.

Barbarus aut Suevo perfusus sanguine Rhenus
 Saucia mœrenti corpora vectet aqua.
Quippe coronatos alienum ad limen amantes
 Nocturnæque canes ebria signa fugæ,
Ut per te clausas sciat excantare puellas,
 Qui volet austeros arte ferire viros.
Talia Calliope, lymphisque a fonte petitis
 Ora Philetæa nostra rigavit aqua.

IV.

Arma Deus Cæsar dites meditatur ad Indos,
 Et freta gemmiferi findere classe maris.
Magna, viri, merces: parat ultima terra triumphos;
 Tigris et Euphrates sub tua jura fluent.

45.] *Suevo.* The good copies give *aevo* or *saevo*. The error was corrected in some of the early editions. The event described is the victory over Ariovistus, the German chieftain, by Julius Cæsar, B.C. 58. See *Bell. Gall.* iv. 1. With *vectet* it seems that *quo* must be supplied, by a very harsh ellipse, from *quibus*, v. 43.

48.] *Ebria signa fugæ.* Hertzberg understands 'spolia ab ebrio amatore nocturnis rixis de puellis recepta;' Kuinoel and others explain it of the rout of the drunken serenaders by more sober rivals or by indignant husbands. Possibly this may have reference to the clever poem 'Disce quid Esquilias' &c. in v. 8, then perhaps completed among other juvenile performances. *Signa* may be referred to the torches and flowers left behind them in their flight.

49.] *Excantare* must be taken in its most literal sense, *cantando excire*, 'to sing them out of their locked apartments.'—*ferire* seems to have been the word conventionally applied to the deceiving a husband. Terence, *Phorm.* i. 1, 13. See v. 5, 44.

52.] *Philetæa aqua.* The sense is, she herself handed me a draught from the same spring whence Philetas had derived his inspiration.

IV. In this spirited elegy the poet predicts success to the expedition contemplated by Augustus against the Parthians A. U. C. 732, but not carried into effect till 734.

1.] *Ad Indos, i. e.* usque ad. Kuinoel wrongly explains it *adversus.*—*deus Cæsar.* See v. 11, 60. Flattery could go no further. Horace pays him the same extravagant, and even to a pagan, almost blasphemous compliment, *Ep.* ii. 1, 16. *Od.* iii. 3, 11, as does Ovid frequently. Such a *προληπτικὴ ἀποθέωσις* shows how deeply Rome was sunk in servility. The blame perhaps lay rather with Julius Cæsar, who permitted and encouraged such extravagant honours. Sueton. *Jul. Cæsar*, § 76, 'Ampliora etiam humano fastigio decerni sibi passus est,—templa, aras, simulacra juxta deos, pulvinar, flaminem, Lupercos, appellationem mensis e suo nomine.' Did he not borrow this from the Egyptian Ptolemies? This appears in fact to be the origin of the Roman *deification* proper, as distinct from 'hero-worship,' which was more nearly connected with devil-worship.

2.] *Gemmiferi maris.* The Indian ocean. See on i. 14, 12. Tibullus, ii. 2, 15, 'Nec tibi gemmarum quicquid felicibus Indis Nascitur, Eoi qua maris unda rubet.'

3.] *Viri.* He addresses and encourages those who were to take part in the expedition. Lachmann was the first to perceive that this was the vocative case. Others altered it to *viro*, supposing it the genitive.

4.] *Sub tua jura fluent.* Sub tuum imperium redigentur, O Auguste. The notion is, as expressed by the accusative, that the two rivers of the east shall unite their waters with the Tiber. See on iv. 9, 52. Nothing can be worse than the correction of Broukhuis, though adopted by Lachmann and Müller, *sub sua jura, i.e.* 'sub debitam ditionem.'

Sera, sed Ausoniis veniet provincia virgis;
  Adsuescent Latio Partha tropæa Jovi.
Ite, agite, expertæ bello date lintea proræ
  Et solitum armigeri ducite munus equi.
Omina fausta cano: Crassos clademque piate;
  Ite et Romanæ consulite historiæ.
Mars pater et sacræ fatalia lumina Vestæ,
  Ante meos obitus sit, precor, illa dies,
Qua videam, spoliis onerato Cæsaris axe,
  Ad vulgi plausus sæpe resistere equos;
Inque sinu caræ nixus spectare puellæ
  Incipiam, et titulis oppida capta legam,

5.] The MSS. have *Sera, sed Ausoniis* &c., and so Lachmann, Jacob, and Hertzberg. *Sera, sed veniet*, as the Greeks would say ὀψὲ μὲν, ἀλλ' ὅμως. Compare iv. 6, 32, 'Parma erit ante meos sera, sed ampla, pedes.' Lachmann rightly explains it, 'ultima terra sera fiet provincia, sed fiet tamen.' Barth and Kuinoel admit the not improbable emendation of Heinsius, *Seres et*, i. e. *Seres quoque*. This is confirmed by the reading of a later copy, *venient*. The Seres (see on v. 3, 8) are mentioned in conjunction with the Indians, Hor. *Od.* i. 12, 53. The nation so called by Virgil, *Georg.* ii. 121, 'Velleraque ut foliis depectant tenuia Seres,' are probably, as implied by the preceding verse, Æthiopians, and not Chinese. The name seems derived from σὴρ, a silk-worm; but not only was cotton (as a raw material) confounded with silk, as may be inferred from the lines of Virgil just referred to, and from Pliny, *N. H.* vi. 17, 20, 'Seres lanicio sylvarum nobiles, perfusam aqua depectentes frondium canitiem, unde geminus feminis nostris labor, reordiendi fila rursumque texendi,' where the first words seem to refer to cotton, the last to unwinding the cocoons of silk,—but, from some perverse notion that the east side of Africa extended to China (Humboldt, *Cosmos*, ii. p. 192), the name Seres was applied to two totally distinct nations. Hence the evident perplexity of Pausanias, lib. vi. cap. 26, 4, οὗτοι μὲν δὴ τοῦ Αἰθιόπων γένους αὐτοί τε εἰσὶν οἱ Σῆρες, καὶ ὅσαι νῆσοι προσεχεῖς αὐτῇ νέμονται, Ἀβασὰ καὶ Σακαία· οἱ δὲ αὐτοὺς οὐκ Αἰθίοπας, Σκύθας δὲ ἀναμεμιγμένους Ἰνδοῖς φασὶν εἶναι. Æschylus also describes the Indians as bordering on (ἀστυγειτονουμένας) the Ethiopians, *Suppl.* 286.

7.] *Proræ* appears to be the dative, though many commentators regard both it and *equi* in the next verse as vocatives. The usual phrase is *dare vela vento* rather than *navi*. The poet addresses in a general way all who were to take part in the expedition. *Expertæ bello*, 'tried in war,' alludes to the naval victory at Actium, in which, in like manner, the poet speaks of 'signa, jam patriæ vincere docta suæ,' v. 6, 24.—*Munus equi* is referred with probability by Hertzberg to the horses provided at the public expense for the Equites: 'omnes Propertius hic alloquitur, quibuscunque equum publicum in bellum ducere licebat.' Some explain it of the horses attached to the triumphal car, as if the victory were already as good as gained; others of a richly caparisoned steed, supposed (but without proof) to have been brought for the use of the Imperator when about to undertake an expedition. Barth takes *munus* for *spolia*.

9.] *Crassos cladem que*. The defeat of the Crassi, father and son, B.C. 53.

11.] 'Vesta, goddess of the sacred fire, which contains the destinies of Rome.'

13.] Lachmann, Jacob, Hertzberg, Keil, and Müller, follow the reading of the MSS. *onerates—axes*. The omission of *et* in the next verse is so harsh, and the correction of Muretus so probable and easy, that with Barth and Kuinoel I have ventured to adopt it. The poet certainly would here have written *et vulgi ad plausus*, though he elsewhere omits the copulative.

15.] *In sinu puellæ*. He had before (ii. 7, 13), declared his aversion to taking any active part in arms.—*titulis* &c. See Tacitus, Ann. ii. 18, 22. Inf. v. 11, 38.

Tela fugacis equi, et braccati militis arcus,
  Et subter captos arma sedere duces.
Ipsa tuam prolem serva, Venus: hoc sit in ævum,
  Cernis ab Ænea quod superesse caput.
Præda sit hæc illis, quorum meruere labores:
  Me sat erit Sacra plaudere posse Via.

V.

Pacis Amor deus est; pacem veneramur amantes.
  Stant mihi cum domina prœlia dura mea:
Nec tamen inviso pectus mihi carpitur auro,
  Nec bibit e gemma divite nostra sitis;
Nec mihi mille jugis Campania pinguis aratur,
  Nec miser æra paro clade, Corinthe, tua.
O prima infelix fingenti terra Prometheo!

17.] *Braccati militis.* See on v. 10, 43. Here however not the Celts but the Parthians are meant, who wore the wide Persian trousers wittily called θύλακοι, 'bags,' by Aristoph. *Vesp.* 1087.—The infinitive *sedere* depends, like the accusatives *tela* and *arcus*, on *spectare* in v. 15, a construction not otherwise remarkable than for the interposition of the finite verb *legam* v. 16. A similar case occurs below, El. 6, 11—13. See the notes on iii. 1, 4, and v. 11, 38.

18.] See on iv. 1, 3. By *sedere sub arma* effigies are meant, placed beneath lofty trophies, as we see in some modern monuments.

19.] *Hoc caput*, Augustus, *sit in ævum*, *vivat*; a popular exclamation.

22.] The reading of the ed. Rheg. is plausible, *sat* for *me*; and so Barth and Kuinoel.

V. This elegant elegy alludes to the same circumstances as the last, the intended expedition into the East. He takes occasion to show the folly of braving the dangers of war for riches, and declares (1) that *his* battles are fought under the standard of Venus, and (2) that when too old for that service he will devote himself to the study of nature.

1—3.] The argument (which neither Lachmann nor Jacob seems to have understood aright) is this: 'Much as all lovers desire peace, I am compelled to wage war, yet not from avarice, but from differences with Cynthia,' *i.e.* my motives *belli gerendi* are very different from those of others about to fight against the Parthians. *Stant mihi prælia*, *h.e.* durant, non facile dirimuntur. Much difficulty has been raised on this word. Some explain it *quiescunt*; Hertzberg, quoting iv. 3, 44, gives the far-fetched explanation, '*stare* pugna dicitur, quum ab utraque parte æquo Marte pugnatum est.' Lachmann, who makes sad havoc of the whole passage 1—6, follows Heinsius in reading *sat mihi*, and in the next line *nec tantum*.

3.] *Carpitur*, vexatur, sollicitatur.

4.] *Nec bibit*, *i.e.* I have no gold and gems to excite in me the desire of possessing more—*gemma* is either for *poculum gemmatum* (*Georg.* ii. 506, 'ut gemma bibat;' Juven. x. 26, 'cum pocula sumes gemmata;' compare *Sat.* v. 38—45), or it may signify a goblet worked out of a single piece of opal, jasper, or chalcedony.—For *bibit* Lachmann gives *bibat*, and in the next verse *aretur*.

6.] The Naples MS. has *aere*, the ed. Rheg. with some later copies *ire*. For *clade* Barth and Kuinoel substitute *classe* from Pucci and the Aldine. On the fondness of the Romans for Corinthian bronze, see Becker, *Gallus*, p. 18—*clade tua* means 'obtained by your destruction,' which was barbarously effected by the consul Mummius B.C. 146.

7.] *Prima terra.* The *princeps lutum* of

Ille parum cauti pectoris egit opus:
Corpora disponens mentem non vidit in arte.
Recta animi primum debuit esse via.
Nunc maris in tantum vento jactamur, et hostem
Quærimus, atque armis nectimus arma nova.
Haud ullas portabis opes Acherontis ad undas:
Nudus ad infernas, stulte, vehere rates.
Victor cum victis pariter miscebitur umbris;
Consule cum Mario, capte Jugurtha, sedes;
Lydus Dulichio non distat Crœsus ab Iro;
Optima mors, parca quæ venit apta die.

Hor. *Od.* I. 16, 13. Human credulity perhaps never went further than in believing that certain lumps of stone, lying in a water-course near Panope in Phocis, were composed of the clay left over and above from the plastic process of Prometheus. Pausanias (x. 4, 3) gravely says, *ταῦτα ἔτι λείπεσθαι τοῦ πηλοῦ λέγουσιν, ἐξ οὗ καὶ ἅπαν ὑπὸ τοῦ Προμηθέως τὸ γένος πλασθῆναι τῶν ἀνθρώπων.* He adds, 'They smell remarkably like the human skin.' The identity of the legend with the creation of Adam is manifest. The Eastern Christians still believe that the first man was made out of red earth at Damascus. (Lepsius, *Discoveries in Egypt*, p. 400).

8.] *Parum cauti pectoris.* In allusion to the etymology of the name from *προμήθεια*. Hertzberg misunderstands the sense, explaining it 'pectori, dum finxisset, parum cavisse.' The poet simply means, that Prometheus executed the work without the care and forethought implied by his name.

10.] *Animi* &c. 'Ante omnia oportuit bonae mentis rationem habere.'—*Barth.* 'If there was one quality more than another which the god of forethought ought to have given to man, it was sound sense and reason.'

11.] *Jactari in mare* is properly to be carried *into* the open sea.—*hostem quærimus* &c. 'not content with repelling attacks at home, we must look for an enemy abroad: not satisfied with the wars on hand, we must add new wars.'

13.] 'And yet riches, when acquired, will profit you nothing in the grave.'

14.] The MSS. agree in *ad infernas—rates*, which is retained by Lachmann, Keil, and Müller. The plural is defended by Lachmann from the mention of *two* ferry-boats for the dead in v. 7, 57. To the correction of Perrey, *ab inferna rate*, it is objected that the preposition is wrongly used. 'Animam *antequam* ad rates pervenerit, *evectam* esse, quo jure dixeris?'—*Hertzberg:* who reads with Schrader *nudus at inferna*; but this is a very incorrect use of *at*, and is not sufficiently defended by i. 6, 22, where the MSS. vary between *at* and *et*. The meaning perhaps is, that whereas we now look for fleets and voyages for making our fortunes, hereafter we shall be stripped of everything, and see only the ships on the infernal river. Thus *vehi ad rates* is simply 'to be ferried over to the fleet.'

15.] The Groning. MS. gives *undis*, whence Barth and Kuinoel read *Indis*, and even Lachmann, who adopts it, calls this 'certissima emendatio.' The same MS. has *miscebimur*, which the above editors also adopt with Lachmann.

18.] Hertzberg, Jacob, Lachmann, and the later editors read *acta* for *apta* from the Naples MS. Lachmann compares iv. 7, 30, 'Ista per humanas mors venit acta manus,' where however the addition of *per manus* makes all the difference. That any editor should be satisfied with Scaliger's explanation of *parca die* by *ἡ πεπρωμένη ἡμέρα* is truly surprising.—*parca dies* is 'a day, or time, of poverty;' and the poet says, that not only is wealth useless when you die, but death comes easiest when it comes *apta*, appropriate and wished for, to relieve you from your poverty. Hertzberg's explanation is far from probable: 'mortem, ut tardissime venerit, atque maxime hominum vitae et diutissime pepercerit, ita optimam esse.' Lachmann reads *Parca die*, which seems scarcely good Latin for *fatali die*, though Jacob gives his approval, and both Keil and Müller follow him. Lachmann indeed compares 'Parcarum dies,' Virg. *Æn.* xii. 150; still this is not strictly parallel, since much of the difficulty lies in the use of the singular.

Me juvat in prima coluisse Helicona juventa,
  Musarumque choris implicuisse manus.
Me juvat et multo mentem vincire Lyæo,
  Et caput in verna semper habere rosa.
Atque ubi jam Venerem gravis interceperit ætas,
  Sparserit et nigras alba senecta comas,
Tum mihi Naturæ libeat perdiscere mores,
  Quis deus hanc mundi temperet arte domum;
Qua venit exoriens, qua deficit, unde coactis
  Cornibus in plenum menstrua luna redit;
Unde salo superant venti; quid flamine captet
  Eurus, et in nubes unde perennis aqua;
Sit ventura dies, mundi quæ subruat arces;
  Purpureus pluvias cur bibit arcus aquas;
Aut cur Perrhæbi tremuere cacumina Pindi,
  Solis et atratis luxerit orbis equis;
Cur serus versare boves et plaustra Bootes;
  Pleïadum spisso cur coit igne chorus;
Curve suos fines altum non exeat æquor,
  Plenus et in partes quattuor annus eat;
Sub terris sint jura deum et tormenta gigantum;
  Tisiphones atro si furit angue caput;
Aut Alcmæoniæ furiæ aut jejunia Phinei;
  Num rota, num scopuli, num sitis inter aquas;

19.] *Me juvat.* 'My pleasure is, (not war, but) love in youth and science in old age.' A similar aspiration after the 'causas rerum' occurs in the magnificent passage, *Georgic*, ii. 475, seq.

24.] The Groning. and Naples MSS. give *integras*; a reading worthy of some consideration.

25.] *Tum*, emphatic; then and not till then.

27.] *Qua*, supply *ratione*; or perhaps like the Greek use of ᾗ for ᾗ ὁδῷ, '*how it comes*,' viz. by what course or direction.

29.] *Quid captet*, what it aims at; what it desires to do. Barth compares Virg. *Georg*. i. 462, *quid cogitet humidus auster*.

31.] Lachmann and others read *si ventura*, and in v. 39, *si jura deum*, in both cases against the authority of the MSS. It is not probable that *si* would have been altered by the copyists. See the note on v. i. 88.

33.] *Perrhæbi Pindi.* Æsch. *Suppl.* 252, ὁρίζομαι δὲ τήν τε Περραιβῶν χθόνα, Πίνδου τε τἀπέκεινα, Παιόνων πέλας, where see the note. It is not known whether any particular earthquake is here alluded to. Barth thinks it is the same as that in iv. 13, 53. But perhaps mountains generally are meant, by a common usage of poets.—*luxerit*, from *lugeo*, but inf. ix. 20 from *luceo*. Notice here the alternation of subjunctive with indicative, as in Persius, *Sat*. iii. 66 seqq.

36.] *Spisso igne.* The apparent proximity to each other of the stars in that constellation presents to the naked eye a confused appearance. Barth and Kuinoel give Heinsius' emendation *imbre*.

39.] *Gigantum* is said to be wanting in the Naples MS. Müller reads *nocentum*, after Haupt.

41.] *Alcmæoniæ Furiæ.* 'An Alcmæon ob Eriphylen matrem interfectam a Furiis agitetur.'—*Kuinoel.*

Num tribus infernum custodit faucibus antrum
  Cerberus, an Tityo jugera pauca novem;
An ficta in miseras descendit fabula gentes,
  Et timor haud ultra quam rogus esse potest.
Exitus hic vitæ superet mihi: vos, quibus arma
  Grata magis, Crassi signa referte domum.

VI.

Dic mihi de nostra, quæ sentis, vera puella:
  Sic tibi sint dominæ, Lygdame, dempta juga.
Num me lætitia tumefactum fallis inani,
  Hæc referens, quæ me credere velle putas?
Omnis enim debet sine vano nuntius esse,
  Majoremque timens servus habere fidem.
Nunc mihi, si qua tenes, ab origine dicere prima
  Incipe; suspensis auribus ista bibam.
Siccine eam incomptis vidisti flere capillis?
  Illius ex oculis multa cadebat aqua?
Nec speculum strato vidisti, Lygdame, lecto?

44.] *Pauca*, 'Et num Tityo jugera novem sint pauca.'—*Barth*; who compares Tibull. i. 3, 75, 'porrectusque novem Tityos per jugera terræ.'

45.] *Ficta fabula*. The Epicurean philosophy. Compare with this passage, iii. 26, 53.

VI. This assumes the form of a dialogue between the poet and Cynthia's slave Lygdamus. The latter is called upon to report faithfully his mistress' disposition towards Propertius, who had deserted her on some disagreement having arisen between them, and to act as mediator in bringing about a reconciliation, should both parties prove equally desirous of it. This is one of the more obscure, and perhaps corrupt of the poet's productions.

3.] *Num*. This is clearly the right reading, preserved by Porci. The Naples MS. gives *non*, the Gron. MS. *dum*.—*tumefactum*, like [illegible] Æsch. *Agam.* 207, 1647, 'puffed up with vain hopes.'—*num fallis* is said in a threatening voice: 'are you thinking of telling me a false tale? You will deceive me at your peril. For, as every messenger ought to report the truth, so especially should a slave with the fear of punishment impending over him.' Hertzberg prefers: 'omnis servus debet verus nuntius esse,' &c.—*timens* is the reading of all the good copies.—*metu* is the useless correction of Muretus. In the preceding verse the ed. Rheg. has *sine vanis esse relator*; a remarkable reading, but probably a gloss.—*sine vano* might be defended, as the Greeks used [illegible] for [illegible], Æsch. *Ag.* 812. Lachmann, failing to see the meaning and connexion of this distich, incloses it within brackets as spurious. He also reads, with a few of the inferior copies, *sine vanis esse relator*. The order is, 'omnis nuntius debet esse sine vano,' *i. e.* carere mendacio. Lygdamus (v. 8, 37), though Cynthia's servant, seems to have been in the confidence of Propertius. The expression *fidem habere* is unusual in the sense of 'to prove faithful,' 'to have truthfulness.' More commonly it signifies 'to have credit,' *i. e.* to be believed, as in iv. 23, 4.

9.] *Siccine*. The MSS. have *si* or *sic*, or *sicut*. The Aldine gives the true reading.

11.] *Nec speculum* &c. 'Was there no mirror lying (as usual) on the bed, indicating that her toilet was a matter of anxious care?'

Ornabat niveas nullane gemma manus?
Ac mæstam teneris vestem pendere lacertis?
Scriniaque ad lecti clausa jacere pedes?
Tristis erat domus, et tristes sua pensa ministræ
Carpebant, medio nebat et ipsa loco?
Humidaque impressa siccabat lumina lana,
Rettulit et querulo jurgia nostra sono?
'Hæc te teste mihi promissa est, Lygdame, merces?
Est pœnæ servo rumpere teste fidem.
Ille potest nullo miseram me linquere facto,
Æqualem nulla dicere habere domo.
Gaudet me vacuo solam tabescere lecto:
Si placet, insultet, Lygdame, morte mea.
Non me moribus illa, sed herbis improba vicit:
Staminea rhombi ducitur ille rota.
Illum turgentis ranæ portenta rubetæ
Et lecta exectis anguibus ossa trahunt,

13.] *Ac mæstam* the Naples MS., *et mæstam* MS. Gron., and so Lachmann and Müller. *Et mæstam* Keil.—*vestem*, the tunica manicata, not buttoned or laced up, but hanging loose from the elbow. These questions are evidently asked in an excited and hurried tone, the point of them all being to know if Cynthia seemed disconsolate at the poet's absence. He here returns to the infinitive depending on *vidisti*. See above, El. 4, 17.—*scrinia*, not the *capsa* or manuscript-case, but the casket or dressing-case for the toilet; if the opinion of the commentators be correct.

17.] *Lana*, viz. with a piece of the wool which she was spinning.

18.] *Retulit jurgia nostra*, *i.e.* 'related to her maids the dispute she had had with me.'

19.] Lygdamus here proceeds to relate what Cynthia had said to him about the poet, and her anxiety to learn if he still loved her. 'Were you a witness (she asked), when he promised me this reward of my constancy? He must certainly feel it, if he has broken that promise made in your presence. Yet now he has the heart to desert me without any fault of mine (*nullo facto*), and the boldness to assert, what is but too clearly false, that he has no other mistress to hold an equal place in his affections.' There is considerable difficulty in these verses. For *æqualem* Barth gives *ac qualem* from Scaliger. The verse is perhaps corrupt. Hertzberg suspects *atque aliam* to be the true reading. Barth and Kuinoel make vv. 21—3 interrogative. Lachmann more correctly prints them with marks of interjection, and so Müller, who reads *multa* for *nulla*. The sense appears to be, 'potest dicere se nulla domo habere æqualem mihi.'

23.] *Gaudet* &c. 'No! he is pleased to think that I pine in solitude. Let him, if he likes, rejoice over my death.' *Morte mea* is an instance of the lax use of the ablative so common with Propertius. It is perhaps better to regard it as governed by the *sense* of *insultet*, *i.e.* superbiat, gaudeat, than as an ablative for a dative, on which idiom see v. 8, 10.

25—30.] She accuses her rival of having drawn away the poet, not by superior accomplishments, but by magic arts. See v. 7, 72, 'Si te non totum Doridos herba tenet.'

28.] *Anguibus*. 'Similiter apud Horatium, *Sat.* I. 8, 42, 'variæ quoque dente colubræ,' *i.e.* *lectis* anguium ossibus, non omnibus, veneficæ utuntur.'—*Jacob.* Barth reads *unguibus*, with Broukhusius. Lachmann gives *ex structis ignibus*, a bad reading made up of his own and Heinsius' conjecture. — *trahunt*, ἕλκουσι, a word technically used to imply the irresistible force of magic arts.

Et strigis inventæ per busta jacentia plumæ,
  Cinctaque funesto lanea vitta viro.
Si non vana canunt mea somnia, Lygdame, testor,
  Pœna erit ante meos sera, sed ampla, pedes.
Putris et in vacuo texetur aranea lecto;
  Noctibus illorum dormiet ipsa Venus.'
Quæ tibi si veris animis est questa puella,
  Hac eadem rursus, Lygdame, curre via,
Et mea cum multis lacrimis mandata reporta;
  Iram, non fraudes esse in amore meo;
Me quoque consimili impositum torquerier igni
  Jurabo et bis sex integer esse dies.
Quod mihi si tanto felix concordia bello
  Extiterit, per me, Lygdame, liber eris.

VII.

Ergo sollicitæ tu causa, Pecunia, vitæ;

29.] *Busta jacentia*, 'ruined tombs.' Others understand the extinct ashes of funeral piles. Hor. *Epod.* v. 19, 'et uncta turpis ova ranæ sanguine, Plumamque nocturnæ strigis,' &c. The strix was probably the screech-owl; but as it was a night bird, and therefore indistinctly seen, the ancients fancied it was a sort of harpy generated by magic art. See Ovid, *Fast.* vi. 131—142. Inf. v. 8, 17.

30.] All the MSS. give *viro*. Heinsius conjectured *toro*. These two words are thought to have been confused also in ii. 9, 16, 'Scyria nec viduo Deidamia viro.' Hertzberg alone retains the vulgate, understanding it of the 'imago funesta,' or image of the party to be enthralled by the charm; see Virg. *Ecl.* viii. 73. Hor. *Sat.* i. 8, 30, 'Lanea et effigies erat, altera cerea' (speaking of witches at their incantation). *Cincta* is for *circumdata*, by a rare use. But verbs of this nature are susceptible of a double construction. Barth has *vinctaque*, Lachmann *vinctaque*, because 'vitta cingebatur torus, non toro vitta.' See on v. 10, 5.

32.] *Pœna erit.* 'Ante meos pedes procumbet, nempe Propertius, veniamque sero rogabit; tunc pœnas de eo exigam amplissimas, gravissimas.'—*Kuinoel.*

33.] This verse is from *Od.* xvi. 34, 'Ὀδυσσῆος δέ που εὐνὴ Χήτει ἐνευναίων κάκ' ἀράχνια κεῖται ἔχουσα.—*dormiet Venus*, 'iners languescet.'—*Kuinoel.*

35.] *Quæ tibi* &c. The reply of Propertius. 'Well! if these were the grounds of the complaints against me, and if they were made not in pettishness but in sincerity, go back at once and tell her, that though I am angry with her, I have not wronged her by my love.'—*Veris animis*, *i. e.* vero affectu. Tac. *Ann.* xiv. 1, 'Formam scilicet displicere, et triumphales avos, an fecunditatem et verum animum?'

36.] *Eadem.* On the dissyllable see v. 7, 7.

40.] See note on ii. 9, 7, *integer*, *i. e.* λέκτρων ἄθικτος. *Esse* is for *fuisse*, and implies the duration of time. He means to assure Cynthia, that her suspicions of his infidelity since their rupture are vain. The change of construction is remarkable: *jurabo me torqueri, et integer esse.*

41.] The Naples MS. has *quod nisi et tanto*, whence Müller reads *Quodsi in e tanto*, which is perhaps right. Lachmann proposed *quod mihi si e tanto* &c.

42.] *Extiterit*, 'shall have resulted from.'—*per me*, *ἐμοῦ ἕκατι*, quantum mea opera fieri potest. See supra v. 2.

VII. This is one of the most beautiful poems of Propertius. The pathos is only equalled by the elegance of the versification. It is on the death of a young friend named Pætus, who was drowned in a voyage to Egypt undertaken for some

Per te immaturum mortis adimus iter.
Tu vitiis hominum crudelia pabula præbes;
Semina curarum de capite orta tuo.
Tu Pætum ad Pharios tendentem lintea portus
Obruis insano terque quaterque mari.
Nam dum te sequitur, primo miser excidit ævo,
Et nova longinquis piscibus esca natat;
Et mater non justa piæ dare debita terræ
Nec pote cognatos inter humare rogos;
Sed tua nunc volucres astant super ossa marinæ;
Nunc tibi pro tumulo Carpathium omne mare est.
Infelix Aquilo, raptæ timor Orithyiæ,
Quæ spolia ex illo tanta fuere tibi?
Aut quidnam fracta gaudes, Neptune, carina?
Portabat sanctos alveus ille viros.
Pæte, quid ætatem numeras? quid cara natanti
Mater in ore tibi est? non habet unda deos.
Nam tibi nocturnis ad saxa ligata procellis

mercantile purpose, which gives the poet occasion to inveigh against the avarice of man. It is strange that Scaliger should have been so little able to appreciate a poetical narrative as to have attempted a new arrangement of the verses throughout the entire elegy. Lachmann truly judges of the result; 'omnia transponendo nihil effecit, nisi ut minus quam antea cohærerent.'

1.] Vulgo *Vita es*. The Naples MS. omits *es*, the addition of which is certainly no improvement to the verse.

2.] *Crudelia*, cruda, ὠμά, *i.e.* by causing so much bloodshed.

4.] *De capite tuo*. Pecunia is here personified. Perhaps there is an allusion to Athene born from the head of Jupiter. See on iv. 18, 2.

5.] *Pharios portus*, *i.e.* Alexandria.

8.] 'Cur *nova* esca, nemo explicuit; scilicet *longinquis* piscibus.'—*Hertzberg*. The food was *strange* because the man came from a far-distant land,—a merely poetical image.

9.] *Piæ terræ*. The epithet partly refers to the idea expressed in the following verses. The earth holds, as it were, in a parental embrace, the deceased members of one family. But with the earth are associated the dead who are buried there. Properly speaking, the mother would pay 'justa debita piis Manibus.'

10.] *Pote*. It is evident that this is not the neuter, but stands for *poti*, i.e. *potis est*. Compare *mage* for *magis*, *amabere* for *amaberis* &c., and see ii. 1, 46.

11.] *Astant* &c. Cf. Ovid, *Heroid*, x. 123, 'ossa superstabunt volucres inhumata marinæ.'

14.] *Ex illo*, Pæte. To carry off the maid had some excuse; but what prize was a poor boy? The whole of this passage has great tenderness and beauty.

16.] *Sanctos viros*, *i.e.* deorum cultores, non sacrilegos, perjuros, &c. Compare *Od.* viii. 565. Æsch. *Theb.* 598, ἢ γὰρ ξυνεισβὰς πλοῖον εὐσεβὴς ἀνὴρ ναύταισι θερμοῖς καὶ πανουργίᾳ τινὶ ὄλωλεν ἀνδρῶν σὺν θεοπτύστῳ γένει.

17.] *Ætatem numeras*, *i.e.* upbraid heaven with cutting off so young a life.—*non habet unda deos*. 'The briny wave cannot hear your prayers.'

19.] *Nam*. For if the sea could have felt pity, it would not have so imperilled the ship by wearing the ropes against the rocks. The *vincula* are the *retinacula*, Ovid, *Her.* 18, 11, *πεῖσμα*, *Od.* xiii. 100. Kuinoel joins *detrita ad saxa*, and understands it of undergirding the ship; in which he merely follows Barth and his immediate

Omnia detrito vincula ſune cadunt.
Sunt Agamemnonias testantia litora curas,
Quæ notat Argynni pœna †minantis aquæ.
Hoc juvene amisso classem non solvit Atrides,
Pro qua mactata est Iphigenia mora.
Reddite corpus humo, positaque in gurgite vita
Pætum sponte tua, vilis arena, tegas.
Et quotiens Pæti transibit nauta sepulcrum,
Dicat: Et audaci tu timor esse potes.
Ite, rates curvas et leti texite causas!
Ista per humanas mors venit acta manus.

predecessors. It is better to take the words in their natural order, *ad saxa ligata*, *i. e.* ad saxosum litus. They had endeavoured to moor the ship in some sheltered bay, but the ropes were chafed by the sharp rocks and would not hold. We are not concerned with the good or bad seamanship of such an attempt. Perhaps the storm arose *after* the ship had been so moored. It was *nocturna procella*, and ships were moored in the evening, Theocr. xiii. 32.

22.] This obscure verse has been variously altered and interpreted. The common reading is *minantis aquæ*, and the MSS. offer no variety of importance, except that the MS. Gron. gives *nota argivis*. Hertzberg undertakes to show that his reading, *Quæ notat Argynni pœna Athamantiadæ*, is the genuine one; it is certainly ingenious, and is adopted by both Keil and Müller. Scaliger from a late copy read *natantis aquæ*, the sense then being 'there are certain shores rendered remarkable for the punishment of Argynnus drowned (or wrecked) in the sea.' Others read *natantis aquas.*—*notat*, infamat. The legend was that Agamemnon, enamoured of a beautiful youth, Argynnus, caused his death by pursuing him to the banks of the Cephisus. See Athen. xiii. p. 603. Martial, *Ep.* vii. 15, 5. It seems to have been a duplicate of the well-known story of Hylas. Hertzberg however is probably right in supposing that our poet followed some account which represented him as lost at sea; otherwise there is no parallel with the case of Pætus. He might have supported his opinion by observing that *litora*, not *ripa*, is used. The scene of Pætus' shipwreck was the same as that of Argynnus before him.

23—4.] Jacob considers this distich the interpolation of some scholiast. Without being necessary, it is a natural addition to amplify the narrative and to express the greatness of the loss, and by implication, that of Pætus also. Lachmann reads *his* for *hoc*.

25—6.] It is not clear to whom the imperative *reddite* is addressed. I agree with Barth that Aquilo and Neptune are meant (13—15), rather than with Hertzberg, who understands *æquorei dii*. For the very existence of the latter is denied in v. 18. Perhaps indeed 25—28 should be transposed to follow 70, where they would come in very appropriately. This was suggested by Scaliger, and he has been followed by Müller. In other respects the sense of these two lines is sufficiently evident: 'now that the water has taken his life, the body may surely be spared for burial in the sand,'—*sponte tua*, *i. e.* in the absence of any friendly hand. In addressing the sand, he applies the same epithet *vilis*, though not a complimentary one, which he would have done had he asked the boon of 'a little valueless sand' from another. The reader will scarcely approve the poetical taste which induced Lachmann to read thus: 'Reddite corpus humo positumque in gurgite, venti, Pætum; sponte tua, vilis arena, tegas.' Jacob's brief note is excellent; 'prædam habetis; corpus reddite.' But his reading of v. 25, from the Naples MS., is far from satisfactory: 'Reddite corpus humo! posita est in gurgite vita!' He is followed however by Müller, who makes the last clause a parenthesis.

29.] The MSS. have *curvæ*, which was corrected by Passerat.

30.] *Ista*, 'that death which you provoke is brought on by human hands;' *i. e.* do not blame fate, or the gods.

Terra parum fuerat: fatis adjecimus undas;
  Fortunæ miseras auximus arte vias.
Ancora te teneat, quem non tenuere Penates?
  Quid meritum dicas, cui sua terra parum est?
Ventorum est, quodcumque paras: haud ulla carina
  Consenuit; fallit portus et ipse fidem.
Natura insidians pontum substravit avaris;
  Ut tibi succedat, vix semel esse potest.
Saxa triumphales fregere Capharea puppes,
  Naufraga cum vasto Græcia tracta salo est.
Paullatim socium jacturam flevit Ulixes,
  In mare cui soliti non valuere doli.
Quod si contentus patrio bove verteret agros,
  Verbaque duxisset pondus habere mea,
Viveret ante suos dulcis conviva Penates,
  Pauper, at in terra, nil ubi flere potest.
Non tulit hic Pætus stridorem audire procellæ,
  Et duro teneras lædere fune manus,
Sed thyio thalamo aut Oricia terebintho

31.] Most editors read *parum fuerat fatis;* but the stop comes better at the cæsura of the verse. *Fatis, i. e.* to the many ways of death already existing. This is a clever distich.

32.] 'We have added by art to the many roads to misery which Chance had already prepared for us.' Barth and Kuinoel read *Naturæ*, and *Fortuna* in v. 37, the unwarrantable alteration of Broukhusius.

37.] I follow Jacob, Keil, and Müller in admitting *insidians* from the Naples MS. and ed. Rheg. The others have *insidias*, which is in itself a good reading, taken in apposition with *pontum*. The sense is: 'It was for the very purpose of ensnaring them that Nature spread out the sea as a smooth and enticing path for the avaricious.' He adds: 'success awaits you scarcely once in your many attempts.' And he illustrates the dangers of the sea by memorable instances of shipwreck.

39.] *Triumphales, i.e.* they were wrecked as it were close to their home and in the very arms of victory. See on v. 1, 115.

42.] The MSS. give *soli*, which Jacob retains. *Soliti* was the conjecture of Lipsius, and is found in one of the later copies. Müller would prefer *solum*. The sense is, 'the usually successful arts and contrivances of Ulysses failed to secure him against losses by sea.'

44.] *Verba mea.* 'The sentiment which I now express in words.' On the change of tenses in *verteret* and *duxisset* see i. 17, 20. Lachmann reads *O si contentus* &c.

46.] Jacob's correction, admitted with great praise by Hertzberg, and adopted by both Keil and Müller, is ingenious and probable, 'nil ubi flare potest,' *i. e.* 'ubi venti nihil possunt.' Still, it is a strange expression, 'on terra firma, *where nothing can blow*,' for 'far from stormy waves.' On the other hand, the vulgate gives a simple and satisfactory sense, 'poor indeed, but with no cause for sorrow.' A prose writer could have said, 'ubi nihil esset quod flere posset.' Probably also he would have used *sed* instead of *at*.

47.] *Non tulit hic.* 'While he remained on land, he had not to endure,' &c. 'Si Pætus in terra manere sustinuisset, non hic pericula et labores ei ferenda erant, sed omnibus vitæ cultioris deliciis lente frui licebat.'—*Hertzberg*. Lachmann reads *non tulit hoc Pætus, stridorem* &c.

49.] *Thyio.* This word is an adjective from *θύον*, or *θυία*, which is generally supposed to have been a kind of cedar, but it is more probably a species of arbor vitæ,

Effultum pluma versicolore caput.
Huic fluctus vivo radicitus abstulit ungues,
  Et miser invisam traxit hiatus aquam;
Hunc parvo ferri vidit nox improba ligno;
  Pætus ut occideret tot coiere mala.
Flens tamen extremis dedit hæc mandata querellis,
  Cum moribunda niger clauderet ora liquor:
Di maris Ægæi quos sunt penes æquora, Venti,
  Et quæcumque meum degravat unda caput,
Quo rapitis miseros primæ lanuginis annos?
  Attulimus longas in freta vestra manus.
Ah miser alcyonum scopulis affligar acutis;
  In me cæruleo fuscina sumpta deo est.
At saltem Italiæ regionibus advehat æstus:

the *Thuja articulata* of Linnæus, a native of the mountains in the N.W. of Africa, and the timber of which exhales a fragrant odour. The terebinth, or turpentine tree, (*pistacia terebinthus*), is of large size and stately growth, and is not uncommon in Palestine and many of the Greek islands. It is not one of the coniferæ, but bears a fruit like a small cherry. Sir Charles Fellows (*Travels in Asia Minor*) compares it with our ash. Our word *turpentine* is a corruption of *terebinthine*. Pucci gives *thyio in thalamo*, and so Jacob. Barth and Kuinoel *thyio thalamo*.—*Oricia*, see i. 8, 20. The MSS. give *abie*, which Keil retains. Lachmann makes a desperate effort to correct a verse about which very little doubt can exist, and reads *sed Cnidio calamo*.

50.] *Effultum*, sc. *erat*. The MSS. have *et fultum*, which Lachmann retains. Mr. Wratislaw reads *et fultus*.—*pluma versicolor* seems naturally to refer to cushions made of dyed feathers; but Hertzberg regards *plumas* as here used for the sofa or coverlet itself. Possibly a sort of *pulvinus* was composed of coloured feathers strung or matted together. On the *plumarii*, or feather-sewers (a craft by no means lost in our times) see a curious dissertation in Becker's *Gallus*, p. 287—90, where the present passage is discussed.

51—4.] The sense is, there were several causes which conspired to drown Pætus; (1) his hands were hurt so that he could not swim effectively: (2) he was nearly choked by swallowing sea-water; (3) the plank he grasped was too small; (4) it was dark. For *vivo* (*i.e.* adhuc spiranti) which is the MSS. reading, some plausibly edit *vivas*, to which Hertzberg fancifully objects that it adds unnecessarily to the shocking picture. *Vivo* is, however, rather *otiose*. The poet perhaps had in view the shipwreck of Ulysses, *Od.* v. 434, θρασειάων ἀπὸ χειρῶν ῥινοὶ ἀπέδρυφθεν.

52.] Lachmann reads *et miserum invita traxit hiatus aqua*. It is hardly necessary to add that *miser hiatus* is = *miseri hominis hiantis*. Cf. v. 68. Or thus: 'miserum os hiantis Pæti invisam aquam hausit.'

54.] *Tot mala*, as if more than ordinary means were required to extinguish such a life.

57.] Dii maris, *et* venti, et quæcunque unda &c.

60.] *Longas manus*. The expression is obscure, as it does not appear what is the point of the appeal. Hertzberg understands 'pulcras, proceras,' which gives a very weak meaning. I incline to Barth's view, 'integras autem,' in allusion to v. 51. Kuinoel follows Scaliger in the far-fetched idea that 'puras, innocentes,' are meant, because the ancients thought that perjury was often punished by the mutilation of a limb. Becker (ap. Hertz.) quotes Ovid, *Am.* iii. 3, 3, 'Quam longos habuit nondum jurata capillos, Tam longos postquam numina læsit habet.'

61.] *Affligar* Lachmann and Müller, with MS. Gron.

63.] *Evehat* is the reading of the good copies (MS. Naples *evenat*). This might mean, perhaps, ἐξενέγκοι, 'throw me ashore on Italian land.' Lachmann and others give *advehat* from Scaliger's correction.

Hoc de me sat erit si modo matris erit.
Subtrahit hæc fantem torta vertigine fluctus;
Ultima quæ Pæto voxque diesque fuit.
O centum æquoreæ Nereo genitore puellæ,
Et tu materno tacta dolore Thetis,
Vos decuit lasso supponere brachia mento;
Non poterat vestras ille gravare manus.
At tu, sæve Aquilo, numquam mea vela videbis;
Ante fores dominæ condar oportet iners.

VIII.

Dulcis ad hesternas fuerat mihi rixa lucernas,
Vocis et insanæ tot maledicta tuæ.
Cur furibunda mero mensam propellis, et in me
Proicis insana cymbia plena manu?
Tu vero nostros audax invade capillos,
Et mea formosis unguibus ora nota;
Tu minitare oculos subjecta exurere flamma,
Fac mea rescisso pectora nuda sinu.
Nimirum veri dantur mihi signa caloris;
Nam sine amore gravi femina nulla dolet.
Quæ mulier rabida jactat convicia lingua,

64.] Sat mihi erit, si hoc quod de me restat, matris erit, *i.e.* si corpus in matris manus veniet.

68.] The MSS. have *Thetis*, which Hertzberg retains. Most editions read *Theti* with Pucci. These four lines (67—70) contain a most beautiful and pathetic appeal. Müller, who here inserts 25—8, incloses 69—70 as a parenthesis, in order that *reddite corpus* &c. may refer to *puellæ* and *Thetis*.

VIII. In this clever and spirited elegy the poet assures Cynthia that so far from being offended with her for her violent bearing in a recent quarrel, he considers it as the strongest proof of her affection. This is said with a view to retaining her favour against the claims of a rival who is briefly addressed with considerable bitterness at the conclusion.

1.] *Hesternas.* Other readings are *externas* and *extremas*. Barth and Kuinoel give the latter: 'sub auroram jam deficiente lucerna,' in the words of Ovid.—*dulcis* rixa is sufficiently explained by v. 5.

3.] For *cur* Pucci gives *cum*. Barth and Kuinoel *dum*, after Broukhuis. As the quarrel had happened the night before, he speaks of it as if still present: 'I ask why do you act with such violence towards me? Yet do more if you will: it is a proof of your love.' The repetition of *insana*, v. 2 and 4, implies hasty composition.

7.] *Oculos exurere*, 'to burn out my eyes,' by thrusting a torch in my face. These personal assaults, which in our times are nearly confined to the lowest and most abandoned, appear to have been ordinary events among very respectable Roman lovers. Cynthia's character is in no respect amiable: see particularly v. 6, 51, seq.

11.] The MSS. give *gravida*. The editors agree in admitting the emendation of Scaliger. It is probable that these verses (11—16) describe the actual conduct of Cynthia on several occasions. The apo-

Et Veneris magnæ volvitur ante pedes,
Custodum gregibus circa se stipat euntem,
  Seu sequitur medias, Mænas ut icta, vias,
Seu timidam crebro dementia somnia terrent,
  Seu miseram in tabula picta puella movet;—
His ego tormentis animi sum verus aruspex,
  Has didici certo sæpe in amore notas.
Non est certa fides, quam non injuria versat.
  Hostibus eveniat lenta puella meis!
Immorso æquales videant mea vulnera collo;
  Me doceat livor mecum habuisse meam.
Aut in amore dolere volo, aut audire dolentem;
  Sive meas lacrimas, sive videre tuas,
Tecta superciliis si quando verba remittis,
  Aut tua cum digitis scripta silenda notas.

doxis occurs in v. 17. The sense is: 'When a woman abuses her lover, passionately supplicates Venus, appears in public with so many attendants that he cannot have access to her, or runs like a frantic Bacchante down the middle of the street, or who is restless from dreams or starts at the sight of a female portrait,—I can only interpret this excitement as betokening strong affection on her part.'

13.] The MSS. Gron. and Naples have *circa se stipat*. Pucci gives *circum*. Barth and Kuinoel *seu quam se stipat*. Jacob (from Perrey) *circum quæ stipat*, which he strangely explains of the woman surrounding the man with attendants, lest her rivals should speak to him. Hertzberg edits *circa seu stipat*, and so Keil and Müller; and lastly, Lachmann has *circum se stipat*, inserting *et* before *gregibus*. Hertzberg appears to acquiesce in Jacob's view. I have preferred the reading of the best copies, understanding '(et quæ) circa stipat se euntem' &c. A similar omission of *et* see inf. 9, 34.

18.] *Certo in amore*, 'in the case of a constant affection.' Barth and Kuinoel give *certas* from inferior copies.

19.] 'That attachment is not to be relied on, which is not moved to resentment by a wrong.' These words cannot signify 'si puella amatorem nulla injuria afficit,' as Kuinoel supposes. — *versat* is *agitat*, *vexat*, and the *injuria* is either a real or a supposed wrong, *i.e.* the wrong of preferring another to her.—*lenta*, 'indifferent,' 'apathetic.'

21.] *Immorso*. Hertzberg's explanation is probably correct: 'æquales non morsi collo ipsi videant me vulneratum.' We have *æqualis* for 'a rival' sup. 6, 22. The apparent emphasis on *me* in the following verse certainly favours the antithesis. Barth has *in morso*: others derive *immorsus* from *immordeo*.—*livor*, a weal, bruise, or blue mark.

23—4.] 'I do not like apathy in true love; I would either feel pain myself, or know that my mistress is pained. On one side, at least, let us have reality.'

25—6.] Lachmann considers these two verses as spurious: a summary course he is too apt to pursue when he is not satisfied with the poet's meaning. He cites two very similar lines from Ovid, *Her.* xvii. 81, 'ah quoties digitis, quoties ego tecta notavi Signa supercilio pæne loquente dari!' Hertzberg devotes two pages of notes to their explanation, but fails to elicit any natural sense. The meaning is this: 'Love is nothing worth when it brings pain to neither side. A little jealousy is inseparable from true affection. I like to hear complaints from my mistress; or if she cannot complain openly in the presence of a rival, to see silent tears and secret tokens of her disapprobation and dislike to his presence.' Writing on the table imaginary letters, or with a finger dipped in wine, was a frequent practice under similar circumstances. It is probable that Cynthia had really acted thus, to the gratification of the poet when he was dreading the success of a

Odi ego, quum numquam pungunt suspiria somnos.
Semper in irata pallidus esse velim.
Dulcior ignis erat Paridi, cum Graia per arma
Tyndaridi poterat gaudia ferre suæ.
Dum vincunt Danai, dum restat barbarus Hector,
Ille Helenæ in gremio maxima bella gerit.
Aut tecum, aut pro te mihi cum rivalibus arma
Semper erunt: in te pax mihi nulla placet.
Gaude, quod nulla est æque formosa; doleres,
Si qua foret; nunc sis jure superba licet.
At tibi, qui nostro nexisti retia lecto,
Sit socer æternum, nec sine matre domus.
Cui nunc si qua data est furandæ copia noctis,
Offensa illa mihi, non tibi amica dedit.

IX.

Mæcenas, eques Etrusco de sanguine regum,

rival. *Notare scripta* is rather a remarkable inversion for *scribere notas*. Müller thinks some lines have dropped out before 25, expressive of hope that the poet may be restored to favour; and he marks a *lacuna* accordingly.

27.] *Quum*. So Jacob and Hertzberg from Pucci. The MS. Gron. has *quæ*, the Naples MS. *quem*. Lachmann, Barth, and Kuinoel edit *quos*, which is not likely to be the true reading. Compare v. 15, and i. 3, 27. *Odi* is used absolutely; *ἀποστρέφομαι*.

29.] The sense is, 'difficulties and obstacles only enhance the enjoyment.' For *Graia* the MSS. give *grata*, which was corrected by Palmer.

31.] *Restat*, *i.e.* resistit.

32.] *Maxima*, longe majora quam illi.

35.] This verse, as Hertzberg well observes, contains a more serious expostulation than his somewhat playful assertion in the former part of the elegy, that he is gratified by her violence: 'Consider yourself fortunate that there is no other as handsome as yourself; otherwise it may be that your pride would tempt me to leave you.'

37.] The MSS. of Propertius agree in *tendisti*, but the editors adopt *nexisti* from Priscian and Diomede the grammarians, the latter of whom has 'Mæcenas; *nexisti retia lecto*,' while the former quotes our poet. There appears to be no authority for the unreduplicated form of perfect, *tendi*.

38.] *Socer*. A father-in-law is naturally severe against the faithless husband of his daughter. Is it therefore to be inferred that the poet's rival was a married man?

39.] *Cui*, *i.e.* nam tibi. 'If she has granted you favours, 'tis merely to spite me, not through regard for you.' An amiable sentiment, certainly. *Furari noctem* implies stealing an opportunity, and in some degree exonerates Cynthia by laying the blame on the rival.

40.] *Offensa*. The Naples MS. has *offensam*, which reading arose from not understanding the right accusative (copiam noctis) to *dedit*.

IX. The poet pays a judicious and elegant compliment to Mæcenas, who had urged him to write heroic verse, by proposing to himself to follow the example of that great man. For while the highest honours of the state were within his reach, he contented himself with the title of Eques. The argument much resembles ii. 1, and it cannot be doubted that the poet received frequent and urgent requests from his patron to try another style of

Intra fortunam qui cupis esse tuam,
Quid me scribendi tam vastum mittis in æquor?
Non sunt apta meæ grandia vela rati.
Turpe est, quod nequeas, capiti committere pondus,
Et pressum inflexo mox dare terga genu.
Omnia non pariter rerum sunt omnibus apta,
Fama nec ex æquo ducitur ulla jugo.
Gloria Lysippo est animosa effingere signa;
Exactis Calamis se mihi jactat equis.
In Veneris tabula summam sibi ponit Apelles;
Parrhasius parva vindicat arte locum.

composition. Whether this desire arose from his own indifference to amatory elegiac compositions, or from a wish to see all the poetic talent of the age devoted to the praises of Cæsar, it is not important to determine.

2.] *Intra fortunam*, 'limites fortunæ tuæ non egredi, contentum esse sorte tua.'—*Barth*. Compare Tacitus, *Ann.* iii. 30.

5.] *Quod nequeas.* Though the mind naturally supplies *ferre*, it is perhaps more correct to regard the verb *nequeo* as used transitively, like *posse aliquid.* Certainly Barth is wrong in understanding *fero committere.*

6.] Jacob reads *pressum* with Pucci. Hertzberg approves of this, but retains the vulgate. Their reason is, that *dare terga* being, as it were, an established expression for *effugere*, was not likely to have been used in this instance for *declinare* or *submittere tergum*. But the objection arises from being the 'slave of words' rather than looking at the sense of the passage as a whole. The addition of *pressum* and *inflexo genu* absolutely fixes the sense of *dare terga*, ἐνδιδόναι, 'to give in;' indeed, the notion of *flight* could hardly occur to a reader engaged in contemplating the bearer of a heavy burden. On the other hand, *pressum dare terga* for 'totis simul viribus fractis concidere' seems an unheard-of expression.

7.] *Omnia rerum*, sc. *genera.*

8.] There is a perplexing variety of readings in this verse. The MS. Gron. gives 'Flamma nec eco ducitur ulla jugo:' the Naples MS. has *flamma*, but otherwise as in the text. The ed. Rheg. 'Flamma nec ex æquo ducitur illa rogo.' One of the inferior MSS. gives *palma* and *clauditur*. *Fama* is from Pucci. If the reading given above be genuine, it seems best to follow Kuinoel in explaining *æquo jugo* by '*pari jugo*,' to which the preceding *pariter* in some degree seems to point, but much more so the tenour of the whole passage. 'To be renowned,' says the poet, 'you must stand alone. You must have no rival, no yoke-fellow attached to the same car.' Lachmann, with the approval of Jacob, understands 'a gentle hill,' 'mons summum facilis,' comparing v. 10, 4, 'Non juvat ex facili lecta corona jugo.' To say nothing of the harshness of the oxymoron, 'a level hill,' or of the unusual sense which Hertzberg assigns to it, 'the same hill with any other,' (diversa sunt juga unde diversæ famæ ducuntur,') the metaphor of the yoke seems so appropriate in itself and so naturally suggested by the epithet, that it certainly would have first presented itself to the mind of a reader. Barth's explanation is no better than the others: 'Idem nomen eademque laus non manat ex eodem fonte, ex eadem arte.'

9.] *Animosa*, 'spirited,' 'expressive.' He was a famous worker in bronze, and was fond of representing Hercules and his supposed descendant Alexander.—Calamis was chiefly renowned for the finish he gave to equestrian statuary; but it is evident from Pausanias, who frequently describes his works, that he did not confine himself to this department of the art. On the use of *mihi*, see i. 6, 8.

11.] *Summam sibi ponit*, regards as his *chef d'œuvre*, as we say; lit. places his highest effort, or effect, in his picture of Venus. 'Summam artis suæ in Veneris tabula positam ipse Apelles judicat.'—*Lachmann.*

12.] *Parva arte*, i. e. in small groups, or, as we say, cabinet pictures. Pliny, *N. H.* xxxv. 10, distinctly says 'pinxit et *minoribus tabellis* libidines, eo genere petu-

Argumenta magis sunt Mentoris addita formæ;
At Myos exiguum flectit acanthus iter.
Phidiacus signo se Juppiter ornat eburno;
Praxitelen propria vindicat urbe lapis.
Est quibus Eleæ concurrit palma quadrigæ;
Est quibus in celeres gloria nata pedes.
Hic satus ad pacem; hic castrensibus utilis armis:
Naturæ sequitur semina quisque suæ.
At tua, Mæcenas, vitæ præcepta recepi,
Cogor et exemplis te superare tuis.

lantis joci se reficiens.' He also states in the same passage that this artist was the first who attended to minute details,—'argutias vultus, elegantiam capilli, venustatem oris,' which may perhaps be included in the meaning of *parva ars*. That Hertzberg should approve Lachmann's conjecture, *forum* for *locum*, on the strength of the above passage, is surprising. Without having recourse to Jacob's explanation, 'qui locum sibi vindicat, reliquos omnes inde depellit,' we may naturally and easily supply *inter summos pictores*, or those artists just enumerated.

13.] *Argumenta*. Not single figures, but subjects involving groups. 'Historiæ fabulæque sculptæ, emblemata insculpta.' *Barth*. Hertzberg well quotes the following from Quintilian, v. 10, 10, 'Vulgoque paullo numerosius opus dicitur argumentosum.'—*formæ*, his model, or design.

14.] *Myos*. The MSS. corruptly give *myros*, *miros*, or *mores*. On this artist see Pausan. i. 28, 2. Like Mentor, his practice was toreutic (cælatum opus). 'His acanthus,' says the poet, 'carves in short and delicately crisp foliage,' viz. round the handles of vases and goblets.

15.] *Ornat se* is a harsh, but not unintelligible expression for *ornatur*. This is, in fact, a Propertian idiom, as *domum se sustulit*, v. 1, 9; *ara se vindicat*, ib. 9, 66. The notion is, that the god condescends to exhibit to man his most graceful form in the Olympian statue made by Phidias. Hertzberg is too refined in his explanation. He thinks Phidiacus Jupiter is the ideal god, as conceived in the artist's mind, and afterwards embodied in wood or stone. Lachmann gives up the verse as hopeless, and according to his custom incloses it with brackets as spurious.

16.] This verse is difficult. For *propria* Broukhusius conjectured *Paria*, and so Barth, Kuinoel, and Lachmann.—*lapis propria urbe* (oriundus) seems to mean the native Pentelic marble of Athens, (of which place Praxiteles was a citizen), as opposed to the imported marbles of Paros. This marble is said to 'claim him for its own,' as if his hand alone could do justice to it. Hertzberg proposes *venditat*, and *patria* for *propria*, i.e. 'unice commendat, jactat hunc;' but the verb is not a poetical one.

17.] *Est quibus*, ἔστιν οἷς, a bold and perhaps unique Græcism.—*concurrit*, simul currit, *comitatur*; i.e. 'there are some whom the victory of the chariot always attends,' or perhaps, 'to whom it is congenial.' Hertzberg, too intent on finding new and curious meanings, protests against the above, and says, 'palma aurigæ acrius nitenti advolare a metis et obviam concurrere egregie fingitur.'

18.] Kuinoel, who is never happy without his hypallage, explains this verse by 'quibus celeres pedes in gloriam nati.' Hertzberg is more scholarlike in his view: 'Hoc ait; gloriam quidem omnibus illis, qui eam qualicunque modo assequuntur, natam esse; indolem tantum differre, qua comparetur. Itaque aut ingenio aut manibus aut adeo pedibus eam tribui et his partibus (sive in has partes), prout quisque excellat, natam videri.' The literal sense is, 'There are others to whom glory was born for their swiftness of foot;' Gr. [illegible], in other words, 'whom glory was destined to await in the foot-race.'

21.] *Tua vitæ præcepta*, 'ad quæ tu vitam tuam dirigis.'—*Hertzberg*. *cogor* is explained by the same editor as implying the will was greater than the ability on the part of Mæcenas to remain in privacy. The sense seems rather to be, 'I am forced, by natural inferiority, to go beyond you in the example you set,' viz. since you have the genius to succeed in your undertakings, which I have not.

Cum tibi Romano dominas in honore secures
  Et liceat medio ponere jura foro,
Vel tibi Medorum pugnaces ire per hostes,
  Atque onerare tuam fixa per arma domum,
Et tibi ad effectum vires det Cæsar, et omni
  Tempore tam faciles insinuentur opes;
Parcis, et in tenues humilem te colligis umbras;
  Velorum plenos subtrahis ipse sinus.
Crede mihi, magnos æquabunt ista Camillos
  Judicia, et venies tu quoque in ora virum,
Cæsaris et famæ vestigia juncta tenebis:
  Mæcenatis erunt vera tropæa fides.
Non ego velifera tumidum mare findo carina:
  Tuta sub exiguo flumine nostra mora est.
Non flebo in cineres arcem sedisse paternos

23.] *Cum*, i.e. *cum enim* &c., the apodosis being at v. 29. It is more probable that *ponere* is to be supplied to the word *secures* than *ponere* literally interpreted, 'statuere, ut faciant lictores cum in foro cum securibus apparent.'—*Barth.* *ponere jura* like our phrase 'to lay down the law,' would thus be used in a somewhat different sense, of those who have supreme authority to legislate for others. Compare v. 4, 11; iv. 11, 46. It is a nice question, in cases like the present, whether the verb actually bears two meanings or a second verb is left to be mentally suggested by the first. Cf. iv. 7, 29.

25.] *Medorum hostes*, i.e. hostes qui ex Media constant. Or the 'enemies of the Medes' may mean the Parthian or Bactrian peoples. Hertzberg seems to approve Lachmann's tasteless conjecture *astus*, i. e. 'astutam Parthorum fugam,' v. 54. Müller reads *hastas*, after Markland.

28.] *Insinuentur*, in sinum tuum fundantur.

31.] 'This resolve of yours will be placed on a level with the great Camilli, and you as well as they shall live in posterity.' The plural is used, because there were several of the same name, though only one was particularly illustrious.

34.] *Fides*. His fidelity to Cæsar. It may be inferred from this passage that Mæcenas was not personally fond of military exploits.

35.] This verse is wanting in the Naples MS., and the rare licence of the short *o* in *findo* has made some critics doubt its genuineness.

36.] *Nostra mora*. 'Moram de loco dicit, non de tempore.'—*Lachmann.* The MS. Gron. has *ratis*, which is a correction; but it alone preserves *tuta;* the others have *tota*, which Jacob in an unusually long note defends. But what is there either obscure or objectionable in the poet saying, 'I lie safe under shelter of a little stream'? The metaphor is obviously borrowed from one who anchors near the mouth of a river into which he may run for shelter in a storm. The Greeks called this ὕφορμον. Lachmann is altogether wrong in the following remark: 'Propertium recte se *sub flumine* morari dicere, cum pars navigii sub aqua sit.'

37.] *Non flebo* &c. 'I do not intend to sing in mournful strains the destruction of Thebes and Troy.' 'Paterni cineres sunt cineres bellis civilibus conflati. Nam *paternus* est *patrius*, i.e. ad patriam pertinens. Hor. *Od.* i. 20, 6, 'paterni fluminis ripa.' Inf. v. 2, 2, 'Accipe Vertumni signa paterna dei.''—*Hertzberg:* who admits the conjecture of Passerat, *septem* for *semper*. So also Keil and Müller. The latter word implies that in several engagements neither side gained any advantage. But there is much probability in the correction, which Jacob also approves: 'septem ab utraque parte cecidisse duces, eaque dici *prœlia*, non est quod moneam.' Barth supposes the proverb Καδμεία νίκη to have been in the poet's mind.

Cadmi, nec semper prœlia clade pari;
Nec referam Scæas et Pergama Apollinis arces,
Et Danaum decimo vere redisse rates,
Mœnia cum Graio Neptunia pressit aratro
Victor Palladiæ ligneus artis equus.
Inter Callimachi sat erit placuisse libellos,
Et cecinisse modis, Dore poeta, tuis.
Hæc urant pueros, hæc urant scripta puellas;
Meque Deum clament, et mihi sacra ferant.
Te duce vel Jovis arma canam, cæloque minantem
Cœum et Phlegræis Oromedonta jugis;
Celsaque Romanis decerpta Palatia tauris
Ordiar, et cæso mœnia firma Remo;
Eductosque pares silvestri ex ubere reges;
Crescet et ingenium sub tua jussa meum.
Prosequar et currus utroque ab litore ovantes,

41.] *Pressit aratro*, *i.e.* effecit, ut 'imprimeret muris hostile aratrum exercitus insolens.' The wooden horse is called 'the work of Pallas' from *Od.* viii. 493, τὸν Ἐπειὸς ἐποίησεν σὺν Ἀθήνῃ. Broukhuis reads *arces* here and *artes* in v. 39, in both places followed by Barth and Kuinoel, as also in his useless correction *undevicesimo* for *decimo*.

44.] Keil and Müller, with Lachmann and Jacob, edit *Coi poeta* from Pucci. The MSS. give *dure*, whence Scriverius ingeniously conjectured *Dore*, which Barth, Kuinoel, and Hertzberg rightly adopt, the allusion being to Philetas. Compare *Britanna* for Britannica, ii. 1, 76, *Lydus* for Lydius, v. 9, 48. So *Parthus*, *Indus*, for *Parthicus* &c.

45.] *Hæc urant*. The Gron. and Naples MSS. *hæc currant*. The reading of Barth and Kuinoel, *hæc pueri currant* (*currant pueri*, Barth) is from Pucci. The verse is rightly printed in the edition of 1488.

47.] *Te duce*. Not *te jubente*, but *te praeeunte*, 'when you live less modestly, then I will write more boldly.'

48.] *Oromedonta*. The MSS. agree in this form of the word, which occurs also in Theocritus, vii. 46, except that the Naples MS. (according to Müller) gives *oromedonta*. The uncertainty of the etymology renders it suspicious, and Hertzberg is probably right in restoring *Eurymedonta* from *Od.* vii. 58, on the suggestion of Huschk. The other form, however, though a corrupt one, is possibly as old as Propertius.

49.] *Celsa Palatia*, a poetic exaggeration, as in v. 9, 3, 'venit ad ductos pecorosa Palatia montis.'—*firma*, firmata.

51.] *Ordiar*. The future seems to be used, because his historic poems in the fifth book were juvenile performances which he does not now take into account.

52.] *Crescet sub tua jussa*, *i.e.* altius ascendet donec sub tua jussa venerit, ut Cæsaris res gestas canat. The expression is a brief one, but not very obscure. It may be compared with *acta in partes*, v. 60, [illegible]. So 'in castra reponere,' v. 4, 37. Compare *sub tua jura fluet*, iv. 4, 4. Hertzberg's comment is as follows: 'Hoc ait, se non aliter suum scribendi institutum mutaturum esse, nisi cum Mæcenas vivendi rationem mutaverit. Tum demum illo duce majora se ausurum.' But it is not easy to assent to his view, that *sub tua jussa* means, 'si sub tuum imperium carmine perventum foret;' *i.e.* 'if my epic were to be continued from the foundation of the city to your times.' What *imperium* had Mæcenas? Or what authority is there for this use of *jussa*?

53.] *Utroque ab litore*. From the extreme east to the extreme west inclusive; the whole Roman empire. The same phrase occurs in *Georgic* iii. 33.—*Prosequar*, *i.e.* carmine: but there is a sort of play on the word.

Parthorum astutæ tela remissa fugæ;
Castraque Pelusi Romano subruta ferro,
Antonique graves in sua fata manus.
Mollis tu cœptæ fautor cape lora juventæ,
Dexteraque inmissis da mihi signa rotis.
Hoc mihi, Mæcenas, laudis concedis; et a te est,
Quod ferar in partes ipse fuisse tuas.

X.

Mirabar quidnam misissent mane Camenæ,
Ante meum stantes sole rubente torum.
Natalis nostræ signum misere puellæ,
Et manibus faustos ter crepuere sonos.
Transeat hic sine nube dies, stent aëre venti,
Ponat et in sicco molliter unda minas.
Adspiciam nullos hodierna luce dolentes,
Et Niobes lacrimas supprimat ipse lapis.
Alcyonum positis requiescant ora querellis;
Increpet absumptum nec sua mater Ityn.

54.] *Remissæ fugæ*, 'unstrung for a crafty flight,' *i.e.* to be used against the enemy by suddenly turning round. Virg. *Georg.* iii. 31, 'fidentemque fuga Parthum versisque sagittis.'

55.] *Castra Pelusi.* Lachmann, Barth, and Kuinoel read *claustra*, the conjecture of Lipsius. Pelusium was regarded as commanding access to Egypt by land, and was therefore destroyed by Octavian. *Castra* here means the garrison or fort: more commonly *castellum*.

57—60.] The meaning of the concluding verses is this: 'Though disinclined to write historical poems, still if you my patron insist upon it, and will engage to regard them favourably if unequal to your expectations, I will consent, conscious that at least you cannot deny me the credit of having taken the side of humility, like yourself.'—*quod ferar*, 'that I shall be said to have myself joined your side,' in partes tuas accessisse. 'Hos honores mihi habendos tu solus concedis, quod tuum exemplum secutus res magnas non affectare prædicabor.'—*Lachmann*; who transposes the last distich after v. 46.

58.] *Immissis rotis*, 'when my car is in full career.' A metaphor from the circus, where the drivers received signs of encouragement from the spectators, and partisans of the factions, *fautores*.

X. This charming little poem seems to have been sent as a birthday compliment to Cynthia. It breathes a fondness which could only have found such expression in sincerity: nor must we measure its morality by any other than a heathen standard.

4.] *Ter crepuere*, *i.e.* by clapping their hands thrice they made a joyous sound, or brought tidings of a happy event, the birth-day of my dear girl. For *misere* we should have expected *tulere*.

6.] *In sicco*, ἐν χέρσῳ, ποτὶ ξερὸν ἠπείροιο, *Od.* v. 402. When there is a storm, the whole shore is wet; in a calm the sand is dry to the water's edge. Pliny, *Ep.* ii. 17, 27, 'ipso litore—quod non nunquam longa tranquillitas mollit, sæpius frequens et contrarius fluctus indurat.'

8.] Hertzberg reads *Niobe* with the Naples MS., comparing, though hardly parallel, *Lernæ palus*, iii. 18, 48, and Hom. *Il.* xxiv. 617, ἔνθα λίθος περ ἐοῦσα θεῶν ἐκ κήδεα πέσσει. Jacob gives *Niobes* from MS. Gron. and Pucci. The others *Niobæ*.

Tuque, o cara mihi, felicibus edita pennis,
  Surge, et poscentes justa precare Deos.
Ac primum pura somnum tibi discute lympha,
  Et nitidas presso pollice finge comas.
Dein qua primum oculos cepisti veste Properti,
  Indue, nec vacuum flore relinque caput;
Et pete, qua polles, ut sit tibi forma perennis,
  Inque meum semper stent tua regna caput.
Inde coronatas ubi ture piaveris aras,
  Luxerit et tota flamma secunda domo,
Sit mensæ ratio, noxque inter pocula currat,
  Et crocino nares murreus ungat onyx.
Tibia nocturnis succumbat rauca choreis,
  Et sint nequitiæ libera verba tuæ;
Dulciaque ingratos adimant convivia somnos;
  Publica vicinæ perstrepat aura viæ.
Sit sors et nobis talorum interprete jactu,
  Quem gravibus pennis verberet ille Puer.
Cum fuerit multis exacta trientibus hora,

11.] *Pennis*, *i.e.* omine, 'born with a lucky omen.' So the Greeks use πτερόν. See on Æsch. *Ag.* 267.

12.] *Poscentes*, scil. invocari. Compare ii. 1, 11, and Ovid, *Fast.* i, ult. 'Ad pia propensos vota vocate deos.'—*justa precare*, *i.e.* talia quæ concessuri sint dii. Or perhaps *justa poscentes*, should be joined, 'the gods who are expecting from you the worship that is due.'

13.] *Somnum discute*. Some understand this of the usual washing in running water to avert the ill effects of a dream (Persius, ii. 16). But the poet seems to have nothing more in view than the common-place, though very elegantly expressed, details of everyday life; 'rise, say your prayers, wash yourself, and put on that silk tunic (see on i. 2, 2; ii. 1, 5) which I admired when I first saw you.'—*finge* &c., 'put into shape those glossy locks by the pressure of your finger.'

17—18.] This beautiful distich is wanting in the Naples MS. probably on account of *caput* ending v. 16.

19.] *Piaveris*, 'when you have performed the holy rite with incense on the festooned altar.' *Piare* is a favourite word with the poet.—*luxerit* (luceo), because favourable omens were derived from the brightness of the flame.

22.] *Crocino*, κροκίνῳ, sc. unguento, essence of saffron. On the word *murreus* see v. 5, 26.—*onyx* was properly a kind of marble; here used for the gallipot itself. So Hor. iv. 12, 16, 'nardi parvus onyx eliciet cadum.'—*ungat*, unguenti odore afficiat.

23.] *Succumbat*. 'Deficiat tibicen et impar sit saltationibus nimis productis.'—*Barth.* 'Let the hoarse piper give in, wearied with the nightly dance, and let there be free expression of the warmth of your amorous feelings' (*nequitiæ*).

26.] *Publica aura*, *i.e.* non modo privata domus intus strepat, sed exterior aura viæ in qua populus versatur. The sense is, 'let the noise of our convivial party be heard by the people in the streets; lit. 'let the very air in the public streets near the house ring with the festive sounds.' The expression is a singular one, and the more so because *publica* in point of sense belongs rather to *viæ*.

28.] *Sit sors* &c. 'Let us try our luck too by a throw of the dice to tell us (*interprete*) which of the company is smitten by the heavy wings of the boy-god' (Cupid). By *gravibus pennis* he means that the blow is heavily felt, Κύπρις γὰρ οὐ φορητὸς ἢν πολλὴ ῥυῇ, Eur. *Hipp.* 443, and so Plato speaks of φέρειν τὸ νοῦ

Noctis et instituet sacra ministra Venus,
Annua solvamus thalamo sollemnia nostro,
Natalisque tui sic peragamus iter.

XI.

Quid mirare, meam si versat femina vitam,
Et trahit addictum sub sua jura virum,
Criminaque ignavi capitis mihi turpia fingis,
Quod nequeam fracto rumpere vincla jugo?
Venturam melius præsagit navita noctem:
Vulneribus didicit miles habere metum.
Ista ego præterita jactavi verba juventa;
Tu nunc exemplo disce timere meo.
Colchis flagrantis adamantina sub juga tauros

πτεροφύτορ' ἀνάγκην, *Phædr.* p. 252, c. The custom alluded to is that described in Hor. *Od.* i. 27, 10. See also Becker's *Gallus*, p. 129, &c. The *triens*, according to the same authority, contained four *cyathi*, or ladles-full; the *sextarius* being divided into twelve parts, like the *as*.

30.] Construe *noctis sacra*, 'when Venus our attendant shall bring on the nightly mysteries,' *i. e.* of lovers.

31.] 'Ipsis igitur natalibus Cynthiæ amores junxerant; eoque ipso die puella, uno anno ante tunicam ostrinam induta, dum ad Vestæ precatum it, Propertii oculos ceperat (III. 21, 26). Vides, cur preces et sacra nunc quoque dii poscant.'—*Hertzberg.* This is surely a gratuitous assumption. All that the poet says is this: 'let us finish the birthday with mutual endearments,' &c. Barth appears to interpret the concluding verse aright; '*peragere iter natalis* est celebrare diem natalem cum longus est. Iter natalis dicitur, ut alibi iter lucis, mortis, vitæ.' Lachmann, who reads *ter* for *sic*, from the MS. Gron., assigns a widely different and less becoming sense to the passage.

XI. This elegy, addressed probably to one of those friends who had endeavoured to draw him away from his unworthy attachment, commences with a justification of his conduct, by showing that the greatest heroes have been equally enslaved. Having quoted among other instances the example of Antony and Cleopatra, he runs off in rather a desultory but splendidly poetical strain to compliment Cæsar on having rid Rome of one whom he seems to have regarded as a sort of female monster. See lib. v. 6, and compare especially Horace, *Od.* i. 37. One might conjecture that our poet here attempted to gratify Mæcenas by giving a specimen of his capability for historic subjects. Kuinoel has a fancy that two elegies are combined in one, and places a mark of separation at v. 28. In the ed. Rheg. the division is fixed at v. 21.

2.] *Addictum*, *i. e.* as an insolvent debtor is formally made over to a creditor, to be sold as a slave *trans Tiberim*. Cf. v. 32.

5.] *Noctem*. This reading is given as a conjecture by Pucci. The good copies have *mortem*, which Müller retains. The sense is, 'As a sailor knows by experience the approach of a storm and its accompanying dangers, better than a landsman, and a wounded soldier has more cause to fear the conflict, so does a lover more clearly foresee the risks and the difficulties of contending against Cupid.'

7.] *Ista* &c. 'What you say to me, I used to say in my youth' (viz. that it was easy to get rid of love's yoke); but let my example now teach you to fear lest you should yourself some day find it to be far otherwise.

9.] The poet proceeds to say, that Medea, Omphale, and others, (for he mentions the *women* rather than the *men*, as more aptly introductory to the chief point of the poem, the case of Cleopatra), exercised a powerful influence on the most renowned heroes, Jason, Hercules, Ninus; nay, that gods and heroes (27) were equally

Egit, et armigera prœlia sevit humo,
Custodisque feros clausit serpentis hiatus,
Iret ut Æsonias aurea lana domos.
Ausa ferox ab equo quondam oppugnare sagittis
Mæotis Danaum Penthesilea rates;
Aurea cui postquam nudavit cassida frontem,
Vicit victorem candida forma virum.
Omphale in tantum formæ processit honorem,
Lydia Gygæo tincta puella lacu,
Ut, qui pacato statuisset in orbe columnas,
Tam dura traheret mollia pensa manu.
Persarum statuit Babylona Semiramis urbem,
Ut solidum cocto tolleret aggere opus,
Et duo in adversum missi per mœnia currus,

susceptible. But the argument is not clearly stated; for in the case of Medea and Semiramis he describes what they did, leaving the reader to trace out the connexion of their acts with the love of those heroes.—*adamantina juga*, a mere poetical expression for *strong* and *unbending*. The material Hertzberg with others regards as iron or steel. I have suggested on v. 11, 4, that the word originally meant *basalt*.

10.] *Prœlia sevit*, 'sparsit dentes draconis, unde nati armati inter se dimicarunt.'—*Barth*.

13.] The legend was, that Penthesilea, queen of the Amazons, having come to assist the Trojans, was slain by Achilles, who on removing her war-cap or helmet was enraptured by her beauty. This was a not uncommon subject with the painters of the early Greek vases. According to Homer, *Il.* iii. 189, the Amazons seem to have fought against the Trojans at a time anterior to the Trojan war.—For *quondam* Lachmann and others give *contra*, which is only found in one of the inferior MSS. —*virum*, *i.e.* the man felt and acknowledged the beauty of the woman.

15.] *Cassida*. A rare form of the nominative, for which Hertzberg's note will supply the student with sufficient authority. Dr. Donaldson (*Varronianus*, p. 155) quotes *cassila* as the ancient Etruscan word. The use of *nudavit*, *i.e.* strepitu fecit ut nudaretur, belongs to an idiom pointed out on iv. 22, 22.

17.] *Omphale et in* Lachmann, Barth, Kuinoel from a single copy of inferior note. The hiatus, though remarkable, appears genuine. Common as an open vowel is when the ictus falls on it, there are but few instances of it under the present circumstances.—*in tantum formæ honorem processit*, ἐς τοσοῦτον ἀφίκετο κάλλους, tam formosa fuit.

18.] *Gygæo lacu*. See Herod. i. 93. Γυγαίη λίμνη was the name even in Homer's time, *Il.* ii. 865. It was called after Gyges king of Lydia, in which country it was situated. On *tincta* see on i. 6, 32. Barth rightly explains 'lota.'

19.] *Statuisset* should rather be *statuerat*; but the relative clause is affected by *ut traheret*.

21.] The poet, in mentioning Semiramis, leaves that part of her history which he must have had in mind without even an allusion. She is said to have been the wife of one of the king's generals, but to have inspired the king (Ninus) with such a passion that he obtained her, as David did Bathsheba, by putting her husband to death. It was by her counsels, it is said, that the Assyrians were enabled to take Bactra after a long siege. The building of Babylon &c. is here spoken of as an instance of the influence obtained by women in carrying out the greatest works, such as their husbands would never have effected alone.

23.] Lachmann and Hertzberg rightly admit *missi* from the Naples and Gron. MSS. Jacob gives *misit* from Pucci, and so Kuinoel. Barth *immissi*, on what authority does not appear.

Ne possent tacto stringere ab axe latus.
Duxit et Euphratem medium, qua condidit arces,
Jussit et imperio surgere Bactra caput.
Nam quid ego heroas, quid raptem in crimine divos?
Juppiter infamat seque suamque domum.
Quid? modo quæ nostris opprobria vexerat armis,
Et famulos inter femina trita suos?
Conjugis obsceni pretium Romana poposcit
Mœnia, et addictos in sua regna patres.
Noxia Alexandrea, dolis aptissima tellus,
Et totiens nostro, Memphi, cruenta malo,
Tres ubi Pompeio detraxit arena triumphos!

24.] *Ne possent.* For *ita ut non possent;* an incorrect usage where the *consequence* and not the *purpose* is expressed. The meaning is, two chariots could be driven past each other on the top of the wall without collision. See Herod. i. 179.—*ab* may be considered as redundant, as in iv. 2, 23.

25.] *Medium.* See Herod. i. 180.

26.] Lachmann reads *subdere*, the conjecture of the elder Burmann. Müller adopts, Hertzberg and Jacob approve without admitting it. It does not indeed accord with history to represent Bactra as the head of the Assyrian empire at that or any other time. But Hertzberg remarks on the uncertainty and the difficulty of reconciling conflicting Eastern legends; and he concludes that our poet probably followed authors now lost. It is more natural and reasonable to refer the statement to the want of accurate information on Eastern history and geography. We may acquiesce in Barth's brief comment, 'voluit urbem primariam esse totius imperii;' *surgere* not being put for *aedificari*, but implying subsequent aggrandisement.

27.] *Raptem in crimine*, 'assail the gods under the same charge.' So MSS. Gron., Naples; *crimina* Pucci. Barth and Hertzberg alone defend the former. It is, however, fully as good, while it has more authority, and was more likely to have been changed to *crimina* by the transcribers than the converse. On *raptem* Hertzberg remarks: 'Judiciale verbum proprie est *raptare*. Hinc in accusandi et convitiandi notionem transiit.' In the acrostich argument to the Amphitryo of Plautus we have 'Iovem raptant pro moechis.'—*infamat*, viz. by his amours.

29.] The best copies have *vexerit*.

30.] *Trita*, a coarse insinuation, that Cleopatra was too familiar with her own slaves and eunuchs. Hor. *Od.* i. 37, 9, 'contaminato cum grege turpium morbo virorum.'

31.] Lachmann reads *conjugi et*, Müller, Barth, and Kuinoel *conjugii*, both against the MSS., which agree in *conjugis*. The sense is, 'As the price to be paid by her debased and degenerate husband Antony she demanded Rome itself.' In other words, she made Antony promise to subject Rome to her dominions. 'Pretium conjugis, quod conjux dat.'—*Jacob*. Compare v. 4, 56, 'dos tibi non humilis prodita Roma venit.' Barth rightly observes, 'alludit ad matrimonium per coemptionem,' *i.e. per aes et libram*. See Becker, *Gallus*, p. 167. Antony was 'emancipatus feminae,' sold to a woman, Hor. *Epod.* 9, 12. The reader will observe that the popular notion of Cleopatra's beauty, elegance, and fascinations, is not borne out by the account of Propertius, who regards her simply as a lewd and abandoned woman, lost to all sense of shame, or even decency.

34.] *Totiens*, i.e. the murder of Pompey on the shore by the treachery of Ptolemy, the siege of Julius Cæsar in the Alexandrine war, and the factions in favour of Antony.

35.] *Detraxit tres triumphos.* The shore itself, where he fell, is said to have stripped him of his former glories. There is, perhaps, an allusion to gladiators; see on iv. 14, 17. The *three* triumphs are the victories over Iarbas, the Pirates, and Mithridates.—*arena*, the African shore, where Pompey was killed by his freedman Pothinus at his own request, Mart. *Ep.* v. lxix.

Tollet nulla dies hanc tibi, Roma, notam.
Issent Phlegræo melius tibi funera campo,
Vel tua si socero colla daturus eras.
Scilicet incesti meretrix regina Canopi,
Una Philippeo sanguine adusta nota,
Ausa Jovi nostro latrantem opponere Anubim,
Et Tiberim Nili cogere ferre minas,
Romanamque tubam crepitanti pellere sistro,
Baridos et contis rostra Liburna sequi,
Fœdaque Tarpeio conopia tendere saxo,

36.] *Notam.* He speaks of the death of Pompey as a national disgrace, either because he was compelled to fly from his country, or because sufficient vengeance was not exacted for his murder. It is clear that his sympathies were strongly on the side of that great and unfortunate general. Lachmann transfers this verse to the place of v. 40, which he inserts in this place, lest the poet should seem to reflect on Augustus. He is sufficiently refuted by Hertzberg. Lachmann's supposition is, that the termination of both verses with *nota* led to the accidental change. There might have been some plea in this, had the two pentameters been separated by a less interval. A still more extravagant transposition has been made by the same critic placing vv. 67—8 after v. 46.

37.] *Phlegræo campo, i.e.* he had better have died in the battle of Pharsalia. Compare Juvenal, x. 283, 'Provida Pompeio dederat Campania febres Optandas; sed multæ urbes et publica vota Vicerunt' &c. There was a *Phlegræan* (*i.e.* volcanic) district in Thessaly as well as that better known by the name in Campania, the scene of the conflict with the giants. See Strabo, *Excerpt.* lib. vii. 12.

38.] *Socero.* Julius Cæsar, whose daughter Julia Pompey had married. 'You had better,' says the poet, 'have entrusted your life and safety to Cæsar after your defeat by him on the field of Pharsalia.'

39.] *Incesti,* viz. because more than one of the Ptolemies married their own sisters.

40.] All the good copies have *sanguine adusta.* Passeratius gives *sanguini,* which Jacob admits. The meaning of the poet is rather obscure, 'branded on us by the race of Philip,' *i.e.* by the Ptolemies. Cf. v. 11, 74, 'hæc cum et cineri spirat inusta meo.' The following is Hertzberg's view: '*Nota adusta* ad omnem periodum pertinet inde a v. 39—46. Turpis reginæ ausa et minæ, Romani nominis contemptio, hæc *una nota* est, quam sanguis Philippeus adussit. Cui autem, nisi Romæ?' He rightly observes, after Lachmann, that the simpler sense of the verse, 'the sole (or peculiar, *unica*) disgrace indelibly marked upon the Ptolemies,' who boasted their descent from the kings of Macedonia, is not borne out by history, since that royal house was far from immaculate in many of its members. Without however regarding *nota* in apposition with what follows, we may understand it thus: 'that sole blot on our fair name which the race of Philip has ever been able to leave.' It is clear that the poet is offended at the *impudence* of Cleopatra fighting with his countrymen, and that he regards this fact alone as an ignominy hardly atoned for by her signal defeat. His detestation of the Egyptians generally is evinced by the spite with which he ridicules Isis, iii. 25, 4.

41.] *Ausa,* supply *est.*

44.] *Sequi, insequi,* 'to endeavour to overtake the sharp-prowed Liburnian galleys by a barge propelled with a pole.' This is bitter irony in disparagement of the Egyptian fleet.

45.] It is rather singular that the mosquito-curtains, now so commonly used in Italy, should have excited the wrath of the Romans so greatly in the Augustan age; see Hor. *Epod.* ix. 16. The circumstance of its being a foreign innovation was perhaps enough to rouse their anger; for such feelings are common among narrow-minded people to this day. It is hardly necessary to add that we derive our word *canopy* from it, which a recent writer on etymology has deduced from *cannabis,* 'hemp.' It is probable that the 'conopium' which gave such offence was a peculiar sort of tent, and not a mere curtain; still less, as some have thought, used as an Egyptian standard.

Jura dare et statuas inter et arma Mari!
Quid nunc Tarquinii fractas juvat esse secures,
Nomine quem simili vita superba notat,
Si mulier patienda fuit? Cape, Roma, triumphum,
Et longum Augusto salva precare diem.
Fugisti tamen in timidi vaga flumina Nili;
Accepere tuæ Romula vincla manus.
Brachia spectavi sacris admorsa colubris,
Et trahere occultum membra soporis iter.
'Non hoc, Roma, fui tanto tibi cive verenda,'
Dixit, 'et assiduo lingua sepulta mero.'
Septem urbs alta jugis, toto quæ præsidet orbi,
Femineas timuit territa Marte minas!
Nunc ubi Scipiadæ classes, ubi signa Camilli,

46.] *Ausa—jura dare.* 'She aspired to legislate at Rome.' Hertzberg well observes, on the authority of Dio, that τὸ ἐν Καπιτωλίῳ δικάσαι was a real wish repeatedly expressed by the Egyptian Queen.—On *jura dare* see v. 11, 18.—*arma Mari*, *i.e.* the arms and trophies taken by Marius and placed in the capitol.—*statuas* must not be connected with the same genitive, as Hertzberg well observes that before Julius Cæsar's statue was erected, none but kings, with the single exception of Brutus, were allowed that honour.

48.] *Quem—notat.* Whose life of pride made him notorious by the just title of Superbus.

51.] *Timidi Nili.* As if the river feared to receive her, lest it should experience Cæsar's wrath. See v. 6, 63.

52.] *Romula vincla*, like *Herculis pila*, sup. iv. 3, 7.

53.] On the metrical licence see on v. 4, 48. It may be questioned if *brachia* was not pronounced as a dissyllable. The death of Cleopatra, commonly attributed to an asp, is of doubtful authority. Strabo, lib. xvii. cap. i. gives another, but scarcely more probable account: λαβὼν (Καῖσαρ) ἐξ ἐφόδου τὴν πόλιν, ἠνάγκασε τὸν μὲν Ἀντώνιον ἑαυτὸν διαχειρίσασθαι, τὴν δὲ Κλεοπάτραν ζῶσαν ἐλθεῖν εἰς τὴν ἐξουσίαν. μικρὸν δ᾽ ὕστερον κἀκείνη ἑαυτὴν ἐν τῇ φρουρᾷ διεχειρίσατο λάθρα δήγματι ἀσπίδος, ἢ φαρμάκῳ ἐπιχρίστῳ· λέγεται γὰρ ἀμφότερα. The commentators suppose, on the testimony of Plutarch, *Anton.* cap. 86, that an effigy of Cleopatra was carried in the triumph. The disappointment of the victor at not being able to exhibit the living reality is expressed v. 6, 63—6.

54.] *Occultum soporis iter.* 'Pro ipso sopore tacite adrepente dictum.'—*Hertzberg.* *trahere*, perhaps for *contrahere*, 'I saw the sleep of death contract her limbs;' or, as others understand it, 'I saw her limbs take in the subtle poison that caused the sleep of death.' The exact construction of *trahere* is not clear.

55—6.] Jacob explains this distich, with the approval of Hertzberg:—'Hoc tanto cive non ego, O Roma, timenda fui, nec Antonius vinositate delirans.' This is quite satisfactory. The dying words of the unfortunate and much-abused queen are here made to pay Augustus a compliment: 'You need not, Romans! have brought me to this. There was no danger from me while Cæsar was your protector.'—*sepulta*, cf. 'mentem lymphatam Mareotico,' Hor. *Carm.* i. 37, 14. On *cive* Barth rightly remarks, 'quia *civilis* videri volebat Augustus. Cf. Ovid, *Trist.* iv. 4, 13.'—With this ablative absolute compare *parva urbe*, v. 1, 83.—*fui* is from Pucci; the MSS. give *fuit*. The reading of Barth, Lachmann, and Kuinoel, *non hæc, Roma, fuit*, and *nec ducis assiduo* &c. is said to be found in some copies; but *nec* appears to be from Heinsius' conjecture.

57-8.] These lines are ironical. 'What! Rome fear a woman's threats?' &c. Perhaps we should read *timeat*. The latter verse is wanting in the Naples MS.—*toto*, see i. 20, 35.

67 seqq.] The absence of any verb, and the difficulty of supplying one even in the

Aut modo Pompeia, Bospore, capta manu?
Hannibalis spolia et victi monumenta Syphacis
Et Pyrrhi ad nostros gloria fracta pedes?
Curtius expletis statuit monumenta lacunis;
At Decius misso prœlia rupit equo;
Coclitis abscissos testatur semita pontes;
Est cui cognomen corvus habere dedit.
Hæc di condiderunt, hæc di quoque mœnia servant:
Vix timeat, salvo Cæsare, Roma Jovem.
Leucadius versas acies memorabit Apollo.
Tantum operis belli sustulit una dies
At tu, sive petes portus, seu, navita, linques,
Cæsaris in toto sis memor Ionio.

mind, may be thought to show the poetic ardour and glow of patriotism with which the whole of this fine passage was written off. The very recurrence of *monumenta* in v. 61, indicates a *furor scribendi*. There is however no reason to suppose the word corrupt in the former verse, with Lachmann, who objects that 'monumenta ob Syphacem devictum nulla Scipioni posita fuerunt.' For *monumentum* is anything which reminds us (*monet*) of an event. Mr. Wratislaw thinks this couplet is in apposition with 'septem urbs alta jugis,' and places only a comma at *minas*. The general sense will thus be, 'Here, in our Capitol, are the tokens of many victories won over mightier enemies than an Egyptian queen. Rome can boast of her Curtii, and her Decii, devoted heads, her Cocles and her Corvinus,—and she has now a Cæsar,' &c. Müller marks a *lacuna* after v. 60. It is better perhaps to transfer 57—8 to follow 58, and so place an interrogation at 60. The sense thus becomes quite simple, 'How Rome must have descended from her former greatness!' And *hæc dii condiderunt* &c. means that even yet we need not despair, for we still have Cæsar for our preserver. Barth preserves the order of this distich, which has been variously transposed by others, and thus explains the sense. 'Fuit ingens olim Africani et Camilli et Pompeii gloria, terra marique parta: sed nunc in ore hominum esse desiit, et quodammodo evanuit, postquam Augustus prœlio Actiaco Antonium et Cleopatram vicit. Hanc victoriam celebrant omnes, et in posterum memorabunt, aliarum pæne obliti.'

58.] *Bosphore* is the reading of the Naples and Gron. MSS. The construction appears to be, 'aut ubi sunt signa capta Pompeio apud te, O Bospore?' It is not impossible that *Bospore* was intended as an ablative or locative, like *Tibure*, inf. 16, 2. Lachmann unnecessarily reads *capte*. Others adopt the false reading *Bosporo* from the ed. Rheg. and some of the later copies. But Lachmann rightly observes that a Greek word formed from πόρος could not have a neuter plural like *Ismara*, *Mænala*, *Gargara*, which imply an obsolete form in *-um*.—*capta*, viz. in the recent Mithridatic War.

65.] *Coclitis semita*. A pathway so called seems to have remained in honour of that hero's exploits at the Sublician bridge even to the Augustan age.—For *est* the MSS. give *et*.

67.] *Condiderunt*. The MSS. give *condiderant*, which Jacob attempts to defend, and Keil also retains.

70.] *Tantum operis* &c. 'So much of military achievement has a single day taken from the victors.' That is, one day has eclipsed all their warlike deeds.

72.] The poet bids every sailor to feel grateful to Augustus for his glorious victory at Actium. The Leucadian Apollo here mentioned, like Apollo Actius, had a temple on the promontory of that name, not far from the scene of the naval engagement.

XII.

Postume, plorantem potuisti linquere Gallam,
  Miles et Augusti fortia signa sequi?
Tantine ulla fuit spoliati gloria Parthi,
  Ne faceres Galla multa rogante tua?
Si fas est, omnes pariter pereatis avari,
  Et quisquis fido prætulit arma toro!
Tu tamen injecta tectus, vesane, lacerna
  Potabis galea fessus Araxis aquam.
Illa quidem interea fama tabescet inani,
  Hæc tua ne virtus fiat amara tibi;
Neve tua Medæ lætentur cæde sagittæ,
  Ferreus aurato neu cataphractus equo:
Neve aliquid de te flendum referatur in urna.
  Sic redeunt, illis qui cecidere locis.
Ter quater in casta felix, o Postume, Galla;

XII. This truly beautiful elegy is addressed to a friend under the real or feigned name of Postumus, who was then engaged in the expedition of Ælius Gallus in Arabia, and had left his wife, who would seem to be related to the Gallus of i. 5, and therefore a connexion of the poet's, to lament his long absence from home. Some have thought that the same parties are addressed in the fine epistle v. 3, under the names of Arethusa and Lycotas; but Hertzberg doubts this (*Quæst.* p. 22), and apparently with good reason: see introductory note to the latter. Ælius Gallus was prefect of Egypt, and was the first who penetrated with a Roman army into Arabia, A.U.C. 730, but he was compelled to retreat with the loss of many of his men. One of the same name is mentioned in Tac. *Ann.* v. 8, A.U.C. 784, but can hardly be the same person.

3.] *Tantine.* Compare iv. 20, 4, 'Tantine, ut lacrimes, Africa tota fuit?' The *aoristic* use of *spoliati*, (when an action is contemplated as prospectively accomplished), is noticed by Hertzberg, who compares 'ascensis Bactris,' v. 3, 63.

4.] *Ne faceres, rogante* &c. i.e. ut Gallæ tuæ preces sperneres, hortantis ne eam relinqueres.

5.] *Avari.* He indirectly upbraids him with leaving his wife from mere motives of gain.

6.] *Fido toro.* His dislike of military service is frequently expressed, as ii. 7, 14; v. 3, 19, &c. On the *lacerna* see v. 3, 18.

8.] *Araxis.* This seems a kind of typical Eastern river with Propertius (like the *Eridanus* of earlier times). He probably, as Mr. Wratislaw suggests, and as appears from v. 3, 35—7, knew but little of the geography of Asia. Thus he calls Babylon the capital of the Persians, sup. 10, 21. More than one river seems called the 'Araxes' by Herodotus.

10.] *Amara tibi.* See on i. 3, 16. So πικρὴν Αἴγυπτον, *Od.* xvii. 448. Supply *metuens ne* &c.

12.] *Aurato equo* is the ablative after *lætetur*. *Ferreus* is opposed to *auratus*. The Parthian, with his barbed horse in chain mail, would exult in the gilded trappings of his more luxurious but less hardy opponent. Virg. *Æn.* xi. 770, 'spumantemque agitabat equum, quem pellis ahenis In plumam squamis auro conserta tegebat.' Hor. *Od.* iii. 6, 11, de Parthis: 'et adjecisse prædam Torquibus exiguis renidet.'—*arato* and *armato* are unnecessary conjectures. On the word *cataphractus* see Tacit. *Ann.* iii. 43; *Hist.* i. 79. Livy, xxxvii. 40. Jacob thinks that the poet had in view the characters of Glaucus and Diomede, *Il.* vi. 236.

Moribus his alia conjuge dignus eras.
Quid faciet nullo munita puella timore,
Cum sit luxuriæ Roma magistra suæ?
Sed securus eas. Gallam non munera vincent,
Duritiæque tuæ non erit illa memor.
Nam quocumque die salvum te fata remittent,
Pendebit collo Galla pudica tuo.
Postumus alter erit miranda conjuge Ulixes.
Non illi longæ tot nocuere moræ;
Castra decem annorum, et Ciconum manus, Ismara capta,
Exustæque tuæ mox, Polypheme, genæ,
Et Circæ fraudes, lotosque, herbæque tenaces,
Scyllaque, et alternas scissa Charybdis aquas,
Lampeties Ithacis veribus mugisse juvencos,—
Paverat hos Phœbo filia Lampetie,—
Et thalamum Æææ flentis fugisse puellæ,
Totque hiemis noctes, totque natasse dies,
Nigrantisque domos animarum intrasse silentum,

16.] *Moribus his*, 'with such a cold and unloving disposition you did not deserve such a wife as Galla.'

17.] *Quid faciet.* 'What can you expect will become of a wife, when the fear of her husband is removed, and when Rome is her residence, the very hot-bed of vice, and the teacher to others of its own profligacy.' However (he adds, to allay the alarm his remark was calculated to arouse) you need not fear for Galla.' Lachmann, Keil, and Müller prefer the reading of some corrected copies, *suæ*, for the vulg. *tuæ*.

22.] *Pudica*, not an otiose epithet, but *salva pudicitia inter tot probra*.

25.] *Ciconum mons, Ismara, Calpe* is the reading of all the authentic copies; and so both Jacob and Hertzberg have edited the passage, on the plea that Propertius may have followed accounts now lost of the wanderings of Ulysses. Yet, as the following incidents are wholly from the *Odyssey*, and as the fight with the Cicones and the capture of their city Ismarus are actually recorded, *Od.* ix. 39, it seems unreasonable to doubt the correction of Fontaine, which Lachmann and Kuinoel have admitted, and so also Müller. Calpe (Gibraltar) seems utterly out of place in speaking of the Thracians and of the Cyclops, both the subjects of the ninth book of the *Odyssey*. There was, it seems, an obscure tradition that Ulysses visited Spain, and founded a city '*Ὀδύσσεια*, *Ulysippo*, or Lisbon, (Strabo, iii. p. 398); and Asciburgium, or *Asburg*, in Holland (Tac. *Germ.* 3); but it does not seem probable that our poet should attach the same weight to it as to the Homeric narrative, which he evidently has in view. Hertzberg endeavours to found an argument on the events not being in the same order as they are recorded in the *Odyssey*, whence he infers that our poet followed Philetas rather than Homer. For the same reason he thinks, with others, that *Ææa puella*, v. 31, is Calypso, and not Circe; an opinion by no means certain, since according to Homer, Circe dwelt in the island *Æa* or *Ææa*, Calypso in Ogygia. Nor is it a conclusive argument that Circe has just been mentioned, v. 27. Perhaps indeed Propertius had no very accurate knowledge of the *Odyssey*, and made the slight mistake of confounding Calypso and Circe, who are but duplicate descriptions of an enchantress half human, half divine.

27.] *Tenaces*, keeping them away from their homes.

31.] *Natasse*. A word peculiarly applied to shipwrecked mariners. See iv. 17, 22.

Sirenum surdo remige adisse lacus,
Et veteres arcus leto renovasse procorum,
Errorisque sui sic statuisse modum.
Nec frustra, quia casta domi persederat uxor.
Vincit Penelopes Ælia Galla fidem.

XIII.

Quæritis, unde avidis nox sit pretiosa puellis,
Et Venere exhaustæ damna querantur Opes.
Certa quidem tantis causa et manifesta ruinis:
Luxuriæ nimium libera facta via est.
Inda cavis aurum mittit formica metallis,
Et venit e rubro concha Erycina salo,
Et Tyros ostrinos præbet Cadmea colores,
Cinnamon et multi pastor odoris Araba.
Hæc etiam clausas expugnant arma pudicas,

35.] *Renovasse*, to have brought again into use a long disused bow by killing the suitors, *Od.* xxii. The infinitives all depend on *non illi nocuit*, from sup. 24.

37.] *Nec frustra*, sc. *non nocuere*, v. 24, unless perhaps it is simpler and easier to supply *hoc omnis perpessus est*. Hertzberg objects to the former; but he is for ever dwelling on *words*, when the general sense is far from obscure. The poet means nothing more than 'it was not for nothing that he escaped so many dangers: he was rewarded by returning to a faithful wife.'

38.] The MSS. give *Lælia* or *Lelia*, but agree in *vincit*, for which Lachmann and others have edited *vincet*. But the sense is, that Galla surpasses in her devotion and fidelity even Penelope.

XIII. Directed against the avarice of women, and probably suggested by the importunity of Cynthia. A very elegant poem, in which the simplicity of primitive life is contrasted with the profligacy of Rome. See on iii. 24, 28.

1.] *Pretiosa*, pretio sc. muneribus emenda. So *Thais pretiosa Menandri*, v. 6, 43. —*Venere* is from Pucci and one late copy. The Naples MS. has *et Veneream exhausto*. *Veneream* is also in MS. Gron. and ed. Rheg., nor is this reading indefensible, *damna* being regarded as in apposition, *i.e.* *damni causam*. On the frequent personification of Opes and Πλοῦτος, see Æsch. *Agam.* 1306. Supra, iv. 7, 1.

5.] *Inda*, for Indica. See on ii. 1, 76. The allusion is to the well-known story in Herod. iii. 102, so ingeniously explained by Humboldt, *Cosmos*, vol. ii. note 205.—*concha Erycina*, 'the shell of Venus,' probably pearls. Others read *Erythræa*. It is impossible to determine with accuracy the particular shell or material here meant. Venus, however, as the goddess born from the sea, is represented as riding in a giant shell, (*concha* was the mystic symbol of the sex), and Hertzberg quotes 'conchas Cytheriacas,' from Martial ii. 47, 2. Why the Indian Ocean was called 'the Red Sea,' from which the more limited term of modern geography is derived, appears to be unknown. May it not have meant the *Eastern* sea, which 'Aurora suis rubra colorat equis,' inf. 16? Cf. Tibull. iv. 2, 20.

8.] *Pastor Arabs.* The Nomade Arabians.—*pastor multi odoris*, as Martial calls him *messor Arabs*, Ep. iii. 65, 5. See Herod. iii. 107. He enumerates, as Barth observes, 'quatuor genera luxuriæ; aurum, gemmas, purpuram, unguenta.' Cinnamon was probably obtained from Ceylon (Taprobane) or East Africa; but the productions of India, Africa, and Arabia are often confounded by the ancients. See Humboldt, *Cosmos*, vol. ii. pp. 206-7, (note 243).

9.] *Etiam clausas expugnant.* A metaphor from a beleaguered city retiring within its closed gates. For *clausas* Müller reads *nymphas*, 'brides,' the Naples MS.

Quæque gerunt fastus, Icarioti, tuos:
Matrona incedit census induta nepotum,
Et spolia opprobrii nostra per ora trahit.
Nulla est poscendi, nulla est reverentia dandi;
Aut si qua est, pretio tollitur ipsa mora.
Felix Eois lex funeris una maritis,
Quos Aurora suis rubra colorat equis.
Namque ubi mortifero jacta est fax ultima lecto,
Uxorum fusis stat pia turba comis,
Et certamen habent leti, quæ viva sequatur
Conjugium; pudor est, non licuisse mori.
Ardent victrices et flammæ pectora præbent,
Imponuntque suis ora perusta viris.
Hic genus infidum nuptarum; hic nulla puella
Nec fida Evadne, nec pia Penelope.

having the reading *nifeas* superscribed by the same hand.

10.] Jacob and Hertzberg read *Hæcque* from Pucci; an unusual and unpleasing combination. The Gron. and Naples MSS. give *quæque*, which Lachmann, Barth, and Kuinoel adopt.—*gerunt* for *terunt* is adopted by the best editors from Guiet. Compare Tac. *Ann.* xi. 37, 'tantum inter extrema superbiæ gerebat' (*superbia egebat* MS. Med.) Lachmann retains *terunt*, the sense of which can only be, 'et eas, quæ *terunt*, deterunt, imminuunt, fastus tuos, O Penelope.' 'Fastum alicujus terere est—facere ne quis tantopere superbiat.'—*Barth.*

11.] *Census induta nepotum.* 'Wearing on her person whole fortunes of spendthrifts.' Hertzberg endeavours to show from a single passage (Ovid, *Met.* vii. 739), that *census* was properly used for *noctis merces*.—*Spolia opprobrii*, i.e. per opprobrium et dedecus suum parta.

13—14.] 'Omnes jam mulieres Romæ *poscunt munera*, omnes jam promiscue et passim sui *dant copiam*. Aut si contra accidit et *mora* injicitur, ne castiorem ideo crede puellam, quæ delicias agit; avarior enim tantum est: aurum ostende, *ipsa mora* tolletur.'—*Hertzberg.* The context seems to show that *poscere* and *dare* are correlative terms, as he is speaking of gifts. The poet means, I think, that the giver is as reckless as the party who asks; and any hesitation in giving—any *avaritia*—is *bought off*, i.e. by making it compulsory to give as a return for something received. People buy even gifts; which from their very nature ought not to be bought.

15—22.] This touching and extremely beautiful passage is interesting as showing the antiquity of the Suttee, that strange and fanatical custom of burning alive widows in India. Ælian, *Var. Hist.* vii. 18, Παρὰ Ἰνδοῖς αἱ γυναῖκες τὸ αὐτὸ πῦρ ἀποθανοῦσι τοῖς ἀνδράσιν ὑπομένουσι. Φιλοτιμοῦνται δὲ περὶ τούτου αἱ γυναῖκες τοῦ ἀνδρὸς καὶ ἡ κλήρῳ λαχοῦσα συγκαίεται. Nor can we doubt that the legend of Evadne leaping into the pyre of her husband Capaneus, I. 15, 21, Eur. *Suppl.* 1046, was derived from an early Indian tradition. See Herod. v. 5.

16.] *Colorat.* "Eastern and western relations determined the whole thermic meteorology of the Greeks. The parts of the earth towards the sun-rising were regarded as near to the sun, or *sun-lands*. 'The God in his course colours the skin of man with a dark sooty lustre, and parches and curls his hair.' (Theodectes)." Humboldt, *Cosmos*, vol. ii. p. 160.

18.] Barth and Kuinoel give *pactis* for *fusis*, from the MS. Gron.

21.] *Victrices*, i.e. quæ amoris certamine vicerunt.

23.] *Nulla—nec.* Lachmann compares iii. 10, 5, 'Nulla neque ante tuas orietur rixa fenestras' &c.

24.] *Euhadne* Müller, *Evadne* Lachmann and others.

Felix agrestum quondam pacata juventus,
  Divitiæ quorum messis et arbor erant.
Illis munus erat decussa Cydonia ramo,
  Et dare puniceis plena canistra rubis;
Nunc violas tondere manu, nunc mixta referre
  Lilia virgineos lucida per calathos;
Et portare suis vestitas frondibus uvas,
  Aut variam plumæ versicoloris avem.
His tum blanditiis furtiva per antra puellæ
  Oscula silvicolis empta dedere viris.
Hinulei pellis totos operibat amantes,
  Altaque nativo creverat herba toro,
Pinus et incumbens lentas circumdabat umbras,
  Nec fuerat nudas pœna videre deas.
Corniger atque dei vacuam pastoris in aulam
  Dux aries saturas ipse reduxit oves;
Dique deæque omnes, quibus est tutela per agros,
  Præbebant vestris verba secunda focis:

25.] *Pacata*, *i.e.* pacis studiosa. Lachmann. With these beautiful verses compare Tacit. *Ann.* iii. 26, 'Vetustissimi mortalium, nulla adhuc mala libidine, sine probro, scelere, eoque sine pœna aut coercitionibus agebant;' and especially Juven. vi. 1—12. Lucretius, v. 962.

27.] Barth and Kuinoel give *illis pompa fuit* from Pucci; an improbable reading.

30.] *Virgineos.* Lachmann and Kuinoel *vimineos*, the plausible conjecture of Palmer. The latter epithet, however, though appropriate, is so obvious and common-place, that Propertius may reasonably be thought to have preferred the former, whether in the sense of *novos*, *intactos*, or for *virginum calathos*, like 'virgineæ urnæ,' ii. 1, 67, which Hertzberg compares.

32.] Jacob reads *pluricoloris* from the ed. Rheg. The others give *versicoloris*, which is probably genuine. In the Naples MS. it is *viricoloris*, in MS. Gron. *varicoloris*.

35.] *Hinulei* is the conjecture of Scaliger. The MSS. have *atque hinuli*, *atque hucculis* or *hoculi*. The form *hinulus*, with the first syllable short, is unknown. Müller supposes the *ei* in *hinulei* was mistaken for a dipthong, *i.e.* the archaic form of *hinuli*, and thus *atque* was added by some transcriber.—For *totos* he also reads *stratos* with Baehrens. The sense seems simple and appropriate, that a skin was large enough to cover up both. This is a satire on the *stragula* and the *pluma* of the modern Roman beds.

37.] Jacob reads *latas* from the ed. Rheg. Barth, Kuinoel, and Lachmann admit *latas* from the Aldine. There is not the slightest ground, except the love of altering the text, for rejecting *lentas*; the *pliant* boughs of the pine formed a bower over them. This is just what most of the pines do; the stone pine (pinus pinea) might indeed be said to lend *latas* umbras, but not *incumbere*, at least in the sense of drooping to the ground.—*Nec pœna fuerat*, *i. e.* et impune licebat.

39.] *Dei pastoris.* The reading appears rather doubtful, though the good copies here agree. Barth and Kuinoel give *Idæi* from the Aldine, the conjecture of Volscus, (1482). Lachmann reads *inque dies*. Jacob and Hertzberg regard *deus pastor* as Apollo. Perhaps it is indefinitely used, since in those golden times the gods commonly conversed with men, as the next distich implies.

42.] *Vestris focis*, *i.e.* O agrestes. Nothing is more frequent in the Propertian elegies than this sudden apostrophe, as has already been observed. The sense is, the gods used to speak kind and encouraging words at the simple sacrifices offered to

'Et leporem, quicumque venis, venaberis, hospes,
'Et si forte meo tramite quæris avem;
'Et me Pana tibi comitem de rupe vocato,
'Sive petes calamo præmia, sive cane.'
At nunc desertis cessant sacraria lucis:
Aurum omnes victa jam pietate colunt.
Auro pulsa fides, auro venalia jura,
Aurum lex sequitur, mox sine lege pudor.
Torrida sacrilegum testantur limina Brennum,
Dum petit intonsi Pythia regna dei;
At mons laurigero concussus vertice diras
Gallica Parnasus sparsit in arma nives.
Te scelus accepto Thracis Polymestoris auro
Nutrit in hospitio non, Polydore, pio.
Tu quoque ut auratos gereres, Eriphyla, lacertos,
Dilapsis nusquam est Amphiaraus equis.
Proloquar: atque utinam patriæ sim vanus aruspex!
Frangitur ipsa suis Roma superba bonis.

their honour. Barth gives Scaliger's correction *sertis*, viz. as participle of *sero*. The beautiful lines which follow are taken from an epigram of Leonidas of Tarentum, which is fortunately preserved:

Εὐάγρει, λαγοθῆρα, καὶ εἰ πετεηνὰ διώκων
Ἰξευτὴς ἥκεις τοῦθ' ὑπὸ δισσὸν ὄρος,
Κἀμὲ τὸν ὑλωρὸν ἀπὸ κρημνοῖο βόασον
Πᾶνα· συναγρεύω καὶ κυσὶ καὶ καλάμοις.

The *calamus* in v. 46 is the fowler's rod; the *arundo* of v. 2, 33. See Martial xiv. 206.

Non tantum calamis, sed cantu fallitur ales,
Callida dum tacita crescit arundo manu.

and also lib. ix. 54.

50.] *Mox*, *i.e.* sequetur aurum. 'Homines ad recte agendum vel legibus vel pudore ingenuo ducuntur. Jam leges auro sublatæ. Mox vel pudor sequetur, qui quamvis hominibus a natura insitus sit, a legibus tamen certum firmamentum habet et vinculum.'—*Hertzberg*.

51.] *Torrida limina*. He gives an example of sacrilegious avarice and impiety and its punishment. Brennus had endeavoured to plunder the temple at Delphi, but was driven away by a sudden earthquake and hailstorm, with thunder and lightning, which the poet speaks of as having struck the temple itself. See Cic. *de Div.* i. § 81; Pausanias, i. cap. 4, and x. cap. 23, who says that Brennus himself and 6000 men were killed in the fight with the Phocians, and 10,000 by the storm and earthquake, and as many more by famine. Professor Geddes says (*Philological Uses of the Celtic Tongue*, p. 19), "The leader whom the Gauls poured down upon Rome in 390 B.C. bore among the Romans the name of Brennus, and this is still the Gaelic word for 'judge' and 'judgment,' *Breithamas*, proving that the Gauls were under a social organisation, where the office of a King was not so much to lead in war as to dispense judgment and administer justice. It is strange to find the same name appearing also in the leader of the irruption into Greece a century later, down upon Delphi, a portion of which band afterwards became the occupants of Galatia, in the heart of Asia Minor."

54.] *Gallica in arma*, *i.e.* in Gallos hostes. The MS. Gron. gives *ora*, which most editors seem to have preferred. See on v. 4, 34.

59.] *Utinam sim vanus aruspex*. 'I hope I may be mistaken in my forebodings.' The Groning. and Naples MSS. give *verus*, which could only mean [illegible]; 'utinam cives mei vera dicentem audiant!' Lachmann compares Livy, xxi. 10, where Hanno says, 'falsus utinam vates sim!'

Certa loquor, sed nulla fides: neque enim Ilia quondam
  Verax Pergameis Mænas habenda malis.
Sola Parim Phrygiæ fatum componere, sola
  Fallacem patriæ serpere dixit equum.
Ille furor patriæ fuit utilis, ille parenti;
  Experta est veros irrita lingua deos.

XIV.

Multa tuæ, Sparte, miramur jura palæstræ,
  Sed mage virginei tot bona gymnasii,
Quod non infames exercet corpore ludos

62.] *Ilia Mænas*. Cassandra. See on Æsch. *Ag*. 1183. The punishment inflicted on her by Apollo was that she should never be believed though she predicted the truth. Compare inf. v. 1, 51, 'Pergameæ sero rata carmina vatis.' The sense is, Ut illa Trojanis, sic ego Romanis de rebus falsa loqui visus sum.—*habenda*, i. e. *fuit* or *videbatur*.

63.] 'She alone declared that Paris was bringing ruin on his country.'—*fatum componere* is explained 'perniciem afferre, struere;' but Hertzberg will have it that the poet simply meant *sepelire*, as i. 22, 3, 'patriæ sepulcra,' *fatum Phrygiæ* being used for *mortuam Phrygiam*. Perhaps the building of the fleet is meant, which was ἀρχέκακος, pregnant with fate to Troy.—*equum*, the wooden horse.

65.] *Fuit utilis, i.e.* revera fuit utilis, quanquam spretus nihili factus est; which is equivalent to saying, 'fuisset utilis, si auditus esset.'—'*irrita lingua*, Cassandræ, non credita, verum deum habuit, vaticinata est vera et exitu comprobata.'—*Barth*. The poet evidently meant to express this sentiment: 'her words, though despised and regarded as vain at the time, proved in the end to have been dictated by divine inspiration.' The voice of a prophet is rightly said 'to have true gods' who inspire it. *Experta est* is used, because their veracity was only known by the result; and *irrita* implies a delusion which could only be removed *experiendo*. Jacob prefers to understand it thus: 'Dii et dono et fide adempta veri fuerunt.' Hertzberg: 'At quamvis veros exinde deos suos eventu postea probaverit, irrita tamen erat, eodem quo ego nunc modo.'

XIV. Though there can be little doubt that a new elegy commences here, the transcriber of the Naples MS. seems to have found it in his copy continuous with the last; and we may observe, as in many other instances, a connexion of subject which shows that the two poems must be regarded as a pair, or the latter as a sequel to the former. For he here speaks of the simplicity of Spartan manners as conducive to chastity, and contrasts the free and unrestrained intercourse of the sexes with the jealous custody of Roman matrons. Kuinoel follows those who imagine the poet to have written this after a tour in Greece (see below, El. 21); but the education of the Spartan women was so notorious that he may at least as probably have read of it in books as witnessed it. It would appear indeed from the account given by Seneca, *De Benefic*. v. cap. 3, that the poet speaks rather of what once was than of the contemporaneous customs of the Spartans. Euripides, *Androm*. 595 seqq., inveighs with much bitterness against the Spartan custom, and says it was the cause of all immorality.

3.] Hertzberg alone defends the reading of all the MSS., *laudes*. The other editors acquiesce in Scaliger's conjecture, *ludos*.—*exercere laudes corpore* for *ostendo prestare* is scarcely defensible even in a *durus poeta* like Propertius; added to which *non infamis laus* for *honesta*, seems scarcely a Latin expression. Jacob hazards a conjecture that the sense may be, 'laudandos esse Lacedæmones, qui iactari nudas suas puellas voluissent, quum laudes easdem Romani infames haberent.' The only way of defending the vulgate would be to understand *laudes* for *virtutem* or *res bene gestas*; in Greek, ἀσκεῖν ἀρετήν. It is not without hesitation that I have rejected

Inter luctantes nuda puella viros;
Cum pila velocis fallit per brachia jactus,
  Increpat et versi clavis adunca trochi,
Pulverulentaque ad extremas stat femina metas,
  Et patitur duro vulnera pancratio.
Nunc ligat ad cæstum gaudentia brachia loris,
  Missile nunc disci pondus in orbe rotat.
Gyrum pulsat equis, niveum latus ense revincit,
  Virgineumque cavo protegit ære caput;
Qualis Amazonidum nudatis bellica mammis
  Thermodontiacis turba lavatur aquis;
Et modo Taygeti, crines adspersa pruina,
  Sectatur patrios per juga longa canes;

the vulgate. But both Keil and Müller, as well as Lachmann, adopt *ludos*. Hertzberg's explanation is this: 'Apud nos quidem lusus, quam nuda puella inter viros luctando quæreret, infamis esset, illic vero minime; atqui hoc illud est, quod mihi ex illorum institutis perplacet.'—It is important here to remind the student, that *nudus* properly means 'lightly clad.'

4.] Various corrections and interpretations of this verse have been proposed. Scaliger's emendation, *veloci jactu*, has been adopted by Barth and Kuinoel; and certainly it removes the difficulty, though it has but little probability. Jacob regards *velocis jactus* as the genitive, 'ea pila, quæ velociter huc illuc volare docta nos fallat.' The MS. Groning. however gives *celeres*, which Müller accepts, while Hertzberg and Lachmann regard *velocis* as the accusative dependent on *fallit*.' The former explains thus: 'ipsa pila dicitur jactus suos fallere, dum per brachia expulsa cursum suum, quem quodammodo promisisse videbatur, subito alio flectat,' comparing iii. 26, 36. Perhaps we may compare Nausicaa's unsuccessful throw, *Od.* vi. Ἀμφιπόλου μὲν ἅμαρτε, βαθείῃ δ' ἔμβαλε δίνῃ. See also *Od.* viii. 374. The reader will find a valuable *excursus* on the *pila* in Becker's *Gallus*, p. 398—404. On *per* for *inter*, see iv. 1, 4.

6.] The game of the *trochus*, or hoop, is involved in considerable obscurity. The reader will refer to the *Dictionary of Antiquities*, where illustrations are given from antique gems. It was 'a bronze ring, and had sometimes bells attached to it.' The instrument by which it was propelled was a hooked wire, here called *clavis adunca*. Iron hoops may be seen at the present day driven precisely in this manner.

7.] *Ad extremas metas*, 'cursu confecto.'—*Barth*. 'When the female all covered with dust (after the foot-race) stands at the pillar at the end of the course, and courageously bears the pain of wounds received in the hard scuffling-match.' Hertzberg regards the particular game here mentioned as a kind of rhetorical exaggeration, since it appears from Seneca *De Benef.* v. 31, that it was not practised by the Spartans.

11.] *Gyrum pulsare* (πωλεῖν, ἱππαστεῖν), is here used for galloping round the turns in the stadium. Lachmann refers to Ovid, *Met.* vi. 219, 487, for *pulsare campum* or *spatium*, and to a note of Burmann's on the *Anthol. Lat.* iii. 15, 15, p. 468, in illustration of 'gyrus' for *spatium curriculi*.

13.] Not only does the Spartan virgin engage in the above laborious and manly exercises, but she bathes in the Eurotas as the Amazons in their native Thermodon. The awkward punctuation of Lachmann, Jacob, and Hertzberg, viz. 'Thermodontiacis turba, lavatur, aquis,' is so artificial that I have preferred to understand *lavatur* (in Eurota), *qualis turba Am. lavatur* in Thermodonte.

15.] *Taygeti*, Ταϋγέτου, probably a corruption of τηλαυγέτου, 'the far-off mountain.'

16.] *Patrios.* Cf. Soph. *Ajax*, 8, κυνὸς Λακαίνης ὥς τις εὔρινος βάσις. Virg. *Georg.* iii. 405, 'veloces Spartæ catulos acremque Molossum.'

Qualis et Eurotæ Pollux et Castor arenis,
 Hic victor pugnis, ille futurus equis;
Inter quos Helene nudis capere arma papillis
 Fertur, nec fratres erubuisse deos.
Lex igitur Spartana vetat secedere amantes,
 Et licet in triviis ad latus esse suæ;
Nec timor aut ulla est clausæ tutela puellæ,
 Nec gravis austeri pœna cavenda viri.
Nullo præmisso de rebus tute loquaris
 Ipse tuis; longæ nulla repulsa moræ.
Non Tyriæ vestes errantia lumina fallunt,
 Est neque odoratæ cura molesta comæ.
At nostra ingenti vadit circumdata turba,
 Nec digitum angusta est inseruisse via.
Nec quæ sint facies, nec quæ sint verba rogandi,
 Invenias: cæcum versat amator iter.
Quod si jura fores pugnasque imitata Laconum,
 Carior hoc esses tu mihi, Roma, bono.

17.] The Naples and Groning. MSS. give *habenis*, Pucci *ad undas*, which Jacob alone prefers. *Arenis* is the conjecture of Volscus (1488). The word is very often spelt *harena* in MSS. The poet's meaning in 17—20 is rather confused in the expression. He intended to say, 'et capit arma inter viros, qualis Helene inter fratres deos,' *i.e.* nec magis pudore afficitur, quam si inter fratres certet. Lachmann reads *interque hos* v. 19, but the meaning is essentially the same.—*arenis* is aptly used in reference to the pugilistic and equestrian contests in which they engaged near the Eurotas. See iv. 11, 35.

21.] *Vetat secedere*, *i.e.* in publico versari jubet, non secreto agere, non vulgi oculis se subtrahere.

25.] *Nullo præmisso.* Without sending a servant before to announce your intended visit.—*longæ moræ* is the dative: 'No refusal follows your long and patient waiting for admission.'

27.] The Spartan maid does not, like the Roman, wear Tyrian purple to *deceive the mistaken eye*. There is no difficulty in this: fine dress seems to promise a fine form, but the eye is often disappointed in looking at the former without finding the latter.

28.] *Comæ.* This is the conjecture of Canter, and has been adopted by all but Hertzberg, who reads *adoratæ—domi* from the Naples MS., and explains it 'de salutantium molesta ubique amatori turba.' All the copies agree in *domi*,—a strange reading, and certainly not like a corruption of *comæ*. Hertzberg proposes, 'Est neque odora canum cura molesta domi,' comparing v. 5, 73, 'Et canis in nostros nimis experrecta dolores.' Few will approve this. If *domi* be genuine, it would be easier to take it adverbially, [illegible], and understand *adoratæ puellæ*.

30.] *Nec digitum* &c. A hyperbolical expression. The pathway is so crowded with attendants, that so far from being allowed access, you could not insert even a finger among them: *via* is the usual ablative of Propertius: see on i. 17, 23, the sense being, 'cum tam densa sit ac frequens via qua ambulat.'

31.] *Facies rogandi*, 'What imploring look to assume without being detected.' The *facies*, as Hertzberg shows, is not that of the girl, but the lover's. 'What to say, or with what face to say it, 'tis not easy to find.'

34.] For *Laconum* in the preceding v. the Naples MS. has the singular reading *lanum*; one proof among many that we must not put too much confidence in that ancient and generally excellent copy.—*hoc bono*, propter hoc bonum.

XV.

Sic ego non ullos jam norim in amore tumultus,
  Nec veniat sine te nox vigilanda mihi;
Ut mihi prætextæ pudor est velatus amictu,
  Et data libertas noscere amoris iter,
Illa rudes animos per noctes conscia primas
  Imbuit heu nullis capta Lycinna datis.
Tertius haud multo minus est cum ducitur annus;
  Vix memini nobis verba coisse decem.
Cuncta tuus sepelivit amor, nec femina post te
  Ulla dedit collo dulcia vincla meo.
Testis erit Dirce tam vero crimine sæva,

XV. The poet intercedes with Cynthia in behalf of a female slave called Lycinna, who seems to have been harshly treated by her on suspicion of some connexion clandestinely continued between them. His object is, by explaining the circumstances, to reassure Cynthia of his constancy.

3.] *Velatus.* Kuinoel *elatus*, from Guyet. This passage presents considerable difficulties, in whatever way we attempt either to explain or to correct the vulgate. The more obvious punctuation is that adopted by Barth and Kuinoel, viz., a full stop at the end of v. 4; 'So may I never be crossed in love, as it is true that' &c. The later editors seem to be right in placing only a comma at *amoris iter*, and understanding it thus: 'So may I never more be crossed in love (as what I now say is true). When my boyish modesty had been veiled by the toga virilis, (*i.e.* hidden and concealed under the plea of manhood now attained) and I found no longer any restraint imposed on my inclinations, then first I became acquainted with Lycinna.' Lachmann explains, 'rubor pudens in petalis (hæc sunt *amictus* rosæ) se in sinum dicitur expandere vel solvere;' and he compares Statius, *Silv.* ii. 1, 136, 'sola verecundo deerat prætexta decori.' Now the *prætexta* is said to have been sometimes laid aside, and the toga libera taken, soon after fourteen, or the age of puberty: though it is probable (Hertzberg, *Quæst.* p. 17), that sixteen was the usual age; see Becker, *Gallus*, pp. 195—7. At this period, therefore, we may assume the connexion to have commenced. But how unusual an expression is this, 'when the bashfulness of the prætexta was concealed by the amictus?' Hertzberg has good reason to doubt if the latter word, in the sense of the toga virilis, can be opposed to the former, since *amictus* is quite a general term for any outer garment. (See, however, Ovid, *Fast.* vi. 623, compared with 570). He therefore proposes to read 'Ut mihi prætexti pudor est elatus amictus,' the Naples MS. giving *prætexti* and *amictus*. *Elatus* is 'dead and buried,' as in v. 9, 'Cuncta tuus *sepelivit* amor.' Without feeling quite satisfied with this, I incline to it as better than any explanation that has been proposed, especially as it has the best MS. authority in its favour, the word *elatus* excepted. Kuinoel construes *prætextæ amictu*, and comments thus: 'postquam posui cum prætexta pudorem.' In this case *cum* could hardly have been omitted. Barth takes *velatus amictu* as a mere metaphor, 'when I had learned to cover up, and set aside, my modesty;' 'postquam pudor puerilis, quem habui in toga prætexta, obrutus a me amictu, adeoque neglectus et abjectus fuit.' On which we remark, that this explanation of *ut* by *postquam* does not suit the full stop at *amoris iter*.

6.] *Tertius* &c. 'The sense is, 'tertius annus ducitur cum (ex quo) memini' &c., or, 'ex quo, quantum memini, vix inter nos decem verba coierunt.' Or supply *eo* or *eo tempore*, *et* vix memini &c.

11.] *Testis erit.*—*erat* Lachmann, who remarks, after others, that it is not clear of what fact Dirce is appealed to as a witness. Barth understands, 'testis erit mulierum adversus pellices iram vehementissimam et acerrimam esse, quæ tam crudelem se præstitit in vero crimine, (*crimen verum*

Nycteos Antiopen accubuisse Lyco.
Ah quotiens pulchros ussit regina capillos,
Molliaque immites fixit in ora manus!
Ah quotiens famulam pensis oneravit iniquis,
Et caput in dura ponere jussit humo!
Sæpe illam immundis passa est habitare tenebris,
Vilem jejunæ sæpe negavit aquam.
Juppiter, Antiopæ nusquam succurris habenti
Tot mala? corrumpit dura catena manus.
Si deus es, tibi turpe tuam servire puellam:
Invocet Antiope quem nisi vincta Jovem?
Sola tamen, quæcumque aderant in corpore vires,
Regales manicas rupit utraque manu.
Inde Cithæronis timido pede currit in arces.
Nox erat, et sparso triste cubile gelu.
Sæpe vago Asopi sonitu permota fluentis
Credebat dominæ pone venire pedes;
Et durum Zethum et lacrimis Amphiona mollem
Experta est stabulis mater abacta suis.

opponit suo quod a Cynthia fingebatur tantum), videlicet cum ipsi nunciatum fuisset, Antiopen Nyctei filiam cum Lyco viro suo in lecto cubuisse.' We must therefore, it would seem, construe *tam vere*, and take *accubuisse* as depending on *criminis*. Still, *tam vere criminis* might mean 'quod tam verum erat quam falsum est quod mihi obicitur.' Hertzberg more simply explains 'testis erit mihi contra Cynthiam.' The story of Dirce is this. Antiope was daughter of Nycteus, and had been married to Lycus, her uncle, king of Thebes. From her were born, by Zeus, Amphion and Zethus. Lycus having repudiated Antiope and married Dirce, the jealousy of the latter induced her to treat Antiope with the greatest indignity. At last however she escaped, and succeeded in informing her step-sons of her cruel treatment; who accordingly avenged her by killing both Lycus and Dirce. The story is given, with some varieties, by Pausanias, ii. v. § 2, who follows Homer, *Od.* xi. 200. This account represents her as the daughter of the river Asopus, and ravished by Epopeus. Apollodor. iii. 5, 5, Ἀντιόπην δὲ ᾐκίζετο Λύκος καθείρξας, καὶ ἡ τούτου γυνὴ Δίρκη· λαθοῦσα δέ ποτε, τῶν δεσμῶν αὐτομάτως λυθέντων, ἧκεν ἐπὶ τῶν παίδων ἔπαυλιν, δεχθῆναι πρὸς αὐτῶν θέλουσα. Οἱ δὲ, ἀναγνωρισάμενοι τὴν μητέρα, τὸν μὲν Λύκον κτείνουσι, τὴν δὲ Δίρκην δήσαντες ἐκ ταύρου θανοῦσαν ῥίπτουσιν εἰς κρήνην τὴν ἀπ' ἐκείνης καλουμένην Δίρκην. The moral of the story is, to warn Cynthia of the fate of one who had acted with unmerited severity towards a rival.

14.] Jacob, Keil, and Müller adopt the unpoetical reading of the ed. Rheg. and Naples MS., *immitius*.

17.] For *habitare* Müller conjectures *latitare*.

21.] Jacob gives *servare* (interrogatively) from the Groning. MS. The others edit *servire*, rightly, in my judgment.

23.] *Sola*. 'Non adjuta a Jove.'—*Barth*. 'Yet all unassisted as she was, by exerting all the strength she had left in her body, she broke with both hands the fetters put on her by the King and his Queen.'

30.] *Abacta*, sc. a Zetho.—*suis*, sibi debitis, quæ *sua* esse, ut mater, putaverat. Hertzberg remarks that *durum Zethum* ought to have come after *Amphiona mollem*, as *abacta* refers directly to the former. The metrical difficulty of the verse will sufficiently account for the arrangement adopted.

Ac veluti magnos cum ponunt æquora motus,
  Eurus ubi adverso desinit ire Noto,
Litore sic tacito sonitus rarescit arenæ;
  Sic cadit inflexo lapsa puella genu.
Sera tamen pietas; natis est cognitus error;
  Digne Jovis natos qui tueare senex,
Tu reddis pueris matrem, puerique trahendam
  Vinxerunt Dircen sub trucis ora bovis.
Antiope, cognosce Jovem: tibi gloria Dirce
  Ducitur, in multis mortem habitura locis.
Prata cruentantur Zetho, victorque canebat
  Pæana Amphion rupe, Aracynthe, tua.
At tu non meritam parcas vexare Lycinnam;
  Nescit vestra ruens ira referre pedem.

31—35.] Hertzberg says on this passage, 'Locum a criticis vario vexatum—interpunctione *persanavimus*.' The reader of taste shall form his own opinion on this new 'interpunctio.'

Ac veluti, magnos cum ponunt æquora motus,
  —Eurus in adversum desinit ire Notum,—
Litore et tacito sonitus rarescit arenæ,
  Sic—cadit inflexo lapsa puella genu—
Sera, tamen pietas.

To the present editor it seems truly surprising that both Keil and Müller should accept the parenthetic construction of the last verse. Nor is that adopted by Jacob much better. There is, no doubt, an obscurity, or perhaps impropriety, in the simile; but *anything* is better than such violent 'interpunctiones.' Kuinoel is perhaps hardly justified in calling it 'præclara comparatio;' but the sinking down of the wearied mother after her earnest appeal for admission, and the altercation consequent upon the request, is not inaptly illustrated by the silence of the worn-out elements after a storm. With Lachmann and Müller I read *ubi adverso—Noto*, the Naples MS. giving *sub adverso Notho*. See v. 5, 24. The others edit *in adversum notos* with the majority of the good copies. Keil has *Eurus et adverso* &c.

33.] The Groning. MS. has *et*, the Naples MS. *sic*. Müller reads *littore et tacito*, Keil and Lachmann *litore sub tacito*. We should not say, 'the waves subside if the sound of the breakers ceases,' but 'the sound ceases if the waves subside.' Pucci gives *quum*, probably an explanation of *si*. *Sic tacito* is to be closely connected, *i.e.* desinentibus, cessantibus ventis tandem silente.

35.] *Sera tamen pietas.* There is some ellipse: '(the conduct of the sons was indeed cruel) *yet* affection showed itself at last.' Indeed, *tamen* is said in respect of *durum Zethum* and *aperta stabulis mea*. The discovery of their relationship was made by an old shepherd, who had educated the youths, and whom the poet apostrophises in ver. 36.

38.] *Sub ora*, to the head or horns of a bull, so as to be tossed and gored to death. A beautiful fresco of this subject was found at Pompeii; but Dirce is there tied to the bull by a rope round its body.

39.] *Cognosce Jovem.* 'Vim Jovis et opem agnosce.'—*Kuinoel*.

41.] Pucci gives *Zeto*, whence Lachmann ingeniously conjectured *leto*. But the dative in the sense of *prata Zethi* is quite defensible. The locality was perhaps so called after the event. He (as Jacob remarks) took upon himself the sterner part both in rejecting the mother and afterwards avenging her wrongs, while Amphion sate him down and played a pæan on his lyre. *Aracynthus* was a mountain on the confines of Attica; perhaps confused with the 'Αραχναῖον αἶπος of Æschylus, *Ag.* 309. But Dr. Smith says (*Classical Dictionary* in v.) 'A mountain on the S.W. coast of Ætolia near Pleuron, sometimes placed in Acarnania. Later writers erroneously make it a mountain between Bœotia and Attica, and hence mention it in connection with Amphion the Bœotian hero. Prop. iv. 13, 41. Virg. *Ecl.* ii. 24.'

44.] *Vestra*, 'the anger of yon jealous woman.'

Fabula nulla tuas de nobis concitet aures:
  Te solam et lignis funeris ustus amem.

XVI.

Nox media, et dominæ mihi venit epistola nostræ
  Tibure: me missa jussit adesse mora,
Candida qua geminas ostendunt culmina turres,
  Et cadit in patulos lympha Aniena lacus.
Quid faciam? obductis committam mene tenebris,
  Ut timeam audaces in mea membra manus?
At si distulero hæc nostro mandata timore,
  Nocturno fletus sævior hoste mihi.
Peccaram semel, et totum sum pulsus in annum:
  In me mansuetas non habet illa manus.

45.] *Concitet*, moveat, i. e. noli credere falsis de me fabulis.

XVI. The poet is supposed to soliloquise on a letter he has just received from his mistress at Tibur. He weighs the inconvenience against the obligation to obey, and concludes with a touching picture of his funeral, supposing that some accident should happen on the journey.

1—2.] The editors generally place a colon at *nostræ*, and make *adesse Tibure* to signify *ad Tibur venire*. Jacob, who thinks the poet was summoned, not from Rome to Tibur, but from Tibur to Rome, defends the ablative by Ovid, *Met.* ii. 512, 'Quæritis, ætheriis quare Regina deorum Sedibus huc adsim.' The sense must then be *adesse Romæ a Tibure*. Perhaps indeed *Tibure adesse* may mean 'to be at Tibur.' Hertzberg observes, that in v. 3—4 a description of Tibur itself is clearly intended; therefore the poet is to go *to* that town. Jacob, feeling this objection to his view, says, 'monumentum aliquod Romanum describunt, quod a quodam lacu Aquæ Aniensis haud procul aberat; illic inventurum Cynthiam esse.' But it seems on the whole better to adopt the punctuation of Hertzberg, by which all obscurity and difficulty is at once removed. 'A letter came from Tibur to say I was wanted there immediately.'

3.] The topography of Tibur is learnedly illustrated by Hertzberg. The white cliff, of the formation called travertin, the ravine of the Anio, which there dashes rapidly into a wide basin, and the prominent landmarks on each side of the bank described as *geminæ turres*, were familiar objects to every Roman, and could only apply to that place.

4.] *Lympha*. Hertzberg prefers *Nympha* from the Naples MS. and ed. Rheg. It is well known that the words are identical; nor does a long note seem necessary, to prove that whatever is presided over by a deity may be called by the name of that deity, as *Ceres* and *Bacchus* often signify *bread* and *wine*.

6—8.] The danger of a night journey in the neighbourhood of Rome, from the roads being infested with banditti, is forcibly expressed. See Juven. iii. 305, x. 20.—For *distulero hæc* some prefer *hæc distulero* from the Groning. MS. and ed. Rheg. On this Lachmann makes a curious remark, which the reader will do well to verify for himself: 'Amant poetæ hæc futura ultima vocali liquefacta ponere.'—*nostro timore*, from personal fear, fear for myself. Hertzberg attempts to connect *nostro mandata timore*, for *nobis timentibus*, as *nostro gemitu* i. 21, 3. This seems as far-fetched as it is unnecessary.

8.] *Fletus*, i. e. the consequences to myself of disobeying her behest: ἐλπίζειν, as Barth observes.

9.] *Peccaram semel*, 'I had offended only once,' or had neglected to go when summoned on one single occasion, 'and I was cast off for a whole year.'—*totum in annum*, i. e. the year 729, according to Hertzberg's calculation, *Quæst.* p. 16.

Nec tamen est quisquam, sacros qui lædat amantes.
Scironis media sic licet ire via.
Quisquis amator erit, Scythicis licet ambulet oris;
Nemo adeo, ut noceat, barbarus esse volet.
Luna ministrat iter; demonstrant astra salebras;
Ipse Amor accensas percutit ante faces.
Sæva canum rabies morsus avertit hiantis:
Huic generi quovis tempore tuta via est.
Sanguine tam parvo quis enim spargatur amantis
Improbus? exclusis fit comes ipsa Venus.
Quod si certa meos sequerentur funera casus,
Talis mors pretio vel sit emenda mihi.
Adferet huc unguenta mihi, sertisque sepulcrum
Ornabit custos ad mea busta sedens.
Di faciant, mea ne terra locet ossa frequenti,
Qua facit assiduo tramite vulgus iter.
Post mortem tumuli sic infamantur amantum;
Me tegat arborea devia terra coma,
Aut humet ignotæ cumulus vallatus arenæ;
Non juvat in media nomen habere via.

11—16.] He here alludes to the popular notion that a lover bore a charmed life: see v. 1, 147—9. Tibull. i. 2, 27, 'Quisquis amore tenetur, eat tutusque sacerque Qualibet; insidias non timuisse decet.'—*sic*, *i.e.* si quis amat, is from Pucci. The MSS. have *sitiat* or *scitiat*.

15.] '*Percutit* omnes. Corrigunt *præcutit*; non recte; nam *præcutit* facem is, qui præcedens percutit; hic autem Amor percutit *ante*.'—*Jacob*. *Percutere* is properly said of those who in carrying links strike the lighted end against a wall to knock off the accumulated ashes. See i. 3, 10, Ovid, *Am.* i. 2, 12, 'Vidi ego jactatas mota face crescere flammas, Et vidi nullo concutiente mori.' The accusative after *ministrat* (*i.e.* præbet, commodat iter), is supported by Lachmann from Virgil (*Georg.* iv. 146), Seneca, and Statius; and therefore to read *equis* for *iter* in v. 15, with Barth and Kuinoel, from one late copy, would be most unreasonable.

18.] *Huic generi*, scil. amatorum.

19.] *Parvo sanguine*, *i.e.* insignificant, *vili*, as offering no prize to recompense the murderer. Müller reads *tam parva*, after Fischer, and even, *suis* for *exclusis* in the pentameter, on the same authority. Both seem to me most needless alterations.

20.] *Exclusis*. The meaning of this word is obscure. Lachmann pronounces it 'ineptissimum,' and reads *et cæcos*. Hertzberg understands *exclusis amatoriis hominibus*, which is the most plausible explanation. The context rather suggests *exclusis amatorum comitata*. Perhaps however the poet had in mind the double danger both of the journey thither and the return when the lover had been refused admittance.

21.] *Meos casus*, death by being waylaid. *Certa funera*, 'si funera sibi parata fore certo sciat.'—*Lachmann*.

22.] *Vel sit emenda*, digna etiam esset quam emerem pretio.

23.] *Huc*, sc. ad funera. Lachmann and others read *hac* with Guyet, but against the authority of the MSS.

29.] Keil and Müller, with Jacob and Lachmann, read *aut humer ignotæ cumulis* &c. The MSS. present various corruptions; the Naples MS. gives *humeri* and *cumulis*, the MS. Gron. *humer* (? so Hertzberg) *humet* according to Jacob, and *tumulus*: the ed. Rheg. *humet*. The epithet

XVII.

Nunc, o Bacche, tuis humiles advolvimur aris:
  Da mihi pacato vela secunda, pater.
Tu potes insanæ Veneris compescere fastus,
  Curarumque tuo fit medicina mero.
Per te junguntur, per te solvuntur amantes:
  Tu vitium ex animo dilue, Bacche, meo.
Te quoque enim non esse rudem testatur in astris
  Lyncibus ad cælum vecta Ariadna tuis.
Hoc mihi, quod veteres custodit in ossibus ignes,
  Funera sanabunt, aut tua vina, malum.
Semper enim vacuos nox sobria torquet amantes,
  Spesque timorque animum versat utroque meum.
Quod si, Bacche, tuis per fervida tempora donis
  Accersitus erit somnus in ossa mea,
Ipse seram vites, pangamque ex ordine colles,
  Quos carpant nullæ, me vigilante, feræ.
Dummodo purpureo spument mihi dolia musto,

vallatus applied to *tumulus* would be superfluous, if not inappropriate; and the person buried would hardly be said *vallari cumulis arenæ*, which is applicable rather to one fenced round with a mound than to a dead body covered by it.

XVII. This spirited poem bears internal evidence of having been written, like Horace's *Evoe! recenti mens trepidat metu*, under the inspiration of the god himself who is addressed. Having been excluded by Cynthia, the poet consoles himself with wine; and the concluding distich would seem to indicate that he was now becoming tired of the servitude which in El. xxiv. he finally abjures.

2.] Lachmann and Barth adopt the reading of the MS. Groning., *bacchato*. But the whole point of the poem is to ask for ease and comfort from the god of wine. The word in the text is also adapted to the simile borrowed from a calm sea.

5.] As on the one hand affection is warmed and love promoted, so on the other quarrels arise and separations result from wine.

6.] *Vitium*, 'this weakness,' 'ægritudinem animi.'—*Barth*.

7.] *Rudem*, amoris expertem.

9.] *In ossibus*. Cf. v. 4, 70, 'Nam Vesta—culpam alit et plures condit in ossa faces.'—*aut tua vina*, *i.e.* if your wine will not heal it, nothing but death will.

12.] There is some doubt as to the true reading of this verse. The Groning. MS. gives *animum versat utrinque metum*; the Naples MS. and ed. Rheg. *animo versat utroque modo*. I am inclined to think that *utroque* is genuine, and that the other ablatives are corruptions arising from an attempt to adapt some substantive to the supposed pronoun. I therefore follow Kuinoel and Lachmann rather than Barth and Jacob, who give *versat utroque modo*, and so also Keil and Müller. Hertzberg has *versat utrinque metum*. Mr. Wratislaw, *utrinque*. The sense is, 'As a sober night is always dismal to a lover who lies *vacuo toro*, and as my mind is distracted at present between hope and the fear of disappointment, therefore I will have recourse to wine.'

13.] Construe *donis per fervida tempora*, sc. *fusis*, 'by wine acting on my feverish brow.' Compare 'hoc sollicitum caput,' inf. 42.

15.] *Pangam*, disponam, conseram, distinguam.—*me vigilante*, *i.e.* quos custodiam ne carpant feræ.

17—20.] 'Provided only I have a never-failing supply of grape juice, I will

Et nova pressantis inquinet uva pedes,
Quod superest vitæ, per te et tua cornua vivam,
Virtutisque tuæ, Bacche, poeta ferar.
Dicam ego maternos Ætnæo fulmine partus,
Indica Nysæis arma fugata choris;
Vesanumque nova nequidquam in vite Lycurgum,
Pentheos in triplices funera grata greges,
Curvaque Tyrrhenos delphinum corpora nautas
In vada pampinea desiluisse rate,
Et tibi per medium bene olentia flumina Naxon,

ever be your votary and the poet of your valourous deeds.' Jacob and Hertzberg seem to have rightly transferred the full stop usually placed at *pedes* v. 18, to *ferar* v. 16, since the condition in *dummodo* refers rather to what follows than to *ipse seram vites* &c.

19.] *Cornua.* One of the attributes of Bacchus was *κερασφόρος*. See Tibull. ii. 1, 3; Plutarch, *Isid.* § 35, who identifies the god with Osiris. The true explanation seems to be that the bull was the common Eastern symbol of vitality and physical power, whence it so commonly occurs in the Assyrian sculptures. According to Plutarch, *Symposiac.* lib. ix. ii. § 3, ἄλφα was the Phœnician name of the ox, which may be supposed to have stood first in a phonetic alphabet as the most important gift of Earth. Now the grape was so naturally associated with the ox, as being one of the most essential vegetable products of the soil, that we need not be surprised at Bacchus being painted with horns. Corn, wine, and cattle, were the three staple commodities of the early settlers, and closely associated in their mythology.

21.] *Ætnæo fulmine.* Eurip. *Bacch.* Σεμέλη λοχευθεῖσ' ἀστραπηφόρῳ πυρί. This legend also is easily explained: in fact, Strabo gave the true interpretation of it long before philology was thought of as a science. The vine, it is well known, delights in volcanic soils, on the potash and sulphur of which it feeds; hence the grape was called the offspring of eruptions. Strabo, lib. xiii. iv.: τινὲς δὲ εἰκότως πυριγενῆ τὸν Διόνυσον λέγεσθαί φασιν, ἐκ τῶν τοιούτων χωρίων τεκμαιρόμενοι. *Idem*, lib. v. cap. 4, (speaking of Vesuvius, which in his time was not an active volcano), τάχα δὲ καὶ τῆς εὐκαρπίας τῆς κύκλῳ τοῦτ' αἴτιον, ὥσπερ τῇ Κατάνῃ φασὶ, τὸ κατατεφρωθὲν μέρος ἐκ τῆς σποδοῦ τῆς ἀνενεχθείσης ὑπὸ τοῦ Αἰτναίου πυρὸς, εὐάμπελον τὴν γῆν ἐποίησεν· ἔχει μὲν γὰρ τὸ λιπαῖνον καὶ τὴν ἐκπυρουμένην βῶλον, καὶ τὴν ἐκφέρουσαν τοὺς καρπούς.

23.] *Vesanum in vite*, 'acting madly in the case of the vine,' *i.e.* in his treatment of it, by a well-known idiom. Various accounts of this Thracian king are given: the epithet *nova* implies that he opposed the introduction of the grape, or, perhaps, some particular variety of it. He is said to have gone mad and to have cut his own knee, or, according to others, to have killed his own son, in attempting to destroy the vines. See *Iliad*, vi. 130: Soph. *Ant.* 955. Apollodor. iii. 5, 1, Λυκοῦργος δὲ, παῖς Δρύαντος, Ἠδωνῶν βασιλεὺς, οἱ Στρυμόνα ποταμὸν παροικοῦσι, πρῶτος ὑβρίσας ἐξέβαλεν αὐτόν.—Ὁ δὲ, μανεὶς, Δρύαντα τὸν παῖδα, ἀμπέλου νομίζων κλῆμα κόπτειν, πελέκει πλήξας, ἀπέκτεινε, καὶ ἀκρωτηριάσας αὐτὸν, ἐσωφρόνησε.

24.] *In triplices greges.* Barth supplies *divisa*, which is certainly better than Kuinoel's '*funera grata in triplices greges* pro, triplicibus gregibus.'—*grata*, *i.e.* Baccho. Compare Eur. *Bacch.* 680, ὁρῶ δὲ θιάσους τρεῖς γυναικείων χορῶν, ὧν ἦρχ' ἑνὸς μὲν Αὐτονόη, τοῦ δευτέρου μήτηρ Ἀγαύη σή, τρίτου δ' Ἰνὼ χοροῦ.

25—6.] This story is beautifully told in one of the Homeric Hymns to Bacchus. See also Ovid, *Met.* iii. 630 seq.—*delphinum corpora*, mutatos in delphinas.

27.] *Flumina*, i.e. *dicam*, v. 21. 'Dicam vini flumina per medium Naxon tibi effluxisse.' The tradition was that at Naxos there was a spring of pure wine; a legend expressive of abundance of the grape. Eur. *Bacch.* 707, καὶ τῇδε κρήνην ἐξανῆκ' οἴνου θεός. It was in this fertile and beautiful island, also called *Dia*, that Bacchus met Ariadne mourning for the perfidious Theseus, and that the wedding ceremony was held, which is here alluded to.

Unde tuum potant Naxia turba merum.
Candida laxatis onerato colla corymbis
Cinget Bassaricas Lydia mitra comas;
Levis odorato cervix manabit olivo,
Et feries nudos veste fluente pedes.
Mollia Dircææ pulsabunt tympana Thebæ;
Capripedes calamo Panes hiante canent;
Vertice turrigero juxta dea magna Cybelle
Tundet ad Idæos cymbala rauca choros.
Ante fores templi crater antistitis auro
Libatum fundens in tua sacra merum.
Hæc ego non humili referam memoranda cothurno,
Qualis Pindarico spiritus ore tonat.
Tu modo servitio vacuum me siste superbo,
Atque hoc sollicitum vince sopore caput.

XVIII.

Clausus ab umbroso qua ludit Pontus Averno,

30.] *Cinget* and the following futures mean *in meo carmine*. Cf. 39. — *Lydia mitra*. Hertzberg considers this to have been a peculiar form of the head-dress, with pendants covering the cheeks. See v. 7, 62, and *ibid.* 5, 72.

32.] *Nudos pedes*. Bacchus seems to have been thus represented from the custom of treading grapes. 'Tinge novo mecum dereptis crura cothurnis,' Virg. *Georg.* ii. 8. The *vestis fluens* alluded to is the long palla. See iii. 23, 16, and on v. 6, 76.

36.] The MSS. give *fundet*. There can be no doubt of the truth of Scaliger's correction, though Jacob hesitates to admit it. The transposition of *cymbala* and *tympana*, on account of their respective epithets, is mere trifling with the text, and it is surprising that Lachmann should have followed Burmann in the alteration. The *tympana* are 'soft,' i.e. yielding to the blow, because made of stretched hide; the *cymbala* are 'harsh' from their noisy clang. On the other hand, as Hertzberg observes, *mollia cymbala* is an absurdity.

37.] *auro*, supply *factus erit*.

41.] *Siste* &c., [illegible], 'fac me carere servitio mihi a Cynthia imposito.'

XVIII. On the death of Marcellus, son of C. Marcellus and Octavia, sister of Augustus, which event took place at Baiæ, B.C. 23, when he was in his 20th year (v. 15). The celebrated passage in the *Æneid*, vi. 860 seq., commemorates and immortalizes his memory. From a mistaken notion that the poet speaks of him in v. 9 as having been accidentally drowned, it has been erroneously inferred that suspicion of foul play on the part of Livia was entertained. The silence of Suetonius on the subject of his death is remarkable; but there is no reason to doubt that it was caused by the incautious or excessive use of the bath, added, perhaps, to the enervating effects of the sea air: see on v. 9.

1.] The MSS. and edd. give *ludit*, 'chafes and ripples,' which has been retained by the recent editors, except Hertzberg, who reads *alludit*, the conjecture of Canter, i.e. 'where the sea washes Baiæ.' But the elision is not metrically elegant, and perhaps it is better to take *stagna* in apposition to *Pontus*, i.e. *ubi sunt stagna*. The Lucrine lake, it is well known, was connected with the Avernian (*Georg.* ii. 161), by a cutting through the intervening ridge, so as to form a connected series of docks or harbours, called the Julian Port, the outer sea, or bay of Naples, being kept out by the natural barrier of the via Herculis, see i. 11, 12. The lake Avernus

Fumida Baiarum stagna tepentis aquæ,
Qua jacet et Trojæ tubicen Misenus arena,
Et sonat Herculeo structa labore via,
Hic, ubi, mortales dextra cum quæreret urbes,
Cymbala Thebano concrepuere deo,—
At nunc, invisæ magno cum crimine Baiæ,

is called *umbrosus*, because the overhanging sides were formerly covered with a verdure which imparted a gloomy and dismal aspect to a lake which was already regarded as 'uncannie,' and *umbrarum locus* (*Æn.* vi. 390). So *umbrosi rogi* in v. 11, 8, are the shadow-haunted tombs. Strabo, v. cap. 4, περικλείεται δ' ὁ Ἄορνος ὀφρύσιν ὀρθίαις, ὑπερκειμέναις πανταχόθεν πλὴν τοῦ εἴσπλου, νῦν μὲν ἡμέρως ἐκπεπονημέναις, πρότερον δὲ συνηρεφέσιν ἀγρίᾳ ὕλῃ μεγαλοδένδρῳ καὶ ἀβάτῳ, αἳ κατὰ δεισιδαιμονίαν κατάσκιον ἐποίουν τὸν κόλπον. The Lucrine lake extended nearly up to Baiæ (πλατύνεται μέχρι Βαϊῶν, Strabo) whence it is here in a manner identified with the hot sulphur baths of that watering place. *Pontus* must therefore be understood of the Lucrine lake, not of the outer sea. It is *clausus*, as divided by a strip of land from Avernus. Hertzberg has a suspicion that *Avernus* is here put for *Lucrinus*, and that *Pontus* is the bay of Naples, shut out by the via Herculis. Strabo, in fact, distinctly says that Artemidorus considered the Lucrine lake to be the Avernus.—The topography of the place is known from ancient accounts; but the nature of the ground has been greatly changed, both by the alteration of the coast line and by the *Monte Nuovo* rising up in a single night, Sept. 19, 1538, in the site of the Lucrine lake, which thus disappeared. See Humboldt, *Cosmos*, vol. i. p. 229. It is probable that the via Herculis was in part at least artificial, as Agrippa, who executed the above great work, is said by Strabo to have repaired it (ἐπισκευάσαι). See Ritter on Tac. *Ann.* xiv. 8. 'Lucrino addita claustra,' *Georg.* ii. 161.

2.] *Fumida.* The copies and earlier edd. give *humida*. Scaliger's emendation admits of no doubt. Ovid, *A. A.* i. 256, 'Quid referam Baias, prætextaque litora velis, Et quæ de calido sulphure fumat, aquam?'

3.] *Misenus.* See i. 11, 4; Virg. *Æn.* vi. 162, seq.—*sonat*, *i.e.* 'maris vehementioris appulsu,' as Hertzberg rightly explains. Others understand *equorum ungulis*. But Strabo says it was only as wide as a carriage road, and not easily crossed even on foot. It was, in fact, a long and narrow trap dyke, which could hardly have been used for horses or even mules, especially as there was, of course, an entrance through it into the Lucrine Lake.

5.] I have adopted *mortales* (for *mortalis*) from the Naples and Groning. MSS. The nominative, as Hertzberg shows, is objectionable for two reasons; first, the very next line speaks of Hercules as *deus*, not *homo*; secondly, he was at all events not *mortalis*, even in the condition of *homo* on earth.—*quærere mortales urbes* is opposed to *cælum adire*, implied in *deo*. Both Keil and Müller however, and also Mr. Wratislaw, read *mortalis*. It is not quite clear whether *Thebanus deus* is Hercules or Bacchus; and on this depends the sense of *quæreret*. The addition of *dextra*, 'by prowess of hand,' seems to fix the sense to Hercules and his conquests. If we read *mortalis*, the meaning will be, 'on the spot where the Theban god was worshipped for conquering cities as a human hero on earth.' From his legendary exploits in this part of Italy the town of Herculaneum derived its name. He was also the patron, as Hertzberg observes, of hot springs, and hence was additionally honoured at Baiæ, as well as at Tibur (v. 7, 82). Hence, too, there is a peculiar force in *hostis deus*, v. 8, as if the patron god had abandoned the springs and some noxious deity had occupied his place. Dr. Livingstone, writing from Central Africa, says, the Manyema people 'call the spirit of evil, who resides in the deep, *Mulambu*. A hot fountain near Bambarre is supposed to belong to this being, the author of death by drowning and other misfortunes.'

7.] The anacoluthon in the opening verses presents no serious difficulty; the distich 7—8 containing one of those sudden apostrophes so characteristic of Propertius. The apodosis is at v. 9. 'Where Baiæ is, —formerly favoured by the presence of a god, but now having a less benign influence, —here,' &c. The name of Marcellus, it will be observed, is suppressed.

Quis deus in vestra constitit hostis aqua?—
His pressus Stygias vultum demisit in undas,
Errat et in vestro spiritus ille lacu.
Quid genus, aut virtus, aut optima profuit illi
Mater, et amplexum Cæsaris esse focos?
Aut modo tam pleno fluitantia vela theatro,
Et per maternas omnia gesta manus?
Occidit, et misero steterat vigesimus annus:
Tot bona tam parvo clausit in orbe dies.
I nunc, tolle animos, et tecum finge triumphos,
Stantiaque in plausum tota theatra juvent.
Attalicas supera vestes, atque omnia magnis
Gemmea sint ludis: ignibus ista dabis.
Sed tamen huc omnes, huc primus et ultimus ordo:

9.] *His pressus*, i.e. *stagnis*, sup. 2. This verse is commonly misinterpreted to signify that the youth was drowned in the bay of Baiæ. But it is evident that this is a gratuitous supposition. Such an explanation leaves it doubtful to what *his* refers: in fact it is only by supplying *aquis*, that such a sense could be elicited. By saying that Marcellus died oppressed and overcome by the baths at Baiæ, he explains why that watering-place was now *invisa cum magno crimine*. Mr. Wratislaw, referring *his* to *his Baiis*, naturally finds a difficulty in *vestro lacu*, and proposes *hic*. It is hard to say if 'demittere vultum in Stygias aquas' is a general term for dying, or has reference to dipping the head and face in sulphur-waters supposed to be infested with a demon. Lachmann, Barth, and others read *demersit*, which would rather require *in undis*. Hertzberg rightly explains *pressus* by *oppressus*, *afflictus*, showing from Cic. *Ep. ad Fam.* ix. 12, that the climate of Baiæ was considered very relaxing and unwholesome. Strabo too calls the volcanic vapours [illegible].

10.] This fine verse is certainly not improved by Lachmann's punctuation, 'Errat et in vestro, spiritus, ille, lacu.' He is right, however, as to the sense. Marcellus 'flits a spirit' in those fatal waters. The Avernian lake was the very abode of ghosts, νεκυομαντεῖον, Strabo, v. cap. 4.

12.] *Amplexum esse*.—*amplexo* Barth and Kuinoel, but against the good copies. What availed it, the poet asks, that he was connected with the house of Cæsar? 'Amplexus vero erat Augusti focos non tantum adoptione, sed etiam sponsaliis celebratis ante deos Penates cum Julia, Augusti filia.'—*Barth*.

13.] The sense is thus given by Hertzberg: 'Quid referam Marcelli ipsius gesta, quid præterea omnia illa, quæ ejus nomine mater gesserit?' Octavia had conducted the duties of her son as Ædile, when he was unable through illness to attend to them. The theatre of Marcellus was erected by Augustus in the name of his nephew. See Tac. *Ann.* iii. 64; Sueton. *Oct.* § 29. 'Quædam etiam opera sub nomine alieno, nepotum scilicet et uxoris sororisque, fecit: ut porticum basilicamque Caii et Lucii; item porticus Liviæ et Octaviæ, theatrumque Marcelli.'—*Modo tam pleno* seems more correct than *modo fluitantia*, i.e. quæ nuper fluitare vidimus. To the same gift he alludes in v. 19, *Attalicas supera vestes*. See v. 5, 24. The *vela* were the *awnings*, (*sinuosa vela*, v. 1, 15), graphically described in the old theatre by Lucretius, iv. 76 seqq., where they are also called *vela*, different perhaps from *aulæa*, *Georg.* iii. 25.

16.] *Dies*, i.e. the brief life of Marcellus.

17.] *I nunc*. Addressed ironically to any vain believer in human glory.

20.] The MSS. agree in *ista*. Jacob and Lachmann, apparently by an oversight, print *uste*, which is also given by Kuinoel from a late MS., though not by Barth. The reading is decidedly inferior, as it ought rather to have been *cremanda*. On the contrary, *ista*, 'those riches and honours of yours,' happily expresses the perishable and worthless nature of them.

21.] *Huc*, sc. tendimus. The Naples and Gron. MSS. have *hac*, which Lach-

Est mala, sed cunctis ista terenda via est.
Exoranda canis tria sunt latrantia colla;
Scandenda est torvi publica cymba senis.
Ille licet ferro cautus se condat et ære,
Mors tamen inclusum protrahit inde caput.
Nirea non facies, non vis exemit Achillem,
Crœsum aut, Pactoli quas parit humor, opes.
Hic olim ignaros luctus populavit Achivos,
Atridæ magno cum stetit alter amor.
At tibi nauta, pias hominum qui traicit umbras,
Huc animæ portet corpus inane tuæ,
Qua Siculæ victor telluris Claudius et qua
Cæsar ab humana cessit in astra via.

mann reads in both places, sc. 'hoc omnes coguntur facere.'—*ordo* perhaps refers to the different ranks as arranged in the theatre.—*tamen* implies some ellipse: '(invisa quidem est mors) sed tamen' &c. This sentiment in fact is expressed in the pentameter.

25.] *Ille*, 'this (*i.e.* any) man may hide his body in iron and brass; yet Death will come and force him to put out his head.' The figure is perhaps derived from a snail or tortoise concealed in a shell.

29.] *Ignaros*, sc. imprudentes, causam mali nescientes. *Alter amor* is the love of Chryseis; whence Clytemnestra taunts her husband with having been Χρυσηΐδων μείλιγμα τῶν ὑπ' Ἰλίῳ, *Ag.* 1414. Lachmann gives *altus amor*, and refers *magno stetit* to the Greeks, not to Agamemnon himself. Hertzberg thus paraphrases: 'quo tempore A. iterum amore male mulctatus est;' observing that in all his loves Agamemnon was unfortunate. As *populavit* is stronger than *exemit*, it is likely that *luctus* is the grief of Achilles for the loss of Briseis; which grief caused the loss, by war and pestilence, of so many of the Greeks. 'Talis tantusque est hic luctus ob Marcellum extinctum, qualis quantusque Græcorum fuit, publicus nempe, non privatus.'—*Barth.*

32.] Müller, with Lachmann and Kuinoel reads *suæ* for *tuæ*, which latter is found in all the copies. The passage is obscure, and has been variously altered and explained. The common reading is, 'At tibi, nauta, pias hominum qui trajicis umbras, Huc animæ portent corpus inane tuæ.'. Hertzberg has a rather tedious note of four pages upon it: '*Tuæ animæ* are explained 'tui venti, tua flamina, O Charon,' as Pucci interpreted it: *tibi*, *i.e.* 'tuo dicto obedientes.' *Corpus inane* is for *umbram mortui*, the confusion between the soul and the body being, as elsewhere remarked, very common in the Latin poets. This explanation of the vulgate is the best that has been proposed. Few however will consider it satisfactory. In the former edition I proposed the reading now given in the text, and it has been adopted by Mr. Wratislaw; *i.e.* 'Tibi, O Marcelle, huc portet Charon corpus inane animæ tuæ, (sc. vita defunctum). Qua,' &c. (see v. 7, 60). The natural mistake of connecting *tibi*, *O nauta*, necessarily led to the corruption of *trajicit* to *trajicis*.—Lachmann quotes 'corpus inane animæ' from Ovid, *Met.* ii. 611, and xiii. 488. So Hor. *Od.* iii. 11, 26, 'inane lymphæ dolium.'

33.] *Claudius*, *i.e.* Claudius Marcellus, conqueror of Syracuse B.C. 212. To him Ovid alludes, *Fast.* iv. 873, 'Utque Syracusas Arethusidas abstulit armis Claudius, et bello te quoque cepit, Eryx,' &c. The meaning of the whole passage is thus given by Hertzberg: 'Hoc Charontem obsecrat, ut Marcellum eo advehat, qua via ad sedes beatorum ducat. Has quondam avum Claudium consiste, has divum Cæsarem ingressum ulterius etiam astra petisse.' *Humana via* is the road which all must tread, *i.e.* death, according to the same authority: but why not *ab hominum conversatione*? *In astra* must of course be understood of Julius Cæsar alone: *qua* (agit or vivit) Claudius, *i.e.* in Elysium, is to be supplied in the former part of the verse.

XIX.

Objicitur totiens a te mihi nostra libido;
  Crede mihi, vobis imperat ista magis.
Vos, ubi contempti rupistis frena pudoris,
  Nescitis captæ mentis habere modum.
Flamma per incensas citius sedetur aristas,
  Fluminaque ad fontis sint reditura caput,
Et placidum Syrtes portum et bona litora nautis
  Præbeat hospitio sæva Malea suo,
Quam possit vestros quisquam reprehendere cursus,
  Et rabidæ stimulos frangere nequitiæ.
Testis, Cretæi fastus quæ passa juvenci
  Induit abiegnæ cornua falsa bovis;
Testis Thessalico flagrans Salmonis Enipeo,
  Quæ voluit liquido tota subire deo.
Crimen et illa fuit patria succensa senecta
  Arboris in frondes condita Myrrha novæ.
Nam quid Medeæ referam quo tempore matris
  Iram natorum cæde piavit amor?
Quidve Clytæmnestræ, propter quam tota Mycenis

XIX. The poet endeavours to prove that the passions of the female sex are stronger and less under control than in men.

5.] *Sedetur*. The potential of *sedare*. Kuinoel reads *sedaret* from the Palatine MS., which however is manifestly wrong, the verb being active.

7.] *Syrtes*, the plural, to which *præbeant* is to be supplied.

8.] *Malea*. Pucci observes that Virgil shortens the second syllable, *Æn.* v. 193, 'Maleæque sequacibus undis.' The Greek is Μάλεια and Μαλέα. It seems certain that the diphthong ει as well as αι is susceptible of being pronounced short before a vowel. So Æschylus uses [illegible], *Ag.* 972, and we have *Æschylie* in iii. 26, 41.

9.] *Reprehendere*, cohibere, retinere.

10.] *Rabidæ* Müller, from the corrected copies, for *rapidæ*, which Lachmann and Keil retain. The strong words *flagrans* (13) and *succensa* (15) justify the correction.

12.] See v. 7, 57, 'mentitæ ligneæ monstra bovis.'—*cornua*, i.e. formam bovis.

13.] *Salmonis*. See on I. 13, 21.

14.] *Subire*, se subdere.

15.] *Crimen*. For *criminosa*, by a Greek use, as *μίασμα*, *στύγημα* &c. applied to persons. Compare I. 11, 30, 'Ah pereant Baiæ, crimen amoris, aquæ.'—*patris succensa senecta*, 'flagrans amore patris senis Cinyræ.'—*Kuinoel*. See Ovid, *Met.* x. 298.

17.] *Medeæ*, sc. crimen. The same word must be supplied in v. 19. The construction is, 'cum Medeæ amor piavit (explevit) matris iram (sc. in Creusam) cæde natorum suorum:' when the love of a mother was so far overcome by her infatuated attachment that she killed her own children. *Matris iræ* is the resentment she felt as a mother, on the father of her children deserting her for another. And this is contrasted with the conflicting emotion, *amor conjugis*. Jacob considers the construction to be; 'quid referam quo tempore Medeæ amor matris iram piavit.' But this leaves the genitive *Clytæmnestræ* unprovided for except by supplying *amor*. Lachmann reads *Clytæmnestra*, in the nominative, which however leaves some ellipse to be supplied.

Infamis stupro stat Pelopea domus?
Tuque o Minoa venumdata, Scylla, figura,
Tondens purpurea regna paterna coma.
Hanc igitur dotem virgo desponderat hosti:
Nise, tuas portas fraude reclusit Amor.
At vos, innuptæ, felicius urite tædas:
Pendet Cretæa tracta puella rate.
Non tamen immerito Minos sedet arbiter Orci:
Victor erat quamvis, æquus in hoste fuit.

XX.

Credis eum jam posse tuæ meminisse figuræ,
Vidisti a lecto quem dare vela tuo?
Durus, qui lucro potuit mutare puellam!

21.] *Tuque O* &c. *i.e.* tu quoque, O Scylla, venumdata es, capta, Minois pulcritudine. On this Propertian use of *figura* see i. 4, 9. Scylla, daughter of Nisus king of Megara, (sometimes wrongly confounded with Scylla the marine monster, as in v. 4, 39) sold herself and her country to Minos, king of Crete, by cutting off a certain purple lock of her father's hair. See Æsch. *Cho.* 616 &c. Pausan. *Att.* I. xix. 4: ἐν ταύτῃ τὴν Νῖσον ἔχει λόγος, τρίχας ἐν τῇ κεφαλῇ οἱ πορφυρᾶς εἶναι, χρῆναι δὲ αὐτὸν ἐπὶ ταύταις ἀποκαρείσαις τελευτᾶν. Ὡς δὲ οἱ Κρῆτες ἦλθον ἐς τὴν γῆν, τὰς μὲν ἄλλας ᾕρουν ἐξ ἐπιδρομῆς τὰς ἐν τῇ Μεγαρίδι πόλεις, ἐς δὲ τὴν Νίσαιαν καταφεύγοντα τὸν Νῖσον ἐπολιόρκουν· ἐνταῦθα τοῦ Νίσου λέγεται θυγατέρα ἐρασθῆναι Μίνω, καὶ ὡς ἀπέκειρε τὰς τρίχας τοῦ πατρός.

22.] *Tondens.* 'Cum purpurea coma patris Nisi regnum simul tondens et excidens.'—*Barth.* Perhaps we should read *purpuream comam*, to which *regna* would stand in apposition; 'comam a qua pendebat regni salus.' See on iv. 13, 2. Keil and Müller read *tondes.* It is easy to supply either *crimine es* or *testis es* from 13, 14.

23.] *Hanc dotem*, *i.e.* prodendæ patriæ. Compare v. 4, 56, 'Dos tibi non humilis prodita Roma venit.'

25.] *Felicius urite*, *i.e.* may your marriages have a happier result.

26.] *Tracta rate.* She was tied to the rudder of Minos' ship.

27.] Though a conqueror, he showed his justice even in the case of an enemy, *i.e.* in avenging even an enemy by punishing her who had betrayed him. Pindar (*Pyth.* ii. 73) gives a similar reason for Rhadamanthys being a judge in Hades, because he was sensible and not deceived by guiles and flatteries.

XX. Barth is of opinion that this difficult elegy is one of the earliest of the poet's compositions; and he places the date at A.U.C. 723, while Hertzberg assigns A.U.C. 732. He shrewdly observes, that the name *Cynthia* does not occur in it; and it is certainly not easy to understand vv. 9 and 13 otherwise than as implying the commencement of their intimacy (in 726). Lachmann and Jacob indeed, as well as Keil and Müller, follow Scaliger in beginning a new elegy after ver. 10, and transposing the distich 13, 14, before 11, 12. If we adopt the latter almost necessary correction, there is no want of continuity in the ordinary arrangement. Having invited Cynthia (or Hostia) to accept his protection and regard, he immediately proceeds to arrange the terms as if he were *ipso facto* her recognised lover. Such a fragmentary and unfinished address of ten lines is not rashly to be attributed to the poet. Who the faithless rival alluded to in v. 1—2 may have been, is unknown.

2.] *Dare vela a lecto.* ἐκ τῶν ἁβροτίμων προκαλυμμάτων ἔπλευσεν, Æsch. *Ag.* 700.

Tantine, ut lacrimes, Africa tota fuit?
At tu, stulta, deos tu fingis, inania verba!
Forsitan ille alio pectus amore terat.
Est tibi forma potens, sunt castæ Palladis artes,
Splendidaque a docto fama refulget avo.
Fortunata domus, modo sit tibi fidus amicus.
Fidus ero: in nostros curre, puella, toros.
Nox mihi prima venit; primæ data tempora noctis
Longius in primo, Luna, morare toro;
Tu quoque, qui æstivos spatiosius exigis ignes,
Phœbe, moraturæ contrahe lucis iter.
Fœdera sunt ponenda prius, signandaque jura,
Et scribenda mihi lex in amore novo.

4.] *Tantine* is the reading of Pucci: the MSS. give *tantisne in lacrimis*, except that *in* is omitted in the MS. Gron. Jacob has *tantine in lacrimis*, which he explains 'inter lacrymas,' and so Keil; Hertzberg *tantine, his lacrimis*, &c. *i. e.* 'hac lacrimante;' Lachmann *Tantisne in lacrimis Africa grata fuit?* Barth *Tantisne in lucris* &c. and lastly, Kuinoel, with Heinsius, *Tantine ut lacrymas* &c. Müller, after Heinsius, *tantine, ut lacrimes*. Of these various attempts I prefer that of Müller, which gives the easiest and most natural sense. Compare sup. 12, 3, 'tantine ulla fuit spoliati gloria Parthi?'

5.] *At tu* &c. 'But you, simpleton, console yourself by fancying that there are gods who will avenge his perfidy; vain belief! while he meanwhile is perhaps cherishing another.' Hertzberg condemns this simple explanation, which is due to Kuinoel, and prefers the following: 'Tu deos veros esse et quales deos esse decet (perjurii vindices) falso tibi persuades. At illi perfidiam non curant,' &c. while *verba fingis* he takes in a different sense, 'verba componis, ne perfidum credere amatorem sustineas.' Lachmann gives *vera* for *verba*, and he is followed by Müller. Jacob says: 'sensus est: et deos et inania promissa tu fingis;—ille istius deos, per quos juraverat, promissaque, quæ dederat, vera fingens, quum essent inania, se ipsa fefellit.'

6.] *Terat*, consumat, vexet suum pectus &c.

7.] *Forma potens*, cf. II. 5, 28, 'Cynthia forma potens, Cynthia verba levis.'—*Palladis artes*, see on I. 2, 27. On the *doctus avus*, whom some have supposed to be the poet Hostius, Hertzberg has a not very convincing discussion, *Quæst.* pp. 38—9, where he insists that Cynthia (*i. e.* Hostia) must have been born of *libertini*, but makes no attempt to account for the strong expressions *splendida fama* and *docto avo*. The *avus* in question may probably have been celebrated as an actor or musician on the stage; for the highly laudatory words of the poet may fairly be regarded as the language of compliment. Nothing whatever is known of Cynthia's parentage.

10.] One of the inferior MSS. gives *sinus*, which is certainly more elegant than the vulgate, and is adopted by Barth and Kuinoel. Had the poet already conferred the name Cynthia on his mistress, he would probably have written 'Cynthia curre' for 'curre puella.'

12.] *Moraturæ lucis*, *i. e.* the day which would in the natural course of events linger on. Compare 'Luna moraturis sedula luminibus,' I. 3, 32; and 'victura rosaria Pæsti,' v. 5, 61. The idea, which is most poetically expressed, perhaps is taken from the legend in Plautus, *Amphitr.* 113, 'et hæc ob eam rem nox est facta longior, Dum cum illa quacum vult voluptatem capit,' sc. Jupiter.

13.] The connexion is, 'nox *enim* prima venit' &c. For *data* Lachmann, Keil, and Müller give *data*, with the Naples MS.

15—20.] 'The marriage rite has first to be duly solemnised.' This, as Jacob supposes, is mentioned as a reason why the day should be shortened and the night protracted. If this be right, *prius* in 15 means that before the night has passed the marriage ceremonies have to be gone through, *i. e.* the *novus amor* to be con-

Hæc Amor ipse suo constringet pignera signo;
Testis sidereæ tota corona deæ.
Quam multæ ante meis cedent sermonibus horæ,
Dulcia quam nobis concitet arma Venus!
Namque, ubi non certo vincitur fœdere lectus,
Non habet ultores nox vigilanda deos,
Et quibus imposuit, solvit mox vincla libido:—
Contineant nobis omina prima fidem!
Ergo, qui pactas in fœdera ruperit aras,
Pollueritque novo sacra marita toro,
Illi sint, quicumque solent in amore dolores,
Et caput argutæ præbeat historiæ;

consummated. The allusion to the marriage is of course allegorical; he means, 'We must first make a formal engagement to live faithfully to each other.' Such compacts appear to have been really made among the Romans, where *justum matrimonium* was out of the question. It has been shown on ii. 7, 1, that Propertius could not legally have married Cynthia if he had wished.

17.] *Signo*. So Juvenal, alluding to the shameless marriage of Messalina with Silius, x. 336, 'veniet cum signatoribus auspex.' As the marriage is not a real, but only a pretended one, so the signatures and the witnesses are impossible personages. But all these ideas are exquisitely rendered, and it would be difficult to find more beautiful verses. For *tota* all the copies give *torta*, which Hertzberg alone retains, explaining it of the apparent revolution of the heavens, and comparing *Æn.* v. 738, 'torquet medios nox humida cursus,' and Ovid, *Met.* ii. 71, 'cœlum—Sideraque alta trahit celerique volumine torquet.' As a matter of poetical taste, one would prefer *tota*, as there is something fine in calling *all* the 'consola sidera' to witness the contract.—*sidereæ deæ*, i. e. *noctis*.

19.] *Quam multæ* &c. 'How many hours must pass in talk,—must be *talked away*—before,' &c. Barth and Kuinoel read *cedant*; the latter even interprets *quam ante* in reference to *fœdera sunt ponenda prius*, making vv. 17, 18, parenthetical. Lachmann follows Scaliger in transposing this couplet to precede 15. Thus *namque* in 21 is left to explain *testis* etc. in 18.

21.] *Namque* &c. 'For, when no marriage-tie as yet exists, the gods will not bring punishment on a night spent in talk.' If the order of this very obscure distich is right, the reference must be to the delay alluded to in 19—20. Some from inferior copies give *nec violanda*, which must mean *adulterina*.

23.] *Non* is the reading of all the good copies, and is retained by Jacob and Hertzberg. 'And besides, mere passion (apart from legal marriage) soon breaks the tie between those on whom it has fastened it. In *our* case may these first rites prove the means of preserving our good faith!' Only inferior MSS. give *mox*. Jacob supposes the order of the words to be: 'quibus libido vincula imposuit, iis (una) nox solvit (ea),' adding, 'quo nihil potest dici melius.' But this is a complexity of construction which no language will bear, if it is to convey intelligible sentiments. It is more probable that *mox solvit* forms an antithesis with *contineant*,—*omina prima*, i. e. auspicia quasi nuptialia.

25.] *Pactas in fœdera*, 'pledged in attestation of the contract.' The Groningen MS. gives *actas in fœdere*. Barth and Kuinoel *factas* from a late copy. *Ergo* introduces the terms of the mutual agreement: 'Accordingly, let us pledge ourselves as follows; May he who violates,' &c., where the words *qui ruperit* are applied by the poet to his own case.

28.] *Argutæ historiæ*. 'La nouvelle galante.'—*Barth*. Hertzberg also correctly understands 'the *gossip* of the neighbourhood.'

Nec flenti dominæ patefiant nocte fenestræ:
  Semper amet, fructu semper amoris egena.

XXI.

Magnum iter ad doctas proficisci cogor Athenas,
  Ut me longa gravi solvat amore via.
Crescit enim assidue spectando cura puellæ:
  Ipse alimenta sibi maxima præbet amor.
Omnia sunt tentata mihi, quacumque fugari
  Possit: at ex omni me premit ipse deus.
Vix tamen aut semel admittit, cum sæpe negavit;
  Seu venit, extremo dormit amica toro.
Unum erit auxilium; mutatis Cynthia terris

29.] 'Nec flenti (illi) patefiant dominæ fenestræ.' Compare the beautiful lines in lib. v. 7, 15—18. Jacob inclines to the reading of the Groningen MS. *patefacta*, understanding *sint* from v. 27.

XXI. It is altogether uncertain whether the journey to Athens here spoken of was ever really made, or even really contemplated. It may have been a mere threat, —a *ruse* to alarm the jealousy of Cynthia. The argument bears some resemblance to the various passages in the first book (i. 1, 30; *ib.* 6 and 15), where he speaks of travelling as a remedy for love. Hertzberg is inclined to suspect that the same journey is here referred to: but observes (*Quæst.* p. 26), that if he had really made the tour of Athens and Asia, some allusion to it might have been looked for in the following elegies. It seems more probable that he was becoming anxious to shake off Cynthia, though he disguises his real feelings here; see however inf. El. 24. We may perhaps surmise, that the poet, who has elsewhere frequently arranged his elegies in connected couplets, purposely placed the present after the preceding, that the commencement of his love might be contrasted with the valediction—for such it virtually is—he has resolved to pronounce.

3.] *Spectanti* Müller, the Naples MS. giving *spectandi*.

6.] *Ex omni*, sc. parte; as 'omnia rerum (genera)' sup. 9, 7.—*ipse deus*, *i. e.* the very god who compels me to gaze, afflicts and distresses me by the sight. *Ille* for *ipse* is only found in the later copies. Müller reads *iste*.

7.] *Negarit* Müller, with the Naples MS.

8.] *Amica.* This is the reading of all MSS. and early edd. Scaliger proposed *amicta*, (in the sense of *operta* iii. 6, 6, and *vestita ibid.* 18), which the obsequious Broukhusius (Broeckhuisen) pronounces 'ex tripode dictum;' and he is followed by Lachmann, Barth, Kuinoel, and the recent editors. Hertzberg places only a comma after *deus* (v. 6), and makes it the subject to *admittit* and *negavit*, thus ingeniously introducing some sort of necessity for a new nominative *amica*. But I cannot persuade myself that this was the poet's meaning. *Amicta* is certainly probable, though the word is rather unusual in the precise sense to be conveyed; compare 'pudor est velatus amictu,' sup. 15, 3; 'vestita cubaris,' iii. 7, 17, and 'tunica duxit operta moram' *ib.* 6. But *amica*, if taken with *admittit* and the following verbs, and not with *dormit* alone, has nothing objectionable in itself. *Venit* is understood by some as a *verbum amatorium* for *copiam dat sui*. Lachmann more probably regards it as opposed to *admittit*, *i. e.* whether I go to her or she to me.—*extremo toro*, i. e. *extrema sponda*, Hor. *Ep.* iii. 22, for the bed had a raised ledge (*pluteus*) on one side, the outer part being called *sponda*; which explains *fractus utroque toro*, iii. 8, 4. See Becker, *Gallus*, p. 291, and inf. v. 8, 68.

9.] Hertzberg rightly follows Lachmann in regarding *Cynthia* as the nominative rather than the vocative: 'Cum Cynthiam non amplius videbo, non amabo amplius.' —*quantum*, *i. e.* quam procul Cynthia ab oculis, tam procul amor ex animo.

Quantum oculis, animo tam procul ibit amor.
Nunc agite, o socii, propellite in æquora navim,
Remorumque pares ducite sorte vices;
Jungiteque extremo felicia lintea malo:
Jam liquidum nautis aura secundat iter.
Romanæ turres et vos valeatis amici,
Qualiscumque mihi tuque puella vale.
Ergo ego nunc rudis Hadriaci vehar æquoris hospes,
Cogar et undisonos nunc prece adire deos.
Deinde per Ionium vectus cum fessa Lechæo
Sedarit placida vela phaselus aqua,
Quod superest, sufferte pedes, properate laborem,
Isthmos qua terris arcet utrumque mare.
Inde ubi Piræi capient me litora portus,
Scandam ego Theseæ brachia longa viæ.
Illic vel studiis animum emendare Platonis

12.] *Pares sorte vices*, 'draw lots for your turns at the oar in couples.' Virg. Æn. iii. 509, 'Sternimur optatæ gremio telluris ad undam, *Sortiti remos*.' It seems that they drew lots (1) who should be paired, and (2) in what order they should relieve each other. But the sense may be, 'pull the equal pairs of oars in your allotted places.'

13.] *Extremo*, summo malo; *i.e.* hoist all sail, put on all the canvass, as we say.

16.] One MS. is said to give *tuque Johanna vale*. The scribe was evidently thinking of his own Cynthia.

19.] *Lechæo*. One of the harbours of Corinth on the side of the Sinus Corinthiacus. The isthmus had to be crossed by travellers to Athens, and a boat taken on the other side, or the rest of the journey was performed by land. Hertzberg seems to understand v. 21 in the latter sense. It may however refer only to crossing the isthmus; for v. 23 seems rather to imply his sailing into the Piræus, though Jacob says 'ad terrestre iter ea oratio' (sc. Piræi litora portus) 'optime vertitur.' In truth it is ambiguous, for *litora* might refer equally to the ship touching the shore, and to the traveller who merely approaches the port by land. The isthmus is only three or four miles in the narrowest part.

23.] Lachmann alone prefers the reading of the Groning. MS. *me lintea portus*. But he candidly adds, 'utra lectio verior sit, non possum dicere.'

25.] It is not easy to comprehend on what grounds almost every commentator has felt difficulties about this passage. 'When arrived at Athens,' says the poet, 'I shall improve my mind by the study of Plato, Epicurus, or Menander.' Nothing can be simpler, no resolve more prudent and reasonable. 'But,' says one, 'Epicurus was not *doctus*; besides, *docte Menandre* occurs just below. We should read *dux Epicure*.' Another will have it that *studiis Platonis* and *studium Demosthenis* cannot have been written by the poet; and therefore corrects *spatiis* or *stadiis*. Even Lachmann was so far led away by these hypercritical objections, that he has enclosed vv. 25—8 in brackets as spurious: and Hertzberg adds, 'fortasse rectius abessent;' a verdict from which we may be allowed to dissent. See the remark on El. 8, 4, supra. Some have maintained that *studia Platonis* cannot literally signify 'the study of Plato;' to which Hertzberg replies that the words mean 'studia, quibus Plato vacabat.' Lastly, the objection that *vel—vel* cannot be used as disjunctives, has perhaps but little force in a poet like Propertius. Granting that the use is not strictly correct (see on ii. 8, 11), can a modern editor guarantee that a Roman poet never by any possibility did or could write inaccurately? I can only say, that I do not agree with Hertzberg in explaining *vel studiis* as equivalent to *etiam studiis*.

Incipiam, aut hortis, docte Epicure, tuis.
Persequar aut studium linguæ, Demosthenis arma,
Librorumque tuos, docte Menandre, sales;
Aut certe tabulæ capient mea lumina pictæ,
Sive ebore exactæ, seu magis ære manus;
Aut spatia annorum, aut longa intervalla profundi,
Lenibunt tacito vulnera nostra sinu;
Seu moriar, fato, non turpi fractus amore;
Atque erit illa mihi mortis honesta dies.

XXII.

Frigida tam multos placuit tibi Cyzicus annos,

Müller edits the passage thus: 'illis aut studiis animum emendare Platonis Incipiam' &c., and (in 28) 'libaboque tuos, scite Menandre, sales.' In this I have no desire to follow him. Lachmann's note is excellent, and the examples he quotes show that the Romans used (1) aut—, aut—, vel; (2) non—, nec—, aut—, vel —; (3) non—, aut—, vel—. But of vel —, aut—, he can adduce no instance. Who shall venture to condemn the present passage, even if a ἅπαξ λεγόμενον, unless we moderns are to prescribe laws for the ancients? These details admit only of observation, not of being reduced to fixed rules. All who write or speak in living languages do so intuitively, and without the consciousness of any formal restraint: and we are by no means sure that we exactly realise the Roman feelings of propriety in speaking.

27.] *Persequar*, 'I will pursue,' 'attain for myself.' Perhaps the word means something more than *sequar*, since we know from v. 1, 134, that the poet was intended for the bar in early life. The Groning. MS. has *prosequar*, a very good reading.

28.] Jacob follows Lachmann in placing a stop after *librorumque*, and understanding *studium*, to which *tuos sales* may stand in opposition, as *arma* in the preceding verse. There is nothing more than a poetical enallage in *tuos sales librorum*.

30.] *Manus.* A bold expression for *manuum opera*.

32.] *Tacito sinu*, 'in a quiet nook;' 'in silent retirement.' Possibly he may mean 'animi tranquillitate,' the ablative of the means. Barth seems to understand it 'in their quiet bosom,' *i.e.* retirement. Cf. Tac. *Agric.* § 4, 'in hujus sinu indulgentiaque educatus.' *Ibid.* § 30, 'nos—recessus ipse ac sinus famæ in hunc diem defendit.' Heinsius reads *situ*.—*situs* is properly 'the being let alone,' and thence the consequences of it, neglect, decay, dirt, &c. A similar word is *sinus*, also perhaps from *sinere*, ἐᾶν. But a *nook* is a *fold* or *bend*; whence *sinus*.

33.] *Fractus*, &c. 'Or, if I am to die, it will at least be by a natural death, and not through grief at being the victim of a discreditable attachment.' '*Recte*' (says Hertzberg) 'contuleris Britannorum *heart-broken*.' From the epithet *turpi* we may infer that this elegy was not addressed 'ad Cynthiam,' as most editors have thought, probably from regarding *Cynthia* in v. 9, as the vocative. Nor does v. 16 militate against the view that it is designed to inform his friends of the intended journey and its motives. For he there takes leave of her in common with other persons and other objects.

XXII. This elegy is addressed to the same friend as i. 6, &c., and is an exhortation that he should return to Rome after a long residence at the noble and picturesque city of Cyzicus on the Propontis (sea of Marmara). He had followed his uncle to Asia in the capacity of legatus (see on i. 6, 34), and after his year of office had expired, remained for the sake of pleasure and improvement in that country. The chief point of the poem is the *laudes Italiæ*, much in the same strain as the well-known passage, *Georgic* ii. 136, &c.

Tulle, Propontiaca qua fluit Isthmos aqua,
Dindymus, et sacræ fabricata juvenca Cybelæ,
Raptorisque tulit qua via Ditis equos.
Si te forte juvant Helles Athamantidos urbes,
Nec desiderio, Tulle, movere meo:
Tu licet aspicias cælum omne Atlanta gerentem,
Sectaque Persea Phorcidos ora manu,
Geryonis stabula, et luctantum in pulvere signa

2.] *Fluit Isthmos.* For the connexion of the island on which the city stood with the continent was only by a bridge. He means that the access to it was over water, not solid earth.

3.] *Dindymus.* A mountain of this name, close to the city, was famous for the worship of the Asiatic goddess Rhea or Cybele, like that of the same name in Phrygia.—*juvenca* is the conjecture of Vossius, and has been admitted by most of the later editors for *inventa*. The particular allusion cannot be fully explained from deficiency of direct testimonies: but as the identity of Rhea or Cybele with Isis or Io is unquestionable, and as the cow was the Indian as well as the Egyptian symbol of Earth, there can be no difficulty in supposing that a famous statue of Cybele under this form existed at Cyzicus. Hertzberg observes that the impress of a cow is frequent on Cyzicenian coins. The MSS. give *sacræ*. Pucci wrote on the margin of the ed. Rheg., 'Dindyma qua Argivum fabricata inventa Cybele est,' but whether from his MS. or his conjecture is uncertain. Müller after Haupt gives *sacra fabricata e vite Cybebe* (MS. Naples *Cibele*). Hertzberg reads 'Dindyma sacra Rheæ, et fabricata juvenca Cybelæ,'—but his reasons scarcely seem to justify so wide a departure from the copies. He is probably right in regarding *Cybelæ* as the dative, since our poet prefers the Greek form of the genitive in *es*. Lachmann accordingly has edited *Cybebes*.

4.] No other record of Proserpine having been carried down to Hades at Cyzicus exists, except a single passage quoted by Hertzberg from the Latin anthology. Among the endless affinities of the ancient deities, due perhaps in great part to the confusion of Semitic and Indo-germanic legends with various local modifications of belief, Proserpine, Isis, and Io, and therefore Cybele, become eventually identified as personifications of the moon. Hence we may expect to find the worship of Proserpine connected with that of Cybele.

5—16.] The whole of this passage forms one connected sentiment, of which this is the brief outline: 'However much you may be pleased with the beauties of art and nature by the Hellespont, and however little, in consequence, you may care to return to your friends; know, that if you were to visit all the wonders of the world, Italy would be found to equal any of them.' Lachmann places a comma at *equos*, a full stop at *meo*. He gives the sense thus: 'Dum tibi Cyzicus placuit, si te Dindymus forte juvat et Hellesponti urbes, qua Ditis raptoris equos via tulit.'

7.] *Licet aspicias.* 'Though you may love to gaze on the statues of Atlas, Perseus, and Hercules,' &c. Humboldt contends that the ancient Atlas is the magnificent volcano now known as the Peak of Teneriffe, which is 12,172 feet above the sea, and generally has its snow-capped cone enveloped in clouds. The highest of the Atlas mountains in the N.W. of Africa rises to 11,400 feet; but it does not appear to have been the original giant of the Hesiodean mythology. See *Aspects of Nature*, vol. i. p. 144.

9.] *Signa.* Not, as Hertzberg thinks, any *statues*, but *vestigia*, the marks fancifully supposed to be left by the wrestling heroes. The event was said to have taken place in Mauretania. Pliny, *N. H.* v. 1. But it is more probable that the poet means the works of art preserved at Cyzicus. It will be observed that where he speaks of actual travels in the following verses, he confines himself to reasonable distances from that city. To send his friend to the extreme west, and then back to Asia, is an improbable arrangement. On the oxen of Geryon see v. 9, 2.—I have preferred the form *Geryonis* (Gr. Γηρυόνης, Æsch. *Ag.* 870), the reading of the Naples and Groningen MSS., to *Geryonæ* or *Geryonei*, the former of which is commonly adopted from the ed. Rheg.

Herculis Antæique, Hesperidumque choros,
Tuque tuo Colchum propellas remige Phasim,
Peliacæque trabis totum iter ipse legas,
Qua rudis Argoa natat inter saxa columba
In faciem proræ pinus adacta novæ,
Et si, qua Ortygiæ visenda est ora Caystri,
Et qua septenas temperat unda vias;
Omnia Romanæ cedent miracula terræ:
Natura hic posuit, quidquid ubique fuit.
Armis apta magis tellus, quam commoda noxæ,
Famam, Roma, tuæ non pudet historiæ.
Nam quantum ferro, tantum pietate potentes
Stamus; victrices temperat ira manus.
Hic Anio Tiburne fluis, Clitumnus ab Umbro
Tramite, et æternum Marcius humor opus;
Albanus lacus et socia Nemorensis ab unda,

10.] *Antæique.* With the elision in this verse compare i. 5, 32, 'non impune illa rogata venit.'

12.] *Ipse*, sc. quod olim heroes legebant.

13.] *Argoa columba*, *i.e.* cum columba Argoa adeuset. (Hertzberg). See on iii. 16, 39.

14.] *In faciem* &c. 'Arbor, rudis antea, redacta in formam navigii novi.'—*Barth.*

15.] *Ortygiæ* is probably the dative of place, 'at Ortygia.' 'Et si navigaveris, qua memorabilis Caystri ora juxta Ephesum tendit.'—*Hertzberg.* 'Qua Caystri ora est, tam vicina illa Ortygiæ, ut huic videnda sit.'—*Lachmann.* 'Ortygia's shore of (or on) Cayster' may be defended by 'Libyæ Jovis antrum,' v. 1, 103. The reading is doubtful: most of the copies give *origæ* or *origo*, but some of the earliest editions have *ogygiæ*, *origiæ*, or *gygæi*. Kuinoel prints a verse which will not even scan; *Et si qua Gygæi* &c. Müller, 'et sis, qua Ortygiæ et visenda est ora Caystri.' Ortygia was the ancient name for Ephesus, or rather of a grove near that city, connected with the worship of Diana and Latona. The reading adopted from Vossius by Barth, *Ortygii—Caystri* is not improbable, as the river might have been called *Ortygian* from the vicinity of the grove, though an objection has been raised, that it was not on the very bank of that river, but of the Cenchrius.

16.] '*Temperare* propria significatione liquor Nili dicitur, qui denuo semper per vias suas effunditur, novasque aquas prioribus addit, et has suis miscet.' *Hertzberg.* This explanation is too artificial: the poet probably only meant 'reduces his speed and volume by dividing his waters into seven channels.' It is not, perhaps, certain, that the Nile is here spoken of. Barth suggests that the Rhesus, a river of the Troad, may be meant, which Strabo describes as having seven mouths. Yet few readers, unless the context clearly determined the matter, could hesitate to refer the familiar expression to the famous Nile.

19.] *Commoda noxæ*, 'damno inferendo; magis vincunt quam nocent Romani.'—*Barth.*

21.] *Pietate*, 'patriotism.'

22.] *Ira temperat*, *i.e.* ira facile remissa temperat victoriam.' 'Ira in hostem, simul ac victum videmus, cessat et manus a sæviendo retrahit.'—*Lachmann.* 'Sic ex studio brevitatis interdum loquuntur poetæ, ut dicant rem fieri ab aliquo, a quo nihil impedimenti interponitur, quo minus fiat.' (Editor's note on Æsch. *Suppl.* 612). Others understand 'postquam vicimus quamvis irati manibus temperamus.'

23.] *Hic*, 'in Italia.'—*Barth.*

24.] *Marcius humor.* See on iv. 2, 12.

25.] The Naples and Groningen MSS. give *socii*, whence Hertzberg reads 'Albanusque lacus, socii Nemorensis et unda,' (*et* for *ab* from MS. Gron.) explaining *socii* as equivalent to *propinqui.* The two lakes, the former said to be of immense depth,

Potaque Pollucis lympha salubris equo.
At non squamoso labuntur ventre cerastæ,
Itala portentis nec fluit unda novis;
Non hic Andromedæ resonant pro matre catenæ,
Nec tremis Ausonias, Phœbe fugate, dapes;
Nec cuiquam absentes arserunt in caput ignes,
Exitium nato matre movente suo;
Penthea non sævæ venantur in arbore Bacchæ;
Nec solvit Danaas subdita cerva rates;
Cornua nec valuit curvare in pellice Juno,
Aut faciem turpi dedecorare bove:
Arboreasque cruces Sinis, et non hospita Graiis

and believed to be an extinct crater, now *Lago di Albano*, certainly cannot with truth be said (as Lachmann asserts) to have a common source. But it is so probable that Propertius records some tradition to that effect, that it seems rash to depart from the reading generally received. There has always been, as there still is, a popular tendency to connect deep waters, whose sources are unknown, by underground communications with other lakes. Barth and Kuinoel also give *Albanusque lacus*, which is found in two or three corrected copies. *Nemorensis* is now *Nemi*.

26.] *Lympha*. The Naples MS. has *nympha*. The pond in the forum Romanum, called *Lacus Juturnæ*, is here meant, from which Castor and Pollux are said to have watered their horses after the battle at Lake Regillus, Ovid, *Fast.* i. 707. The enthusiasm with which the Latin poets enumerate the rivers and springs and aqueducts can only be understood by remembering the great scarcity of wholesome water over a large district of lower Italy.

27.] *At non* &c. Compare Virg. *Georg.* ii. 140 seqq., 'hæc loca non tauri spirantes naribus ignem Invertere satis immanis dentibus hydri' &c.

29.] *Andromedæ*. . 'For Andromeda through her mother's fault.' See on v. 7, 66.

30.] *Ausonias dapes*. The banquet of Thyestes. The sense is, 'You have not to fear an Italian banquet as you were horrified by that in Greece.'

31.] The story of Althæa, who threw on the fire the fatal log of wood, the δαλὸς ἥλιξ of Æsch. *Cho.* 607, by which the death of her son Meleager was caused. Pausan. *Phocic.* x. cap. 31, Τὸν δὲ ἐπὶ τῷ δαλῷ λόγον, ὡς δοθείη μὲν ὑπὸ Μοιρῶν τῇ Ἀλθαίᾳ, Μελεάγρῳ δὲ οὐ πρότερον ἔδει τὴν τελευτὴν συμβῆναι, πρὶν ἢ ὑπὸ πυρὸς ἀφανισθῆναι τὸν δαλόν, καὶ ὡς ὑπὸ τοῦ θυμοῦ καταπρήσειεν αὐτὸν ἡ Ἀλθαία, τοῦτον τὸν λόγον Φρύνιχος ὁ Πολυφράδμονος πρῶτος ἐν δράματι ἔδειξε Πλευρωνίαις·

'Ἐκ κρυερὸν γὰρ οὐκ ἤλυξεν μόρον
Ὠκεῖα δέ νιν φλὸξ κατεδαίσατο
Δαλοῦ περθομένου
Ματρὸς ὑπ' αἰνᾶς κακομηχάνου.'

—*absentes ignes* is elegantly used, because, ordinarily, fire can only damage the persons of those in contact.

33.] *In arbore*, i. e. sedentem. See Eur. *Bacch.* 1093.

34.] *Subdita cerva*, the substitution of a deer for Iphigenia when laid on the altar at Aulis.

36.] *Bove*, for *bovis figura*, in allusion to Io. See iii. 20, 17. Æsch. *Suppl.* 299, βοῦν τὴν γυναῖκ' ἔθηκεν Ἀργεία θεός.

37.] *Arboreasque* Lachmann. With *cruces* the commentators usually supply *valuit curvare* from v. 35. But this, as Barth observed before Hertzberg, will not explain the accusative *saxa*, nor could *curvare curvatas trabes* be tolerated. We must therefore supply *non valuit habere* or *adhibere*, as Lachmann suggests. Müller marks the loss of some lines before this verse, in which he supposes the labours of Hercules to have been described.—*in sua fata*, because the robber was killed as he had killed others, by being tied to fir-trees which were bent together and then let go. Hence he was called πιτυοκάμπτης. The *saxa* are the Scironian rocks, which are interposed awkwardly enough, since *in sua fata* must refer, not to Sciron, but to Sinis. Perhaps the poet confused the two stories, since both robbers were

Saxa, et curvatas in sua fata trabes.
Hæc tibi, Tulle, parens, hæc est pulcherrima sedes;
Hic tibi pro digna gente petendus honos.
Hic tibi ad eloquium cives, hic ampla nepotum
Spes et venturæ conjugis aptus amor.

XXIII.

Ergo tam doctæ nobis periere tabellæ,
Scripta quibus pariter tot periere bona!
Has quondam nostris manibus detriverat usus,
Qui non signatas jussit habere fidem.
Illæ jam sine me norant placare puellas,
Et quædam sine me verba diserta loqui.
Non illas fixum caras effecerat aurum:
Vulgari buxo sordida cera fuit.
Qualescumque, mihi semper mansere fideles,
Semper et effectus promeruere bonos.
Forsitan hæc illis fuerant mandata tabellis:
'Irascor, quoniam es, lente, moratus heri.
An tibi nescio quæ visa est formosior? an tu

killed by Theseus. See however iv. 16, 12. Hertzberg understands the rocky Isthmus where Sinis dwelt. Pausan. ii. 1, 4: *ἔστι δὲ ἐπὶ τοῦ Ἰσθμοῦ τῆς ἀρχῆς, ἔνθα ὁ λῃστὴς Σίνις λαμβανόμενος πιτύων ἦγεν ἐς τὸ κάτω σφᾶς. Τούτῳ διεφθάρη τρόπῳ καὶ αὐτὸς ὑπὸ Θησέως ὁ Σίνις.*

40.] *Pro digna gente.* 'Ambiendi tibi sunt honores et magistratus capiendi prout nobilitas gentis tuæ postulat.'—*Barth.* Tullus was therefore yet a youth, and an aspirant to the usual routine of offices in the city. The concluding verse shows that he was not yet married.

41.] *Ad eloquium.* 'To whom you may exhibit your eloquence, and for whom you may profitably employ it.'

XXIII. This little poem stands alone in the writings of Propertius. It is a playful lament on the loss of his *tabellæ*,—thin tablets of wood, covered with wax, and hinged together, used for the transmission of messages by post,—and concludes with the offer of a reward for their recovery.

2.] *Tot bona.* For the book was lost in returning from Cynthia, and with it therefore the answer she had sent. Or perhaps he had written in it some verses, which he playfully calls *bona*.

3.] *Usus detriverat manibus*, poetically for *manus detriverant usu*.

4.] *Non signatas*, 'Even without being sealed.' 'Namque amica Propertii noverat illas ita, ut signo nihil opus esset.'—*Barth.* For the method of folding and tying these missives the reader may consult Becker's *Gallus*, p. 329.

5.] *Sine me.* 'They were as effectual as my presence in appeasing the anger of my mistresses.' The good copies agree in *puellas*: Lachmann and his predecessors give *puellam* from corrected MSS. Elsewhere, however, (as iii. 20, 67), he boasts of a plurality of female acquaintances. Compare Martial, xiv. 8, 'Nondum legerit hos licet puella; Novit quid cupiant vitelliani.'

9.] *Qualescumque*, sc. fuerunt. Supr. El. 21, 16, 'Qualiscunque mihi tuque puella vale.' Lib. v. 1, 1, 'hoc, quodcunque vides, hospes.'—*promeruere*, 'they won for me.'

13.] *An tibi* &c. 'Was the cause of your coming indifference (*lente*), or because

Non bene de nobis crimina ficta jacis ?'
Aut dixit: 'Venies hodie, cessabimus una:
Hospitium tota nocte paravit Amor.'
Et quæcumque volens reperit non stulta puella,
Garrula cum blandis dicitur hora dolis.
Me miserum, his aliquis rationem scribit avarus,
Et ponit duras inter ephemeridas!
Quas si quis mihi rettulerit, donabitur auro.
Quis pro divitiis ligna retenta velit ?
I puer, et citus hæc aliqua propone columna,
Et dominum Esquiliis scribe habitare tuum.

XXIV.

Falsa est ista tuæ, mulier, fiducia formæ,
Olim oculis nimium facta superba meis.

you preferred the charms of another, or because you are spending your time in getting up false charges against me?' The third reason should rather be, 'that you are listening to charges against me;' and perhaps for *jacis* we should read *rapis*.

14.] The MSS. give *non bona*. All the editors have admitted *non bene*, from one late copy and two of the early edd. Jacob quotes *bene* from the Naples MS.

17.] *Volens*. This is the correction of Broukhusius for *dolens*, which is clearly against the sense.

18.] *Dicitur*, i.e. condicitur, indicitur,' 'when with winning wiles she appoints an hour for a chat.' This reading was restored by Lachmann from the MS. Groning. The others have *ducitur*. Kuinoel reads *ducitur hora jocis*, the last word from Heinsius. But a little consideration will show that this is far from the poet's meaning, and indeed from common sense. Cynthia would not write 'while the time was passing in jokes,' but she would add 'such persuasive and complimentary expressions as a clever girl can devise when she invites to an interview.' *Blandi doli* may be understood of stealthy or clandestine meetings; or 'dolosæ blanditiæ,' *ἀπάται ἐρωτικαί*.

20.] *Duras ephemeridas*, 'his clumsy ledgers;' or, perhaps, his heartless accounts.' Hertzberg refers *duras* to the thick and heavy clasped books in which the miser kept his daily reckonings. Ovid has copied this passage, *Am.* i. 12, 25.

22.] *Ligna* is from Pucci. The others have *signa*.

23.] *Columna*, pila, a public post or column, perhaps before a bookseller's shop. See Hor. *Sat.* i. 4, 71, and *Epist. ad Pison.* 373.

XXIV. Kuinoel pronounces this elegy 'ingenuo sitore commendabilis.' One almost regrets to find the poetry of a romantic attachment dispelled by an unfeeling and unexpected farewell, conveying at once a taunt (v. 8), and a boast that the lover has escaped from a great danger. But we cannot forget that Cynthia was really in fault; the concluding elegy shows that the separation had cost the poet a pang, and contains a fair apology for his apparently harsh conduct. It will be observed that this elegy has a particular reference to the introductory one of the first book: to which it therefore forms a *palinodia*.

2.] *Oculis meis*. The meaning is a little obscure. Kuinoel explains 'oculorum judicio,' Hertzberg 'oculis quasi spoliis quibusdam superba,' as a lover's eyes are said *capi*, to be captivated. But this seems to be less consistent with what follows; the admission that he had seen her with partial eyes. Hence the sense must rather be supplied thus: 'made conceited by the charms which my partial eyes discovered in you, and which found expression in my impassioned verse.'

Noster amor tales tribuit tibi, Cynthia, laudes;
  Versibus insignem te pudet esse meis.
Mixtam te varia laudavi sæpe figura,
  Ut, quod non esses, esse putaret amor.
Et color est totiens roseo collatus Eoo,
  Cum tibi quæsitus candor in ore foret.
Quod mihi non patrii poterant avertere amici,
  Eluere aut vasto Thessala saga mari,
Hæc ego, non ferro, non igne coactus, et ipsa
  Naufragus Ægæa verba fatebor aqua.
Correptus sævo Veneris torrebar aheno;
  Vinctus eram versas in mea terga manus.
Ecce coronatæ portum tetigere carinæ,
  Trajectæ Syrtes, ancora jacta mihi est.
Nunc demum vasto fessi resipiscimus æstu,
  Vulneraque ad sanum nunc coiere mea.
Mens Bona, si qua dea es, tua me in sacraria dono.

4.] *Te pudet esse*, i.e. pudet me te insignem esse, &c.

5.] *Varia figura*, i.e. variis pulchritudinis partibus, elementis. See ii. 3, 9, seqq.—*ut* &c., for *ita ut*, 'so that love fancied you were what you were not,' or that your artificial charms were real ones. The connexion and meaning are not clear, and Müller thinks a distich has been lost after 4, beginning with *et*. Perhaps *mixtam* means *compositam*, partly real and partly made up. Barth compares Theocr. vi. 18, ἦ γὰρ ἔρωτι πολλάκις ὦ Πολύφαμε, τὰ μὴ καλὰ καλὰ πέφανται.

7.] *Roseo Eoo*. 'The blush of morning.' *Georgic*. i. 288, 'Aut cum sole novo terras irrorat Eous.'

9.] *Patrii amici*. Compare i. 1, 25, *ib*. 9, and for *ferro* and *igne*, a metaphor from surgery, *ib*. 27.

12.] Hertzberg alone retains the reading of all the copies, *verba fatebor*. The others admit the probable conjecture of Passerat, *vera fatebor*. The words would then allude to the fine elegy, i. 17, where he bewails his absence from Cynthia in the midst of a storm. 'Without being forced into the confession by violent remedies, but merely moved by the danger of a shipwreck, I acknowledged to you that I loved you, *torreri me Veneris aheno*.' There is not, perhaps, much difficulty in understanding *et ipsa* for *ne ipsa*, i.e. continuing the negative sense, 'nor even by shipwreck' &c. The reading in the text may be thus explained: 'As for that enthralment which I once said neither my friends nor even magic arts could prevent,—all this I will now confess to have been *mere words*, and that without being put to the torture which I then had to endure; nay, even though again in such danger of a shipwreck as formerly called forth all those tender expressions.' This is nearly the sense as given by Hertzberg. By the words *naufragus* &c. he means to say, 'Place me in like danger again, and see if I will use the same language towards Cynthia.' Others place a full stop at *mari* and a colon at *foret* in ver. 8. In that case *quod* (9) will mean 'which infatuation of believing in your beauty.'

15.] *Coronatæ*. Cf. *Georgic*. i. 303, 'Ceu pressæ cum jam portum tetigere carinæ, Puppibus et læti nautæ imposuere coronas.'

19.] *Dono*, I hereby make an offering of myself, as a *tabula votiva* for having escaped as it were a moral shipwreck. Barth and Kuinoel adopt the needless correction of Heinsius, *condo*.—*Condere in aliquid* is a construction familiar to Propertius, as ii. 1, 42, 'in Phrygios condere nomen avos;' iv. 19, 16, 'Arboris in frondes condita Myrrha novæ.' But the same Grecism explains *donare in aliquid*. 'Ipsum se pro donario vel ἀναθήματι donat Bonæ Menti.' *Lachmann*. Mens Bona, as Hertzberg well

Exciderant surdo tot mea vota Jovi.

XXV.

Risus eram positis inter convivia mensis,
  Et de me poterat quilibet esse loquax.
Quinque tibi potui servire fideliter annos:
  Ungue meam morso sæpe querere fidem.
Nil moveor lacrimis: ista sum captus ab arte.
  Semper ab insidiis, Cynthia, flere soles.
Flebo ego discedens, sed fletum injuria vincet.
  Tu bene conveniens non sinis ire jugum.
Limina jam nostris valeant lacrimantia verbis,
  Nec tamen irata janua fracta manu.
At te celatis ætas gravis urgeat annis,

observes, is not an abstract idea personified by the fancy of the poet, but a real goddess worshipped as such by the Romans, and possessing a temple. See Ovid, *Fast.* vi. 241, and compare *Am.* i. 2, 31.

20.] *Exciderant.* 'I dedicate myself to you, since all my vows *had been* slighted by Jupiter before I had recourse to you (*i.e.* to Reason) for liberating me.' Others have proposed *exciderint*, or *exciderunt*. The ed. Rheg. has *exciderunt*. See on v. 7, 15, 'Jamne tibi *exciderant* vigilacis furta suburæ?'

XXV. The subject of the last is continued, and more explicit reasons are given for the poet's resolution to resign all connexion with Cynthia. Lachmann and Jacob, following the suggestion of Pucci, print this elegy in continuation with the preceding. It is however probable that the present is a reply to her expostulations and tears on receiving the last.

1.] *Risus eram.* Hertzberg regards *risus* as the substantive, *γέλως*, and so Kuinoel had explained it. As the pluperfect of *rideor* it is less suited to the sense. He would have said *ridebar*.

3.] *Quinque annos*, *i.e.* from the year 726 to the beginning of 732, according to the careful chronology of Hertzberg (*Quæst.* p. 16), who includes in his reckoning the year of separation mentioned iv. 16, 9, 'Peccaram semel, et totum sum pulsus in annum,' which seems to have been A.U.C. 729. That the word *fideliter* must not be taken in the sense we are wont to attach to it, as implying *exclusive* devotion to one, has been before observed, and is clear from admissions frequently made in the foregoing elegies. So *fidem*, v. 7, 53.

6.] *Ab insidiis.* The *motive* for crying is generally an artful one. Such is the force of *ab*. In the preceding verse, *ab arte*, the mode and the agent are mentally confused, *a te captus sum arte lacrimandi*.

7.] *Flebo ego*, *i.e.* ego quoque.

8.] *tu* &c., 'It is *you* (not I) who do not allow the pair to be well-matched in the journey through life.'

9.] *Lacrimantia.* Compare i. 17—44, where the door is spoken of as susceptible of feelings of compassion. So concise however is the language of our poet, that he may have meant, 'lacrimis perfusa inter verba querentis.'—*nec tamen*, see on iii. 20, 52. 'Et januam quam, iratus quamvis, nolui manu frangere, *h.e.* pulsando.'

11.] *Celatis*, 'tacite adlabentibus,' Kuinoel. Rather, *dissimulatis*.—The imprecation, bad as it is and cruel in a former lover to utter it, must be taken for what it is worth in the mouth of a Roman lover, to whom it came almost as a form and a matter of course, poetically at least. See v. 5, 75.

13—16.] Lachmann and Hertzberg follow the best MSS. in reading *cupias*, *patiare*, and *quereris*. Jacob and the other two later editors prefer the future on the authority of Pucci, (the Groning. MS. having *cupies*). The optative seems better to agree with *has diras*, v. 17.

Et veniat formæ ruga sinistra tuæ.
Vellere tum cupias albos a stirpe capillos,
Ah, speculo rugas increpitante tibi;
Exclusa inque vicem fastus patiare superbos,
Et quæ fecisti, facta queraris anus.
Has tibi fatalis cecinit mea pagina diras.
Eventum formæ disce timere tuæ.

14.] The MSS. have *a speculo*. Barth reads *et*, Kuinoel *at*.—*ah* is often written *a* in the copies. *Et speculo*, i. e. vel ipso speculo, is a good reading, but is found only in the corrected MSS. The meaning is, that when you look into the mirror during the process of pulling out the grey hairs, you will be startled to see how wrinkled you have got.

18.] *Eventum formæ*. 'Quod formæ tuæ eveniet, rugas intelligit et canos cumque his conjunctum contemptum.'—*Barth*.

PROPERTII

LIBER QUINTUS.

I.

HOC, quodcumque vides, hospes, qua maxima Roma est,
  Ante Phrygem Ænean collis et herba fuit;
Atque ubi Navali stant sacra Palatia Phœbo,

The elegies in this book are of a miscellaneous character, and of dates varying between A.U.C. 726 and 738. They are all good, each differing in subject and character, and of the highest value and interest for their large stores of legendary and archæological lore. At the same time they are full of difficulties, and demand, as they fairly deserve, a long and careful study. It is the opinion of Lachmann, in which Hertzberg concurs, that they were not published during the life of the poet, but collected and edited by his friends; and he thinks that they are generally in a more rude and imperfect state than the others. There are indications without doubt (see on 67 inf., and on ii. 57 inf.) of a re-arrangement and correction of previously written poems; but it is likely enough that the author undertook the task himself when he had risen to fame. From the fifth elegy Ovid would seem to have borrowed the idea of his *Ibis*, and also his *Ars Amatoria;* from the third,—a most beautiful composition,—his *Epistles*, from the first, second, ninth and tenth, his *Fasti*. However this may be, it is certain that not a few of these posthumous poems are of surpassing beauty, and a very high order of poetical merit. There is a marked difference in style between this book and the first, especially in the studied use, in the first, of long words at the end of the pentameters.

I. This difficult elegy, as far as v. 70, is supposed by Hertzberg to have been designed as a proœmium to a book of Roman Fasti, undertaken by the poet, probably in the year of the city 726, and just before his love for Cynthia, in imitation of the Αἴτια of Callimachus. To the same work probably belong El. 2, 4, 9 and 10, all of which are among his earliest performances. The latter part of the present elegy was evidently added after his attachment had commenced (inf. 140), and was meant as a kind of apology for not pursuing the historic style of composition further, but devoting himself to amatory versification. (See iv. 3, 5). Hence the *hospes* addressed in v. 1, originally represented an imaginary stranger to whom the poet was pointing out the antiquities of the city; the idea of making him speak in the character of a Babylonian Seer may have subsequently suggested itself. But it is more likely that the two persons are not the same.

1.] The MSS. have *quam* for *qua*. The mistake arose from supposing *quam maxima* was an intensive superlative. 'This small site, where now is mighty Rome, before Æneas came from Phrygia (Troy) was a grassy hill.'—*quodcumque*, as it may appear in your eyes, either large or small. So Lucret. ii. 16, 'qualibus in tenebris vitæ quantisque periclis Degitur hoc ævi, quodcunque est.' See also sup. iv. 23, 9.—*Phrygem*, see iv. 13, 63.

3.] *Navali Phœbo*. 'Significat ædem Apollinis in monte Palatino, quam Augustus A.U.C. DCCXXVI propter navalem ad Actium de Antonio et Cleopatra reportatam victoriam Apollini, cui hanc victoriam navalem tribuebat, extruxerat.'—*Kuinoel*. See on v. 6, init. The *Navalis Phœbus* of the Palatine was the local *Actius Apollo* whom Augustus thus honoured by transferring his cultus to Rome. See Æn. viii.

Evandri profugæ concubuere boves.
Fictilibus crevere deis hæc aurea templa,
Nec fuit opprobrio facta sine arte casa,
Tarpeiusque pater nuda de rupe tonabat,
Et Tiberis nostris advena bubus erat.
Quo gradibus domus ista Remi se sustulit, olim
Unus erat fratrum maxima regna focus.
Curia, prætexto quæ nunc nitet alta Senatu,
Pellitos habuit, rustica corda, patres.
Buccina cogebat priscos ad verba Quirites:

704.—*Palatia*, as usual, includes the Palatine hill itself, as well as merely the buildings upon it. Compare 'pecorosa palatia' inf. v. 9, 3. Tibull. ii. 5, 25, 'sed tunc pascebant herbosa palatia vaccæ.' Martial, i. 70, 5.

4.] *Profugæ*, 'exiled,' as 'profugos Penates' inf. 39. For the story of Evander and his prophetic mother Carmentis, see Ovid, *Fast*. i. 470 seqq.

5.] *Crevere*, as inf. 56, 'qualia creverunt mœnia lacte tuo,' means that from humble beginnings, a mere shed (*casa*) for clayen gods, the present gilded temple of Jupiter Capitolinus arose. Perhaps a structure of green boughs or turf is meant as the original shrine. Cf. Tib. ii. 5, 25, 'sed tunc pascebant herbosa Palatia vaccæ, Et stabant humiles in Jovis arce casæ.' Ovid, *Fast*. i. 203, 'frondibus ornabant quæ nunc Capitolia gemmis,' and 202, 'Inque Jovis dextra fictile fulmen erat.' We have *casa* similarly used inf. 9, 28 and 56.—*opprobrio*, sc. *illis*.

7.] *Nuda de rupe*. The temple of Jupiter Tonans (as distinct from Capitolinus) stood on the Arx, above the Tarpeian rock. The poet means, that he formerly thundered from the bare rock, in all the majesty of nature, and had no temple at all on the spot. Virg. *Æn*. viii. 347, 'hinc ad Tarpeiam sedem et Capitolia ducit, Aurea nunc, olim silvestribus horrida dumis.' Juvenal, xiii. 78, speaks of swearing 'per Tarpeia fulmina.'

8.] *Advena*, 'the Tiber rolled his waters from afar (only) for our oxen,' not for the inhabitants of a mighty city. Ovid has this phrase more than once, *e.g*. *Fast*. ii. 68, 'qua petit æquoreas advena Tibris aquas,' *ib*. iii. 524, 'haud procul a ripis, advena Tibri, tuis.' Also v. 288, 'et pereunt lentas, advena Nile, tuas;' and a similar sentiment occurs *ibid*. 641, 'et quam nunc gentes Tiberim noruntque timentque, Tunc etiam pecori despiciendus eram.' The notion seems derived from the water, in passing from its source into the sea, visiting different places in its course.

9—10.] *Quo*, 'eo loco, in quo nunc stat domus (casa) Romuli, olim fratres habebant unius foci commune regnum, et magnum quidem.' The word *domus* is used improperly in reference to the humble cottage which was still traditionally pointed to as the 'casa Romuli,' but poetically as the residence of kings. 'One hearth-stone was a large kingdom for two brothers' is a happy expression. Compare sup. iii. 7, 8, 'et ipse Stramineæ posset dux habitare casæ.' *Fast*. i. 199, 'dum casa Martigenam capiebat parva Quirinum.' *Ib*. iii. 183, 'quæ fuerit nostri, si quæris, regia nati, Aspice de canna straminibusque domum.' *Æn*. viii. 654, 'Romuleoque recens horrebat regia culmo.'—*se sustulit gradibus* means that the *casa* had 'mounted up' on steps to a higher place of dignity, viz. from its original site in the valley near the Circus, to the Palatine. Hertzberg thinks the *gradus* here mentioned are the *βαθμοὶ* of Plutarch, Romul. § 20, and the *Scalæ Caci* of Solinus.

11.] *Curia*, the new senate-house built and consecrated by Augustus, which did not stand on the site of the old Curia Hostilia.—*prætexto*, prætextato, in reference to the purple border on the senatorial toga, as *nitet* is said of the 'nitida toga,' or clean white woollen mantle. The old senate-house had 'skin-clad fathers, clownish minds,' whom the poet describes, in the following distich, as summoned to their parliament (*ad verba*) by the shepherd's horn, and 'often to have had no other meeting-place than a meadow.'—*centum illi*, 'the original hundred appointed by Romulus.'

Centum illi in prato sæpe Senatus erat.
Nec sinuosa cavo pendebant vela theatro,
Pulpita sollemnes non oluere crocos.
Nulli cura fuit externos quærere divos,
Cum tremeret patrio pendula turba sacro,
Annuaque accenso celebrare Parilia fœno,
Qualia nunc curto lustra novantur equo.
Vesta coronatis pauper gaudebat asellis,
Ducebant macræ vilia sacra boves.
Parva saginati lustrabant compita porci,

15.] *Vela*, the awnings of the theatre of Marcellus. See on iv. 18, 13.—*pulpita* &c., 'nor was the stage made fragrant with the saffron used on great days,' or festive occasions when unusual displays were made. Saffron-water was sprinkled about the theatre to cool the air and to afford a refreshing smell. Ovid, *Fast.* i. 343, 'Nec fuerant rubri cognita fila croci,' (where *fila* are the dried pistils of *crocus sativus*, the *spica Cilissa* of 6, 74, inf.) Martial, *Ep.* v. 25, 'rubro pulpita nimbo spargere, et effuso permaduisse croco.' Ovid, *A. A.* i. 103, 'Tum neque marmoreo pendebant vela theatro, Nec fuerant liquido pulpita rubra croco,'—a passage perhaps borrowed from this.

18—20.] *Nulli* &c. 'No one then cared to look for foreign gods, when the crowd hung in anxious suspense over their native rites, or to celebrate the annual Parilia with lighted hay, for expiations such as are still kept up with the blood of a dock-tailed horse.' By *externi dii*, ἔπακτοι θεοί, the worship of Isis with other Syrian and Egyptian gods, more or less lately introduced, is meant.—*tremeret pendula* is a comment on the most probable meaning of *superstitio*, 'the standing over an object of awe' (*e.g.* a *puteal* or a *bidental*), or the exhibition of any sacred rite or mystery.

19.] *Parilia*, or *Palilia* (*l* and *r* being convertible) was the old festival kept in honour of the country goddess *Pales*, probably the female of the god Φάλης, Ar. *Acharn.* 263, and the origin of *Palatium*. The poet seems to say that, rude and simple as the ceremony was, viz. that of jumping through lighted bonfires placed at intervals, it was not known at the earliest period. See Inf. i, 77. Ovid *Fast.* iv, 720 seqq. Persius, i. 72, 'fumosa Palilia fœno.' It is probable that it was a symbolic record of a kind of Moloch-worship, in which victims were burnt alive to the demon-spirits,—for such, alas! was primitive religion.—*curto equo*, like *curto mulo*, Hor. *Sat.* i. 6, 105. Certain expiatory rites (lustra) were performed with the blood of the October horse; which rites are said *novari*, *i.e.* solemniter fieri, after the old fashion. The horse was killed for the purpose six months beforehand, and the tail was cut off that the blood might drop on the altar of Vesta, from which it was removed in a concrete form to be used as a *suffimen*, mixed with other substances enumerated by Ovid, *Fast.* iv. 733, 'Sanguis equi suffimen erit, vitulique favilla: Tertia res, duræ culmen inane fabæ.' By *novantur* it is meant that the rites are renewed and kept up every year, as, it is clear from the passage in Ovid, was really the case. The blood of the horse, perhaps, had some relation to sun-worship, since that was the victim offered by the Persians to the sun, Ovid, *Fast.* i. 385.

21.] *Coronatis asellis*. On the feast of Vesta, or the fifth before the Ides of June, a procession took place in honour of that goddess, in which the prominent figure was an ass decked with strings of loaves. Ovid, *Fast.* vi. 313, 'Ecce coronatis panis dependet asellis, Et velant scabras florida serta molas.' *Ibid.* v. 347, 'Quem tu, Diva, memor de pane monilibus ornas.' The origin of the custom is explained at length in that passage.—*macræ boves*, 'poorly-fed cows conveyed the homely altar-fittings,' εὐτελῆ ἱερά. By ἱερεῖα, ἱερὰ, and *sacra*, not only the victims, but all the implements and *instrumenta* of a sacrifice are usually meant.

23.] *Compita*, 'the cross-roads, then but small, were consecrated (or exorcised) by the blood of home-fed porkers, and the shepherd offered the inwards of a ewe to the notes of a reed pipe.' The sense is, that the feast of the Compitalia to the Lares (*Fast.* v. 140) was then celebrated

Pastor et ad calamos exta litabat ovis.
Verbera pellitus sætosa movebat arator,
Unde licens Fabius sacra Lupercus habet.
Nec rudis infestis miles radiabat in armis:
Miscebant usta prœlia nuda sude.
Prima galeritus posuit prætoria Lycmon,
Magnaque pars Tatio rerum erat inter oves.
Hinc Titiens Ramnesque viri Luceresque coloni,

on a small scale, and with cheap and humble victims only. Perhaps there is an allusion to the costly *suovetaurilia* of later times.—*ad calamos*, in place of the *tibia* (αὐλὸν) used in the ceremony.—*litabat*, *ἐκαλλιερεῖτο*, a word not easy to render in English; *litare* is to make an offering acceptable to the gods, as *Fast.* iv. 630, 'pontifices, forda sacra litate bove.' Mart. *Ep.* x. 73, 6, 'non quacunque manu victima cæsa litat.' Pers. *Sat.* ii. 75, 'farre litabo.'

25.] *Pellitus*, 'decked with pieces of goat-skin to imitate Pan.'—*setosa verbera* are the blows inflicted with thongs of raw goats' hide by the Luperci on all whom they met in the streets, and especially on the women. This was regarded as a cause of prosperity and fecundity. Ovid, *Fast.* ii. 31, 'Mensis ab his (*i.e. februis*) dictus, secta quia pelle Luperci Omne solum lustrant, idque piamen habent.' See also *ib.* 427—455, and lib. v. 102. The festival is described in detail, *ib.* ii. 267, &c. I add an interesting passage from Plutarch, *Quæst. Rom.* § lxviii. *Διὰ τί κύνα θύουσιν οἱ Λούπερκοι; (Λούπερκοι δ' εἰσὶν οἱ τοῖς Λουπερκαλίοις γυμνοὶ διαθέοντες ἐν περιζώμασι, καὶ καθικνούμενοι σκύτει τῶν ἀπαντώντων) πότερον ὅτι καθαρμός ἐστι τῆς πόλεως τὰ δρώμενα, καὶ τὸν μῆνα Φεβρουάριον καλοῦσι, καὶ νὴ Δία τὴν ἡμέραν ἐκείνην Φεβράτην, καὶ φέβραριν τὸ τῶν σκυτῶν εἴδει καθικνεῖσθαι, τοῦ ῥήματος τὸ καθαίρειν σημαίνοντος; τῷ δὲ κυνὶ πάντες, ὡς ἔπος εἰπεῖν, Ἕλληνες ἐχρῶντο καὶ χρῶνταί γε μέχρι νῦν ἔνιοι σφαγίῳ πρὸς τοὺς καθαρμούς.* The Lupercalia having fallen into disuse were restored by Augustus, Sueton. *Oct.* § 31.

26.] *Unde*, ex quo more.—*licens*, 'lewd,' the conduct of these men in the performance of a phallic ceremony not being very modest or refined. They are the 'nudi Luperci' of *Æn.* viii. 663, and the name would seem to indicate some primitive worship *ad arcendos lupos*, for keeping the wolves from the flocks placed under the protection of Pan. They were divided into two classes, the Fabii and the Quintilii, called (it was said) after the gens of their respective founders, the followers of Romulus and Remus. See *Fast.* ii. 377, 'Risit, et indoluit Fabios potuisse Remumque Vincere; Quintilios non potuisse suos.' So the priests of Hercules were divided into *Potitii* and *Pinarii*, Livy, i. 7.

27.] *Nec rudis* &c. 'Rude was the soldier then, nor in offensive armour did he shine: they joined in the fight without covering, and with no weapons but a charred stake.'—*nuda*, ἀτευχῆ, without the protection even of a target. *Æn.* vii. 523, 'non jam certamine agresti, Stipitibus duris agitur sudibusve præustis.'

29.] *Lycmon*, or *Lygmon*, (al. *Lirmon*, *Lucmo*), seems either a general name for an Etruscan chief or noble, or the *eponym* hero of the *Lucumones* or *Luceres*, (be they Latians or Etrurians). Compare *Lycomedius*, inf. 2, 51. *Galeritus* means 'clad in the rustic cap of wolf-skin.' *Æn.* vii. 688, 'fulvosque lupi de pelle galeros Tegmen habent capiti.' The sense appears to be, that the first regular camp, with separate quarters for the general, was introduced by the Luceres, with some attempt at protective armour as a covering for the head; and Titus Tatius, himself a warrior, was too much engaged in settling disputes among his shepherd people to give up his whole time to war.

31.] *Hinc* &c. 'Yet, small as these beginnings were, it was from them that the three tribes of the Titienses, Ramnes, and Luceres arose, and that Romulus ended in driving four white steeds in triumph to the Capitol,' viz. after his victory over the Cæninenses, inf. 10, 9, Livy, i. 10.—*Titiens* (al. *Tities*) seems intended as the nominative singular of *Titientes* or *Titienses*, the 'warriors' (*Varronianus*, p. 26). The *Ramnes* contain the same root as Romulus, Remus, Roma, ficus Ruminalis &c. (Donaldson, *Varron.* p. 60, suggests the Lithuarian *rauma*, 'a dug,' which certainly best

Quattuor hinc albos Romulus egit equos.
Quippe suburbanæ parva minus urbe Bovillæ
Et, qui nunc nulli, maxima turba Gabi,
Et stetit Alba potens, albæ suis omine nata,
Hac †ubi Fidenas longe erat ire via.
Nil patrium nisi nomen habet Romanus alumnus:
Sanguinis altricem non pudet esse lupam.
Huc melius profugos misisti, Troia, penates.
O quali vecta est Dardana puppis ave!

suits our idea of 'to ruminate,' or 'make milk;' others *groma*, *gruerus*, *srouma*, 'stream-town,' but it is all guess). There is much difficulty in the antithesis *viri* and *coloni*. The sense cannot be 'fighting-men' and 'farmers,' because the Lucumo is said to have made the first camp. Therefore, *coloni* probably means *fresh*, viz. that the Luceres came last and were added on, as new settlers, to the Roman and Sabine tribes. It is to be observed that Ovid, *Fast.* iii. 131, makes the first syllable of *Luceres* long, 'Quin etiam partes totidem Titiensibus idem, Quosque vocant Ramnes, Luceribusque dedit.'

33.] *Quippe* seems to give the reason why Romulus could triumph over towns which afterwards became almost part of Rome. Bovillæ was indeed about ten miles distant; yet Ovid also, *Fast.* iii. 667, applies the same epithet, 'Orta suburbanis quædam fuit Anna Bovillis.' Müller marks the loss of some verses before this, which he thus explains: 'When Rome was small, Bovillæ was less in its immediate neighbourhood (*minus suburbana*) than it now is, when the imperial city has so much encroached on the towns and villages near.' The order of the words certainly suggests the construe of *parva minus urbe*. May this be the ablative of quality, and mean that formerly Bovillæ, now small, and a mere suburb, was once 'of a less small and insignificant size,' *i.e.* relatively? It was then thought a *great* place, because there was no larger city to contrast with it. This sense exactly suits the next verse, 'And Gabii, now nothing, was a large people.' Müller however, rather ingeniously, transposes 34 and 36, and here reads 'Atque ibi Fidenas longe erat isse via,' in this sense; 'it was then a long journey from Rome to Fidenæ, which now seems close at hand.' Others read *parva eminus urbe*; but I think Propertius would certainly have used *procul*, not *eminus*.—It is hardly necessary to add that Gabii, once an important Alban or Latin town, was at this time almost deserted, Hor. *Ep.* i. 11, 7.

36.] *Hac* &c. 'Alba stood on the road which brought you to Fidenæ by a long route.' If this be genuine, the sense can only be, that Alba stood on the road to Fidenæ, which in fact lay in an opposite direction from Rome. This is not likely to have ever been the case; but as a poetical hyperbole it may mean that a journey even to Fidenæ was then thought a serious matter. I have marked the passage however as doubtful both in sense and in the reading. The Naples MS. gives *isse* for *ire*.

37.] *Nil patrium* &c. 'Nomen tantummodo a Romulo usurpant; sanguinem, *i.e.* indolem a Martis lupa habent.'—*non pudet*, gloriantur se a lupa nutritos esse, utpote gentem marte validam. This is said to show how and why the neighbouring towns were so soon absorbed in Rome, and why Rome still delights in its conquests.

39.] *Melius*, felicius, quam si Græcis præda cessissent.—*Barth.* *huc*, sc. in tam bellicosam terram.—*quali ave*, quam bono omine. Hor. *Od.* i. 15, 6, 'mala ducis avi domum.' *Hoc* simply expresses admiration. Hertzberg and others read *O*, against the good copies.—*Dardana puppis*, the ship that brought Æneas, who is virtually described under *illam* in the next verse. It was a favourable circumstance, says the poet, and an omen of her future destinies, that Troy did not lose *all* her citizens by the stratagem of the wooden horse, but that Æneas escaped with his father Anchises and a handful of followers. The vowel is shortened before *sp* as in iv. 11, 53, 'brachia spectavi,' inf. v. 4, 48, 'tu cave spinosi rorida terga jugi,' where we trace the French pronunciation, *épine*, in the liquefaction of the *s*. So also in *σκέπαρνον*, *σμάραγδος*, *Scamander* &c., and *στέγειν*, *σφάλλειν*, compared with *tegere*, *fallere*. See also v. 5, 17.

Jam bene spondebant tunc omina, quod nihil illam
  Læserat abiegni venter apertus equi,
Cum pater in gnati trepidus cervice pependit,
  Et verita est humeros urere flamma pios.
Tunc animi venere Deci Brutique secures,
  Vexit et ipsa sui Cæsaris arma Venus,
Arma resurgentis portans victricia Trojæ:
  Felix terra tuos cepit, Iule, deos!
Si modo Avernalis tremulæ cortina Sibyllæ
  Dixit Aventino rura pianda Remo,
Aut si Pergameæ sero rata carmina vatis
  Longævum ad Priami vera fuere caput,
Vertite equum, Danai, male vincitis: Ilia tellus
  Vivet, et huic cineri Juppiter arma dabit.
Optima nutricum nostris lupa Martia rebus,
  Qualia creverunt mœnia lacte tuo!
Mœnia namque pio conor disponere versu:

44.] *Flamma.* See the fine account in *Æn.* ii. 721.—*pios*, 'filial.'

46.] *Vexit arma.* An elegant compliment to the victorious arms of Augustus, derived from the tale of Thetis bringing the arms of Achilles, and the probably older tale of the Nereids conveying the arms of Peleus as a marriage present from the gods. For *vexit* Müller proposes *auxit*, which seems to me entirely to destroy the point and beauty of the passage.—*portans*, 'in bringing the victorious arms of the Troy that was destined to rise again out of its own ashes, *i.e.* in Rome, Venus brought the arms which were to be used by her own Cæsar in his expeditions.'

49.] 'Romam felicis fata manent, si vere Sibylla gemellos reges et auspicari et condere Urbem jussit.' *Hertzberg.*—*pianda*, *i.e.* ad capiendum auspicium. Florus, i. 1, 'Gemini erant: uter auspicaretur et regeret, adhibuere piacula.' *Idem.*—*Aventino* is perhaps the ablative of place, 'on the Aventine;' or we might read *Aventini rura*. The Sibyl is called *Avernalis* from her residence at Cumæ near the Avernian lake, on which see iv. 18, 1, *Æn.* iii. 412. *cortina*, the seat or cover of the prophetic tripod, originally, it is probable, intended to receive and inclose the volcanic gases which were supposed to be the breath of the spirits below. See *Æn.* iii. 92, 'neque te Phœbi cortina fefellit.'

51.] *Sero rata*, 'too late found true.' The simple sense is, 'aut si vera cecinit Cassandra, in fatis esse ut Troja resurgeret.' See on iv. 13, 62.—*ad Priami caput*, viz. predicting that her father's murder by Neoptolemus would be avenged. The apodosis is at *Vertite equum, Danai.* 'If prophecies were true, that Rome should be a second Troy, then the Greeks were wrong in seeking the old Troy, because they would be conquered in their turn by the new one.' This is the sense of *male vincitis*. Müller regards *vertite—dabit* as Cassandra's speech, to which he prefixes 87, 88 inf., transposed to this place. I cannot see the least appropriateness or probability in such an arrangement.

56.] *Qualia*, ἡλίκα, 'to what a size have grown walls from your milk,' *i. e.* built by one nourished from the wolf's teat. A harsh expression; cf. sup. 5.—With this verse, as I believe, the original, or first draught of the poem ended. We now proceed with the verses of a man made vain by success, and marked by an egotism from which the earlier verses are free. I think too that in 67—70 I detect verses which were at first designed as a general proœme to his ballads on Roman history, but which were, in the subsequent recension, misplaced or interpolated in the wrong place, precisely like the lines concluding the *Vertumnus* (inf. 2, 59—64).

57.] *Mœnia* is repeated from the preceding verse, like *arma* in 47.—*disponere*

Hei mihi, quod nostro est parvus in ore sonus!
Sed tamen exiguo quodcumque e pectore rivi
Fluxerit, hoc patriæ serviet omne meæ.
Ennius hirsuta cingat sua dicta corona:
Mi folia ex hedera porrige, Bacche, tua,
Ut nostris tumefacta superbiat Umbria libris,
Umbria Romani patria Callimachi.
Scandentes si quis cernet de vallibus arces,
Ingenio muros æstimet ille meo.
Roma, fave, tibi surgit opus, date candida cives
Omina et inceptis dextera cantet avis.
Sacra diesque canam et cognomina prisca locorum:
Has meus ad metas sudet oportet equus.
Dicam: Troia cades et Troica Roma resurges, 87
Et maris et terræ longa sepulcra canam. 88
'Quo ruis inprudens, vage, dicere sacra, Properti? 71

is 'to describe,' by arranging in parts, or in a methodical way, and so is nearly a synonym of *describere*. So Lucret. iii. 420, 'digna tua pergam disponere carmina cura.' *pio* is here 'affectionate.' Müller, who thinks the vulgate reading absurd, and denies that *disponere* can have this sense, edits on his own conjecture 'Munere namque pio conor disponere versus.'

61.] *Ennius* &c. The poet says he will devote his talents to the praise of his country, leaving however rough heroics to others, and preferring the soft and smooth elegiac verse. Müller marks *dicta* with an obelus.—*hedera*, partly as the type of smoothness, partly in reference to the 'doctarum hederæ præmia frontium.' To these are opposed the thorny or prickly crown of Ennius. Cf. Ovid, *Trist.* ii. 259, 'sumpserit Annales, nihil est hirsutius illis.' Supra iv. 1, 19, 'Mollia, Pegasides, date vestro serta poetæ; Non faciet capiti dura corona meo.' Hertzberg: 'hirsutæ coronæ dum mollius folium opponere poeta vult, sponte se præbuit hedera, cujus æquæ natura vel in proverbium abiit. Hederam suam Bacchus sequutus est. Quem deum—ut poetarum lyricorum et elegiacorum patronum hic quoque, quamvis majora ausurus, jure Propertius veneratur.'

64.] The poet calls himself the Roman Callimachus in accordance with the sentiments before expressed, iv. 1, 1, &c.

65.] *Scandentes*, i.e. *ascendentes*, surgentes.—*arces* are the same as *muros*, the natural precipices on which his native town arose. See below, v. 125.—*quisquis* Müller, from MS. Naples, for *si quis*.

66.] *Æstimet ingenio meo.* 'Let him measure their greatness and importance by my genius,' or by their being my birthplace. *Ingenio* is the ablative of price, as Hertzberg almost unnecessarily remarks. Compare inf. 126, 'Murus ab ingenio notior ille tuo.'

67—70.] As above remarked (on 56), it is probable that these verses really formed a general *proœmium*, to which purpose they are singularly appropriate. Rome is asked to favour the work, and a favourable omen is asked to attend the undertaking. Add to these four verses the obscure distich, 87-8, 'dicam Troja cades' &c., and we have a statement of the general subject, much like that in the opening lines of the *Fasti*, e.g. 7, 8, 'Sacra recognosces annalibus eruta priscis, Et quo sit merito quæque notata dies.'—*longa sepulcra*, longinquas mortes, the deaths of the heroes in their return from Troy.

70.] *Has ad metas.* 'This is the goal which my steed must toil to reach.' Cf. *Georg.* iii. 202, 'hic vel ad Elei metas et maxima campi Sudabit spatia.' Müller here marks the loss of some verses, and Lachmann makes a space or break in the poem; but the abruptness does not show the passage to be faulty. No sooner has the poet announced his in-

Non sunt ab dextro condita fila colo.
Aversis Charisin cantas, aversus Apollo:
Poscis ab invita verba pigenda lyra.
Certa feram certis auctoribus: aut ego vates
Nescius ærata signa movere pila.
Me creat Archytæ soboles Babylonius Horos,
Horon et a proavo ducta Conone domus.
Di mihi sunt testes non degenerasse propinquos,
Inque meis libris nil prius esse fide.
Nunc pretium fecere deos et fallitur auro

tention, and the aim which he has in view, than his ardour is checked by the serious warning of an Astrologer, who extols his own infallibility in his art somewhat vauntingly, and at considerable length, in order to gain credit for his prediction that the contemplated historical poem will prove a failure. This is, of course, only an expedient on the part of the poet to apologize for his supposed unfitness for the task. There is no reason whatever to identify the Astrologer with the *hospes* in ver. 1. The Romans were greatly influenced by astrological predictions. See, for instance, Persius, *Sat.* v. 45 seqq., Tac. *Ann.* iv. 58, and inf. on 83 (after 106).

Ibid. *Imprudens*, 'thoughtless,' 'without foreseeing the consequences.'—*vage*, desultory, restless, not keeping to one theme or subject. For *sacra* the best copies give *fata* or *facta*. Lachmann and Müller adopt the former. *Sacra* certainly suits the sense better, as it takes up the word in ver. 69, '*Sacra*, did you say? That is not a thread for you to twist, nor for your lute to play.'

72.] *Condita*, 'not put together from a lucky distaff,'—in allusion perhaps to the thread spun by the Fates. For the masculine *colus* see inf. ix. 47.

73.] *Charisin* has no MS. authority, and is the conjecture of Heinsius. The Naples MS. gives *aversis lacrimas*, the Groningen *aversis lacrimis*. Müller proposes *aversis rythmis*, Lachmann *aversis Latium*. Pucci *aversis musis*, which Jacob adopts. Cf. Martial, *Ep.* viii. 62, 'Scribit in aversa Picens epigrammata charta, Et dolet, averso quod facit illa deo.'

75.] *Aut ego*, i.e. 'or put me down as one who does not know how to use the astrolabe.' Jacob and Keil give *haud*, from Pucci, Müller *haut*.—*signa movere*, to move the planets in concentric rings on the Astrolabe. *Pila*, which I before interpreted a hollow sphere round which the planets were made to move as in an orrery, I now think, from having seen one, must be the astrolabe, which is a flat circular disk with moving segments so contrived as to mark conjunctions and opposition of the planets.

77.] There is some uncertainty here about the reading. In the first line the MSS. vary between *orops* and *horos*, for which Pucci gives *Oron*; in the second all give *oron* or *horon*. The sense appears to be, 'me creavit Horus, et Horon creavit domus Cononis.' Lachmann understands, 'me Horum creat Horops et,' &c., and so Müller.—'Nec nunc ansis quærendum, quomodo Archytæ Tarentini gentem cum Cononis Alexandrini et Hori Chaldæi componas. Satis erat homini gloriabundo clara mathematicorum nomina undique corrasa tanquam paterna et avita jactare.' *Hertzberg*.—*creat* for *creavit*, as inf. v. 121, *edit* for *edidit*.

79.] *Degenerasse*. This verb is followed by an accusative in Ovid *Met.* vii. 543; *ex Pont.* iii. 1, 45; quoted by Kuinoel. In the same sense, the Greeks say καταισχύνειν γένος.—*fide*, 'their declaring the truth, whether favourable or not, to those who consult me.' This was doubtless the boastful profession of the impostors in the art.

81.] *Pretium fecere deos*, 'Now-a-days they have turned the gods to profit.' The nominative to be supplied is, the pretenders to astrology; the Babylonian having just boasted of his own *fides*.—*fallitur auro Jupiter*, 'for gold they misrepresent Jupiter;' i.e. these pretenders, for money, will falsely announce the will of the gods to those who consult them. See below on 11, 60.

Juppiter, obliquæ signa iterata rotæ.
Dixi ego, cum geminos produceret Arria natos,
(Illa dabat natis arma vetante deo)
Non posse ad patrios sua pila referre Penates:
Nempe meam firmant nunc duo busta fidem.
Quippe Lupercus, equi dum saucia protegit ora,
Heu sibi prolapso non bene cavit equo:
Gallus at, in castris dum credita signa tuetur,
Concidit ante aquilæ rostra cruenta suæ.
Fatales pueri, duo funera matris avaræ,
Vera, sed invito contigit ista fides.
Idem ego, cum Cinaræ traheret Lucina dolores
Et facerent uteri pondera lenta moram,
Junonis facito votum inpetrabile, dixi:
Illa parit: libris est data palma meis.
Hoc neque harenosum Libyæ Jovis explicat antrum

82.] *Obliquæ rotæ signa.* The sphere or globe is called *rota*, and the epithet expresses that the axis is deflected from the perpendicular, so that the ecliptic or plane of the sun cuts it transversely. Claudian, *Epigr.* xxv. 'Fallaces vitreo stellas componere mundo, Et vaga Saturni sidera sæpe queri, Venturumque Jovem paucis promittere nummis, Cureti genitor noverat Urania.' The invention was attributed to Archimedes: Ovid, *Fast.* vi. 277, 'Arte Syracosia suspensus in aere clauso Stat globus, immensi parva figura poli.' The *signa iterata* appear to be the signs of the zodiac repeatedly consulted and considered,—as we should say, *hackneyed.* See inf. 3, 7. It seems best to supply *sunt.*

89.] *Dixi ego.* 'I predicted (viz. which was more than these impostors could have done) when Arria was escorting her twin sons to the war, against the will of the gods, that it was impossible they should return alive to their home.' This prophecy, like that following about Cinara in labour (100), was a pretty safe guess, and probably the examples are given merely to satirize the art.—*producere* is *προπέμπειν*, to give a complimentary escort. So Ovid, *Her.* 13, 141—3, 'Arma dabit, dumque arma dabit, simul oscula sumet,—producetque virum.'

94.] *Sibi non bene cavit.* In endeavouring to save his horse who had been wounded in the head, he took no care of his own safety after his horse had fallen, and he had no steed to mount. To avoid the repetition *equi—equo*, Heinsius proposed *Lupercus apro.*

95.] *Credita* (sibi) *signa*, as the bearer of the eagle of the legion. *Signum* more commonly means the vexillum of a cohort. In *rostra cruenta* there is a play on the double sense, derived from the habits of a bird of prey.

97.] *Avaræ*, either she had coveted the *stipendium*, or had sent them to war in the hope of spoils. Müller ingeniously proposes *Martis avari.* But there is pathos in the widowed mother too late bewailing her loss, and blaming herself as the cause of it. Lachmann makes the genitive depend on *pueri;* but *funera* means 'deaths,' 'losses,' as 'funera Tantalidos,' iii. 23, 14.

98.] *Ista* seems rather improperly used, and is best taken in the sense of *hæc.*—*fides*, 'this fulfilment of the prediction came true, but I was sorry that it happened so.'

101.] *Facito* for *facite* is Burmann's correction. Lachmann reads *votum facite.*—*Junonis*, i.e. Lucinæ. Kuinoel and Barth read *Junoni* with Scaliger. Lachmann defends the genitive by *vota deum solvere* in *Æn.* xi. 4.

103.] *Hoc* &c. As above remarked, there must be irony in making the Astrologer say 'That is more than the oracle of Jupiter Ammon could tell you.' The point of what follows is to magnify astrology to the disparagement of all other kinds of divination.—*Libyæ Jovis antrum*,

Aut sibi commissos fibra locuta deos,
Aut si quis motas cornicis senserit alas,
Umbrave quæ magicis mortua prodit aquis.
Aspicienda via est cæli verusque per astra
Trames et ab zonis quinque petenda fides, 108
Felicesque Jovis stellæ Martisque rapacis 83
Et grave Saturni sidus in omne caput, 84
Quid moveant Pisces animosaque signa Leonis, 85
Lotus et Hesperia quid Capricornus aqua. 86
Exemplum grave erit Calchas: namque Aulide solvit
Ille bene hærentes ad pia saxa rates:
Idem Agamemnoniæ ferrum cervice puellæ
Tinxit, et Atrides vela cruenta dedit:

'the prophetic voices of Jupiter in Libya.' See on iv. 22, 15, 'Ortygiæ visenda est ora Caystri.' Pind. *Pyth.* iv. 56, Νείλοιο πρὸς πῖον τέμενος Κρονίδα, 'the fertile oasis of Jupiter near the Nile;' where also the temple of Ammon is meant.

106.] *Prodit*, declarat. Some kind of *νεκυομαντεία*, necromancy, or what modern superstition calls 'spirit-rapping,' was probably practised at the Avernian lake. Lachmann and Müller read *umbrave quæ*, the Naples MS. having *umbrane quæ*.

107.] *Verus per astra trames*, 'the true path that lies through the stars,' or, as we should say, 'the only road to truth is through astrology.' It is best perhaps to supply *petendus est*. The variant *versus* for *verus* is worth attention; cf. *Georg.* i. 238, 'via secta per ambas, Obliquus qua se signorum verteret ordo.' The allusion here clearly is to a globe with the five zones (*Georg.* i. 233), in which the equator is intersected by the ecliptic.—After this verse I have inserted four lines which are at least appropriate in this place, (reading *stellæ* for *stellas*, with Scaliger), while in their usual order they are well-nigh unintelligible. The meaning now is clear; if one wants to know the future, one must take the horoscope of a person, and observe what the constellations or planets under which he was born portend for good or evil. Compare Persius, *Sat.* v. 50, 'Saturnumque gravem nostro Jove frangimus una.'

83—6.] 'Even the good and bad planetary influences, and what the Pisces &c. portend,—all this is now a mere matter of traffic with the pretenders.'—In the punctuation and explanation of this obscure passage I have departed widely from both Jacob and Hertzberg. It must be remembered that the astrologers (*Chaldæi* or *Mathematici*) obtained great and dangerous influence in Rome under the Emperors. Even Tacitus appears to have believed in the science: *Ann.* iv. 58. See also vi. 22, 'Plurimis mortalium non eximitur quin primo cujusque ortu ventura destinentur: sed quædam secus quam dicta sint cadere *fallaciis ignara dicentium.*' Juvenal, vi. 553, 'Chaldæis sed major erit fiducia; quicquid Dixerit astrologus, credent a fonte relatum Hammonis; quoniam Delphis oracula cessant' &c. Augustus was a believer in the art. Suet. *Oct.* § 94, 'Tantam mox fiduciam fati Augustus habuit, ut thema suum vulgaverit, nummumque argenteum nota sideris Capricorni, quo natus est, percusserit.' Tiberius had Chaldæans with him at Capreæ, Juv. x. 94.

85.] *Animosa* (iv. 9, 9), is perhaps an astrologer's term, in reference to the supposed courage or spirit of the animal.

109.] *Exemplum grave*, 'a serious warning,' viz. of the danger of trusting seers rather than astrologers. Agamemnon, misled by Calchas, let his fleet sail from Aulis when it would have been well detained (bene hærentes) at rocks which asked not, as Diana did, the death of a child, Iphigenia.—*pia saxa*, like *pia porta*, inf. 7, 87, having regard and reverence for loved objects. Cic. *de Div.* i. 16, § 29, 'Agamemnon, quum Achivi cœpissent *inter sese strepere, aperteque artem obterere extispicum, Solvere imperat secundo rumore adversaque avi.*'

Nec rediere tamen Danai: tu diruta fletum
  Supprime et Euboicos respice, Troia, sinus.
Nauplius ultores sub noctem porrigit ignes
  Et natat exuviis Græcia pressa suis.
Victor Oiliade, rape nunc et dilige vatem,
  Quam vetat avelli veste Minerva sua.
Hactenus historiæ: nunc ad tua devehar astra:
  Incipe tu lacrimis æquus adesse novis.
Umbria te notis antiqua Penatibus edit,
  (Mentior? an patriæ tangitur ora tuæ?)

113.] 'Dry your eyes, O Troy, when you turn them to view the destruction of the Grecian fleet off the south-eastern promontory of Eubœa, and see yourself thus avenged.' The sense is, Calchas had promised a safe return, but his prediction was proved by the event to have been false. Nauplius, the father of Palamedes, to avenge himself on the Greeks for the loss of his son, held up lights off the dangerous promontory of Caphareus, by which the Greek pilots were deceived and the vessels wrecked. Compare iv. 7, 39, 'Saxa triumphales fregere Capharea puppes, Naufraga cum vasto Græcia tracta salo est.' Virg. *Æn.* xi. 260, 'Euboicæ cautes, ultorque Caphareus.' Pausan. iv. 36, 3, *ἐοίκασι δὲ αἱ ἀνθρώπειαι τύχαι καὶ χωρία τέως ἄγνωστα ἐς δόξαν προηχέναι. Καφηρέως γὰρ ἐστιν ὄνομα τοῦ ἐν Εὐβοίᾳ, τοῖς σὺν Ἀγαμέμνονι Ἕλλησιν ἐπιγενομένου χειμῶνος ἐνταῦθα, ὡς ἐκομίζοντο ἐξ Ἰλίου.*

116.] *Et natat &c.* 'The Grecian fleet floats helpless on the water (is waterlogged), overweighted with sacrilegious spoils.' For this sense of *natat* see iii. 17, 24, and iv. 12, 32. It seems better to understand it thus than to refer it to the efforts of the crew to save themselves by swimming. The story is taken from the ancient tale of the *Νόστοι*, like the account of the storm in the Agamemnon and at the beginning of the Troades.

117.] *Oiliade*, Ajax the son of Oïleus. The initial *O* represents the digamma. Lachmann needlessly reads *Iliade victor*. Pindar has the form Ἰλιάδα for Ϝιλιάδα in *Ol.* ix. 112.—*dilige*, choose as your consort. Ajax, son of Oïleus, had ravished Cassandra in the very temple of Pallas, and though she had taken refuge by clasping the sacred statue. See *Æn.* i. 40, and the fine passage in ii. 403, &c.—*veste sua*, in allusion to the peplus, which was placed on the *βρέτας*, or ancient statue of Pallas in the Parthenon; the same usage being supposed to exist at Troy, by a common practice of the poets. This scene, the rape of Cassandra from the Palladium, is one of the commonest of the designs on Greek Vases. The sense is, 'Go, now, Ajax, commit sacrilege,—and suffer the just consequences of it.' This use of the imperative is common when the speaker dares or challenges another to brave a certain risk: so *i nunc, ite &c.* iv. 7, 29, and 18, 17. The calamities of the voyage homewards were attributed to this act of Ajax. See on Æsch. *Agam.* 336.

119.] *Historiæ.* 'So far for history. Now I will come (lit. down the course of time) to *your* destinies. Prepare yourself to hear with patience a new subject of grief.'—*novis*, different from the old tale of Troy.

122.] *Mentior.* 'Am I speaking falsely, or do I hit (with my art) the border of your native land?' Cf. Æsch. *Ag.* 1165, *ἥμαρτον, ἢ θηρῶ τι, τοξότης τις ὥς;*—*qua &c.*, 'it is the place where dank *Mevania* (*Bevagna*) sheds its dews on the low-lying plain, and the Umbrian tarn basks with its waters in the summer sun.' The *lacus Umber* seems to be the sources of the river Clitumnus, described by Pliny in a well-known and beautiful letter, *Ep.* viii. 8, 'eluctatus (fons) quem facit gurgitem *lato gremio patescit* purus et vitreus.' Those who have seen the sources of the 'New River' near Ware, will understand the description. But Pliny adds that its waters are intensely cold, 'rigor aquæ certaverit nivibus.' Poetically, perhaps, rather than truly, it is said to be warmed by the summer sun. But the form *intepeo* (for *intepesco*) is suspected. Müller reads *si tepet*, but he does not condescend to explain what sense he thus attaches to the passage.

Qua nebulosa cavo rorat Mevania campo,
  Et lacus æstivis intepet Umber aquis,
Scandentisque Asisi consurgit vertice murus,
  Murus ab ingenio notior ille tuo.
Ossaque legisti non illa ætate legenda
  Patris et in tenues cogeris ipse Lares:
Nam tua cum multi versarent rura juvenci,
  Abstulit excultas pertica tristis opes.
Mox ubi bulla rudi demissa est aurea collo,
  Matris et ante deos libera sumpta toga,
Tum tibi pauca suo de carmine dictat Apollo
  Et vetat insano verba tonare foro.
At tu finge elegos, fallax opus, hæc tua castra,
  Scribat ut exemplo cetera turba tuo.
Militiam Veneris blandis patiere sub armis
  Et Veneris pueris utilis hostis eris.
Nam tibi victrices quascumque labore parasti,

125.] *Asisi* for *Asis* is the almost certain correction of Lachmann and Haupt. *Asisium*, or *Asisi*, one of the many hill-towns of Italy, was the birthplace of the poet, and is better known in modern times as that of St. Francis. With the vanity of one who had now made a fame, Propertius puts his own biography into the mouth of the pseudo-astrologer.

127.] It appears from iii. 26, 55, that Propertius was born of impoverished parents, not conspicuous for their ancestry. See also iii. 16, 21. That he was, however, *ingenuus* is clear from the mention of the *aurea bulla* v. 131. Of his parentage and *gens* next to nothing is known. See Hertzberg, *Quæst.* pp. 12—14.

130.] *Pertica*, the measuring-rod, or *perch*, by which the unjust distribution of confiscated lands was made to the veterans of Octavian in the year 713, an event so well known from the first Eclogue of Virgil.—*excultas*, 'highly tilled;' cf. Martial, *Ep.* i. 85, 1.

131.] *Bulla aurea.* The pendant or amulet worn round the neck of infants, and retained till the age (16) for taking the toga virilis, (libera toga, v. 132). This bulla was of gold if the parents were patrician, and of leather if they were in humble life. Juven. v. 164, 'Etruscum puero si contigit aurum, Vel nodus tantum, et signum de paupere loro.' Hence the ecclesiastical document called 'a bull,' derives its name from the seal appended to it. *Dimissa* is rightly read in the Naples MS. *Demissa* is retained by Müller.

132.] *Matris deos.* His father being dead, the Lares are called his mother's gods. We know from Persius, *Sat.* v. 31, that such was the custom: 'Bullaque succinctis Laribus donata pependit.' See Becker, *Gallus*, p. 183.

133.] *Tum tibi* &c. The sense is, 'then you began to write verses, and refused to be brought up as a lawyer.' Of course, all this is attributed to the influence of Apollo. Whether the next distich contains the words of the god or of the astrologer, is not very clear.

135]. *Fallax opus*, 'disappointing though the work may be.' Or perhaps, as Lachmann explains it, 'quod in fraudibus et fallaciis versatur,' 'intended to deceive.'—*hæc* &c., 'this is your field, to furnish a model for inferior poets to follow.'—*turba*, ὄχλος τῶν ποιητῶν. So iv. 1, 12, 'scriptorumque meas turba secuta rotas.'

138.] *Utilis*, you will serve the Cupids as a fit person to practice on.

139.] *Victrices palmas*, victorias, or de victorem. 'One girl will make vain, or baffle, all the victories you may have gained over love.' The sentiment is expanded in the next couplet; 'you may boast that you have resisted the charms of many, but Cynthia will catch you at last.'

Eludet palmas una puella tuas:
Et bene cum fixum mento discusseris uncum,
Nil erit hoc, rostro te premet ansa suo.
Illius arbitrio noctem lucemque videbis:
Gutta quoque ex oculis non nisi jussa cadet.
Nec mille excubiæ nec te signata juvabunt
Limina: persuasæ fallere rima sat est.
Nunc tua vel mediis puppis luctetur in undis,
Vel licet armatis hostis inermis eas,
Vel tremefacta cavo tellus diducat hiatum:
Octipedis Cancri terga sinistra time.

II.

Quid mirare meas tot in uno corpore formas?
Accipe Vertumni signa paterna dei.

142.] *Ansa*, the handle, or knop, of the hook by which a body was dragged ignominiously from the place of execution. 'Sejanus ducitur unco Spectandus,' Juven. x. 66. Hor. *Carm.* i. 35, 19, 'Nec severus Uncus abest liquidumve plumbum.' Ovid, *Ibis*, 167, 'Carnificisque manu, populo plaudente traheris, Infixusque tuis ossibus uncus erit.' The notion intended probably is, that when the sharp hook would not hold in a lacerated or putrified corpse, some use was made of the other end for pushing, shoving, or thrusting it along, which is the literal sense of *premet*; but this is only a conjectural explanation of a very obscure passage. The general sense may be, 'you may get away from her now and then, but she will beat you in the end.' The MSS. give *nostro* and *ansa*, and inf. 146 *prima*, which were emended by Pucci.

143.] *Arbitrio*, by her permission alone you will be allowed to sleep, or be awake, or even to cry. Compare i. 3, 11, 'Non tibi jam somnos, non illa relinquet ocellos.'

145.] *Nec* &c. 'Nor, though she thus holds you in thrall, will you keep her faithful to you.'—*persuasæ*, cui persuasum est; cf. Ovid, *Ars. Am.* 679, 'Jamdudum persuasus erit; miserebitur ultro.'

147.] 'You need not now dread shipwreck, battles, or earthquakes; your fate will come from a woman born under the constellation Cancer,' and therefore *rapax*. This is almost a proverbial way of predicting a certain end, as when we say, 'That man was not born to be drowned.' See iii. 19, 12; iv. 16, 11 seqq., and Tibull. i. 2, 27, 'Quisquis amore tenetur, eat tutusque sacerque Qualibet.' There is some satire perhaps on the mystic language of the astrologers in *terga cancri*. The allusion may be to Cynthia's avaricious demands, iii. 7, and iv. 13.

149.] Lachmann and others read *cavo hiatu*, with MS. Gron., and this would be satisfactory enough with *deducat*, 'carry you down in its yawning gulf.' Perhaps there were two readings, *cavum diducat hiatum*, (like *diducere rictum*, Juv. x. 230), and *cavo deducat hiatu*. As the text stands in the best editions, *tremefacta cavo* must be construed, *i.e. utero concussa*.

II. A mythological account of the god Vertumnus, who is introduced as the *persona loquens*. Vertumnus was a kind of harlequin god, who in accordance with his name was made to take different costumes at different festivals and seasons.

2.] *Vertumni*. Another form, found in the best copies, is *Vortumni*, which seems to point to *Vortumni*. Compare *Portumnus* and *Portuna*. The word is from an old participle of *verto* or *vorto*, i.e. *vortomenus*. Similarly *Autumnus* for *auctomenus*, 'the year as it gets old.' It is well known that a duality of sexes characterized the oldest mythology, whence we find *Liber* and *Libera*, (Tac. *Ann.* ii. 41), *Jupiter* and *Juno*, (*i.e.* Jovino), *Janus* and *Diana*, *Helios* and *Selene*, &c. The origin of the name

Tuscus ego et Tuscis orior, nec pœnitet inter
  Prœlia Volsanos deseruisse focos.
Hæc me turba juvat, nec templo lætor eburno:
  Romanum satis est posse videre forum.
Hac quondam Tiberinus iter faciebat, et aiunt
  Remorum auditos per vada pulsa sonos:
At postquam ille suis tantum concessit alumnis,

Fortuna, otherwise called Fors (for *Vorts*), (the *Fortis Fortuna* of *Fasti* vi. 773), must be sought in the peculiar attributes of Chance,—uncertainty, fickleness, and revolutionary caprice. Hence she is painted with a wheel: see Ritter on Tac. *Ann.* iii. 71; supra, ii. 8, 7—8. According to Pausanias, lib. iv. cap. 30, § 3, 4, the Messenians represented their Τύχην as πόλον ἔχουσαν ἐπὶ τῇ κεφαλῇ. Fortuna was worshipped as Nursia or Nortia (Nevortia, Juven. x. 74) at Vulsinii, and hence she is clearly identified with Vertumnus. Some derived Vertumnus from *ver*, and so made him the husband of Pomona, from a fancied analogy of Vertumnus to Auctumnus. Varro (*L. L.* § 74), writes 'et arae Sabinam linguam olent, quae Tati regis voto sunt Romae dedicatae: nam ut Annales dicunt, vovit Opi,—Vortumno.' But the semi-Greek form of the name points to a Tyrrhenian origin, *verto* being an Umbrian or indigenous word inflected on the Pelasgic model. Compare *Varroniana*, p. 386. A writer in Dr. Smith's smaller Classical Dictionary does not seem justified in saying: 'The story of the Etruscan origin seems to be sufficiently refuted by his genuine Roman name, and it is much more probable that the worship of Vertumnus was of Sabine origin.'—*signa paterna*, 'the proofs of the parentage or paternity, *i.e.* of the native land, of the god Vertumnus.' He means the proofs, such as those adduced inf. 49 seqq. But *paternus* and *patrius* are not synonyms, though here confused.

3.] *Inter prœlia*, when the early wars of Rome with the Sabines were in progress. See inf. v. 51.

4.] The MSS. vary between *volsanos*, *volsinos*, and *volsanios*, each of which forms, as usual in similar cases, finds an advocate in one or other of the editors. *Volsiniis* occurs in Tac. *Ann.* iv. 1, and in Juvenal, *Sat.* iii. 190, with the first *i* short, whence *Volsinios* was conjectured by Heinsius. Barth and Lachmann give *Volsanos*, which, according to Hertzberg, is also approved by Müller. But he now reads *Volsanios*.

5.] *Hæc turba*, *i. e.* frequentissimus hic vicus.—*juvat*, in a double sense: I like Rome, and I like to see the people, and therefore I would not have them hid from my sight. The statue of Vertumnus, apparently not inclosed in a shrine (*nec templo lætor eburno*), was placed in the vicus Tuscus, otherwise called, as Hertzberg shows in a very elaborate note, vicus turarius, (Hor. *Epist.* ii. 1, 269, 'vicum vendentem thus et odores,') from a confusion between *Tuscus* and *turarius* or *thurarius*. Varro, v. 46, distinctly says, 'ab eis (sc. Tuscis) dictus vicus Tuscus, et ibi ideo Vortumnum stare, quod is deus Etruriæ princeps.' Thus parts of English cities were called *the Jewry* from being assigned for the habitation of Jews. The vicus Tuscus led from the Velabrum into the Forum Romanum (see v. 4, 12), and appears to have commanded a view of it.

7.] The first reason the god assigns for his name is that the part of Rome called the Velabrum (from *vela*, inf. 9, 6) was formerly covered with water, and was recovered by *turning* the course of the river. Ovid, *Fast.* vi. 405—10, 'Qua Velabra solent ad Circum ducere pompas, Nil præter salices crassaque canna fuit.—Nondum conveniens diversis iste figuris Nomen ab averso ceperat amne Deus' (*Vertumnus* quasi *Vertamnus*).—*hac*, δεικτικῶς, pointing to the Velabrum lying below.—*Tiberinus*, the river-god, who was supposed to have walked on the oozy shallows.

9.] *Concessit*, 'gave up so much ground to the children whom he fed with his waters,' as κουροτρόφος. Lucret. v. 1370, 'inque dies magis in montem succedere silvas cogebant, infraque locum concedere cultis.' In the pentameter I have written *Vertamnus* (as in 12 *Vertamnus*) in place of the ordinary form. It is evident that the poet discusses the origin of the name according to different ways of spelling and pronouncing it. Hence in 21 and 47 it is equally clear that *Vertumnus* was derived from *vertere in omnes*, and in 54 from *vertere amnes in fugam*.

Vertumnus verso dicor ab amne deus.
Seu, quia vertentis fructum præcepimus anni,
Vertanni rursus creditur esse sacrum.
Prima mihi variat liventibus uva racemis,
Et coma lactenti spicea fruge tumet.
Hic dulces cerasos, hic auctumnalia pruna
Cornis et æstivo mora rubere die.
Insitor hic solvit pomosa vota corona,
Cum pirus invito stipite mala tulit.
Mendax fama noces: alius mihi nominis index:
De se narranti tu modo crede deo:
Opportuna mea est cunctis natura figuris;
In quamcumque voles, verte; decorus ero.
Indue me Cois, fiam non dura puella:
Meque virum sumpta quis neget esse toga?
Da falcem et torto frontem mihi comprime fœno,

11.] Another theory of the name is propounded, and enlarged upon by a description of the changes of fruit in the autumn.—*præcepimus*, 'we take the first tribute of,'—a *præceptio* of the fruits, as it were. The plural refers to the citizens generally, not to the god, who throughout uses the singular. They are said to take the early samples of garden-produce and offer them on the feast of Vertumnus, the perfect tense representing the aoristic sense 'præcipere solemus.' It seems needless to alter this into *præcerpimus*, with Fea, whom Müller follows.—*rursus*, *sc.* 'for this other reason.'—*sacrum*, i. e. *tempus* or *festum*; 'the time of the first tasting is considered the Feast of Vertumnus.' The MSS. give *credidit*, which was corrected by Pucci.

13.] *Prima* &c. This explains what is meant by the *præceptio*. 'The first bunch of grapes that changes its colour is mine (lit. 'does so for me'); and the first spiky ear that swells with milky grain,' *i.e.* in which the milky grain begins to enlarge.—*variat*, verti incipit; here intransitive, as in ii. 5, 11, 'non ita Carpathiæ variant Aquilonibus undæ.' The Greek is ὑποπερκάζειν, *Od.* vii. 126. Soph. *Frag.* 239, 6, καὶ πλίσσεταί γε κἀποπερκοῦται βότρυς.

15.] *Hic*, before my statue, to which the first ripe fruits (*dulces*) were duly brought.

16.] *Rubere*. Like the blackberry, the mulberry is green, scarlet, or black in different stages of ripening. Æsch. *Frag. Cress.* 107, λευκοῖς τε γὰρ μόροισι καὶ μελαγχίμοις καὶ μιλτοπρέπτοις βρίθεται ταὐτοῦ χρόνου.

17.] Another kind of change, the success of which is attributed to the god, is that produced by grafting; though, of course, a pear-stock will not bear apples any more than an elm will bear acorns, as Virgil fancied, *Georg.* ii. 72.—*pomosa corona* may mean either a string of young apples or a garland of apple-blossoms.

19.] *Noces*, 'you do me injustice.' The popular notions about the origin of the name *Vertumnus* are all wrong; the real derivation is from *verti in omnes figuras*.—*mihi*, *i.e.* alium habeo nominis indicem, sc. meipsum. Perhaps however *tibi* should be read, addressed, like the following *tu*, to the reader, or more simply still, to *Fama*, who is thus referred to the god himself for the account she is to give of him. Whether *modo crede* should be construed, or *deo modo dum de se narrat*, is uncertain.

21—2.] In *cunctis* and *verte* the name *Vertumnus* is implied, as inf. 47. The intervening verses describe the varieties of guise assumed by the god.

23.] *Cois*, see i. 2, 2, and ii. 1, 5.—*non dura*, no awkward girl, but of natural and easy gait.

25.] *Falcem*. Give me a sickle (or scythe) and a hayband round my brows, and you will swear I have been mowing

  Jurabis nostra gramina secta manu.
Arma tuli quondam et, memini, laudabar in illis:
  Corbis in imposito pondere messor eram.
Sobrius ad lites: at cum est imposta corona,
  Clamabis capiti vina subisse meo.
Cinge caput mitra, speciem furabor Iacchi:
  Furabor Phœbi, si modo plectra dabis.
Cassibus impositis venor: sed harundine sumpta
  Faunus plumoso sum deus aucupio.
Est etiam aurigæ species Vertumnus et ejus,
  Traicit alterno qui leve pondus equo.
Suppetat hoc, pisces calamo prædabor, et ibo
  Mundus demissis institor in tunicis.
Pastor me ad baculum possum curvare vel idem

gram.' The whole of this passage should be compared with Ovid, *Met.* xiv. 641—51.

27.] *Arma*, see 3 and 53.—*laudabar*, as sup. *decorus eram*;—*in illis*, as Gr. *ἐν ὅπλοις*, dressed as a warrior. The use of *in* is the same in the pentameter, where *corbis* is the reaper's basket or hamper in which the ears of corn were placed, the straw being left standing.

29.] *Sobrius*, *οὐκ εἰμὶ πάροινος*, 'I am not easily provoked to a drunken brawl.' He can assume the guise of a *comissator* or *κωμαστής*, and appear as if wine had got into his head. Plaut. *Amphitryo*, 999, 'capiam coronam mi in caput, adsimulabo me esse ebrium.'

33.] *Harundine*, the fowler's jointed rod, tipped with bird-lime and so constructed that it could be suddenly darted out to a considerable length; the *calamus* of iv. 13, 46. Martial, ix. 54, 3, 'aut crescente levis traheretur harundine præda, Pinguis et implicitas virga teneret aves.'—*aucupio*, 'for bird-catching,' 'for taking feathered game.'

35.] 'Vertumnus assumes also the guise of a charioteer, and of one who throws his light weight from one horse to another in the circus.'—*leve pondus* is the accusative, not the nominative in apposition to *qui*, as Lachmann thought. Barth rightly supplies 'scil. corporis sui.' So *pedes traicere* inf. 4, 78. The practice alluded to is much like that which is still commonly exhibited, viz., feats of agility on horseback at full speed. The horses were called *equi desultorii*. Kuinoel refers to Sueton. *Jul. Cæsar*, 39, 'quadrigas bigasque et equos desultorios agitaverunt nobilissimi juvenes.' The celebrated and curious passage in Hom. *Il.* xv. 680 shows that this exhibition sometimes took place on the high roads.

37.] *Suppetat hoc*, *i.e.* modo fiat mihi copia hujus rei. Compare inf. 5, 9.

38.] *Mundus*, 'spruce and tidy.'—*demissis tunicis*, non succinctus. The latter implied hurry, exertion, and indifference to personal appearance. The pedlar (*institor*) would seem to have found great favour in Roman families, and to have had interested motives in dressing so as to please female eyes. Compare Hor. *Od.* iii. 6, 30; *Epod.* xvii. 20; Ovid, *Art. Am.* i. 421; *Remed. Amor.* 306. The proper office of the *institor* seems to have been to dispose of goods on commission, much in the way practised by our commercial travellers.

39.] All the good copies give *pastorem ad baculum possum curvare*; a reading with which Jacob expresses no desire to quarrel. Hertzberg also retains it, and thinks *pastorem curvare* is not more harsh than *implere pastorem*, 'to fulfil the part of a shepherd,' like 'censorem implere,' Vell. Paterc. ii. 95. So also Müller and Keil. I still think this reading is nonsense, and I doubt if Mr. Wratislaw mends the matter by reading 'pastorem ad baculum possum curvare,' *i.e.* 'curvum pastorem agere.' I have therefore adopted, with Kuinoel, the excellent conjecture of Ayrmann, in defence of which Kuinoel well observes, that on ancient gems shepherds are usually represented as leaning on their staffs, and he quotes from Ovid, *Trist.* iv. 1, 11, 'Fossus ut incubuit baculo saxove residit Pastor.'

Sirpiculis medio pulvere ferre rosam.
Nam quid ego adiciam, de quo mihi maxima fama est,
  Hortorum in manibus dona probata meis?
Cæruleus cucumis tumidoque cucurbita ventre
  Me notat et junco brassica vincta levi.
Nec flos ullus hiat pratis, quin ille decenter
  Impositus fronti langueat ante meæ.
At mihi, quod formas unus vertebar in omnes,
  Nomen ab eventu patria lingua dedit.
Et tu, Roma, meis tribuisti præmia Tuscis,
  Unde hodie vicus nomina Tuscus habet,
Tempore quo sociis venit Lycomedius armis,
  Atque Sabina feri contudit arma Tati.
Vidi ego labentes acies et tela caduca,

40.] *Medio pulvere*, which some take for *media arena*, and explain of the custom of selling roses to the spectators in the circus, Hertzberg and others more probably understand for *media aestate*. 'Hortorum villicam vel adeo puellam rusticam tibi finge aestate per vias pulverulentas canistras (canistra) florum plenas Romam portantem.'—*Hertzberg*, who perhaps presses the sense of *medio pulvere* too closely. The custom of sending flowers to sell in the city is mentioned *Georg.* iv. 134, 'Primus vere rosam, atque autumno carpere poma.' The *sirpiculus* was a hamper or flower-basket, alluded to perhaps in iv. 13, 30. Varro (the worst of etymologists) says, perhaps rightly, v. § 137, 'Falces *sirpiculae* vocatae ab sirpando, id est ab alligando,' and again § 139, 'sirpea, quod virgis sirpatur, id est colligando implicatur.'

41.] *Nam quid* &c., 'quid quod hortorum dona ponuntur in manibus meis,' *i.e.* accedit quod &c.—*maxima fama*, because Vertumnus was associated with Pomona.—*dona probata*, the choice produce of the garden, including fruits and vegetables, but the latter here seem chiefly meant.

43.] *Caeruleus*, in respect of its bluish or glaucous bloom. So Lucretius has 'olearum caerula plaga,' v. 1374.—*me notat*, insignem facit; in a good, or at least, indifferent sense. Cf. iv. 7, 22, 'qua notat Argynni poena natantis aquas.'

45.] *Ille* seems to mean *et ille*; as inf. 7, 92, 'nos vehimur' is *nos quoque*. Compare however *ibid.* 76.—*pratis* is opposed to *hortorum*; 'nay, even the first flowers of the fields are put to wither on my brow.'

47.] *In omnes*, see sup. on 21.—*patria*, the language of my adopted country, the Roman.

49.] *Et tu, Roma.* 'As I was called *Vertumnus* from *verti in omnia*, so *Vicus Tuscus* was called from the *Tusci*.'—*unde*, *i.e.* 'nam ab iis' &c.

51.] The good copies agree in *Lycomedius*. Kuinoel and Lachmann admit Burmann's conjecture, *Lucumonius*. See on v. 1, 29. The historical incident referred to by the poet is the assistance lent to the Romans against the Sabines by the Tuscans under Caeles Vibenna, whence the *vicus Tuscus* was believed to have derived its name, and the tribe of the Luceres seems to have sprung. Tacitus, *Ann.* iv. 65, 'Caelium (montem) appellitatum a Caele Vibenna, qui dux gentis Etruscae cum auxilium tulisset, sedem eam acceperat a Tarquinio Prisco, seu quis alius regum dedit: nam scriptores in eo dissentiunt. Cetera non ambigua sunt, magnas eas copias per plana etiam ac foro propinqua habitavisse, unde Tuscum Vicum e vocabulo advenarum dictum.' A people called Lucomedi, the same in fact as the Luceres, are recorded by Festus and Paul the deacon, quoted by Hertzberg; but of a leader so called, no mention occurs except in the present passage. There seems an allusion to λύκος or λυκεῖος, as suggestive of fierceness.

53.] *Vidi ego.* See sup. 27.—*tela caduca*, *irrita*, weapons that fell short of the mark.

Atque hostes turpi terga dedisse fugæ.
Sed facias, divum sator, ut Romana per ævum
Transeat ante meos turba togata pedes.
Sex superant versus: te, qui ad vadimonia curris,
Non moror: hæc spatiis ultima meta meis.
Stipes acernus eram, properanti falce dolatus,
Ante Numam grata pauper in urbe deus.
At tibi, Mamurri, formæ cælator ahenæ,
Tellus artifices ne terat Osca manus,
Qui me tam docilis potuisti fundere in usus.
Unum opus est, operi non datur unus honos.

III.

Hæc Arethusa suo mittit mandata Lycotæ,

54.] *Hostes*, i.e. Sabinos. As they were *versi in fugam*, it is probable that the name Vertumnus is again alluded to.

56.] *Ante meos pedes*. The way to the Circus maximus, which stood in the low ground between the Palatine and Aventine hills, from the Forum Romanum, was by the Vicus Tuscus and the Velabrum, so that crowds of people were constantly passing the statue of Vertumnus. — *Togata*, peaceful or civilian.

57.] *Ad vadimonia*. Here used for any urgent and important business. Juv. iii. 213, 'differt vadimonia prætor.' Any one in a hurry, says the poet, may pass over the remaining six verses, as merely supplementary. It may be conjectured, from the unusual and awkward way in which the last six lines are connected with the preceding, that the present elegy was at first commenced with the words 'Stipes acernus eram' &c. See sup. on i. 67, and compare Horace, *Sat*. i. 8, 1. 'Olim truncus eram ficulnus,' &c.

58.] *Ultima meta*, 'the last heat;' cf. sup. i. 70, 'has meus ad metas sudet oportet equus.'—*spatiis*, as in *Georg*. i. 512, means the courses run, each up-and-down, δίαυλος, being a 'spatium.'

61.] Mamurius Veturius was a famous sculptor or modeller in the time of Numa. Ovid, *Fast*. iii. 383, speaking of the ancilia: 'Mamurius, morum fabræne exactior artis Difficile est illud dicere, clausit opus.' With Müller and the Naples MSS., we should read *Mamurri* in the present passage, as Ovid shortens the *u*.

62.] *Osca*. It is not very clear whether the poet meant generally *Itala*, as Müller (quoted by Hertzberg) thinks, or *Campana*, as the latter prefers, or lastly, whether any antithesis is intended between the aboriginal Oscans and the Etrurian or Pelasgic settlers. Possibly (as in *Lycomedius* sup.) there is a fanciful allusion to *opifex* in *Osci* or *Opici*. The name would seem to be connected with *Mamers*, the Oscan word for Mars; see *Varronianus*, p. 80. The general sense however is clear: 'may the earth spare the skilful hands that made me,' i.e. may it be light to your remains.

63.] *Fundere*, χωνεύειν, whence, of course, our word *foundry*. There is this difference between *fundere* and *conflare* (inf. v. 7, 47), that the former is to cast a new statue &c., the latter to melt down an old one.—*docilis* is here in a passive sense, 'readily assumed:' the mind of the poet was perhaps rather 'me docilem in tot usus,' 'who had the skill to cast me fit for being turned into so many uses.' Hence *non unus honos operi*; it is praised under whichever of its attributes it is viewed.

III. This elegy, which Kuinoel rightly styles 'mollitissimum carmen,' as much resembles Ovid's Heroides as the two preceding are like the style of the Fasti. Under the feigned names of Arethusa and Lycotas it is generally thought that Ælia Galla and her husband Postumus are meant. See on iv. 12, which also treats

Cum totiens absis, si potes esse mea.
Si qua tamen tibi lecturo pars oblita deerit,
Hæc erit e lacrimis facta litura meis:
Aut si qua incerto fallet te littera tractu,
Signa meæ dextræ jam morientis erunt.
Te modo viderunt iteratos Bactra per ortus,
Te modo munito Neuricus hostis equo,
Hibernique Getæ, pictoque Britannia curru,
Ustus et Eoa discolor Indus aqua.
Hæcne marita fides et pactæ gaudia noctes,
Cum rudis urgenti brachia victa dedi?
Quæ mihi deductæ fax omen prætulit, illa
Traxit ab everso lumina nigra rogo,

of Cæsar's expedition to the East. Hertzberg doubts the identity of the parties (*Quæst.* lib. 1, cap. v. p. 22), because he thinks it improbable that feigned names should be used after the real ones had been given. A more plausible argument lies in the curious fact, pointed out by Bentley on Hor. *Od.* ii. 12, 13, that when the Roman writers employed feigned names, they selected such as were of the same rhythm as the real ones, *i.e.* metrically convertible. Whether this was a law, or merely a common practice, may perhaps fairly be questioned. The similarity of circumstances detailed in the two elegies strongly suggests that the persons are the same. The date 734 is assigned by Hertzberg to the present elegy, *Quæst.* p. 228.

3.] *Si qua tamen* &c. Ovid expresses this idea with not less beauty, *Her.* iii. 3, 'Quascunque aspicies, lacrimæ fecere lituras; Sed tamen et lacrimæ pondera vocis habent;' and *ibid.* xi. 1, 'si qua tamen cæcis errabunt scripta lituris, Oblitus a dominæ cæde libellus erit.'—*hæc* is emphatic: '*this* is not the ordinary erasure of letter-writers' &c.

5.] *Aut si* &c. 'Or, if you fail to read any letter from its unsteady stroke, this shall be a sign that death was even now upon my hand.'

7.] *Iteratos*, 'more than once visited;' in allusion perhaps to the sending troops and supplies for the second Parthian expedition to revenge the death of Crassus (inf. 6, 83). Compare *signa iterata* sup. i. 62, and Hor. *Carm.* i. 7, 32, 'cras ingens iterabimus æquor.' Müller marks the passage as corrupt, the Naples MS. omitting the words *Bactra per ortus.*—*Neuricus* is the conjecture of Jacob, adopted by Hertzberg and Müller, for *hericus* or *ericus*. Lachmann and the older editors read *Sericus* after Beroaldus. Keil gives *Noricus*. The Neuri were a Sarmatian people, mentioned by Strabo, vii. 3, § 14, Herod. iv. 17, and elsewhere. *Munito equo* refers to the cataphractæ or mail-clad Sarmatian cavalry, Tac. *Hist.* i. 79. See sup. iv. 12, 12.

9.] *Picto curru.* Cf. ii. 1, 76, 'esseda cælatis siste Britanna jugis.'—*Eoa aqua*, 'ad aquam Eoam,' *Lachmann*. This seems the best and simplest explanation; 'the sun-burnt swarthy Indian by the eastern sea.' The far north, west, and east are mentioned under the names *Getæ*, *Britanni*, and *Indi*. The ancient idea, that the sun rose from the far-distant eastern ocean, and burnt black the natives of that region, is a fair subject for a poet to adopt. Others take *Indus* for the name of the river, which makes it hard to explain *ustus* and *discolor*. Müller, with Barth and Kuinoel, read *eoo discolor Indus equo;* one objection to which is, that *equo* thus ends two consecutive pentameters.

11.] *Pactæ et mihi gaudia noctis* is the plausible conjecture of Müller for *et parce avia noctes* (MS. Naples), or *et pactæ mihi noctes* (MS. Gron.) The ordinary texts give *hæ pactæ sunt mihi noctes*, after Pucci and Beroaldus. I formerly gave *et sic pactæ* &c. Mr. Shilleto suggests *et pactæ tam mihi noctes*, *Cum rudis* &c. For *avia* Haupt proposed *aveia*, a word but little used by elegiac writers. It occurs however iii. 21, 39.

13—14.] *Quæ mihi* &c. 'The torch which preceded me as an omen of my marriage drew its dismal light from some

Et Stygio sum sparsa lacu, nec recta capillis
  Vitta data est: nupsi non comitante deo.
Omnibus heu portis pendent mea noxia vota:
  Texitur haec castris quarta lacerna tuis.
Occidat, immerita qui carpsit ab arbore vallum
  Et struxit querulas rauca per ossa tubas,
Dignior obliquo funem qui torqueat Ocno,

burnt-out pyre.'—*nigra*, fuliginosa, not burning clear and bright, which was a good omen, sup. iv. 10, 20. Such fires are called *nigri* and *atri*, *e.g.* Hor. *Carm.* iv. 12, 26; *Æn.* xi. 186. The Romans had a great dread of connecting in any way the rites of marriage and of burial. They did not marry during the Feralia, whence Ovid writes (*Fast.* ii. 561), 'Conde tuas, Hymenaee, faces, et ab ignibus atris aufer: habent alias moesta sepulcra faces.' See *ibid.* v. 487. They also thought much of lighting a torch from a lucky source. Ovid, *Her.* ii. 117—120, 'Pronuba Tisiphone thalamis ululavit in illis,—Suntque sepulcrali lumina mota face.'

15.] *Stygio*. The water used for sprinkling was not fresh from the stream, but came from the Avernian lake. The chaplet too was placed awry on my head, and this was an unlucky omen. The god Hymen, invoked in the marriage song, 'Hymen ades, o Hymenaee,' did not come when he was called, and so I was married without his attendance.'

17.] *Portis*. Hertzberg appears to be right in understanding the city gates, at which altars and shrines of the *Lares viales* were placed, and before which written vows for the safety of the absent were suspended. In this case, her vows (*i.e.* promises of offerings) for Lycotas' return from service were *noxia*, rather injurious than otherwise; not favourably received by the gods. 'Quae magis nocent quam juvant, reditu non impetrato.'—*Barth*. In Cic. *de Legg.* ii. 23, § 58, mention is made of an altar in the temple of Honour without the Colline Gate.

18.] *Quarta lacerna*. That her vows for his return had not been heard, was shown by his now being absent for the fourth year on service. The custom of wives and their maidens weaving these military cloaks for their husbands in the camp, is alluded to in Livy i. 26, 'soror—cognito super humeros fratris paludamento sponsi quod ipsa confecerat, solvit crines.' *Fast.* ii. 746, 'Mittenda est domino, nunc nunc properate, puellae, Quam primum nostra facta lacerna manu.'

19.] *Occidat*, 'perish he who first invented the implements of war!'—*vallum*, the stake carried by the Roman soldier for fencing the camp.—*immerita* (inf. 4, 23) ἀναιτίῳ, not to be blamed as the cause of war; perhaps, deserving of a better fate; or, which never should have been used for such a purpose.—*querulas per ossa*, uttering its hoarse notes through lengths of hollow bone. The leg-bone (tibia) seems anciently to have been so used, and it is said to be so still. The North American Indians make whistles out of the bones of their enemies. Among the arms taken from the natives of Dewangiri, Bhootan, was a trumpet made out of a human thigh-bone (*Illustrated News*, June 24, 1865). A New Zealand chief is said to have made a flute out of the thigh-bone of his enemy. Compare Ar. *Acharn.* 863, τοῖς ὀστίνοις φυσῆτε τὸν πρωκτὸν κυνός. Callim. *H. Dian.* 214, οὐ γάρ πω νέβρεια δι' ὀστέα τετρήναντο.

21.] *Dignior*. 'More worthy was he than the lollard Ocnus to twist the rope merely to provide a lasting supply of food for the hungry ass.'—*obliquo*, λεχρίῳ, not sitting straight, but turning on one side so as not to see the ass at his elbow. This seems to have been either a well-known fable or a common subject for wall-painters. The general sense is, 'Dignior, qui funem torqueat, etiam quam Ocnus ipse, qui obliquus et transversus operi incumbit, dum asinus ad latus ignaro funem comedit:'—the inventor of war ought to have been the personification of useless toil and trouble, rather than Ocnus in the picture. Pausan. *Phocic.* lib. x. cap. 29, 1, (speaking of certain paintings at Delphi): μετὰ δὲ αὐτοὺς ἀνήρ ἐστι καθήμενος, ἐπίγραμμα δὲ Ὄκνον εἶναι λέγει τὸν ἄνθρωπον· πεποίηται μὲν πλέκων σχοινίον, παρέστηκε δὲ θήλεια ὄνος ἐπεσθίουσα τὸ πεπλεγμένον ἀεὶ τοῦ σχοινίου. Τοῦτον εἶναι τὸν Ὄκνον φιλεργόν φασιν ἄνθρωπον, γυναῖκα δὲ ἔχειν δαπανηράν· καὶ ὁπόσα συλλέξαιτο ἐργαζόμενος, οὐ πολὺ ἐν ὕστερον ὑπὸ ἐκείνης ἀνήλωτο. — οἷα

Æternusque tuam pascat, aselle, famem.
Dic mihi, num teneros urit lorica lacertos?
  Num gravis imbelles atterit hasta manus?
Hæc noceant potius, quam dentibus ulla puella
  Det mihi plorandas per tua colla notas.
Diceris et macie vultum tenuasse: sed opto,
  E desiderio sit color iste meo.
At mihi cum noctes induxit vesper amaras,
  Si qua relicta jacent, osculor arma tua.
Tum queror in toto non sidere pallia lecto,
  Lucis et auctores non dare carmen aves.
Noctibus hibernis castrensia pensa laboro
  Et Tyria in radios vellera secta suos,
Et disco, qua parte fluat vincendus Araxes,
  Quot sine aqua Parthus milia currat equus,
Conor et e tabula pictos ediscere mundos,

δὴ καὶ ὑπὸ Ἰώνων, ὁπότε ἴδοιέν τινα πονοῦντα ἐπὶ οὐδενὶ ἔργων φέροντι, ὑπὸ τούτων εἰρημένον, ὡς ὁ ἀνὴρ οὗτος συνάγει τοῦ Ὄκνου τὴν θώμιγγα. Pliny, *N. H.* lib. xxxv. 11, § 137, 'piger qui appellatur Ocnos, spartum torquens quod asellus rodit.'

23—4.] *Dic mihi.* 'Tell me, does the corslet chafe those tender arms, or the heavy spear gall those too delicate hands? I would rather these should hurt you than that any girl should leave on your neck marks that I should have to deplore,' viz. the 'livor Quem facit impresso mutua dente Venus,' Tibull. i. 6, 14. Inf. 5, 39, 'semper habe morsus circa tua colla recentes, Litibus alternis quos putet esse datos.'—*urit*, so Hor. *Epist.* i. 13, 6, 'si te forte meæ gravis uret sarcina chartæ.'

27.] 'I am told too that you look thin and wan: I only hope that paleness of yours comes from a longing for me,' not from ill-health or over-fatigue.

29.] *Amaras*, cf. i. 1, 33, 'in me nostra Venus noctes exercet amaras.' Ovid, 'nunc et amara dies et noctis amarior umbra est.' *si qua* &c., 'if any arms left in the house lie about, I kiss them as yours.'

31.] *In toto lecto*, see on i. 14, 21. She complains that the coverlet (the χλαῖνα, often used for this purpose), does not rest on the whole bed, but only on half of it, *i.e.* that one occupant of it is absent. I think this is a more probable explanation than that she complains of its slipping off the bed, which in itself would be a trifling incident. Cf. i. 14, 21, 'et miserum toto juvenem versare cubili.'—*aves*, the cocks do not announce the coming dawn by crowing.

34.] *In radios suos*, 'cut in lengths to fit their shuttles.' In weaving patterns of different coloured wool, several shuttles would be used, each charged with a certain quantity of dyed worsted. The MSS. have *gladios*, which was corrected by Perrey. For *gladius* is the *batten*, or σπάθη (Æsch. *Cho.* 224), used for pressing the wool close. *Tyria*, of sea-purple dye; but there were many different hues in use. Cf. inf. 51.

35.] Perhaps *sunt disco* &c., viz. as one of the employments of the long winter-nights. 'I try to make out in what part of the East the Araxes flows, that is to be conquered by your arms, and how many miles the Parthian steed runs without water' (*i.e.* must run to get water). The Arab horse is second only to the camel in his endurance of thirst.

37.] *Conor* is the reading of Hertzberg for *cogor*, after Broukhusius. The words are sometimes confused, and *cogor* could only express the truism, that as she was not with her husband in the east, she was obliged to have recourse to the map. By 'pictos mundos' she seems to mean 'pictas mundi (*i.e.* orbis) partes.' The πίναξ of Herod. v. 49 shows how early this device was invented; and only a few centuries have elapsed since anything approaching to accuracy in map-making was attained. Some blunders in the map of Dicæarchus are pointed out by Cicero, *Ep. ad Att.* vi. 2, 3.

Qualis et hæc docti sit positura dei,
Quæ tellus sit lenta gelu, quæ putris ab æstu,
Ventus in Italiam qui bene vela ferat.
Adsidet una soror, curis et pallida nutrix
Peierat hiberni temporis esse moras.
Felix Hippolyte nuda tulit arma papilla
Et texit galea barbara molle caput.
Romanis utinam patuissent castra puellis!
Essem militiæ sarcina fida tuæ,
Nec me tardarent Scythiæ juga, cum pater altas
†Africus in glaciem frigore nectit aquas.
Omnis amor magnus, sed aperto in conjuge major:
Hanc Venus, ut vivat, ventilat ipsa facem.
Nam mihi quo Pœnis tibi purpura fulgeat ostris

38.] *Positura* is a Lucretian word. The sense seems to be, 'And how this world of ours has been arranged in its parts by the wise Creator.'—*docti dei*, τοῦ σοφοῦ πάντων δημιουργοῦ. That she does not mean the geography of the east alone, seems shown by the use of *hæc* instead of *ista*.

39.] *Lenta*, 'numbed,' 'stiff,' 'frost-bound;' opposed to *putris*, as 'adhesive' to 'loose and friable;' *putre solum*, *Georg.* ii. 204, and *ibid.* 250, 'haud unquam manibus jactata fatiscit, Sed picis in morem ad digitos lentescit habendo.'—*ventus* &c., in reference to the hoped-for return of her husband by the first favourable wind.

42.] *Peierat*, 'falsely swears.' Though she knows it is not true, yet, for the purpose of consoling me, my nurse assures me the continued delay is caused solely by the sailing-season not yet having arrived.

43.] *Felix* &c. 'Happy was the queen of the Amazons who could bear arms with exposed breast' (the *one* breast, as from ἀ and μα(ζός)), 'and barbarian as she was, cover a woman's head with the dog-skin cap. O that the camp were open to Roman wives too! A faithful companion to your train would I make.' The sense is, 'She, as an Eastern Queen, had a freedom to serve in the wars which is denied to us Roman girls.'—*fida*, virtuous amid all the allurements of a camp. On the exclusion of Roman wives from the service, see on ii. 7, 16. Ovid, *Her.* iii. 68, 'non ego sum classi sarcina magna tuæ,' says Briseis to Achilles.

48.] The reading of the MSS. *Africus* must be considered doubtful. Assuming that the winds are sometimes personified, and that 'pater Boreas,' 'Zephyrus' &c. might even be justified on the idea of their life-giving influence, yet the *south-west wind* would hardly be the wind to freeze the rivers of Scythia. It may be replied (1) that local meteorology may be very exceptional; (2) that Propertius may speak in ignorance of or indifference to exact eastern geography; (3) that *Africus* is used indefinitely for any wind. These considerations have sufficient weight to make the rejection of the vulgate somewhat rash. The best correction, I think, that has been made is *aprico* for *Africus*; 'when Jupiter freezes the deep rivers by clear cold frost.' Müller reads *ætheris*, which he thinks 'pæne necessarium' to explain 'altas aquas.' But he forgets that *æther* is always associated with fire and upper bright air, never with rain. Lachmann reads *Arctos*, Schneidewin and Haupt *Tetricus*, neither of which seem to have much probability.

49.] *Aperto in conjuge*, 'in the case of an acknowledged and lawful husband,' κουρίδιος πόσις. Kuinoel, after Burmann, reads *deserto in conjuge*. The alliteration in the next line seems intentional. It is a beautiful verse, the metaphor being taken from swinging to and fro, or fanning, a piece of charcoal or any feeble flame,—perhaps a torch or link.

51.] Hertzberg, Keil, Müller, and others place the question at *quo?* 'What is it to me to be handsomely dressed? For your eyes alone let the costly Tyrian hues glow, and my hands wear clear crystal gems.' But it seems simpler to understand

Crystallusque meas ornet aquosa manus?
Omnia surda tacent, rarisque adsueta kalendis
Vix aperit clausos una puella lares,
Glaucidos et catulæ vox est mihi grata querentis:
Illa tui partem vindicat una toro.
Flore sacella tego, verbenis compita velo,
Et crepat ad veteres herba Sabina focos.
Sive in finitimo gemuit stans noctua tigno,
Seu voluit tangi parca lucerna mero,
Illa dies hornis cædem denuntiat agnis,

it thus: 'What is it to me that you have fine clothes and that I wear fine gems? All is dull and silent without you' &c. Lachmann, Barth, and Kuinoel read *si fulgent* after Heins; but this should be *si fulget*. The Naples MS. gives *te* for *tibi*, and the Groningen MS. *tuas* for *meas* in the pentameter; and this reading is preferred by Hertzberg, while Barth and others give *suas*. On *crystallus aquosa* see iii. 15, 12. Whether the *pila*, or hand-ball of rock crystal is meant, or a crystal ring, or even a diamond (*adamas*), is very uncertain. The feminine seems to follow the analogy of ἡ λίθος in the sense of 'precious stone.'—*aquosa* may mean 'with water in it' (the *pila*), or 'clear as water,' or lastly, 'congealed from water,' according to the ideas prevalent about the origin of rock-crystal.

53.] *Raris Kalendis*, 'only now and then on the first of the month.' So Martial, *Ep.* iv. 66, 3, 'Idibus et raris togula est excussa Kalendis.' Kuinoel adopts the needless alteration of Schrader, 'lanigeque assueta colendis.' The *clausi Lares* refers to the *lararium*, the shrine or closet in which the Lares were inclosed, something after the fashion of our altar-triptychs, perhaps. To the Roman mind, the shutting up of the Lar Familiaris was a symbol of complete desolation in a house.

55.] *Et* (perhaps *at*) seems to mean 'et sola vox catulæ' &c. Martial has a very pretty epigram, i. 110, on a lap-dog called Issa, which slept on its master's bed.—*tui partem* means 'vindicat sibi partem quam tu debebas (solebas) capere in toro.' Hertzberg explains it 'non omne mariti munus, sed partem tantum;' and this may be right.

58.] *Herba Sabina*, the Savine or Juniper, seems to have been used in φίλτρα or love-potions, and an omen was derived from its crackling sound when burnt as a charm on the hearth. Ovid, *Fast.* i. 343, 'Ara dabat fumos herbis contenta Sabinis.' *compita*, at the shrines of the *Lares viales*, perhaps.

59—62.] 'If an owl has whooped, or the lamp has spluttered, the omen is followed by a sacrifice, either to avert evil portended by the one, or to ensure the good promised by the other.' The owl was counted *inter diras aves* by the Romans, and has been regarded with awe in every age. See iv. 6, 29.

60.] *Tangi mero*. An omen was derived from the spluttering of a wick, which was called 'sneezing.' *Anthol. Gr. A.* 130, ἤδη, φίλτατε λύχνε, τρὶς ἔπταρες· ἦ τάχα τερπνὴν Ἐς θαλάμους ἥξειν Ἀντιγόνην προλέγεις. Kuinoel appositely quotes Ovid, *Heroid.* xix. 151, 'Sternuit et lumen (posito nam scribimus illo), Sternuit, et nobis prospera signa dedit. Ecce merum nutrix faustos instillat in ignes; Crasque erimus plures, inquit, et ipsa bibit:'—but it is singular that he should have stopped at the third line, whereas the fourth shows that if the lamp spluttered, an arrival was expected. The wine was poured by way of acknowledgment of the omen, and as a libation, and also, perhaps, because it made the lamp splutter the more. Compare the modern custom of predicting a guest from the tea-leaves at the bottom of a cup.

61.] *Hornis*, *hovernis*, spring (or yearling) lambs. If a lucky omen occurs, it is followed up at once by a sacrifice, and the butchers, with their sacrificial dress (called *limus*) tucked up for the work, are eager after fresh perquisites,—a portion of the meat being sent to them after duly performing the sacrifice. The *popa* was employed to fell the victim, the *cultrarius* to cut the throat. Persius has 'popa venter,' *Sat.* vi. 74.

Succinctique calent ad nova lucra popæ.
Ne, precor, ascensis tanti sit gloria Bactris,
Raptave odorato carbasa lina duci,
Plumbea cum tortæ sparguntur pondera fundæ,
Subdolus et versis increpat arcus equis.
Sed, tua sic domitis Parthæ telluris alumnis
Pura triumphantis hasta sequatur equos,
Incorrupta mei conserva fœdera lecti.
Hac ego te sola lege redisse velim,
Armaque cum tulero portæ votiva Capenæ,
Subscribam 'salvo grata puella viro.'

IV.

Tarpeium nemus et Tarpeiæ turpe sepulcrum

63.] *Tanti*, sc. ut vitam perdas.—*ascensis*, as if Bactra was an acropolis. It is said to have stood at the foot of the mountain range known as the Hindoo Koosh. *odorato*, from the notion that the east was the region of perfumes, and that the great potentates always used them.—*carbasa lina*, the colours, or standard, of embroidered linen cloth. The *spolia opima* may perhaps be meant (inf. 10, 5). The combination *carbasa lina* is strange: probably all that Propertius knew was that *carbasus* was an eastern word, and it is pretty clear that he here uses it as an adjective. Virgil, *Æn.* xi. 776, has 'sinus crepantes carbaseos,' where *crepantes* may refer to the thick and rustling material. It is said to be the Sanscrit *Karpasa*, 'cotton.' Inf. 11, 54, 'exhibuit vivos carbasus alba focos.'

66.] *Versis equis.* The Parthian pretended flight, and then suddenly turned on his enemy and discharged arrows at him. See iii. 1, 13.

67.] *Sed* &c. Do not care for glory, but think only of, and try to requite, the virtuous love of your wife. She adds, 'So may the virgin spear follow the horses in the triumphal car, after the conquest of the Parthians.' The *pura hasta* was a pointless wand presented as a badge of honour to those who had first distinguished themselves in the wars. It is like the 'winning the spurs' in our ages of chivalry. Compare *Æn.* vi. 760, 'hic juvenis pura qui nititur hasta.'

71.] *Portæ Capenæ*, i.e. to the temple of Mars *ad portam*. Ovid, *Fast.* vi. 191, 'Lux eadem Marti festa est, quem prospicit extra Appositum Tectæ Porta Capena viæ.' It was the custom for wives to offer arms in this way on the safe return of their lords. Ovid, *Her.* i. 27, 'grata ferunt Nymphæ pro salvis dona maritis.' The four simple words that end this beautiful elegy form a most effective conclusion. The verb, it is needless to add, is usually omitted in this formula, as in the verse 'Æneas hæc de Danais victoribus arma,' and even in much earlier Greek dedications. Ἱέρων—τῷ Διὶ Τυρρανὰ ἀπὸ Κύμας is the inscription on a helmet about B.C. 475 (Donaldson's *Pindar*, p. 86). Sup. iii. 20, 44, 'scribam ego, Per magnum salva puella Jovem.'

IV. The legend of Tarpeia, who betrayed the capitol to Titus Tatius, king of the Sabines, for whom she had conceived an affection. See Ovid, *Fast.* i. 260; Livy, i. 2. Tacit. *Ann.* xii. 24, 'Forum Romanum et Capitolium non a Romulo sed a Tito Tatio additum urbi credidere.' Roman pride, of course, clung to the legend or tradition that the Capitol was betrayed to the Sabine king. This is one of the most beautiful of the elegies, and was doubtless composed for the work on the Fasti already alluded to. The date is uncertain, but it is one of the early poems.

1.] *Turpe sepulcrum*, infamem sepulturam, inf. v. 91.—*limina capta Jovis*, 'the capture of the fortress where now stands the temple of Jupiter Capitolinus.' He is called *antiqui* in contrast with the more modern temple: cf. sup. 1, 5.

Fabor et antiqui limina capta Jovis.
Lucus erat felix hederoso conditus antro,
  Multaque nativis obstrepit arbor aquis,
Silvani ramosa domus, quo dulcis ab æstu
  Fistula poturas ire jubebat oves.
Hunc Tatius fontem vallo præcingit acerno,
  Fidaque suggesta castra coronat humo.
Quid tum Roma fuit, tubicen vicina Curetis
  Cum quateret lento murmure saxa Jovis,
Atque ubi nunc terris dicuntur jura subactis,
  Stabant Romano pila Sabina foro?
Murus erant montes: ubi nunc est Curia septa,
  Bellicus ex illo fonte bibebat equus.
Hinc Tarpeia deæ fontem libavit: at illi
  Urgebat medium fictilis urna caput.

3.] *Lucus felix*, a thriving or luxuriant grove; the *Tarpeii luci*, inf. 8, 31.—*conditus antro*, 'inclosed within an ivy-clad ravine,' i.e. the sides of which were clothed with ivy. *Consitus antro* Barth, Kuinoel, and Lachmann, from inferior copies; and this Jacob approves.—*Antrum* is here used as 'Partheniis in antris' i. 1, 11, and *ibid.* 2, 11, 'surgat et in solis formosius arbutus antris.' Virgil, *Æn.* viii. 347, describes the Tarpeia sedes as 'olim sylvestribus horrida dumis.'

4.] *Obstrepit*, 'makes music to the rippling of a natural spring.' Cf. i, 17, 46.—*nativis*, not conducted by pipes from an aqueduct: see iv. 2, 12.

6.] *Poturas*, more usually *potum ire*.

7.] *Hunc fontem*. Hertzberg considers this to have been a small mountain stream, running down the gorge between wooded banks, and collected in a pond at the bottom, from which 'bellicus equus bibebat' v. 14. From the spring-head Tarpeia drew water v. 15, so that it is clear that it was not in the occupation of the Sabines. By *hunc fontem* he seems to mean the pond itself at the bottom of the hill, which Tatius secured for his own use by fencing it in front with palisades. Hertzberg quotes the following important passage from Plutarch, *Num.* 13, τὴν δὲ πηγὴν ἣ κατάρδει τὸ χωρίον, ὕδωρ ἱερὸν ἀπέδειξε ταῖς Ἑστιάσι παρθένοις, ὥστε λαμβανούσαις καθ᾽ ἡμέραν ἁγνίζειν καὶ ῥαίνειν τὸ ἀνάκτορον. It was sacred to the Muses, and known as Fons Camenarum.

8.] *Coronat*, 'he makes a secure camp by heaping up the earth into a circular agger, or ring-fence.' A clever verse, in which every word has a special meaning.

9.] *Curetis*, Κουρῆτες, Quirini; *Quirinus* and *Cures* being, perhaps, but different names for the chief town of the Sabines. Here, it would seem, as in *Lycmon* sup. 1, 29, the poet makes *Cures*, *Curetis*, the eponym title of the Sabine fighting-men. Cf. Ovid, *Fast.* ii. 477, 'sive quod hasta curis priscis est dicta Sabinis.'—*lento*, 'lingering,' 'long-drawn,' echoing against the rocks where now stands the temple of Jupiter.

12.] *Romano foro*. As above remarked, from Tacitus, the Forum Romanum was believed originally to have belonged to the Sabines.

13.] *Murus*. There was no other wall but the mountains,—no *agger*, no *Roma Quadrata*, no *pomœrium*.—*Curia*, the Curia Hostilia at the foot of the Capitoline hill. *ex illo fonte*, 'from a spring (or pond) on that spot,' viz. that inclosed by a palisade by Tatius, sup. 7. From this spring, but at its source, or at some point on the hill-side, Tarpeia on one occasion drew water in her urn for the service of Vesta. Then first she saw Tatius, and fell in love at the sight of his kingly bearing and comely form.

16.] *Urgebat*, premebat, ἔπιεζε.—*fictilis*, the terra-cotta urn used by Vestals. So *Fast.* iii. 14 (of the Vestal Silvia), 'ponitur e summa fictilis urna coma.' Pers. *Sat.* ii. 60, 'aurum—vestalesque urnas et Tuscum fictile mutat.'

Et satis una malæ potuit mors esse puellæ,
Quæ voluit flammas fallere, Vesta, tuas?
Vidit harenosis Tatium proludere campis
Pictaque per flavas arma levare jubas:
Obstupuit regis facie et regalibus armis,
Interque oblitas excidit urna manus.
Sæpe illa immeritæ causata est omina lunæ,
Et sibi tingendas dixit in amne comas:
Sæpe tulit blandis argentea lilia Nymphis,
Romula ne faciem læderet hasta Tati:
Dumque subit primo Capitolia nubila fumo,
Rettulit hirsutis brachia secta rubis,
Et sua Tarpeia residens ita flevit ab arce

17.] *Una.* As the punishment of a faithless Vestal was to be buried alive, this cruel fate is called 'many deaths,' like the Greek *μυριάκις* or *πολλάκις τεθνάναι*. So Hor. *Carm.* iii. 27, 37, quoted by Barth, 'levis una mors est Virginum culpæ.'—*voluit fallere*, *θέλει* or *ἔτλη προδοῦναι*, 'consented to betray.' The remark anticipates the statement, that she fell in love with the royal barbarian whom she saw exercising on the level sand, and raising his arms, from his superior height, over the crested helmets of his officers around him.—*per*, i.e. *inter*, as in iv. 1, 4.

22.] *Excidit*, cf. inf. 7, 96, 'inter complexus excidit umbra meos.' The sense merely is, that she forgot to take again into her hands the urn that she had lifted from her head.

23—6.] *Causata est*, *προφασίζετο*, 'often she pleaded as an excuse (viz. for going to the spring) some ominous appearance of the moon, when the moon was not to be blamed, and declared that she must dip her hair in the water. Often too she brought silver lilies to the gentle nymphs of the spring, that the spear of Romulus might not harm the handsome face of her Tatius.' Compare Tibull. i. 3, 17, 'aut ego sum causatus aves aut omina dira.' Tac. *Ann.* i. 47, 'mox hiemem aut negotia vario causatus primo prudentes, dein vulgum, diutissime provincias fefellit.' *immeritæ*, sup. 3, 19. The 'omens' were, of course, pretended; but eclipses, which were attributed to sorcery, were always dreaded, Tac. *Ann.* i. 28. The dipping the head in running water was done *avertendi ominis gratia*. Pers. *Sat.* ii. 16, 'hæc sancte ut poscas, Tiberino in gurgite mergis Mane caput bis terque, et noctem flumine purgas.'

26.] *Romula*, for *Romulea*, like 'Romula vincla' in iv. 11, 52. The meaning appears to be, that while she professed to be making a pious offering to the Naiad nymphs, she accompanied it with a prayer that they would protect her Tatius, who had taken the spring under his own care, sup. 7. Hence this visit also to the spring was made under false pretences.

27.] *Subit*, ascendit.—*primo fumo* may mean the early evening smoke, when the fires were lighted for cooking the evening meal. Virg. *Ecl.* i. 83, 'et jam summa procul villarum culmina fumant, Majoresque cadunt longis de montibus umbræ.' If the morning smoke is meant, we must suppose she had been absent all night, which is unlikely, or at least, that she had gone out very early.—*rubis*, because the hill-side was *spinosus*, inf. 48.

29.] *Ita*, in the following terms (31—46). Barth and Müller extend the speech or soliloquy of the maid to ver. 66; but the address in ver. 48 should be regarded as distinct, since *flevit* is inapplicable to the command there given.—*vulnera*, the wounds of love, which, as they were destined to cause the betrayal of the Arx to the Sabines, were not to be tolerated, *οὐ συγγνωστά*, by the god of the neighbouring height (Jupiter Tarpeius, or Capitolinus, sup. 1, 6—7), especially in a Vestal. Compare inf. 86, 'Sed Jupiter unus decrevit pœnis invigilare tuis.' Lachmann and Hertzberg prefer to make *patienda* the nominative; 'she, who ought not to have been admitted to the Arx from which her complaints were made.'

Vulnera, vicino non patienda Jovi:
'Ignes castrorum et Tatiæ prætoria turmæ
Et formosa oculis arma Sabina meis,
O utinam ad vestros sedeam captiva Penates,
Dum captiva mei conspicer ora Tati.
Romani montes et montibus addita Roma
Et valeat probro Vesta pudenda meo.
Ille equus, ille meos in castra reponet amores,
Cui Tatius dextras collocat ipse jubas.
Quid mirum in patrios Scyllam sævisse capillos,
Candidaque in sævos inguina versa canes?
Prodita quid mirum fraterni cornua monstri,
Cum patuit lecto stamine torta via?
Quantum ego sum Ausoniis crimen factura puellis,
Improba virgineo lecta ministra foco!
Pallados extinctos si quis mirabitur ignes,

32.] *Formosa oculis meis.* They were *picta arma* sup. 20, and would have been thought barbaric and the reverse of beautiful by less prejudiced Roman eyes.

34.] *Ora*, 'provided only that I might gaze a captive on the face of my Tatius.' A beautiful sentiment. The Naples MS. gives *ore Tati*, the Groning. MS. *arma Tati*. As in i. 3, 16, and iv. 13, 54, *ora* and *arma* have been interchanged by the transcribers, who here seem to have copied *arma* from 32 sup. Compare inf. 6, 32—4.

35.] Tarpeia now speaks as if she had formed a desperate resolve to make at once for the enemy's camp, and to bid good-bye to Rome and her service of the goddess.—*addita*, mountains lately covered with wood, *collis et herba*, sup. 1, 2, now crowned with buildings that add to their height.—*pudenda*, like *verba pigenda* sup. 1, 74, and *barba pudenda* inf. 8, 26, 'Vesta, whom I ought to be ashamed of for my crime.'

37.] *Meos amores* is explained *me amantem*; 'that horse and none other shall take me back to the camp (*i.e.* where my heart has long been), whose mane my Tatius with his own hand arranges on the right side of the neck.' But I am now inclined to think *meos amores* means Tatius himself; and thus she wishes she were the horse whose happy lot it was to bear his master back to the camp. Müller approves the conjecture of Broukhusius, *reportet* for *reponet*.

38.] *Dextras.* Virgil, *Georgic*, iii. 86, 'densa juba, et dextro jactata recumbit in armo.'

39—42.] She now recals cases of broken faith through the force of love, and says she can feel and understand the strength of the motive. 'What wonder is it that Scylla should have betrayed her father, and Ariadne her brother the Minotaur, by giving Theseus a clue to guide him out of the labyrinth?' For the legend of Scylla see iv. 19, 21. Propertius has confounded the Homeric monster (the cuttle-fish) with the daughter of Nisus, king of Megara; but other poets have done the same. See Virg. *Ecl.* vi. 74, 'Scyllam Nisi, quam fama secuta est, Candida succinctam latrantibus inguina monstris.' Ovid, *Fast.* iv. 500, and *Ars. Am.* i. 331.

41.] *Cornua*, 'the horned monster her brother,' the Minotaur.—*lecto stamine*, 'by the clue which he took up as he went along.' This is the literal and perhaps primary sense of *legere*, as in 'legere litus,' 'flumina' &c. Ovid, *Her.* x. 103, 'nec tibi quæ reditus monstrarent, fila dedissem, Fila per adductas sæpe recepta manus.'

43.] *Quantum* &c. A feeling of remorse at her resolve comes over her mind: 'But then what a cause of reproach I am about to bring on Italian maidens, for having been chosen to serve the altar of the goddess, unworthy wretch that I am!'

45.] *Pallados.* The Palladium (*Fast.* vi. 421 seqq.) is sometimes confounded with Vesta, in whose temple the image,

Ignoscat: lacrimis spargitur ara meis.
Cras, ut rumor ait, tota pugnabitur urbe:
Tu cape spinosi rorida terga jugi.
Lubrica tota via est et perfida; quippe tacentes
Fallaci celat limite semper aquas.
O utinam magicæ nossem cantamina Musæ!
Hæc quoque formoso lingua tulisset opem.
Te toga picta decet, non quem sine matris honore
Nutrit inhumanæ dura papilla lupæ.
Sive hospes, pariamve tua regina sub aula,

brought from Troy, was preserved. Ovid, *Trist.* iii. 1, 29, 'hic locus est Vestæ, qui Pallada servat et ignem.'—*ignoscat*, 'let him make allowance for, let him pardon, the seeming negligence; the altar was wet with my tears and the fire would not burn.' A truly poetical idea.

47.] Tarpeia now makes the resolve. She will betray the citadel at all hazards, and she chooses a day when the guards are on holiday and their attention will not be directed to the enemy's movements (inf. 81). At present, she gives the very opposite reason, viz. the prospect of a general fight on the morrow. It is not easy to reconcile the two, especially as 'convenit hostem' in 81 seems to indicate her first actual meeting with Tatius. In either case however the time named would be suitable to the attempt. But does *tu cape* (or *tu cave*) refer to Tatius, or is she exhorting herself? I rather suspect the latter, even though *te* in 53 is certainly addressed to him. She must either invite him to ascend the hill for an interview, or herself to descend for the same purpose. Then *cape*, the reading of the copies, is altered into *cave* by every editor but Hertzberg. In the latter case, we may compare inf. 5, 6, 'virgo, tale iter omne cave,' and understand 'beware how you ascend the back of the thorn-clad hill, for the whole path is dangerous and slippery from the hidden streamlet.' On the other hand, *cape*, if addressed to herself, will mean the thorny path already familiar to her, and the same as that mentioned sup. 28, 'rettulit hirsutis brachia secta rubis.' And thus also *lubrica* and *perfida* will have a very significant and appropriate *double entendre*; 'the road is one of danger and perfidy,' *i.e.* of betrayal, and 'one that is slippery and treacherous to the feet.' Reading, then, with the MSS., *tu cape*, she will mean 'take that path, but remember that it is a dangerous one.' Of course, *cape* or *cave* may be conceived as spoken to Tatius in his absence; but it is a pointless thing to give a special direction where one knows it cannot be heard.

50.] *Aquas.* Either the spring before alluded to (15), or a hot sulphureous spring which, according to Ovid, was sent forth by the god Janus expressly to stop the ascent of the Sabines:

'Oraque, qua pollens ope sum, fontana reclusi,
Sumque repentinas ejaculatus aquas.
Ante tamen madidis subjeci sulpura venis,
Clauderet ut Tatio fervidus humor iter.'

—On the short vowel before *spinosi*, see sup. 1, 41.—*limite*, cf. inf. 9, 60, 'hæc lympha puellis Avia secreti limitis una fluit.'

51.] *Utinam &c.* 'Would that, like Medea, I knew the incantations of magic song! Then would my tongue too, like her's, bring aid to my handsome knight.'

53.] *Te.* 'You, barbarian and enemy though they call you, the robe of victory should grace: not him who, born of an unhonoured mother (a faithless Vestal), was nurtured by the hard teat of a she-wolf that had nothing of the human in it.' Martial, *Ep.* x. 48, 14, 'hœdus inhumani raptus ab ore lupi.' Cf. sup. 1, 38, 'sanguinis altricem non pudet esse lupam.'

55.] The MSS. read *sic hospes pariamve tua* &c., which Müller retains, but marks as corrupt, after Lachmann. So also Barth and the older editors. Mr. Wratislaw thinks the vulgate may stand for *sive—sive*, 'Whether it be as a guest (*i. e.* concubine) or as a queen (*i.e.* legitimate wife) that I bear children within your palace.' Hertzberg reads 'sic, hospes, patriæve tua regina sub aula;' Jacob, with Pucci, 'si conjux, pariamve tua' &c. I think *sive—pariamve* is sufficiently defended by 5, 19, 'exornabat opus verbis, seu blanda pararet Saxosamve terat sedula culpa viam.'

Dos tibi non humilis prodita Roma venit.
Si minus, at, raptæ ne sint inpune Sabinæ,
Me rape, et alterna lege rependo vices.
Commissas acies ego possum solvere; nuptæ,
Vos medium palla fœdus inite mea.
Adde, Hymenæe, modos; tubicen fera murmura conde;
Credite, vestra meus molliet arma torus.
Et jam quarta canit venturam buccina lucem,
Ipsaque in Oceanum sidera lapsa cadunt.
Experiar somnum; de te mihi somnia quæram:
Fac venias oculis umbra benigna meis.
Dixit, et incerto permisit brachia somno,
Nescia væ furiis accubuisse novis.
Nam Vesta, Iliacæ felix tutela favillæ,
Culpam alit, et plures condit in ossa faces.

57.] *Si minus* &c. 'If these terms please you not, then carry me off as a reprisal for the rape of the Sabine women. The good copies have *si*, not '*sin* minus,' as Barth and Kuinoel have edited.

59.] *Solvere*, as inf. 8, 88, 'tuto solvimus arma toro.' The sense is, 'It is in *my* power, *i.e.* not that of the generals, to separate the armies engaged in the fight.' This is what the Sabine women were said to have done, expressing their willingness to remain with their Roman conquerors, *Fast.* iii. 217 seqq.—*nuptæ*, 'ye Sabine brides,' viz. in whose cause this war is being waged.—*palla mea*, nuptiis meis; the ablative implying the means whereby the treaty was to be effected. The *palla* seems to have been used as a marriage-dress. Hertzberg cites Ovid, *Her.* 21, 162, 'et trahitur multo splendida palla croco.'—*medium fœdus* means simply a treaty between the two contending parties; 'a *mediating* treaty,' perhaps.

61.] *Tubicen*. Let us have the *tibia* for the marriage strain, and not the *tuba* with its war-notes wild.—*meus torus*, again for 'nuptiæ meæ.' This, she says, will be no rape, but a voluntary marriage on my part.—*vestra arma*, the contest about you,—'my *marriage* (a surer bond than a *rapina* for reprisal) shall allay the anger of those who would reclaim you or retain you by force of arms.'—*molliet*, solvet, compescet, καταλύσει μάχην.

63—6.] A beautiful passage. Weary with watching, excitement, and grief, she lies down by her altar for repose. I may be allowed to cite a few lines from my 'Verse Translations from Propertius:'

'Now the fourth bugle calls the coming morn;
The very stars sink paled before the dawn.
Come sleep, come pleasing visions of the night;
Come thou, kind shade, and bless my longing sight!
She spoke, and sank with wearied arms to rest?
Unlooked-for demons still her sleep infest:—
Vesta, blest guardian of the Trojan fires,
Burns in her bones, and kindles fierce desires.'

65.] *De te*, cf. Martial, *Ep.* vii. 54, 1, 'semper mane mihi de me tua somnia narras.'—*fac venias*, like *fac transeas*, inf. 11, 68; *fac sentire*, 5, 34.—*benigna*, in angelic form, as we should say; not as a 'goblin damned.'

67.] *Incerto*, 'fitful.'—*permisit brachia*, a formula of complete submission, as *dare manus, brachia victa*, sup. 3, 12.—*accubuisse*, 'little thinking she had lain down near one (Vesta) who would be to her a fresh cause of passion.' Vesta, whom Tarpeia had wronged, now becomes to her a *Furia* and a vengeful power, though the *kindly* guardian of the sacred fire.' Perhaps indeed we should read *succubuisse*, 'that she had given way to a passion that would bring a fresh curse,' *i.e.* her death by violence. Müller, after Lachmann and the older editors, reads *ex furiis*, the MSS. giving *nefariis*. Jacob, whom Hertzberg follows, proposed *ve*.—*condit in ossa*, viz. as the goddess of fire, 'subdit ossibus ignem.'

Illa ruit, qualis celerem prope Thermodonta
  Strymonis abscisso fertur aperta sinu.
Urbi festus erat, dixere Parilia patres,
  Hic primus cœpit mœnibus esse dies,
Annua pastorum convivia, lusus in urbe,
  Cum pagana madent fercula deliciis,
Cumque super raros fœni flammantis acervos
  Traicit immundos ebria turba pedes.
Romulus excubias decrevit in otia solvi
  Atque intermissa castra silere tuba.
Hoc Tarpeia suum tempus rata convenit hostem:
  Pacta ligat, pactis ipsa futura comes.
Mons erat ascensu dubius festoque remissus:
  Nec mora, vocales occupat ense canes.
Omnia præbebant somnos: sed Juppiter unus
  Decrevit pœnis invigilare tuis.
Prodiderat portæque fidem patriamque jacentem,

71.] *Ruit*, μεγάροιο διέσσυτο μαινάδι ἴση, *Il.* xxii. 460.—*illa* is used superfluously, as sup. 2, 45, inf. 6, 63.—*Strymonis* is usually taken for an Amazon, on account of the locality (Æsch. *Prom.* 744) on the river Thermodon. More probably a Thracian Bacchante was meant, especially as Propertius often shows vague notions of geography.—*sinu*, the folds of the dress, προστέρνοι στολμοί, Æsch. *Cho.* 27, which were torn off in the mad excitement of the race.

73.] *Festus erat*, supply *dies* from the next verse. This is better than, with Lachmann and Haupt, to inclose *dixere—mos* in a parenthesis.—*dixere*, indixerant; the burghers had given notice of a general holiday on the feast of the Parilia or Palilia (sup. 1, 19).—*primus cœpit esse*, a poetical way of saying 'hic primus dies fuit condendis mœnibus,' or 'primus dies, quo cœperunt esse mœnia.'

76.] *Pagana fercula*, 'when the platters of the shepherds in the *pagi*, or hill fastnesses, are moistened with richer fare,' lit. with more oil in them than usual. The 'uncta patella' (Pers. *Sat.* iv. 17), and 'madidi penates' (Mart. *Ep.* vii. 27, 5), are opposed to 'siccos cibos,' ξηρὸς σῖτος, ordinary dry fare,—our phrase 'dry bread.'

77.] *Raros*, 'placed at intervals.' See sup. on 1, 19.—*immundos pedes*, 'their grimy feet,' is a certain correction of *immundas dapes*, an error arising, as Hertzberg supposes, from the mind of the transcriber being fixed on the *fercula* preceding.

80.] *Intermissa*, 'discontinued for a time,' viz. for the day's holiday. So 'intermissa custodiis loca,' Livy, xxiv. 35.

81.] *Suum*, thinking their time was her time; judging that her chance of having an interview with Tatius was now a good one.—*ligat*, 'she makes the compact a binding one by promising herself to take a part in the fulfilment of it.' The bargain is to be null and void unless she is there at the appointed time to open the gates. Thus *comes pactis* is a short way of saying 'adfutura cum pacta rata fient.'

83.] *Remissus*, 'left unguarded.' 'Nam loca natura munitissima ideoque ascensu difficillima, maxime negligi ab oppugnatis solent.'—*Hertzberg.*

84.] *Occupat*, *i.e.* Tatius; he silences the dogs by striking them with his sword before they could give tongue; φθάνει ὑλακτεῖν.

85.] *Omnia*, the holiday, the good cheer, the wine &c.—*unus*, *i.e.* as the other guards were asleep, Jupiter resolved that he at least would keep awake to punish the traitress. Barth, Lachmann, and others give *suis*, but against the good copies. Sudden apostrophes are a remarkable feature in the style of Propertius.

87.] *Portæ fidem*, portæ custodiam. Her father was in fact the warder, but she would naturally have an easy task in be-

Nubendique petit, quem velit ipse, diem.
At Tatius (neque enim sceleri dedit hostis honorem)
'Nube,' ait, 'et regni scande cubile mei.'
Dixit, et ingestis comitum super obruit armis.
Hæc, virgo, officiis dos erat apta tuis.
A duce Tarpeio mons est cognomen adeptus:
O vigil, injustæ præmia sortis habes.

V.

Terra tuum spinis obducat, lena, sepulcrum,
Et tua, quod non vis, sentiat umbra sitim,
Nec sedeant cineri Manes, et Cerberus ultor

traying it. Livy, i. 11, 'Sp. Tarpeius Romanæ præerat arci. Hujus filiam virginem auro corrumpit Tatius, ut armatos in arcem accipiat. Aquam forte ea tum sacris extra mœnia petitum ierat. Accepti obrutam armis necavere, seu ut vi capta potius arx videretur, seu prodendi exempli causa, ne quid usquam fidum proditori esset.'—*jacentem*, 'somno,' perhaps; 'vino somnoque sepultam,' *Barth.*—*ipse*, she leaves it to Tatius to name the day. Hertzberg and Barth retain the MSS. reading *ipsa*. The difference is not very important, but the best editors agree in accepting *ipse*.

89.] *Hostis*, though an enemy, he had a noble soul, and would not give credit to treachery. Propertius had a patriotic zeal which was superior to the charms of women. Hence of Tarpeia the Vestal, not less than of Cleopatra the Queen, he speaks in terms of bitter reproach, as sup. iv. 11, 29 and 39, inf. 6, 22 &c.

90.] *Scande cubile*, a poetical way of saying 'become my queen,' or, 'be this your royal bed,' the place where you will lie.

91.] *Armis*. Livy, i. 11, and Ovid, *Fast.* i. 261, represent Tarpeia to have been bribed by the golden bracelets of the Sabines, and then treacherously killed by the weight of their shields.—*virgo*, i.e. as a faithless Vestal such a death, to be buried alive, was a befitting end. But *dos* may have reference to the Sabine *armillæ* as her marriage portion.—*officiis*, your services in betraying to them the capital. Cf. sup. 66.

93.] *Tarpeio*. The sense seems to be, that from the father, not from the daughter, the Tarpeian rock obtained its name. Thus the warder, *vigil*, though he lost a daughter, which was *injusta sors* to one who had not deserved it, yet obtained the honour in question. Keil, Müller, and Mr. Wratislaw read *Tarpeia*, and *injuste*, with Lachmann, who explains the verse thus: 'Tarpeia culpæ sui præmia immerito accepit, monte Tarpeio ab ea nomen adepto.'

V. This difficult but rather important poem in part resembles the *Ibis* of Ovid, and is yet more plainly imitated by that poet in *Amor.* i. 8, as Kuinoel has observed. It contains a malediction on an old *lena* called Acanthis (ver. 61), who appears to have incurred the resentment of our poet for some reasons unknown to us, and perhaps unconnected with his love for Cynthia. It is probable too that Ovid borrowed the idea of his *Art of Love* from vv. 21—60. And to the same verses he alludes when he says (*Trist.* ii. 461), speaking of Tibullus, 'Multaque dat talis furti præcepta, docetque Qua nuptæ possint fallere ab arte viros.'—Invenies eadem blandi præcepta Properti,'—lines which Lachmann has too hastily used as a proof that not all Propertius' writings have come down to us (*Praef.* p. xxi.)

1.] *Spinis*, in allusion to the name Acanthis; 'thorny in life, may you be thorny also in death.'—*quod non vis*, which you, as a tippler, would specially dislike. Compare the propensities of the *lena* in Plautus, *Curcul.* i. 2.

3.] *Nec sedeant*. 'May your shade not rest on your grave, and may vengeful Cerberus scare those foul old bones by his hungry bark.' The notion of the ghost flitting restlessly over the tomb seems as old as literature. See Eur. *Hec.* 37;

Turpia jejuno terreat ossa sono,
Docta vel Hippolytum Veneri mollire negantem,
Concordique toro pessima semper avis,
Penelopen quoque neglecto rumore mariti
Nubere lascivo cogeret Antinoo.
Illa velit, poterit magnes non ducere ferrum
Et volucris nidis esse noverca suis.
Quippe et, Collinas ad fossam moverit herbas,
Stantia currenti diluerentur aqua.
Audax cantatæ leges imponere lunæ
Et sua nocturno fallere terga lupo,
Posset ut intentos astu cæcare maritos,
Cornicum immeritas eruit ungue genas,

Æsch. *Pers.* 686; Plat. *Phæd.* p. 81, c, ψυχὴ—περὶ τὰ μνήματά τε καὶ τοὺς τάφους κυλινδουμένη, περὶ ἃ δὴ καὶ ὤφθη ἄττα ψυχῶν σκιοειδῆ φαντάσματα. Inf. 11, 8. *Ibid.* 25, 'Cerberus et nullas hodie petat improbus umbras.'

5—8.] *Docta* &c. 'One who had skill enough to reconcile the reluctant Hippolytus to the goddess of love, and who ever brought the worst luck on a well-assorted marriage' (*i.e.* by causing groundless jealousies), 'would have forced even a Penelope to give up all concern to hear news of her husband, and to marry the amorous Antinous.' See *Od.* xiv. 126 seqq.—*concordi*, ὁμόφρονας αὐτὰς, Pind. *Ol.* vi. init. Eur. *Med.* 15, ὅταν γυνὴ πρὸς ἄνδρα μὴ διχοστατῇ.—*avis*, as 'mala ducis avi domum' &c., Hor. *Carm.* i. 15, 5.

9—10.] *Velit*, si velit, as 'suppetat hoc' sup. 2, 37, 'moverit' inf. 11 &c. 'Should she desire it, the magnet could lose its power of attracting iron, and a bird could play the step-dame to its own nest,' *i.e.* by turning out of it its own callow young.

11.] The 'Colline herbs' were supposed to have a special magic power, because near the Porta Collina was the 'Campus Sceleratus,' said to have been the cemetery for the Vestal Virgins who were doomed to be buried alive. So the grave-yard on the Esquiliæ was used, Hor. *Sat.* i. 8, 22.—*moverit*, 'let her but apply to the magic trench the rank weeds from the Colline field, and solid rocks would melt away in flowing water.' Compare a fine passage on the supposed power of witchcraft, Tibull. i. 2, 43—54.—*stantia*, 'res solidissimæ et firmæ liquescerent, mutata ipsa rerum natura.'—*Barth.* So Horace has 'stat nive candidum Soracte,' 'stat glacies iners' &c.

13—16.] The construction of these lines is nearly the same as 5—8. 'Daring as she was in forcing the enchanted moon to obey her spells, and in disguising her own form by that of a night-prowling wolf, her custom was, in order to blind by her craft the keen-eyed husbands, to gouge out the eyes of poor harmless ravens with her nail.' This is a very curious passage. See Becker, *Gallus*, p. 120. The ancient and singular superstition that witches could change themselves into other forms, especially into that of the *were-wolf*, and so become *versipelles*, is not yet extinct. I myself remember a whole village in a panic because an old woman was said to have been seen in the form of a white hare, and at another time in that of a white pigeon. See Herod. iv. 105, κινδυνεύουσι δὲ οἱ ἄνθρωποι οὗτοι γόητες εἶναι, λέγονται γὰρ ὑπὸ Σκυθέων καὶ Ἑλλήνων—ὡς ἔτεος ἑκάστου ἅπαξ τῶν Νευρῶν ἕκαστος λύκος γίνεται ἡμέρας ὀλίγας, καὶ αὖτις ὀπίσω ἐς ταὐτὰ κατίσταται. For the use of *fallere* compare inf. 11, 80, 'cum venient, siccis oscula falle genis.' Virg. *Æn.* i. 684, 'tu faciem illius noctem non amplius unam Falle dolo.'—For *posset ut* the MSS. give *posset et*, which Lachmann and Jacob retain, placing a full stop at the end of the verse.

16.] *Genas*, *i.e.* oculos. The notion was, that if the eyes of a crow were added to a love-potion (like the 'eye of newt,' in Shakespeare's *Macbeth*), they would draw away, by a sort of mesmeric influence, or in some way neutralise by their superior brightness, the vigilance of the husband's eye.

Consuluitque striges nostro de sanguine et in me
  Hippomanes fetæ semina legit equæ.
Exornabat opus verbis, seu blanda perurat
  Saxosamve terat sedula culpa viam:
'Si te Eoa, Doryxenium, juvat aurea ripa,
  Et quæ sub Tyria concha superbit aqua,
Eurypylique placet Coæ textura Minervæ

17—18.] For *striges* I suspect that we should read *strigas*. The strigæ (the modern Italian *streghe*) were a kind of bird-witch, supposed to carry off and kill or lacerate infants in their cradle. (See my note on Ovid, *Fast.* vi. 131). Plautus, *Pseud.* 820, 'non condimentis condiunt, sed strigibus, Vivis convivis intestina quæ exedint.' It appears from this, that though the short ĕ before *striges* may be defended (sup. 4, 48), we might here read 'consuluit strigas.'—*de sanguine*, 'nece,' 'caede.'—*Kuinoel.*—Virg. *Georgic.* iii. 280, 'hippomanes, quod sæpe malæ legere novercæ, Miscueruntque herbas et non innoxia verba.'

19—20.] *Exornabat* Kuinoel, Barth and Lachmann. The more recent editors retain *exorabat*, the MSS. reading; but the phrase *opus exorare* conveys no intelligible meaning, naturally at least. On the other hand *exornare* is like the Greek κοσμεῖν ἔργα 'to dress up exploits' by the graces of poetry, music &c. The passage is difficult, and variously explained and read, some giving *perreret* for *perurat* on conjecture, *lympha* for *culpa* from one or two inferior MSS., and varying between *seu* of the good copies and *seu*, *saxosamque* and *saxosamve*. The sense seems to be this: 'she dressed up (or glozed over) her vile work by specious words, whether the seductive crime (*blanda culpa*) fires the victim, or slowly (*sedula*) wears its way in a stony heart.' For *seu—ve* = *seu—sive*, see sup. iv. 55. The metaphor seems taken from the opposite effects of water and fire, the one wearing away a stone drop by drop, the other setting ablaze the fuel it touches; and these effects are transferred to phlegmatic or excitable constitutions. With *perurat* supply *puellæ animum* or *ingenium*, *viam* belonging only to *terat*. The emended reading *viam perreret teritque*, which allows the retention of the MSS. reading *saxosamque*, of course refers only to the slow effects of water; and thus *viam* forms the object to both verbs alike.

21—62.] These lines contain the infamous advice of the old woman to some young girl, who is here named (according to a common Greek usage of forming the ὑποκόρισμα of a harlot by a neuter diminutive) *Doryxenium*, Δορυξένιον. The MSS. have *dorozantheum*, or *dorozantum*, with some varieties, all of which are confessedly corrupt. My own conjecture, *Doryxenium*, I find has been anticipated by Jacob. Hertzberg considers *Dorozantum*, 'ignotum populi Indici nomen;' and Keil and Müller adopt this. Turnebus perceived that the name of a girl was required by the sense; but he proposed one of unintelligible formation, *Dorozanium*, which Lachmann prefers, therein following Barth. The sense is, 'If you wish for the gold of the east, or Tyrian purple,' &c. By the indefinite term *aurea ripa*, we may understand the eastern shore of the Erythræan sea, the ancient Ophir, *ripa* being used improperly, as conversely *litus* in i. 2, 13. Hertzberg raises the objection, that Cynthia in particular is here meant. But where is the proof? The poet is describing in general terms the insidious arts which the old woman practised on her youthful victims. Nor is *nostra amica*, v. 63, conclusive in his favour, since *his* may very well mean 'his atque talibus.'

22.] *Concha*. Our poet speaks of the shell that furnishes the sea-purple (a species of whelk) as if its purple hue were visible in the water, which of course is not the case; so that we must regard *superbit* as a poetical hyperbole.

23.] *Eurypyli*. The double genitive is not so rare as to cause any reasonable perplexity. See sup. i. 103. 'Eurypylus's texture of Coan art,' is not more strange than 'so and so's Manchester cotton' would sound to our ears. Eurypylus was an ancient king of Cos. *Il.* ii. 677. See on i. 2, 2. Hertzberg makes *Eurypyli* the genitive after *Coæ*, which is scarcely good Latinity.

24.] *Putria signa*. 'Tattered fragments of tapestry cut from divans which belonged to Attalus,' king of Pergamus, whose wealth

Sectaque ab Attalicis putria signa toris,
Seu quæ palmiferæ mittunt venalia Thebæ,
 Murreaque in Parthis pocula cocta focis,
Sperne fidem, provolve deos, mendacia vincant,
 Frange et damnosæ jura pudicitiæ.
Et simulare virum pretium facit: utere causis:
 Major dilata nocte recurret amor.
Si tibi forte comas vexaverit utilis ira,
 Post modo mercata pace premendus erit.
Denique ubi amplexu Venerem promiseris empto,
 Fac simules puros Isidis esse dies.
Ingerat Apriles Iole tibi, tundat Amycle

was inherited by the Roman people. Hertzberg thinks that *signa* are the designs in overlaid wood, ivory, or tortoise-shell, so often mentioned in connexion with the ancient *spondæ* or sofas. This is not improbable in itself, as the Romans were extremely fond of collecting articles of *vertu*. But the eastern method of covering settees with rich embroidery is not to be overlooked. Ælian, *Var. Hist.* viii. 7, (speaking of an entertainment given by Alexander), καὶ ἑκάστη κλίνη ἀργυρόπους ἦν, ἡ δὲ αὐτοῦ χρυσόπους. Καὶ κατέστρωντο πᾶσαι ἁλουργοῖς καὶ ποικίλοις ἱματίοις ὑφῆς βαρβαρικῆς μεγατίμων.—For *putria* compare Plaut. *Rudens*, 1321, 'tramas putidas,' 'rotten woof.' Hor. *Sat.* ii. 3, 118, 'cui stragula vestis, Blattarum ac tinearum epulæ, putrescat in arca.' Martial, *Ep.* v. 62, 6, 'nulla tegit fractos nec inanis culcita lectos, Putris et abrupta fascia reste jacet.'

26.] The peculiar ware called *murrea* or *murrhine vases*, a manufacture now lost, is well known from frequent allusion to it, to have been highly prized by the Romans. According to Pliny, xxxvii. 2, quoted by Kuinoel, Parthia was one of the places where it was made. Supposed specimens of it exist in many museums. The fabric of those generally exhibited appears to be glass. The *Dictionary of Antiquities* says, 'Most recent writers are inclined to think that they were true Chinese porcelain,' and the present passage is adduced in support of the opinion. Martial also speaks of 'myrrhina picta,' xiii. 110. See also *ibid.* ix. 59, 14. Becker, *Gallus*, p. 304, on the authority of Pliny, *N.H.* xxxvii. 2, 8, considers the true murrhine vases to have been made of fluor spa, and regards those mentioned in the text as imitations.

27.] *Provolve deos.* 'Eos pedibus velut proculca, a sacrariis proturba, exquisite pro, contemne deos.'—*Kuinoel.* The general sense from v. 21 is, 'If you expect your wishes to be gratified, you must not be scrupulous.'

> 'Spurn faith, despise divine and human laws;
> Break virtue's precepts; 'tis a losing cause.'

29.] The obvious sense of this verse, 'it pays too to pretend that you are a married woman,' seems preferable to Hertzberg's explanation: 'simulatio amatorem pretium *facit*, *i.e.* efficit ut ex viro lucrum facias,' for which he quotes 'Nunc pretium fecere deos,' sup. v. 1, 81. The pretended difficulty thrown in the way of the lover would of course induce him to give larger bribes.—*utere causis*, 'make the best use of reasons for refusal,' *i.e.* by rejecting him on the particular occasion make him more importunate, and so more liberal in his offers.

31.] 'All the better for you if he ruffles your hair in anger: you will make him pay for peace, and so keep a tight rein over him for the future.' Hertzberg places a comma after *vexaverit*, and understands 'utilis (erit) ira.'

34.] *Fac simules*, cf. sup. 4, 66.—*Isidis*, the correction of Beroaldus, is adopted by the best editors for *sideris*, the sacred festival of Isis, on which *secubitus*, or the separation of the sexes, was rigidly enforced. Ovid, *Amor.* i. 8, 73, 'Sæpe nega noctes, capiti modo finge dolorem, Et modo quæ causas præbeat, Isis erit.' Hertzberg thinks *sideris dies* may mean *dies Saturni*, 'Saturday,' the *sabbata* of the Jews, Pers. *Sat.* v. 180. Tibull. i. 3, 18, 'Saturni aut sacram me tenuisse diem.'

35.] *Ingerat*, 'force upon your notice.' Tac. *Ann.* i. 72, 'nomen patris patriæ Tiberius, a populo sæpius ingestum, repu-

Natalem Maiis Idibus esse tuum.
Supplex ille sedet: posita tu scribe cathedra
Quidlibet: has artes si pavet ille, tenes.
Semper habe morsus circa tua colla recentes,
Litibus alternis quos putet esse datos.
Nec te Medeæ delectent probra sequacis
(Nempe tulit fastus ausa rogare prior),
Sed potius mundi Thais pretiosa Menandri,
Cum ferit astutos comica mœcha Getas.
In mores te verte viri: si cantica jactat,
I comes et voces ebria junge tuas.
Janitor ad dantes vigilet: si pulset inanis,
Surdus in obductam somniet usque seram.
Nec tibi displiceat miles non factus amori,
Nauta nec attrita, si ferat æra, manu,

disvit.' Pers. *Sat.* v. 177, 'donec ingens large Rixanti populo.' The sense is, 'Let your maids come in one after the other and remind you, in his presence, that you expect a present.'—*Apriles*, either *Kalendas* or *Idus*; an unusual ellipse. There may be an allusion to a ceremony performed to the statue of Venus by the *meretrices*, mentioned in *Fast.* iv. 133 seqq. See also *Ars Am.* i. 417, 'Magna superstitio tibi sit natalis amicæ, Quaque aliquid dandum est, atra sit illa dies.' On both these occasions the lover, of course, was expected to be liberal.—*tundat*, 'din into you,' as if you had forgotten it.—*Maiis* for *malis* the later editions; *Mais* Müller.

37.] *Supplex* &c. Here the art is to be tried of pretended indifference. 'Suppose that he sits a suppliant for your favour. Well, take your easy chair and write anything you please. If he shows fear of these arts, then you have him.'—*quidlibet* seems to show that the mere act of writing, *i.e.* the inattention thereby implied to the lover's request, rather than the penning of an invitation to a rival, is meant.—*cathedra* was the chair especially in use by women. —*tenes*, ἔχεις, ἔχεις αὐτόν.

39.] *Morsus.* Next *jealousy* is to be roused. 'Affect to have marks upon your face left by some lover's fray, that he may think you have been too familiar with his rival.' See sup. 3, 25.

41.] *Nec te* &c. 'And be not too forward or free in your taunts and reproaches, or you will alienate his affections.'—*sequacis*, 'persecuting,' 'importunate.' The epithet does not seem to refer to the character in the play of Euripides, though *probra*, in its literal sense, suits it well enough. Perhaps the poet meant *sequitia*, 'amorousness.' See Eur. *Med.* 285.—*nempe*, cf. inf. 11, 6; 'in fact, she gained for herself dislike by being too forward in asking.'

43.] *Sed potius.* 'Rather be the high-priced Thais of the elegant Menander, when the girl in the comedy makes the cunning Getan slaves to fall in love with her.'—*ferit*, a metaphor from gladiators. So in iv. 3, 50, 'Qui volet austeros arte ferire viros.' In Plautus, *Trinum.* 247, 'ibi illa pendentem ferit;' perhaps the punishment of slaves is alluded to, though *ferit* means 'capit,' 'fascinates.'—*comici*, κομψοῦ, neat and eloquent in expression.

45—6.] 'Accommodate yourself to your lover's humours, and be merry when he is so disposed.' So Hor. *Epist.* i. 18, 40, 'nec, cum venari volet ille, poemata panges.'—*jactat*, 'if he sports (or spouts) love-ditties, accompany him.'

47—58.] 'Above all things take care the lover brings money or presents. Never mind who he is; look only to what he offers.'—*ad dantes*, 'at the call of those who give,'—not to himself as a bribe for opening the door, but to the inmate whom the lover seeks.—*inanis*, 'empty-handed.' *surdus*, 'let him pretend not to hear, and go on sleeping over (leaning on) the bar drawn across the door.' A graphic picture of one who doggedly refuses to wake up when he is wanted. See Becker, *Gallus*, p. 281.

Aut quorum titulus per barbara colla pependit,
  Cretati medio cum saluere foro.
Aurum spectato, non quæ manus adferat aurum.
  Versibus auditis quid nisi verba feres?
[Quid juvat ornato procedere, vita, capillo
  Et tenues Coa veste movere sinus?]
Qui versus, Coæ dederit nec munera vestis,
  Istius tibi sit surda sine ære lyra.
Dum vernat sanguis, dum rugis integer annus,
  Utere, ne quid cras libet ab ore dies.
Vidi ego odorati victura rosaria Pæsti
  Sub matutino cocta jacere Noto.'
His animum nostræ dum versat Acanthis amicæ,
  Per tenuem ossa mihi sunt numerata cutem.

51.] *Titulus.* 'Do not reject even a slave, who has stood on the *catasta* with a paper round his neck, setting forth age, abilities, country, &c., and whose chalked feet have danced to show his agility and muscular power,' (*i.e.* do not spurn one who was once a slave, but now is a rich *libertus*). The same practice prevailed till lately, if it does not still continue, in the slave-markets of South America. The *gypsati pedes* are mentioned also by Martial and Tibullus ii. 2, 59, and allude to a custom of so marking *foreign* slaves by way of distinction. This appears from Juvenal, i. 111, 'Nuper in hanc urbem pedibus qui venerat albis.' The MSS. give *celati*, whence Jacob, Hertzberg, Keil and Müller, with the Aldine, read *cælati*, which they explain 'tattooed.' But first, it is very doubtful whether such were ever exhibited in the slave-market; and secondly, it seems strange to call such a man 'engraved,' or 'embossed.' I have therefore adopted with Lachmann the ingenious conjecture of Passerat. See Becker, *Gallus*, p. 200, who remarks that only the inferior class of slaves were thus exposed in the market.

54.] As *verba dare* is 'to cheat,' so *verba ferre* may mean 'to be cheated;' but with the double meaning 'you will get nothing but words,' *i.e.* nothing more substantial.

55—6.] All the MSS. here insert a distich from i. 2, 1—2, which Lachmann and Kuinoel omit with Scaliger, to the great indignation of Hertzberg, who calls it 'nervos totius elegiæ.' These verses may indeed have been a marginal quotation added by some copyist; but they may also have been repeated by the poet,—though not, perhaps, in very good taste,—to apply the remark more pointedly to his own case. The sense is, 'He who gives no better present than mere compliments, is not to be listened to, however fine his poetry may be.'—*sine ære*, *i.e.* si sine oblato ære sonet. The ed. Rheg. gives *sine arte*, which Kuinoel adopts.

59—62.] 'Make the best use of your youthful charms, and remember that they are not lasting.'—*vernat*, *florens*, the bloom of life.—*libet*, carpat, decerpat.

61.] *Victura*, 'which would have lived longer,' *i.e.* killed before their time. An elegant usage; compare 'luna moraturis sedula luminibus,' i. 3, 32.—*cocta*, 'withered,' 'shrivelled.' The *Notus* is perhaps what is called the *Sirocco*, though this, properly speaking, is the S.E.

63.] *Versat*, 'plies,' 'keeps in suspense.' So Hor. *Sat.* i. 8, 19, 'carminibus quæ versant atque venenis Humanos animos.'—*his*, 'by the foregoing precepts;' meaning especially that about admitting only the rich.

64.] This verse is thus given in the MSS. and early editions; 'per tenues ossa sunt numerata cutes,' which Keil retains. Müller gives 'Ossa inter tenues sunt' &c. Kuinoel, Barth, and Lachmann omit it altogether, as being thrust in by some copyist to fill up a lacuna. If genuine, it is not easy to restore the metre with anything like certainty. Of two conjectures, I prefer that of Jacob. Hertzberg edits *per tenues ossa has*, &c., which is not only (as

Sed cape torquatæ, Venus o regina, columbæ
Ob meritum ante tuos guttura secta focos.
Vidi ego rugoso tussim concrescere collo,
Sputaque per dentes ire cruenta cavos,
Atque animam in tegetes putrem expirare paternas:
Horruit algenti pergula curta foco.
Exequiæ fuerant rari furtiva capilli
Vincula et immundo pallida mitra situ,
Et canis in nostros nimis experrecta dolores,
Cum fallenda meo pollice clatra forent.
Sit tumulus lenæ curto vetus amphora collo:

he admits) unrhythmical, but retains the unusual plural *cutes*, in which the corruption seems partly to lie. The sense is, 'While Acanthis was thus lecturing Cynthia on the art of frustrating a lover's hopes, I was pining away with desire.' Cf. i. 9, 29, 'qui non ante patet, donec manus attigit ossa.'

65—6.] 'But, thank Venus, I have lived to pay her a tribute for delivering me from such a hag,' &c.—*torquata columba*, a pretty expression for a ring-dove. Kuinoel quotes Ovid, *Fast.* i. 452, 'Uritur Idaliis alba columba focis.' 'Torquatus palumbus' occurs in Martial, xiii. 67.

67—70.] A curious and not pleasing, though powerful, description of death by consumption, as it would seem. 'I have lived to see the cough get more choking in that skinny neck, and the blood-tinged spittle pass through the hollows between her teeth;—I have seen her gasp out that foul breath in the beggarly rags that her father wore, while she lay shivering before the fireless hearth in a narrow out-house.' The *teges* was a coarse mat worn by mendicants, as appears from Juven. *Sat.* 5, 8, 'nusquam pons et tegetis pars Dimidia brevior?' Mart. *Ep.* xi. 56, 5, 'et teges et cimex et nudi sponda grabati.' *Ibid.* 32, 2, 'de bibula sarta palude teges;' and ix. 92, 3, 'dat tibi securos vilis tegeticula somnos.' Plautus calls it 'tegillum,' *Rud.* 576. For *pergula*, a kind of lean-to of wood, built on to a house, see Rich's *Companion to the Dictionary* in v., and Becker, *Gallus*, p. 268. Perhaps this, or something like it, is the 'posticulum' or 'back-house' in Plaut. *Trin.* 194. The *pergula* itself is said *horrere* by a common figure, meaning, of course, the occupant of it. The MSS. give *percula* or *pocula curva*. Lachmann, with Barth and Kuinoel, read *tegula curta* after Pucci; cf. inf. 7, 26.

71—4.] *Exequiæ*, here the dress in which she was laid out. 'They buried her in the band she had stolen to bind her thin grey hairs, and in a cap from which the colour had faded from untidy dirt; the dog too was there, that had too often been wakeful to my vexation, when the latch had to be stealthily lifted by the pressure of my thumb.' There is mixed comedy and pathos in the description, which is at once heartless and clever. The poet vents his spite even upon the poor little dog, which was her only friend in life and her only mourner at her grave.—*mitra*, iii. 21, 15, a kind of night-cap or folded kerchief, once coloured, now dim, ἐξίτηλος, through the dirt of neglect, *situs*.—*clatra*, the MSS. give *cultra* or *castra*. The Romans hardened the dental, as in *tus*, *θεν*, *cœlitus*, for the termination *θεν*.

75.] *Tumulus*. 'May the old bawd have no more costly tomb than an old wine-jar with a broken neck; and may a vigorous wild fig-tree narrow her grave by its growth above it.' Nothing more, perhaps, is meant than that some such cheap and worthless monument should mark her grave, as would encourage the passer-by to pelt it with stones, as a half-broken pot would do. This was considered a special insult; compare Eur. *El.* 324, πέτροισι λεύει μνῆμα λάϊνον πατρός. There may also (as sup. ver. 2) be an allusion to the old woman's fondness for drink. The caprificus, generally spoken of as destructive of tombs (Juv. x. 145) by forcing its way through the joints of the stones, seems here to have reference to the roots penetrating into the grave beneath which it grows.

Urgeat hunc supra vis, caprifice, tua.
Quisquis amas, scabris hoc bustum cædite saxis,
Mixtaque cum saxis addite verba mala.

VI.

Sacra facit vates: sint ora faventia sacris,
Ut cadat ante meos icta juvenca focos.
Hedra Philotæis certet Romana corymbis,

77.] Jacob and Hertzberg give *cædite*, the MS. reading being *edite*, which Keil and Müller retain. The correction may easily have been made by copyists in reference to the singular, *quisquis amas*; and the same motive will account for the MS. Groning. giving in the short verse *adjice* for *addite*.

78.] *Verba mala.* 'Pelt the tomb not only with stones, but with imprecations.' Thus the Greeks say *θείνειν* or *βάλλειν ἔπεσιν*, and so Arist. *Ach.* 686, *ἐν τάχει παίει ξυνάπτων στρογγύλοις τοῖς ῥήμασι*, 'with his words rounded like balls for throwing.'

VI. This very fine elegy is the earliest, and perhaps in some sense the most detailed and authentic, record of the great battle of Actium. Like the *Persae* of Æschylus, compared with the later and more popularised account of the battle of Salamis in Herodotus, it is of value beyond its mere poetic merit. It contains a splendid eulogy on Augustus for his victory over Antony and Cleopatra, B.C. 31, in thanksgiving for which he had rebuilt on the spot a temple to Apollo Actius (*navalis Phœbus* v. 1, 3), and instituted games to be celebrated every five years, or rather, remodelled the ancient *Actia* which were held every three years. Sueton. *Octav.* § 18, 'Quoque Actiacæ victoriæ memoria celebratior et in posterum esset, urbem Nicopolim apud Actium condidit, ludosque *illic* quinquennales constituit; et ampliato vetere Apollinis templo locum castrorum, quibus fuerat usus, exornatum navalibus spoliis, Neptuno ac Marti consecravit.' *Ibid.* § 29, 'Publica opera plurima extruxit, —templum Apollinis in Palatio, ædem Tonantis Jovis in Capitolio.' The reader will not confound these two distinct monuments of the victory. Hertzberg considers that there were two local games, *i.e.* at Actium and at the temple on the Palatine, the latter of which are here meant. There is some obscurity on this point: perhaps the Actia were transferred to Rome, while a semblance of the old institution was kept up at Actium. The word *illic* will be noticed in the former extract from Suetonius. The present elegy, as Barth observes, seems to have been intended as an *ἐπινίκιον* on the occasion of these games, A.U.C. 738, being held for the fourth time.

1.] *Sacra facit, θύει ἐπινίκια.* The poet represents himself as a priest about to perform a sacrifice; and hence in the succeeding verses he borrows metaphors strictly derived from sacrificial usages.' On which Hertzberg well observes, 'In allegoria, quam decem primos versus obtinet, magnopere cavendum est, ne ad vivum resecare metaphoras, neve quæ singula significent, anxie quærere velimus. Quid enim juvenca, quid costum, quid laneus orbis, quid denique lymphæ translatione soluta in carmine significent, putidum est explorare.'

2.] I have given *ut cadat* for *et cadat*, on the ground that the sacrificial custom was to command silence for the killing of the beast, immediately after which a joyful sacrificial shout was raised.

3.] The sense is, 'Let Roman verses vie with the elegiac renown of Philetas of Cos.' But the reading is rather doubtful. The good copies give *cera Philippeis*. Most editors adopt *serta* from Scaliger; cf. iii. 26, 37. Haupt reads *ara*; but nothing seems to me so probable as *Hedra*, which is found in one of the later MSS. Compare sup. i. 62, 'mi folia ex hedera porrige, Bacche, tua.' So *aspris* for *asperis*, *Æn.* ii. 379, *poplo* for *populo*, Plaut. *Amphitr.* 101.—*Philetaeis* is the certain correction of Beroaldus. See on iv. 1, 1. In v. 4, Callimachus of Cyrene is meant, the flow of whose verses is compared with lustral water, *χέρνιψ*, used for the purposes of the sacred rites. To drink of certain springs was thought inspiring to a poet; cf. sup. iv. 3, 6; Pindar, *Ol.* vi. 85; *Isth.* v. 74.

Et Cyrenæas urna ministret aquas.
Costum molle date et blandi mihi turis honores,
Terque focum circa laneus orbis eat.
Spargite me lymphis, carmenque recentibus aris
Tibia Mygdoniis libet eburna cadis.
Ite procul fraudes, alio sint aere noxæ:
Pura novum vati laurea mollit iter.
Musa, Palatini referemus Apollinis ædem:
Res est, Calliope, digna favore tuo.
Cæsaris in nomen ducuntur carmina: Cæsar
Dum canitur, quæso, Juppiter ipse vaces.
Est Phœbi fugiens Athamana ad litora portus,
Qua sinus Ioniæ murmura condit aquæ,
Actia Iuleæ pelagus monimenta carinæ,

6.] *Laneus orbis* is the vitta or infula, the woollen chaplet, which is generally seen sculptured on the sides of Roman altars. See Virg. *Ecl.* viii. 65, and *Dict. of Antiq.* in v. ara.

7.] *Spargite.* This too was a Greek custom at a sacrifice; see *Arist. Pax* 972. *recentibus*, *νεοδμήτοις*, newly built of turf.

8.] Lachmann, Kuinoel, and Jacob write *Cadis* as a proper name, after Scaliger. According to Strabo, xii. p. 220, a town of Phrygia was so named, and as the Phrygians were also called Mygdones, the music may be supposed to have been played Φρυγιστί. But Hertzberg more probably regards it as a continuation of the same metaphor, by which the notes of the tibia are compared with the libation of wine from a jar or cask at a sacrifice. He aptly quotes Pindar, *Nem.* iii. 78, where the idea of *πόμ' ἀοίδιμον* is carried out through several verses. Compare also *νέκταρ χυτόν, Μουσᾶν δόσιν*, *Ol.* vii. 7. We may therefore translate, 'and let the pipe pour forth music from Phrygian stores at the altars of fresh turf.'

9.] *Fraudes*, like *noxæ*, here signifies generally all that is bad and unworthy to be present at a sacrifice. See Aristoph. *Pax* 968. Perhaps from Callimachus, *ἑκὰς ἑκὰς ὅστις ἀλιτρός*.—*alio sint aere*, a common method of deprecating any evil, 'let it go where it likes if only it does not stay here.'

10.] *Mollit*, because the road is strewed thick with leaves.—*novum iter*, 'panegyricum hic elegiacum.' *Hertzberg.* — *pura laurea* seems so called in reference to Apollo's attribute *φοῖβος*, and it is also mentioned as the plant of victory.

11.] *Referemus*, 'our theme shall be the building, *i.e.* the cause of building, the temple of the Palatine Apollo.' Barth cites Ovid, *A. A.* iii. 389, 'visite laurigero sacrata Palatia Phœbo; Ille Parætonias mersit in alta rates.' (*Parætonias*, *i.e.* Ægyptias; so called from a town on the north coast of Africa).

14.] *Vaces*, sc. carmine; 'consent for a time not to be honoured in our verse.'

15.] *Athamana litora*, 'the shores of Epirus,' of which the Ἀθαμᾶνες were a people. See on v. 1, 36. The construction of the passage cannot be explained better than in the words of Hertzberg: 'ipse sinus eleganti appositione et *pelagus* dicitur (est enim maris pars), et *monumenta* carinæ Iuleæ, et *via facilis* nautis. Monumentum autem omne est, quo alicujus rei admonemur. *Actia* denique attributum vocis *monumenta*, cum proprie ad *pelagus* deberet referri.' Translate, 'a wide expanse of water that records (by the temple on its shore) the exploits of the Julian fleet at Actium, and a roadway that gives no trouble to sailors' vows,' *i.e.* from its open and easy access. The plural *monumenta* is worthy of remark, as being used in this sense by Tacitus, *Ann.* iii. 23, 72, and iv. 7. The *sinus Ambracius* is meant, which is of considerable size, (about 25 miles long by 10 wide) otherwise *pelagus* is properly used of the open sea, as *mare* and *pontus* express inland seas, and *oceanus* the great circumambient external ocean. See Tac. *Ann.* ii. 53.

Nautarum votis non operosa via.
Huc mundi coiere manus: stetit æquore moles
Pinea, nec remis æqua favebat avis.
Altera classis erat Teucro damnata Quirino,
Pilaque feminea turpiter acta manu:
Hinc Augusta ratis plenis Jovis omine velis
Signaque jam patriæ vincere docta suæ.
Tandem acies geminos Nereus lunarat in arcus,
Armorum radiis picta tremebat aqua,
Cum Phœbus linquens stantem se vindice Delon
(Nam tulit iratos mobilis una Notos)
Astitit Augusti puppim super, et nova flamma
Luxit in obliquam ter sinuata facem.

19.] *Mundi manus.* Antony's fleet was composed partly of Egyptian auxiliaries, partly of eastern nations. Kuinoel refers to Virg. *Æn.* viii. 687, 'Ægyptum viresque Orientis et ultima secum Bactra vehit.' cf. v. 705.—*moles pinea*: see ibid. viii. 691. The notion is, that the fleet, from the size of its ships, seemed to stand motionless on the sea like some rock or mountain, though built of buoyant fir-wood. Virg. *Æn.* vi. 471, 'nec magis incepto vultum sermone movetur Quam si dura silex aut stet Marpesia cautes.'—*nec æqua* &c., 'at non æque bonum utrique classi erat augurium.' 'The one fleet (Antony's) was under the ban of the Troy-descended Romulus, and so were the darts that were basely directed against Rome by a woman's hand.'—*turpiter*, because it was discreditable in a woman to join a war in (as the poet considered it) an unholy cause.—*damnata*, alluding to the custom of solemnly denouncing in the senate the enemies of the Roman people. Compare iii. 7, 38, 'Actis damnatis æquora militibus.'

23.] *Jovis omine*, the favourable breeze was regarded as sent by Ζεὺς οὔριος.—*hinc*, 'on our side.'

24.] *Vincere docta.* In the various victories Augustus had already obtained by land: compare v. 39. The dative is acquisitively used.

25.] The disposition of the opposing fleets in two crescent-shaped lines is represented as entrusted to the god of the sea. Martial, *Lib. Spectac.* 28, 7, perhaps alludes to this in his account of a Naumachia in the Amphitheatre; 'Dumque parat sævis ratibus fera prælia Nereus, Abnuit in liquidis ire pedester aquis.'—*radiis*, 'the sheen of the arms.' Lachmann reads *armorum et radiis*. The battle is just about to commence, when Apollo arrives from Delos, and takes his place on the ship of Augustus in the form of a wavy flame on the poop. I have endeavoured to explain the allusion in the note on Æsch. *Agam.* 647. See Humboldt, *Cosmos*, vol. ii. note 90.

28.] The MSS. have *unda*, but the MS. Gron. with a dot under the *d*, showing that it should be erased. Jacob, Hertzberg, and Müller edit *una*; Lachmann, with Barth and Kuinoel, admit the improbable conjecture of Broukhusius, *ante*. The idea is, that Phœbus had so firmly fixed the island, which was the only one that had ever been otherwise than fixed, and liable to be borne to and fro by the angry winds, that he now left it fearlessly to take care of itself in his absence.—*se vindice*, 'under threat of his vengeance,' means that he would have punished it for *not* standing, by finally reducing it to the former condition of instability. Or perhaps (as inf. 41) 'under his protection.' Hence '*nam tulit*' &c., *i.e. pertulit, perpessa est*, 'bore the brunt of.' Or should we read *iratis mobilis unda notis*, 'the water carried it before the winds?'

30.] *Ter sinuata.* Not *tripartita*, but 'thrice deflected from a straight line, after the fashion of a torch held aslant;' by which the flame is curved upwards. Lucian, περὶ τῶν ἐπὶ μισθῷ συνόντων, p. 652, ridicules the idea of a god ἐπὶ τῆς πρύμνης καθεζόμενον ἢ πρὸς τοῖς πηδαλίοις ἑστῶτα καὶ πρός τινα ἠϊόνα μαλακὴν ἀπευθύνοντα τὴν ναῦν, &c.

Non ille attulerat crines in colla solutos
  Aut testudineæ carmen inerme lyræ,
Sed quali aspexit Pelopeum Agamemnona vultu,
  Egessitque avidis Dorica castra rogis,
Aut qualis flexos solvit Pythona per orbes
  Serpentem, imbelles quem timuere †lyræ.
Mox ait 'o longa mundi servator ab Alba,
  Auguste, Hectoreis cognite major avis,
Vince mari: jam terra tua est: tibi militat arcus,
  Et favet ex humeris hoc onus omne meis.
Solve metu patriam, quæ nunc te vindice freta
  Imposuit proræ publica vota tuæ.
Quam nisi defendes, murorum Romulus augur
  Ire Palatinas non bene vidit aves.
Et nimium remis audent; proh turpe Latinis
  Principe te fluctus regia vela pati.

31.] This noble and spirited passage describes the character under which Apollo appeared: not as the god of music, waving his *intonsos crines*, but as the god of war and destruction, armed with bow and quiver.

33.] We may either understand 'sed (venerat) quali vultu,' or 'sed (attulerat) vultum, quali' &c. Müller reads *ad testudinea* &c. This alludes to the pestilence described in Homer as having been sent by Apollo against the Greeks, *Il.* i. 40—50. *egerere castra* is a metaphor from digging out and carrying away earth or rubbish: hence to clear or empty by removing the dead to the pyres without,—αἰεὶ δὲ πυραὶ νεκύων καίοντο θαμειαί. Cf. Pers. v. 69, 'ecce aliud cras Egerit hos annos.'

35.] *Aut qualis* &c. 'Or as when he disabled the serpent Python (the monster snake of Delphi) in all his twining coils.' This is the subject of one of Turner's greatest pictures, now in the National Gallery.

36.] *Imbelles lyræ.* A sufficiently bold expression for the Muses, to whom the snake which Apollo scotched had been an object of terror. See on iii. 18, 18. But the termination of this verse has probably been repeated by mistake from 32 (see iii. 18, 18), and we should here read either *deæ* or *chori*. Müller reads, on his own conjecture, *imbelles quem tacuere lyræ*. The only way of explaining the vulgate is to regard it as a short phrase for 'Musæ non arma sed lyras gestantes.'

37.] *Ab Alba*, like 'pastor ab Amphryso,' *Georgic.* iii. 2.—*cognite*, ἐξετασθείς, whose exploits have proved you to be greater than even your Trojan ancestors.

40.] *Hoc omne onus*, *i.e.* pharetram.

42.] *Vota*, viz. in the form of *coronæ* or *tabellæ*.

43.] *Auctor* is the reading of Lachmann and Kuinoel, after Bentley on *Hor.* iii. 3, 66. The correction is too obvious to deserve the praise of ingenuity; and the great name of the critic to whom it is due has given it (as in so many other cases) a weight to which its merits do not entitle it. The very next verse shows the vulgate to be correct.—*augur murorum* is briefly put for *cum muris augurio cæperit*. The sense is, 'If you, Augustus, do not now save Rome, it will have been founded *male avi*, contrary to the belief of all the world.' Compare sup. 1, 49—54.

44—6.] These obscure verses are explained in various ways, according to the punctuation adopted. That of Hertzberg is somewhat harsh and awkward: 'regia vela nimium audent pati fluctus Latinis remis;' or, in his own words, 'nimium turpe est, quod naves reginæ, Te principe, Romani remigii ope fluctibus committere se audent.' He admits that *vela* for *naves* is somewhat objectionable when coupled closely with *remis*, but throws the blame

Nec te, quod classis centenis remiget alis,
  Terreat: invito labitur illa mari:
Quodque vehunt proræ Centaurica saxa minantis,
  Tigna cava et pictos experiere metus.
Frangit et attollit vires in milite causa;
  Quæ nisi justa subest, excutit arma pudor.
Tempus adest, committe rates: ego temporis auctor
  Ducam laurigera Julia rostra manu.'
Dixerat, et pharetræ pondus consumit in arcus:
  Proxima post arcus Cæsaris hasta fuit.
Vincit Roma fide Phœbi: dat femina pœnas:
  Sceptra per Ionias fracta vehuntur aquas.
At pater Idalio miratur Cæsar ab astro:

on the poet. I prefer the following: 'turpe est Romanis, quibus tu es princeps, fluctus maris, quod sub ipsorum ditione est, pati naves reginæ Cleopatræ;' the antithesis lying in the words *princeps* and *regina*; for *rex* was a forbidden word, so to speak, under the empire. For *pro* the MSS. give *prope*, which Müller retains, reading *es* with some late copies for *et*.—The sentence *et nimium remis audent*, seems to imply that Antony's ships first rowed forward for the conflict; perhaps also, that they placed too much confidence in their oars, and too little in the aid of a god.

47.] *Remiget* means, 'do not be frightened because you think that each ship in the fleet rows with a hundred oars' (the Homeric sense of *πτερά*). Perhaps *remiget* should be read, like *vehunt* in 49; which implies the objective fact that it was so.—*invito mari*, 'the very sea it rides on is against it.' There appears to have been rather rough water at the battle of Actium: see Martial, *Ep.* iv. 11, 6, (Antoni nomen) 'obruit Actiaci quod gravis ira freti.'

49.] 'And as for the prows carrying figures which seem to be heaving stones as large as those hurled by the Lapithæ against the Centaurs,—why, you will find them to be mere *μορμολυκεῖα*, painted boards.' *Centaurus* is the reading of Barth and Kuinoel after Guyet; which alters the sense materially against the authority of all the copies. Hertzberg observes that real stones used as missiles against the enemy might be meant, quoting Dio l. 33, and Virg. *Æn.* viii. 693, 'Tanta mole viri turritis navibus instant,' but that the pentameter verse seems conclusive against it. Probably they were painted figures, as we know from Virg. *Georg.* iv. 289, that the Egyptians had this custom, 'Et circa *pictis* vehitur sua rura phaselis.' And perhaps (as in *Æn.* x. 195) one of the ships was called *The Centaur*. Is *vehunt* used intransitively for *vehuntur*, as we say, 'the ship *rides* on the waves?' Compare *vector*, 'a rider,' inf. 7, 84, and the examples of *vehere* for *equitare* supplied by the Dictionaries.

52.] *Subest*, *ὑπάρχει*. 'It is the cause which weakens or raises the courage in a soldier; if there is no justice in it from the first, his arms fall *from* his hands through his own sense of shame.' "'Tis the cause makes all, Degrades or hallows valour in its fall.'—*Byron*.

54.] *Laurigera manu*. Elegantly used, as if Apollo were about to put a crown of victory on the conquering prows.—*temporis auctor*, *ἐγὼ ὁ τὸν καιρὸν ὑποδείξων*, viz. the time for commencing the action.

57.] *Fide Phœbi*, ex promissis, v. 39, 40.

58.] *Sceptra fracta*, *i.e.* victa classis.—*vehuntur*, 'rides,' or perhaps 'is towed,' viz. as a prize taken.

59.] Barth and Kuinoel read *mirатus* from the Aldine, and *es* for *et* or *est* in the pentameter, after Markland, in which latter both Lachmann and Hertzberg agree. The 'Idalian star' from which the deified Julius regarded with admiration the exploits of his adopted son, does not mean any particular star (much less the planet Venus), but the epithet relates to his supposed descent from the goddess. See the commentators on *Julium sidus*, Hor. *Od.* i. 12, 47, on which passage Orelli, observing that mention is made of Julius Cæsar only

'Sum deus, et nostri sanguinis ista fides.'
Prosequitur cantu Triton, omnesque marinæ
Plauserunt circa libera signa deæ.
Illa petit Nilum cymba male nacta fugaci
Hoc unum, jusso non moritura die.
Dii melius! quantus mulier foret una triumphus,
Ductus erat per quas ante Jugurtha vias.
Actius hinc traxit Phœbus monimenta, quod ejus
Una decem vicit missa sagitta rates.
Bella satis cecini: citharam jam poscit Apollo
Victor et ad placidos exuit arma choros.
Candida nunc molli subeant convivia luco,
Blanditiæque fluant per mea colla rosæ,
Vinaque fundantur prælis elisa Falernis,
Terque lavet nostras spica Cilissa comas.
Ingenium potis irritat Musa poetis:

twice by Horace, and thrice by Virgil, is not correct in stating that he is nowhere spoken of by Propertius. See also sup. iv. 15, 34. The sense of v. 60 is, 'I am a god, and this victory of yours is a guarantee that you are born of my race.' *Fides* is so used sup. 1, 98.

61.] *Triton*, cf. Hom. *Il.* xiii. 27, βῆ δ' ἐλάαν ἐπὶ κύματ', ἄταλλε δὲ κήτε' ὑπ' αὐτοῦ πάντοθεν ἐκ κευθμῶν, οὐδ' ἠγνοίησεν ἄνακτα. Mart. *Lib. Spect.* 28, 5, 'Vidit in æquoreo ferventes pulvere currus, Et domini Triton ipse putavit equos.'

62.] *Libera signa.* 'Nunc demum, postquam apud Actium debellatum est, non amplius ab Antonio oppugnata, vere *libera* dicuntur.'—*Hertzberg*.

63.] *Illa*, 'the queen on her part;' cf. sup. 4, 71, and 5, 9. Keil reads *ipsa*. For *nixa* I have ventured to read *nacta*, by which *hoc unum* obtains something like an intelligible syntax. 'She gained this one advantage, though unfairly, by the speed of her galley, that she was not destined to die on the very day that her conqueror had ordered.' He should properly have said *non moriendum sibi esse*,—*jusso die*, constituto a victore. The only exception to her complete defeat was that she eluded the conqueror's hands and put an end to her own existence.

65.] *Dii melius*, sc. nobis consuluerunt. The sense is, 'Heaven willed it otherwise, and no doubt for the best: for a woman would have made but a sorry figure as a captive in a triumph, which had before been graced by such a great king and so illustrious an enemy as Jugurtha.'—*quantus*, quantillus. Perhaps the mark of a question should be placed at *vias*.

68.] *Ejus sagitta.* So *Æn.* viii. 704, 'Actius hæc cernens arcum intendebat Apollo Desuper' &c. Sup. 55. The hyperbole is extravagant, of course.

69.] *Citharam*, viz. which he had laid aside during the fight, sup. 32.

71.] *Luco.* The poet, who in the commencement of the elegy had assumed the character of a priest, now speaks of the banquet which (says Hertzberg) the college of priests used to partake of in the sacred grove after the sacrifice had been offered. See the commentators on 'Saliares dapes.' Hor. *Od.* i. 37, 2, and on 'Pontificum cœnis,' *ib.* ii. 14, 28. Kuinoel reads *ludo* after Heinsius. In the pentameter verse, *rosæ* is the genitive, as Hertzberg points out after others. See on v. 5, 40.

71—2.] *Candida* &c. 'Let the white-robed banqueters now enter the turf-clad grove, and the soft caress of the rose (or, chaplets of dainty roses) droop freely over my neck.' Lachmann's emendation, *blandæ utrimque fluant*, has little to commend it.

74.] *Spica Cilissa*, used by Ovid, *Fast.* i. 76, for the saffron of Corycus in Cilicia. See sup. 1, 15.

75.] I have adopted Scaliger's reading *irritat* for *irritet*, since not the wish, but

Bacche, soles Phœbo fertilis esse tuo.
Ille paludosos memoret servire Sicambros,
Cepheam hic Meroen fuscaque regna canat,
Hic referat sero confessum fœdere Parthum:
Reddat signa Romi, mox dabit ipse sua:
Sive aliquid pharetris Augustus parcet Eois,
Differat in pueros ista tropæa suos.
Gaude, Crasse, nigras si quid sapis inter harenas:
Ire per Euphraten ad tua busta licet.
Sic noctem patera, sic ducam carmine, donec
Iniciat radios in mea vina dies.

VII.

Sunt aliquid Manes: letum non omnia finit,

the statement of a fact seems conveyed, that wine stimulates the poet's genius. The vulgate might however mean, 'Let us try the effect of wine in inspiring our minds.' And Lachmann prefers this, rejecting Scaliger's emendation.

76.] *Fertilis*, γόνιμον Arist. *Ran.* 96, 'suggestive.' The intimate connection between Bacchus and Apollo in the patronage of poetry explains *Phœbo tuo*. Thus Parnassus was sacred to both deities. Juvenal (7, 64) speaks of poets as inspired 'dominis Cirrhæ Nysæque.' Tibullus, iii. 4, 44, 'casto nam rite poetæ Phœbusque et Bacchus Pieridesque favent.' Ovid, *Am.* i. 3, 11, 'At Phœbus, comitesque novem, vitisque repertor, Hoc faciunt.' Here, however, the poet is implied under the name of the god himself.

77.] 'Let one poet celebrate (viz. in recitations at the *[illegible]*) the emperor's victory over the Germans, another his Ethiopian conquests, and a third his expedition against the Parthians to recover the lost standards of Crassus.'—*dabit*, cf. inf. 10, 12. *Meroe* is a well-known island formed by the Nile, Herod. ii. 29. Strabo xvi. 4, xvii. 1, here called *Cephean* from Cepheus king of Ethiopia, the father of Andromeda.

79.] *Confessum*, i. e. Romanorum potentiam, et se ab iis probe victum esse.

81—2.] 'If Augustus does not entirely quell the rebel Parthians, may it be for the purpose of leaving his sons something to conquer.' Caius and Lucius Cæsar, the sons of his daughter Julia by M. Agrippa, adopted by Augustus, are here meant. See Ovid, *A. A.* i. 177.

83.] *Nigras harenas*, the alluvial plains watered by the Euphrates; though properly speaking these did not extend up to Parthia. Virg. *Georg.* iii. 241, 'Et viridem Ægyptum nigra fecundat arena.'—*si quid sapis*, i.e. if there is any consciousness in Hades, if your Manes can know that you have been avenged. Similarly iii. 4, 42, 'Nonnihil ad verum conscia terra sapit.'

84.] *Ire licet*. The way to the east is now opened by the Roman arms. Some light is thrown on this passage by Tacit. *Ann.* ii. 58, 'Inter quæ ab rege Parthorum Artabano legati venere. Miserat amicitiam ac fœdus memoraturos, et cupere renovari dextras, daturumque honori Germanici ut ripam Euphratis accederet.'

VII. This elegy also is of very great pathos and beauty, and is in all respects a most instructive and interesting poem. The ghost of Cynthia, in all the horrors of a half-burnt body from the funeral pile, appears to the poet when asleep and dreaming of her, and upbraids him in affecting words with his heartless neglect of her in death. From the concluding elegies of the fourth book the reader is prepared for the part Propertius was likely to take in the matter. Her continued profligacy had in fact at length effectually estranged him. Yet it seems singular that he should record the just complaints of the deceased against himself, unless impelled to do so by remorse. It was evidently composed immediately after the obsequies, but the exact date cannot be determined.

1.] *Sunt aliquid Manes*. 'There are then such things as spirits:' ἦν ἄρα τι

Luridaque evictos effugit umbra rogos.
Cynthia namque meo visa est incumbere fulcro,
Murmur ad extremæ nuper humata viæ,
Cum mihi somnus ab exequiis penderet amoris,
Et quererer lecti frigida regna mei.
Eosdem habuit secum, quibus est elata, capillos,
Eosdem oculos: lateri vestis adusta fuit,
Et solitum digito beryllon adederat ignis,
Summaque Lethæus triverat ora liquor:
Spirantisque animos et vocem misit: at illi
Pollicibus fragiles increpuere manus:
'Perfide nec cuiquam melior sperande puellæ,
In te jam vires somnus habere potest?
Jamne tibi exciderant vigilacis furta Suburæ

ψυχή, compare *Il.* xxiii. 103; *Od.* xi. 218; Juv. 2, 149. The doctrine of the immortality of the soul was perhaps not more sincerely held by the majority of well-informed pagans than the legends of Tartarus and future judgment connected with it. Of its separate existence, apart from the body, and its spiritual essence, the Romans understood perhaps less than the Greeks. See on v. 11, 1. The poet's scepticism is evinced by iv. 5, 45.—*evictos rogos*, i.e. qui Manes domare non possunt. 'The grisly ghost flies free from the pyre that has failed to destroy it.' Æsch. *Cho.* 315, τέκνον, φρόνημα τοῦ θανόντος οὐ δαμάζει πυρὸς μαλερὰ γνάθος.—*effugit*, elapsa est.

4.] *Murmur*, strepitum prætereuntis populi, according to Hertzberg, which becomes a faint murmur in the *extrema via*, the remoter parts; where, we may suggest from the tenour of the poem, the poor and despised were buried, while such of the more wealthy as were not interred *suo agro* had their graves close to the road-way, that all might ejaculate *sit tibi terra levis* &c.—*Murmur* is by others, more correctly, I think, explained of the waters of the Anio, on the banks of which the via Tiburtina ended. See inf. 85—6. *Marmor ad extremæ* &c. is an obvious suggestion, 'hard by the milestone;' yet this could only have a local meaning which we are not warranted in assuming. In either case *humata* refers to burying the cinerary urn, for which the more correct expression is *sepulta* (Becker, *Gallus*, p. 516).

5.] *Exequiis amoris*, 'my buried love.' Compare i. 17, 20, 'Ultimus et posito staret amore lapis,' and Theocr. 23, 43, κἤμα δέ μοι κοίλανον, ὅ μευ κρύψει τὸν ἔρωτα, passages which Lachmann has well quoted in defence of the MS. reading. Barth and Kuinoel give *amoris* after Broukhusius.

7.] The dissyllabic *eosdem* is remarkable; *idem* and *isdem* for *iidem* and *iisdem* are familiar; *ii* is a monosyllable iii. 16, 35. The initial *e* was pronounced as our *y*. Compare 'hoc eodem ferro' ii. 8, 26; 'hac eadem via' iv. 6, 36. Most of the copies here give *hosdem*. So ἕως Soph. *Ajac.* 1114.

8.] *Vestis.* 'Her appearance was the same as in life, but the tunic was scorched on her side (lit. 'burnt on to it'), and the beryl that she used to wear was blistered on her finger.' It appears from inf. 48, and from the evidence of gems which have evidently passed through the fire (one of which I have seen), that the jewels were placed on the pyre with the body, though sometimes recovered from the ashes.

10.] *Lethæus liquor.* Kuinoel appears to be right in explaining this of the pallor or blackness of the lips, as if she had sipped the waters of Lethe before she returned to earth.

11—12.] *animos* &c. 'The energy of her words and the sounds she uttered were those of one living; but the frail hands rattled in the finger-joints.' Cf. sup. 3, 66, 'subdolus et versis increpat arcus equis.'

14.] *Jam*, 'so soon.' So the ghost of Patroclus says in *Il.* xxiii. 69, εὕδεις, αὐτὰρ ἐμεῖο λελασμένος ἔπλευ, Ἀχιλλεῦ.

15.] The MSS. have *exciderant* (not *exciderunt*), which seems to be correct. See

Et mea nocturnis trita fenestra dolis?
Per quam demisso quotiens tibi fune pependi,
  Alterna veniens in tua colla manu!
Sæpe Venus trivio commissa est, pectore mixto
  Fecerunt tepidas pallia nostra vias.
Fœderis heu taciti! cujus fallacia verba
  Non audituri diripuere Noti.
At mihi non oculos quisquam inclamavit euntis;
  Unum impetrassem, te revocante, diem.
Nec crepuit fissa me propter harundine custos,
  Læsit et obiectum tegula curta caput.
Denique quis nostro curvum te funere vidit,
  Atram quis lacrimis incaluisse togam?

iv. 24, 20. 'Had you already forgotten, when you fell asleep, our stealthy meetings in the Suburra?' This part of Rome was disreputable (Pers. *Sat.* v. 32), and it may be adduced among other proofs of Cynthia's low birth and character.

21—2.] *Fœderis* seems a genitive of exclamation, in imitation of a well-known Greek idiom. 'Alas for the plighted love that found no utterance; for the words, destined but to deceive, were wafted away by winds that would not hear them.' The notion is, that the promised pledges came to nothing, because they were never expressed in audible words.

23.] It requires some sagacity to choose between *inclamavit*, the reading of the Naples MS., and *inclinavit*, which most editors have adopted from MS. Gron. and ed. Rheg. Hertzberg, Keil, and Müller admit the former, and Jacob also approves of it, observing that the pentameter verse has no allusion to closing the eyes, but evidently implies an earnest appeal to the dying, when the eyes are *natantes* (*i.e.* labentes, deficientes), to stay yet awhile with the friends who sit by the couch. The action is natural; and Jacob observes 'posse autem amore, desiderio, voto retineri fugientem animam putarunt multi.' See iii. 19, 16, 'Si modo damnatum revocaverit aura puellæ, Concessum nulla lege redibit iter.' It was the custom, when the eyes of the deceased *had been closed* (so says Becker, *Gallus*, p. 505), to set up a loud clamour or wailing, to recal the departing spirit, if the person should only be in a trance. When no hope remained, they said *conclamatum est*. Does not the present passage show that the *clamor* took place also *in articulo mortis*? In fact, this is clear from Ovid, *Trist.* iii. 3, 43, quoted by Becker himself, and from Lucret. iii. 598, 'ubi jam trepidatur, et omnes extremum cupiunt vitæ reprendere vinclum.'

25.] Much has been written, and not a few conjectures have been proposed on these two verses, which Lachmann, Jacob, and others have transferred to follow v. 20 or v. 18, (Jacob in the latter instance suggesting *ac crepuit* for *nec crepuit*). But the objection to *denique*, that it shows 'ante exequias actam esse rem,' is easily removed by Hertzberg, who remarks that it is 'non temporis, sed ordinis vocabulum.' The arrangement in fact is quite a natural one: (1) nemo morientem inclamavit. (2) Mortuum nemo assedit. (3) Nemo vidit te atram togam indutum.—The *custos* here mentioned was appointed to watch by the body till it was carried to the pyre (*elatum*), and he seems to have occasionally sounded a shrill note with a pipe, in case the apparently dead should only be in a trance, and so might possibly be aroused to consciousness. This is stated on the authority of Pliny, quoted by Servius on *Æn.* vi. 218.

26.] *Tegula curta.* Instead of a cushion, a broken tile was used to prop the head on the *lectus*, or funeral bier, which head was cut (*læsa*) by being rudely *jammed against it*, (*obiectum*).

27.] *Curvum*, bent, weighed down with grief. Lachmann adopts the improbable alteration of Passerat, *furvum*, in the sense of *pullatum*.

Si piguit portas ultra procedere, at illuc
  Jussisses lectum lentius ire meum.
Cur ventos non ipse rogis, ingrate, petisti?
  Cur nardo flammæ non oluere meæ?
Hoc etiam grave erat, nulla mercede hyacinthos
  Inicere et fracto busta piare cado?
Lygdamus uratur, candescat lamina vernæ;—
  Sensi ego, cum insidiis pallida vina bibi;—
At Nomas arcanas tollat versuta salivas:
  Dicet damnatas ignea testa manus.
Quæ modo per viles inspecta est publica noctes,
  Hæc nunc aurata cyclade signat humum;
Et graviora rependit iniquis pensa quasillis,

30.] 'If you would not attend me to the pyre, at least you might have given orders that the bearers (vespillones) should carry the bier (sandapila) without such indecent haste.' It was a common custom for the friends to accompany the body only as far as the city gate. The bearers perhaps hastened their steps after this, just as with us a hearse or a mourning coach moves quicker when it has passed through a town.—*illuc*, *saltem*, 'at least as far as the gate.' Barth reads *illud*.

31.] *Ipse*, present in person at the funeral.—*ventos petisti*, Hom. *Il.* xxiii. 208, ἀλλ' Ἀχιλεὺς Βορέην ἠδὲ Ζέφυρον κελαδεινὸν ἐλθεῖν ἀρᾶται, καὶ ὑπίσχεται ἱερὰ καλά.

32.] *Nardo*, the precious perfume generally translated *spikenard*, and supposed by some to have been oil of cloves. It is said to have been the produce of a species of valerian from the mountains of India.

34.] I have placed a mark of interrogation at *cado*, the simplest sense of the passage being a continuation of the reproach in the same strain: 'Was this too a trouble to you, to throw on my pyre hyacinths at no cost, and to propitiate the fire by breaking over it a crock of wine?' (viz. as a libation to the element; see sup. 3, 60). Compare *Fast.* v. 426, 'compositique nepos busta piabat avi.' Propertius is fond of the word *piare* in various senses.

35.] This Lygdamus was Cynthia's confidential slave; see iv. 6, 2. The sense is, 'You ought to put Lygdamus to the ordeal of the hot iron on suspicion of poisoning my wine, and thus give at least a late proof of your regard by avenging my death.'—*lamina*, the hot plate, μύδρους αἴρειν χεροῖν, Soph. *Antig.* 264.—*sensi*, 'I felt the deadly effects as soon as I drank the poisoned wine that was handed to me by his treachery.' Sudden attacks of illness were generally attributed to the influence of some drug. The wine is called *pallida*, from producing a sudden paleness when drunk. So *livida adipata*, Juv. vi. 631.

37.] 'Let Nomas, who was an accomplice in the plot, only lay aside her cunning trick of spitting on them, and the hot tile will declare her hands to be guilty.' The supposed benefit of spitting on the hand was magical rather than physical, this being a common method of averting harm. It seems that Nomas had undergone the trial before, but had been declared innocent in consequence, as is now hinted, of having had recourse to an unfair expedient.

39.] Cynthia here charges the poet with having taken into his favour and dressed in fine clothes some woman of low degree, who punishes with jealous severity any of Cynthia's faithful handmaids who presume to say a word or do a deed in compliment to their departed mistress.—*inspecta est*, *i.e.* ut prostibulum.

40.] *Cyclade*, a light flowing dress like our 'muslin shawl,' with gold embroidery round the edges. (See Rich, *Companion to Dict.* in v.) The proper dress of the meretrix was the toga.

41.] *Quasillis*, wool-baskets, ταλάροις, Tibull. iv. 10, 3, 'sit tibi cura togæ potior pressumque quasillo Scortum, quam Servi filia Sulpicia.' (See Rich, in v. *Qualus*).—*de facie*, sc. quam pulchra fuerit.

Garrula de facie si qua locuta mea est;
Nostraque quod Petale tulit ad monumenta coronas,
Codicis immundi vincula sentit anus;
Cæditur et Lalage tortis suspensa capillis,
Per nomen quoniam est ausa rogare meum.
Te patiente meæ conflavit imaginis aurum,
Ardenti e nostro dotem habitura rogo.
Non tamen insector, quamvis mereare, Properti:
Longa mea in libris regna fuere tuis.
Juro ego Fatorum nulli revolubile carmen,
Tergeminusque canis sic mihi molle sonet,
Me servasse fidem. Si fallo, vipera nostris
Sibilet in tumulis et super ossa cubet.
Nam gemina est sedes turpem sortita per amnem,
Turbaque diversa remigat omnis aqua.
Una Clytæmnestræ stuprum vehit, altera Cressæ

44.] The *codex* was a clog tied to the foot, in this case to keep her from visiting the tomb. See Juvenal, *Sat.* ii. 57.

45.] *Suspensa capillis.* It is not clear whether this should be taken together, 'hung up by her hair,' or, in a modified sense, *capillis correpta*; or whether with Burmann and Kuinoel we must understand 'flagella ex capillis tanquam in funem contortis facta.' The excessive cruelty of mistresses to their maids is very touchingly described by Juvenal, vi. 490—5, and in a beautiful epigram by Martial, ii. 66.

47.] *Conflavit*, nova domina tua. See on v. 2, 68.—*dotem habitura*, 'hoping to obtain a dowry from the very flames of the pyre,' *i.e.* by rescuing from the fire the portrait set in gold. The notion seems to be, that riches would bring no luck, derived from such a source; see sup. 3, 14. Cynthia therefore was consumed with her own jewellery, as the beryl ring, v. 9, and her likeness, perhaps in a gem or cameo, according to a common but barbaric usage of depositing or consuming with the body the most favourite possessions in life. But must we not infer from this passage that the attendants sometimes filched trinkets from the pyre as perquisites for themselves?

51.] *Nulli revolubile*, 'which cannot be untwisted,' *i.e.* the weird song sung by the Parcæ as they spin the thread, and which is not to be unspun. The phrase *texere*, *ducere*, *deducere versus* &c. is almost as common as it is with *filum*. Compare v. 1, 72. The MS. Groning. gives *revocabile*.

53.] *Fidem*, 'my promise to be yours.' *Fidelity*, in the stricter sense, she could not profess.—*si fallo*, compare inf. 11, 27.

55.] *Sortita*, 'allotted.' This word, both here and inf. 11, 20, appears to bear a passive sense. See on i. 2, 5. The construction as explained by Hertzberg is somewhat complex and harsh: 'nam turba omnis gemina (sc. in duas partes divisa) sedes per fluvium sortita est, et diversa aqua remigat.' If the transitive sense be insisted on, it will be better to take *gemina* adverbially (sc. as equivalent to an adverb, δίχα) which however amounts nearly to the same thing. In either case the meaning is clear: 'all who are rowed across are conveyed either to Elysium or to penal abodes, the one in an opposite direction from the other.'—*diversa aqua* perhaps means, that some go up, others down the stream, *omnis turba* meaning the οἱ πολλοί, the dead in general.—*per amnem* seems to mean *trans amnem*.

57.] The MSS. give *una* and *altera*, which has every appearance of being genuine, though rather difficult to explain. For it is argued that Clytæmnestra, the murderer of her husband, and Pasiphae from whose unnatural appetite the Minotaur sprung, were only fit to keep company in going *one* road, and that the opposite to the Elysian. Hence for *altera* various corrections have been proposed; *utraque*,

Portat mentitæ lignea monstra bovis.
Ecce, coronato pars altera vecta phaselo,
Mulcet ubi Elysias aura beata rosas,
Qua numerosa fides, quaque æra rotunda Cybebes,
Mitratisque sonant Lydia plectra choris:
Andromedeque et Hypermnestre, sine fraude maritæ,
Narrant historias pectora nota suas,—
Hæc sua maternis queritur livere catenis
Brachia, nec meritas frigida saxa manus;
Narrat Hypermnestre magnum ausas esse sorores,
In scelus hoc animum non valuisse suum.
Sic mortis lacrimis vitæ sanamus amores.
Celo ego perfidiæ crimina multa tuæ.

unaque, arteque, unaque, ac rate &c. Hertzberg reads, 'Unda Clytæmnestræ stuprum vehit altera, Cressæ Portat,' &c. in which he maintains that the asyndeton is not only excusable but even laudable. Müller marks both verses as corrupt, but proposes 'unda Clytæmnestræ stuprum et vehit altera Cressæ Portans' &c. The true interpretation seems to be this: the good go one way, the bad another: these are the two great divisions, the heaven or the hell, as it were, of the pagan mythology. But, as there are degrees of punishment, so Clytemnestra is conveyed in a different boat and by a different course from the destination of Pasiphae. They are not both bad enough or good enough to be conveyed in the same boat. The *pars altera*, v. 59, has nothing to do with the sub-division of the damned implied by *una et altera aqua*, i.e. *cymba*.

58.] The construction is, 'altera vehit Cressæ stuprum, mentitæ (πλασσομένης) lignea monstra bovis.'

59.] *Coronato*, in reference, perhaps, to the Delian mission-ship, θεωρίς. Plat. *Phæd.* p. 57, c, ἐπειδὰν ὁ ἱερεὺς τοῦ Ἀπόλλωνος στέψῃ τὴν πρύμναν τοῦ πλοίου.—*aura*, the soft breeze usually mentioned in connection with Elysium. Pind. *Ol.* ii. 71; Hom. *Od.* iv. 567.—*mitratis*, the turbaned choirs; cf. sup. 5, 72. Ar. *Ran.* 154—7.

> 'But see, one bay-wreathed bark the blest conveys,
> Where fragrant air 'mid flowers Elysian plays;
> Where lutes resound, where tinkling cymbals ring,
> And mitred choirs to Lydian minstrels sing.'
>
> *Verse-Translations* &c., p. 47.

61.] *Quaque æra rotunda*. This is the certain emendation of Scaliger and Turnèbe for the MS. reading *qua queror* (or *quærar*) *ad unda*.

63.] *Sine fraude maritæ*, 'those guileless wives,' viz. as contrasted with Clytemnestra.—For *pectora* Müller reads *fœdera*, retaining the MSS. reading *historiæ suæ*. Being unable to see the sense of this, I have ventured to edit *historias*, believing that the dative has been introduced to make the construction depend on *nota*. But *nota* means *nota famæ*, insignis, illustris. Compare sup. 1, 12, 'pellitos habuit, rustica corda, patres.' I formerly read, with Hertzberg and Lachmann, *Narrant, historiis pectora nota suis*.

65.] *Maternis catenis*. Because the reason of her being chained to the rock, to be devoured by the sea monster, was the pride of her mother Cassiope in contending with the Nereids in beauty. Apollodor. ii. 4, 3. See iv. 22, 29, 'Non hic Andromedæ resonant pro matre catenæ.' *Sua maternis* is only found in the MS. Groning. The other copies have *summa æternis*, which Jacob thinks may fairly be said of Andromeda as a constellation. But what has that to do with her personality in Elysium?

67.] *Magnum*, μέγα, δεινόν. See Hor. *Carm.* iii. 1, 30 seqq.; Æsch. *Prom.* 880.

69.] 'Thus among the shades we heal the wounds inflicted by earthly love, while we weep over each other's griefs.' Or more literally, 'Our loves in life by tears in death we heal'—a beautiful sentiment. *Mortis lacrimæ* is briefly used for *lacrimæ inter inferos profusæ*.

70.] *Celo ego*. The *ego* is emphatic: 'unlike the heroines who console themselves by relating their loves, *I* say nothing (in Hades) of your perfidy to me.'

Sed tibi nunc mandata damus, si forte moveris,
  Si te non totum Chloridos herba tenet:
Nutrix in tremulis ne quid desideret annis
  Parthenie: potuit, nec tibi avara fuit.
Deliciæque meæ Latris, cui nomen ab usu est,
  Ne speculum dominæ porrigat illa novæ.
Et quoscumque meo fecisti nomine versus,
  Ure mihi: laudes desine habere meas.
Pelle hederam tumulo, mihi quæ pugnante corymbo
  Mollia contortis alligat ossa comis.
Pomosis Anio qua spumifer incubat arvis,
  Et numquam Herculeo numine pallet ebur,
Hic carmen media dignum me scribe columna,

72.] Müller has restored *Chloridos* from the Naples MS., for the vulg. *Doridos*. Chloris is the *nova domina* alluded to in v. 39, who is here said to have captivated Propertius by magic arts, or some hag in her employ; as if Cynthia was unwilling to believe that his regard for her could have vanished except by some such artifices. Compare iv. 6, 25.

74.] *Potuit*, tibi facilis fuit;—*nec avara*, *i. e.* nec nimia mercede id fecit. Cf. Theocr. xiv. 47, *αἱ δὲ Λύκος νῦν πάντα, Λύκῳ καὶ νυκτὸς ἀνῳκται*.

76.] *Porrigat*, 'hold out at arm's length.' So 'porrigit ignem,' sup. 1, 115.—*illa*, see sup. 2, 45.

77.] *Meo nomine*, 'on my account,' 'about me.' The first book, inscribed *Cynthia*, can hardly be meant; for why should that only be destroyed? Besides, *quoscumque* implies *all* that he had written about her. In the short verse *meas laudes* is *τὴν δι' ἐμὲ δόξαν*, 'credit devolving upon you through me.'

79.] *Pelle* &c. 'Clear from my tomb the ivy which in chains Of straggling stems my gentle bones retains.'—*mollia*, 'slight,' 'womanly,' as 'molle caput' sup. 3, 44. To prevent the grave of a relative from being overgrown with weeds is a common and natural dictate in our own minds. But the notion that ivy impeded the free egress of the spirit, which seems here intended, is a very singular one.

81.] Jacob here received (with all the later editors except Hertzberg) the correction of Broukhusius, *Pomosis Anio qua spumifer*, for *ramosis Anio qua pomifer*. Cf. iv. 16, 4, 'qua cadit in patulos lympha Aniena lacus.' *Arva* are the orchards for which Tibur was celebrated; Hor. *Od.* I. 7, 14, 'Tiburni lucus, et uda mobilibus pomaria rivis.' *Sat.* II. 4, 70, 'Picenis cedunt pomis Tiburtia succo.'

82.] *Herculeo numine*, 'by the favour of Hercules,' who was worshipped at Tibur, whence 'Herculeum Tibur,' iii. 24, 5. He was the patron of hot springs in general; see iv. 17, 5. The ancients imagined that ivory never turned to a dingy yellow, but remained white, from the air impregnated by sulphureous exhalations. See Martial, iv. 62, 'Tibur in Herculeum migravit nigra Lycoris, Omnia dum fieri candida credit ibi;' and *ib.* viii. 28, 11, 'Lilia tu vincis, nec adhuc delapsa ligustra, Et Tiburtino monte quod albet ebur.' Also lib. vii. 13. The white-faced Saxon is apt to misunderstand the classical idea of *pallor*, which implies the greenish-yellow or bilious tint peculiar to olive complexions. Hence Ovid compares it to the sere leaves in autumn, *Fast.* vi. 150. Hence also Homer's *ὦχρός δέ μιν εἷλε παρειάς*, *ἐμὲ δὲ χλωρὸν δέος ᾕρει* &c. Thus 'ivory becoming *pale*' meant ivory losing its whiteness. Horace indeed (*Epod.* vii. 15), has 'pallor albus;' but also 'pallor luteus,' *ib.* x. 16, and 'tinctus viola pallor,' *i.e.* of the yellow pansy, *ib.* iii. 10, 14. *Candor* (as iv. 21, 8), is always spoken of as a peculiar beauty.

83.] *Columna*, the square cippus, inscribed at half height with the couplet.—*vector*, like *gestator*, Mart. *Ep.* iv. 64, 19, here means 'a rider,' either on horseback or in a car. We may infer from this that loiterers on the way stopped to read the tombs.

'In Tibur's earth here golden Cynthia lies,
  Thy banks, O Anio, now the more we prize.'

Sed breve, quod currens vector ab urbe legat:
HIC TIBURTINA JACET AUREA CYNTHIA TERRA.
ACCESSIT RIPÆ LAUS, ANIENE, TUÆ.
Nec tu sperne piis venientia somnia portis:
Cum pia venerunt somnia, pondus habent.
Nocte vagæ ferimur; nox clausas liberat umbras;
Errat et abiecta Cerberus ipse sera.
Luce jubent leges Lethæa ad stagna reverti.
Nos vehimur; vectum nauta recenset onus.
Nunc te possideant aliæ; mox sola tenebo;
Mecum eris, et mixtis ossibus ossa teram.
Hæc postquam querula mecum sub lite peregit,
Inter complexus excidit umbra meos.

85-6.] This beautiful epitaph—to which the expression *aurea Cynthia*, i.e. *cara*, *pretiosa*, lends such a charm, (compare an epigram on Homer attributed to Pisistratus, *Ἡμέτερος γὰρ κεῖνος ὁ χρύσεος ἦν πολιήτης*), is given by Hertzberg as it stands in the MSS. *Tiburtina jacet hac*, &c. The Naples MS. giving 'Sed Tiburna jacet hic,' &c. where *sed* appears to have been added to fill up the metre. But there is weight in Jacob's reasoning, 'Si Tiburtina Cynthia erat, non brevi hoc monumento honor Anieni accedebat, sed loco natali.' Which Hertzberg thus answers: 'non hic honorem Anieni accessisse poeta dicit, quod Tiburtina illa fuerit, sed quod aurea puella et per secula carminibus amici immortalis illic sepulta sit.' *Accessit* is rather ambiguous, as it does not necessarily imply that Cynthia came there from another place, but only that additional charm was gained by her remains lying near the Anio. The beautiful was brought to the beautiful, and so the beauty was now double. The question is of some importance, because if the MSS. be right, the verse determines the birthplace of Cynthia, of which there is no hint in any other place. See iv. 16, 2.—*Anienus* is the River-god, who represents the river itself. Similarly Tiberinus for Tiberis v. 2, 7.

87.] *Piis portis*, 'the gates (of Hades) that send news of those we love.' The gates of horn are evidently meant, through which true dreams were believed to be transmitted. Virg. *Æn.* vi. 894, 'Sunt geminæ somni portæ, quarum altera fertur Cornea, qua veris facilis datur exitus umbris,' &c. *pia somnia* may be understood of dreams or visions of relatives, having some message of affection to communicate; compare *pia saxa*, sup. 1, 110.

88.] *Pondus habent*. Perhaps the rather obscure word in Hom. *Od.* xix. 565, *ἐλεφαίρονται*, 'are light and fickle,' is alluded to.

90.] *Abiecta*, sc. *a postibus*. See sup. 5, 48; *inf.* 11, 26.

92.] *Nos vehimur*, i.e. *nos quoque*.—*recenset*, 'he counts his crew, so that not one can escape,' as a shepherd counts his sheep. Virg. *Ecl.* iii. 34.

95.] *Sub lite* is a remarkable expression, to which it is hard to find a parallel, unless perhaps in the Greek *αὐγαῖς ὑπὸ θεσπεσίαις*, Pind. *Isth.* v. 44.—*excidit*, see sup. 4, 22. *Fast.* v. 476, 'Lubrica prensantes effugit umbra manus.' Virg. *Æn.* ii. 793. Hom. *Od.* xi. 207, *τρὶς δέ μοι ἐκ χειρῶν σκιῇ εἴκελον ἢ καὶ ὀνείρῳ Ἔπτατ'*. A beautiful and appropriate ending of a most interesting and well-written poem.

VIII.

Disce, quid Esquilias hac nocte fugarit aquosas,
  Cum vicina novis turba cucurrit agris.
Lanuvium annosi vetus est tutela draconis,
  Hic ubi tam raræ non perit hora moræ,
Qua sacer abripitur cæco descensus hiatu,
  Qua penetrat,—virgo, tale iter omne cave!
Jejuni serpentis honos, cum pabula poscit
  Annua, et ex ima sibila torquet humo.
Talia demissæ pallent ad sacra puellæ,

VIII. The poet gives a lively account of the manner in which he had retaliated on Cynthia for her infidelity, and how she had detected him, and of her summary vengeance. The provocation is sufficiently manifest: the fault was the greater on her side (v. 16).

1.] *Esquilias.* That Propertius lived there we know from iv. 23, 24. It was called *aquosas* from its springs and marshy slopes, which were favourable to the growth of the *esculeta* or oak-groves from which the name was derived. See Varro, *L. L.* v. § 49. So *Viminalis* from *vimen*, ib. § 51. Cælius was originally *Querquetulanus* from its *quercetum*, Tac. *Ann.* iv. 65. It is curious that these hills of Rome should have been named from their vegetation; and the circumstance confirms the poet's statements in v. 4, 3, &c.—*hac nocte*, 'last night,' as the Greeks say νυκτὶ τῇδε, or ἐν νυκτὶ τῇ νῦν, Soph. *Ant.* 16.

2.] *Novis agris.* Mæcenas had converted a cemetery which formerly existed there into a suburban park. See Hor. *Sat.* I. 8, 14, 'Nunc licet Esquiliis habitare salubribus atque Aggere in aprico spatiari, qua modo tristes Albis informem spectabant ossibus agrum.' The sense is, 'Hear now the cause that last night scared all the marshy Esquiline, and set the folk who live near the new park running to see what was the matter.'—After the first couplet, perhaps, should follow that which now stands 19—20 inf.

3.] *Lanuvium.* This place was celebrated for the cultus of Juno Sospita, and for the presiding divinity of a serpent. See Ælian, *Nat. Anim.* xi. 16; Cic. *de Div.* I. § 36.—*tutela* means not only 'patronage,' but the thing or person protected, as Ovid, *Trist.* i. 10, 1, 'Est mihi, sitque precor, flavæ tutela Minervæ Navis, et a picta casside nomen habet.'

4.] *Hic ubi* &c. 'Hic ubi spectaculum tam rarum, quippe non nisi semel quotannis obvium, non perit, sed avide arripitur a spectatoribus.' *Barth.*—*mora* is for *tempus commorandi*, as Hertzberg observes. 'Here, where the season of an amusement so rarely to be enjoyed (*annua*, inf. 8) is not thrown away.'—*mora*, see inf. 78. For *hic* we might suggest *hac*, repeated inf. 15, with a colon at *draconis*.

5—8.] *Hiatu*, sup. 1, 149. 'Where the descent into the sacred cave is rapidly made through a dark opening, into which the tribute to the hungry snake finds its way (beware, maids! of all such ways as this), when he demands his yearly food, and hisses from the depths of the earth as he moves his coils.'—The ceremony, which is similar to one long kept up in this country, by making girls pass through holes or apertures in walls &c., is evidently of phallic origin, the serpent being a phallic symbol. Like the tales about Cerberus, Typhœus, Echidna, &c., either the hissing or rumbling heard in volcanic caves, or some trick easily put on the credulous, will sufficiently account for the story here told.

6.] *Qua penetrat*, ubi demittitur, inicitur, *honos serpentis*, γέρας, donum, placamentum, μελιτοῦττα. Barth and Kuinoel give *penetral* from the conjecture of Scaliger. The allusion in *cave, virgo!* is to the popular notion that the successful return from the serpent's cave was a proof of chastity, and the bantering which would follow the experiments no doubt made this a favourite and much-frequented festival.

9—10.] 'Such are the rites to which girls descend pale with fear into the cave, when their hands (i.e. holding out the food) are rashly trusted in the snake's mouth.'—*demissæ*, sup. 5, 17.

Cum temere anguino creditur ore manus.
Ille sibi admotas a virgine corripit escas:
Virginis in palmis ipsa canistra tremunt.
Si fuerint castæ, redeunt in colla parentum;
Clamantque agricolæ: Fertilis annus erit.
Huc mea detonsis avecta est Cynthia mannis:
Causa fuit Juno, sed mage causa Venus.
Appia dic, quæso, quantum te teste triumphum
Egerit, effusis per tua saxa rotis,
Turpis in arcana sonuit cum rixa taberna;
Si sine me, famæ non sine labe meæ.
Spectaclum ipsa sedens primo temone pependit,
Ausa per impuros frena movere locos.

10.] *Creditur ore.* A remarkable use of the ablative in a locative sense. See i. 17, 22. It does not seem philosophical to say that the ablative can be used in these cases for the dative: but it is not very easy on any other theory to explain *carmine cessit*, iii. 26, 64; or *insultet morte*, iv. 6, 24. Dr. Donaldson (*Varronianus*, p. 282, ed. 2) has some remarks on the confusion of form in the dative, locative, and ablative of nouns; but these instances are more decisive than any which he quotes. Lachmann retains the reading of the best copies, *tremere*. We might suggest *tenera*.

11.] *Admotas a virgine*, 'if offered by a maid, he greedily seizes the food.' Otherwise, according to Ælian, it was rejected.

12.] *Canistra.* The basket containing the food sometimes shook from the nervousness of the person undergoing the test; and this was regarded as a good omen.

15.] *Detonsis*, 'clipped,' that is, trimmed as to tails and manes. On the word *mannus* see the commentators on Hor. *Od.* iii. 27, 7. The MSS. have *ab annis*, which was corrected by Beroaldus.

16.] A very witty verse. The ostensible motive was the worship of Juno; the real one, to spend the day with a favoured rival of the poet's.

18.] *Per tua saxa.* The Appian road was paved with large blocks, whence Hor. *Sat.* i. 5, 6, 'nimis est gravis Appia tardis,' 'too jolting for those who would take a journey easily.' To drive in a dashing style over this pavement was the ambition of a smart Roman; for carriages were not allowed in the streets of the city. Hor. *Epod.* iv. 14, 'et Appiam mannis terit.'—*effusis rotis*, ἀνέδην, ἀπεχαλινωμένως. This verb is applied to the passage over obstacles without check, as Persius, i. 64, 'ut per leve severos *effundat* junctura ungues.'

19—20.] This couplet, as above remarked, would come in better after ver. 2. 'When a disgraceful brawl raised a disturbance in an out-of-the-way tavern, if without me, yet not without a slur on my character.' Whether this *taberna* was the place mentioned inf. 35 seqq., is not clear; nor how the poet can justly say the brawl was 'sine me.' Perhaps he means, that he did not intend to provoke it.

21.] This also is an expressive verse. She leant forward, *pependit*, over the pole (prima parte temonis, πρώτῳ ῥυμῷ, *Il.* vi. 40), *spectaclum*, so as to attract the attention of all to herself and her skilful driving over rough parts of the road, *impuros locos*. The figure seems borrowed from charioteers in the circus.—*pependit*, cf. *Æn.* v. 147, 'aurigæ—proni in verbera pendent.' Cynthia, it would seem, took a turn at the reins herself, to exhibit her courage and steady hand, whence *ausa*. The very words *frena movere* (ἀνεῖν χαλινόν) bear the sense of 'driving at *full* speed.'—*purus*, like καθαρός, is sometimes used of clear, unimpeded ground. So Ovid. *Fast.* iii. 581, 'Est prope piscosos lapidosi Crathidis amnes *Purus ager*.'—Q. Curtius, iii. 4, 8, 'Cydnus—leni tractu a fontibus labens, *puro solo* excipitur.' Kuinoel and others wrongly understand 'loca sordida,'—'byways and alleys.' But no one who wishes to display his equipage selects such places.

Serica nam taceo volsi carpenta nepotis
  Atque armillatos colla Molossa canes,
Qui dabit immundæ venalia fata saginæ,
  Vincet ubi erasas barba pudenda genas.
Cum fieret nostro totiens injuria lecto,
  Mutato volui castra movere toro.
Phyllis Aventinæ quædam est vicina Dianæ,
  Sobria grata parum; cum bibit, omne decet.
Altera Tarpeios est inter Teïa lucos,
  Candida, sed potæ non satis unus erit.
His ego constitui noctem lenire vocatis,
  Et Venere ignota furta novare mea.
Unus erat tribus in secreta lectulus herba.
  Quæris concubitus? inter utramque fui.
Lygdamus ad cynthos, vitrique æstiva supellex,
  Et Methymnæi Græca saliva meri.

23.] *Serica nam taceo.* The elegant correction of Beroaldus for *sirice* or *sirige nam ceple* or *tacte.* *Carpentum* was a two-wheeled vehicle, peculiarly used by women (like the ἁρμάμαξα of the Greeks) and on state occasions; whence it is called *serica*, lined or curtained with silk. Tac. *Ann.* xii. 42, 'Suum quoque fastigium Agrippina extollere altius; carpento Capitolium ingredi, qui mos sacerdotibus et sacris antiquitus concessus venerationem augebat feminæ.' Juv. *Sat.* viii. 146, 'Præter majorum cineres atque ossa volucri Carpento rapitur pinguis Damasippus.'—*vulsi nepotis*, 'the close-shaved fop.' *Nepos* expresses what we call 'a fast man.' The pulling out (iv. 25, 13,) or otherwise removing hair (*depilatio*) of straggling and irregular growth was a frequent practice with effeminate Romans, and was considered disreputable. Hence Suetonius (*Cæs.* § 45,) 'circa corporis curam morosior, ut non solum tonderetur, sed velleretur etiam, ut quidam exprobraverunt.'

24.] *Armillatos.* Some have fancied that Cynthia's bracelets were transferred to the dogs' necks; an absurd idea. The word is derived from *armus*, and properly means that which pertains to the shoulders. Hence, applied to human beings, armillæ are not *bracelets* but *armlets*, *i.e.* rings on the upper part of the arm, just below the shoulders, as they are still worn by many savage tribes. *Molossa* agreeing with *colla* is a singular construction. Müller reads *Molosso* (*molosso* MS. Naples). The dogs, or hounds, belonged to the *servos*, and had ornamental collars on, called perhaps in ridicule, 'armillæ.'

25.] 'A wretch who will one day (viz. when he has run through all his property), sell himself to be trained and coarsely fed for a gladiator, where the beard he will have to be ashamed of (*i.e.* of which he has such a dislike) will outgrow and get the mastery over the cheeks now so finely scraped.'—*pudenda*, sup. 4, 36.

29.] *Aventinæ Dianæ.* The temple of the goddess on the Aventine. Ovid, *Fast.* iii. ult, 'Aventino Luna colenda jugo.' Hor. *Carm. Sæc.* 69, 'Quæque Aventinum tenet Algidumque,' &c.—With this verse a new elegy commences in the MSS.

31.] *Tarpeios lucos.* See sup. 4, 3.

33—4.] 'By inviting these I made an appointment to dismiss dull care for one night, and to repeat my former stealthy meetings by trying a new mistress.'—*furta*, see sup. 7, 15.

35.] *In secreta herba*, *i.e.* in the viridarium, or conservatory in the centre of the peristyle. See Becker, *Gallus*, p. 251. This custom is still kept up in Spanish houses, where the inner court is planted with orange-trees and fragrant shrubs. Compare Tibull. iii. 3, 15, 'et nemora in domibus sacros imitantia lucos.'

36.] *Concubitus.* He evidently speaks of the triclinium, as he proceeds to describe the entertainment.

37—8.] 'We had Lygdamus to serve the wine, and we had a light summer-

Nile tuus tibicen erat, crotalistria Phyllis,
  Et facilis spargi munda sine arte rosa.
Nanus et ipse suos breviter concretus in artus
  Jactabat truncas ad cava buxa manus.
Sed neque suppletis constabat flamma lucernis,
  Recidit inque suos mensa supina pedes.
Me quoque per talos Venerem quaerente secundos,
  Semper damnosi subsiluere canes.
Cantabant surdo, nudabant pectora caeco:
  Lanuvii ad portas (hei mihi!) solus eram;
Cum subito rauci sonuerunt cardine postes,

service of glass, and wine from Methymna with the Greek smack of turpentine.' The *vinum picatum* derived a flavour from the rosin that lined the jars internally, and this peculiar flavour was still more prevalent in the Greek wines. Hence in Arist. *Ach.* 190, the σταμνία, which are samples of wine, are said (in one sense) ὄζειν πίττης.—Compare Pers. vi. 24, 'nec tenuem sollers turdarum nosse salivam.'

39.] There does not seem to be any ground for the alteration of Scaliger, *Niliotes tibicen*, though it has been received by Kuinoel, Lachmann, and Müller.—*crotalistria* is the emendation of Turnèbe; the MSS. give a word more or less corrupted, *choralistria*, *choralistria*. The part of the κροταλίστρια was to beat time with castanets (κρόταλα ὀστράκινα) of terra cotta or box-wood (*cava buxa*, v. 42).

40.] *Facilis spargi rosa*, 'good-natured to be pelted with roses.' Hertzberg may be right in regarding *rosa* as the ablative, and referring *facilis* to Phyllis. He compares 'simplex munditiis' of Horace, and remarks that the amusement of tossing flowers (perhaps pulled from the chaplets) was common in company of this description. Thus *munda sine arte* is 'tidily, but not artistically dressed.' Otherwise we might translate 'roses neatly tied in bunches for throwing them easily about.' So Hor. *Carm.* iii. 19, 21, 'parcentes ego dexteras Odi; sparge rosas.' The poet seems to prefer the use of *rosa* in the singular. Compare 'blanditiae rosam,' v. 6, 72; 'verna rosa,' iv. 5, 22; 'ferre rosam,' v. 2, 40. So Ovid uses *flos* for *flores*, *Fast.* v. 211—2, and Tibullus has even 'innumeram ovem,' ii. 2, 42.

41.] *Nanus et* &c. 'A dwarf too, shrunk up into his own limbs, flung out his shortened hands to the hollow box-wood castanets.' The action meant is the *gesticulatio* (Livy, vii. 2) to the *crotalistria*. Thus the *bellus homo* in Martial, *Ep.* iii. 63, 6, among other accomplishments 'movet in varios brachia volsa modos.' The MSS. give *magnus*, corrected by Beroaldus. Hertzberg observes that two bronze effigies of dwarfs, with castanets precisely in the attitude here described, have been found at Herculaneum. On these *pumiliones* see Becker's *Gallus*, p. 211. Augustus had the good sense to discountenance the fashionable folly. Suet. *Oct.* § 83, 'pumilos atque distortos et omnes generis ejusdem, ut ludibria naturae malique ominis, abhorrebat.'

43—4.] *Sed neque.* 'But the flame did not burn steady though the lamp was filled with oil, and the top of the table fell with its face uppermost upon its own feet.' The unsteady (or spluttering) flame was an omen of an arrival, sup. 3, 60.—*in suos pedes* can only mean that the *mensa* or *abacus* was moveable, and slid off from its frame, *trapezophora*. See my note on Martial, *Ep.* 367, and 476, 7. Becker, *Gallus*, p. 296, who might have made important use of this passage. The sense is, 'in spite of all attempts at merriment, unlucky omens disturbed our sport, and ill-success with the dice added to my chagrin.'

46.] *Damnosi*, 'losing,' supra, 5, 28. Plaut. *Capt.* 73; *Curcul.* 356.—*subsiluere*, 'fell so that aces always came uppermost.' The highest throw was *Venus*, when all the four dice turned up different numbers; the lowest *canis*, when the player threw four aces. See Becker's *Gallus*, p. 500.

48.] *Solus.* 'My mind was solely with Cynthia at Lanuvium.'—*solus* for *solummodo*, or *totus*.

Et levia ad primos murmura facta Lares.
Nec mora, cum totas resupinat Cynthia valvas,
  Non operosa comis, sed furibunda decens.
Pocula mi digitos inter cecidere remissos,
  Pallucrantque ipso labra soluta mero.
Fulminat illa oculis et quantum femina sævit:
  Spectaclum capta nec minus urbe fuit.
Phyllidos iratos in vultum conicit ungues;
  Territa vicinas Teïa clamat aquas.
Lumina sopitos turbant elata Quirites,
  Omnis et insana semita nocte sonat.
Illas direptisque comis tunicisque solutis
  Excipit obscuræ prima taberna viæ.
Cynthia gaudet in exuviis, victrixque recurrit,
  Et mea perversa sauciat ora manu,
Imponitque notam collo, morsuque cruentat,
  Præcipueque oculos, qui meruere, ferit.
Atque ubi jam nostris lassavit brachia plagis,
  Lygdamus ad pluteí fulcra sinistra latens
Eruitur, geniumque meum prostratus adorat;—

50.] *Levia*, 'faint sounds were heard as of one talking at the entrance of the house,' i.e. demanding admission from the *janitor*.

52.] *Operosa* (iv. 2, 12, sup. 6, 18), 'not elaborately decked or attired in her hair, but all dishevelled as she was.'—*Furibunda decens*, 'beautiful in her rage.'—The *valvæ* were double or jointed doors, like window shutters, which folded back, whence *resupinat*: *totas* is added, because in entering quietly it was usual to open only one side, or flap.

54.] *Pallucrantque*. The change of tense suggests the omission of *que*. Probably he wrote *palluerunt*, pronounced as a trisyllable.—*ipso mero* is for *inter ipsum vinum*, 'in the very act of drinking.' See on v. 10, supra.

56.] *Spectaclum*, 'a scene.'

57.] The margin of MS. Gron. has *ignes*, which seems to have been suggested by *aquas* in the next verse. But it was a strange action even for Cynthia to throw the lamp in Phyllis' face; and *iratos* could thus only be taken for *irata*. On the other hand, compare iv. 8, 7, 'Tu minitare oculos subjecta exurere flamma,' which will allow us to explain *conjicit* 'thrusts in her face.' Still this reading is not necessary; for experience shews that on any sudden panic people are willing enough to cry out 'fire!' and others to bawl for 'water!'—*vicinas*, the Esquiline hill being 'aquosum,' sup. 1.

60.] *Insana nocte*, 'the nightly brawl.' Cf. iv. 10, 26, 'publica vicinæ perstrepat aura viæ.' Kuinoel has *voce sonat*, as usual against the best MSS.

61.] *Illas* &c. 'They, with hair all pulled about and tunics all loose, find shelter in the first shop in the gloomy alley.'

63.] *Recurrit*, sc. ad me. 'Having put them to flight, she runs back and wounds my face with vixenish hand.' On *gaudere in* &c. see ii. 4, 18, where however 'gaudeat in puero' perhaps rather belongs to the idiom pointed out on i. 13, 7, so that *in* may here stand for *inter*. Cf. Catull. 22, 17; Lucret. iii. 72.

65.] *Notam*, sup. 3, 26. 'She leaves a mark on my neck by biting till the blood starts, but especially she strikes my eyes, which were the real delinquents.'

69.] *Latens*, 'who had been lying concealed.'—*eruitur*, for *eruitur*, was restored

Lygdame, nil potui: tecum ego captus eram.
Supplicibus palmis tum demum ad fœdera veni,
  Cum vix tangendos præbuit illa pedes,
Atque ait: Admissæ si vis me ignoscere culpæ,
  Accipe, quæ nostræ formula legis erit.
Tu neque Pompeia spatiabere cultus in umbra,
  Nec cum lascivum sternet arena forum.
Colla cave inflectas ad summum obliqua theatrum,
  Aut lectica tuæ sidat aperta moræ.
Lygdamus in primis, omnis mihi causa querellæ,
  Veneat, et pedibus vincula bina trahat.
Indixit leges. Respondi ego: Legibus utar.
  Riserat imperio facta superba dato.
Dein quemcumque locum externæ tetigere puellæ,
  Suffiit; at pura limina tergit aqua.
Imperat et totas iterum mutare lacernas,

by Lachmann from the Naples MS., which also gives *protractus*, a reading not inferior to the vulgate.—*fulcra pluteri* seem to be the legs supporting the raised board or ledge,—as we should say, the back of the sofa,—in other words, the hinder legs of the triclinium.—The Lygdamus here mentioned must have been the poet's slave, as she demands his punishment, v. 80, and therefore the person mentioned sup. 7, 35, and iv. 6, 2, may be regarded as lent to Cynthia, on the principle often acted on by Cicero and Atticus, κατὰ τὸ τῶν φίλων.

70.] *Tecum*, *i.e.* I was taken captive like yourself.

72.] *Cum vix*, 'when at last'—for so *vix* may frequently be rendered—'she allowed me to embrace and kiss her feet.'

74.] *Quæ erit*, i.e. *quæ sit*, or *futura sit*.

75.] 'You shall never walk in full dress under Pompey's piazza,'—*i.e.* to attract or be attracted,—'nor be a spectator of the gladiators in the forum.' Compare iii. 14, 8, 'Quænam nunc porticus illam excipit?' This verse seems to have been copied by Martial, xi. 47, 'Cur nec Pompeia lentus spatiatur in umbra?'—*arena* is here literally meant, 'when sand shall strew the forum *for* the combat.' Ovid, *Trist.* ii. 282, 'Martia cum durum sternet arena forum.'

77.] *Summum theatrum.* The higher and therefore more remote seats, where the women sate apart.' Sueton. *Oct.* § 44, 'Feminis ne gladiatores quidem, quos promiscue spectari solemne olim erat, *nisi ex superiore loco* spectare concessit. Solis Virginibus Vestalibus locum in theatro separatim et contra prætoris tribunal dedit. Athletarum vero spectaculo muliebre secus omne adeo summovit, ut pontificalibus ludis pugilum par postulatum distulerit in sequentis diei matutinum tempus, edixeritque, mulieres ante horam quintam venire in theatrum non placere.'

78.] The MSS. give *sudet*. (The Naples MS. *sidet* according to Jacob and Lachmann; but Hertzberg says, '*sudet omnes*.') The sense is, 'let not the lectica be left open for your amusement.' See sup. 4.

82.] *Dato*, concesso sibi a me.

84.] The MSS. have *sufficiat pura*, or *sufficat pura*.—*sufficit: et pura* is the reading of the ed. Rheg. It is hard to choose between *suffiit, et* and *suffit, at* (Hertzberg). The latter is certainly nearer the MS. reading. Jacob has edited *suffit, et a pura* from Puccl. Müller, *suffit et pura*.

85.] *Totas mutare lacernas*, 'to change again (*i.e.* as I had just put one on) the mantle with its hood.' It is difficult to render the plural, which implies 'the set,' or cloak with its appendages. Compare Martial, *Ep.* ii. 29, 3, and iv. 61, 5, 'milibus decem dixti Emptas lacernas munus esse Pompullæ.' The *Lacerna* was the garment which the Romans threw over the toga, and which differed but little from the

Torque meum tetigit sulphuris igne caput.
Atque ita, mutato per singula pallia lecto,
Respondi, et tuto solvimus arma toro.

IX.

Amphitryoniades qua tempestate juvencos
Egerat a stabulis, o Erythea, tuis,
Venit ad eductos pecorosa Palatia montes,
Et statuit fessos fessus et ipse boves,
Qua Velabra suo stagnabant flumine, quaque

pensula. See Becher's *Gallus*, p. 420. The Naples MS. has *lucernas*, 'quod puto verius esse,' says Jacob.

56.] *Sulphuris* (al. *sulfuris*), used in expiation or lustration; Hom. *Od.* xxii. 482; Ovid, *Fast.* iv. 740, 'tactaque fumanti sulphure balet ovis.'

57.] *Per singula pallia*, 'the bedding having been changed sheet by sheet.' See on v. 3, 31. These passages show that more than one of these coverlets were occasionally used.

58.] All the MSS. have *respondi et toto*. Both Jacob and Hertzberg have adopted from Puccii *despondi, et tuto*. Kuinoel has *et spondis*, Lachmann and Barth *et sponda et*. *Respondi* is ὑπήκουσα, 'I complied with her request.' Müller marks the verse as corrupt, but suggests *res paria* for *respondi*. By *totus* he may mean *utrumque torum*, sup. iii. 8, 4, and v. 3, 31, 'in toto non sidere pallia lecto,' viz. that peace was made by occupying the couch together. Compare sup. 4, 59 and 62, 'solvere acies' and 'mollist arma.'—*tuto toro* may well mean, 'rendered harmless by the purification employed, and the change of the *pallia*,' or perhaps, 'not again disturbed by a brawl.' Barth and Kuinoel read *movimus arma* from Heinsius. It does not seem to have occurred to these emendators, that poets purposely avoid hackneyed expressions.

IX. This poem contains the legend of the foundation and dedication by Hercules of the Ara Maxima (Livy, i. 7), which women were forbidden to approach, and is evidently one of those composed for the work on Roman Fasti already mentioned. Incidentally other stories are introduced, as the origin of the Velabrum, the Forum Boarium, and the Sabine title of Hercules, *Sancus*, v. 74.

2.] *Erythea.* An island on the s.w. coast of Spain, where Geryon kept his herds. Hence Ovid calls them 'boves Erytheidas,' *Fast.* i. 543. 'Erytheida praedam,' *ib.* v. 649. Strabo, lib. iii. cap. 2, ἐοίκασι δ' οἱ παλαιοὶ καλεῖν τὸν Βαῖτιν (the Guadalquiver) Ταρτησσόν, τὰ δὲ Γάδειρα (Cadiz) καὶ τὰς πρὸς αὐτὴν νήσους Ἐρύθειαν.—Ἐρατοσθένης δὲ τὴν συνεχῆ τῇ Κάλπῃ (Gibraltar) Ταρτησσίδα καλεῖσθαί φησι, καὶ Ἐρύθειαν νῆσον εὐδαίμονα. See also Herod. iv. 8, from which it is clear that Erythea was the Isle de Leon, on which Cadiz stands. The legend probably arose from the Greeks wishing to obtain from Spain a superior breed of cattle; and Pausanias, who is often ingenious in interpreting a myth, perceived this, lib. iv. cap. 36, § 2, Ἡρακλεῖ κατὰ δόξαν τὴν ἐν Ἰβηρίᾳ βοῶν προσέταξεν Εὐρυσθεὺς ἐλάσαι τῶν Γηρυόνου βοῶν τὴν ἀγέλην· φαίνεται δὲ καὶ Ἔρυξ τότε ἐν Σικελίᾳ δυναστεύων ὁρμὴν οὕτως ἔχων ἐς τὰς βοῦς τὰς ἐξ Ἐρυθείας ἔρωτα, ὥστε καὶ ἐπάλαισε πρὸς τὸν Ἡρακλέα.

3.] *Ad eductos.* The MSS. give *et adductos*, or *et ad victos*, from the latter of which the common reading *ad invictos* was devised by the early editors. Lachmann conjectured *eductos*, i.e. editos, which Hertzberg and Müller have adopted. The correction is a probable one. Compare 'celsa Palatia,' iv. 9, 49. Though *educere* is generally applied to works of art, as *Aen.* vi. 178, 'aramque sepulcri Congerere arboribus, caeloque educere certant,' and 'eductae turres,' Tac. *Ann.* xii. 16, it occurs in Lucan ii. 428, of the Apennine ridge, 'educto dorso' (quoted by Hertzberg).—On *pecorosa*, pecoribus plena, i.e. depasta, see v. 1, 4.—*nemorosa* is a reading of less MS. authority.

5.] *Velabra.* The low part of the city called the Velabrum is here derived from

Nauta per urbanas velificabat aquas.
Sed non infido manserunt hospite Caco
Incolumes: furto polluit ille Jovem.
Incola Cacus erat, metuendo raptor ab antro,
Per tria partitos qui dabat ora focos.
Hic, ne certa forent manifestæ signa rapinæ,
Aversos cauda traxit in antra boves;
Nec sine teste deo: furem sonuere juvenci,
Furis et implacidas diruit ira fores.
Mænalio jacuit pulsus tria tempora ramo
Cacus; et Alcides sic ait: Ite boves,
Herculis ite boves, nostræ labor ultime clavæ,
Bis mihi quæsitæ, bis mea præda, boves,
Arvaque mugitu sancite boaria longo:
Nobile erit Romæ pascua vestra forum.
Dixerat, et sicco torret sitis ora palato;
Terraque non ullas feta ministrat aquas.

vela, on the theory that it was once, like the place called Λίμναι at Athens, stagnant water. See on v. 2, 8. Varro, *L. L.* v. § 43—4, 'Olim paludibus mons (Aventinus) erat ab reliquis disclusus, itaque ex urbe advehebantur ratibus: quojus vestigia, quod ea, qua tum vehebantur, etiam nunc dicitur Velabrum.'—'Velabrum a vehendo. Velaturam facere etiam nunc dicuntur, qui id mercede faciunt.'

7.] *Sed non.* 'But they did not long remain safe under so faithless a host as Cacus: for he played the thief and violated the sanctity of the asylum of Jupiter.' He was the θεὸς ἐγχώριος, though his seat was rather the Capitol than the Palatine. Hercules had accepted the hospitality of this Cacus, which had been proffered with a view to the theft. The word may be identical with κακὸς, *i. e.* κακοεργὸς, the Devastator. He was the Roman type of Typhoeus or Chimæra, a volcanic agent who sent up fire and smoke through several vents at the same time. See the fine account in *Æn.* viii. 190, seqq. Ovid also represents Cacus as fire-breathing, but not as three-headed, *Fast.* i. 572.

9.] *Incola.* MSS. *incola.* Schrader and Kuinoel *accola.*—*raptor ab antro*, like *doctor ab arte*, inf. x. 9; *mundi servator ab Alba*, sup. 6, 37.

12.] Ovid has nearly the same verse, *Fast.* i. 550, 'Traxerat aversos Cacus in antra feros.'

13.] *Nec* (*i. e.* nec tamen) *sine teste deo.* *Deus* is the god of hospitality (v. 5) who gave testimony of the theft by making the cattle in the cave low in recognition of the rest as they passed.

14.] *Et.* The conjunction implies the immediate consequence. Kuinoel reads *at*, with Heinsius.—*implacidas*, ἀπραεῖς, hostiles. Hor. *Carm.* iv. 14, 10, 'Genaunos, implacidum genus.'

15.] *Ramo.* Cf. i. 1, 13, 'Hylaei percussus vulnere rami.'

19.] *Sancite.* The sense is, inaugurate the site of, or supply a precedent after which the Forum Boarium may reasonably be called in future times. One might suppose the poet had in mind βοὸς rather than βόες. The Naples MS. gives *bovaria*, which Müller has adopted; the MS. Gron. *boaria*, with the letter *v* erased.

20.] *Nobile*, a chief or principal forum. After this verse (if nothing has been lost) we must suppose the act of building and dedicating the Ara Maxima, on the recovery of the lost oxen, to have taken place. For inf. 68, Hercules speaks of it as already constructed.

22.] *Feta ministrat* may be taken as equivalent to *parit*, or *parvas praebet.* 'Terra nunc feta non erat Herculi, neque potum ministrabat.'—*Hertzberg.* 'The teeming earth (*i. e.* that had given pasture to the cattle) supplies no water for him.' Cf. sup. 6, 4, 'et Cyrenaeas urna ministret aquas.'

Sed procul inclusas audit ridere puellas,
  Lucus ubi umbroso fecerat orbe nemus;
Femineæ loca clausa deæ fontesque piandos,
  Impune et nullis sacra retecta viris.
Devia puniceæ velabant limina vittæ,
  Putris odorato luxerat igne casa,
Populus et longis ornabat frondibus ædem,
  Multaque cantantis umbra tegebat aves.
Huc ruit in siccam congesto pulvere barbam,
  Et jacit ante fores verba minora deo:
'Vos precor, o luci sacro quæ luditis antro,
  'Pandite defessis hospita fana viris.
'Fontis egens erro, circaque sonantia lymphis,

24.] The conjecture of Heinsius, *ubi* for *ab*, appears to deserve more notice than it has received from the later editors. The correction is so obvious, and so much improves the sense, while on the other hand 'lucus fecerat nemus ab orbe' is such an unusual construction, that I have not hesitated to reject the old reading. Similarly *ubi* has been corrupted, from the elision of *i*, in iv. 15, 32.

25.] *Fontes piandos.* 'Qui sacrificiis adhibentur.' *Hertzberg*: who compares 'sacra piare' i. 1, 20. Barth explains, 'viris expiandos si inde biberint.' Unless the water itself was purified and as it were consecrated before being used for aspersion, it could not be called *pianda*. Propertius is fond of using this verb, which is a metrically convenient one, but not very definite in its meaning. The accusative, it will be observed, does not depend directly on *fecerat*, but some participle like *continens* must be mentally supplied with *nemus*.

26.] The goddess alluded to is Bona Dea, and the connexion of her cultus by women exclusively with that of Demeter in the Thesmophoria cannot reasonably be doubted. They are called 'rites not to be revealed (or, that never had been revealed) with impunity to any male.'

27.] *Vittae.* 'The doorway of the sequestered retreat was veiled by scarlet fillets.' This, like the Greek *εἰρεσιώνη* placed over doors, seems to have indicated an asylum, or the offer of hospitality. See inf. on v. 62.—*putris casa*, 'innuitur sacrarium vetustate fere collapsum, ut apud Hor. *Epist.* i. 10, 49, 'fanum putre Vacunae.''—*Kuinoel.* The word is connected with *πύθεσθαι*, and signifies the decomposition and softening caused by time and exposure, as *putris navis*, iii. 17, 7, *putria signa*, sup. 5, 24. It is but rarely used (as in Ovid, *Fast.* i. 379), in the sense which the English derivative bears.—*casa*, i.e. sacellum, as in v. 1, 6. 'The time-worn shrine had been lit up with fragrant fire.'

29.] *Populus*, the tree sacred to Hercules, and so giving as it were an omen of his reception.—*multa umbra*, ἀμφιλαφής, its ample shade (or, the shade of many trees) gave shelter to singing birds.

32.] *Minora deo.* 'Beneath the language of a god,' 'undignified for a god to utter.' He condescended to petition as a mere mortal, being not yet deified.

33.] *Luditis.* This refers to *ridere* v. 23.—*antro*, 'this bower.' Cf. sup. 4, 3.—*fana* is Scaliger's correction. The Naples MS. gives *vana*, the MS. Gron. and ed. Rheg. *antra*, whence Pucci suggested *tegna*.—*viris*, 'even males (sup. 26), if weary, have a claim on your hospitality.'

35.] *Sonantia.* The ellipse of *loca* is unusual; nor is Hertzberg's remark quite to the point, that with adjectives involving the sense of the substantive, such as *declivia, plana, aperta, lubrica*, &c. the latter may be omitted. He more aptly quotes Ovid, *Met.* v. 405, 'Perque lacus altos et olentia sulphure fertur.'—*quae* must be understood as *quamquam*, Gr. καὶ ταῦτα. 'A wanderer I, perishing for drink, while all round the sound of water is heard' (*i.e.* there is plenty for all), 'and all I ask is as much of it from the stream as I can take in the hollow of my hand.' Cf. sup. 1, 146, 'persuasae fallere rima sat est.'

'Et cava suscepto flumine palma sat est.
'Audistisne aliquem, tergo qui sustulit orbem?
'Ille ego sum: Alciden terra recepta vocat.
'Quis facta Herculeæ non audît fortia clavæ,
'Et numquam ad †natas irrita tela feras,
'Atque uni Stygias homini luxisse tenebras?
'Accipite; hæc fesso vix mihi terra patet.
'Quod si Junoni sacrum faceretis amaræ,
'Non clausisset aquas ipsa noverca suas.
'Sin aliquam vultusque meus sætæque leonis
'Terrent, et Libyco sole perusta coma,
'Idem ego Sidonia feci servilia palla
'Officia, et Lydo pensa diurna colo;
'Mollis et hirsutum cepit mihi fascia pectus,
'Et manibus duris apta puella fui.'
Talibus Alcides; at talibus alma Sacerdos,
Puniceo canas stamine vincta comas;
'Parce oculis, hospes, lucoque abscede verendo:
'Cede agedum, et tuta limina linque fuga.
'Interdicta viris metuenda lege piatur,

40.] *Natas* can hardly be the true reading; but no probable conjecture has been proposed. The Naples MS. gives *adverias*. It may be remarked generally how much less successful conjectural emendation is when applied to the Latin than to the Greek classics. *Varias*, *vastas*, *saevas*, *tenias*, *notas* have been suggested; but none of these is quite satisfactory. Can the poet have attempted to represent the Grecism πρὸς τὰ ἀεὶ ἀπογεγενημένα θηρία, 'darts that never failed against any creature that ever was born?'—I have given *audit* for *audit*.

42.] This verse recurs after v. 66. If genuine in both places, it would seem to have resulted rather from haste or oversight in composing than to be 'summa cum indignationis vi repetitus,' as Hertzberg thinks. Müller with Barth and Kuinoel omits it here, after Scaliger, thus leaving an awkward lacuna in the text. Lachmann also follows them. The sense is, 'Take me in; let it not be said that this is the only corner in the world that, after all my labours in clearing it of monsters, refuses to receive me when weary.'

43.] 'Why, even if you had been offering a sacrifice to Juno, my step-mother and implacable enemy, and not to Bona Dea, she would not thus cruelly have denied me water.' Jacob and Müller follow Lachmann in reading *Quid, si* &c. interrogatively.

47.] 'I am the same hero who in the service of Omphale was dressed as a woman in Tyre-dyed robe and spun wool.' See Ovid, *Her.* 9, 60, &c. and supra iv. 11, 17—20.—*colus* here and v. 1, 72, is masculine, if the MSS. are to be trusted. There seem to have been two forms, *hæc colus*, of the *u* declension, and *hic colus*.—L. Barth and Lachmann read *colu*.

49.] *Fascia*. The Greek στρόφιον, somewhat resembling the modern use of stays. See Rich's Dict. *in v.*

50.] *Manibus duris*. 'And, hard as my hands were, I made a handy girl'—*apta*, sc. pensis trahendis, habilis. So sup. 2, 23, 'fiam non dura puella.'

52.] *Puniceo stamine*. The vitta, which confined the woollen infula to the brows. The purple or scarlet colour, denoting sacrificial or priestly dignity, (Æsch. *Eum.* 982) is retained in modern ecclesiastical costumes.

55.] *Metuenda lege interdicta*, i.e. by the penalty of blindness. Hence 'parce

'Quæ se summota vindicat ara casa.
'Magno Tiresias aspexit Pallada vates,
'Fortia dum posita Gorgone membra lavat.
'Di tibi dent alios fontes: hæc lympha puellis
'Avia secreti limitis una fluit.'
Sic anus; ille humeris postes concussit opacos,
Nec tulit iratam janua clausa sitim.
At postquam exhausto jam flumine vicerat æstum,
Ponit vix siccis tristia jura labris.
'Angulus hic mundi nunc me mea fata trahentem
'Accipit; hæc fesso vix mihi terra patet.
'Maxima quæ gregibus devota est Ara repertis,

oculis hospes,' 'have regard for your eyesight,' v. 53. *Piare aram* is to purify, ἁγνίζειν, an altar before commencing the sacrifice: here the reference seems to be to the expiations which would be necessary on the violation of it.—*tuta fuga*, 'while yet you can retire in safety.' Compare iv. 10, 19, and sup. 1, 50.—*vindicat se*, 'asserts its own sanctity,' viz. a temere accedentibus viris.

57.] Hertzberg alone has ventured to retain the reading of all the good copies, *magnum*. With better critical judgment, as I think, Lachmann and the recent editors have admitted *magno*, though the avowedly corrected reading of an interpolated copy. The epithet *magnum* is superfluous and insipid, whereas *magno*, *i.e.* pretio, is all but required by the sense. Were any argument wanting, it would be supplied by the verse of Callimachus, evidently copied by Propertius, *Lav. Pall.* 102, μισθῷ τοῦτον ἰδεῖν μεγάλῳ, sc. γυμνὴν τὴν Παλλάδα. See also *ibid.* 75.

58.] *Posita Gorgone*, after having divested herself of the ægis (the goat-skin folded round the chest). See ii. 2, 8.

60.] *Hæc—fluit*. 'This particular spring in a retired course far from the high road flows only for the use of women.' There was some superstition connected with this: see *Hes.* Ἔργ. 751, μηδὲ γυναικείῳ λουτρῷ χρόα φαιδρύνεσθαι ἀνέρα.—*limitis*, see sup. 4, 50, 'fallaci celat limite semper aquas.' The MSS. have *fluit*, which Jacob retains. *Fluit* is the correction of Fruter.

61.] *Concussit*. Hercules was represented in comedy as knocking violently at doors and bursting them open, κενταυρικῶς, Ar. *Ran.* 38 (where Dionysus is imitating the customs of Hercules).—*clausa*, 'though closed to him, it could not withstand his angry demands for drink.'

64.] This verse may be interpreted in two very different ways: either 'he scarcely puts reluctant control on his thirsty lips,' *i.e.* can scarcely stop drinking; or, 'he lays down severe laws even before drying his lips,' alluding to v. 69. The latter is probably right. Compare 'ponere jura,' iv. 9, 24.—In this, as in most of the legends of Hercules, a strong admixture of comedy is perceptible.

65—6.] The meaning is, 'Thus then my destiny has brought me to this obscure corner of the world, and here I am doomed to be refused a cup of water.' The sentiment is that of a king who should find himself spurned from a cottage door, and implies conscious merit and just indignation. See sup. 42.—*trahentem*, not *ultro*, but in the performance, or working out, of my destiny.

67.] *Gregibus repertis* is the ablative absolute, not the dative after *devota*, (*i.e.* promissa si reperisset) as Hertzberg shows. *Devovere*, he observes, is used of victims, not of places, when in the sense of promising something on the fulfilment of a desire. The sense is, 'hæc ara, quæ post receptas boves nunc mihi dicata est, et a parva maxima facta est' &c. For the altar was not newly built, but only enlarged by him; it was the same altar of the Bona Dea which the women had in charge; and as they had excluded males from approaching it, so now in retaliation he decrees that women in future shall not be allowed access. (This enlarging of old altars, we may remark, was an ancient custom; see Thucyd. vi. 54, *ad fin.*) There is some uncertainty whether this altar was dedi-

'Ara per has,' inquit, 'Maxima facta manus,
'Hæc nullis umquam pateat veneranda puellis,
'Herculis eximii ne sit inulta sitis.'
Sancte pater salve, cui jam favet aspera Juno;
Sancte, velis libro dexter inesse meo.
Hunc, quoniam manibus purgatum sanxerat orbem,
Sic Sanctum Tatiæ composuere Cures.

X.

Nunc Jovis incipiam causas aperire Feretri,

cated by Hercules to Jupiter, in thanksgiving for recovering his oxen, or whether *suo numini*, as a memorial of himself, and as conscious of his own divinity. But it appears, as Hertsberg demonstrates at length, that the two actions were distinct: the first is briefly alluded to by Ovid, *Fast.* i. 579, 'Immolat ex illis taurum tibi Jupiter unum Victor;' the latter was an institution of a new cultus, that of the Potitii and Pinarii, with a view to his own future deification.

70.] *Sitis*, the refusal of drink to the thirsty Hercules.

71.] *Sancte Pater*. The invocation of the poet, that Hercules may be propitious to his verse. Whether here we read *Sance*, and in v. 74 *Sancum*, or with Jacob, Müller, and Hertsberg retain the MS. reading in both places, we cannot doubt that allusion is intended to the Sabine title of Hercules, *Sancus*. Dr. Donaldson (*Varronianus*, p. 6) considers Sancus to have been an Umbrian deity; which is much the same thing, as the Sabines were of Umbrian origin. He thinks that the word meant 'revered.' Other names for the same god were *Fidius* (whence *Medius Fidius*, 'may Fidius (son) of Jove help me') and *Semo*. Ovid, *Fast.* vi. 213, 'Quærebam Nonas Sanco Fidiove referrem, An tibi, Semo pater: cum mihi Sancus ait, Cuicumque ex illis dederis, ego munus habebo; Nomina trina fero; sic voluere Cures.' Varro, *L. L.* v. § 66, 'Ælius Dium Fidium dicebat Diovis filium, ut Græci Διόσκορον Castorem, et putabat hunc esse Sancum ab Sabina lingua, et Herculem a Græca.' Here it is evident that the poet wishes to derive the title from *sancire*. Cf. sup. In fact the word was written, as Hertsberg shows, *Sancus*, *Sangus*, and *Sanctus*.—*Cui jam favet Juno*, i.e. cui jam, ut in cœlum recepto, iram remisit.' He had wedded Hebe, the daughter of Juno.

72.] *Inesse* is the reading of all the copies. Kuinoel and others give *adesse*. The former word conveys the prayer that the hero will be *in* the poem, by the inspiration of his divinity.

73.] For *hunc* Müller reads *huic*, Lachmann *nunc*. The sense is, '(I say Sancte), for this very god, since he had cleared the world of crime, the chief city of the Sabines consecrated, *for these benefits*, as the Purifier.'—*sic*, ἐπὶ τούτοις.—*composuere*, ἱδρύσαντο, templo dedicavere. See ii. 6, 5, 'quæ delectas potuit componere Thebas.'

X. The poet in the present elegy endeavours to assign the origin of the obscure title Jupiter Feretrius. Whether the restoration of the temple of this deity by Octavianus, which probably took place while Propertius was quite a youth, had any part in suggesting the subject, or whether it was written simply in reference to his work on the Roman Fasti, is uncertain, and is a matter of no great importance. The commencement, '*Nunc* incipiam *causas*' &c., seems to point to the latter. The poem undoubtedly bears the impress of a juvenile performance, and has perhaps as little merit as anything remaining to us from the same pen. The word *feretrius* is clearly Greek, φερέτριος, and certainly cannot be derived from *ferire*, (inf. 46,) but is rather from *ferre*, either in the sense of φέρειν or φέρεσθαι.

1.] *Causas*, the origin of the name. Compare inf. 45. In using the word, (with which Ovid also opens his *Fasti*, 'Tempora cum causis' &c.) allusion is probably made to the Αἴτια of Callimachus.—Hertsberg's objection, that *causas aperire* is incorrect, seems futile, since the sense itself suggests *causas*.

Armaque de ducibus trina recepta tribus.
Magnum iter ascendo, sed dat mihi gloria vires:
Non juvat e facili lecta corona jugo.
Imbuis exemplum primæ tu, Romule, palmæ
Hujus, et exuvio plenus ab hoste redis,
Tempore quo portas Cæninum Acronta petentem
Victor in eversum cuspide fundis equum.
Acron Herculeus Cænina ductor ab arce,
Roma, tuis quondam finibus horror erat.
Hic spolia ex humeris ausus sperare Quirini
Ipse dedit, sed non sanguine sicca suo.
Hunc videt ante cavas librantem spicula turres
Romulus, et votis occupat ante ratis:
Juppiter, hæc hodie tibi victima corruet Acron.
Voverat: et spolium corruit ille Jovi.
Urbis virtutisque parens sic vincere suevit,
Qui tulit aprico frigida castra Lare.
Idem eques et frenis, idem fuit aptus aratris,

4.] *E facili jugo.* This is elegantly said in reference to *ascendo* in v. 3. The sentiment is the same as in the well-known lines of Lucretius, 'Avia Pieridum peragro loca,' &c., and is expressed by the proverb, χαλεπὰ τὰ καλά.

5.] *Imbuis*, 'you impart,' or furnish. More usually, *aliquem aliquo*, and properly used of the first dye or colour (Mart. viii. 51, 17, 'imbuat egregium digno mihi nectare munus'). The root is probably the same as in βάπτω and βαφή.—*hujus palmæ*, of the *spolia opima*, or arms taken by a Roman general (or as some will have it, see sup. 3, 61, by a common soldier,) with his own hand from the leader of the hostile forces.

6.] The best copies have *cænino* or *cæniso*, which are mere varieties in reading rather than in writing *cænio*. The common reading, *cæninis*, which Kuinoel and Barth give, seems to have proceeded from the school of Italian emendators. The form *cæninum* appears of questionable authority. Compare however *delicium*, Martial, i. 8.

7.] Acron, king of the Cæninenses, a Sabine people, and as such boasting his descent from Hercules (see on v. 71 of the preceding elegy), was killed by Romulus (Livy, i. 10), who carried his arms as the primitiæ of war to the capitol, 'fabricato ad id apte ferculo,' *i. e.* φερέτρῳ, whence the historian supposes the title to be derived.

8.] *In eversum equum.* 'Hasta Romuli prostravit equitem, et equum simul fusum resupinavit.'—*Barth.* So sup. 1, 94, 'heu sibi prolapso non bene cavit equo.' 'You threw (or pitched) him with your spear upon the horse that had fallen under him' (or, that had been overthrown by the shock).

9.] *Ab arce.* See sup. 9, 9.

12.] *Ipse dedit.* Cf. sup. 6, 60, 'reddat signa Remi, mox dabit ipse sua.'

14.] *Occupat*, is beforehand with him, anticipates him in making vows that were *rata*, accepted by the gods, *non irrita*. So 'vocales occupat ense canes,' sup. 4, 84. Ovid, *Fast.* i. 575, 'occupat Alcides,' 'Hercules closes with Cacus and strikes him first.'

17.] *Sic vincere*, *i.e.* by determination to win at all hazards; by making a solemn engagement to do so. Or, by saying he would do a thing, and doing it.

18.] *Aprico Lare.* 'Who bore the cold of the camp without the shelter of a tent,' *i.e.* non sub tecto, and 'patiens pulveris atque solis' in castris.

Et galea hirsuta compta lupina juba,
Picta neque inducto fulgebat parma pyropo;
Præbebant cæsi baltea lenta boves.
Cossus at insequitur Veientis cæde Tolumni,
Vincere cum Veios posse laboris erat,
Nec dum ultra Tiberim belli sonus; ultima præda
Nomentum et captæ jugera terna Coræ.
O Veii veteres, et vos tum regna fuistis,
Et vestro posita est aurea sella foro:
Nunc intra muros pastoris buccina lenti
Cantat, et in vestris ossibus arva metunt.
Forte super portæ dux Veius adstitit arcem,
Colloquiumque sua fretus ab urbe dedit.

20.] *Et galea.* 'His cap or helmet was of wolf-skin with its shaggy hair combed into shape,' not the plumed helmet of the later time. Cf. sup. 1, 29, and 4, 20, 'Nor was his shield,' he continues, 'overlaid with plates of pinchbeck; and slaughtered oxen afforded him a tough leather belt.' With the *galea lupina* compare the *καταῖτυξ* of Hom. *Il.* x. 258. With *compta*, though the construction is a little abrupt, it is best to supply *erat*.

21.] *Pyropo.* Ovid, *Met.* 11, 2, 'Clara micante auro flammasque imitante pyropo.' According to Pliny, *N. H.* xxxiv. 20, *pyropus* was a mixed metal of gold and brass. —*Hertzberg.*

23.] *Insequitur, i. e.* as the second instance of *spolia opima*. For the narrative, see Livy, iv. 20; Virg. *Æn.* vi. 842. The *at*, as usual, introduces a change of subject. For its position compare sup. 1, 95. Tolumnius was killed by Cornelius Cossus in the war subsequent upon the outrage committed by the people of Fidenæ on four Roman ambassadors in the year 438 B.C. Since at this period the Roman arms were widely extended, it has been suggested by Passerat to transpose vv. 25, 26, so as to follow 22. To say that B.C. 438, Nomentum and Cora, (Plaut. *Capt.* 881), towns within a few miles of Rome, were the limits of Roman victory, and that war had not yet been heard beyond the Tiber, is, as Hertzberg remarks, 'non *ὑπερβολή*, sed mendacium.' The blame is conveniently thrown on the youthful carelessness of the poet, otherwise there is much to recommend the proposed change in the text, especially as 'O Veii veteres' so naturally follows v. 24.—In *jugera terna* Niebuhr, quoted by Hertzberg, thinks that allusion is made to the triple division of captured territory between the three original tribes of Rome. The best copies give *terra Coræ* or *Coras*.

27.] *O vehi veteres*, MS. Gron., whence Jacob, Lachmann, Hertzberg, Keil, give *O Veii* for *Et Veii*, the reading of Kuinoel and the earlier editions. *Heu Veii veteres!* Müller. The immense city of Veii was so completely destroyed after its capture by Camillus that hardly a vestige remained in the time of Augustus; and its site has only recently been determined with certainty.

28.] *Aurea sella.* The official seat of the king, the position of which in the forum indicated the ancient office of deciding suits, long performed by the kings in person until a vicegerent was found necessary. But as even in our country a judge is the representative of the sovereign, as exercising the power over life and death; so the prætor at Rome was possessed of curule dignity; see Livy i. 20.

29.] *Buccina* (sup. 1, 13), the horn of the lazy shepherd sounds on the spot once enclosed by walls, and reapers gather the harvests from fields enriched by the bones of your buried heroes. A fine passage.

31.] *Forte* &c. 'It chanced that the commander of Veii had taken his stand on the Gate Tower, and held parley with the enemy from his own citadel, confident in its strength.'—*fretus, i. e.* confidenter; unless with Hertzberg we understand *urbe fretus sua, ab urbe dedit*.

Dumque aries murum cornu pulsabat aheno,
  Vinea qua ductum longa tegebat opus,
Cossus ait: Forti melius concurrere campo.
  Nec mora fit: plano sistit uterque gradum.
Di Latias juvere manus: desecta Tolumni
  Cervix Romanos sanguine lavit equos.
Claudius a Rheno trajectos arcuit hostes,
  Belgica cum vasti parma relata ducis
Virdumari. Genus hic Rheno jactabat ab ipso,
  Nobilis e rectis fundere gaesa rotis.
Illi virgatis jaculantis ab agmine braccis

34.] *Vinea longa*, the penthouse or mantlet which covered the long earth-work; the shed raised over the *vallum* on which the ram was worked.—Jacob, Hertzberg, Lachmann, and the later editors, follow the Naples MS. in reading *qua ductum*. Barth and Kuinoel give *Vineaque inductum* with the MS. Gron. and ed. Rheg.

35.] *Forti*, sub. *viro*, 'For a *brave* man it were better to give a meeting on the plain. Nor is there delay on his own part; each takes his stand on the level ground.' The taunt implied in *forti* made the *dux Veius* ashamed of ensconcing himself longer in his tower.

39.] The third instance of winning the spolia opima. Marcus Claudius Marcellus was five times consul, for the first time in 222 B.C. when he conquered the Insubres near Milan, and slew Britomart (Virdomarus or Virdumarus) with his own hand. This is the hero mentioned in iv. 18, 33, and so finely celebrated by Virgil, *Æn.* vi. 856, 'Aspice ut ingreditur spoliis Marcellus opimis,' &c.—For *a Rheno* Barth, Kuinoel, and Müller read *Eridanum*, the conjecture of Guyet. There does not seem sufficient reason for departing from the MSS., as the enemy are rightly said *a Rheno* (in Italiam) *trajecti*.

40.] *Cum*, quo tempore, *relata*, reportata est &c.—*cui* Kuinoel and Müller, with Guyet and Heinsius.—*vasti*, 'huge,' πελώρου. A rather rare sense of the word; cf. 'vastos leones,' iii. 10, 21; 'vasta trabe,' Pers. *Sat.* v. 141.

41.] *Brenno*, Heinsius, which Jacob calls 'admodum probabilis.' There would, however, be less point in tracing his descent from Brennus, than from the mythical river-god. And Hertzberg sensibly remarks, 'Nihil poetis Latinis frequentius quam heroum originem a diis patriis, fluvialibus imprimis, repetere.'—*rectis* is the reading of the good copies, (*erectis*, according to Hertzberg, in the Naples MS.) which has been altered to *e tectis* by Lipsius, and this has been admitted by Barth and Kuinoel. Keil and Müller retain *rectis*, the latter with an obelus. Hertzberg explains *recta rota* to mean the chariot *managed* by the driver at the same time that he hurls his javelin; quoting Caesar *de B. Gall.* iv. 33. But, 'to deal darts from ruled wheels' is a singular sort of terseness, besides that *rectus* generally loses its primary sense of *ruled* for the secondary adjectival one. I think *e recto curru* is naturally equivalent to the ὀρθὸν δίφρον of Soph. *Electr.* 742, and may be rendered, 'from the car driven safely at full speed,' i.e. not yet overthrown in the heat of the contest. Compare Pind. *Pyth.* v. 30, ἀκηράτοις ἡνίαις.

43.] This verse is considered by most of the editors as hopelessly corrupt, and has been variously corrected *maculanti sanguine braccas*, *jaculanti abrupta braccis* (Hertzberg), and *jaculantis ab inguine braccis*. Perhaps we may venture to explain it thus: 'illi, nempe Claudio, torquis decidit ab gula Virdumari jaculantis ab agmine virgatis braccis, i.e. dum braccas indutus jaculatur ab agmine suo.' Some consider *illi* an old form of the genitive; an unnecessary hypothesis.—The *virgatae bracae* of the Celts were probably striped like the tartan plaids of the modern Gaels. Virg. *Æn.* viii. 659, 'Aurea caesaries ollis atque aurea vestis; Virgatis lucent sagulis; tum lactea colla Auro innectuntur; duo quisque Alpina coruscant Gaesa manu, scutis protecti corpora longis.' Diodor. *Sic.* v. 30, init., ἐσθῆσι δὲ χρῶνται (οἱ Γαλάται) καταπληκτικαῖς, χιτῶσι μὲν βαπτοῖς χρώμασι παντοδαποῖς διηνθισμένοις καὶ ἀναξυρίσιν, ἃς ἐκεῖνοι βράκας προσαγ-

Torquis ab incisa decidit unca gula.
Nunc spolia in templo tria condita; causa Feretri,
Omine quod certo dux ferit ense ducem.
Seu quia victa suis humeris hæc arma ferebant,
Hinc Feretri dicta est ara superba Jovis.

XI.

Desine, Paulle, meum lacrimis urgere sepulcrum:
Panditur ad nullas janua nigra preces.
Cum semel infernas intrarunt funera leges,
Non exorato stant adamante viæ.
Te licet orantem fuscæ deus audiat aulæ;
Nempe tuas lacrimas litora surda bibent.

[illegible].—*ab agmine*, *i.e.* covered by his comrades in the line, not alone and in the open field. The *torquis*, or Celtic torque, identical with the ornament sometimes found in the bogs and peat-mosses of Great Britain, derived its name from being made of twisted gold wire. The epithet *unca* refers to the hook and eye by which the collar was clasped round the throat, and which are seen in the specimens preserved in our museums.

46.] *Omine certo*, with an omen that had its fulfilment in the name.

47.] *Seu*, *i.e.* sive a *feriendo*, seu potius a *ferendo*.

XI. This elegy may fairly be regarded as the masterpiece of the poet's genius. It is a splendid composition, full of pathos and eloquent appeal, and is on the whole worthy of the almost extravagant praises which Barth and Kuinoel have bestowed upon it. It assumes the form of an address from a deceased wife, Cornelia, to her husband Lucius Æmilius Paulus, who was Censor in the year B.C. 22. Cornelia was the daughter of Scribonia, formerly wife of P. Cornelius Scipio, but subsequently married to Augustus. See Tac. *Ann.* ii. 27; Sueton. *Oct.* 62. She was divorced by the latter on his marriage with Livia. He appears indeed to have left her from her unamiable temper; 'pertæsus,' says Suetonius, 'ut scribit, morum perversitatem ejus.' This is the latest of the poet's extant writings, the date being A.U.C. 738, as appears from v. 66.

1.] *Urgere*, 'to press,' *i.e.* to vex, or weary with your tears. So Hor. *Od.* ii. 9, 9, 'Tu semper urges flebilibus modis Mysten ademptum.'—*Sepulcrum* is here for *Manes*. The confusion of bodily and spiritual ideas, and therefore of terms, so observable in this elegy, and generally in the Latin poets, is a natural consequence of the materialism of the ancient mythology. Thus *funera* v. 3, *rogos* v. 8, *ossa* v. 20 and 58, are used of the ghost of the deceased, from which the poet cannot detach the notion of a continued bodily existence in the other world; which is the more perplexing, as he does not forget the annihilation of the earthly corpse on the pyre, v. 10. See sup. 7, 1. 'The practical tendency of the Roman mind made them regard all realities as necessarily palpable.' (*Varronianus*, p. 304). Conversely, iii. 4, 32, we have, 'Accipiat *Manes* parvula testa meos,' where he means *cineres*.

2.] *Panditur*, *i.e.* ad emittendum mortuum. So Hades is called *πυλάρτης κρατερὸς*, *Od.* xi. 277. The door of the tomb, (or rather, sepulchral chamber,) is the barrier, as it were, between life and death.

3.] 'Cum semel sub inferorum ditione venerint mortui, clausi sunt et quasi firmantur exitus adamante nullis precibus amovendo.' We might conjecture *[illegible]*.—*stant viæ adamante*, for 'adamas stat non exorandus in viis.' 'Adamant' seems to mean 'basalt,' *Στυγὸς μελανοκάρδιος πέτρα*, Ar. *Ran.* 470.

6.] *Nempe*. A form of *namque*, as *quispiam* is a form of *quisquam*. And this sense is sufficiently appropriate here, if we suppose some ellipse, ('but you will not gain your object,') for the sand that cannot

Vota movent Superos,—ubi portitor æra recepit,
  Obserat umbrosos lurida porta rogos.
Sic mœstæ cecinere tubæ, cum subdita nostrum
  Detraheret lecto fax inimica caput.
Quid mihi conjugium Paulli, quid currus avorum
  Profuit, aut famæ pignora tanta meæ?
Num minus immites habuit Cornelia Parcas?
  En sum, quod digitis quinque levatur, onus.
Damnatæ noctes, et vos vada lenta paludes,
  Et quæcumque meos implicat unda pedes,
Immatura licet, tamen huc non noxia veni.
  Det pater hinc umbræ mollia jura meæ.

hear you will drink up your tears, and thus they will never reach the god whom they were intended to soften.' Compare sup. 1, 92, and 5, 42. The sense is, 'the god may be willing, on his part, to hear you, but the laws of fate are superior to his will, and inexorable.' There seems to have been something ominous to the Roman mind in representing Pluto as cruel and relentless. They preferred to speak of him as the Greeks did of the Eumenides.

7.] 'Superi tantummodo moventur precibus, non item inferi. Nam cum semel Charon naulum, sc. obolum accepit, Orci porta continet et includit sepultos.' For the obscure epithet *herbosos*, the reading of all the good copies, Jacob and Müller have adopted *umbrosos* from Pucci. Lachmann and Hertzberg adhere to the MSS., and it certainly seems at first sight improbable that so simple a word as *umbrosos* should have been altered to *herbosos*. The latter is explained by Barth: '*herbosi rogi* vel mortui dicuntur, quorum sepulcris spirantes croci aliique flores bene olentes ingerebantur.' But *umbrosos* is the more appropriate word in the sense of 'haunted by the shade;' see on iv. 17, 1. Some one may have altered it to *herbosos*, who supposed the shade of trees was meant.—*lurida*, 'grisly;' cf. sup. 7, 2, 'luridaque evictos effugit umbra rogos.'

9.] 'Such was the burden of the funeral strain,' *i.e.* the mournful notes of the tuba in the procession proclaimed this doctrine. Similarly iii. iv. 20, 'Nec tuba sit fati vana querela mei.' See on ii. 7, 12. The following verse must be literally understood: 'when the lighted pile was consuming my remains, and withdrawing my head from the bier.' See on v. 7, 26; iii. 2, 3.

13.] *Habui*, Jacob, with Barth, Kuinoel, and Lachmann; who remarks 'quod sine dubio verum est.' So also Keil and Müller. Hertzberg has *habuit* with the best MSS. Compare inf. v. 43—4. In the next verse *en* for *et* has been admitted by all from the MS. Gron., to which we are also indebted for alone preserving *num minus* for *non minus*. The well-known passage of Juvenal, 'Expende Hannibalem' &c., will occur as a parallel to v. 14.

15.] *Damnatæ noctes*, 'darkness of the damned,' 'noctes inferorum ubi damnati sunt,' *Kuinoel*. 'Figura Propertii maxime familiari,' *Hertzberg*. See on i. 16, 42.

16.] *Implicat*, 'entangles,' a metaphor from a rope entwined round the feet of one who endeavours to escape. Compare *Georg.* iv. 478, 'tardaque palus inamabilis unda Alligat, et novies Styx interfusa coercet.'

17.] Præmatura morte extingui eos credebant qui grave quoddam commisissent crimen. Itaque criminis suspicionem a se amoliri Cornelia studet.' *Kuinoel*.—In v. 18, *hinc* is the reading of the MS. Gron. (the Naples MS. has unfortunately lost a leaf, including v. 17—76).—*hinc* Jacob with Pucci: *hic*, Kuinoel, Lachmann, Müller, Hertzberg. *Hinc* seems almost necessary to the sense, *i.e.* propter innocentiam meam. Hertzberg understands *pater hic* as Jupiter infernus; which does not read very poetically.—*Jura dare*, as Hertzberg proves by abundant examples, is never used for *jus dicere* or *judicare*, but for *leges constituere*. The sense therefore of this verse is, 'may Pluto accordingly

Aut si quis posita judex sedet Æacus urna,
  In mea sortita vindicet ossa pila.
Assideant fratres, juxta Minoida sellam
  Eumenidum intento turba severa foro.
Sisyphe, mole vaces; taceant Ixionis orbes;
  Fallax Tantaleo corripiare liquor;
Cerberus et nullas hodie petat improbus umbras,
  Et jaceat tacita lapsa catena sera.

impose lenient conditions on my shade for its residence in Orcus.' *Dare jus* is either to decide a question at issue, as judge, or to confer the power of deciding on another, as Tac. *Ann.* iv. 15.

19—21.] These verses are exceedingly difficult. From Hertzberg's commentary upon them, extending over seven octavo pages, the following interpretation may be extracted; and it is on the whole perhaps the best that has been proposed: 'Or, if I am to undergo a trial (my asserted innocence not being taken for granted), and if there be indeed an Æacus to judge the dead, let him punish my shade according to its deserts by the appointment of a jury (by drawing from the urn the names of the *judices*); and let Minos and Rhadamanthus act as assessors, while near the chair of the former the Furies stand as lictors:' (rather perhaps as accusers; see Æsch. *Eumen.* 565, seq.) In this complicated allusion to the judicial forms of the prætor's court, the reader will observe:—(1) That Æacus is the *quæsitor* (*Æn.* vi. 430) who appoints the jury by putting the names to be drawn, written on a ballot (*pila*), into an urn. (2) That the jury are supposed to be taken from the shades of the dead. (3) That *vindicare in aliquem* can only mean *to punish*, as Tac. *Ann.* iv. 15, 'in Caium Silanum vindicatum erat;' and that this sense in fact suits the context best, *aut* (v. 19) implying 'or, if I am guilty,' &c. (4) That *sortita pila* is the same as *sortiendis judicibus*, the participle being used in a passive signification: see on i. 2, 5; v. 7, 55. 'Sic igitur dispositam judicii quodammodo scenam puta, ut in medio tribunali Æacus quæsitor sedeat; ab utraque parte Minos et Rhadamanthus assessores; hinc in subselliis judices selecti, illinc (juxta Minoida sellam) Eumenides ad exequenda judicia paratæ.' *Hertzberg.*—Jacob reads *judicet*, with the Groningen and Hamburg MSS. Müller, *in mea sortita* &c., which does not read poetically.

21.] *Minoida sellam*, Lachmann, Jacob, Hertzberg, with the best copies. *Minois sella, et*, Barth and Kuinoel, with Scaliger and the succeeding editors. Müller reads, with Lachmann, *juxta et Minoida sellam*, the only way of construing which is 'assideant Eumenides juxta fratres et sellam Minois,' or (as Lachmann puts it) 'juxta Minoem ejusque fratres.' The MS. Gron. has *juxta Minoida sellam*. The ed. Rheg. gives *juxta Minois sella*. There is no difficulty in admitting the Greek accusative of Μινωΐς. See iii. 16, 27.

22.] *Intento foro*, 'in the listening court.' In continuation of this idea the poet proceeds to speak of the infernal punishments.—*severa*, 'with fixed looks.'

24.] *Tantaleo*. Jacob reads *Tantalide*, one of the inferior MSS. having *Tantaleo*. But the patronymic is very unsatisfactory. *Tantaleo corripiare ore* is the conjecture of Auratus, which Hertzberg calls 'blanda,' and Kuinoel and Müller admit into the text. *Tantaleus* is perhaps as probable as any correction. 'May the delusive water in which Tantalus stands be caught by him at last.' *Od.* xi. 582, καὶ μὴν Τάνταλον εἰσεῖδον χαλέπ' ἄλγε' ἔχοντα, ἑσταότ' ἐν λίμνῃ, ἡ δὲ προσέπλαζε γενείῳ. Sup. iii. 8, 5, 'vel tu Tantalea moveare ad flumina sorte, Ut liquor arenti fallat ab ore sitim.' Hertzberg is inclined to acquiesce in the lengthened form of the name, and retains the vulgate with Lachmann. If this be the true reading, it must represent the Greek form Ταντάλεος from Ταντάλειος, like Τυνδαρέου for Τυνδάρεω, *Od.* xi. 298, and Πανδαρέου for Πανδάρεω, *ib.* xix. 518.

26.] *Et*, perhaps *set* or *sed*. 'May the relentless dog this day attack none of the shades, but may his chain fall from the silent door-bar (*i.e.* to which he is tied) and lie quietly on the ground.'—*tacita*, because the bar is no longer jerked by his straining the chain and barking at the ghosts.

Ipsa loquor pro me. Si fallo, pœna sororum
  Infelix humeros urgeat urna meos.
Si cui fama fuit per avita tropæa decori,
  Afra Numantinos regna loquuntur avos.
Altera maternos exæquat turba Libones,
  Et domus est titulis utraque fulta suis.
Mox, ubi jam facibus cessit prætexta maritis,
  Vinxit et acceptas altera vitta comas,
Jungor, Paulle, tuo, sic discessura, cubili:
  In lapide huic uni nupta fuisse legar.
Testor majorum cineres tibi, Roma, verendos,
  Sub quorum titulis, Africa, tonsa jaces,

27.] *Loquor*, Lachmann with MS. Gron. and ed. Rheg. Jacob, Kuinoel, and Müller *loquar*. The verses which follow, to the end of the poem, must be regarded as the speech addressed to the infernal court before whom she is arraigned. This appears from v. 99, 'Causa perorata est.' But the poet has not maintained the *persona loquens* with perfect consistency, as the appeal to her children (v. 63), and still more, her advice respecting their conduct towards their stepmother, and to her husband (v. 73), have nothing to do with a defence. In fact, there is a confusion throughout both as to locality and the subject-matter. The poet would seem to have been so carried away by his theme as to have forgotten that his heroine was on her trial, and by no means in a position to lecture her family from below. Mr. Wratislaw says, 'Cornelia in the lower world is supposed to see her friends lamenting at her tomb, and at the end of her defence before her judges calls them as witnesses to her character.'—*si fallo*, cf. sup. 7, 53.

30.] *Afra*. This is the certain correction of Scaliger for *Æra*. The allusion is to Scipio Africanus (*i.e.* P. Cornelius Scipio Æmilianus Minor, the younger son of Lucius Æmilius Paulus) who obtained the agnomen of *Numantinus* from Numantia in Spain. Ovid, *Fast*. i. 595, 'Hunc Numidæ faciunt, illum Messana superbum; Ille Numantina traxit ab urbe notam.' His father Lucius Æmilianus was surnamed *Macedonicus* from his victory and triumph over Perses or Perseus, B.C. 168. Cornelia here boasts of her descent on the father's side.—*altera turba*, the ancestry on the mother's side, *exæquat*, ἐξισοῖ, pares facit paternis, Libones. The latter were members of the Scribonia gens, Cornelia's mother bearing this nomen, v. 55.—*fulta*, both families alike rest on their titles, so as not to come to extinction or obscurity.

33.] *Prætexta*, the maiden dress, laid aside at marriage. The form of the *vitta* (riband or head-band) was also different for the wife and the virgin. See v. 3, 15, 'nec recta capillis Vitta data est,' &c.—*acceptas comas* is the MS. reading; Kuinoel's *aspersas* is from a corrected copy. *Capere crines* was the phrase used for 'taking up' the maiden's long locks. See Plaut. *Mostell*. i. 3, 69, 'soli gerundum censes morem, et capiundos crines.' *Mil. Glor*. 792, 'ut matronarum modo Capite compto crines vittasque habeat adsimuletque se Tuam esse uxorem.' Callim. *H. ad Cer*. 5, μὴ παῖς μηδὲ γυνὰ μηδ' ἃ κατεχεύατο χαίταν.

35.] *Sic discessura*, *i.e.* not destined to enter into a second marriage.—*Hertzberg*.

36.] Jacob and Hertzberg retain, with Barth, the MS. reading *hoc*. Lachmann, Kuinoel, and Müller edit *huic*. And this seems more likely to be true, since *in lapide hoc*, which Hertzberg explains 'in lapide hujus, i.e. meo,' is to a degree strained and unnatural; while the obvious sense implies an unmeaning appeal to the epitaph δεικτικῶς.—*legar* is here the future.

38.] Under the inscription at the base of a statue or trophy commemorating the exploits of Scipio Africanus, we must suppose a symbolical sculpture of Africa to have been placed, represented as a woman (or female slave or captive) with hair shorn in token of grief. See iii. 6, 46. The custom is familiar to us at the present day by such monuments as those in St. Paul's and Westminster Abbey, the only difference

Et Persen, proavi simulantem pectus Achillis,
Quique tuas proavus fregit, Achille, domos:
Me neque censuræ legem mollisse, nec ulla
Labe mea vestros erubuisse focos.
Non fuit exuviis tantis Cornelia damnum:
Quin erat et magnæ pars imitanda domus.
Nec mea mutata est ætas; sine crimine tota est:
Viximus insignes inter utramque facem.
Mi natura dedit leges a sanguine ductas,
Ne possem melior judicis esse metu.
Quælibet austeras de me ferat urna tabellas:
Turpior assessu non erit ulla meo,
Vel tu, quæ tardam movisti fune Cybellen,

being that in the latter case the order is usually reversed, the *titulus* being beneath the effigy. Mr. Wratislaw thinks that coins rather than monuments are here alluded to.

39.] For *et Persen* Lachmann reads *Te, Persen*, and in the pentameter *proavo* for *proavus*. The construction may be either *et* (testor) *Persen et eum qui fregit* &c., or *et* (testor) *proavum, qui fregit Persen et tuas domos, Achille*; which Mr. Wratislaw prefers.

40.] *Proavus*, L. Æmilius Paullus, the conqueror of Perses, and ancestor of Cornelia's husband. *Achille* is the vocative, on the principle that Greek names in *es* (Pericles &c.) were inflected in Latin mostly after the *e* declension.

41.] 'That my husband was not compelled to relax the severity of the Censorship through any fault of mine which he would have had to punish.' Lit. 'that I did not relax,' for *non fuisse me causam cur molliret* &c. She here answers a charge which seems to have been unjustly brought against her, of having by some misconduct disgraced herself and her ancestry. The ancients had a theory that high birth was closely allied with natural virtue; τὸ γὰρ εὐγενὲς ἀναφέρεται πρὸς αἰδῶ.—For *vestros* Müller reads *nostros*. Compare inf. v. 67. —*mollisse*, cf. sup. 4, 62.

43—4.] 'Cornelia did not detract from such high honours as her family can show; nay, great as was the house of which she was a member, she was herself even a pattern of virtue in it.'

46.] *Utramque facem*, the marriage and the funeral torch. Ovid, *Her.* 21, 172, 'Et face pro thalami fax mihi mortis erit.' —*insignes*, the observed and admired of all.

47.] *A sanguine ductas*. Cf. Eur. *Hipp.* 79, ὅσοις διδακτὸν μηδέν, ἀλλ' ἐν τῇ φύσει τὸ σωφρονεῖν εἴληχεν ἐς τὰ πάνθ' ὁμῶς.

48.] *Ne possem* &c. 'Ita ut tum, cum viverem, non possem melior esse metu, quia per naturam eram optima.'—*Barth.*

49.] The *urna* here mentioned is different from that in v. 19, being the one into which the votes of acquittal and condemnation were dropped. The sense is, 'Let any jury you please pass their severest sentence on me, still no one, however virtuous, will be disgraced by contact with me,' *i.e.* by being classed with me. The sense is well given by Hertzberg: 'Non, siqua uno ordine locoque mecum censetur, turpior inde videbitur.' *Qualibet urna* for *quilibet judex*. Hertzberg thinks that reference is made to several urns being used to collect the votes of the jury *per decurias*. Kuinoel with the emendators gives *quamlibet*, against all the copies.

51.] *Cybellen*. See on v. 7, 61. The legend of Claudia is this:—She was a Vestal Virgin, and being unjustly suspected of having violated her vows, was favoured with a miraculous attestation to her virtue by drawing a ship, containing the image of Cybele, off a shoal in the Tiber, with her own hands, after numbers of men had made the same effort in vain. See Ritter on Tac. *Ann.* iv. 64, who quotes from Orelli an ancient inscription commemorative of the above event, *Navis Salviæ*. The story is told in Ovid, *Fast.* iv. 300—27; Livy, xxix. 14; Suetonius, *Tib.* § 2.—*tardam*, when stranded in the Tiber.—*turrita*, see Lucret. ii. 606.—*rara*, cf. i. 17, 16.

Claudia, turritæ rara ministra deæ;
Vel cui, commissos cum Vesta reposceret ignes,
Exhibuit vivos carbasus alba focos.
Nec te, dulce caput, mater Scribonia, læsi.
In me mutatum quid, nisi fata, velis?
Maternis laudor lacrimis urbisque querellis,
Defensa et gemitu Cæsaris ossa mea.
Ille sua nata dignam vixisse sororem
Increpat; et lacrimas vidimus ire deo.
Et tamen emerui generosos vestis honores,
Ne mea de sterili facta rapina domo.
Tu, Lepide, et tu, Paulle, meum post fata levamen,
Condita sunt vestro lumina nostra sinu.
Vidimus et fratrem sellam geminasse curulem;
Consule quo facto tempore rapta soror.
Filia, tu specimen censuræ nata paternæ,
Fac teneas unum, nos imitata, virum.
Et serie fulcite genus. Mihi cymba volenti

53.] *Reposceret*, 'claimed as a deposit committed to her care.' Æmilia was also a Vestal, who was accused of letting the sacred fire go out; when she lighted a piece of her embroidered garment from the apparently cold ashes.

54.] *Carbasus*. See sup. 3, 64.

55.] *Mater Scribonia*. She had been the wife of Augustus, but divorced; see introduction to the present elegy. This explains the allusions in v. 58—9. For the notorious Julia was the daughter of Scribonia by Augustus, and therefore half-sister of Cornelia.

58.] *Defensa*. Kuinoel well remarks that some aspersions seem to have been cast on Cornelia, by which her reference to the chaste but suspected Vestals in v. 51—4 becomes peculiarly appropriate.

59.] *Sua nata dignam*. An instance of the gross adulation of the age. On *deo*, *i.e.* Cæsari, see iv. 4, 1.—*Increpat viriam*, mortuam esse queritur.

61.] *Et tamen*, viz. quamvis immatura morte rapta, sup. 17.—*vestis honores*, the presentation of an embroidered vestment, perhaps in imitation of the Greek peplus. This seems to have been a privilege connected with the jus trium liberorum. But nothing definite appears to be recorded on the subject.

65.] The brother of Cornelia, Publius Cornelius Scipio, was ædile and prætor (both curule offices), and consul B.C. 16, which is therefore the date of Cornelia's death, if reliance can be placed on any interpretation of the obscure pentameter, v. 66. If it be not a brief or rather a confused way of expressing 'qui cum consul factus esset, eo tempore rapta est soror ejus,' (*i.e.* ego rapta sum), or, *cujus consulatus tempore rapta est soror*, we must understand *tempore* with Hertzberg as the ablative of the instrument, rather than with others for *opportune*. Müller, after Lachmann, reads 'Consul quo factus tempore, rapta soror,' which is at best awkward, if it means 'quo tempore is factus est consul, eo tempore rapta est soror.'

67.] 'Filia nata ut sis specimen censuræ paternæ, ut censuram patris moribus tuis exprimas.'—*Kuinoel*.

68.] *Fac teneas*. See sup. 4, 66; and 6, 34.

69.] *Serie fulcite*. Cf. sup. 32. Pliny, *Ep.* iv. 21, 3, 'cui nunc unus ex tribus liberis superest, domumque pluribus adminiculis paulo ante fundatam desolatus fulcit ac sustinet.' So 'pluribus munimentis insistere,' Tac. *Ann.* i. 3.

Solvitur, aucturis tot mea fata meis.
Hæc est feminei merces extrema triumphi,
Laudat ubi emeritum libera fama rogum.
Nunc tibi commendo, communia pignora, natos.
Hæc cura et cineri spirat inusta meo.
Fungere maternis vicibus pater. Illa meorum
Omnis erit collo turba ferenda tuo.
Oscula cum dederis tua flentibus, adjice matris.
Tota domus cœpit nunc onus esse tuum.
Et si quid doliturus eris, sine testibus illis:
Cum venient, siccis oscula falle genis.
Sat tibi sint noctes, quas de me, Paulle, fatiges,
Somniaque in faciem credita saepe meam.

70.] The MSS. have *malis*, which Pucci thus explains: 'tot malis aucturis mea fata, quod insequi poterant mala, quæ præverti moriens.' This is so unsatisfactory, that I have followed Hertzberg and Müller in admitting Lachmann's conjecture *meis*. The sense will then be, 'I die resigned now that so many of my children survive me to perpetuate my memory.' *Mea fata* signifies *meam sortem*, which would derive additional lustre from the glory and virtue of her descendants.—*malis* may have been written by transcribers who objected to the close occurrence of *mea* and *meis*.

71—2.] A noble sentiment finely expressed. 'This is the highest glory of a woman, to leave behind her a fair fame among those who are free to speak of her as she deserves.'—*emeritum rogum*, in its simplest sense, means nothing more than *defunctam vita mulierem*, according to the familiar use of *emeritus* applied to things done with, past and gone, and become unserviceable. Hertzberg interprets it 'plane meritum, *i.e.* laudari meritum,' comparing *emerui* v. 61, and *emeritis* for *valde meritis*, Ovid, *Ep. ex Pont.* I. 7, 61. It is difficult to decide: Propertius is apt to be so lax in his use of words that *laudare emeritum rogum* may have been intended for *vitam bene emeritam post fatum laudare*.

74.] 'This care lives as it were branded in my very bones.' The impression must therefore be deep to survive the pyre. The passage from Cicero, *Verr.* 1, 44, quoted by Hertzberg after Broukhusius, is remarkably apposite: 'Cur hanc dolorem cineri ejus atque ossibus inussisti?' The conclusion of the poem from v. 73 is exquisitely beautiful, full as it is of affection, tenderness, and truthfulness to nature. I add here a few lines from 'Verse-Translations' &c.—

'Take now these dearest pledges of my love;
To them a father and a mother prove.
To thee, their care, the precious charge returns;
This care still lives, and in my ashes burns.
To thy dear neck my children all must cling,
On thee henceforth a double burden bring.
And when your weeping little ones you see,
And kiss them, kiss them yet again for me.
In sighing, let them not perceive your sighs;
In greeting, with dry cheeks your grief disguise.
Enough, for me the livelong nights to pine,
Dream of delusive shapes, and think them mine.'

76.] *Turba*, cf. iii. 23, 4.—*erit ferenda*, sup. 6, 32.

80.] *Oscula falle*, 'abstersis lacrymis, dolore occultato, et fac, ne fleverisse te sentiant.'—*Hertzberg*; who refers *oscula* to the children's kiss, not to the father's. But there seems no reason why we may not understand 'falle eos, osculando siccis genis,' *i.e.* 'give a feigned cheerfulness to your kisses,' 'disguise your real feelings by a cheerful kiss;' since *fallere aliquid* is to do anything falsely or with a disguised action. So 'fallere terga lupo,' v. 5, 14, to assume a form which is not your real one; 'fallitur Jupiter,' *ib.* 1, 61, 'Jupiter is made a liar.' The same editor rightly, as I think, places a colon instead of a comma at the end of the preceding verse, the sense being *ne dolens* (sc. dolori indulgens) *coram illis*.

82.] *In faciem meam* &c. 'Vain dreams, taken for visions of me,' *passypsiva*, or, in the words of Hertzberg, 'ita credita, ut facies mea tibi apparere videatur.'

Atque ubi secreto nostra ad simulacra loqueris,
  Ut responsuræ singula verba jace.
Seu tamen adversum mutarit janua lectum,
  Sederit et nostro cauta noverca toro,
Conjugium, pueri, laudate et ferte paternum;
  Capta dabit vestris moribus illa manus.
Nec matrem laudate nimis; collata priori
  Vertet in offensas libera verba suas.
Seu memor ille mea contentus manserit umbra,
  Et tanti cineres duxerit esse meos,
Discite venturam jam nunc sentire senectam,
  Cœlibis ad curas nec vacet ulla via.
Quod mihi detractum est, vestros accedat ad annos:
  Prole mea Paullum sic juvet esse senem.
Et bene habet: nunquam mater lugubria sumpsi;
  Venit in exequias tota caterva meas.
Causa perorata est. Flentes me surgite testes,

83.] *Nostra ad simulacra*, 'to my portrait;' imagine that it will answer you, and realise from it that which it only represents.

85.] *Mutarit janua lectum*, for 'seu lectus genialis mutatus sit ex adverso januæ.' Propertius frequently treats the means or cause by which anything is done, as the agent which effects it, of which Hertzberg has collected a great number of examples, *Quæst.* lib. ii. § 28, p. 153. The sense is, 'If a new marriage-bed shall have been placed in the atrium opposite to the door,' *i. e.* a new bride introduced. Lit. 'If the door shall have got a new *lectus* opposite to it.' 'Genialis hic lectus cuique domum intranti signum erat conjugum par in ea habitare; nam muliere mortua vel post divortium cum ea factum, tollebatur.' Orelli on Hor. *Ep.* I. 1, 87. Becker (*Gallus*, p. 247) regards *adversus* as a synonym of *genialis*. See also *ibid.* p. 166.

86.] *Cauta*, 'suspicious,' 'reserved.' The epithet is meant to imply, in a gentle manner consistently with Cornelia's amiable character, the proverbial attributes of a *noverca*, severity and jealousy.

87.] *Laudate*, *alvēre*, 'acquiesce in,' 'speak kindly of.' Müller marks this word as corrupt, and suggests *placati ferte*.

93.] *Sentire*, 'learn to mark the least symptoms of his approaching age,' and so to anticipate his wants and weaknesses.—*jam nunc* is to be construed with *sentire*, i. e. *præsentire*.

> 'But if my ashes still he holds so dear,
> And still my memory honours with a tear,
> Learn to anticipate his coming age,
> And let no cares a widower's thoughts engage.'
> *Verse-Translations &c.*

The reading of Shrader, adopted by Kuinoel and Müller, *lenire*, would be satisfactory enough, if only the poet had thought fit to use it. But some critics put themselves in the position of a master correcting a schoolboy's exercise rather than confine themselves to detecting the interpolations and errors of transcribers.

96.] *Sic*, by your being all spared till his old age. May the happiness he finds in you cause him to feel pleasure in his declining years.

98.] *Tota caterva* = *omnis turba meorum*, sup. 75.

99.] *Causa perorata est*. See supra on v. 27. The poet, who seems to have forgotten that Cornelia was not arraigned before Æacus to talk of family matters, here recals the position in which he had placed her. Who the witnesses are whom she invites to speak in her favour before the infernal tribunal, she leaves uncertain. The allusion is to the custom of the courts, by which witnesses were called after the defence. But there seems no particular reference intended to *testor majorum cineres*,

Dum pretium vitæ grata rependit humus.
Moribus et cælum patuit; sim digna merendo
Cujus honoratis ossa vehantur equis.

v. 97. As she considers her defence complete, and leaves no doubt to be entertained of her innocence, she uses the words *flentes me* rather than *dicentes pro me*; and regards the reward bestowed upon her by the 'grateful earth' (*i.e.* while her memory is still cherished on earth,) as conferred at once, even while the witnesses are lamenting her loss to those above.

101.] 'Some have even ascended to the gods by their virtues: all that I aspire to is, that my shade may have a triumphal entry into rest.' Such appears to be the true meaning of these obscure verses. For *equis* the Naples MS. and ed. Rheg. give *aquis*, whence Lachmann, Müller and Kuinoel, with Heinsius, edit *avis*, understanding it of laying her bones in the sepulchre of her honoured ancestors. But the verb *vehantur* is strongly in favour of *equis*. *Vehi avis* could hardly mean *ad avos*; and unless *vehi* is used of Charon's boat (as sup. 7 ad fin.), we should expect *ferantur*. The idea of a triumphal procession and a car of honour, *carpentum*, so familiar to the mind of a Roman, is borrowed to express Cornelia's joyful conveyance to the regions of Elysium, as Hertzberg, with his usual good sense, has shown against the improbable fancies and alterations of his predecessors. There is perhaps an allusion to a curious Roman custom mentioned by Plutarch, *Quaest. Rom.* § lxxix, Διὰ τί τοῦ θριαμβεύσαντος, εἶτα ἀποθανόντος καὶ καέντος, ἐξῆν ὀστέον λαβόντας εἰς τὴν πόλιν εἰσφέρειν καὶ κατατίθεσθαι, &c.

INDEX OF PROPER NAMES,

(CORRECTED FROM KUINOEL'S EDITION).

B.

C.

D.

V.

X.

Z.

INDEX II.

INDEX III.

S.

T.

U.

V.

W.

Z.

APPENDIX.

Since the foregoing sheets were printed, some remarks by Professor Ellis, on certain obscure passages in Propertius, have appeared in the "Professorial Dissertations for 1871—2," issued by University College, London.

In ii. 2, 11—12, he accepts the correction of Turnebe, *Brimo* for *primo*, and says that "no one at the present day will doubt that this is right." I think this is rather strong: between the MSS. readings *satis—primo*, and the conjecture *Sais—Brimo* there is rather a serious difference. There is some difficulty in proving that *Brimo* was a title of Proserpine; difficulty in the wide separation of the epithet from the name; difficulty also in identifying the Egyptian name of Athene or Minerva, *Sais*, with Brimo or Proserpine. Prof. Ellis suggests that *Sais* may mean "of Saos in Thrace or Samothrace," where Hecate is thought to have been worshipped. Another suggestion of his is that we should read *satius* for *satis;* "satius fuerat Brimo composuisse latus, ut fertur, Mercurio," and this for "satius fuerat Mercurium concubuisse Brimo quam violantem Cynthiam,"—(meaning, I presume, *quam violasse Cynthiam*). Independently of the very unsatisfactory sense, I doubt if this syntax of *satius fertur* would even be correct Latinity.

I fear the passage is well-nigh hopeless. If *Brimo* be right, I think *satis* is the corruption of some epithet to *undis*. (I suppose *salsis* is not physically true). If *Sais* is genuine, I should prefer to retain (as I have edited) *primo*, which suits *virgineum*, in respect of the 'primus concubitus.' Perhaps *primum* was avoided for the sake of euphony.

In iii. 4, 1, Mr. Ellis suggests *Atusa* for the corrupt MS. reading *Etrusca*. He finds on a unique coin the name of the 'Ατουσιεῖς, an Assyrian city, with the badge of an arrow and a palm branch.

In iii. 24, 50, Mr. Ellis defends *deligere* (which I have retained against the proposed alteration *deripere*), by showing that *delegere* and *ablegere* in Tac. *Ann.* i. 22, sometimes meant 'to remove,' 'do away with.' (The dictionaries however recognise only *delegare* and *ablegare*. An example of *deligere* in this sense is cited from Virg. *Æn.* v. 717).

In iv. 22, 15, for the corrupt *orige* he proposes *Corycii*, as an epithet to *Caystri*. It is difficult however to see what connexion there can be between a river in Lydia and a town in Cilicia.

In vol. i. no. 2 (pp. 152—5) of the *Journal of Philology*, Mr. Wratislaw has given his view of a few of the more difficult passages in our poet. In iii. 5, 29, he would retain *nunc ad te, mea lux*, supplying *ibo*, and regarding *veniat mea navis, an sidat vadis* as equivalent to *sive—sive*. I think this rather far-fetched, especially as, under the latter condition, (viz. the ship settling in the shoals), *ad te ibo* could hardly be said; unless indeed the poet meant that he would then swim to the shore.

In iii. 26, 72, Mr. Wratislaw thinks the sense of the pentameter is parenthetical: "Happy are you, Virgil, in your love affairs. To this ungrateful girl of mine Tityrus himself (*i. e.* Virgil) may sing, and sing in vain."

In iv. 9, 25, he takes precisely the same view of *Medorum ire per hostes* as I have done, viz. that the hostile Parthians are meant, who had conquered the Medes.

I must beg the reader to pardon a few slight and unimportant misprints, which have escaped eyes that are not as good as they were. Such are,—

Plat. Symph. for *Plat. Symp.*, p. 10, note 21.
Pagase for *Pagasæ*, p. 45, note 17.
Asis for *Asiâ*, p. 48, note 9.
portray for *pourtray*, p. 58, note 42.
fermosam for *formosam*, p. 108, note 24.
Amphiarae for *Amphiaraæ*, p. 137, note 39.
pinguis for *pinguis*, p. 227, note 33.
Carpenæ for *Capenæ*, p. 235, note 71.
Typhœus for *Typhoeus*, p. 263, note 5.
ἐπιχώριον for *ἐπιχώριον*, p. 270, note 7.

THE END.

www.ingramcontent.com/pod-product-compliance
Lightning Source LLC
Chambersburg PA
CBHW030807230426
43667CB00008B/1106

* 9 7 8 3 7 4 2 8 0 7 5 2 6 *